ISBN 978-1-330-54758-8

PIBN 10076928

HISTORY

OF

THE REFORMATION IN EUROPE

IN THE TIME OF CALVIN.

BY J. H. MERLE D'AUBIGNÉ, D.D.

AUTHOR OF THE
'HISTORY OF THE REFORMATION OF THE SIXTEENTH CENTURY' ETC.

'Les choses de petite durée ont coutume de devenir fanées, quand elles ont passé leur temps.
'Au règne de Christ, il n'y a que le nouvel homme qui soit florissant, qui ait de la vigueur, et dont il faille faire cas.'

CALVIN.

VOL. IV.

ENGLAND, GENEVA, FRANCE, GERMANY, AND ITALY.

LONDON:

LONGMANS, GREEN, AND CO.

1866.

PREFACE.

THIS VOLUME narrates the events of an important epoch in the Reformation of England, Switzerland, France, Germany, and Italy. From the first the author purposed to write a *History of the Reformation in Europe*, which he indicated in the title of his work. Some persons, misled by the last words of that title, have supposed that he intended to give a mere biography of Calvin: such was not his idea. That great divine must have his place in this history, but, however interesting the life of a man may be, and especially the life of so great a servant of God, the history of the work of God in the various parts of Christendom possesses in our opinion a greater and more permanent interest.

Deo soli gloria. Omnia hominum idola pereant!

In the year 1853, in the fifth volume of his *History of the Reformation of the Sixteenth Century*, the author described the commencement of the reform in England. He now resumes the subject where he had left off, namely, after the fall and death of Wolsey. The following pages were written thirteen years ago, immediately subsequent to the publication of the fifth volume; they have since then been revised and extended.

The most important fact of that epoch in Great Britain is the act by which the English Church resumed its independence. It was attended by a peculiar circumstance. When Henry VIII. emancipated his people from the papal supremacy, he proclaimed himself head of the Church. And hence, of all Protestant countries, England is the one in which Church and State are most closely united. The legislators of the Anglican Church understood afterwards the danger presented by this union, and consequently declared, in the Thirty-seventh Article (*Of the Civil Magistrates*), that, 'where they attributed to the King's Majesty the chief government, they gave not to their princes the ministering of God's Word.' This did not mean that the king should not preach; such an idea did not occur to any one; but that the civil power should not take upon itself to determine the doctrines of the divine Word.

Unhappily this precaution has not proved sufficient. Not long since a question of doctrine was raised with regard to the *Essays and Reviews*, and the case having been carried on appeal before the supreme court, the latter gave its decision with regard to important dogmas. The Privy Council decided that the denial of the plenary inspiration of Scripture, of the substitution of Christ for the sinner in the sacrifice of the cross, and of the irrevocable consequences of the last judgment, was not contrary to the profession of faith of the Church of England. When they heard of this judgment, the rationalists triumphed; but an immense number of protests were made in all parts of Great Britain. While we feel the greatest respect for the persons and intentions of the members of the judicial committee of the Privy Council, we venture to ask whether this judgment be not subversive of the fundamental principles of the Anglican Church; nay more (though in this we may be wrong), is it not a violation of the English Constitution, of which the Articles of Religion form part? The fact is the more serious as it was accomplished notwithstanding the opposition (which certainly deserved to be taken into consideration) of the two chief spiritual conductors of the Church—the Archbishop of Canterbury, Primate of all England, and the Archbishop of York, both members of the council. Having to describe in this volume the historical fact in which the evil originated, the author is of opinion that he ought to point out respectfully but frankly the evil itself. He does so with the more freedom because he believes that he is in harmony on this point with the majority of the bishops, clergy, and pious laymen of the English Church, for whom he has long felt sincere respect and affection.

But let us not fear. The ills of the Church must not prevent our acknowledging that at no time has evangelical Christianity been more widely extended than in our days. We know that the Christians of Great Britain will not only hold firm the standard of faith, but will redouble their efforts to win souls to the Gospel both at home and in the most distant countries. And if at any time they should be compelled to make a choice—and either renounce their union with the civil power, or sacrifice the holy doctrines of the Word of God—there is not (in our opinion) one evangelical minister or layman in England who would hesitate a moment on the course he should adopt.

England requires now more than ever to study the Fathers of the Reformation in their writings, and to be animated by their spirit. There are men in our days who are led astray by strange imaginations, and who, unless precautions be taken against their errors, would overturn the glorious chariot of Christian truth, and plunge it into the abyss of superstitious Romanism or over the abrupt precipice of incredulity. On one side, scholastic doctrines (as transubstantiation for instance) are boldly professed in certain Protestant churches; monastic orders, popish rites, candles, vestments of the fourteenth century, and all the mummeries of the Middle Ages are revived. On the other side, a rationalism, which though it still keeps within bounds is not the less dangerous on that account, is attacking the inspiration of Scripture, the atonement, and other essential doctrines. May we be permitted to conjure all who have God's glory, the safety of the Church, and the prosperity of their country at heart, to preserve in its integrity the precious treasure of God's Word, and to learn from the men of the Reformation to repel foolish errors and a slavish yoke with one hand, and with the other the empty theorems of an incredulous philosophy.

I would crave permission to draw attention to a fact of importance. A former volume has shown that the spiritual reformation of England proceeded from the Word of God, first read at Oxford and Cambridge, and then by the people. The only part which the king took in it was an opposition, which he followed out even to the stake. The present volume shows that the official reformation, the reform of abuses, proceeded from the Commons, from the most notable laymen of England. The king took only a passive part in this work. Thus neither the internal nor the external reform proceeded from Henry VIII. Of all the acts of the Reformation only one belongs to him: he broke with the pope. That was a great benefit, and it is a great honour to the king. But could it have lasted without the two other reforms? We much doubt it. The Reformation of England primarily came from God; but if we look at secondary causes, it proceeded from the people, and not from the sovereign. The noble vessel of the political constitution, which had remained almost motionless for centuries, began to advance at the first breath of the Gospel. Rationalists and papists, notwithstanding all their hopes, will never deprive Great Britain of the Reformation accomplished by the Word of God; but if England were to lose the Gospel, she would at the same time lose her liberty. Coercion under the reign of popery or excesses under the reign of infidelity, would be equally fatal to it.

A distinguished writer published in 1858 an important work in which he treated of the history of

England from the fall of Wolsey.* We have great
pleasure in acknowledging the value of Mr. Froude's
volumes; but we do not agree with his opinions
with respect to the character of Henry VIII. While
we believe that he rendered great services to England as a king, we are not inclined, so far as his
private character is concerned, to consider him a
model prince, and his victims as criminals. We differ
also from the learned historian in certain matters of
detail, which have been partly indicated in our notes.
But everyone must bear testimony to the good use
Mr. Froude has made of the original documents which
he had before him, and to the talent with which the
history is written, and we could not forbear rejoicing as we noticed the favourable point of view
under which, in this last work of his, he considers the
Reformation.

After speaking of England, the author returns to
the history of Geneva; and readers may perhaps
complain that he has dwelt longer upon it than is con-
sistent with a general history of the Reformation. He
acknowledges that there may be some truth in the
objection, and accepts his condemnation in advance.
But he might reply that according to the principles
which determine the characteristics of the Beautiful,
the liveliest interest is often excited by what takes
place on the narrowest stage. He might add that
the special character of the Genevese Reform, where
political liberty and evangelical faith are seen triumph-

* *History of England from the Fall of Wolsey to the Death of Queen
Elizabeth,* by J. A. Froude.

ing together, is of particular importance to our age.
He might say that if he has spoken too much of
Geneva, it is because he knows and loves her; and
that while everybody thinks it natural for a botanist,
even when taking note of the plants of the whole
world, to apply himself specially to a description of
such as grow immediately around him; a Genevese
ought to be permitted to make known the flowers
which adorn the shores upon which he dwells, and
whose perfume has extended far over the world.

For this part of our work we have continued to
consult the most authentic documents of the sixteenth
century, at the head of which are the Registers of
the Council of State of Geneva. Among the new
sources that we have explored we may mention an
important manuscript in the Archives of Berne,
which was placed at our disposal by M. de Stürler,
Chancellor of State. This folio of four hundred
and thirty pages contains the minutes of the sittings of
the Inquisitional Court of Lyons, assembled to try Baudichon de la Maisonneuve for heresy. To avoid swell-
ing out this volume, it was necessary to omit many
interesting circumstances contained in that document; we should have curtailed them even more
had we not considered that the facts of that trial
did not yet belong to history, and had remained for
more than three centuries hidden among the state-
papers of Berne.* De la Maisonneuve was the chief
layman of the Genevese Reformation—*the captain of*

---

* M. Gaberel has quoted some passages of this manuscript which concern Geneva, in the first volume of his History of the Genevese Church.

the Lutherans, as he is frequently called by the witnesses in their depositions. The part he played in
the Reformation of Geneva has not been duly appreciated. No doubt the excess of his qualities, particularly of his energy, sometimes carried him too far;
but his love of truth, indomitable courage, and indefatigable activity make him one of the most prominent
characters of the Reform. The name of Maisonneuve
no longer exists in that city; but a great number of
the most ancient and most respected families descend
from him, either in a direct or collateral line.*

Another manuscript has brought to our knowledge
the chief mission of the embassy which solicited
Francis I. to set Baudichon de la Maisonneuve at
liberty. The head of that embassy was Rodolph of
Diesbach: M. Ferdinand de Diesbach, of Berne, has
had the kindness to place the manuscript records of
his family at our disposal; and the circumstance
that we have learnt from them does not give a very
exalted idea of that king's generosity.

The project of Francis I. and of Melanchthon, described in the portion of the volume devoted to
France and Germany, and the important letters
hitherto unknown in our language, which are given
there, appear worthy the attention of enlightened and
serious minds.

---

* M. Charles Eynard, a friend of the Author's, has communicated to
him some genealogies of the descendants of Baudichon de la Maisonneuve, in which, besides a great number of Genevese names, are
found those of some foreign families,—Constant-Rebecque in Holland;
the de Gasparins, de Staëls, and other families of note in France, who
descend from Baudichon de la Maisonneuve through the Neckers.

We conclude with Italy. We could have wished to describe in this volume Calvin's journey to Ferrara, and even his arrival at Geneva; but the great space given to other countries did not permit us to carry on the Genevese Reformation to that period. Two distinguished men, whose talents and labours we respect, M. Albert Rilliet, of Geneva, and M. Jules Bonnet, of Paris, have had a discussion about Calvin's transalpine expedition. M. Rilliet's essay (*Deux points obscurs de la vie de Calvin*) was published as a pamphlet, and M. Bonnet's answer (*Calvin en Italie*) appeared in the *Revue Chrétienne* for 1864, p. 461 sqq., and in the *Bulletin de la Société de l'Histoire du Protestantisme Français* for 1864, p. 183 sqq. M. Rilliet denies that Calvin ever visited the city of Aosta, and M. Bonnet maintains that he did. Data are unfortunately wanting to decide a small number of secondary points; but the important fact of Calvin's journey *through Aosta*, seems beyond a doubt, and when we come to this epoch in the reformer's life, we will give such proofs—in our opinion incontestible proofs—as ought to convince every impartial mind.

Before describing Calvin's residence at Ferrara, the author had to narrate the movement which had been going on in Italy from the beginning of the Reformation. Being obliged to limit himself, considering the extent of his task, he had wished at first to exclude those countries in which the Reformation was crushed out, as Italy and Spain. On studying more closely the work there achieved, he could not make up his mind to pass it over in silence. Among the oldest

editions of the books of that period which he has
made use of is a copy of the works of Aónio Paleario
(1552), recently presented by the Marquis Cresi, of
Naples, to the library of the School of Evangelical
Theology at Geneva. This volume wants thirty-two
leaves (pp. 311 to 344), and at the foot of p. 310
is the following manuscript note: *Quæ desunt pagellæ
sublatæ fuerunt de mandato Rev. Vicarii Neap.*; 'the
missing pages were torn out by order of the Reverend
Vicar of Naples.' This was an annoyance to the
author, who wished to read those pages all the more
because the inquisition had cut them out. Happily
he found them in a Dutch edition belonging to Professor André Cherbuliez.

Some persons have thought that political liberty
occupied too great a space in the first volume of this
history; we imagined, however, that we were doing a
service to the time in which we live, by showing
the coexistence in Geneva of civil emancipation and
evangelical reform. On the continent, there are men
of education and elevated character, but strangers
to the Gospel, who labour under a mistake as to
the causes which separate them from Christianity.
In their opinion it arises from the circumstance
that the Church whose head is at Rome is hostile
to the rights of the people. Many of them have
said that religion might be strengthened and perpe-
tuated by uniting with liberty. But is it not united
with liberty in Switzerland, England, and the United
States of America? Why should we not see everywhere, and in France particularly, as well as in the

countries we have just named, religion which respects the rights of God uniting with policy which respects the rights of the people? It is not the Encyclic of Pius IX. that the Gospel claims as a companion, it is liberty. The Gospel has need of liberty, and liberty has need of the Gospel. The people who have only one or other of these two essential elements of life are sick; the people who have neither are dead.

'The greatest imaginable absurdity,' says one of the eminent philosophers and noble minds of our epoch, M. Jouffroy, 'would be the assertion that this present life is everything, and that there is nothing after it. I know of no greater in any branch of science.' Might there not, however, be another absurdity worthy of being placed by its side? The same philosopher says that, so far as regards our state after this life, 'science and philosophy have not, after two thousand years, arrived at a single accepted result.'* Consequently, by the side of the absurdity which M. Jouffroy has pointed out, we confidently place another, as the second of 'the greatest imaginable absurdities,' namely, that which consists in believing, after two thousand years of barren labours, that there is another way besides Christianity to know and possess the life invisible and eternal. The essential fact of the history of religion and the history of the world: *God manifest in the flesh,* is the ray from heaven which reveals that life to us, and procures it for us. We know that a wind of incre-

---

* See the works of M. Jouffroy, and the *Revue des Deux Mondes* for 15th March, 1865.

dulity has scattered over barren sands many noble
souls who aspire to something better, and for whom
Christ has opened the gates of eternity; but let us
hope that their fall will be only temporary, and that
many, enlightened from on high, turning their eyes
away from the desert which surrounds them, and
lifting them towards heaven, will exclaim: *I will
arise and go to my Father.*

We must, as Jouffroy says, 'recommence our investigations;' but, 'first of all,' he adds, 'we must
confess the secret vice which has hitherto rendered
all our exertions powerless.' That secret vice consists in considering the question in an intellectual
and theoretical point of view only, while it is absolutely necessary to grapple with it in a practical
way, and to make it an individual fact. The matter
under discussion belongs to the domain of humanity,
not of philosophy. It does not regard the understanding alone, but the conscience, the will, the heart
and the life. The real vice consists in our not recognising, within us, the evil that separates us from God,
and, without us, the Saviour who leads us to Him.
The royal road to learn and possess life invisible and
eternal is the knowledge and possession of that Son
of Man, of that Son of God, who said with authority:
I AM THE WAY, THE TRUTH, AND THE LIFE; NO MAN
COMETH UNTO THE FATHER BUT BY ME.

MERLE D'AUBIGNÉ.

LA GRAVELINE, EAUX VIVES, GENEVA:
    May 1866.

CONTENTS

OF

THE FOURTH VOLUME.

———◆◇◆———

BOOK VI.

ENGLAND BEGINS TO CAST OFF THE PAPACY.

———

CHAPTER I.

THE NATION AND ITS PARTIES.

(Autumn 1529.)

CHAPTER II.

PARLIAMENT AND ITS GRIEVANCES.

(November 1529.)

CHAPTER X.

SEPARATION OF THE KING AND QUEEN.

(MARCH TO JUNE 1531.)

CHAPTER XI.

THE BISHOPS PLUNDER THE CLERGY AND PERSECUTE THE PROTESTANTS.

(SEPTEMBER 1531 TO 1532.)

CHAPTER XII.

THE MARTYRS.

(1531.)

CHAPTER XIII.

THE KING DESPOILS THE POPE AND THE CLERGY.

(MARCH TO MAY 1532.)

CHAPTER XIV.

CHAPTER XV.

CHAPTER XVI.

CHAPTER XVII.

CHAPTER XVIII.

CHAPTER XIX.

CHAPTER XX.

ENGLAND SEPARATES GRADUALLY FROM THE PAPACY.

(1533.)

CHAPTER XXI.

PARLIAMENT ABOLISHES THE USURPATIONS OF THE POPES IN ENGLAND.

(JANUARY TO MARCH 1534.)

BOOK VII.

MOVEMENTS OF THE REFORMATION IN ENGLAND, AT GENEVA, AND IN FRANCE, GERMANY, AND ITALY.

CHAPTER. I.

THE BISHOP ESCAPES FROM GENEVA NEVER TO RETURN.

(JULY 1533.)

CHAPTER II.

TWO REFORMERS AND A DOMINICAN IN GENEVA.

(JULY TO DECEMBER 1533.)

CHAPTER III.

FAREL, MAISONNEUVE, AND FURBITY IN GENEVA.

(DECEMBER 1533 TO JANUARY 1534.)

CHAPTER IV.

THE TOURNAMENT.

(JANUARY TO FEBRUARY 1534.)

CHAPTER V.

THE PLOT.

(JANUARY AND FEBRUARY 1534.)

CHAPTER VI.

A FINAL EFFORT OF ROMAN-CATHOLICISM.

(FEBRUARY 10 TO MARCH 1, 1534.)

CHAPTER VII.

FAREL PREACHES IN THE GRAND AUDITORY OF THE CONVENT AT RIVE.

(MARCH 1 TO APRIL 25, 1534.)

CHAPTER XII.

SENTENCE OF DEATH.

(JULY 1534.)

CHAPTER XIII.

NIGHT OF THIRTY-FIRST OF JULY AT GENEVA.

(JULY 1534.)

CHAPTER XIV.

AN HEROIC RESOLUTION AND A HAPPY DELIVERANCE.

(AUGUST AND SEPTEMBER 1534.)

CHAPTER XV.

THE SUBURBS OF GENEVA ARE DEMOLISHED AND THE ADVERSARIES MAKE READY.

(SEPTEMBER 1534 TO JANUARY 1535.)

CHAPTER XVI.

THE KING OF FRANCE INVITES MELANCHTHON TO RESTORE UNITY AND TRUTH.

(END OF 1534 TO AUGUST 1535.)

CHAPTER XVII.

WILL THE ATTEMPT TO ESTABLISH UNITY AND TRUTH SUCCEED?

(AUGUST TO NOVEMBER 1535.)

CHAPTER XVIII.

THE GOSPEL IN THE NORTH OF ITALY.

(1519 TO 1536.)

CHAPTER XIX.

THE GOSPEL IN THE CENTRE OF ITALY.

(1520 TO 1536.) .

CHAPTER XX.

THE GOSPEL AT NAPLES AND AT ROME.

(1520–1536.)

HISTORY

OF THE

REFORMATION IN EUROPE

IN THE TIME OF CALVIN.

ERRATUM.

Page 626, line 16, *for* and to purify *read* and purify.

ᴛʜᴇ ɴᴀᴛɪᴏɴ ᴀɴᴅ ɪᴛs ᴘᴀʀᴛɪᴇs.

(Aᴜᴛᴜᴍɴ 1529.)

ENGLAND, during the period of which we are about to treat, began to separate from the pope and to reform her Church. In the history of that country the fall of Wolsey divides the old times from the new.

The level of the laity was gradually rising. A certain instruction was given to the children of the poor; the universities were frequented by the upper classes, and the king was probably the most learned prince in Christendom. At the same time the clerical level was falling. The clergy had been weakened and corrupted by its triumphs, and the English, awakening with the age and opening their eyes at last, were

HISTORY

OF THE

REFORMATION IN EUROPE

IN THE TIME OF CALVIN.

BOOK VI.

ENGLAND BEGINS TO CAST OFF THE PAPACY.

CHAPTER I.

THE NATION AND ITS PARTIES.

(AUTUMN 1529.)

ENGLAND, during the period of which we are about to treat, began to separate from the pope and to reform her Church. In the history of that country the fall of Wolsey divides the old times from the new.

The level of the laity was gradually rising. A certain instruction was given to the children of the poor; the universities were frequented by the upper classes, and the king was probably the most learned prince in Christendom. At the same time the clerical level was falling. The clergy had been weakened and corrupted by its triumphs, and the English, awakening with the age and opening their eyes at last, were

disgusted with the pride, ignorance, and disorders of
the priests.

While France, flattered by Rome calling her its
eldest daughter, desired even when reforming her doctrine to preserve union with the papacy; the Anglo-
Saxon race, jealous of their liberties, desired to form
a Church at once national and independent, yet remaining faithful to the doctrines of Catholicism.
Henry VIII. is the personification of that tendency,
which did not disappear with him, and of which it
would not be difficult to discover traces even in later
days.

Other elements calculated to produce a better reformation existed at that time in England. The Holy
Scriptures, translated, studied, circulated, and preached
since the fourteenth century by Wickliffe and his
disciples, became in the sixteenth century, by the publication of Erasmus's Testament and the translations
of Tyndale and Coverdale, the powerful instrument of
a real evangelical revival, and created the scriptural
reformation.

These early developments did not proceed from
Calvin, he was too young at that time; but Tyndale,
Fryth, Latimer, and the other evangelists of the reign
of Henry VIII., taught by the same Word as the reformer of Geneva, were his brethren and his precursors. Somewhat later, his books and his letters to Edward VI., to the regent, to the primate, to Sir W. Cecil
and others, exercised an indisputable influence over
the reformation of England. We find in those letters
proofs of the esteem which the most intelligent persons of the kingdom felt for that simple and strong
man, whom even non-protestant voices in France

have declared to be 'the greatest Christian of his age.'*

A religious reformation may be of two kinds: internal or evangelical, external or legal. The evangelical reformation began at Oxford and Cambridge almost at the same time as in Germany. The legal reformation was making a beginning at Westminster and Whitehall. Students, priests, and laymen, moved by inspiration from on high, had inaugurated the first; Henry VIII. and his parliament were about to inaugurate the second, with hands occasionally somewhat rough. England began with the spiritual reformation, but the other had its motives too. Those who are charmed by the reformation of Germany sometimes affect contempt for that of England. 'A king impelled by his passions was its author,' they say. We have placed the scriptural part of this great transformation in the first rank; but we confess that for it to lay hold upon the people in the sixteenth century, it was necessary, as the prophet declared, that kings should be its nursing-fathers, and queens its nursing-mothers.† If diverse reforms were necessary, if by the side of German cordiality, Swiss simplicity and other characteristics, God willed to found a protestantism possessing a strong hand and an outstretched arm; if a nation was to exist which with great freedom and power should carry the Gospel to the ends of the world, special tools were required to form that robust organisation, and the leaders of the people—the commons, lords, and king—were each to play their part. France had

---

* These letters will be found in Bonnet's *Lettres Françaises de Calvin*, i. pp. 261, 305, 332, 345, 374. *Zurich Letters*, ii. pp. 70, 785, &c.
† Isaiah xlix. 23.

nothing like this: both princes and parliaments opposed the reform ; and thence partly arises the difference between those two great nations, for France had
in Calvin a mightier reformer than any of those whom
England possessed.   But let us not forget that we are
speaking of the sixteenth century.   Since then the
work has advanced; important changes have been
wrought in Christendom ; political society is growing daily more distinct from religious society, and
more independent; and we willingly say with Pascal,
' Glorious is the state of the Church when it is supported by God alone !'

Two opposing elements—the reforming liberalism
of the people, and the almost absolute power of the
king—combined in England to accomplish the legal
reformation.   In that singular island these two rival
forces were often seen acting together ; the liberalism
of the nation gaining certain victories, the despotism
of the prince gaining others; king and people agreeing
to make mutual concessions.   In the midst of these
compromises, the little evangelical flock, which had no
voice in such matters, religiously preserved the treasure entrusted to it : the Word of God, truth, liberty,
and christian virtue.   From all these elements sprang
the Church of England.   A strange Church some call it.
Strange indeed, for there is none which corresponds so
imperfectly in theory with the ideal of the Church, and,
perhaps, none whose members work out with more
power and grandeur the ends for which Christ has
formed his kingdom.

Scarcely had Henry VIII. refused to go to Rome to
plead his cause, when he issued writs for a new parliament (25th September, 1529).   Wolsey's unpopularity

had hitherto prevented its meeting: now the force of circumstances constrained the king to summon it. When he was on the eve of separating from the pope, he felt the necessity of leaning on the people. Liberty is always the gainer where a country performs an act of independence with regard to Rome. Permission being granted in England that the Holy Scriptures should regulate matters of religion, it was natural that permission should also be given to the people and their representatives to regulate matters of state. The whole kingdom was astir, and the different parties became more distinct.

The papal party was alarmed. Fisher, bishop of Rochester, already very uneasy, became disturbed at seeing laymen called upon to give their advice on religious matters. Men's minds were in a ferment in the bishop's palace, the rural parsonage, and the monk's cell. The partisans of Rome met and consulted about what was to be done, and retired from their conferences foreseeing and imagining nothing but defeat. Du Bellay, at that time bishop of Bayonne, and afterwards of Paris, envoy from the King of France, and eye-witness of all this agitation, wrote to Montmorency: 'I fancy that in this parliament the priests will have a terrible fright.'[*] Ambitious ecclesiastics were beginning to understand that the clerical character, hitherto so favourable to their advancement in a political career, would now be an obstacle to them. 'Alas!' exclaimed one of them, 'we must off with our frocks.'[†]

Such of the clergy, however, as determined to

---

[*] Le Grand, *Preuves du Divorce*, p. 378.

[†] 'Il nous faudra jeter le froc aux orties.'—Ibid.

remain faithful to Rome gradually roused themselves.
A prelate put himself at their head. Fisher, bishop
of Rochester, was learned, intelligent, bold, and
slightly fanatical; but his convictions were sincere,
and he was determined to sacrifice everything for the
maintenance of catholicism in England. Though discontented with the path upon which his august pupil
King Henry had entered, he did not despair of the future, and candidly applied to the papacy our Saviour's
words: *The gates of hell shall not prevail against it.*

A recent act of the king's increased Fisher's hopes:
Sir Thomas More had been appointed chancellor.
The Bishop of Rochester regretted indeed that the
king had not given that office to an ecclesiastic, as
was customary; but he thought to himself that a layman wholly devoted to the Church, as the new chancellor was, might possibly in those strange times be
more useful to it than a priest. With Fisher in the
Church, and More in the State (for Sir Thomas, in
spite of his gentle *Utopia*, was more papistical and
more violent than Wolsey), had the papacy anything
to fear? The whole Romish party rallied round these
two men, and with them prepared to fight against
the Reformation.

Opposed to this hierarchical party was the political
party, in whose eyes the king's will was the supreme
rule. The dukes of Norfolk and Suffolk, president
and vice-president of the Council, Sir William Fitz-
William, lord-admiral, and those who agreed with
them, were opposed to the ecclesiastical domination,
not from the love of true religion, but because they
believed the prerogatives of the State were endangered
by the ambition of the priests, or else because, seeking

honour and power for themselves, they were impatient at always encountering insatiable clerks on their path.

Between these two parties a third appeared, on whom the bishops and nobles looked with disdain, but with whom the victory was to rest at last. In the towns and villages of England, and especially in London, were to be found many lowly men, animated with a new life—poor artisans, weavers, cobblers, painters, shopkeepers—who believed in the Word of God and had received moral liberty from it. During the day they toiled at their respective occupations ; but at night they stole along some narrow lane, slipped into a court, and ascended to some upper room in which other persons had already assembled. There they read the Scriptures and prayed. At times even during the day, they might be seen carrying to well-disposed citizens certain books strictly prohibited by the late cardinal. Organised under the name of ' The Society of Christian Brethren,' they had a central committee in London and missionaries everywhere, who distributed the Holy Scriptures and explained their lessons in simple language. Several priests, both in the city and country, belonged to their society.

This Christian brotherhood exercised a powerful influence over the people, and was beginning to substitute the spiritual and life-giving principles of the Gospel for the legal and theocratic ideas of popery. These pious men required a moral regeneration in their hearers, and entreated them to enter, through faith in the Saviour, into an intimate relation with God, without having recourse to the mediation of the clergy ; and those who listened to them, enraptured at hearing of truth, grace, morality, liberty, and of the Word of God, took the teachings to heart. Thus began a new era. It has been asserted that the Reformation entered England by a back-door. Not so; it was the true door these missionaries opened, having even prior to the rupture with Rome preached the doctrine of Christ.* Idly do men speak of Henry's passions, the intrigues of his courtiers, the parade of his ambassadors, the skill of his ministers, the complaisance of the clergy, and the vacillations of parliament: we too shall speak of these things; but above them all there was something else, something better—the thirst exhibited in this island for the Word of God, and the internal transformation accomplished in the convictions of a great number of its inhabitants. This it was that worked such a powerful revolution in British society.

In the interval between the issuing of the writs and the meeting of parliament, the most antagonistic opinions came out. Conversation everywhere turned on present and future events, and there was a general feeling that the country was on the eve of great changes. The members of parliament who arrived in London gathered round the same table to discuss the questions of the day. The great lords gave sumptuous banquets, at which the guests talked about the abuses of the Church, of the approaching session of parliament, and of what might result from it.† One would mention some striking instance of the avarice of the priests; another slyly called to mind the strange privilege which permitted them to commit with impunity

---

* 'Certain preachers who presumed to preach openly or secretly in a manner contrary to the catholic faith.'—Foxe, *Acts*, iv. p. 677.

† Le Grand, *Preuves du Divorce*, Du Bellay to Montmorency, p. 374.

certain sins which they punished severely in others. 'There are, even in London, houses of ill-fame for the use of priests, monks, and canons.* And,' added others, 'they would force us to take such men as these for our guides to heaven.' Du Bellay, the French ambassador, a man of letters, who, although a bishop, had attached Rabelais to his person in the quality of secretary, was frequently invited to parties given by the great lords. He lent an attentive ear, and was astonished at the witty and often very biting remarks uttered by the guests against the disorders of the priests. One day a voice exclaimed: 'Since Wolsey has fallen, we must forthwith regulate the condition of the Church and of its ministers. We will seize their property.' Du Bellay on his return home did not fail to communicate these things to Montmorency: 'I have no need,' he says, 'to write this strange language in cipher; for the noble lords utter it at open table. I think they will do something to be talked about.' †

The leading members of the Commons held more serious meetings with one another. They said they had spoken enough, and that now they must act. They specified the abuses they would claim to have redressed, and prepared petitions for reform to be presented to the king.

Before long the movement descended from the sphere of the nobility to that of the people: a sphere always important, and particularly when a social revolution is in progress. Petty tradesmen and artisans spoke

---

* 'Communis pronuba inter presbyteros, fratres, monacos et canonicos.' —Hall, *Criminal Causes*, p. 28.

† 'Je crois qu'ils vont faire de beaux miracles.'—Le Grand, *Preuves*, p. 374.

more energetically than the lords. They did more than speak. The apparitor of the Bishop of London having entered the shop of a mercer in the ward of St. Bride, and left a summons on the counter calling upon him to pay a certain clerical tax, the indignant tradesman took up his yard-measure, whereupon the officer drew his sword, and then, either from fear or an evil conscience, ran away. The mercer followed him, assaulted him in the street, and broke his head. The London shopkeepers did not yet quite understand the representative system; they used their staves when they should have waited for the speeches of the members of parliament.

The king tolerated this agitation because it forwarded his purposes. There were advisers who insinuated that it was dangerous to give free course to the passions of the people; and that the English, combining great physical strength with a decided character, might go too far in the way of reform, if their prince gave them the rein. But Henry VIII. possessing an energetic will, thought it would be easy for him to check the popular ebullition whenever he pleased. When Jupiter frowned, all Olympus trembled.

CHAPTER II.

PARLIAMENT AND ITS GRIEVANCES.

(NOVEMBER 1529.)

ON the morning of the 3rd of November, Henry went in his barge to the palace of Bridewell; and, having put on the magnificent robes employed on great ceremonies, and followed by the lords of his train, he proceeded to the Blackfriars church, in which the members of the new parliament had assembled. After hearing the mass of the Holy Ghost, king, lords, and commons met in parliament; when, as soon as the king had taken his seat on the throne, the new chancellor, Sir Thomas More, explained the reason of their being summoned. Thomas Audley, chancellor of the Duchy of Lancaster, was appointed Speaker of the lower house.

Generally speaking, parliament confined itself to passing the resolutions of the government.   The Great Charter had, indeed, been long in existence, but until now it had been little more than a dead letter.   The Reformation gave it life.   'Christ brings us out of bondage into liberty by means of the Gospel,' said Calvin.*   This emancipation, which was essentially spiritual, soon extended to other spheres, and gave an impulse to liberty throughout all Christendom.

* In Johannem, viii. 36.

Even in England such an impulse was needed. Under the Plantagenets and the Tudors the constitutional machine existed, but it worked only as it was directed by the strong hand of the master. Without the Reformation, England might have slumbered long.

The impulse given by religious truth to the latent liberties of the people was felt for the first time in the parliament of 1529. The representatives shared the lively feelings of their constituents, and took their seats with the firm resolve to introduce the necessary reforms in the affairs of both Church and State. Indeed, on the very first day several members pointed out the abuses of the clerical domination, and proposed to lay the desires of the people before the king.

The Commons might of their own accord have applied to the task, and by proposing rash changes have given the Reform a character of violence that might have worked confusion in the State; but they preferred petitioning the king to take the necessary measures to carry out the wishes of the nation; and accordingly a petition respectfully worded, but in clear and strong language, was agreed to. The Reformation began in England, as in Switzerland and in Germany, with personal conversions. The individual was reformed first; but it was necessary for the people to reform afterwards, and the measures requisite to success could not be taken in the sixteenth century without the participation of the governing powers. Freely therefore and nobly a whole nation was about to express to their ruler their grievances and wishes.

On one of the first days of the session, the Speaker and certain members who had been ordered to accompany him proceeded to the palace. 'Your highness,' they began, 'of late much discord, variance, and debate hath arisen, and more and more daily is likely to increase and ensue amongst your subjects, to the great inquietation, vexation, and breach of your peace, of which the chief causes followingly do ensue.'*

This opening could not fail to excite the king's attention, and the Speaker of the House of Commons began boldly to unroll the long list of the grievances of England. 'First, the prelates of your most excellent realm, and the clergy of the same, have in their convocations made many and divers laws without your most royal assent, and without the assent of any of your lay subjects.

'And also many of your said subjects, and specially those that be of the poorest sort, be daily called before the said spiritual ordinaries or their commissaries, on the accusement of light and indiscreet persons, and be excommunicated and put to excessive and impostable charges.

'The prelates suffer the priests to exact divers sums of money for the sacraments, and sometimes deny the same without the money be first paid.

'Also the said spiritual ordinaries do daily confer and give sundry benefices unto certain young folks, calling them their nephews or kinsfolk, being in their minority and within age, not apt nor able to serve the cure of any such benefice . . . whereby the said ordinaries accumulate to themselves large sums of money, and the poor silly souls of your people perish without doctrine or any good teaching.

* MS. petition in Record Office: Froude, *History of England*, i. pp. 208, 214.

' Also a great number of holydays be kept throughout this your realm, upon the which many great,
abominable, and execrable vices, idle and wanton
sports be used, which holydays might by your majesty be made fewer in number.

' And also the said spiritual ordinaries commit
divers of your subjects to ward, before they know
either the cause of their imprisonment, or the name
of their accuser.' *

Thus far the Commons had confined themselves to
questions that had been discussed more than once ;
they feared to touch upon the subject of heresy before
the Defender of the Roman Faith. But there were
evangelical men among their number who had been
eye-witnesses of the sufferings of the reformed. At
the peril, therefore, of offending the king, the Speaker
boldly took up the defence of the pretended heretics.

' If heresy be ordinarily laid unto the charge of the
person accused, the said ordinaries put to them such
subtle interrogatories concerning the high mysteries
of our faith, as are able quickly to trap a simple unlearned layman. And if any heresy be so confessed
in word, yet never committed in thought or deed,
they put the said person to make his purgation. And
if the party so accused deny the accusation, witnesses
of little truth or credence are brought forth for the
same, and deliver the party so accused to secular
hands.'

The Speaker was not satisfied with merely pointing
out the disease : ' We most humbly beseech your
Grace, in whom the only remedy resteth, of your good-

---

* Petition of the Commons : Froude's *England*, i. pp. 208–216.

ness to consent, so that besides the fervent love your Highness shall thereby engender in the hearts of all your Commons towards your Grace, ye shall do the most princely feat, and show the most charitable precedent that ever did sovereign lord upon his subjects.'

The king listened to the petition with his characteristic dignity, and also with a certain kindliness. He recognised the just demands in the petition of the Commons, and saw how far they would support the religious independence to which he aspired. Still, unwilling to take the part of heresy, he selected only the most crying abuses, and desired his faithful Commons to take their correction upon themselves. He then sent the petition to the bishops, requiring them to answer the charges brought against them, and added that henceforward his consent would be necessary to give the force of law to the acts of Convocation.

This royal communication was a thunderbolt to the prelates. What! the bishops, the successors of the apostles, accused by the representatives of the nation, and requested by the king to justify themselves like criminals! . . . Had the Commons of England forgotten what a priest was? These proud ecclesiastics thought only of the indelible virtues which, in their view, ordination had conferred upon them, and shut their eyes to the vices of their fallible human nature. We can understand their emotion, their embarrassment, and their anger. The Reformation which had made the tour of the Continent was at the gates of England; the king was knocking at their doors. What was to be done? they could not tell. They assembled,

and read the petition again and again.   The Archbishop
of Canterbury, and the bishops of London, Lincoln,
St. Asaph, and Rochester carped at it and replied to
it.   They would willingly have thrown it into the
fire—the best of answers in their opinion; but the
king was waiting, and the Archbishop of Canterbury
was commissioned to enlighten him.

Warham did not belong to the most fanatical party;
he was a prudent man, and the wish for reform had
hardly taken shape in England when, being uneasy
and timid, he had hastened to give a certain satisfaction to his flock by reforming abuses which he had
sanctioned for thirty years.*   But he was a priest, a
Romish priest; he represented an inflexible hierarchy.
Strengthened by the clamours of his colleagues, he
resolved to utter the famous *non possumus*, less
powerful, however, in England than in Rome.

'Sire,' he said, ' your Majesty's Commons reproach
us with uncharitable behaviour. . . . On the contrary, we love them with hearty affection, and have
only exercised the spiritual jurisdiction of the Church
upon persons infected with the pestilent poison of
heresy.   To have peace with such had been against
the Gospel of our Saviour Christ, wherein he saith,
I came not to send peace, but a sword.

'Your Grace's Commons complain that the clergy
daily do make laws repugnant to the statutes of your
realm.   We take our authority from the Scriptures of
God, and shall always diligently apply to conform our
statutes thereto; and we pray that your Highness
will, with the assent of your people, temper your

---

* 'Within these ten weeks, I reformed many other things.'—Froude,
i. 233, *Reply of the Bishops.*

Grace's laws accordingly; whereby shall ensue a most sure and hearty conjunction and agreement.

'They accuse us of committing to prison before conviction such as be suspected of heresy. . . . Truth it is that certain apostates, friars, monks, lewd priests, bankrupt merchants, vagabonds, and idle fellows of corrupt intent have embraced the abominable opinions lately sprung up in Germany; and by them some have been seduced in simplicity and ignorance. Against these, if judgment has been exercised according to the laws of the Church, we be without blame.

'They complain that two witnesses be admitted, be they never so defamed, to vex and trouble your subjects to the peril of their lives, shames, costs, and expenses. . . . To this we reply, the judge must esteem the quality of the witness, but in heresy no exception is necessary to be considered, if their tale be likely. This is the universal law of Christendom, and hath universally done good.

'They say that we give benefices to our nephews and kinsfolk, being in young age or infants, and that we take the profit of such benefices for the time of the minority of our said kinsfolk. If it be done to our own use and profit, it is not well; but if it be bestowed to the bringing up and use of the same parties, or applied to the maintenance of God's service, we do not see but that it may be allowed.'

As for the irregular lives of the priests, the prelates remarked that they were condemned by the laws of the Church, and consequently there was nothing to be said on that point.

Lastly, the bishops seized the opportunity of taking

the offensive: 'We entreat your Grace to repress heresy. This we beg of you, lowly upon our knees, so entirely as we can.'*

Such was the brief of Roman Catholicism in England. Its defence would have sufficed to condemn it.

* *The Answer of the Ordinaries.* Record Office MS. Froude, i. p. 225.

CHAPTER III.

REFORMS.

(END OF 1529.)

THE answer of the bishops was criticised in the royal residence, in the House of Commons, at the meetings of the burgesses, in the streets of the capital, and in the provinces, everywhere exciting a lively indignation. 'What!' said they, 'the bishops accuse the most pious and active Christians of England— men like Bilney, Fryth, Tyndale, and Latimer—of that idleness and irregularity of which their monks and priests are continually showing us examples. To no purpose have the Commons indisputably proved their grievances, if the bishops reply to notorious facts by putting forward their scholastic system. We condemn their practice, and they take shelter behind their theories; as if the reproach laid against them was not precisely that their lives are in opposition to their laws. "The fault is not in the Church," they say. But it is its ministers that we accuse.'

The indignant parliament boldly took up the axe, attacked the tree, and cut off the withered and rotten branches. One bill followed another, irritating the clergy, but filling the people with joy. When the legacy dues were under discussion, one of the members drew a touching picture of the avarice and cruelty of the priests. 'They have no compassion,' he said; 'the children of the dead should all die of hunger and go begging, rather than they would of charity give to them the silly cow which the dead man owed, if he had only one.' There was a movement of indignation in the house, and they forbade the clergy to take any mortuary fees when the effects were small.

'And that is not all,' said another; 'the clergy monopolise large tracts of land, and the poor are compelled to pay an extravagant price for whatever they buy. They are everything in the world but preachers of God's Word and shepherds of souls. They buy and sell wool, cloth, and other merchandise; they keep tanneries and breweries. . . . How can they attend to their spiritual duties in the midst of such occupations?' The clergy were consequently prohibited from holding large estates or carrying on the business of merchant, tanner, brewer, &c. At the same time plurality of benefices (some ignorant priests holding as many as ten or twelve) was forbidden, and residence was enforced. The Commons further enacted that any one seeking a dispensation for non-residence (even were the application made to the pope himself) should be liable to a heavy fine.

The clergy saw at last that they must reform. They forbade priests from keeping shops and taverns, playing at dice or other games of chance, passing through towns and villages with hawks and hounds, being present at unbecoming entertainments, and spending the night

* Foxe, *Acts*, iv. p. 611.

in suspected houses.* Convocation proceeded to enact severe penalties against these disorders, doubling them for adultery, and tripling them for incest. The laity asked how it was that the Church had waited so long before coming to this resolution; and whether these scandals had become criminal only because the Commons condemned them?

But the bishops who reformed the lower clergy did not intend to resign their own privileges. One day when a bill relating to wills was laid before the upper house, the Archbishop of Canterbury and all the other prelates frowned, murmured, and looked uneasily around them.† They exclaimed that the Commons were heretics and schismatics, and almost called them infidels and atheists. In all places, good men required that morality should again be united with religion; and that piety should not be made to consist merely in certain ceremonies, but in the awakening of the conscience, a lively faith, and holy conduct. The bishops, not discerning that God's work was then being accomplished in the world, determined to maintain the ancient order of things at all risks.

Their efforts had some chance of success, for the House of Lords was essentially conservative. The Bishop of Rochester, a sincere but narrow-minded man, presuming on the respect inspired by his age and character, boldly came forward as the defender of the Church. 'My lords,' he said, 'these bills have no other object than the destruction of the

---

* 'Quod non pernoctent in locis suspectis. Mulierum colloquia suspecta nullatenus habeant.'—Wilkins, *Concilia*, iii. pp. 717, 722, &c.

† 'The Archbishop of Canterbury and all the bishops began to frown and grunt.'—Foxe, *Acts*, iv. p. 612.

Church; and if the Church goes down, all the glory
of the kingdom will fall with it.   Remember what
happened to the Bohemians.   Like them, our Commons cry out, "Down with the Church!"   Whence
cometh that cry?   Simply from lack of faith. . . .
My lords, save the country, save the Church.'

This speech made the Commons very indignant;
some members thought the bishop denied that they
were Christians.   They sent thirty of their leading
men to the king.   ' Sire,' said the Speaker, ' it is an
attaint upon the honour of your Majesty to calumniate
before the upper house those whom your subjects
have elected.   They are accused of lack of faith, that
is to say, they are no better than Turks, Saracens,
and heathens.   Be pleased to call before you the
bishop who has insulted your Commons.'

The king made a gracious reply, and immediately
sent one of his officers to invite the Archbishop of
Canterbury, the Bishop of Rochester, and six other
prelates to appear before him.   They came quite uneasy as to what the prince might have to say to them.
They knew that, like all the Plantagenets, Henry VIII.
would not suffer his clergy to resist him.   Immediately the king informed them of the complaint
made by the Commons, their hearts sank and they
lost courage.   They thought only how to escape the
prince's anger, and the most venerated among them,
Fisher, having recourse to falsehood, asserted that
when speaking about ' lack of faith,' he had not thought
of the Commons of England, but of the Bohemians
only.   The other prelates confirmed this inadmissible
interpretation.   This was a graver fault than the
fault itself, and the unbecoming evasion was a defeat

to the clerical party from which they never recovered. The king allowed the excuse, but he afterwards made the bishops feel the little esteem he entertained for them. As for the House of Commons, it loudly expressed the disdain aroused in them by the bishops' subterfuge.

One chance of safety still remained to them. Mixed committees of the two houses examined the resolutions of the Commons. The peers, especially the ecclesiastical peers, opposed the reform by appealing to usage. ' Usage ! ' ironically observed a Gray's-inn lawyer; ' the usage hath ever been of thieves to rob on Shooter's Hill, *ergo* it is lawful and ought to be kept up ! ' This remark sorely irritated the prelates; ' What ! our acts are compared to robberies ! ' But the lawyer, addressing the Archbishop of Canterbury, seriously endeavoured to prove to him that the exactions of the clergy in the matter of probates and mortuaries were open robbery. The temporal lords gradually adopted the opinions of the Commons.

In the midst of these debates, the king did not lose sight of his own interests. Six years before, he had raised a loan among his subjects; he thought parliament ought to relieve him of this debt. This demand was opposed by the members most devoted to the principle of the Reformation ; John Petit, in particular, the friend of Bilney and Tyndale, said in parliament : ' I give the king all I lent him; but I cannot give him what others have lent him.' Henry was not however discouraged, and finally obtained the act required.

The king soon showed that he was pleased with the Commons. Two bills met with a stern opposition

from the Lords; they were those abolishing plural-
ism and non-residence. These two customs were so
convenient and advantageous that the clergy determined not to give them up. Henry, seeing that the
two houses would never agree, resolved to cut the
difficulty. At his desire eight members from each
met one afternoon in the Star Chamber. There was
an animated discussion; but the lay lords, who were
in the conference, taking part with the Commons, the
bishops were forced to yield. The two bills passed
the Lords the next day, and received the king's assent.
After this triumph the king adjourned parliament in
the middle of December.

The different reforms that had been carried through
were important, but they were not the Reformation.
Many abuses were corrected, but the doctrines remained unaltered; the power of the clergy was
restricted, but the authority of Christ was not increased; the dry branches of the tree had been
lopped off, but a scion calculated to bear good fruit
had not been grafted on the wild stock. Had
matters stopped here, we might perhaps have obtained a Church with morals less repulsive, but not
with a holy doctrine and a new life. But the Reformation was not contented with more decorous forms,
it required a second creation.

At the same time parliament had taken a great
stride towards the revolution that was to transform the
Church. A new power had taken its place in the
world: the laity had triumphed over the clergy. No
doubt there were upright catholics who gave their
assent to the laws passed in 1529; but these laws were
nevertheless a product of the Reformation. This it

was that had inspired the laity with that new energy,
parliament with that bold action, and given the liberties of the nation that impulse which they had wanted
hitherto.   The joy was great throughout the kingdom; and while the king removed to Greenwich to
keep Christmas there 'with great plenty of viands,
and disguisings and interludes,' the members of the
Commons were welcomed in the towns and villages
with public rejoicings.*   In the people's eyes their representatives were like soldiers who had just gained a
brilliant victory.   The clergy, alone in all England,
were downcast and exasperated.   On returning to
their residences the bishops could not conceal their
anguish at the danger of the Church.†   The priests,
who had been the first victims offered up on the altar
of reform, bent their heads.   But if the clergy foresaw days of mourning, the laity hailed with joy the
glorious era of the liberties of the people, and of the
greatness of England.   The friends of the Reformation went further still: they believed that the
Gospel would work a complete change in the world,
and talked, as Tyndale informs us, 'as though the
golden age would come again.'‡

* Foxe, *Acts*, iv. p. 614.
† 'The great displeasure of spiritual persons.'—Ibid.
‡ Tyndale's *Works*, i. p. 481.

CHAPTER IV.

ANNE BOLEYN'S FATHER BEFORE THE EMPEROR AND THE POPE.

(WINTER OF 1530.)

BEFORE such glorious hopes could be realised, it was necessary to emancipate Great Britain from the yoke of Romish supremacy. This was the end to which all generous minds aspired; but would the king assist them?

Henry VIII. united strength of body with strength of will: both were marked on his manly form. Lively, active, eager, vehement, impatient, and voluptuous—whatever he was, he was with his whole soul. He was at first all heart for the Church of Rome; he went barefoot on pilgrimages, wrote against Luther, and flattered the pope. But before long he grew tired of Rome without desiring the Reformation: profoundly selfish, he cared for himself alone. If the papal domination offended him, evangelical liberty annoyed him. He meant to remain master in his own house, the only master, and master of all. Even without the divorce, Henry would possibly have separated from Rome. Rather than endure any contradiction, this singular man put to death friends and enemies, bishops and missionaries, ministers of state and favourites—even his wives. Such was the prince whom the Reformation found king of England.

History would be unjust, however, were it to maintain that passion alone urged him to action. The question of the succession to the throne had for a century filled the country with confusion and blood. This Henry could not forget. Would the struggles of the Two Roses be renewed after his death, occasioning perhaps the destruction of an ancient monarchy? If Mary, a princess of delicate health, should die, Scotland, France, the party of the White Rose, the Duke of Suffolk, whose wife was Henry's sister, might drag the kingdom into endless wars. And even if Mary's days were prolonged, her title to the crown might be disputed, no female sovereign having as yet sat upon the throne. Another train of ideas also occupied the king's mind. He enquired sincerely whether his marriage with the widow of his brother was lawful. Even before its consummation, he had felt doubts about it. But even his defenders, if there are any, must acknowledge that one circumstance contributed at this time to give unusual force to these scruples. Passion impelled the king to break a holy bond: he loved another woman.

Catholic writers imagine that this guilty motive was the only one: it is a mistake, for the two former indisputably occupied Henry's mind. As for parliament and people, the king's love for Anne Boleyn affected them very little: it was the reason of state which made them regard the divorce as just and necessary.*

A congress was at that time sitting at Bologna with

---

* 'All indifferent and discreet persons judged that it was right and necessary.'—Hall, *Chronicles of England*, p. 784.

great pomp.* On the 5th of November, Charles V. having arrived from Spain, had entered the city, attended by a magnificent suite, and followed by 20,000 soldiers. He was covered with gold, and shone with grace and majesty. The pope waited for him in front of the church of San Petronio, seated on a throne and wearing the triple crown. The emperor, master of Italy, which his soldiers had reduced to the last desolation,† fell prostrate before the pontiff, but lately his prisoner. The union of these two monarchs, both enemies of Henry VIII., seemed destined to ruin the King of England and thwart his great affair.

And yet not long before, an ambassador from Charles V. had been received at Whitehall: it was Master Eustace Chappuis, who had already discharged a mission to Geneva.‡ He came to solicit aid against the Turks. Henry caught at the chance: he imagined the moment to be favourable, and that he ought to despatch an embassy to the head of the empire and the head of the Church. He sent for the Earl of Wiltshire, Anne Boleyn's father; Edward Lee, afterwards archbishop of York; Stokesley, afterwards bishop of London, and some others. He told them that the emperor desired his alliance, and commissioned them to proceed to Italy and explain to Charles V. the serious motives that induced him to separate from Catherine. 'If he persists in his opposition to the divorce,' continued Henry, 'threaten him, but in covert terms. If the threats prove useless, tell him plainly

---

* 'Congressus iste magna cum pompa fiet.'—*State Papers*, vii. p. 209. We must not confound this congress with the one held later in this city. See antea, vol. ii. book ii. chap. xxv. xxvi. xxix.

† Letter from Sir H. Carew to Henry VIII.: *State Papers*, vii. 225.

‡ Antea, vol. i. ch. ix.

that, in accord with my friends, I will do all I can to restore peace to my troubled conscience.' He added with more calmness: 'I am resolved to fear God rather than man, and to place full reliance on comfort from the Saviour.'* Was Henry sincere when he spoke thus? No one can doubt of his sensuality, his scholastic catholicism, and his cruel violence: must we also believe in his hypocrisy? He was no doubt under a delusion, and deceived himself on the state of his soul.

An important member was added to the deputation. One day when the king was occupied with this affair, Thomas Cranmer appeared at the door of his closet with a manuscript in his hand. Cranmer had a fine understanding, a warm heart, a character perhaps too weak, but extensive learning. Captivated by the Holy Scriptures, he desired to seek for truth nowhere else. He had suggested a new point of view to Henry VIII. 'The essential thing,' he said, 'is to know what the Word of God teaches on the matter in question.' 'Show me that,' exclaimed the king. Cranmer brought him his treatise, in which he proved that the Word of God is above all human jurisdiction, and that it forbids marriage with a brother's widow. Henry took the work in his hand, read it again and again, and praised its excellence. A bright idea occurred to him. 'Are you strong enough to maintain before the bishop of Rome the propositions laid down in this treatise?' said the king. Cranmer was timid, but convinced and devoted. 'Yes,' he made answer, 'with God's grace, and if your Majesty commands it.' 'Marry, then,' exclaimed Henry with delight,

* Instruction to Wiltshire : *State Papers*, vii. p. 230.

' I will send you.'* Cranmer departed with the others
in January 1530.

While Henry's ambassadors were journeying slowly,
Charles V., more exasperated than ever against the
divorce, endeavoured to gain the pope.   Clement
VII., who was a clever man, and possessed a certain
kindly humour, but was at heart cunning, false, and
cowardly, amused the puissant emperor with words.
When he learnt that the King of England was sending
an embassy to him, he gave way to the keenest sorrow.
What was he to do? which way could he turn ?   To
irritate the emperor was dangerous ; to separate England from Rome would be to endure a great loss.
Caught between Charles V. and Henry VIII., he
groaned aloud: he paced up and down his chamber
gesticulating ; then suddenly stopping, sank into a
chair and burst into tears.   Nothing succeeded with
him : it was, he thought, as if he had been bewitched.
What need was there for the King of England to send
him an embassy ?   Had not Clement told Henry
through the Bishop of Tarbes : ' I am content the
marriage should take place, provided it be without
my authorisation.' †   It was of no use : the pope
asked him to do without the papacy, and the king
would only act with it.   He was more popish than
the pope.

To add to his misfortunes, Charles began to press
the pontiff more seriously, and yielding to his impor-
tunities, Clement drew up a brief on the 7th of March,
in which he commanded Henry ' to receive Catherine
with love, and to treat her in all things with the

---

* Foxe, *Acts*, viii. p. 9.   † Le Grand, *Preuves*, p. 400.

affection of a husband.' * But the brief was scarcely written when the arrival of the English embassy was announced. The pope in alarm immediately put the document back into his portfolio, promising himself that it would be long before he published it.

As soon as the English envoys had taken up their quarters at Bologna, the ambassadors of France called to pay their respects. De Gramont, bishop of Tarbes, was overflowing with politeness, especially to the Earl of Wiltshire. ' I have shown much honour to M. de Rochford,' he wrote to his master on the 28th of March. ' I went out to meet him. I have visited him often at his lodging. I have fêted him, and offered him my solicitations and services, telling him that such were your orders.' † Not thus did Clement VII. act : the arrival of the Earl of Wiltshire and his colleagues was a cause of alarm to him. Yet he must make up his mind to receive them : he appointed the day and the hour for the audience.

Henry VIII. desired that his representatives should appear with great pomp, and accordingly the ambassador and his colleagues went to great expense with that intent.‡ Wiltshire entered first into the audience-hall : being father of Anne Boleyn, he had been appointed by the king as the man in all England most interested in the success of his plans. But Henry had calculated badly : the personal interest which the earl felt in the divorce made him odious both to Charles and Clement. The pope, wearing his

* 'Reginam complectendo, affectione maritali tractet in omnibus.'—Le Grand, *Preuves*, p. 451.

† Ibid. p. 399.

‡ 'Esso Conte habi commissione far una grossa spesa.'—*Lettre de Joachim de Vaux*, ibid. p. 409.

pontifical robes, was seated on the throne, surrounded
by his cardinals.   The ambassadors approached, made
the customary salutations, and stood before him.
The pontiff, wishing to show his kindly feelings
towards the envoys of the ' *Defender of the Faith*,' put
out his slipper according to custom, presenting it
graciously to the kisses of those proud Englishmen.
The revolt was about to begin.   The earl, remaining
motionless, refused to kiss his holiness's slipper.   But
that was not all : a fine spaniel, with long silky
hair, which Wiltshire had brought from England, had
followed him to the episcopal palace.   When the
bishop of Rome put out his foot, the dog did what
other dogs would have done under similar circumstances : he flew at the foot, and caught the pope
by the great toe.*   Clement hastily drew it back.
The sublime borders on the ridiculous: the ambassadors, bursting with laughter, raised their arms and
hid their faces behind their long rich sleeves.   ' That
dog was a *protestant*,' said a reverend father.   ' Whatever he was,' said an Englishman, ' he taught us
that a pope's foot was more meet to be bitten by
dogs than kissed by Christian men.'   The pope, recovering from his emotion, prepared to listen, and the
count, regaining his seriousness, explained to the
pontiff that as Holy Scripture forbade a man to marry
his brother's wife, Henry VIII. required him to annul
as unlawful his union with Catherine of Aragon.   As
Clement did not seem convinced, the ambassador skilfully insinuated that the king might possibly declare
himself independent of Rome, and place the British

* ' The spaniel took fast with his mouth the great toe of the pope.'—
Foxe, *Acts*, viii. p. 9.

Church under the direction of a patriarch. 'The example,' added the ambassador, 'will not fail to be imitated by other kingdoms of Christendom.' *

The agitated pope promised not to remove the suit to Rome, provided the king would give up the idea of reforming England. Then, putting on a most gracious air, he proposed to introduce the ambassador to Charles V. This was giving Wiltshire the chance of receiving a harsh rebuff. The earl saw it; but his duty obliging him to confer with the emperor, he accepted the offer.

The father of Anne Boleyn proceeded to an audience with the nephew of Catherine of Aragon. Representatives of two women whose rival causes agitated Europe, these two men could not meet without a collision. True, the earl flattered himself that as it was Charles's interest to detach Henry from Francis I., that phlegmatic and politic prince would certainly not sacrifice the gravest interests of his reign for a matter of sentiment; but he was deceived. The emperor received him with a calm and reserved air, but unaccompanied by any kindly demonstration. The ambassador skilfully began with speaking of the Turkish war; then ingeniously passing to the condition of the kingdom of England, he pointed out the reasons of state which rendered the divorce necessary. Here Charles stopped him short: 'Sir Count, you are not to be trusted in this matter; you are a party to it; let your colleagues speak.' The earl replied with respectful coldness: 'Sire, I do not speak here as a father, but as my master's servant,

---

* 'Che l' altri regni questo imitando.'—Le Grand, *Preuves du Divorce,* p. 419.

and I am commissioned to inform you that his conscience condemns a union contrary to the law of
God.' *   He then offered Charles the immediate resti-
tution of Catherine's dowry.   The emperor coldly
replied that he would support his aunt in her rights,
and then abruptly turning his back on the ambassador, refused to hear him any longer.†

Thus did Charles, who had been all his life a crafty
politician, place in this matter the cause of justice
above the interests of his ambition.   Perhaps he
might lose an important ally; it mattered not; before
everything he would protect a woman unworthily
treated.   On this occasion we feel more sympathy for
Charles than for Henry.   The indignant emperor
hastily quitted Bologna on the 22nd or 24th of
February.

The earl hastened to his friend M. de Gramont,
and, relating how he had been treated, proposed that
the kings of France and England should unite in the
closest bonds.   He added, that Henry could not
accept Clement as his judge, since he had himself
declared that he was ignorant of the law of God.‡
'England,' he said, 'will be quiet for three or four
months.   Sitting in the ball-room, she will watch the
dancers, and will form her resolution according as
they dance well or ill.' §   A rule of policy that has
often been followed.

Gramont was prepared to make common cause with
Henry against the emperor ; but, like his master, he

---

* Le Grand, *Preuves*, pp. 401, 454.

† Ibid.

‡ 'He declared himself ignorant of that law.'—*State Papers*, xii. p. 230.

§ Le Grand, *Preuves*, pp. 401, 455.

could not make up his mind to do without the pope. He strove to induce Clement to join the two kings and abandon Charles; or else—he insinuated in his turn—England would separate from the Romish Church. This was to incur the risk of losing Western Europe, and accordingly the pope answered with much concern : 'I will do what you ask.' There was, however, a reserve; namely, that the steps taken overtly by the pope would absolutely decide nothing.

Clement once more received the ambassador of Henry VIII. The earl carried with him the book wherein Cranmer proved that the pope cannot dispense any one from obeying the law of God, and presented it to the pope. The latter took it and glanced over it, his looks showing that a prison could not have been more disagreeable to him than this impertinent volume.* The Earl of Wiltshire soon discovered that there was nothing for him to do in Italy. Charles V., usually so reserved, had made the bitterest remarks before his departure. His chancellor, with an air of triumph, enumerated to the English ambassador all the divines of Italy and France who were opposed to the king's wishes. The pope seemed to be a puppet which the emperor moved as he liked; and the cardinals had but one idea, that of exalting the Romish power. Wearied and disgusted, the earl departed for France and England with the greater portion of his colleagues.

Cranmer was left behind. Having been sent to show Clement that Holy Scripture is above all

* 'A book as welcome to his Holiness as a prison.'—Fuller, *Church History*, p. 182.

Roman pontiffs, and speaks in a language quite opposed to that of the popes, he had asked more than
once for an audience at which to discharge his mission.
The wily pontiff had replied that he would hear him
at Rome, believing he was thus putting him off until
the Greek calends. But Clement was deceived : the
English doctor, determining to do his duty, refused to
depart for London with the rest of the embassy, and
repaired to the metropolis of Catholicism.

CHAPTER V.

DISCUSSIONS CONCERNING THE DIVORCE AT OXFORD AND CAMBRIDGE.

(WINTER OF 1530.)

AT the same time that Henry sent ambassadors to Italy to obtain the pope's consent, he invited all the universities of Christendom to declare that the question of divorce was of divine right, and that the pope had nothing to say about it. It was his opinion that the universal voice of the Church ought to decide, and not the voice of one man.

First he attempted to canvass Cambridge, and as he wanted a skilful man for that purpose, he applied to Wolsey's old servant, Stephen Gardiner, an intelligent, active, wily churchman and a good catholic. One thing alone was superior to his catholicism—his desire to win the king's favour. He aspired to rise like the cardinal to the summit of greatness. Henry named the chief almoner, Edward Fox, as his colleague.

Arriving at Cambridge one Saturday about noon in the latter half of February, the royal commissioners held a conference in the evening with the vice-chancellor (Dr. Buckmaster), Dr. Edmunds, and other influential men who had resolved to go with the court. But these doctors, members of the political

party, soon found themselves checked by an embarrassing support on which they had not calculated :
it was that of the friends of the Gospel. They
had been convinced by the writing which Cranmer
had published on the divorce. Gardiner and the
members of the conference, hearing of the assistance
which the evangelicals desired to give them, were
annoyed at first. On the other hand, the champions of the court of Rome, alarmed at the alliance of
the two parties who were opposed to them, began
that very night to visit college after college, leaving
no stone unturned that the peril might be averted.
Gardiner, uneasy at their zeal, wrote to Henry
VIII.: 'As we assembled they assembled ; as we
made friends they made friends.' *   Dr. Watson, Dr.
Tomson, and other fanatical individuals at one time
shouted very loudly, at another spoke in whispers. †
They said that Anne Boleyn was a heretic, that her
marriage with Henry would hand England over to
Luther ; and they related to those whom they desired
to gain—wrote Gardiner to the king—'many fables,
too tedious to repeat to your Grace.' These 'fables'
would not only have bored Henry, but greatly irritated
him.

The vice-chancellor, flattering himself that he had
a majority, notwithstanding these clamours, called a
meeting of the doctors, bachelors of divinity, and
masters of arts, for Sunday afternoon. About two
hundred persons assembled, and the three parties
were distinctly marked out. The most numerous
and the most excited were those who held for the
pope against the king. The evangelicals were in a

---

* Burnet, *Records,* i.   † 'In the ears of them.'—Ibid. p. 39.

minority, but were quite as decided as their adversaries, and much calmer.   The politicians, uneasy at
seeing the friends of Latimer and Cranmer disposed
to vote with them, would have, however, to accept of
their support, if they wished to gain the victory.
They resolved to seize the opportunity offered them.
'Most learned senators,' said the vice-chancellor,
'I have called you together because the great love
which the king bears you engages me to consult your
wisdom.'   Thereupon Gardiner and Fox handed in
the letter which Henry had given them, and the vice-
chancellor read it to the meeting.   In it the king set
forth his hopes of seeing the doctors unanimous to do
what was agreeable to him.   The deliberations commenced, and the question of a rupture with Rome
soon began to appear distinctly beneath the question
of the divorce.   Edmunds spoke for the king, Tomson
for the pope.   There was an interchange of antagonistic opinions, and a disorder of ideas among many;
the speakers grew warm; one voice drowned another,
and the confusion became extreme.*

The vice-chancellor, desirous of putting an end to
the clamour, proposed referring the matter to a
committee, whose decision should be regarded as that
of the whole university, which was agreed to.   Then
seeing more clearly that the royal cause could not
succeed without the help of the evangelical party, he
proposed some of its leaders—Doctors Salcot, Reps,
Crome, Shaxton, and Latimer—as members of the
committee.   On hearing these names, there was an
explosion of murmurs in the meeting.   Salcot, abbot

---

* 'Et res erat in multa confusione.'—Burnet, *Records*, i. p. 79: Gardiner
to the king.

of St. Benet's, was particularly offensive to the doctors of the Romish party. 'We protest,' they said, 'against the presence in the committee of those who have approved of Cranmer's book, and thus declared their opinion already.' 'When any matter is talked of all over the kingdom,' answered Gardiner, 'there is not a sensible man who does not tell his friends what he thinks about it.' The whole afternoon was spent in lively altercation. The vice-chancellor, wishing to bring it to an end, said: 'Gentlemen, it is getting late, and I invite every one to take his seat, and declare his mind by a secret vote.'* It was useless; no one took his seat; the confusion, reproaches, and declamations continued. At dark, the vice-chancellor adjourned the meeting until the next day. The doctors separated in great excitement, but with different feelings. While the politicians saw nothing else to discuss but the question of the king's marriage, the evangelicals and the papists considered that the real question was this: Which shall rule in England—the Reformation or Popery?

The next day, the names of the members of the committee having been put to the vote, the meeting was found to be divided into two equal parties. In order to obtain a majority Gardiner undertook to get some of his adversaries out of the way. Going up and down the Senate-house, he began to whisper in the ears of some of the less decided; and inspiring them either with hope or fear, he prevailed upon several to leave the meeting.†

* 'To resort to his seat apart, every man's mind to be known secretly.' —Burnet, *Records*, i. p. 80.

† 'To cause some to depart the house.'—Ibid.

The grace was then put to the vote a third
time and passed. Gardiner triumphed. Returning
to his room, he sent the list to the king. Sixteen of
the committee, indicated by the letter A, were favourable to his majesty. 'As for the twelve others,' he
wrote, 'we hope to win most of them by *good means.*'
The committee met and took up the royal demand.
They carefully examined the passages of Holy Scripture, the explanations of translators, and gave their
opinion.* Then followed the public discussion. Gardiner was not without fear: as there might be skilful
assailants and awkward defenders, he looked out for
men qualified to defend the royal cause worthily. It
was a remarkable circumstance that, passing over the
traditional doctors, he added to the defence—of which
he and Fox were the leaders—two evangelical doctors,
Salcot, abbot of St. Benet's, and Reps. He reserved
to his colleague and himself the political part of the
question; but notwithstanding all his catholicism, he
desired that the scriptural reasons should be placed
foremost. The discussion was conducted with great
thoroughness,† and the victory remained with the
king's champions.

On the 9th of March, the doctors, professors, and
masters having met after vespers in the priory hall,
the vice-chancellor said: 'It has appeared to us as
most certain, most in accord with Holy Scripture, and
most conformable to the opinions of commentators,
that it is contrary to divine and natural law for a
man to marry the widow of his brother dying child-

---

* 'S. Scripturæ locorum conferentes, tum etiam interpretum.'—Burnet,
Records, iii. p. 22.

† 'Publicam disputationem matura deliberatione.'—Ibid.

less.'* Thus the Scriptures were really, if not expli-
citly, declared by the university of Cambridge to be
the supreme and only rule of Christians, and the contrary decisions of Rome were held to be not binding.
The Word of God was avenged of the long contempt
it had endured, and after having been put below the
pope's word, was now restored to its lawful place. In
this matter Cambridge was right.

It was necessary to try Oxford next. Here the
opposition was stronger, and the popish party looked
forward to a victory. Longland, bishop of Lincoln
and chancellor of the university, was commissioned
by Henry to undertake the matter; Doctor Bell, and
afterwards Edward Fox, the chief almoner, being
joined with him. The king, uneasy at the results of
the negotiation, and wishing for a favourable decision
at any cost, gave Longland a letter for the university, through every word of which an undisguised
despotism was visible. ' We will and command you,'
he said, ' that ye, not leaning to wilful and sinister
opinions of your own several minds, considering that
we be your sovereign liege lord, and totally giving
your affections to the true overtures of divine learning in this behalf, do show and declare your true
and just learning in the said cause. . . . And we, for
your so doing, shall be to you and to our university
there so good and gracious a lord for the same, as ye
shall perceive it well done in your well fortune to
come. And in case you do not uprightly handle
yourselves herein, we shall so quickly and sharply
look to your unnatural misdemeanour herein, that it

* 'Scrutatis diligentissime Sacræ Scripturæ locis.'—Burnet, *Records,*
iii. p. 22.

shall not be to your quietness and ease hereafter. . . .
Accommodate yourselves to the mere truth; assuring
you that those who do shall be esteemed and set forth,
and the contrary neglected and little set by. . . .
We doubt not that your resolution shall be our high
contentation and pleasure.'

This royal missive caused a great commotion in the
university. Some slavishly bent their heads, for the
king spoke rod in hand. Others declared themselves
convinced by the political reasons, and said that
Henry must have an heir whose right to the throne
could not be disputed. And, lastly, some were convinced that Holy Scripture was favourable to the royal
cause. All men of age and learning, as well as all
who had either capacity or ambition, declared in favour
of the divorce. Nevertheless a formidable opposition
soon showed itself.

The younger members of the Senate were enthusiastic for Catherine, the Church, and the pope.
Their theological education was imperfect; they could
not go to the bottom of the question, but they judged
by the heart. To see a Catholic lady oppressed, to
see Rome despised, inflamed their anger; and if the
elder members maintained that their view was the
more reasonable, the younger ones believed theirs
to be the more noble. Unhappily, when the choice
lies between the useful and the generous, the useful
commonly triumphs. Still, the young doctors were
not prepared to yield. They said—and they were
not wrong—that religion and morality ought not to
be sacrificed to reasons of state, or to the passions of
princes. And seeing the spectre of Reform hidden
behind that of the divorce, they regarded themselves

as called upon to save the Church. ' Alas!' said the royal delegates, the Bishop of Lincoln and Dr. Bell, ' alas! we are in continual perplexity, and we cannot foresee with any certainty what will be the issue of this business.'*

They agreed with the heads of houses that, in order to prepare the university, three public disputations should be solemnly held in the divinity schools. By this means they hoped to gain time. ' Such disputations,' they said, ' are a very honourable means of amusing the multitude until we are sure of the consent of the majority.'† The discussions took place, and the younger masters, arranging each day what was to be done or said, gave utterance to all the warmth of their feelings.

When the news of these animated discussions reached Henry, his displeasure broke out, and those immediately around him fanned his indignation. ' A great part of the youth of our university,' said the king, 'with contentious and factious manners, daily combine together.' . . . The courtiers, instead of moderating, excited his anger. Every day, they told him, these young men, regardless of their duty towards their sovereign, and not conforming to the opinions of the most virtuous and learned men of the university, meet together to deliberate and oppose his Majesty's views. ' Hath it ever been seen,' exclaimed the king, ' that such a number of right small learning should stay their seniors in so weighty a cause?'‡ Henry, in exasperation, wrote to the heads of the

* 'In doubt always.'—*State Papers*, i. p. 377.
† ' Most convenient way to entertain the multitude.'—Ibid.
‡ Burnet, *Records*, iii. p. 26.

houses: '*Non est bonum irritare crabrones.*'   It is not
good to stir a hornet's nest.   This threat excited the
younger party still more: if the term 'hornet' amused
some, it irritated others.   In hot weather, the hornet
(the king) chases the weaker insects; but the noise
he makes in flying forewarns them, and the little ones
escape him.   Henry could not hide his vexation; he
feared lest the little flies should prove stronger than
the big hornet.   He was uneasy in his castle of
Windsor; and the insolent opposition of Oxford pursued him wherever he turned his steps—on the
terrace, in the wide park, and even in the royal
chapel.   'What!' he exclaimed, 'shall this university dare show itself more unkind and wilful than
all other universities, abroad or at home?'*   Cambridge had recognised the king's right, and Oxford
refused.

Wishing to end the matter, Henry summoned the
High-Almoner Fox to Windsor, and ordered him to
repeat at Oxford the victory he had gained at Cambridge.   He then dictated to his secretary a letter to
the recalcitrants: 'We cannot a little marvel that
you, neither having respect to our estate, being your
prince and sovereign lord, nor yet remembering such
benefits as we have always showed unto you, have
hitherto refused the accomplishment of our desire.
Permit no longer the private suffrages of light and
wilful heads to prevail over the learned.   By your
diligence redeem the errors and delays past.

'Given under our signet, at our castle of
Windsor.'†

Fox was entrusted with this letter.

---

* Burnet, *Records*, iii. p. 26.   † Ibid. p. 27.

The Lord High-Almoner and the Bishop of Lincoln immediately called together the younger masters of the university, and declared that a longer resistance might lead to their ruin. But the youth of Oxford were not to be overawed by threats of violence. Lincoln had hardly finished, when several masters of arts protested loudly, some even spoke 'very wickedly.' Not permitting himself to be checked by such rebellion, the bishop ordered the poll to be taken; twenty-seven voted for the king, and twenty-two against. The royal commissioners were not yet satisfied; they assembled all the faculties, and invited the members to give their opinion in turn. This intimidated many, and only eight or ten had courage enough to declare their opposition frankly. The bishop, encouraged by such a result, ordered that the final vote should be taken by ballot. Secresy emboldened many of those who had not dared to speak; and while thirty-one voted in favour of the divorce, twenty-five opposed it. That was of little consequence, as the two prelates had the majority. They immediately drew up the statute in the name of the university, and sent it to the king; after which the bishop, proud of his success, celebrated a solemn mass of the Holy Ghost.* The Holy Ghost had not, however, been much attended to in the business. Some had obeyed the prince, others the pope; and if we desire to find those who obeyed Christ, we must look for them elsewhere.

The university of Cambridge was the first to send in its submission to Henry. The Sunday before Easter (1530), Vice-Chancellor Buckmaster arrived

---

* *State Papers,* i. p. 379, and note.

at Windsor in the forenoon. The court was at chapel, where Latimer, recently appointed one of the king's chaplains, was preaching. The vice-chancellor came in during the service and heard part of the sermon. Latimer was a very different man from Henry's servile courtiers. He did not fear even to attack such of his colleagues as did not do their duty: 'That is no godly preacher that will hold his peace, and not strike you with his sword that you smoke again. . . . Chaplains will not do their duties, but rather flatter. But what shall follow? Marry, they shall have God's curse upon their heads for their labour. The minister must reprove without fearing any man, even if he be threatened with death.' * Latimer was particularly bold in all that concerned the errors of Rome, which Henry VIII. desired to maintain in the English Church. 'Wicked persons (he said), men who despise God, call out, We are christened, therefore we are saved. Marry, to be christened and not obey God's commandments is to be worse than the Turks! Regeneration cometh from the Word of God; it is by believing this Word that we are born again.'†

Thus spoke one of the fathers of the British Reformation: such is the real doctrine of the Church of England; the contrary doctrine is a mere relic of popery.

As the congregation were leaving the chapel, the vice-chancellor spoke to the secretary (Cromwell) and the provost, and told them the occasion of his visit. The king sent a message that he would re-

---

* Latimer, *Sermons* (Parker Soc.), pp. 46, 381.
† Ibid. pp. 126, 471.

ceive the deputation after evening service.   Desirous
of giving a certain distinction to the decision of the
universities, Henry ordered all the court to assemble
in the audience-chamber.   The vice-chancellor presented the letter to the king, who was much pleased
with it.   'Thanks, Mr. Vice-Chancellor,' he said, 'I
very much approve the way in which you have ma-
naged this matter.   I shall give your university tokens
of my satisfaction. . . . You heard Mr. Latimer's   ·
sermon,' he added, which he greatly praised and
then withdrew.   The Duke of Norfolk, going up to
the vice-chancellor, told him that the king desired
to see him the following day.

The next day, Dr. Buckmaster, faithful to the appointment, waited all the morning ; but the king had
changed his mind, and sent orders to the deputy from
Cambridge that he might depart as soon as he pleased.
The message had scarcely been delivered before the
king entered the gallery.   An idea which quite engrossed his mind urged him on : he wanted to speak
with the doctor about the principle put forward by
Cranmer.   Henry detained Buckmaster from one
o'clock until six, repeating in every possible form,
'Can the pope grant a dispensation when the law of
God has spoken ?'*   He even displayed much ill-
humour before the vice-chancellor, because this point
had not been decided at Cambridge.   At last he
quitted the gallery ; and, to counterbalance the sharp-
ness of his reproaches, he spoke very graciously to
the doctor, who hurried away as fast as he could.

* 'An papa potest dispensare.'—Burnet, *Records*, iii. p. 24.

CHAPTER VI.

HENRY VIII. SUPPORTED IN FRANCE AND ITALY BY THE CATHOLICS, AND BLAMED IN GERMANY BY THE PROTESTANTS.

(JANUARY TO SEPTEMBER 1530.)

THE king did not limit himself to asking the opinions of England: he appealed to the universal teaching of the Church, represented according to his views by the universities and not by the pope. The element of individual conviction, so strongly marked in Tyndale, Fryth, and Latimer, was wanting in the official reformation that proceeded from the prince. To know what Scripture said, Henry was about to send delegates to Paris, Bologna, Padua, and Wittemberg: he would have sent even to the East, if such a journey had been easy. That false catholicism which looked for the interpretation of the Bible to churches and declining schools where traditionalism, ritualism, and hierarchism were magnified, was a counterfeit popery. Happily the supreme voice of the Word of God surmounted this fatal tendency in England.

Henry VIII., full of confidence in the friendship of the King of France, applied first to the university of Paris; but Dr. Pedro Garray, a Spanish priest, as ignorant as he was fanatical (according to the English

agents),* eagerly took up the cause of Catherine of
Aragon.   Aided by the impetuous Beda, he obtained
an opinion adverse to Henry's wishes. .

When he heard of it, the alarmed prince summoned
Du Bellay, the French ambassador, to the palace, gave
him for Francis I. a famous diamond fleur-de-lis valued at 10,000*l.* sterling, also the acknowledgments
for 100,000 livres which Francis owed Henry for
war expenses, and added a gift of 400,000 crowns for
the ransom of the king's sons.   Unable to resist such
strong arguments, Francis charged Du Bellay to represent to the faculty of Paris ' the great scruples of
Henry's conscience;'† whereupon the Sorbonne de-
liberated, and several doctors exclaimed that it would
be an attaint upon the pope's honour to suppose him
capable of refusing consolation to the wounded conscience of a Christian.   During these debates, the
secretary took the names, received the votes, and entered them on the minutes.   A fiery papist observing that the majority would be against the Roman
opinion, jumped up, sprang upon the secretary,
snatched the list from his hands, and tore it up.   All
started from their seats, and ' there was great disorder and tumult.'   They all spoke together, each
trying to assert his own opinion; but as no one could
make himself heard amid the general clamour, the
doctors hurried out of the room in a great rage.
' Beda acted like one possessed,' wrote Du Bellay.

Meanwhile the ambassadors of the King of England

* Stokesley to the Earl of Wiltshire, January 16, 1530 : *State Papers*,
vii. p. 227.

† Le Grand, *Preuves du Divorce*, p. 459. This letter is from Du Bellay,
and not from Montmorency, as a distinguished historian has supposed.

were walking up and down an adjoining gallery, waiting for the division. Attracted by the shouts, they ran forward, and seeing the strange spectacle presented by the theologians, and 'hearing the language they used to one another,' they retired in great irritation. Du Bellay, who had at heart the alliance of the two countries, conjured Francis I. to put an end to such 'impertinences.' The president of the parliament of Paris consequently ordered Beda to appear before him, and told him that it was not for a person of his sort to meddle with the affairs of princes, and that if he did not cease his opposition, he would be punished in a way he would not soon forget. The Sorbonne profited by the lesson given to the most influential of its members, and on the 2nd of July declared in favour of the divorce by a large majority. The universities of Orleans, Angers, and Bourges had already done so, and that of Toulouse did the same shortly after.* Henry VIII. had France and England with him.

This was not enough: he must have Italy also. He filled that peninsula with his agents, who had orders to obtain from the bishops and universities the declaration refused by the pope. A rich and powerful despot is never in want of devoted men to carry out his designs.

The university of Bologna, in the states of the Church, was, after Paris, the most important in the Catholic world. A monk was in great repute there at this time. Noble by birth and an eloquent preacher, Battista Pallavicini was one of those independent

---

* The opinions of these universities are given in Burnet's *Records*, i. p. 83.

thinkers often met with in Italy. The English agents applied to him; he declared that he and his colleagues were ready to prove the unlawfulness of Henry's marriage, and when Stokesley spoke of remuneration, they replied: 'No, no! what we have received freely, we give freely.' Henry's agents could not contain themselves for joy: the university of the pope declares against the pope! Those among them who had an inkling for the Reformation were especially delighted. On the 10th June the eloquent monk appeared before the ambassadors with the judgment of the faculty, which surpassed all they had imagined. Henry's marriage was declared 'horrible, execrable, detestable, abominable for a Christian and even for an infidel, forbidden by divine and human law under pain of the severest punishment.* ... The holy father, who can do almost everything,' innocently continued the university, 'has not the right to permit such a union.' The universities of Padua and Ferrara hastened to add their votes to those of Bologna, and declared the marriage with a brother's widow to be 'null, detestable, profane, and abominable.'† Henry was conqueror all along the line. He had with him that universal consent which, according to certain illustrious doctors, is the very essence of Catholicism. Crooke, one of Henry's agents, and a distinguished Greek scholar, who discharged his mission with indefatigable ardour, exclaimed that 'the just cause of the king was approved by all the doctors of Italy.'‡

---

* 'Tale conjugium horrendum esse, execrabile, detestandum, viroque christiano etiam cuilibet infideli prorsus abominabile.'—Rymer, *Acta*, vi. p. 155.

† Burnet, *Records*, iii. p. 87.   ‡ *State Papers*, vii. p. 242.

In the midst of this harmony of catholicity, there was one exception of which no one had dreamt. That divorce which, according to the frivolous language of a certain party, was the cause of the Reformation in England, found opponents among the fathers and the children of the Reformation. Henry's envoys were staggered. ' My fidelity bindeth me to advertise your Highness,' wrote Crooke to the king, ' that all Lutherans be utterly against your Highness in this cause, and have letted [hindered] as much with their wretched poor malice, without reason or authority, as they could and might, as well here as in Padua and Ferrara, where be no small companies of them.'* The Swiss and German reformers having been summoned to give an opinion on this point, Luther, Œcolampadius, Zwingle, Bucer, Grynæus, and even Calvin,† all expressed the same opinion. ' Certainly,' said Luther, ' the king has sinned by marrying his brother's wife; that sin belongs to the past; let repentance, therefore, blot it out, as it must blot out all our past sins. But the marriage must not be dissolved; such a great sin, which is future, must not be permitted.‡ There are thousands of marriages in the world in which sin has a part, and yet we may not dissolve them. *A man shall cleave unto his wife, and they shall be one flesh.* This law is superior to the other, and overrules the lesser one.' The collective opinion of the Lutheran doctors was in conformity

---

* Burnet, *Records*, i. p. 82.

† Calvin's letter or dissertation (*Calvini Epistolæ*, p. 384) harmonises the apparently contradictory passages of Leviticus and Deuteronomy ; but I much doubt if it belongs to this period.

‡ 'Tam grande peccatum futurum permitti non debet.'—Lutheri *Epp.* iv. p. 265.

with the just and Christian sentiments of Luther.* Thus (we repeat) the event which, according to Catholic writers, was the cause of the religious transformation of England, was approved by the Romanists and condemned by the evangelicals. Besides, the latter knew very well that a Reformation must proceed, not from a divorce or a marriage, not from diplomatic negotiations or university statutes, but from the power of the Word of God and the free conviction of Christians.

While these matters were going on, Cranmer was at Rome, asking the pope for that discussion which the pontiff had promised him at their conference in Bologna. Clement VII. had never intended to grant it: he had thought that, once at Rome, it would be easy to elude his promise; it was that which occupied his attention just now. Among the means which popes have sometimes employed in their difficulties with kings, one of the most common was to gain the agents of those princes. It was the first employed by Clement; he nominated Cranmer grand almoner for all the states of the King of England, some even say for all the Catholic world. It was little more than a title, and 'was only to stay his stomach for that time, in hope of a more plentiful feast hereafter, if he had been pleased to take his repast on any popish preferment.'† But Cranmer was influenced by purer motives; and without refusing the title the pope gave him,—since having the task of winning him to the king's side, he would thus have compromised his mission,—he made no account of it, and

---

* Burnet, *Records*, i. p. 88.   † Fuller, *Church History*, p. 182.

showed all the more zeal for the accomplishment of his charge.

The embassy had not succeeded, and they were getting uneasy about it in England. Some of the pope's best friends could not understand his blindness. The two archbishops, the dukes of Norfolk and Suffolk, the marquises of Dorset and Exeter, thirteen earls, four bishops, twenty-five barons, twenty-two abbots, and eleven members of the Lower House determined to send an address to Clement VII. 'Most blessed father,' they began, 'the king, who is our head and the life of us all, has ever stood by the see of Rome amidst the attacks of your many and powerful enemies, and yet he alone is to reap no benefit from his labours. . . . Meanwhile we perceive a flood of miseries impending over the commonwealth.* If your Holiness, who ought to be our father, have determined to leave us as orphans, we shall seek our remedy elsewhere. . . . He that is sick will by any means be rid of his distemper; and there is hope in the exchange of miseries, when, if we cannot obtain what is good, we may obtain a lesser evil. . . . We beseech your Holiness to consider with yourself: you profess that on earth you are Christ's vicar. Endeavour then to show yourself so to be by pronouncing your sentence to the glory and praise of God.' Clement gained time: he remained two months and a half without answering, thinking about the matter, turning it over and over in his mind. The great difficulty was to harmonise the will of Henry VIII., who desired another wife, and that of Charles V.,

* 'Malorum pelagus reipublicæ nostræ imminere cernimus ac certum quoddam diluvium comminari.'—Rymer, *Acta*, vi. p. 160.

who insisted that he ought to keep the old one.
. . . There was only one mode of satisfying both
these princes at once, and that was by the king's
having the two wives together. Wolsey had already
entertained this idea. More than two years before,
the pope had hinted as much to Da Casale: 'Let him
take another wife,' he had said, speaking of Henry.*
Clement now recurred to it, and having sent privately
for Da Casale, he said to him: 'This is what we have
hit upon: we permit his Majesty to have two wives.'†
The infallible pontiff proposed bigamy to a king. Da
Casale was still more astonished than he had been at
the time of Clement's first communication. 'Holy
father,' he said to the pope, 'I doubt whether such
a mode will satisfy his Majesty, for he desires above
all things to have the burden removed from his conscience.'‡

This guilty proposal led to nothing; the king, sure
of the lords and of the people, advanced rapidly in
the path of independence. The day after that on
which the pope authorised him to take two wives,
Henry issued a bold proclamation, pronouncing
against whosoever should ask for or bring in a papal
bull contrary to the royal prerogative 'imprisonment
and further punishment of their bodies according to
his Majesty's good pleasure.' §   Clement, becoming
alarmed, replied to the address : 'We desire as much

* 'Rex aliam uxorem ducat.'—Letter of G. Da Casale, Orvieto,
January 13, 1528.

† 'Ut duas uxores habeat.'—Rome, September 28, 1530. Herbert,
p. 330.

‡ 'An conscientiæ satisfieri posset, quam V. M. imprimis exonerare
cupit.'—Herbert, p. 330.

§ Collier, ii. p. 60.

as you do that the king should have male children;
but, alas! we are not God to give him sons.'*

Men were beginning to stifle under these manœuvres and tergiversations of the papacy : they
called for air, and some went so far as to say that if
air was not given them, they must snap their fetters
and break open the doors.

---

* 'Sed pro Deo non sumus, ut liberos dare possimus.'—Herbert, p. 338.

CHAPTER VII.

LATIMER AT COURT.

(JANUARY TO SEPTEMBER 1530.)

HENRY, seeing that he could not obtain what he asked from the pope, drew nearer the evangelical party in his kingdom. In the ranks of the Reformation he found intelligent, pious, bold, and eloquent men, who possessed the confidence of a portion of the people. Why should not the prince try to conciliate them? They protest against the authority of the pope: good! he will relieve them from it; but on one condition, however—that if they reject the papal jurisdiction they recognise his own. If Henry's plan had succeeded, the Church of England would have been a Cæsareo-papistical Church (as we see elsewhere) planted on British soil; but it was the Word of God that was destined to replace the pope in England, and not the king.

The first of the evangelical doctors whom Henry tried to gain was Latimer. He had placed him, as we have seen, on the list of his chaplains. 'Beware of contradicting the king,' said a courtier to him one day, mistrusting his frankness. 'Speak as he speaks, and instead of presuming to lead him, strive to follow him.' 'Marry, out upon thy counsel!' replied

Latimer; 'shall I say as he says? Say what your conscience bids you. . . . Still, I know that prudence is necessary.

Gutta cavat lapidem non vi sed sæpe cadendo.

The drop of rain maketh a hole in the stone, not by violence, but by oft falling. Likewise a prince must be won by a little and a little.'

This conversation was not useless to the chaplain, who set to work seriously amid all the tumult of the court. He studied the Holy Scriptures and the Fathers, and frankly proclaimed the truth from the pulpit. But he had no private conversation with the king, who filled him with a certain fear. The thought that he did not speak to Henry about the state of his soul troubled him. One day, in the month of November, the chaplain was in his closet, and in the volume of St. Augustine which lay before him he read these words: 'He who for fear of any power *hides the truth*, provokes the wrath of God to come to him, for he fears men more than God.' Another day, while studying St. Chrysostom, these words struck him: 'He is not only a traitor to the truth who openly for truth teaches a lie; but he also who *does not freely pronounce and show the truth* that he knoweth.' These two sentences sank deeply into his heart.* 'They made me sore afraid,' he continued, 'troubled and vexed me grievously in my conscience.' He resolved to declare what God had taught him in Scripture. His frankness might cost him his life (lives were lost easily in Henry's time);

---

* 'I marked them earnestly in the inward parts of mine heart.'— Latimer, *Remains*, p. 298.

it mattered not. ' I had rather suffer extreme punishment,' he said, ' than be a traitor unto the truth.' *

Latimer reflected that the ecclesiastical law, which
for ages had been the very essence of religion, must
give way to evangelical faith—that the form must
yield to the life. The members of the Church
(calling themselves regenerate by baptism) used to
attend catechism, be confirmed, join in worship, and
take part in the communion without any real individual transformation; and then finally rest all together in the churchyard. But the Church, in Latimer's opinion, ought to begin with the conversion of
its members. Lively stones are. needed to build up
the temple of God. Christian individualism, which
Rome opposed from her theocratic point of view, was
about to be revived in Christian society.

The noble Latimer formed the resolution to make
the king understand that all real reformation must
begin at home. This was no trifling matter.
Henry, who was a man of varied information and
lively understanding, but was also imperious, passionate, fiery, and obstinate, knew no other rule than
the promptings of his strong nature; and although
quite prepared to separate from the pope, he detested
all innovations in doctrine. Latimer did not allow
himself to be stopped by such obstacles, and resolved
to attack this difficult position openly.

' Your Grace,' he wrote to Henry, ' I must show
forth such things as I have learned in Scripture, or
else deny Jesus Christ. The which denying ought
more to be dreaded than the loss of all temporal

---

* Latimer, *Remains*, p. 298.

goods, honour, promotion, fame, prison, slander, hurts, banishment, and all manner of torments and cruelties, yea, and death itself, be it never so shameful and painful.* . . . There is as great distance between you and me as between God and man ; for you are here to me and to all your subjects in God's stead ; and so I should quake to speak to your Grace. But as you are a mortal man having in you the corrupt nature of Adam, so you have no less need of the merits of Christ's passion for your salvation than I and others of your subjects have.'

Latimer feared to see a Church founded under Henry's patronage, which would seek after riches, power, and pomp; and he was not mistaken. 'Our Saviour's life was very poor. In how vile and abject a place was the mother of Jesus Christ brought to bed ! And according to this beginning was the process and end of His life in this world. . . . But this He did to show us that his followers and vicars should not regard the treasures of this world. . . . Your Grace may see what means and craft the spirituality imagine to break and withstand the acts which were made in the last parliament against their superfluities.'

Latimer desired to make the king understand who were the true Christians. 'Our Saviour showed his disciples,' continued he, 'that they should be brought before kings. Wherefore take this for a sure conclusion, that where the Word of God is truly preached, there is persecution ; and where quietness and rest in worldly pleasure, there is not the truth.'

---

* Latimer, *Works*, ii. p. 298 (Parker Soc.)

Latimer next proceeded to declare what would give real riches to England. 'Your Grace promised by your last proclamation that we should have the Scripture in English. Let not the wickedness of worldly men divert you from your goodly purpose and promise. There are prelates who, under pretence of insurrection and heresy, hinder the Gospel of Christ from having free course. . . . They would send a thousand men to hell ere they send one to God.' *

Latimer had reserved for the last the appeal he had determined to make to his master's conscience : 'I pray to God that your Grace may do what God commandeth, and not what seemeth good in your own sight; that you may be found one of the members of His Church, and a faithful minister of His gifts, and not,' he added, showing contempt for a title of which Henry was very proud, 'and not a defender of His faith ; for He will not have it defended by man's power, but by His word only.

'Wherefore, gracious king, remember yourself. Have pity on your soul, and think that the day is even at hand when you shall give account of your offiee, and of the blood that hath been shed with your sword. In the which day that your Grace may stand steadfastly, and not be ashamed, but be clear and ready in your reckoning, and to have (as they say) your *quietus est* sealed with the blood of our Saviour Christ, which only serveth at that day, is my daily prayer to Him that suffered death for our sins, which

---

* Latimer, *Works*, ii. p. 306 (Parker Soc.)

also prayeth to His Father for grace for us continually.' *

Thus wrote the bold chaplain. Such a letter from Latimer to Henry VIII. deserved to be pointed out. The king does not appear to have been offended at it: he was an absolute prince, but there was occasionally some generosity in his character. He therefore continued to extend his kindness to Latimer, but did not answer his appeal.

Latimer preached frequently before the court and in the city. Many noble lords and old families still clung to the prejudices of the middle ages; but some had a certain liking for the Reformation, and listened to the chaplain's preaching, which was so superior to ordinary sermons. His art of oratory was summed up in one precept: ' Christ is the preacher of all preachers.'† ' Christ,' he exclaimed, ' took upon Him our sins: not the work of sin—not to do it— not to commit it, but to purge it, and that way He was the great sinner of the world.‡ . . . It is much like as if I owed another man 20,000*l.*, and must pay it out of hand, or else go to the dungeon of Ludgate; and when I am going to prison, one of my friends should come and ask, Whither goeth this man? I will answer for him; I will pay all for him. Such a part played our Saviour Christ with us.'

Preaching before a king, he declared that the authority of Holy Scripture was above all the powers of the earth. ' God,' he said, ' is great, eternal, almighty,

---

* Latimer, *Works*, ii. p. 309 (Parker Soc.)
† Ibid. i. p. 155. ‡ Ibid. p. 223.

everlasting; and the Scripture because of Him is also great, eternal, most mighty, and holy. . . . There is no king, emperor, magistrate, or ruler, but is bound to give credence unto this holy word.'* He was cautious not to put 'the two swords' into the same hand. 'In this world God hath two swords,' he said; 'the temporal sword resteth in the hands of kings, whereunto all subjects—as well the clergy as the laity—be subject. The spiritual sword is in the hands of the ministers and preachers of God's Word to correct and reprove. Make not a mingle-mangle of them. To God give thy soul, thy faith; . . . to the king, tribute and reverence.† Therefore let the preacher amend with the spiritual sword, fearing no man, though death should ensue.'‡ Such language astonished the court. 'Were you at the sermon to-day?' said one of his hearers to a zealous courtier one day. 'Yes,' replied the latter. 'And how did you like the new chaplain?' 'Marry, even as I liked him always—a seditious fellow.'§

Latimer did not permit himself to be intimidated. Firm in doctrine, he was at the same time eminently practical. He was a moralist; and this may explain how he was able to remain any time at court. Men of the world, who soon grow impatient when you preach to them of the cross, repentance, and change of heart, cannot help approving of those who insist on certain rules of conduct. The king found it convenient to keep a great number of horses in abbeys founded for the support of the poor. One day when

---

* Latimer, *Works*, i. p. 85 (Parker Soc.)   † Ibid. p. 295.
‡ Ibid. p. 86.   § Ibid. p. 134.

Latimer was preaching before him, he said, ' A prince ought not to prefer his horses above poor men. Abbeys were ordained for the comfort of the poor, and not for kings' horses to be kept in them.' *

There was a dead silence in the congregation—no one dared turn his eyes towards Henry—and many showed symptoms of anger. The chaplain had hardly left the pulpit, when a gentleman of the court, the lord-chamberlain apparently, went up to him and asked, ' What hast thou to do with the king's horses? They are the maintenances and part of a king's honour, and also of his realm; wherefore, in speaking against them, ye are against the king's honour.' ' To take away the right of the poor,' answered Latimer, ' is against the honour of the king.'   He then added, ' My lord, God is the grand-master of the king's house, and will take account of every one that beareth rule therein.' †

Thus the Reformation undertook to re-establish the rule of conscience even in the courts of princes. Latimer knowing, like Calvin, that ' the ears of the princes of this world are accustomed to be pampered and flattered,' armed himself with invincible courage.

The murmurs grew louder. While the old chaplains let things take their course, the other wanted to restore morality among Christians. The Reformer was alive to the accusations brought against him, for his was not a heart of steel. Reproaches and calumnies appeared to him sometimes like those impetuous winds which force the husbandman to fly hurriedly

* Latimer, *Works*, i. p. 93.   † Ibid.

for shelter to some covered place. 'O Lord!' he exclaimed in his closet, 'these people pinch me; nay,
they have a full bite at me.'* He would have desired to flee away to the wilderness, but he called to
mind what had been done to his Master; 'I comfort
myself,' he said, 'that Christ Himself was noted to be
a stirrer up of the people against the emperor.'

The priests, delighted that Latimer censured the
king, resolved to take advantage of it to ruin him.
One day, when there was a grand reception, and the
king was surrounded by his councillors and courtiers,
a monk slipped into the midst of the crowd, and,
falling on his knees before the monarch, said, 'Sire,
your new chaplain preaches sedition.' Henry turned
to Latimer: 'What say you to that, sir?' The chaplain bent his knee before the prince; and, turning to
his accusers, said to them, 'Would you have me
preach nothing concerning a king in the king's
sermon?' His friends trembled lest he should be
arrested. 'Your Grace,' he continued, 'I put myself
in your hands: appoint other doctors to preach in my
place before your Majesty. There are many more
worthy of the room than I am. If it be your
Grace's pleasure, I could be content to be their
servant, and bear their books after them.† But if
your Grace allow me for a preacher, I would desire
you give me leave to discharge my conscience. Permit me to frame my teaching for my audience.'

Henry, who always liked Latimer, took his part,
and the chaplain retired with a low bow. When

---

* Latimer, *Works*, i. p. 134.

† Ibid. The preacher, when he left the vestry, was followed to the
pulpit by an attendant carrying his books.

he left the audience, his friends, who had watched this scene with the keenest emotion, surrounded him, saying, with tears in their eyes,* 'We were convinced that you would sleep to-night in the Tower.' '*The king's heart is in the hand of the Lord,*' he answered, calmly.

The evangelical Reformers of England nobly maintained their independence in the presence of a catholic and despotic king. Firmly convinced, free, strong men, they yielded neither to the seductions of the court nor to those of Rome. We shall see still more striking examples of their decision, bequeathed by them to their successors.

* Latimer, *Works,* i. p. 135.

CHAPTER VIII.

THE KING SEEKS AFTER TYNDALE.

(JANUARY TO MAY, 1531.)

HENRY VIII., finding that he wanted men like Latimer to resist the pope, sought to win over others of the same stamp. He found one, whose lofty range he understood immediately. Thomas Cromwell had laid before him a book then very eagerly read all over England, namely, the *Practice of Prelates.* It was found in the houses not only of the citizens of London, but of the farmers of Essex, Suffolk, and other counties. The king read it quite as eagerly as his subjects. Nothing interested him like the history of the slow but formidable progress of the priesthood and prelacy. One parable in particular struck him, in which the oak represented royalty, and the ivy the papacy. 'First, the ivy springeth out of the earth, and then awhile creepeth along by the ground till it find a great tree. There it joineth itself beneath alow unto the body of the tree, and creepeth up a little and a little, fair and softly. And at the beginning, while it is yet thin and small, that the burden is not perceived, it seemeth glorious to garnish the tree in the winter, and to bear off the tempests of the weather. But in the mean season it thrusteth roots into the bark of the tree to hold fast withal; and ceaseth not to climb up till it be at the top and above all. And then it sendeth its branches along by the branches of the tree, and overgroweth all, and waxeth great, heavy, and thick; and sucketh the moisture so sore out of the tree and his branches, that it choaketh and stifleth them. And then the foul stinking ivy waxeth mighty in the stump of the tree, and becometh a seat and a nest for all unclean birds and for blind owls, which hawk in the dark and dare not come at the light. Even so the Bishop of Rome at the beginning crope along upon the earth. . . . He crept up and fastened his roots in the heart of the emperor, and by subtilty clamb above the emperor, and subdued him, and made him stoop unto his feet and kiss them another while. Yea, when he had put the crown on the emperor's head, he smote it off with his feet again.'*

Henry would willingly have clapped his hand on his sword to demand satisfaction of the pope for this outrage. The book was by Tyndale. Laying it down, the king reflected on what he had just read, and thought to himself that the author had some striking ideas 'on the accursed power of the pope,' and that he was besides gifted with talent and zeal, and might render excellent service towards abolishing the papacy in England.

Tyndale, from the time of his conversion at Oxford, set Christ above everything: he boldly threw off the yoke of human traditions, and would take no other guide

---

* 'Dominus autem papa statim percussit cum pede suo coronam imperatoris et dejecit eam in terram.'—Tyndale, *Practice of Prelates*, p. 170 (Parker Soc.)

but Scripture only.   Full of imagination and eloquence, active and ready to endure fatigue, he exposed
himself to every danger in the fulfilment of his mission.*   Henry ordered Stephen Vaughan, one of his
agents, then at Antwerp, to try and find the Reformer
in Brabant, Flanders, on the banks of the Rhine, in
Holland . . . wherever he might chance to be ; to
offer him a safe-conduct under the sign-manual, to
prevail on him to return to England, and to add the
most gracious promises in behalf of his Majesty.†

To gain over Tyndale seemed even more important
than to have gained Latimer.   Vaughan immediately
undertook to seek him in Antwerp, where he was said
to be, but could not find him.   'He is at Marburg,'
said one; 'at Frankfort,' said another; 'at Hamburg,'
declared a third.   Tyndale was invisible now as before.
To make more certain, Vaughan determined to write
three letters directed to those three places, conjuring
him to return to England.‡   'I have great hopes,'
said the English agent to his friends, 'of having done
something that will please his Majesty.'   Tyndale, the
most scriptural of English reformers, the most inflexible in his faith, labouring at the Reformation with the
cordial approbation of the monarch, would truly have
been something extraordinary.

Scarcely had the three letters been despatched
when Vaughan heard of the ignominious chastisement

---

* *History of the Reformation of the Sixteenth Century*, vol. v.

† 'Upon the promise of your Majesty, be content to repair into
England.'—Vaughan to Henry VIII.   Cotton MSS. Galba, bk. x. fol. 42.
Bible Ann. i. p. 270.

‡ 'Whatsoever surety he could reasonably desire.' — Vaughan to
Cromwell, ibid. p. 270.

inflicted by Sir Thomas More on Tyndale's brother.* Was it by such indignities that Henry expected to attract the Reformer? Vaughan, much annoyed, wrote to the king (26th January, 1531) that this event would make Tyndale think they wanted to entrap him, and he gave up looking after him.

Three months later (17th April), as Vaughan was busy copying one of Tyndale's manuscripts in order to send it to Henry (it was his answer to the *Dialogue* of Sir Thomas More), a man knocked at his door. ' Some one, who calls himself a friend of yours, desires very much to speak with you,' said the stranger, ' and begs you to follow me.'—' Who is this friend? where is he?' asked Vaughan.—' I do not know him,' replied the messenger, ' but come along, and you will see for yourself.' Vaughan doubted whether it was prudent to follow this person to a strange place. He made up his mind, however, to accompany him. The agent of Henry VIII. and the messenger threaded the streets of Antwerp, went out of the city, and at last reached a lonely field, by the side of which the Scheldt flowed sluggishly through the level country.† As he advanced, Vaughan saw a man of noble bearing who appeared to be about fifty years of age. ' Do you not recognise me?' he asked Vaughan. ' I cannot call to mind your features,' answered the latter. ' My name is Tyndale,' said the stranger. ' Tyndale!' exclaimed Vaughan with delight. ' Tyndale! what a happy meeting!'

---

* *History of the Reformation of the Sixteenth Century,* tom. v. book xx. ch. 15.

† ' He brought me without the gates . . . into a field.'.—Anderson, *Annals of the English Bible,* p. 272.

Tyndale, who had heard of Henry's new plans, had no confidence either in the prince or in his pretended Reformation. The king's endless negotiations with the pope, his worldliness, his amours, his persecution of evangelical Christians, and especially the ignominious punishment inflicted on John Tyndale: all these matters disgusted him. However, having been informed of the nature of Vaughan's mission, he desired to turn it to advantage by addressing a few warnings to the prince. 'I have written certain books,' he said, 'to warn your Majesty of the subtle demeanour of the clergy of your realm towards your person, in which doing I showed the heart of a true subject; to the intent that your Grace might prepare your remedies against their subtle dreams. An exile from my native country, I suffer hunger, thirst, cold, absence of friends, everywhere encompassed with great danger, in innumerable hard and sharp fightings, I do not feel their asperity, by reason that I hope with my labours to do honour to God, true service to my prince, and pleasure to his commons.'*

'Cheer up,' said Vaughan, 'your exile, poverty, fightings, all are at an end; you can return to England.' . . . 'What matters it,' said Tyndale, 'if my exile finishes, so long as the Bible is banished? Has the king forgotten that God has commanded His Word to be spread throughout the world? If it continues to be forbidden to his subjects, very death were more pleasant to me than life.'†

Vaughan did not consider himself worsted. The messenger, who remained at a distance and could hear

* Anderson (Chr.), *Annals of the English Bible*, p. 152.
† Ibid.

nothing, was astonished at seeing the two men in that solitary field conversing together so long, and with so much animation. 'Tell me what guarantees you desire,' said Vaughan: 'the king will grant them you.' 'Of course the king would give me a safe-conduct,' answered Tyndale, 'but the clergy would persuade him that promises made to heretics are not binding.' Night was coming on, Henry's agent might have had Tyndale followed and seized.* The idea occurred to Vaughan, but he rejected it. Tyndale began, however, to feel himself ill at ease.† 'Farewell,' he said, ' you shall see me again before long, or hear news of me.' He then departed, walking away from Antwerp. Vaughan, who re-entered the city, was surprised to see Tyndale make for the open country. He supposed it to be a stratagem, and once more doubted whether he ought not to have seized the Reformer to please his master. 'I might have failed of my purpose,' he said;‡ besides it was now too late, for Tyndale had disappeared.

As soon as Vaughan reached home he hastened to send to London an account of this singular conference. Cromwell immediately proceeded to court and laid before the king the envoy's letter and the Reformer's book. 'Good!' said Henry, ' as soon as I have leisure I will read them both.'§ He did so, and was exasperated against Tyndale, who refused his invitation, mistrusted his word, and even dared to give

---

* 'Lest I would have persued him.'—Anderson, p. 152.

† 'Being something fearful.'—*Ibid.*

‡ Cotton MSS. Titus, bk. i. fol. 6, 7. Anderson, *Annals*, i. p. 273.

§ 'At opportune leisure his Highness would read the content.'—Ibid. p. 275.

him advice. The king in his passion tore off the latter part of Vaughan's letter, flung it in the fire, and entirely gave up his idea of bringing the Reformer into England to make use of him against the pope, fearing that such a torch would set the whole kingdom in a blaze. He thought only how he could seize him and punish him for his arrogance.

He sent for Cromwell; before him on the table lay the treatise by Tyndale, which Vaughan had copied and sent. ' These pages,' said Henry to his minister, while pointing to the manuscript, ' these pages are the work of a visionary: they are full of lies, sedition, and calumny. Vaughan shows too much affection for Tyndale.* Let him beware of inviting him to come into the kingdom. He is a perverse and hardened character who cannot be changed. I am too happy that he is out of England.'

Cromwell retired in vexation. He wrote to Vaughan, but the king found the letter too weak, and Cromwell had to correct it, to make it harmonise with the wrath of the prince.† An ambitious man, he bent before the obstinate will of his master; but the loss of Tyndale seemed irreparable. Accordingly, while informing Vaughan of the king's anger, he added that if wholesome reflection should bring Tyndale to reason, the king was ' *so inclined to mercy, pity, and compassion,*'‡ that he would doubtless see him with pleasure.

---

* ' Ye bear much affection towards the said Tyndale.'—Cotton MSS. Galba, bk. x. fol. 338. Anderson, *Annals*, p. 275.

† The corrections are still to be seen in the original draft, and are indicated in the biographical notice of Tyndale at the beginning of his *Practices* (Parker Society), pp. 46, 47.

‡ *State Papers*, vii. p. 303.

Vaughan, whose heart Tyndale had gained, began to hunt after him again, and had a second interview with him. He gave him Cromwell's letter to read, and when the Reformer came to the words we have just quoted about Henry's compassion, his eyes filled with tears.* 'What gracious words!' he exclaimed. 'Yes,' said Vaughan, 'they have such sweetness, that they would break the hardest heart in the world.' Tyndale, deeply moved, tried to find some mode of fulfilling his duty towards God and towards the king. 'If his Majesty,' he said, 'would condescend to permit the Holy Scriptures to circulate among the people in all their purity, as they do in the states of the emperor and in other Christian countries, I would bind myself never to write again; I would throw myself at his feet, offering my body as a sacrifice, ready to submit if necessary to torture and to death.'

But a gulf lay between the monarch and the Reformer. Henry VIII. saw the seeds of heresy in the Scriptures; and Tyndale rejected every reformation which they wished to carry out by proscribing the Bible. 'Heresy springeth not from the Scriptures,' he said, 'no more than darkness from the sun.'† Tyndale disappeared again, and the name of his hiding-place is unknown.

The King of England was not discouraged by the check he had received. He wanted men possessed of talent and zeal, men resolved to attack the pope. Cambridge had given England a teacher who might be placed beside, and perhaps even above, Latimer and

---

* 'In such wise that water stoode in his eyes.'—*State Papers*, vii. p. 303.
† Tyndale, *Exposition*, p. 141.

Tyndale; this was John Fryth. He thirsted for the truth; he sought God, and was determined to give himself wholly to Jesus Christ. One day Cromwell said to the king, 'What a pity it is, your Highness, 'that a man so distinguished as Fryth in letters and sciences, should be among the sectarians!' Like Tyndale, he had quitted England. Cromwell, with Henry's consent, wrote to Vaughan: 'His Majesty strongly desires the reconciliation of Fryth, who (he firmly believes) is not so far advanced as Tyndale in the evil way. Always full of mercy, the king is ready to receive him to favour; try to attract him chari-'tably, politically.' Vaughan immediately began his inquiries; it was May 1531, but the first news he received was that Fryth, a minister of the Gospel, was just married in Holland. 'This marriage,' he wrote to the king, 'may by chance hinder my persuasion.'* This was not all; Fryth was boldly printing, at Amsterdam, Tyndale's answer to Sir Thomas More. Henry was forced to give him up, as he had given up his friend. He succeeded with none but Latimer, and even the chaplain told him many harsh truths. There was a decided incompatibility between the spiritual reform and the political reform; the work of God refused to ally itself with the work of the throne. The Christian faith and the visible Church are two distinct things. Some (and among them the Reformers) require Christianity—a living Christianity; others (and it was the case of Henry and his prelates) look for the Church and its hierarchy, and care little whether a living faith be found there or not. This

* *State Papers,* vii. p. 302.

is a capital error. Real religion must exist first; and then this religion must produce a true religious society. Tyndale, Fryth, and their friends desired to begin with religion; Henry and his followers with an ecclesiastical society, hostile to faith. The king and the reformers could not, therefore, come to an understanding. Henry, profoundly hurt by the boldness of those evangelical men, swore that as they would not have peace they should have war, . . . war to the knife.

CHAPTER IX.

THE KING OF ENGLAND RECOGNISED AS HEAD OF THE CHURCH.

(JANUARY TO MARCH, 1531.)

HENRY VIII. desired to introduce great changes into the ecclesiastical corporation of his kingdom. His royal power had much to bear from the power of the clergy. It was the same in all Catholic monarchies; but England had more to complain of than others. Of the three estates, Clergy, Nobility, and Commons, the first was the most powerful. The nobility had been weakened by the civil wars; the commons had long been without authority and energy; the prelates thus occupied the first rank, so that in 1529 an archbishop and cardinal (Wolsey) was the most powerful man in England, not even the king excepted. Henry had felt the yoke, and wished to free himself, not only from the domination of the pope, but also from the influence of the higher clergy. If he had only intended to be avenged of the pontiff, it would have been enough to allow the Reformation to act; when a mighty wind blows from heaven, it sweeps away all the contrivances of men. But Henry was deficient neither in prudence nor calculation. He feared lest a diversity of doctrine should engender disturbances in his kingdom. He wished to free him-

self from the pope and the prelates, without throwing
himself into the arms of Tyndale or of Latimer.

Kings and people had observed that the domination
of the papacy, and its authority over the clergy, were
an insurmountable obstacle to the autonomy of the
State. As far back as 1268, St. Louis had declared
that France owed allegiance to God alone; and other
princes had followed his example. Henry VIII,
determined to do more—to break the chains which
bound the clergy to the Romish throne, and fasten
them to the crown. The power of England, delivered from the papacy, which had been its canker-
worm, would then be developed with freedom and
energy, and would place the country in the foremost
rank among nations. The renovating spirit of the
age was favourable to Henry's plans; without delay
he must put into execution the bold plan which
Cromwell had unrolled before his eyes in Whitehall
Park. Henry could think of nothing but getting
himself recognised as head of the Church.

This important revolution could not be accomplished by a simple act of royal authority—in England particularly, where constitutional principles already possessed an incontestable influence. It was
necessary to prevail upon the clergy to cross the
Rubicon by emancipating themselves from Rome.
But how bring it about? This was the subject of
the meditations of the sagacious Cromwell, who, gradually rising in the king's confidence to the place
formerly held by Wolsey, made a different use of it.
Urged by ambition, possessing an energetic character,
a sound judgment, unshaken firmness, no obstacle
could arrest his activity. He sought how he could

give the king the spiritual sceptre, and this was the
plan on which he fixed. The kings of England had
been known occasionally to revive old laws fallen into
desuetude, and visit with heavy penalties those who
had violated them. Cromwell represented to the king
that the statutes made punishable any man who should
recognise a dignity established by the pope in the
English Church; that Wolsey, by exercising the
functions of papal legate, had encroached upon the
rights of the Crown and been condemned, which was
but justice; while the members of the clergy—who
had recognised the unlawful jurisdiction of the pretended legate—had thereby become as guilty as he
had been. 'The statute of *Præmunire*,' he said,
'condemns them as well as their chief.' Henry, who
listened attentively, found the expedient of his Secretary of State was in conformity with the letter of the
law, and that it put all the clergy in his power. He
did not hesitate to give full power to his ministers.
Under such a state of things there was not one
innocent person in England; the two houses of parliament, the privy council, all the nation must be
brought to the bar. Henry, full of 'condescension,'
was pleased to confine himself to the clergy.

The convocation of the province of Canterbury
having met on the 7th of January, 1531, Cromwell
entered the hall and quietly took his seat among the
bishops; then rising, he informed them that their property and benefices were to be confiscated for the
good of his Majesty, because they had submitted to
the unconstitutional power of the cardinal. What
terrible news! It was a thunderbolt to those selfish
prelates; they were amazed. At length some of

them plucked up a little courage. 'The king himself had sanctioned the authority of the cardinal-legate,' they said. 'We merely obeyed his supreme will. Our resistance to his Majesty's proclamations would infallibly have ruined us.'—'That is of no consequence,' was the reply; 'there was the law: you should obey the constitution of the country even at the peril of your lives.' * The terrified bishops laid at the foot of the throne a magnificent sum by which they hoped to redeem their offences and their benefices. But that was not what Henry desired : he pretended to set little store by their money. The threat of confiscation must constrain them to pay a ransom of still greater value. 'My lords,' said Cromwell, 'in a petition that some of you presented to the pope not long ago, you called the king your *soul* and your *head.*† Come, then, expressly recognise the supremacy of the king over the Church,‡ and his majesty, of his great goodness, will grant you your pardon.' What a demand! The distracted clergy assembled, and a deliberation of extreme importance began. 'The words in the address to the pope,' said some, 'were a mere form, and had not the meaning ascribed to them.'—'The king being unable to untie the Gordian knot at Rome,' said others, alluding to the divorce, 'intends to cut it with his sword.' §—'The secular power,' exclaimed the most

* 'They ought to take notice of the constitution at their peril.'—Collyers, ii. p. 61. Burnet, p. 108.

† 'Regia majestas nostrum caput atque anima.'—Collyers, *Records,* p. 8, 30 July, 1530.

‡ 'Ecclesiæ protector et supremum caput.'—Collyers, ii. p. 62.

§ 'Seeing this Gordian knot, to play the noble Alexander.'—Foxe, *Acts,* v. p. 55.

zealous, 'has no voice in ecclesiastical matters. To recognise the king as head of the Church would be to overthrow the catholic faith. . . . The head of the Church is the pope.' The debate lasted three days, and as Henry's ministers pointed to the theocratic government of Israel, a priest exclaimed : 'We oppose the New Testament to the Old ; according to the gospel, Christ is head of the Church.' When this was told the king, he said : 'Very well, I consent. If you declare me *head of the Church* you may add *under God.*' In this way the papal claims were compromised all the more. 'We will expose ourselves to everything,' they said, 'rather than dethrone the Roman pontiff.'

The bishops of Lincoln and Exeter were deputed to beseech the king to withdraw his demand : they could not so much as obtain an audience. Henry had made up his mind : the priests must yield. The only means of their obtaining pardon (they were told) was by their renouncing the papal supremacy. The bishops made a fresh attempt to satisfy both the requirements of the king and those of their own conscience. 'Shrink before the clergy and they are lions,' the courtiers said ; 'withstand them and they are sheep.'—'Your fate is in your own hands. If you refuse the king's demand, the disgrace of Wolsey may show you what you may expect.' Archbishop Warham, president of the convocation, a prudent man, far advanced in years and near his end, tried to hit upon some compromise. The great movements which agitated the Church all over Europe disturbed him. He had in times past complained to the king of Wolsey's usurpations,* and was not far from recog-

* Strype's *Memorials,* i. p. 111.

nising the royal supremacy. He proposed to insert a simple clause in the act conferring the required jurisdiction on the king, namely, *Quantum per legem Christi licet*, so far as the law of Christ permits. 'Mother of God!' exclaimed the king, who, like his royal brother Francis I., had a habit of saying irreverent things, 'you have played me a shrewd turn. I thought to have made fools of those prelates, and now you have so ordered the business that they are likely to make a fool of me. Go to them again, and let me have the business passed without any *quantums* or *tantums*. . . . So far as the law of Christ permits! Such a reserve would make one believe that my authority was disputable.' *

Henry's ministers ventured on this occasion to resist him : they showed him that this clause would prevent an immediate rupture with Rome, and it might be repealed hereafter. He yielded at last, and the archbishop submitted the clause with the amendment to convocation. It was a solemn moment for England. The bishops were convinced that the king was asking them to do what was wrong, the end of which would be a rupture with Rome. In the time of Hildebrand the prelates would have answered No, and found a sympathetic support in the laity. But things had changed ; the people were beginning to be weary of the long domination of the priests. The primate, desirous of ending the matter, said to his colleagues : 'Do you recognise the king as sole protector of the Church and clergy of England, and, so far as is allowed by the law of Christ, also as your

---

* Tytler, *Life of Henry VIII.*, p. 312.

supreme head?' All remained speechless. 'Will
you let me know your opinions?' resumed the archbishop. There was a dead silence. 'Whoever is
silent seems to consent,' said the primate.—'Then we
are all silent,' answered one of the members.* Were
these words inspired by courage or by cowardice?
Were they an assent or a protest? We cannot say.
In this matter we cannot side either with the king or
with the priests. The heart of man easily takes the
part of those who are oppressed; but here the oppressed were also oppressors. Convocation next
gave its support to the opinion of the universities
respecting the divorce, and thus Henry gained his
first victory.

Now that the king had the power, the clergy were
permitted to give him their money. They offered a
hundred thousand pounds sterling, an enormous sum
for those times, nearly equivalent to fifteen times as
much of our money. On the 22nd of March, 1531,
the courteous archbishop signed the document which
at one stroke deprived the clergy of England of both
riches and honour.†

The discussion was still more animated in the convocation of York. 'If you proclaim the king supreme head,' said bishop Tonstal, 'it can only be in
temporal matters.'—'Indeed!' retorted Henry's minister, 'is an act of convocation necessary to determine that the king reigns?'—'If spiritual things are
meant,' answered the bishop, 'I withdraw from

* 'Qui tacet consentire videtur. Itaque tacemus omnes.'—Collyers,
p. 63.

† The act is given in Wilkins, *Concilia*, iii. p. 742, and Rymer,
Fœdera, vi. p. 163.

convocation that I may not withdraw from the Church.'*

' My lords,' said Henry, ' no one disputes your right to preach and administer the sacraments.† Did not Paul submit to Cæsar's tribunal, and our Saviour himself to Pilate's ? ' Henry's ecclesiastical theories prevailed also at York. A great revolution was effected in England, and fresh compromises were to consolidate it.

The king having obtained what he desired, con-descended in his great mercy to pardon the clergy for their unpardonable offence of having recognised Wolsey as papal legate. At the request of the com-mons this amnesty was extended to all England. The nation, which at first saw nothing in this affair but an act enfranchising themselves from the usurped power of the popes, showed their gratitude to Henry; but there was a reverse to the medal. If the pope was despoiled, the king was invested. Was not the func-tion ascribed to him contrary to the Gospel? Would not this act impress upon the Anglican Reformation a territorial and aristocratic character, which would introduce into the Reformed Church the world with all its splendour and wealth? If the royal pre-eminence endows the Anglican Church with the pomps of worship, of classical studies, of high digni-ties, will it not also carry along with it luxury, sine-cures, and worldliness among the prelates? Shall we not see the royal authority pronounce on questions of dogma, and declare the most sacred doctrines in-

---

* ' Ne ab ecclesia catholica dissentire videar, expresse dissentio.'— Wilkins, *Concilia*, iii. p. 745.

† Collyers, ii. p. 64.

different?   A little later an attempt was made to limit the power of the king in religious matters. ' We give not to our princes the ministry of God's Word or the sacraments,' says the thirty-seventh Article of Religion.

CHAPTER X.

SEPARATION OF THE KING AND QUEEN.

(MARCH TO JUNE 1531.)

THE king having obtained so important a concession from the clergy, turned to his parliament to ask a service of another kind—one in his eyes still more urgent.

On the 30th of March, 1531, the session being about to terminate, Sir Thomas More, the chancellor, went down to the House of Commons, and submitted to them the decision of the various universities on the king's marriage and the power of the pope. The Commons looked at the affair essentially from a political point of view; they did not understand that because the king had lived twenty years with the queen, he ought not to be separated from her. The documents placed before their eyes 'made them detest the marriage' of Henry and Catherine.[*] The chancellor desired the members to report in their respective counties and towns that the king had not asked for this divorce of his own will or pleasure, but 'only for the discharge of his conscience and surety of the succession of his crown.'[†]   'Enlighten

---

[*] Lord Herbert, p. 353.   [†] Hall, *Chron. of England*, p. 780.

the people,' he said, ' and preserve peace in the nation with the sentiments of loyalty due to the monarch.'

The king hastened to use the powers which universities, clergy, and parliament had placed in his hands. Immediately after the prorogation, certain lords went down to Greenwich and laid before the queen the decisions which condemned her marriage, and urged her to accept the arbitration of four bishops and four lay peers. Catherine replied sadly but firmly: ' I pray you tell the king I say I am his lawful wife, and in that point I will abide until the court of Rome determine to the contrary.' *

The divorce, which notwithstanding Catherine's refusal was approaching, caused great agitation among the people, and the members of parliament had some trouble to preserve order, as Sir Thomas More had desired them. Priests proclaimed from their pulpits the downfall of the Church and the coming of Antichrist; the mendicant friars scattered discontent in every house which they entered, the most fanatical of them not fearing to insinuate that the wrath of God would soon hurl the impious prince from his throne. In towns and villages, in castles and alehouses, men talked of nothing but the divorce and the primacy claimed by the king. Women standing at their doors, men gathering round the blacksmith's forge, spoke more or less disrespectfully of parliament, the bishops, the dangers of the Romish Church, and the prospects of the Reformation. If a few friends met at night around the hearth, they told strange tales to one another. The king, queen, pope, devil, saints, Crom-

---

* Herbert, p. 354.

well, and the higher clergy formed the subject of their conversation. The gipsies at that time strolling through the country added to the confusion. Sometimes they would appear in the midst of these animated discussions, and prophesy lamentable events, at times calling up the dead to make them speak of the future. The terrible calamities they predicted froze their hearers with affright, and their sinister prophecies were the cause of disorders and even of crimes. Accordingly an act was passed pronouncing the penalty of banishment against them.*

An unfortunate event tended still more to strike men's imaginations. It was reported that the bishop of Rochester, that prelate so terrible to the reformers and so good to the poor, had narrowly escaped being poisoned by his cook. Seventeen persons were taken ill after eating porridge at the episcopal palace; one of the bishop's gentlemen died, as well as a poor woman to whom the remains of the food had been given. It was maliciously remarked that the bishop was the only one who frankly opposed the divorce and the royal supremacy. Calumny even aimed at the throne. When Henry heard of this, he resolved to make short work of all such nonsense; he ordered the offence to be deemed as high-treason, and the wretched cook was taken to Smithfield, there to be *boiled to death*.† This was a variation of the penalty pronounced upon the evangelicals. Such was the cruel justice of the sixteenth century.

While the universities, parliament, convocation, and

---

* Bill against conjuration, witchcraft, sorcerers, &c. Henry VIII. cap. viii.

† Burnet, i. p. 110.

the nation appeared to support Henry VIII., one
voice was raised against the divorce. It was that of
a young man, brought up by the king, and that voice
moved him deeply. There still remained in England some scions of the house of York, and among
them a nephew of that unhappy Warwick whom
Henry VII. had cruelly put to death. Warwick had
left a sister Margaret, and the king, desirous of appeas-
ing the remorse he suffered on account of the tragical
end of that prince, 'the most innocent of men,' * had
married her to Sir Richard Pole, a gentleman of
her own family. She was left a widow with two
daughters and three sons—the youngest, Reginald,
became a favourite with Henry VIII., who destined
him for the archiepiscopal see of Canterbury. ' Your
kindnesses are such,' said Pole to him, ' that a king
could grant no more, even to a son.'† But Reginald, to whom his mother had told the story of the
execution of the unhappy Warwick, had contracted
an invincible hatred against the Tudors. Accordingly,
in despite of certain evangelical tendencies, Pole seeing Henry separating from the pope, resolved to throw
himself into the arms of the pontiff. Reginald, invested with the Roman purple, rose to be president of
the council and primate of all England under Queen
Mary. Elegant in his manners, with a fine intellect,
and sincere in his religious convictions, he was selfish,
irritable, and ambitious: desires of elevation and revenge led a noble nature astray. If the branch of
which he was the representative was ever to recover

---

* ' Omnium innocentissimum.'—Pole, *De Unitate*, p. 57.

† ' Ut nec rex pater principi filio majus dare possit.'—Pole, *De Unitate*,
p. 85.

the crown, it could only be by the help of the Roman pontiffs: henceforward their cause was his. Loaded with benefits by Henry VIII., he was incessantly pursued by the recollection of the rights of Rome and of the White Rose; and he went so far as to insult before all Europe the prince who had been his first friend.

At this time Pole was living at a house in the country which Henry had given him. One day he received at this charming retreat a communication from the duke of Norfolk. 'The king destines you for the highest honours of the English Church,' wrote this nobleman, 'and offers you at once the important sees of York and Winchester, left vacant by the death of Cardinal Wolsey.' At the same time the duke asked Pole's opinion about the divorce. Reginald's brothers, and particularly Lord Montague, entreated him to answer as all the catholic world had answered, and not irritate a prince whose anger would ruin them all. The blood of Warwick and the king's revolt against Rome induced Pole to reject with horror all the honours which Henry offered; and yet that prince was his benefactor. He fancied he had discovered a middle course which would permit him to satisfy alike his conscience and his king.

He went to Whitehall, where Henry received him like a friend. Pole hesitated in distress; he wished to let the king know his thoughts, but the words would not come to his lips. At last, encouraged by the prince's affability, he summoned up his resolution, and in a voice trembling with emotion, said: 'You must not separate from the queen.' Henry had ex-pected something different. Is it thus that his kindnesses are repaid? His eyes flashed with anger, and he laid his hand on his sword. Pole humbled himself: 'If I possess any knowledge, to whom do I owe it, unless to your Majesty? In listening to me, you are listening to your own pupil.'* The king recovered himself, and said, 'I will consider your opinion, and send you my answer.' Pole withdrew. 'He put me in such a passion,' said the king to one of his gentlemen, 'that I nearly struck him. . . . But there is something in the man that wins my heart.'

Montague and Reginald's other brother again conjured him to accept the high position which the king reserved for him; but his soul revolted at being subordinate to a Tudor. He therefore wrote a memoir, which he presented to Henry, and in which he entreated him to submit implicitly the divorce question to the court of Rome. 'How could I speak against your marriage with the queen?' he said. 'Should I not accuse your Majesty of having lived for more than twenty years in an unlawful union?† By the divorce, you will array all the powers against you—the pope, the emperor; and as for the French . . . we can never find in our hearts to trust them. You are at this moment on the verge of an abyss. . . . One step more, and all is over.‡ There is only one way of safety left your grace, and that is submission to the pope.'

Henry was moved. The boldness with which this young nobleman dared accuse him, irritated his pride;

---

* 'Cum me audies, alumnum tuum audies.'—Pole, *De Unitate*, p. 3.

† 'Infra etiam belluarum vitam.'—Ibid. p. 55.

‡ 'The king standeth even upon the brink of the water; all his honour is drowned.'—Ibid.

still his friendship prevailed, and he forgave it. Pole received the permission he had asked to leave England, with the promise of the continued payment of his pension.

Reginald Pole was, as it were, the last link that united the royal pair. Thus far the king had continued to show the queen every respect; their mutual affection seemed the same, only they occupied separate rooms.* Henry now decided to take an important step. On the 14th of July a new deputation entered the queen's apartment, one of whom informed her that as her marriage with Prince Arthur had been duly consummated she could not be the wife of her husband's brother. Then after reproaching her with having, contrary to the laws of England and the dignity of the crown, cited his Majesty before the pope's tribunal, he desired her to choose for her residence either the castle of Oking or of Estamsteed, or the monastery of Bisham. Catherine remained calm, and replied: ' Wheresoever I retire, nothing can deprive me of the title which belongs to me. I shall always be his Majesty's wife.'† She left Windsor the same day, and removed to the More, a splendid mansion which Wolsey had surrounded with beautiful gardens; then to Estamsteed, and finally to Ampthill. The king never saw her again; but all the papists and discontented rallied round her. She entered into correspondence with the sovereigns of Europe, and became the centre of a party opposed to the emancipation of England.

* ' Had he not forborne to come to her bed.'—Lord Herbert, 33, p. 5.
† ' To what place soever she removed, nothing could remove her from being the king's wife.'—Herbert, p. 354.

CHAPTER XI.

THE BISHOPS PLUNDER THE CLERGY AND PERSECUTE THE PROTESTANTS.

(SEPTEMBER 1531 to 1532.)

AS Henry, by breaking with Catherine, had broken with the pope, he felt the necessity of uniting more closely with his clergy. Wishing to proceed to the establishment of his new dignity, he required bishops, and particularly dexterous bishops. He therefore made Edward Lee archbishop of York, and Stephen Gardiner bishop of Winchester; and these two men, devoted to scholastic doctrines, ambitious and servile, were commissioned to inaugurate the new ecclesiastical monarchy of the king of England. Although the pope had hastened to send off their bulls, they declared they held their dignity 'immediately and only' of the king,* and began without delay to organise a strange league. If the king needed the bishops against the pope, the bishops needed the king against the reformers. It was not long before this alliance received the baptism of blood.

But before proceeding so far, the prelates delibe-

---

* 'Immediately and only upon your grace.'—Juramentum. Rymer, *Acta*, vi. p. 169.

rated about the means of raising the 118,000*l.* they had bound themselves to pay the king. Each wished to make his own share as small as possible, and throw the largest part of the burden upon his colleagues. The bishops determined to place it in great measure on the shoulders of the parochial clergy.

Stokesley, bishop of London, began the battle. An able, greedy, violent man, and jealous of his prerogatives, he called a meeting of six or eight priests on whom he believed he could depend, in order to draw up with their assistance such resolutions as he could afterwards impose more easily upon their brethren. These picked ecclesiastics were desired to meet on the 1st of September, 1531, in the chapter-house of St. Paul's.

The bishop's plan had got wind, and excited general indignation in the city. Was it just that the victims should pay the fine ? Some of the laity, delighted at seeing the clergy quarrelling, sought to fan the flame instead of extinguishing it.

When the 1st of September arrived the bishop entered the chapter-house with his officers, where the conference with the eight priests was to be held. Presently an unusual noise was heard round St. Paul's : not only the six or eight priests, but six hundred, accompanied by a great number of citizens and common people, made their appearance. The crowd swayed to and fro before the cathedral gates, shouting and clamouring to be admitted into the chapter-house on the same footing as the select few. What was to be done ? The prelate's councillors advised him to add a few of the less violent priests to those he had already chosen. Stokesley adopted their advice, hoping that the gates and bolts would be strong enough to keep out the rest. Accordingly he drew up a list of new members, and one of his officers, going out to the angry crowd, read the names of those whom the bishop had selected. The latter came forward, not without trouble; but at the same time the excluded priests made a vigorous attempt to enter. There was a fierce struggle of men pushing and shouting, but the bishop's officials having passed in quickly, those who had been nominated hurriedly closed the doors. So far the victory seemed to rest with the bishop, and he was about to speak, when the uproar became deafening. The priests outside, exasperated because their financial matters were to be settled without them, protested that they ought to hold their own purse-strings. Laying hands on whatever they could find, and aided by the laity, they began to batter the door of the chapter-house. They succeeded: the door gave way, and all, priests and citizens, rushed in together.* The bishop's officials tried in vain to stop them; they were roughly pushed aside.† Their gowns were torn, their faces streamed with perspiration, their features were disfigured, and some even were wounded. The furious priests entered the room at last, storming and shouting. It was more like a pack of hounds rushing on a stag than the reverend clergy of the metropolis of England appearing before their bishop. The prelate, who had tact, showed no anger, but sought rather to calm the

---

* 'The rest forced the door, rushed in, and the bishop's servants were beaten and ill-used.'—Burnet, i. p. 110.

† 'They struck the bishop's officers over the face.'—Hall, *Chronicles of England*, p. 783.

rioters. ' My brethren,' he said, ' I marvel not a little why ye be so heady. Ye know not what shall be said to you, therefore I pray you hear me patiently. Ye all know that we be men frail of condition, and by our lack of wisdom have misdemeaned ourselves towards the king and fallen in a *præmunire*, by reason whereof all our lands, goods, and chattels were to him forfeit, and our bodies ready to be imprisoned. Yet his Grace of his great clemency is pleased to pardon us, and to accept of a little instead of the whole of our benefices—about one hundred thousand pounds, to be paid in five years. I exhort you to bear your parts towards payment of this sum granted.' *

This was just what the priests did not want. They thought it strange to be asked for money for an offence they had not committed. ' My lord,' answered one, ' we have never offended against the *præmunire*, we have never meddled with cardinal's faculties.† Let the bishops and abbots pay; they committed the offence, and they have good places.'— ' My lord,' added another, ' twenty nobles ‡ a year is but a bare living for a priest, and yet it is all we have. Everything is now so dear that poverty compels us to say No. Having no need of the king's pardon we have no desire to pay.' These words were drowned in applause. ' No,' exclaimed the crowd, which was getting noisy again, ' we will pay nothing.' The bishop's officers grew angry and came to high words; the priests returned abuse for abuse; and the citizens, delighted to see their ' masters ' quarrelling,

---

* Hall, *Chronicles*.   † Ibid. p. 784.
‡ The noble was worth six shillings and eightpence.

fanned the strife. From words they soon came to
blows. The episcopal ushers, who tried to restore
order, were 'buffeted and stricken,' and even the
bishop's life was in danger. At last the meeting
broke up in great confusion. Stokesley hastened to
complain to the chancellor, Sir Thomas More, who,
being a great friend of the prelate's, sent fifteen
priests and five laymen to prison. They deserved it,
no doubt; but the bishops, who, to spare their super-
fluity, robbed poor curates of their necessaries, were
more guilty still.

Such was the unity that existed between the
bishops and the priests of England at the very time
the Reformation was appearing at the doors. The
prelates understood the danger to which they were
exposed through that evangelical doctrine, the source
of light and life. They knew that all their ecclesiastical pretensions would crumble away before
the breath of the divine Word. Accordingly, not
content with robbing of their little substance the poor
pastors to whom they should have been as fathers,
they determined to deprive those whom they called
heretics, not only of their money, but of their liberty
and life. Would Henry permit this?

The king did not wish to withdraw England from
the papal jurisdiction without the assent of the clergy.
If he did so of his own authority, the priests would
rise against him and compare him to Luther. There
were at that time three great parties in Christendom :
the evangelical, the catholic, and the popish. Henry
purposed to overthrow popery, but without going so
far as evangelism : he desired to remain in catholicism. One means occurred of satisfying the clergy.

Although they were fanatical partisans of the Church, they had sacrificed the pope ; they now imagined that, by sacrificing a few heretics, they would atone for their cowardly submission.   In a later age Louis XIV. did the same to make up for errors of another kind. The provincial synod of Canterbury met and addressed the king : ' Your Highness one time defended the Church with your pen, when you were only a member of it ; now that you are its supreme head, your Majesty should crush its enemies, and so shall your merits exceed all praise.'*

In order to prove that he was not another Luther, Henry VIII. consented to hand over the disciples of that heretic to the priests ; and gave them authority to imprison and burn them, provided they would aid the king to resume the power usurped by the pope.   The bishops immediately began to hunt down the friends of the Gospel.

A will had given rise to much talk in the county of Gloucester.   William Tracy, a gentleman of irreproachable conduct and ' full of good works, equally generous to the clergy and the laity,' † had died praying God to save his soul through the merits of Jesus Christ, but leaving no money to the priests for masses.   The primate of England had his bones dug up and burnt.   But this was not enough : they must also burn the living.

* ' Tanta ejus Majestatis merita quod nullis laudibus æquari queant.' —*Concilia*, M. Brit. p. 742.

† Latimer, *Sermons*, i. p. 46 (Parker Soc.) ; Tyndale, *Op.* iii. p. 231.

CHAPTER XII.

THE MARTYRS.

(1531.)

THE first blows were aimed at the court-chaplain.
The bishops, finding it dangerous to have such a
man near the king, would have liked (Latimer tells
us) to place him on burning coals.* But Henry loved
him, the blow failed, and the priests had to turn to
those who were not so well at court.

Thomas Bilney, whose conversion had begun the
Reformation in England,† had been compelled to do
penance at St. Paul's Cross; but from that time he
became the prey of the direst terror. His backsliding
had manifested the weakness of his faith. Bilney
possessed a sincere and lively piety, but a judgment
less sound than many of his friends. He had not got
rid of certain scruples which in Luther and Calvin
had yielded to the supreme authority of God's Word.‡
In his opinion none but priests consecrated by bishops
had the power to bind and loose.§ This mixture of

---

* 'Ye would have raked in the coals.'—Latimer, *Works*, i. p. 46
(Parker Soc.); Tyndale, *Op.* iii. 231.

† *History of the Reformation of the Sixteenth Century*, vol. v. bk. xviii.
ch. ii. ix. xii.; bk. xix. ch. vii.; bk. xx. ch. xv.

‡ 'A man of a timorous conscience, and not fully resolved touching
that matter of the Church.'—Foxe, *Acts*, p. 649.

§ 'Soli sacerdotes, ordinati ritè per pontifices, habent claves.'—Ibid.

truth and error had caused his fall. Such sincere but imperfectly enlightened persons are always to be met with—persons who, agitated by the scruples of their conscience, waver between Rome and the Word of God.

At last faith gained the upper hand in Bilney. Leaving his Cambridge friends, he had gone into the Eastern counties to meet his martyrdom. One day, arriving at a hermitage in the vicinity of Norwich, where a pious woman dwelt, his words converted her to Christ.* He then began to preach ' openly in the fields ' to great crowds. His voice was heard in all the county ; weeping over his former fall, he said : ' That doctrine which I once abjured is the truth. Let my example be a lesson to all who hear me.'

Before long he turned his steps in the direction of London, and, stopping at Ipswich, was not content to preach the Gospel only, but violently attacked the errors of Rome before an astonished audience.† Some monks had crept among his hearers, and Bilney perceiving them called out : ' *The Lamb of God taketh away the sins of the world.* If the bishop of Rome dares say that the hood of St. Francis saves, he blasphemes the blood of the Saviour.' John Huggen, one of the monks, immediately made a note of the words. Bilney continued : ' To invoke the saints and not Christ, is to put the head under the feet and the feet above the head.' ‡ Richard Seman, the other brother, took down these words. ' Men will come

* 'The anachoress whom he had converted to Christ.'—Foxe, *Acts*, p. 642.

† Herbert, p. 357.

‡ 'Like as if a man should take and strike off the head and set it under the foot, and to set the foot above.'—Foxe, *Acts*, iv. p. 649.

after me,' continued Bilney, ' who will teach the same faith, the true gospel of our Saviour, and will disen‧tangle you from the errors in which deceivers have bound you so long.'   Brother Julius hastened to write down the bold prediction.

Latimer, surrounded by the favours of the king and the luxury of the great, watched his friend from afar.   He called to mind their walks in the fields round Cambridge, their serious conversation as they climbed the hill afterwards called after them ' the heretics' hill,' * and the visits they had paid together to the poor and to the prisoners.†   Latimer had seen Bilney very recently at Cambridge in fear and anguish, and had tried in vain to restore him to peace. ' He now rejoiced that God had endued him with such strength of faith, that he was ready to be burnt for Christ's sake.'

Bilney, drawing still nearer to London, arrived at Greenwich about the middle of July.   He procured some New Testaments, and hiding them carefully under his clothes, called upon a humble Christian named Staple.   Taking them ' out of his sleeves,' he desired Staple to distribute them among his friends. Then, as if impelled by a thirst for martyrdom, he turned again towards Norwich, whose bishop Richard Nix, a blind octogenarian, was in the front rank of the persecutors.   Arriving at the solitary place where the pious ' anachoress ' lived, he left one of the precious volumes with her.   This visit cost Bilney his life. The poor solitary read the New Testament, and lent it to the people who came to see her.   The bishop, hearing of it, informed Sir Thomas More, who had

---

* Latimer, *Remains*, p. xiii.   † Ibid.

Bilney arrested,* brought to London, and shut up in the Tower.

Bilney began to breathe again : a load was taken off him ; he was about to suffer the penalty his fall deserved.   In the room next his was John Petit, a member of parliament of some eloquence, who had distributed his books and his alms in England and beyond the seas.   Philips, the under-gaoler of the Tower, who was a good man, told the two prisoners that only a wooden partition separated them, which was a source of great joy to both.   He would often remove a panel, and permit them to converse and take their frugal meals together.†

This happiness did not last long.   Bilney's trial was to take place at Norwich, where he had been captured : the aged bishop Nix wanted to make an example in his diocese.   A crowd of monks—Augustins, Dominicans, Franciscans, and Carmelites—visited the prison of the evangelist to convert him. Dr. Gall, provincial of the Franciscans, having consented that the prisoner should make use of Scripture,‡ was shaken in his faith ; but, on the other hand, Stokes, an Augustin and a determined papist, repeated to Bilney : 'If you die in your opinions, you will be lost.'

The trial commenced, and the Ipswich monks gave their evidence.   'He said,' deposed William Cade, ' that the Jews and Saracens would have been converted long since, if the idolatry of the Christians had

---

* 'Fit empoigner.'—Crespin, *Actes des Martyrs*, p. 101.

† Strype, p. 313.

‡ 'As he had planted himself upon the firm rock of God's Word.'— Foxe, *Acts*, iv. p. 643.

not disgusted them with Christianity.'—' I heard him say,' added Richard Neale : ' down with your gods of gold, silver, and stone.'—' He stated,' resumed Cade, ' that the priests take away the offerings from the saints and hang them about their women's necks ; and then, if the offerings do not prove fine enough, they are put upon the images again.' *

Every one foresaw the end of this piteous trial. One of Bilney's friends endeavoured to save him. Latimer took the matter into the pulpit, and conjured the judges to decide according to justice. Although Bilney's name was not uttered, they all knew who was meant. The bishop of London went and complained to the king that his chaplain had the audacity to defend the heretic against the bishop and his judges.† ' There is not a preacher in the world,' said Latimer, . ' who would not have spoken as I have done, although Bilney had never existed.' The chaplain escaped once more, thanks to the favour he enjoyed with Henry.

Bilney was condemned, and after being degraded by the priests, was handed over to the sheriff, who, having great respect for his virtues, begged pardon for discharging his duty. The prudent bishop wrote to the chancellor, asking for an order to burn the heretic. ' Burn him first,' rudely answered More, ' and then ask me for a bill of indemnity.' ‡

A few of Bilney's friends went to Norwich to bid him farewell : among them was Parker, archbishop of Canterbury. It was in the evening, and Bilney was taking his last meal. On the table stood some frugal

* Foxe, *Acts*, iv. p. 648.
† Latimer, *Works*, ii. p 330 (Parker Soc.)   ‡ Ibid. p. 650.

fare (ale brew), and on his countenance beamed the joy that filled his soul. ' I am surprised,' said one of his friends, ' that you can eat so cheerfully.'—' I only follow the example of the husbandmen of the county,' answered Bilney, ' who having a ruinous house to dwell in, yet bestow cost so long as they may hold it up.' With these words he rose from the table, and sat down near his friends, one of whom said to him : ' To-morrow the fire will make you feel its devouring fierceness, but God's Holy Spirit will cool it for your everlasting refreshing.' Bilney, appearing to reflect upon what had been said, stretched out his hand towards the lamp that was burning on the table and placed his finger in the flame. ' What are you doing?' they exclaimed.—' Nothing,' he replied ; ' I am only trying my flesh ; to-morrow God's rods shall burn my whole body in the fire.' And still keeping his finger in the flame, as if he were making a curious experiment, he continued : ' I feel that fire by God's ordinance is naturally hot ; but yet I am persuaded, by God's Holy Word and the experience of the martyrs, that when the flames consume me, I shall not feel them. Howsoever this stubble of my body shall be wasted by it, a pain for the time is followed by joy unspeakable.' * He then withdrew his finger, the first joint of which was burnt. He added, ' *When thou walkest through the fire, thou shalt not be burnt.*'† These words remained imprinted on the hearts of all who heard them, until the day of their death, says a chronicler.

---

* Latimer, *Works*, ii. p. 650 (Parker Soc.)

† Isaiah xliii. 2. In Bilney's Bible, which is preserved in the library of Corpus Christi College, Cambridge, this passage (verses 1—3) is marked in the margin with a pen.

Beyond the city gate—that known as the *Bishop's gate*—was a low valley, called the *Lollards' pit* : it was surrounded by rising ground, forming a sort of amphitheatre. On Saturday, the 19th of August, a body of javelin-men came to fetch Bilney, who met them at the prison gate. One of his friends approaching and exhorting him to be firm, Bilney replied : ' When the sailor goes on board his ship and launches out into the stormy sea, he is tossed to and fro by the waves ; but the hope of reaching a peaceful haven makes him bear the danger. My voyage is beginning, but whatever storms I shall feel, my ship will soon reach the port.' *

Bilney passed through the streets of Norwich in the midst of a dense crowd : his demeanour was grave, his features calm. His head had been shaved, and he wore a layman's gown. Dr. Warner, one of his friends, accompanied him ; another distributed liberal alms all along the route. The procession descended into the Lollards' pit, while the spectators covered the surrounding hills. On arriving at the place of punishment, Bilney fell on his knees and prayed, and then rising up, warmly embraced the stake and kissed it. † Turning his eyes towards heaven, he next repeated the Apostles' Creed, and when he confessed the incarnation and crucifixion of the Saviour his emotion was such that even the spectators were moved. Recovering himself, he took off his gown, and ascended the pile, reciting the hundred and forty-third psalm. Thrice he repeated the second verse : ' *Enter not into judgment with thy servant, for in*

---

* Latimer, *Works*, ii. p. 654 (Parker Soc.)
† Foxe, *Acts*, iv. p. 655, note.

thy sight shall no man living be justified.' And then
he added : '*I stretch forth my hands unto thee; my
soul thirsteth after thee.'* Turning towards the executioner, he said : ' Are you ready ? '—' Yes,' was the
reply. Bilney placed himself against the post, and
held up the chain which bound him to it. His friend
Warner, with eyes filled with tears, took a last farewell. Bilney smiled kindly at him and said : ' Doctor,
pasce gregem tuum; feed your flock, that when the
Lord cometh He may find you so doing.' Several
monks who had given evidence against him, perceiving the emotion of the spectators, began to tremble,
and whispered to the martyr : ' These people will
believe that we are the cause of your death, and will
withhold their alms.' Upon which Bilney said to them :
' Good folks, be not angry against these men for my
sake ; even should they be the authors of my death,
it is not they.' * He knew that his death proceeded
from the will of God. The torch was applied to the
pile : the fire smouldered for a few minutes, and then
suddenly burning up fiercely, the martyr was heard
to utter the name of Jesus several times. A strong
wind which blew the flames on one side prolonged his
agony ; thrice they seemed to retire from him, and
thrice they returned, until at length, the whole pile
being kindled, he expired.

A strange revolution took place in men's minds
after this death : they praised Bilney, and even his
persecutors acknowledged his virtues. ' Mother of
Christ,' exclaimed the bishop of Norwich (it was his
usual oath), ' I fear I have burnt Abel and let Cain

---

* Latimer, *Works*, ii. p. 655 (Parker Soc.)

go.' Latimer was inconsolable; twenty years later he still lamented his friend, and one day preaching before Edward VI. he called to mind that Bilney was always doing good, even to his enemies, and styled him ' that blessed martyr of God.' *

One martyrdom was not sufficient for the enemies of the Reformation. Stokesley, Lee, Gardiner, and other prelates and priests, feeling themselves guilty towards Rome, which they had sacrificed to their personal ambition, desired to expiate their faults by sacrificing the reformers. Seeing at their feet a fatal gulf, dug between them and the Roman pontiff by their faithlessness, they desired to fill it up with corpses. The persecution continued.

There was at that time a pious evangelist in the dungeons of the bishop of London. He was fastened upright to the wall, with chains round his neck, waist, and legs. Usually the most guilty prisoners were permitted to sit down, and even to lie on the floor; but for this man there was no rest. It was Richard Bayfield, accused of bringing from the continent a number of New Testaments translated by Tyndale.†　When one of his gaolers told him of Bilney's martyrdom, he exclaimed : ' And I too, and hundreds of men with me, will die for the faith he has confessed.' He was brought shortly afterwards before the episcopal court. ' With what intent,' asked Stokesley, ' did you bring into the country the errors of Luther, Œcolampadius the great heretic, and others of that

---

* ' And toward his enemy so charitable.'—Latimer, *Works*, ii. p. 330 (Parker Soc.)

† *History of the Reformation of the Sixteenth Century*, vol. v. bk. xx. ch. xv.

damnable sect?'—'To make the Gospel known,' answered Bayfield, 'and to glorify God before the
people.' * Accordingly, the bishop, having condemned
and then degraded him, summoned the lord mayor
and sheriffs of London, 'by the bowels of Jesus Christ'
(he had the presumption to say), to do to Bayfield
'according to the *laudable custom* of the famous realm
of England.' † 'O ye priests,' said the gospeller, as if
inspired by the Spirit of God, 'is it not enough that
your lives are wicked, but you must prevent the life
according to the gospel from spreading among the
people?' The bishop took up his crosier and struck
Bayfield so violently on the chest that he fell backwards and fainted.‡ He revived by degrees, and
said, on regaining his consciousness : 'I thank God
that I am delivered from the wicked church of Antichrist, and am going to be a member of the true
Church which reigns triumphant in heaven.' He
mounted the pile ; the flames, touching him only on
one side, consumed his left arm. With his right hand
Bayfield separated it from his body, and the arm fell.
Shortly after this he ceased to pray, because he had
ceased to live.

John Tewkesbury, one of the most respected merchants in London, whom the bishops had put twice to
the rack already, and whose limbs they had broken,§
felt his courage revived by the martyrdom of his
friend. CHRIST ALONE, he said habitually : these two

---

* 'To the intent that the Gospel of Christ might be set forward.'
—Foxe, *Acts*, iv. p. 683.

† Ibid. p. 687.

‡ 'He took his crozier-staff and smote him on the breast.'—Ibid.

§ *History of the Reformation of the Sixteenth Century*, vol. v. bk. xx.
ch. vii.

words were all his theology.   He was arrested, taken
to the house of Sir Thomas More at Chelsea, shut up
in the porter's lodge, his hands, feet, and head being
held in the stocks ; * but they could not obtain from
him the recantation they desired.   The officers took
him into the chancellor's garden, and bound him so
tightly to the *tree of truth*, as the renowned scholar
called it, that the blood started out of his eyes ; after
which they scourged him.†   Tewkesbury remained
firm.

On the 16th of December the bishop of London
went to Chelsea and formed a court.   'Thou art a
heretic,' said Stokesley, 'a backslider ; thou hast incurred the great excommunication.   We shall deliver
thee up to the secular power.'   He was burnt alive
at Smithfield on the 20th of December, 1531.   'Now,'
said the fanatical chancellor, 'now he is uttering cries
in hell !'

Such were at this period the cruel *utopias* of the
bishops and of the witty Sir Thomas More.   Other
evangelical Christians were thrown into prison.   In
vain did one of them exclaim : 'The more they persecute this sect, the more will it increase.'‡   That
opinion did not check the persecution.   'It is impossible,' says Foxe (doubtless with some exaggeration),
'to name all who were persecuted before the time of
Queen Anne Boleyn.   As well try to count the grains
of sand on the seashore !'

* Foxe, *Acts*, iv. p. 689.

† 'And also twisted in his brows with small ropes so that the
blood . . .'—Ibid.

‡ Cotton MS.   Anderson, *Annals of Bible*, i. p. 310.   'It will cause
the sect to wax greater, and those errors to be plenteously sowed in the
realm, than heretofore.'

Thus did the real Reformation show by the blood
of its martyrs that it had nothing to do with the
policy, the tyranny, the intrigues, and the divorce of
Henry VIII. If these men of God had not been
burnt by that prince, it might possibly have been
imagined that he was the author of the transformation
of England; but the blood of the reformers cried
to heaven that he was its executioner.

CHAPTER XIII.

THE KING DESPOILS THE POPE AND THE CLERGY.

(MARCH TO MAY 1532.)

HENRY VIII. having permitted the bishops to execute their task of persecution, proceeded to carry out his own, that of making the papacy disgorge. Unhappily for the clergy, the king could not attack the pope, and they entirely escape the blows. The duel between Henry and Clement was about to become more violent, and in the space of three months (March, April, and May) the Romish Church, stripped of important prerogatives, would learn that, after so many ages of wealth and honour, the hour of its humiliation had come at last.

Henry was determined, above all things, not to permit his cause to be tried at Rome. What would be thought if he yielded? 'Could the pope,' wrote Henry to his envoys, 'constrain kings to leave the charge God had entrusted to them, in order to humble themselves before him? That would be to tread under foot the glory of our person and the privileges of our kingdom. If the pope persists, take your leave of the pontiff and return to us immediately.'— 'The pope,' added Norfolk, 'would do well to reflect if he intend the continuance of good obedience of England to the see apostolic.' *

Catherine on her part did not remain behind : she wrote a pathetic letter to the pope, informing him that her husband had banished her from the palace. Clement, in the depths of his perplexity, behaved, however, very properly : he called upon the king (25th January) to take back the queen, and to dismiss Anne Boleyn from court. Henry spiritedly rejected the pontiff's demand. 'Never was prince treated by a pope as your Holiness has treated me,' he said ; 'not painted reason,† but the truth alone, must be our guide.' The king prepared to begin the emancipation of England.

Thomas Cromwell is the representative of the political reform achieved by that prince. He was one of those powerful natures which God creates to work important things. His prompt and sure judgment taught him what it would be possible to do under a Tudor king, and his intrepid energy put him in a position to accomplish it. He had an instinctive horror of superstitions and abuses, tracked them to their remotest corner, and threw them down with a vigorous arm. Every obstacle was shattered under the wheels of his car. He even defended the evangelicals against their persecutors, without committing himself, however, and encouraged the reading of Holy Scripture; but the royal supremacy, of which he was the originator, was his idol.

The exactions of Rome in England were numerous : the king and Cromwell were content for the moment

* *State Papers,* vol. vii. p. 349.
† Burnet, *Records,* i. p. 100.

to abolish one, the appropriation by the papacy of the first year's income of all ecclesiastical benefices. 'These *annates*,' said Cromwell, 'have cost England eight hundred thousand ducats since the second year of Henry VII.*   If, in consequence of the abolition of annates, the pope does not send a bishop his bull of ordination, the archbishop or two bishops shall ordain him, as in the old times.'   Accordingly, in March 1532, the Lower House agreed to a resolution, which they expressed in these words: *A cest bille les communes sont assentes*, To this bill the Commons assent.

The bishops were overjoyed: they had to incur great expenses for their establishment, and the first money arising from their benefice went to the pope. Their friends used to make them pecuniary advances; but if the bishop died shortly after his enthronisation, these advances were lost.   Some of the bishops, fearing the opposition of the pope, exclaimed: 'These exactions are contrary to God's law. St. Paul bids us withdraw ourselves from all such as walk inordinately. Therefore, if the pope claims to keep the annates, let it please your Majesty and parliament to withdraw the obedience of the people from the see of Rome.'†   The king was more moderate than the prelates: he said he would wait a year or two before giving his assent to the bill.

If the bishops refused the pope his ancient revenue, they refused the king the new authority claimed by the crown, and maintained that no secular power had

---

* This was equivalent to two millions and a half sterling of our money. Burnet, *Records*, ii. p. 96. *Statutes of the Realm*, iii. p. 388.

† Strype, *Eccl. Memor*. i. pt. ii. p. 158.

any right to meddle with them.* ˙Cromwell resisted them, and determined to carry out the reform of abuses. 'The clergy,' said the Commons to the king, 'make laws in convocation without your assent and ours which are in opposition to the statutes of the realm, and then excommunicate those who violate such laws.' † A second time the frightened bishops vainly prayed the king to make his laws harmonise with theirs. Henry VIII. insisted that the Church should conform to the State and not the State to the Church, and he was inexorable. The bishops knew well that it was their union with powerful pontiffs, always ready to defend them against kings, which had given them so much strength in the middle ages, and that now they must yield. They therefore lowered their flag before the authority which they had themselves set up. Convocation did, indeed, make a last effort. It represented that 'the authority of bishops proceeds immediately from God, and from no power of any secular prince, as *your Highness hath shown in your own book most excellently written against Martin Luther.*' But the king was firm, and made the prelates yield at last.‡ Thus was a great revolution accomplished : the spiritual power was taken away from those arrogant priests who had so long usurped the rights of the members of the Church. It was only justice ; but it ought to have been placed in better hands than those of Henry VIII.

* 'There needeth not any temporal power to concur with the same.' —Strype, *Eccl. Memor.* i. p. 202.

† 'Declaring the infringers to incur into the terrible sentence of excommunication.'—Wilkins, *Concilia,* iii. p. 751.

‡ 'The king made them buckle at last.'—Strype, *Eccles. Memorials,* i. p. 204.

Cromwell was preparing a fresh blow that would strike the pontiff's triple crown.   He drew his master's attention to the oaths which the bishops took at their consecration, both to the king and to the pope.   Henry first read the oath to the pope.   'I swear,' said the bishop, 'to defend the papacy of Rome, the regality of St. Peter, against all men.   If I know of any plot against the pope, I will resist it with all my might, and will give him warning.   Heretics, schismatics, and rebels to our holy father I shall resist and perse-cute with all my power.'*   On the other hand, the bishops took an oath to the king at the same time, wherein they renounced every clause or grant which, coming from the pope, might be in any way detri-mental to his Majesty.   In one breath they must obey the pope and disobey him.

Such contradictions could not last : the king wanted the English to be, not with Rome but with England. Accordingly he sent for the Speaker of the Commons, and said to him : 'On examining the matter closely, I find that the bishops, instead of being wholly my sub-jects, are only so by halves.   They swear an oath to the pope quite contrary to that they swear to the crown ; so that they are the pope's subjects rather than mine.†   I refer the matter to your care.'   Par-liament was prorogued three days later on account of the plague ; but the prelates declared that they re-nounced all orders of the pope prejudicial to his Majesty's rights.‡

* 'Prosequar et impugnabo.'—Burnet, *Reformation*, i. p. 250 (Oxford, 1829).

† Burnet, *Hist. Reform.* i. p. 249 (Oxford, 1829).

‡ Wilkins, *Concilia*, iii. p. 354.

The political party was delighted, the papal party confounded. The convents reechoed with rumours, maledictions, and the strangest projects. The monks, during the visits they made in their daily rounds, raved against the encroachments made on the power of the pope. When they went up into the pulpit, they declaimed against the sacrilege of which Cromwell (they said) was the author and the English people the victims.

To the last the English priests had hoped in Sir Thomas More. That disciple of Erasmus had acted like his master. After assailing the Romish superstitions with biting jests, he had turned round, and seeing the Reformation attack them with weapons still more powerful, he had fought against the evangelicals · with fire. For two years he had filled the offiee of lord-chancellor with unequalled activity and integrity. Convocation having offered him four thousand pounds sterling 'for the pains he had taken in God's quarrel,' * he answered: 'I will receive no recompense save from God alone;' and when the priests urged him to accept the money, he said: 'I would sooner throw it into the Thames.' He did not persecute from any mercenary motives; but the more he advanced, the more bigoted and fanatical he became. Every Sunday he put on a surplice and sang mass at Chelsea. The duke of Norfolk surprised him one day in this equipment. 'What do I see?' he exclaimed. 'My lord-chancellor acting the parish clerk . . . you dishonour your office and your king.' †—'Not so,' answered Sir Thomas seriously, 'for I am honouring his master and ours.'

---

* *Thomas More*, by his grandson, p. 187.   † Ibid. p. 193.

The great question of the bishop's oath warned him
that he could not serve both the king and the pope.
His mind was soon made up. In the afternoon of the
16th of May he went to Whitehall gardens, where the
king awaited him, and in the presence of the Duke of
Norfolk resigned the seals.*   On his return home, he
cheerfully told his wife and daughters of his resigna-
tion, but they were much disturbed by it. As for Sir
Thomas, delighted at being freed from his charge, he
indulged more than ever in his flagellations, without
renouncing his witty sayings—Erasmus and Loyola
combined in one.

Henry gave the seals to Sir Thomas Audley, a man
well disposed towards the Gospel: this was preparing
the emancipation of England.   Yet the Reformation
was still exposed to great danger.

Henry VIII. wished to abolish popery and set
catholicism in its place—maintain the doctrine of
Rome, but substitute the authority of the king for
that of the pontiff. He was wrong in keeping the
catholic doctrine ; he was wrong in establishing the
jurisdiction of the prince in the Church. Evangelical
Christians had to contend against these two evils in
England, and to establish the supreme and exclusive
sovereignty of the Word of God. Can we blame them
if they have not entirely succeeded? To attain their
object they willingly have poured out their blood.

* 'In horto suo.'—Rymer, vi. p. 171.

CHAPTER XIV.

LIBERTY OF INQUIRY AND OF PREACHING IN THE
SIXTEENTH CENTURY.

(1532.)

THERE are writers who seriously ascribe the
Reformation of England to the divorce of Henry
VIII., and thus silently pass over the Word of God and
the labours of the evangelical men who really founded
protestant Christianity in that country. As well
forget that light proceeds from the sun. But for the
faith of such men as Bilney, Latimer, and Tyndale,
the Church of England, with its king, ministers
of state, parliament, bishops, cathedrals, liturgy,
hierarchy, and ceremonies, would have been a gallant
bark, well supplied with masts, sails, and rigging, and
manned by able sailors, but acted on by no breath
from heaven. The Church would have stood still. It
is in the humble members of the kingdom of God that
its real strength lies. 'Those whom the Lord has exalted to high estate,' says Calvin, 'most often fall back
little by little, or are ruined at one blow.' England,
with its wealth and grandeur, needed a counterpoise :
the living faith of the poor in spirit. If a people
attain a high degree of material prosperity; if they
conquer by their energy the powers of nature; if
they compel industry to lavish its stores on them;

if they cover the seas with their ships, the more distant countries with their colonies and marts, and fill
their warehouses and their dwellings with the produce of the whole earth, then great dangers encom-
pass them.   Material things threaten to extinguish
the sacred fire in their bosoms; and unless the Holy
Ghost raises up a salutary opposition against such
snares, that people, instead of acting a moralising and
civilising part, may turn out nothing better than a
huge noisy machine, fitted only to satisfy vulgar
appetites.   For a nation to do justice to a high and
glorious calling, it must have within itself the life of
faith, holiness of conscience, and the hope of incorruptible riches.   At this time there were men in England in whose hearts God had kindled a holy flame,
and who were to become the most important instruments of its moral transformation.

About the end of 1531, a young minister, John
Nicholson, surnamed Lambert, was on board one of
the ships that traded between London and Antwerp.
He was chaplain to the English factory at the latter
place, well versed in the writings of Luther and other
reformers, intimate with Tyndale, and had preached
the Gospel with power.   Being accused of heresy by
a certain Barlow, he was seized, put in irons, and sent
to London.   Alone in the ship, he retraced in his
memory the principal events of his life—how he had
been converted at Cambridge by Bilney's ministry;
how, mingling with the crowd round St. Paul's Cross,
he had heard the bishop of Rochester preach against
the New Testament; and how, terrified by the impiety of the priests, and burning with desire to gain
the knowledge of God, he had crossed the sea.   When

he reached England, he was taken to Lambeth, where
he underwent a preliminary examination. He was
then taken to Ottford, where the archbishop had a
fine palace, and was left there for some time in a
miserable hole, almost without food. At last he was
brought before the archbishop, and called upon to
reply to forty-five different articles.

Lambert, during his residence on the Continent,
had become thoroughly imbued with the principles of
the Reformation. He believed that it was only by
entire freedom of inquiry that men could be convinced of the truth. But he had not wandered
without a compass over the vast ocean of human
opinions : he had taken the Bible in his hand, believing firmly that every doctrine found therein is
true, and everything that contradicts it is false. On
the one hand he saw the ultramontane system which
opposes religious freedom, freedom of the press, and
even freedom of reading ; on the other hand protestantism, which declares that every man ought to
be free to examine Scripture and submit to its
teachings.

The archbishop, attended by his officers, having
taken his seat in the palace chapel, Lambert was
brought in, and the examination began.

'Have you read Luther's books?' asked the prelate.

'Yes,' replied Lambert, 'and I thank God that ever
I did so, for by them hath God shown me, and a
vast multitude of others also, such light as the darkness cannot abide.' Then testifying to the freedom
of inquiry, he added : 'Luther desires above all
things that his writings and the writings of all his
adversaries may be translated into all languages, to

the intent that all people may see and know what is said on each side, whereby they may better judge what is the truth. And this is done not only by hundreds and thousands, but by whole cities and countries, both high and low. But (he continued) in England our prelates are so drowned in voluptuous living that they have no leisure to study God's Scripture; they abhor it, no less than they abhor death, giving no other reason than the tyrannical saying of Sardanapalus: *Sic volo, sic jubeo: sit pro ratione voluntas,* So I will, so do I command, and let my will for reason stand.' *

Lambert, wishing to make these matters intelligible to the people, said: ' When you desire to buy cloth, you will not be satisfied with seeing one merchant's wares, but go from the first to the second, from the second to the third, to find who has the best cloth. Will you be more remiss about your soul's health? . . . When you go a journey, not knowing perfectly the way, you will inquire of one man after another; so ought we likewise to seek about entering the kingdom of heaven. Chrysostom himself teaches you this.† . . . Read the works not only of Luther, but also of all others, be they ever so ill or good. No good law forbids it, but only constitutions pharisaical.'

Warham, who was as much opposed then to the liberty of the press as the popes are now, could see nothing but a boundless chaos in this freedom of inquiry. ' Images are sufficient,' he said, ' to keep Christ and His saints in our remembrance.' But

---

* Foxe, *Acts,* v. pp. 184, 185.
† Chrysostom, in opere imperfecto.

Lambert exclaimed: 'What have we to do with senseless stones or wood carved by the hand of man? That Word which came from the breast of Christ Himself showeth us perfectly His blessed will.' *

Warham having questioned Lambert as to the number of his followers, he answered: 'A great multitude through all regions and realms of Christendom think in like wise as I have showed. I ween the multitude mounteth nigh unto the one half of Christendom.' † Lambert was taken back to prison; but More having resigned the seals, and Warham dying, this herald of liberty and truth saw his chains fall off. One day, however, he was to die by fire, and, forgetting all controversy, to exclaim in the midst of the flames: 'Nothing but Jesus Christ.'

There was a minister of the Word in London who exasperated the friends of Rome more than all the rest; this man was Latimer. The court of Henry VIII., which was worldly, magnificent, fond of pleasures, intrigue, the elegances of dress, furniture, banquets, and refinement of language and manners, was not a favourable field for the Gospel. 'It is very difficult,' said a reformer, 'that costly trappings, solemn banquets, the excesses of pride, a flood of pleasure and debauchery should not bring many evils in their train.' Thus the priests and courtiers could not endure Latimer's sermons. If Lambert was for freedom of inquiry, the king's chaplain was for freedom of preaching: his zeal sometimes touched upon imprudence, and his biting wit, his extreme frankness, did not spare his superiors. One day, some honest merchants, who hun-

---

* Foxe, *Acts*, v. p. 203.　　　　　　† Ibid. p. 225.

gered and thirsted for the Word of God, begged him
to come and preach in one of the city churches.
Thrice he refused, but yielded to their prayers at
last.   The death of Bilney and of the other martyrs
had wounded him deeply.   He knew that wild beasts,
when they have once tasted blood, thirst for more,
and feared that these murders, these butcheries, would
only make his adversaries fiercer.   He determined to
lash the persecuting prelates with his sarcasms.
Having entered the pulpit, he preached from these
words in the epistle of the day : *Ye are not under the
law, but under grace.** 'What!' he exclaimed, 'St.
Paul teaches Christians that they are not under the
law. . . . What does he mean? . . . No more law!
St. Paul invites Christians to break the law. . . .
Quick! inform against St. Paul, seize him and take
him before my lord bishop of London! . . . The
good apostle must be condemned to bear a faggot at
St. Paul's Cross.   What a goodly sight to see St.
Paul with a faggot on his back, before my lord in
person seated on his episcopal throne! . . . But no!
I am mistaken, his lordship would not be satisfied
with so little. . . . he would sooner burn him.' †

This ironical language was to cost Latimer dear.
To no purpose had he spoken in one of those churches
which, being dependencies of a monastery, were not
under episcopal jurisdiction : everybody about him
condemned him and embittered his life.   The courtiers talked of his sermons, shrugged their shoulders,
pointed their fingers at him when he approached
them, and turned their backs on him.   The favour of

---

* Romans, vi. 14.

† Latimer, *Works,* ii. p. 326 (Parker Soc.)

the king, who had perhaps smiled at that burst of pulpit oratory, had some trouble to protect him. The court became more intolerable to him every day, and Latimer, withdrawing to his closet, gave vent to many a heavy sigh. ' What tortures I endure!' he said; 'in what a world I live! Hatred ever at work; factions fighting one against the other; folly and vanity leading the dance; dissimulation, irreligion, debauchery, all the vices stalking abroad in open day. . . . It is too much. If I were able to do something . . . but I have neither the talent nor the industry required to fight against these monsters. . . . I am weary of the court.'

Latimer had recently been presented to the living of West Kington, in the diocese of Salisbury. Wishing to uphold the liberty of the Christian Church, and seeing that it existed no longer in London, he resolved to try and find it elsewhere. ' I am leaving,' he said to one of his friends: 'I shall go and live in my parish.'—' What is that you say?' exclaimed the other; ' Cromwell, who is at the pinnacle of honours, and has profound designs, intends to do great things for you. . . . If you leave the court, you will be forgotten, and your rivals will rise to your place.'— ' The only fortune I desire,' said Latimer, ' is to be useful.' He departed, turning his back on the episcopal crosier to which his friend had alluded.

Latimer began to preach with zeal in Wiltshire, and not only in his own parish, but in the parishes around him. His diligence was so great, his preaching so mighty, says Foxe,* that his hearers must either

* Foxe, *Acts*, vii. p. 454.

believe the doctrine he preached or rise against it.
'Whosoever entereth not into the fold by the door,
which is Christ, be he priest, bishop, or pope, is a
robber,' said he. 'In the Church there are more
thieves than shepherds, and more goats than sheep.' *
His hearers were astounded. One of them (Dr.
Sherwood) said to him: 'What a sermon, or rather
what a satire! If we believe you, all the hemp in
England would not be enough to hang those thieves
of bishops, priests, and curates.† . . . It is all exaggeration, no doubt, but such exaggeration is rash, auda-
cious, and impious.' The priests looked about for
some valiant champion of Rome, ready to fight with
him the quarrel of the Church.

One day there rode into the village an old doctor
of strange aspect; he wore no shirt, but was covered
with a long gown that reached down to the horse's
heels, 'all bedirted like a slobber,' says a chronicler.‡
He took no care for the things of the body, in order
that people should believe he was the more given
up to the contemplation of the interests of the soul.
He dismounted gravely from his horse, proclaimed
his intention of fasting, and began a series of long
prayers. This person, by name Hubberdin, the
Don Quixote of Roman-catholicism, went wandering
all over the kingdom, extolling the pope at the
expense of kings and even of Jesus Christ, and
declaiming against Luther, Zwingle, Tyndale, and
Latimer.

---

* 'Plures longe fures esse quam pa tores.'—Foxe, *Acts*, vii. p. 479.

† 'Quibus latronibus suffocandis ne Angliæ totius canavum sufficere
prædicabas.'—Ibid. p. 478.

‡ Strype, i. p. 245.

On a feast-day Hubberdin put on a clerical gown
rather cleaner than the one he generally wore, and
went into the pulpit, where he undertook to prove
that the new doctrine came from the devil—which he
demonstrated by stories, fables, dreams, and amusing
dialogues. He danced and hopped and leaped about,
and gesticulated, as if he were a stage-player, and his
sermon a sort of interlude.* His hearers were surprised and diverted ; Latimer was ˙ disgusted. ' You
lie,' he said, ' when you call the faith of Scripture a
new doctrine, unless you mean to say that it makes
new creatures of those who receive it.'

Hubberdin being unable to shut the mouth of the
eloquent chaplain with his mountebank tricks, the
bishops and nobility of the neighbourhood resolved
to denounce Latimer. A messenger handed him a
writ, summoning him to appear personally before
the bishop of London to answer touching certain excesses and crimes committed by him.† Putting down
the paper which contained this threatening message,
Latimer began to reflect. His position was critical.
He was at that time suffering from the stone, with
pains in the head and bowels. It was in the dead of
winter, and moreover he was alone at West Kington,
with no friend to advise him. Being of a generous
and daring temperament, he rushed hastily into the
heat of the combat, but was easily dejected. ' Jesu
mercy ! what a world is this,' he exclaimed, ' that I
shall be put to so great labour and pains above my
power for preaching of a poor simple sermon ! But we

---

* Strype, i. p. 245.

† ' Crimina seu excessus graves personaliter responsurus.'—Ibid. p. 455.

must needs suffer, and so enter into the kingdom of Christ.' *

The terrible summons lay on the table. Latimer took it up and read it. He was no longer the brilliant court-chaplain who charmed fashionable congregations by his eloquence; he was a poor country minister, forsaken by all. He was sorrowful. ' I am surprised,' he said, ' that my lord of London, who has so large a diocese in which ·he ought to preach the Word in season and out of season,† should have leisure enough to come and trouble me in my little parish . . . wretched me, who am quite a stranger to him.' He appealed to his ordinary; but Bishop Stokesley did not intend to let him go, and being as able as he was violent, he prayed the archbishop, as primate of all England, to summon Latimer before his court, and to commission himself (the bishop of London) to ex- amine him. The chaplain's friends were terrified, and entreated him to leave England; but he began his journey to London.

On the 29th of January, 1532, a court composed of bishops and doctors of the canon law assembled, under the presidency of Primate Warham, in St. Paul's Cathedral. Latimer having appeared, the bishop of London presented him a paper, and ordered him to sign it. The reformer took the paper and read it through. There were sixteen articles on belief in purgatory, the invocation of saints, the merit of pil- grimages, and lastly on the power of the keys which (said the document) belonged to the bishops of Rome,

---

* 'Oportet pati et sic intrare.'—Latimer, *Works*, ii. p. 351 (Parker Soc.)

† ' Tempestive, intempestive, privatim, publice.'—Ibid.

' even should their lives be wicked,' * and other such
topics.   Latimer returned the paper to Stokesley,
saying : ' I cannot sign it.'   Three times in one week
he had to appear before his judges, and each time the
same scene was repeated : both sides were inflexible.
The priests then changed their tactics : they began
to tease and embarrass Latimer with innumerable
questions.   As soon as one had finished, another
began with sophistry and plausibility, and inter-
minable subterfuges.   Latimer tried to make his adversaries keep within the circle from which they were
straying, but they would not hear him.

One day, as Latimer entered the hall, he noticed a
change in the arrangement of the furniture.   There
was a chimney, in which there had been a fire before :
on this day there was no fire, and the fireplace was
invisible.   Some tapestry hung down over it, and the
table round which the judges sat was in the middle of
the room.   The accused was seated between the table
and the chimney.   ' Master Latimer,' said an aged
bishop, whom he believed to be one of his friends,
' pray speak a little louder : I am hard of hearing, as
you know.'   Latimer, surprised at this remark, pricked
up his ears, and fancied he heard in the fireplace the
noise of a pen upon paper.†   ' Ho ho !' thought he,
' they have hidden some one behind there to take
down my answers.'   He replied cautiously to captious
questions, much to the embarrassment of the judges.

Latimer was disgusted, not only with the tricks of

---

* ' Etiam si male vivant.'—Latimer, *Works*, ii. p. 466 (Parker Soc.) ;
and Foxe, *Acts*, vii. p. 450.

† ' I heard a pen walking in the chimney, behind the cloth.'—Latimer,
Sermons, i. p. 294.

his enemies, but still more with their 'troublesome unquietness;'* because by keeping him in London they obliged him to neglect his duties, and especially because they made it a crime to preach the truth. The archbishop, wishing to gain him over by marks of esteem and affection, invited him to come· and see him; but Latimer declined, being unwilling at any price to renounce the freedom of the pulpit. The reformers of the sixteenth century did not contend that all doctrines should be preached from the same pulpit, but that evangelical truth should be freely preached everywhere. 'I have desired and still desire,' wrote Latimer to the archbishop, 'that our people should learn the difference between the doctrines which God has taught and those which proceed only from ourselves. Go, said Jesus, and *teach all things.* . . . What things? . . . *all things whatsoever I have commanded you,* and not *whatsoever you think fit to preach.*† Let us all then make an effort to preach with one voice the things of God. I have sought not my gain, but Christ's gain; not my glory, but God's glory. And so long as I have a breath of life remaining, I will continue to do so.' ‡

Thus spoke the bold preacher. It is by such unshakeable fidelity that great revolutions are accomplished.

As Latimer was deaf to all their persuasion, there was nothing to be done but to threaten the stake. The charge was transferred to the Convocation of

* Foxe, *Acts,* vii. p. 455.

† 'Non dicit omnia quæ vobis ipsis videntur prædicanda.'—Foxe, *Acts,* iii. p. 747.

‡ 'Donec respirare licebit, stare non desinam.'—Ibid.

Canterbury, and on the 15th of March, 1532, he appeared before that body at Westminster. The fifteen articles were set before him. 'Master Latimer,' said the archbishop, 'the synod calls upon you to sign these articles.'—'I refuse,' he answered.—All the bishops pressed him earnestly. 'I refuse absolutely,' he answered a second time. Warham, the friend of learning, could not make up his mind to condemn one of the finest geniuses of England. 'Have pity on yourself,' he said. 'A third and last time we entreat you to sign these articles.' Although Latimer knew that a negative would probably consign him to the stake, he still answered, 'I refuse absolutely.' *

The patience of Convocation was now exhausted. 'Heretic! obstinate heretic!' exclaimed the bishops. 'We have heard it from his own mouth. Let him be excommunicated.' The sentence of excommunication was pronounced, and Latimer was taken to the Lollards' Tower.

Great was the agitation both in city and court. The creatures of the priests were already singing in the streets songs with a burden like this:

Wherefore it were pity thou shouldst die for cold.†

'Ah!' said Latimer in the Martyrs' Tower, 'if they had asked me to confess that I have been too prompt to use sarcasm, I should have been ready to do so, for sin is a heavy load. O God! unto Thee I cry; wash me in the blood of Jesus Christ.' He looked for death, knowing well that few left that tower except for the scaffold. 'What is to be done?' said

* 'Tertio requisitus ut subscriberet, recusavit.'—Wilkins, Concilia, iii. p. 747.

† Strype, Records, i. p. 180.

K 2

Warham and the bishops. Many of them would have handed the prisoner over to the magistrate to do what was customary, but the rule of the papacy was coming to an end in England, and Latimer was the king's chaplain. One dexterous prelate suggested a means of reconciling everything. 'We must obtain something from him, be it ever so little, and then report everywhere that he has recanted.'

Some priests went to see the prisoner: 'Will you not yield anything?' they asked.—'I have been too violent,' said Latimer, 'and I humble myself accordingly.'—'But will you not recognise the merit of works?'—'No!'—'Prayers to the saints?'—'No!' 'Purgatory?'—'No!'—'The power of the keys given to the pope?'—'No! I tell you.'—A bright idea occurred to one of the priests. Luther taught that it was not only permitted, but praiseworthy, to have the crucifix and the images of the saints, provided that it was merely to remind us of them and not to invoke them. He had added, that the Reformation ought not to abolish fast days, but to strive to make them realities.* Latimer declared that he was of the same opinion.

The deputation hastened to carry this news to the bishops. The more fanatical of them could not make up their minds to be satisfied with so little. What! no purgatory, no virtue in the mass, no prayers to saints, no power of the keys, no meritorious works! It was a signal defeat; but the bishops knew that the king would not suffer the condemnation of his chaplain. Convocation decided, after a long discussion,

---

* Luther, *Wieder die himmlischen Propheten,* and *Explication du 6me chapitre de St. Mathieu.*

that if Master Latimer would sign the two articles, he should be absolved from the sentence of excommunication. In fact, on the 10th of April the Church withdrew the condemnation it had already pronounced.*

* 'Fuit absolutus a sententia excommunicationis.'—Wilkins, *Concilia*, iii. p. 747.

CHAPTER XV.

HENRY VIII. ATTACKS THE PARTISANS OF THE POPE AND OF
THE REFORMATION.

(1532.)

THE vital principle of the Reformation of Henry
VIII. was its opposition both to Rome and the
Gospel. He did not hesitate, like many, between
these two doctrines: he punished alike, by exile or by
fire, the disciples of the Vatican and those of Holy
Scripture.

Desiring to show that the resolution he had taken
to separate from Catherine was immutable, the king
had lodged Anne Boleyn in the palace at Greenwich,
although the queen was still there, and had given
her a reception room and a royal state. The crowd
of courtiers, abandoning the setting star, turned
towards that which was appearing above the horizon.
Henry respected Anne's person, and was eager that
all the world should know that if she was not actually
queen, she would be so one day. There was a want
of delicacy and principle in the king's conduct, at
which the catholic party were much irritated, and not
without a cause.

The monks of St. Francis who officiated in the
royal chapel at Greenwich took every opportunity of
asserting their attachment to Catherine and to the

pope. Anne vainly tried to gain them over by her
charms; if she succeeded with a few, she failed with
the greater number. Their superior, Father Forest,
Catherine's confessor, warmly defended the rights
of that unhappy princess. Preaching at St. Paul's
Cross, he delivered a sermon in which Henry was violently attacked, although he was not named. Those
who had heard it made a great noise about it, and
Forest was summoned to the court. ' What will be
done to him?' people asked; but instead of sending
him to prison, as many expected, the king received
him well, spoke with him for half an hour, and ' sent
him a great piece of beef from his own table.'

On returning to his convent, Forest described with
triumph this flattering reception; but the king did
not attain his object. Among these monks there
were men of independent, perhaps of fanatical,
character, whom no favours could gain over.

One of them, by name Peto, until then unknown,
but afterwards of great repute in the catholic world
as cardinal legate from the pope in England,* thinking that Forest had not said enough, determined to
go further. Anne Boleyn's elevation filled him with
anger: he longed to speak out, and as the king
and all the court would be present in the chapel
on the 1st of May, he chose for his text the
words of the prophet Elijah to King Ahab: *The
dogs shall lick thy blood.*† He drew a portrait of
Ahab, described his malice and wickedness, and
although he did not name Henry VIII., certain pas-

* Tyndale, *Treatises*, p. 38; Strype, *Memorials*, i. 257, iii., bk. i. p. 257;
bk. ii. pp. 30, 136.
† 1 Kings xxi. 19.

sages made the hearers feel uncomfortable. At the
peroration, turning towards the king, he said: 'Now
hear, O king, what I have to say unto thee, as of old
time Micaiah spoke to Ahab. This new marriage is
unlawful. There are other preachers who, to become
rich abbots or mighty bishops, betray thy soul, thy
honour, and thy posterity. Take heed lest thou, being
seduced like Ahab, find Ahab's punishment . . . who
had his blood licked up by the dogs.'

The court was astounded; but the king, whose features were unmoved during this apostrophe, waited
until the end of the service, left the chapel as if nothing
had happened, and allowed Peto to depart for Canterbury. But Henry could not permit such invectives
to pass unnoticed. A clergyman named Kirwan was
commissioned to preach in the same chapel on the following Sunday. The congregation was still more numerous than before, and more curious also. Some monks
of the order of Observants, friends of Peto, got into
the rood-loft, determined to defend him. The doctor
began his sermon. After establishing the lawfulness
of Henry's intended marriage, he came to the sermon
of the preceding Sunday and the insults of the preacher.
'I speak to thee, Peto,' he exclaimed, 'who makest thyself Micaiah; we look for thee, but thou art not to be
found, having fled for fear and shame.' There was a
noise in the rood-loft, and one of the Observants named
Elstow rose and called out: 'You know that Father
Peto is gone to Canterbury to a provincial council, but
I am here to answer you. And to this combat I
challenge thee, Kirwan, prophet of lies, who for thy
own vainglory art betraying thy king into endless
perdition.'

The chapel was instantly one scene of confusion: nothing could be heard. Then the king rose: his princely stature, his royal air, his majestic manners overawed the crowd. All were silent, and the agitated congregation left the chapel respectfully. Peto and his friend were summoned before the council. 'You deserve to be sewn in a sack and thrown into the Thames,' said one. 'We fear nothing,' answered Elstow; 'the way to heaven is as short by water as by land.' *

Henry having thus made war on the partisans of the pope, turned to those of the Reformation. Like a child, he see-sawed to and fro, first on one side, then on the other; but his sport was a more terrible one, for every time he touched the ground the blood spurted forth.

At that time there were many Christians in England to whom the Roman worship brought no edification. Having procured Tyndale's translation of the Word of God, they felt that they possessed it not only for themselves but for others. They sought each other's company, and met together to read the Bible and receive spiritual graces from God. Several Christian assemblies of this kind had been formed in London, in garrets, in warehouses, schools and shops, and one of them was held in a warehouse in Bow Lane. Among its frequenters was the son of a Gloucestershire knight, James Bainham by name, a man well read in the classics, and a distinguished lawyer, respected by all for his piety and works of charity. To give advice freely to widows and orphans, to see justice done to the oppressed, to aid poor students,

* Tyndale, *Treatises*, p. 38. Stowe, *Annals*, p. 562.

protect pious persons, and visit the prisons, were his daily occupations. ' He was an earnest reader of Scripture, and mightily addicted to prayer.' *   When he entered the meeting, every one could see that his countenance expressed a calm joy; but for a month past his Bow Lane friends noticed him to be agitated and cast down, and heard him sighing heavily. The cause was this. Some time before (in 1531), when he was engaged about his business in the Middle Temple, this ' model of lawyers ' had been arrested by order of More, who was still chancellor, and taken like a criminal to the house of the celebrated humanist at Chelsea. Sir Thomas, quite distressed at seeing a man so distinguished leave the Church of Rome, had employed all his eloquence to bring him back; but finding his efforts useless, he had ordered Bainham to be taken into his garden and tied to ' the tree of truth.' There the chancellor whipped him, or caused him to be whipped: we adopt the latter version, which is more probable.† Bainham having refused to give the names of the gentlemen of the Temple tainted with heresy, he was taken to the Tower. ' Put him on the rack,' cried the learned chancellor, now become a fanatical persecutor. The order was obeyed in his presence. The arms and legs of the unfortunate protestant were seized by the instrument and pulled in opposite directions: his limbs were dislocated, and he went lame out of the torture-chamber.‡

* Foxe, *Acts*, iv. p. 697.

† Both Strype (*Memorials*, i. p. 35) and Foxe (*Acts*, iv. p. 698) say, *and whipped him*; but More denied it.

‡ ' Sir Thomas More being present himself, till in a manner he had lamed him.'—Foxe, *Acts*, iv. p. 698.

Sir Thomas had broken his victim's limbs, but not his courage; and accordingly when Bainham was summoned before the bishop of London, he went to the palace rejoicing to have to confess his Master once more. 'Do you believe in purgatory?' said Stokesley to him sternly. Bainham answered: '*The blood of Jesus Christ cleanseth us from all sin.*' * 'Do you believe that we ought to call upon the saints to pray for us?' He again answered: '*If any man sin, we have an advocate with the Father—Jesus Christ the righteous.*'†

A man who answered only by texts from Scripture was embarrassing. More and Stokesley made the most alluring promises, and no means were spared to bend him.‡ Before long they resorted to more serious representations: 'The arms of the Church your mother are still open to you,' they said; 'but if you continue stubborn, they will close against you for ever. It is now or never!' For a whole month the bishop and the chancellor persevered in their entreaties; Bainham replied: 'My faith is that of the holy Church.' Hearing these words, Foxford, the bishop's secretary, took out a paper. 'Here is the abjuration,' he said; 'read it over.' Bainham began: 'I voluntarily, as a true penitent returned from my heresy, utterly abjure' . . . At these words he stopped, and glancing over what followed, he continued: 'No, these articles are not heretical, and I cannot retract them.' Other springs were now set in motion to shake Bainham. The prayers of his friends, the threats of his enemies, especially the

* 1 John i. 7.　　　　　　　　　　† Ibid. ii. 1.

‡ Foxe, *Acts*, iv. p. 700.

thought of his wife, whom he loved, and who would be left alone in destitution, exposed to the anger of the world: these things troubled his soul. He lost sight of the narrow path he ought to follow, and five days later he read his abjuration with a faint voice. But he had hardly got to the end before he burst into tears, and said, struggling with his emotion: ' I reserve the doctrines.' He consented to remain in the Roman Church, still preserving his evangelical faith. But this was not what the bishop and his officers meant. ' Kiss that book,' they said to him threateningly. Bainham, like one stunned, kissed the book; that was the sign; the abjuration was looked upon as complete. He was condemned to pay a fine of twenty pounds sterling, and to do penance at St. Paul's Cross. After that he was set at liberty, on the 17th of February.

Bainham returned to the midst of his brethren: they looked sorrowfully at him, but did not reproach him with his fault. That was quite unnecessary. The worm of remorse was preying on him; he abhorred the fatal kiss by which he had sealed his fall; his conscience was never quiet; he could neither eat nor sleep, and trembled at the thought of death. At one time he would hide his anguish and stifle it within his breast; at another his grief would break forth, and he would try to relieve his pain by groans of sorrow. The thought of appearing before the tribunal of God made him faint. The restoration of conscience to all its rights was the foremost work of the Reformation. Luther, Calvin, and an endless number of more obscure reformers had reached the haven of safety through the midst of such tempests. ' A tragedy was being acted in all protestant souls,' says a writer who does not belong to the Reformation—the eternal tragedy of conscience.

Bainham felt that the only means of recovering peace was to accuse himself openly before God and man. Taking Tyndale's New Testament in his hand, which was at once his joy and his strength, he went to St. Austin's church, sat down quietly in the midst of the congregation, and then at a certain moment stood up and said: 'I have denied the truth.' . . . He could not continue for his tears.* On recovering, he said: 'If I were not to return again to the doctrine I have abjured, this word of Scripture would condemn me both body and soul at the day of judgment.' And he lifted up the New Testament before all the congregation. 'O my friends,' he continued, 'rather die than sin as I have done. The fires of hell have consumed me, and I would not feel them again for all the gold and glory of the world.'†

Then his enemies seized him again and shut him up in the bishop's coal-cellar, where, after putting him in irons, they left him for four days. He was afterwards taken to the Tower, where he was scourged every day for a fortnight, and at last condemned as a relapsed heretic.

On the eve of the execution four distinguished men, one of whom was Latimer, were dining together in London. It was commonly reported that Bainham was to be put to death for saying that Thomas à Becket was a traitor worthy of hell. 'Is it worth a

* 'Stood up there before the people in his pew with weeping tears.' —Foxe, *Acts,* iv. p. 702.

† 'He would not feel such a hell again as he did feel.'—Ibid.

man's while to sacrifice his life for such a trifle?' said
the four friends. 'Let us go to Newgate and save
him if possible.' They were taken along several
gloomy passages, and found themselves at last in the
presence of a man, sitting on a little straw, holding a
book in one hand and a candle in the other.* He was
reading; it was Bainham. Latimer drew near him:
'Take care,' he said, ' that no vainglory make you
sacrifice your life for motives which are not worth the
cost.' 'I am condemned,' answered Bainham, ' for
trusting in Scripture and rejecting purgatory, masses,
and meritorious works.'—'I acknowledge that for
such truths a man must be ready to die.' Bainham
was ready; and yet he burst into tears. 'Why do
you weep?' asked Latimer. 'I have a wife,' answered
the prisoner, ' the best that man ever had. A widow,
destitute of everything and without a supporter,
everybody will point at her and say, That is the
heretic's wife.'† Latimer and his friends tried to console him, and then they departed from the gloomy
dungeon.

The next day (30th of April, 1532) Bainham was
taken to the scaffold. Soldiers on horseback surrounded the pile: Master Pave, the city clerk, directed the execution. Bainham, after a prayer, rose
up, embraced the stake, and was fastened to it with a
chain. 'Good people,' he said to the persons who
stood round him, ' I die for having said it is lawful
for every man and woman to have God's book. I die
for having said that the true key of heaven is not that
of the bishop of Rome, but the preaching of the

* Strype, *Annals*, i. p. 372.   † Ibid.

Gospel. I die for having said that there is no other purgatory than the cross of Christ, with its consequent persecutions and afflictions.'—'Thou liest, thou heretic,' exclaimed Pave; 'thou hast denied the blessed sacrament of the altar.'—'I do not deny the sacrament of Christ's body,' resumed Bainham, 'but I do deny your idolatry to a piece of bread.'—'Light the fire,' shouted Pave. The executioners set fire to a train of gunpowder, and as the flame approached him, Bainham lifted up his eyes towards heaven, and said to the town clerk: 'God forgive thee! the Lord forgive Sir Thomas More . . . pray for me, all good people!' The arms and legs of the martyr were soon consumed, and thinking only how to glorify his Saviour, he exclaimed: 'Behold! you look for miracles, you may see one here; for in this fire I feel no more pain than if I were on a bed of roses.' * The primitive Church hardly had a more glorious martyr.

Pave had Bainham's image continually before his eyes, and his last prayer rang day and night in his heart. In the garret of his house, far removed from noise, he had fitted up a kind of oratory, where he had placed a crucifix, before which he used to pray and shed bitter tears.† He abhorred himself: half mad, he suffered indescribable sorrow, and struggled under great anguish. The dying Bainham had said to him: 'May God show thee more mercy than thou hast shown to me!' But Pave could not believe in mercy: he saw no other remedy for his despair than death. About a year after Bainham's martyrdom, he sent his domestics and clerks on different errands, keeping only one servant-maid in the house. As soon

* Foxe, *Acts*, iv. p. 705.   † Ibid.

as his wife had gone to church, he went out himself, bought a rope, and hiding it carefully under his gown, went up into the garret. He stopped before the crucifix, and began to groan and weep. The servant ran upstairs. 'Take this rusty sword,' he said, 'clean it well, and do not disturb me.' She had scarcely left the room when he fastened the rope to a beam and hanged himself.

The maid, hearing no sound, again grew alarmed, went up to the garret, and seeing her master hanging, was struck with terror. She ran crying to the church to fetch her mistress home;* but it was too late: the wretched man could not be recalled to life.

If the deaths of the martyrs plunged the wicked into the depths of despair, it often gave life to earnest souls. The crowd which had surrounded the scaffold of these men of God dispersed in profound emotion. Some returned to their fields, others to their shops or workrooms; but the pale faces of the martyrs followed them, their words sounded in their souls, their virtues softened many hearts most averse to the Gospel. 'Oh! that I were with Bainham!' exclaimed one.† These people continued for some time to frequent the Romish churches, but ere long their consciences cried aloud to them: 'It is Christ alone who saves us;' and they forsook the rites in which they could find no consolation. They courted solitude; they procured the writings of Wickliffe and of Tyndale, and especially the New Testament, which they read in secret, and if any one came near, hid them hastily under a bed, at the bottom of a chest, in the hollow of a tree, or even under stones, until the enemy had retired and they

* Foxe, *Acts*, iv. p. 706.   † Ibid. v. p. 32.

could take the books up again.   Then they whispered about them to their neighbours, and often had the joy of meeting with men who thought as they did.   A surprising change was taking place.   While the priests were loudly chanting in the cathedrals the praises of the saints, of the Virgin, and of the *Corpus Domini*, the people were whispering together about the Saviour *meek and lowly in heart*.   All over England was heard a still, small voice such as Elijah heard, and on hearing it wrapped his face in his mantle and stood silent and motionless, because the Lord was there. Great changes were about to take place.

It is not without a reason that we describe in some detail in this history the lives and deaths of these evangelical men.   We desire to show that the Church in England, as in all the world, is not a mere ecclesiastical hierarchy, in which prelates exercise dominion over the inheritance of the Lord; nor a confused assemblage of men, whose spirit imagines about religion all kinds of doctrines contrary to the revelation from heaven, and whose profession of faith comprehends all the opinions that are found in the nation from catholic scholasticism to pantheistic materialism.   The Church of God, raised above the human systems of the superstitious and the incredulous alike, is the assembly of those who by a living faith are partakers of the righteousness of Christ, and of the new life of which the Holy Ghost is the creator—of those in whom selfishness is vanquished, and who give themselves up to the Saviour to achieve with their brethren the conquest of the world.   Such is the true Church of God; very different, it will be seen, from all those invented by man.

CHAPTER XVI.

THE NEW PRIMATE OF ALL ENGLAND.

(FEBRUARY 1532 TO MARCH 1533.)

A MAN who for more than thirty years had had an important voice in the management of the ecclesiastical affairs of the kingdom now disappeared from the scene to give place to the most influential of the reformers of England. Warham, archbishop of Canterbury, a learned canonist, a skilful politician, a dexterous courtier, and the friend of letters, had made it his special work to exalt the sacerdotal prerogative, and to that end had had recourse to the surest means, by fighting against the idleness, ignorance, and corruption of the priests. He had even hoped for a reform of the clergy, provided it emanated from episcopal authority. But when he saw another reformation accomplished in the name of God's Word, without priests and against the priests, he turned round and began to persecute the reformers and to strengthen the papal authority. Alarmed at the proceedings of the Commons, he sent for three notaries, on the 24th February, 1532, and protested in their presence against every act of parliament derogatory to the authority of the Roman pontiff.[*]

---

[*] 'Protestamur quod nolumus alicui statuto edito in derogationem Romani pontificis consentire.'—Wilkins, *Concilia*, iii. p. 746.

On the 22nd August of the same year, just at the very height of the crisis, 'the second pope,' as he was sometimes called, was removed from his see by death, and the people anxiously wondered who would be appointed to his vacant place.

The choice was important, for the nomination might be the symbol of what the Church of England was to be. Would he be a prelate devoted to the pope, like Fisher; or a catholic favourable to the divorce, like Gardiner; or a moderate evangelical attached to the king, like Cranmer; or a decided re-former, like Latimer? At this moment, when a new era was beginning for Christendom, it was of consequence to know whom England would take for her guide; whether she would march at the head of civilisation, like Germany; or bring up the rear, like Spain and Italy. The king did not favour either extreme, and hesitated between the two other candidates. All things considered, he had no confidence in such men as Longland and Gardiner, who might promise and not fulfil. He wanted somebody less political than the one, and less fanatical than the other—a man separated from the pope on principle, and not merely for convenience.

Cranmer, after passing a few months at Rome, had returned to England.* Then departing again for Germany on a mission from the king, he had arrived at Nuremberg, probably in the autumn of 1531. He examined with interest that ancient city, its beautiful churches, its monumental fountains, its old and picturesque castle; but there was something that

* There is a letter of his dated from Hampton Court, 12th June, 1531.

attracted him more than all these things. Being
present at the celebration of the sacrament, he noticed
that while the priest was muttering the gospel in
Latin at the altar, the deacon went up into the pulpit
and read it aloud in German.* He saw that, although
there was still some appearance of catholicism in
Nuremberg, in reality the Gospel reigned there. One
man's name often came up in the conversations he
had with the principal persons in the city. They
spoke to him of Osiander as of a man of great eloquence.† Cranmer followed the crowd which poured
into the church of St. Lawrence, and was struck
with the minister's talents and piety. He sought his
acquaintance, and the two doctors had many a conversation together, either in Cranmer's house or in Osiander's study; and the German divine, being gained
over to the cause of Henry VIII., published shortly
after a book on unlawful marriages.

Cranmer, who had an affectionate heart, loved to
join the simple meals, the pious devotions, and the
friendly conversations at Osiander's house; he was
soon almost like a member of the family. But although his intimacy with the Nuremberg pastor grew
stronger every day, he did not adopt all his opinions.
When Osiander told him that he must substitute the
authority of Holy Scripture for that of Rome, Cranmer
gave his full assent; but the Englishman perceived
that the German entertained views different from
Luther's on the justification of the sinner. 'What

---

* Cotton MS., Vitellius, bk. xxi. p. 54.

† 'Commendatus primoribus civitatis facundia sua.'--Camerarius,
Melanchthonis Vita, p. 285.

justifies us,' he said, 'is not the imputation of the merits of Christ by faith, but the inward communication of His righteousness.' 'Christ,' said Cranmer, 'has paid the price of our redemption by the sacrifice of His body and the fulfilling of the law; and if we heartily believe in this work which He has perfected, we are justified. The justified man must be sanctified, and must work good works; but it is not the works that justify him.'* The conversation of the two friends turned also upon the Lord's Supper. Whatever may have been Cranmer's doctrine before, he soon came (like Calvin) to place the real presence of Christ not in the wafer which the priest holds between his fingers, but in the heart of the believer.†

In June 1532 the protestant and Roman-catholic delegates arrived at Nuremberg to arrange the religious peace. The celibacy of the clergy immediately became one of the points discussed. It appeared to the chiefs of the papacy impossible to concede that article. 'Rather abolish the mass entirely,' exclaimed the archbishop of Mayence, 'than permit the marriage of priests.' 'They must come to that at last,' said Luther; 'God is overthrowing the mighty from their seat.'‡ Cranmer was of his opinion: 'It is better,' he said, 'for a minister to have his own wife, than to have other men's wives, like the priests.'§ 'What services may not a pious wife do for the pastor

---

* 'It excludeth them from the office of justifying.'—*Homily of Salvation*. Cranmer, *Works*, ii. p. 129 (Parker Soc.)

† 'Christ is corporally in heaven and spiritually in His lively members.'—Cranmer, *On the Lord's Supper*, p. 33.

‡ Lutheri *Opp.* xxii. p. 1808.

§ Cranmer, *Works*, ii. p. 219 (Parker Soc.)

her husband,' added Osiander, 'among the poor, the women, and the children?'

Cranmer had lost his wife at Cambridge, and his heart yearned for affection. Osiander's family presented him a touching picture of domestic happiness. One of its members was a niece of Osiander's wife.* Cranmer, charmed with her piety and candour, and hoping to find in her the virtuous woman who is a crown to her husband, asked her hand and married her, not heeding the unlawful command of those who 'forbid to marry.' †

Still Cranmer did not forget his mission. The king of England was desirous of forming an alliance with the German protestants, and his agent made overtures to the electoral prince of Saxony. 'First of all,' answered the pious John Frederick, 'the two kings (of France and England) must be in harmony with us as to the articles of faith.'‡ The alliance failed, but, at the same moment, affairs took an unexpected turn. The emperor, who was marching against Solyman, desired the help of the King of England, and Granvelle had some talk with Cranmer on the subject. The latter was procuring carriages, horses, boats, tents, and other things necessary for his journey, with the intention of rejoining the emperor at Lintz, when a courier suddenly brought him orders to return to London.§ It was very vexatious. Just as he was on the point of concluding an alliance with the nephew of Queen Catherine, in which the matter of the

---

* 'Hæc erat neptis uxoris Osiandri.'—Godwin, *Annales Angl.* p. 167.
† 1 Timothy iv. 3.
‡ Seckendorff, *Hist. Lutheranismi*, 1532.
§ Cranmer, *Remains*, p. 232.

divorce would consequently be arranged, Henry's envoy had to give up everything. He wondered anxiously what could be the motive of this sudden and extraordinary recall: the letters of his friends explained it.

Warham was dead, and the king thought of Cranmer to succeed him as archbishop of Canterbury and primate of all England. The reformer was greatly moved. 'Alas!' he exclaimed, 'no man has ever desired a bishopric less than myself.* If I accept it, I must resign the delights of study and the calm sweetness of an obscure condition.'† Knowing Henry's domineering character and his peculiar religious principles, Cranmer thought that with him the reformation of England was impossible. He saw himself exposed to disputes without end: there would be no more peace for the most peaceable of men. A brilliant career, an exalted position — he was terrified. 'My conscience,' he said, 'rebels against this call. Wretch that I am! I see nothing but troubles, and conflicts, and insurmountable dangers in my path.'

Upon mature reflection, Cranmer thought he might get out of his difficulty by gaining time, hoping that the king, who did not like delays, would doubtless give the see to another.‡ He sent an answer that important affairs prevented his return to England. Solyman had retreated before the emperor; the latter had determined to pass through Italy to Spain, and had appointed a meeting with the pope at

---

* Cranmer, *Remains*, p. 232.   † Foxe, *Acts*, viii. p. 65.

‡ 'Thinking that he would be forgetful of me in the meantime.' —Cranmer, *Remains*, p. 216.

Piacenza or Genoa.   Henry's ambassador thought it his duty to neutralise the fatal consequences of this interview; and Charles having left Vienna on the 4th of October, Cranmer followed him two days later. The exalted dignity that awaited him oppressed him like the nightmare.   On his road he found neither inhabitants nor food, and hay was his only bed.* Sometimes he crossed battle-fields covered with the carcases of Turks and Christians.   A comet appeared in the east foreboding some tragic event.   Many declared they had seen a flaming sword in the heavens. ' These strange signs,' he wrote to Henry, ' announce some great mutation.' †   Cranmer and his colleagues could not gain the pope to their side.   Several months passed away, during which men's minds became so excited, that the cardinals forgot all decorum.   ' Alas!' says a catholic historian, ' all the time this affair continued, they went to the consistory as if they were going to a play.'‡   Charles V. prevailed at last.

Then came that famous interview (October 1532) between the kings of France and England at Calais and Boulogne, which we have described elsewhere; § and the two princes having come to an understanding, Henry thought seriously of bringing the matter to an end.   Did he marry Anne Boleyn at that time? Everything seems to point in that direction; and if we are to believe some of the most trustworthy historians, the marriage took place in the following month

* ' I found in no town, man, woman, nor child, meat, drink, nor bedding.'—Cranmer, *Remains*, p. 223.

† Ibid. p. 225.

‡ Le Grand, *Histoire du Divorce*, i. p. 229.

§ *History of the Reformation of the Sixteenth Century*, tom. ii. bk. ii. ch. xxi.

of November.* Perhaps it was quite a private wedding, the legal formalities not being completed. Contemporary testimony is at variance, and the point has not been cleared up. In any case, Henry determined to wait before making the marriage public. The conference the pope was about to hold at Bologna with the ambassador of Francis I.; the probability of an interview between the king of France and the pontiff at Marseilles, which might give a new aspect to the great affair; and perhaps the desire to confer about it with Cranmer, for whom he destined the see of Canterbury—seem to have induced the prince to defer the ceremony for a few weeks. He lost no time, however, in summoning the future primate to London.

A report having circulated in Italy, that the king was about to place Cranmer at the head of the English Church, the imperial court treated him with unusual consideration. Charles V., his ministers, and the foreign ambassadors, said openly that such a man richly deserved to hold a high place in the favour and government of the king his master.† About the middle of November, the emperor gave Cranmer his farewell audience; and the latter arrived in England not long after. Not wishing to act in opposition to general usage and clerical opinion, he thought it more prudent to leave his wife for a time with Osiander. He sent for her somewhat later, but she was

---

* This is the date given by Hall, *Chronicles,* fol. 209; Holinshed, *Chronicles,* iii. p. 629; Strype, *Cranmer's Mem.* p. 16; Collyers, ii. p. 71. Others hesitate between November and January (1533); Burnet, i. p. 121; Herbert, p. 368; Benger, p. 336, &c.

† 'They judge him a man right worthy to be high in favour and authority with his prince.'—*State Papers* (Henry VIII.), vii. p. 391.

never presented at court. It was not necessary, and it might only have embarrassed the pious German lady.

As soon as Cranmer reached London, he waited upon the king, being quite engrossed in thinking of what was about to take place between his sovereign and himself. Henry went straight to the point: he told him that he had nominated him archbishop of Canterbury. Cranmer objected, but the king would take no refusal. In vain did the divine urge his reasons: the monarch was firm. It was no slight matter to contend with Henry VIII. Cranmer was alarmed at the effect produced by his resistance. 'Your Highness,' he said, 'I most humbly implore your Grace's pardon.' *

When he left the king, he hurried off to his friends, particularly to Cromwell. The burden which Henry was laying upon him seemed more insupportable than ever. Knowing how difficult it is to resist a prince of despotic character, he foresaw conflicts and perhaps compromises, which would embitter his life, and he could not make up his mind to sacrifice his happiness to the imperious will of the monarch. 'Take care,' said his friends, 'it is as dangerous to refuse a favour from so absolute a prince as to insult him.' But Cranmer's conscience was concerned in his refusal. 'I feel something within me,' he said,† 'which rebels against the supremacy of the pope, and all the superstitions to which I should have to submit as primate of England. No, I will not be a bishop!' He might sacrifice his repose and his happiness, expose

* Foxe, *Acts*, viii. p. 66.   † 'Aliquid intus.'

himself to painful struggles; but to recognise the pope and submit to his jurisdiction was an insurmountable obstacle. His friends shook their heads. 'Your *nolo episcopari*,' they said, 'will not hold against our master's *volo te episcopum esse*.* And after all what is it? Permitting the king to place you at the summit of honours and power. . . . You refuse all that men desire.' 'I would sooner forfeit my life,' answered Cranmer, 'than do anything against my conscience to gratify my ambition.'†

Henry, vexed at all these delays, again summoned Cranmer to the palace, and bade him speak without fear. 'If I accept this office,' replied that sincere man, 'I must receive it from the hands of the pope, and this my conscience will not permit me to do. . . . Neither the pope nor any other foreign prince has authority in this realm.'‡ Such a reason as this had great weight with Henry. He was silent for a little while, as if reflecting,§ and then said to Cranmer: 'Can you prove what you have just said?' 'Certainly I can,' answered the doctor; 'Holy Scripture and the Fathers support the supreme authority of kings in their kingdoms, and thus prove the claims of the pope to be a miserable usurpation.'

Such a statement bound Henry to take another step in his reforms. As he had not yet thought of establishing bishops and archbishops without the pope, he sent for some learned lawyers, and asked them how he could confer the episcopal dignity on Cranmer

---

* 'I am unwilling to be made a bishop.' 'I desire you to be a bishop.' —Fuller, *Eccl. Hist.* bk. v. p. 184.

† Foxe, *Acts*, viii. p. 66.

‡ Cranmer, *Remains*, p. 223.   § Ibid.

without wounding the conscience of the future primate. The lawyers proposed, that as Cranmer refused
to submit to the Roman primacy, some one should be
sent to Rome to do in his stead all that the law required. 'Let another do it, if he likes,' said Cranmer,
'but *super animam suam*, at the risk of his soul. As
for me, I declare I will not acknowledge the authority
of the pope any further than it agrees with the Word
of God; and that I reserve the right of speaking
against him and of attacking his errors.'

The lawyers found bad precedents to justify a bad
measure. 'Archbishop Warham,' they said, 'while
preserving the advantages he derived from the state,
protested against everything the state did prejudicial
to Rome. If the deceased archbishop preserved the
rights of the papacy, why should not the new one
preserve those of the kingdom? . . . Besides (they
added) the pope knows very well that when they
make oath to him, every bishop does so *salvo ordine
meo*, without prejudice to the rights of his order.' *

It having been conceded that in the act of consecration 'the rights of the Word of God' should be
reserved, Cranmer consented to become primate of
England. Henry VIII., who was less advanced in
practice than in theory, all the same demanded of
Clement VII. the bulls necessary for the inauguration
of the new archbishop. The pontiff, only too happy
to have still something to say to England, hastened to
despatch them, addressing them directly to Cranmer
himself. But the latter, who would accept nothing

---

* Bossuet makes this remark when speaking of Cranmer's oath. —
Histoire des Variations, liv. vii. p. 11.

from the pope, sent them to the king, declaring that he would not receive his appointment from Rome.*

By accepting the call that was addressed to him, Cranmer meant to break with the order of the Middle Ages, and reestablish, so far as was in his power, that of the Gospel. But he would not conceal his intentions: all must be done in the light of day. On the 30th of March, 1533, he summoned to the chapter-house of Westminster Watkins, the king's prothonotary, with other dignitaries of the Church and State. On entering, he took up a paper, and read aloud and distinctly: 'I, Thomas, archbishop of Canterbury, protest openly, publicly, and expressly,† that I will not bind myself by oath to anything contrary to the law of God, the rights of the king of England, and the laws of the realm; and that I will not be bound in aught that concerns liberty of speech, the government of the Church of England, and the reformation of all things that may seem to be necessary to be reformed therein. If my representative with the pope has taken in my name an oath contrary to my duty, I declare that he has done so without my knowledge, and that the said oath shall be null. I desire this protest to be repeated at each period of the present ceremony.'‡ Then turning to the prothonotary: 'I beg you to prepare as many copies as may be necessary of this my protest.'

Cranmer left the chapter-house and entered the

---

* 'Quas bullas obtulit tum regi.'—Lambeth MS. No. 1136.

† 'Palam et publice et expresse protestor.'—Wilkins, *Concilia*, iii. p. 757.

‡ 'Quas protestationes in omnibus clausulis et sententiis dictorum juramentorum repetitas et recitatas volo.'—Wilkins, *Concilia*, iii. p. 757.

abbey, where the clergy and a numerous crowd
awaited him.   He was not satisfied with once declaring his independence of the papacy; he desired
to do it several times.   The greater the antiquity of
the Romish power in Britain, the more he felt the
necessity of proclaiming the supremacy of the Divine
Word.   Having put on his sacerdotal robes, Cranmer
stood at the top of the steps of the high altar, and
said, turning towards the assembly: ' I declare that I
take the oath required of me only under the reserve
contained in the protest I have made this day in the
chapter-house.'   Then bending his knees before the
altar, he read it a second time in presence of the
bishops, priests, and people; * after which the bishops
of Lincoln, Exeter, and St. Asaph consecrated him to
the episcopate.

The archbishop, standing before the altar, prepared
to receive the pallium, but first he had a duty to
fulfil: if he sacrificed his repose, he did not intend to
sacrifice his convictions.   For the third time he took
up the protest, and again read it † before the immense
crowd that filled the cathedral.‡   The accustomed
order of the ceremony having been twice interrupted
by an extraordinary declaration, all were at liberty
to praise or blame the action of the prelate as they
pleased.   Cranmer having thus thrice published
his reserves, read at last the oath which the archbishops of Canterbury were accustomed to make to
St. Peter and to the holy apostolic Church of Rome,

* 'Eandem sedulam perlegit.'—Lambeth MS. No. 2106.
† ' Qua protestatione per eundem reverendissimum tertio facta.'—Ibid.
‡ 'In the presence of so much people as the church could hold.'—
Card. Pole.

with the usual protest: *salvo meo ordine* (without prejudice to my order).

Cranmer's triple protest was an act of Christian decision. Some time afterwards he said: 'I made that protest in good faith: I always loved simplicity and hated falseness.' But it was wrong of him to use after it the formula ordinarily employed in consecrations. Doubtless it was nothing more than a form; a form that was imposed by the king, and Cranmer protested against all the bad it might contain: still 'it is necessary to walk consistently in all things,' as Calvin says;* and we here meet with one of those weaknesses which sometimes appear in the life of the pious reformer of England. He ought at no price to have made oath to the pope; that oath was a stain which in some measure tinged the whole of his episcopate. Yet if we were to condemn him severely, we should be forgetting that striking truth—*in many things we offend all.* Cranmer was the first in the breach, and he has claims to the consideration of those who are comfortably established in a position gained by him with so much suffering. The energy with which he thrice proclaimed his independence deserves our admiration. Nevertheless all weakness is a fault, and when that fault is committed in high station it may lead to fatal consequences. The sanctity of the oath taken by churchmen was compromised by Cranmer's act, and we have seen in later times other divines secretly communing with Romish doctrines while appearing to reject popery. There have sometimes been disguised papists in the protestant Church of England.

* 'Il faut marcher rondement en toutes choses.'

After the ceremony the new archbishop returned to his palace at Lambeth. From that hour this patron of letters, a scholar himself, a truly pious man, a distinguished preacher, and of indefatigable industry, never ceased to labour for the good of the Church. He was able to introduce Christian faith into many hearts, and sometimes to defend it against the king's ill-humour. He constantly endeavoured to spread around him moderation, charity, truth, piety, and peace. When Cranmer became primate of all England, on the 30th of March, 1533, in that cathedral of Westminster, the burial-place of kings, the papal order was interred, and it might be foreseen that the apostolic order would be revived. England preserved episcopacy because it was the form under which she had received Christianity in the second century, and because she thought it necessary for the functions of inspection and government in the Church. But she rejected that Roman superstition which makes bishops the sole successors of the apostles, and maintains that they are invested with an indelible character and a spiritual power which no other minister possesses.[*] ' Most assuredly,' said Cranmer, ' at the beginning of the religion of Christ, bishops and presbyters (priests) were not two things, but one only.'[†] He declared that a bishop was not necessary to make a pastor; that not only presbyters possessed this right, but ' *the people also by their election.*' ' Before there were Christian princes, it was the people,' he said, ' who generally elected the bishops and priests.' Cranmer

[*] Concilium Tridentinum, Sessio prima.

[†] Resolutions of certain bishops. Burnet, *Records*, bk. iii. art. 21; Cranmer, *Remains*, p. 117.

was not the only man who professed these principles, which make of the episcopalian and the presbyterian constitution two varieties, having many things in common. The most venerable fathers of the Anglican Church—Pilkington, Coverdale, Whitgift, Fulke, Tyndale, Jewel, Bradford, Becon, and others—have acknowledged the identity of bishops and presbyters. By the Reformation, England belongs not to the papistical system of episcopacy, but to the evangelical system. A public act which would bring back that Church to her holy origin, would be a source of great prosperity to her.

The great reformers of England did not separate from Rome only, but also from the semi-catholicism that was intended to be substituted for it. To them the spirit and the life were in the ministry of the Word of God, and not in rites and ceremonies. By their noble example they have called all men of God to follow them.

CHAPTER XVII.

QUEEN CATHERINE DESCENDS FROM THE THRONE, AND QUEEN
ANNE BOLEYN ASCENDS IT.

(NOVEMBER 1532 TO JULY 1533.)

CRANMER was on the archiepiscopal throne: if
Anne Boleyn were now to take her seat on the
royal throne by the side of Henry, it was the pope's
opinion that everything would be lost. Clement recurred once more to his favourite suggestion of
bigamy, already advised by him in 1528 and 1530.
True, this suggestion could not be acceptable either
to Henry or to Charles V., but that made it all the
better in the eyes of the pontiff: he would then have
the appearance of assenting to the king's plans without running the least risk of seeing them realised.
' Rather than do what his Majesty asks,' he said to one
of the English envoys, ' I would prefer granting him
the necessary dispensation to have two wives: that
would be a smaller scandal.' *

The tenacity with which the pope advised Henry
again and again to commit the crime of bigamy has
not prevented the most illustrious advocates of catholicism from exclaiming that ' to have two wives at once
is a mystery of iniquity, of which there is no example

---

* 'Multo minus scandalosum fuisset, dispensare cum Majestate vestra
super duabus uxoribus.'—Record Office MS.

in Christendom.'* A singular assertion after a cardinal and then a pope had on several occasions advised what they call ' a mystery of iniquity.' Again, for the third time, the king refused a remedy that was worse than the disease.

The pope wished at any price to prevent Rome from losing England; and turning to the other side, he resolved to try to gain over Charles V. and prevail upon him not to oppose the divorce. In order to succeed, Clement determined to undertake a journey to Bologna in the worst season of the year. He started on the 18th of November with six cardinals and a certain number of attendants, and took twenty days to reach that city by way of Perugia. Most of his officers had done everything to dissuade him from this painful expedition, but in vain. The rain fell in torrents; the rivers were swollen and unfordable; the roads muddy and broken up; the mules sank of fatigue one after another; the couriers who preceded him solicited the pope to travel on foot; and at last his Holiness's favourite mule broke its leg. It mattered not: he must oppose the Reformation of England: the poor pontiff, already sick, had but this one idea. But the discomforts of the journey increased: the pope often arrived at inns where there was no bed, and had to sleep among the straw.† At last he reached Bologna on the 7th of December, but in such a plight that, notwithstanding his love for ceremonies, he entered the city furtively.

Another disappointment awaited him. The cardi-

---

* Bossuet, *Hist. des Variations*, liv. vi.
· † ' Compelled to lie in the straw.'—*State Papers* (Henry VIII.), part vii. p. 394.

nal of Ancona died, the most influential member of the Sacred College, and on whom Clement relied to gain over the emperor, who greatly respected him. But this did not cool the pontiff's zeal: 'I am thoroughly decided to please the king in this great matter,'* he said to Henry's envoys, and added: 'To have universal concord between all the princes of Christendom, I would give a joint of my hand.'† In fact Clement set to work and went so far as to tell Charles that, according to the theologians, the pope had no right to grant a dispensation for a marriage between brother and sister; but the emperor was immoveable. The pope then proposed a truce of three or four years between Henry, Francis, and Charles, during which he would convoke a general council, to whom he would remit the whole affair. Francis informed Henry that all this was nothing but a trick.‡

The king, convinced that the pope was trifling with him, no longer hesitated to follow the course which the interests of his people and his own happiness seemed to point out. He determined that Anne Boleyn should be his wife and queen of England also. It was now that, according to the second hypothesis, the marriage took place. Cranmer states in a letter written on the 17th of June, 1533, that he did not perform the ceremony, that he did not hear of it until a fortnight after, and that it was celebrated 'much about

---

* 'Utterly resolve to do pleasure to your Highness.'—Benet to Henry VIII., *State Papers*, pp. 401, 402.

† 'He would it had cost him a joint of his hand.'—Ibid.

‡ 'Your Grace should give no credence thereto, for it is but dissimulation.'—Ibid. p. 422.

Saint Paul's day last'* (25th of January, 1533). Which date must we accept: this, or the 15th of November, given by Hall, Hollinshed, Burnet, and others? Cranmer's language is not precise enough to settle the question.

Whatever may have been the date of the marriage —November or January—it became the universal topic of conversation in the beginning of 1533; people did not speak of it publicly, but in private, some attacking and others defending it. If the members of the Romish party circulated ridiculous stories and outrageous calumnies against Anne, the members of the national party replied that the purity of her life, her moderation, her chastity, her mildness, her discretion, her noble and exalted parentage, her pleasing manners, and (they added somewhat later) her fitness to give a successor to the crown of England, made her worthy of the royal favour.† Men may have gone too far in their reproaches as well as in their eulogies.

This important step on the part of Henry VIII. was accompanied with an explosion of murmurs against Clement VII. 'The pope,' he said, 'wanders from the path of the Redeemer, who was obedient in this world to princes. What! must a prince submit to the arrogance of a human being whom God has put under him? Must a king humble himself before that man above whom he stands by the will of God? No! that would be a perversion of the order God has established.' This is what Henry represented

---

* Cranmer, *Remains*, p. 246.

† 'The purity of her life, her constant virginity.'—Burnet, *Records*, iii. p. 64; see also Wyatt, *Memoirs of Anne Boleyn*, p. 437.

to Francis through Lord Rochford;* but the words
did not touch the King of France, for the emperor
was just then making several concessions to him, and
the evangelicals of Paris were annoying him. From
that hour the cordial feeling between the two monarchs
gradually decreased. England turned her eyes more
and more towards the Gospel, and France towards
Rome. Just at the time when Anne Boleyn was about
to reign in the palaces of Whitehall and Windsor,
Catherine de Medicis was entering those of St. Germain and Fontainebleau. The contrast between the
two nations became daily more distinct and striking:
England was advancing towards liberty, and France
towards the dragonnades.

The divorce between Rome and Whitehall soon became manifest. A brief of Clement VII. posted in
February on the doors of all the churches in Flanders,
in the states of the king's enemy, and as near to
England as possible, attracted a great number of
readers.† 'What shall we do?' said the pontiff to
Henry. 'Shall we neglect thy soul's safety? . . .
We exhort thee, our son, under pain of excommunication, to restore Queen Catherine to the royal honours
which are due to her, to cohabit with her, and to cease
to associate publicly with Anne; and that within a
month from the day on which this brief shall be
presented to thee. Otherwise, when the said term
shall have elapsed, we pronounce thee and the said

* Henry's instructions to the Earl of Rochford are written in
French, probably that they might be shown to Francis.—*State Papers*,
vii. pp. 429–431.

† *State Papers*, vii. p. 421. A note mentions that the document
cannot be found. It is evidently the brief given by Le Grand, *Preuves
du Divorce*, p. 558.

Anne to be *ipso 'facto* excommunicate, and command all men to shun and avoid your presence.' * It would appear that this document, demanded by the imperialists, had been posted throughout Flanders without the pope's knowledge.†

A copy was immediately forwarded to the king by his agents. He was surprised and agitated, but believed at last that it was forged by his enemies.‡ How could he imagine that the pope, just at the very time he was showing the king especial marks of his affection,§ would (even conditionally) have anathematised and isolated him in the midst of his people? Henry sent a copy of the document to Benet, his agent at Rome, and desired him to ascertain carefully whether it did really proceed from the pope or not.

Benet presented the document to Clement as a paper forwarded to him by his friends in Flanders. The latter was 'ashamed and in great perplexity,' wrote the envoy.‖ He then read it again more attentively, stopped at certain passages, and seemed as if he were choking. Having come to the end, he expressed his surprise, and pretended that the copy differed from the original. 'There is one mistake in particular which almost chokes the pope every time it is mentioned,' wrote Benet to Cromwell. This mistake was

---

* 'Te et ipsam Annam, excommunicationis pœna, innodatos declaramus.'—Le Grand, *Preuves*, p. 567.

† 'Granted by the pope at the suits of the imperials.'—*State Papers*, vii. p. 454.

‡ 'He can hardly believe it to be true rather than to be counterfeited.'—Ibid. p. 421.

§ 'In derogation both of justice and the affection lately shown by his Holiness unto us.'—Ibid.

‖ Ibid.

the including Queen Anne Boleyn in the censure, without giving her previous warning, which (they said) was contrary to all the commandments of God. Accordingly Dr. Benet received orders to bring up this mistake frequently in his audiences with the pope; and he did not fail to do so.   At this moment, in which he was about to lose England, the pope was more uneasy at having committed an error of form with regard to Anne Boleyn, than with having struck the monarch of a powerful kingdom with an inter- dict.   There is, besides, no doubt that he dictated the unhappy phrase himself.

Benet and his friends took advantage of the pope's vexation, and even increased it: they communicated the brief to the dignitaries of the Church in Clement's household, and the latter acknowledged that the docu- ment must be offensive to his Majesty of England, and that 'the pope was much to blame.' *   Benet transmitted the pontiff's *errata* to the king, but it was too late: the blow had taken effect.   The in- dignant Henry was about to proceed ostentatiously to the very acts which Rome threatened with her thunders.

Whilst the pope was hesitating, England firmly pursued her emancipation.   Parliament met on the 4th of February, and the boldest language was uttered. 'The people of England, in accord with their king,' said eloquent speakers, 'have the right to decide su- premely on all things both temporal and spiritual; † and certainly the English possess intelligence enough

---

* *State Papers*, vii. p. 454.

† Statute against appeals, 24 Henry VIII. cap. 12; Collyers, *Ch. History*, ii.

for that. And yet, in spite of the prohibitions issued by so many of our princes, we see bulls arriving every moment from Rome to regulate wills, marriages, divorces, everything in short. We propose that henceforward these matters be decided solely before the national tribunals.' The law passed. Appeals, instead of being made to Rome, were to be made in the first instance to the bishop, then to the archbishop, and, if the king was interested in the cause, to the Upper Chamber of the ecclesiastical Convocation.

The king took immediate advantage of this law to inquire of Convocation whether the pope could authorise a man to marry his brother's widow. Out of sixty-six present, and one hundred and ninety-seven who voted by proxy, there were only nineteen in the Upper House who voted against the king. The opposition was stronger in the Lower House; but even this agreed with the other house in declaring that Pope Julius II. had exceeded his authority in giving Henry a dispensation, and that the marriage was consequently null from the very first.

Nothing remained now but to proceed to the divorce. On the 11th of April, two days before Easter, Cranmer, as archbishop, wrote a letter to the king, in which he set forth, that desiring to fill the office of archbishop of Canterbury, 'according to the laws of God and Holy Church, for the relief of the grievances and infirmities of the people, God's subjects and yours in spiritual causes,' * he prayed his Majesty's favour for that office.† Cranmer did not decline the royal

* Wilkins, *Concilia Mag. Britanniæ,* iii. pp. 756–759. Rymer, *Fœdera,* vi. p. 179.

† *State Papers* (Henry VIII.), i. p. 390.

intervention, but he avoided confounding spiritual
with temporal affairs.*

Henry, who was doubtless waiting impatiently for
this letter, was alarmed as he read the words, 'according to the laws of God and Holy Church.' God
and the Church. . . . Well! but what of the king
and the royal supremacy? The primate seemed to
assert the right of acting *proprio motu*, and, while
asking the king's favour, to be doing a simple act of
courtesy. . . . Did the Church of England claim to
take the pontiff's place and station, and leave the
king aside? . . . That was not what Henry meant.
Tired of the pretensions of the pope of Rome, would
he suffer a pope on a small scale at his side? He
intended to be master in his own kingdom—master of
everything. The letter must be modified, and this
Henry intimated to Cranmer.

That day, or the next after the one on which this
letter had been written, there was a great festival at
the court in honour of Anne Boleyn. 'Queen Anne
that evening went in state to her closet openly as
queen,' says Hall. It was probably during this
festival that the king, taking the prelate aside, desired
him to suppress the unwelcome passage. The idea
suggested by an eminent historian, that Cranmer sent
both the letters together to Henry, that he might
choose which he would prefer, seems to me inadmissible. Cranmer, as it would appear, submitted, waiting for better days. On returning to Lambeth, he
recopied his letter, omitting the words which had been
pointed out. Not content with asking the king's

---

* 'Your sufferance and grants.'—*State Papers* (Henry VIII.), i. p. 390.

favour, he desired his *licence*, his authorisation to proceed. He dated his second letter the same day, and sent it to his master, who was satisfied with it.*

This alone did not satisfy Henry: in his reply to the archbishop, he marked still more strongly his intention not to have in England a primate independent of the crown: ' Ye therefore duly recognising that it becometh you not, being our subject, to enterprise any part of your said office *without our licence obtained so to do.* . . . In consideration of these things, albeit we being your king and sovereign, do recognise no superior upon earth but only God; yet because ye be under us, by God's calling and ours, the most principal minister of our spiritual jurisdiction, we will not refuse your humble request.'

This language was clear. Henry VIII. did not, however, claim the arbitrary authority to which the pope pretended: human and divine laws were to be the supreme rule in England, but he, the king, was to be their chief interpreter. Cranmer must understand that. ' To these laws we, as a Christian king,' wrote Henry, ' have always heretofore submitted, and shall ever most obediently submit ourselves.' The ecclesiastical system which Henry VIII. established in England in 1533 was not a free Church in a free State, and there is no reason to be surprised at it.

Cranmer having received the royal licence, set out for Mortloke manor to prepare the act which, for six

---

* The two letters are in the State Paper Office; they are in Cranmer's handwriting, and appear to have been read, both of them, by the king. Our hypothesis touching these letters differs from that of Mr. Froude (*Hist. England*, i. p. 440). *State Papers* (Henry VIII.), i. pp. 390, 391.

years, had kept England and the continent in suspense.
Taking the bishops of Lincoln and Winchester and
some lawyers with him, he proceeded quietly, and
without ostentation, to the priory of Dunstable, five
miles from Ampthill, where Queen Catherine was
staying.   He wished to avoid the notoriety of a trial
held in London.

The ecclesiastical court being duly formed, Henry
and Catherine were summoned to appear before it on
the 10th of May.   The king was present by attorney:
but the queen replied: ' My cause is before the pope;
I accept no other judge.'   A fresh summons was immediately made out for the 12th of May, and as the
queen appeared neither in person nor by any of her
servants, she was pronounced contumacious,* and the
trial went forward.   The king was informed every
night of each day's proceedings, and he was often in
great anxiety.   Some unexpected event, an appeal
from Catherine, the sudden intervention of the pope
or of the emperor, might stop everything.   His
courtiers were on the watch for news.   Anne said
nothing, but her heart beat quick, and the ambitious
Cromwell, whose fortunes depended on the success of
the matter, was sometimes in great alarm.   Cranmer
rested on the declarations of Scripture, and showed
much equity and uprightness during the trial.†   ' I
have willingly injured no human being,' he said.
But he knew the queen had numerous partisans;
they would conjure her, perhaps, to appear before

---

* ' Vere et manifeste contumacem.'—*State Papers* (Henry VIII.),
i. p. 394.

† ' My lord of Canterbury handleth himself very uprightly.'—Ibid.
p. 395.

her judges; there would then be a great stir, and the voice of the people would be heard.* The archbishop could hardly restrain his emotion as he thought of this. He must indeed expect an inflexible resistance on the part of the queen; but in the midst of all the agitation around her, she alone remained calm and resolute. Her hand had grasped the pope's robe, and nothing could make her let it go. ' I am the king's lawful wife,' she repeated; ' I am queen of England. My daughter is the king's child: I place her in her father's hands.'

On Wednesday the 23rd of May, the primate, attended by all the archiepiscopal court, proceeded to the church of St. Peter's priory at Dunstable, in order to deliver the final judgment of divorce. A few persons attracted by curiosity were present; but, although Dunstable was near Ampthill, all of Catherine's household kept themselves respectfully aloof from an act which was to deal their mistress such a grievous blow. The primate, after reciting the decisions of the several universities, provincial councils, and other premises, continued: ' Therefore we, Thomas, archbishop, primate, and legate, having first called upon the name of Christ, and having God altogether before our eyes, do pronounce and declare that the marriage between our sovereign lord King Henry and the most serene Lady Catherine, widow of his brother, having been contracted contrary to the law of God, is null and void; and therefore we sentence that it is not lawful for the said most illustrious Prince Henry and the said most serene Lady Catherine

---

* 'A great bruit and voice of the people.'—Cranmer, *Remains*, p. 342.

to remain in the said pretended marriage.'* The act, drawn up very carefully by two notaries, was imme· diately sent to the king.

The divorce was pronounced, and Henry was free. Many persons gave way to feelings of alarm: they thought that all Europe would combine against Eng- land. ' The pope will excommunicate the English,' said some; ' and then the emperor will destroy them.' But, on the other hand, the majority of the nation desired to have done with a subject which had been agitating their minds during the last seven years. England, getting out of a labyrinth from which she had never expected to find an issue, began to breathe again.

Catherine's marriage was declared to be null: it only remained now to recognise Anne Boleyn's. On the 28th of May, an archiepiscopal court held at Lambeth, in the primate's palace, officially declared that Henry and Anne had been lawfully wedded, and the king had now no thought but how to seal his union by the pomp of a coronation. It would certainly have been preferable had the new queen taken her seat quietly on the throne ; but slanderous reports made it ne- cessary for the king to present his wife to the people in all the splendour of royalty.

At three o'clock in the afternoon of Thursday before Whitsuntide, a magnificent procession started from Greenwich. Fifty barges, adorned with rich banners, conveyed the representatives of the different city companies, and the metropolis joyfully hailed a union that promised to inaugurate a future of light and

---

* 'Non licere in eodem prætenso matrimonio remanere.'—Wilkins, Concilia, iii. p. 759 ; Rymer, Fœdera, vi. p. 182.

faith: it was almost a religious festival. On the banner of the Fishmongers was the inscription, *All worship belongs to God alone*; on that of the Haber-dashers, *My trust is in God only*; on that of the Grocers, *God gives grace*; and on that of the Gold-smiths, *To God alone be all the glory.* The city of London thus asserted, in the presence of the immense crowd, the principles of the Reformation. The lord mayor's barge immediately preceded the galley, all hung with cloth of gold, in which Anne was seated. Near it floated another gay barge, on which a little mountain was contrived, planted with red and white roses, in the midst of which sat a number of young maidens singing to the accompaniment of sweet music. A hundred richly ornamented barques, carrying the nobility of England, brought up the magnificent pro-cession, and a countless number of boats and skiffs covered the river. The moment Anne set her foot on shore at the Tower, a thousand trumpets sounded points of triumph, and all the guns of the fortress fired such a peal as had seldom been heard before.*

Henry, who liked the sound of cannon, met Anne at the gate and kissed her, and the new queen entered in triumph that vast fortress from which, three years later, she was to issue, by order of the same prince, to mount, an innocent victim, the cruel scaf-fold. She smiled courteously on all around; and yet, seized with a sudden emotion, she sometimes trembled, as if, instead of the joyous flowers on which she trod with light and graceful foot, she saw a deep gulf yawning beneath her.

The king and queen passed the whole of the next

---

* Cranmer, *Remains*, p. 245.

day (Friday) at the Tower. On Saturday Anne left
it for Westminster.* The streets were gay with banners, and the houses were hung with velvet and cloth of
gold. All the orders of the State and Church, the
ambassadors of France and Venice, and the officers of
the court, opened the procession. The queen was
carried in a magnificent litter covered with white
cloth shot with gold, her head, which she held modestly
inclined, being encircled with a wreath of precious
stones. The people who crowded the streets were
full of enthusiasm, and seemed to triumph more than
she did herself.

The next day, Whit-Sunday, she proceeded for the
coronation to the ancient abbey of Westminster,
where the bishops and the court had been summoned
to meet her. She took her seat in a rich chair, whence
she presently descended to the high altar and knelt
down. After the prescribed prayers she rose, and the
archbishop placed the crown of St. Edward upon her
head. She then took the sacrament and retired; the
Earl of Wiltshire, her father, trembling with emotion,
took her right hand . . . he was at the pinnacle of
happiness, and yet he was uneasy. Alas! a caprice
of the man who had raised his daughter to the throne
might be sufficient to hurl her from it! Anne herself,
in the midst of all these pomps, greater than any ever

---

* Mr. Froude says that Anne went to the Tower on the 19th of May,
and that she quitted it for Westminster on the 31st, so that she resided
there for eleven days (*History of England*, i. pp. 450, 451). That appears
hardly probable, and is in contradiction to Cranmer's narrative, where we
read : 'Her grace came to the Tower on Thursday at night. ... Friday
all day the king and queen tarried there. .... The next day, which was
Saturday, the knights rid before the queen's grace towards Westminster.'
—*Letters*, p. 245.

seen before at the coronation of an English queen, could not entirely forget the princess whose place she had now taken. Might not she be rejected in her turn? . . . In such a thought there was enough to make her shudder.

Anne did not find in her marriage with Henry the happiness she had dreamt, and a cloud was often seen passing across those features once so radiant. The idol to which this young woman had sacrificed everything—the splendour of a throne—did not satisfy her longings for happiness: she looked within herself, and found once more, as queen, that attraction towards the doctrine of the Gospel which she had felt in the society of Margaret of Valois, and which, amid her ambitious pursuits, had been almost extinguished in her heart. She discovered that for those who have everything, as well as for those who have nothing, there is only one single good—God himself. She did not probably give herself up entirely to Him, for her best impressions were often fugitive; but she took advantage of her power to assist those who she knew were devoted to the Gospel. She petitioned for the pardon of John Lambert, who was still in prison, and that faithful confessor of Jesus Christ settled in London, where he began to teach children Latin and Greek, without however neglecting the defence of truth.*

Two women had for some time attracted the eyes of all England—the one who was ascending the throne, and the other who was descending from it. Nothing awakens the sympathy of generous souls more than misfortune, and particularly innocence in misfortune;

* 'Lambert delivered . . . by the coming of Queen Anne.'—Foxe, *Acts,* v. p. 225.

and accordingly Catherine's fate will always excite
a lively interest, even in the ranks of protestantism.
We must not forget, however, that Catherine's cause
was that of the old times and of the Roman papacy;
and that Anne's cause was identified with that light,
liberty, and new life which have distinguished modern times. It is true, Catherine died in disgrace,
but in peace, surrounded by her women, her officers,
her faithful servants; while the youthful Anne, separated from her friends, alone on a scaffold, praying
God to bless the prince who put her to death, had
her head cruelly cut off by the hangman's sword.
If on the one side there was innocence and divorce, on
the other there was innocence and martyrdom.

The king, who had informed Catherine through
Lord Mountjoy of the archiepiscopal sentence, officially
communicated his divorce and marriage to the various
crowned heads of Europe, and particularly to the king
of France, the emperor, and the pope. The latter
on the 11th of July annulled the sentence of the Archbishop of Canterbury, declared the king's marriage
with Anne Boleyn unlawful, and threatened to excommunicate both, unless they separated before the end
of September. Henry angrily commanded his theologians to demonstrate that the bull was a nullity, recalled his ambassador, the Duke of Norfolk, and said
that the moment was come for all monarchs and all
Christian people to withdraw from under the yoke of
the bishop of Rome. 'The pope and his cardinals,'
he wrote to Francis I., 'pretend to have princes, who
are free persons, at their beck and commandment.
Sire, you and I and all the princes of Christendom
must unite for the preservation of our rights, liberties,

and privileges; we must alienate the greatest part of Christendom from the see of Rome.'*

But Henry had scholastic prejudices which made him fall into the strangest contradictions. While he was employing his diplomacy to isolate the pope, he still prayed him to declare the nullity of his marriage with Catherine.† It is not at the court of this prince that we must look for the real Reformation: we must go in search of it elsewhere.

* 'To the clear alienation of a great part of Christendom from that see.'—*State Papers*, vii. p. 477.

† 'That the matrimony was and is naught.'—Ibid. p. 498.

CHAPTER XVIII.

A REFORMER IN PRISON.

(AUGUST 1532 TO MAY 1533.)

ONE of the leading scholars of England was about to seal the testimony of his faith with blood. John Fryth had been one of the most brilliant stars of the university of Cambridge. 'It would hardly be possible to find his equal in learning,' said many. Accordingly Wolsey had invited him to his college at Oxford, and Henry VIII. had desired to place him among the number of his theologians. But the mysteries of the Word of God had more attraction for Fryth than those of science: the wants of conscience prevailed in him over those of the intellect, and neglecting his own glory, he sought only to be useful to mankind.* A sincere, decided, and yet moderate Christian, preaching the Gospel with great purity and love, this man of thirty seemed destined to become one of the most influential reformers of England. Nothing could have prevented his playing the foremost part, if he had had Luther's enthusiastic energy or Calvin's indomitable power. There were less strong, but perhaps more amiable features in his character; he taught with gentleness

* 'Serving for the common utility'—Tyndale to Fryth, *Works*, iii. p. 74.

those who were opposed to the truth, and while many, as Foxe says,* 'take the bellows in hand to blow the fire, but few there are that will seek to quench it,' Fryth sought after peace. Controversies between protestants distressed him. 'The opinions for which men go to war,' he said, 'do not deserve those great tragedies of which they make us spectators. Let there be no longer any question among us of Zwinglians or Lutherans, for neither Zwingle nor Luther died for us, and we must be one in Christ Jesus.'† This servant of Christ, meek and lowly of heart, like his Master, never disputed even with papists, unless obliged to do so.‡

A true catholicism which embraced all Christians was Fryth's distinctive feature as a reformer. He was not one of those who imagine that a national Church ought to think only of its own nation; but of those who believe that if a Church is the depositary of the truth, she is so for all the earth; and that a religion is not good, if it has no longing to extend itself to all the races of mankind. There were some strongly marked national elements in the English Reformation: the king and the parliament; but there was also a universal element: a lively faith in the Saviour of the world. No one in the sixteenth century represented this truly catholic element better than Fryth. 'I understand the Church of God in a wide sense,' he said. 'It contains all those whom we regard as members of Christ. It is a net thrown into the sea.'§

---

* Foxe, *Acts*, v. p. 10.

† Tyndale and Fryth, *Works*, iii. p. 421.

‡ 'He would never seem to strive against the papists.'—Foxe, *Acts*, v. p. 9.

§ Fryth, *A Declaration of Baptism*, p. 287.

This principle, sown at that time as a seed in the
English Reformation, was one day to cover the world
with missionaries.

Fryth, having declined the brilliant offers the king
had made to him through Cromwell and Vaughan,
joined Tyndale in translating and publishing the Holy
Scriptures in English. While labouring thus for
England, an irresistible desire came over him to circulate the Gospel there in person. He therefore quitted
the Low Countries, returned to London, and directed
his course to Reading, where the prior had been his
friend. Exile had not used him well, and he entered
that town miserably clothed, and more like a beggar
than one whom Henry VIII. had desired to place near
him. This was in August 1532.

His writings had preceded him. Having received,
when in the Netherlands, three works composed in
defence of purgatory by three distinguished men—
Rastell, Sir Thomas More's brother-in-law, More himself, and Fisher, bishop of Rochester—Fryth had replied to them: ' A purgatory! there is not *one* only,
there are *two*. The first is the *Word of God*, the
second is the *cross of Christ*: I do not mean the cross
of wood, but the cross of tribulation. But the lives
of the papists are so wicked that they have invented
a third.'*

Sir Thomas, exasperated by Fryth's reply, said with
that humorous tone he often affected, ' I propose to
answer the good young father Fryth, whose wisdom is
such that three old men like my brother Rastell, the
bishop of Rochester, and myself are mere babies when

* See Tyndale and Fryth, *Works,* iii. p. 91. Preface to the Reader.

confronted with father Fryth alone.'* The exile having returned to England, More had now the opportunity of avenging himself more effectually than by his jokes.

Fryth, as we have said, had entered Reading. His strange air and his look as of a foreigner arriving from a distant country attracted attention, and he was taken up for a vagabond. 'Who are you?' asked the magistrate. Fryth, suspecting that he was in the hands of enemies of the Gospel, refused to give his name, which increased the suspicion, and the poor young man was set in the stocks. As they gave him but little to eat, with the intent of forcing him to tell his name, his hunger soon became insupportable.† Knowing the name of the master of the grammar-school, he asked to speak with him. Leonard Coxe had scarcely entered the prison, when the pretended vagabond all in rags addressed him in correct latinity, and began to deplore his miserable captivity. Never had words more noble been uttered in a dungeon so vile. The head-master, astonished at so much eloquence, compassionately drew near the unhappy man and inquired how it came to pass that such a learned scholar was in such profound wretchedness. Presently he sat down, and the two men began to talk in Greek about the universities and languages. Coxe could not make it out: it was no longer simple pity that he felt, but love, which turned to admiration when he heard the prisoner recite with the purest accent those noble lines of the *Iliad* which were so applicable to his own case:—

---

* Anderson, *Annals of the Bible*, i. p. 338.   † Foxe, *Acts*, v. p. 5.

Sing, O Muse,
The vengeance deep and deadly ; whence to Greece
Unnumbered ills arose ; which many a soul
Of mighty warriors to the viewless shades
Untimely sent.*

Filled with respect, Coxe hurried off to the mayor,
complained bitterly of the wrong done to so remarkable a man, and obtained his liberation.   Homer saved
the life of a reformer.

Fryth departed for London and hastened to join the
worshippers who were accustomed to meet in Bow
Lane.   He conversed with them, and exclaimed : ' Oh!
what consolation to see such a great number of believers walking in the way of the Lord!'† These
Christians asked him to expound the Scriptures to
them, and, delighted with his exhortations, they exclaimed in their turn : ' If the rule of St. Paul were
followed, this man would certainly make a better
bishop than many of those who wear the mitre.' ‡ Instead of the crosier he was to bear the cross.

One of those who listened was in great doubt relative
to the doctrine of the Lord's Supper; and one day,
after Fryth had been setting Christ before them as the
food of the Christian soul through faith, this person
followed him and said : ' Our prelates think differently :
they believe that the bread transformed by consecration becomes the flesh, blood, and bones of Christ;
that even the wicked eat this flesh with their teeth,
and that we must adore the host. . . . What you

---

* Earl of Derby's Translation.

† He added : ' Now have I experience of the faith which is in you.'—
Tyndale and Fryth, *Works,* iii. p. 257.

‡ Ibid. p. 324.

have just said refutes their errors, but I fear that I
cannot remember it. Pray commit it to writing.'
Fryth, who did not like discussions, was alarmed at the
request, and answered: 'I do not care to touch that
terrible tragedy;'* for so he called the dispute about
the Eucharist.   The man having repeated his request,
and promised that he would not communicate the
paper to anybody, Fryth wrote an explanation of
the doctrine of the Sacrament and gave it to that
London Christian, saying: 'We must eat and drink
the body and blood of Christ, not with the teeth, but
with the hearing and through faith.'   The brother
took the treatise, and, hurrying home with it, read it
carefully.

In a short time every one at the Bow Lane meeting
spoke about this writing.   One man, a false brother,
named William Holt, listened attentively to what was
said, and thought he had found an opportunity of destroying Fryth.   Assuming a hypocritical look, he
spoke in a pious strain to the individual who had the
manuscript, as if he had desired to enlighten his faith,
and finally asked him for it.   Having obtained it, he
hastened to make a copy, which he carried to Sir
Thomas More, who was still chancellor.

Fryth soon perceived that he had tried in vain to
remain unknown: he called with so much power
those who thirsted for righteousness to come to Christ
for the waters of life, that friends and enemies were
struck with his eloquence.   Observing that his name
began to be talked of in various places, he quitted
the capital and travelled unnoticed through several

---

* Tyndale and Fryth, *Works*, iii. p. 321.

counties, where he found some little Christian congregations whom he tried to strengthen in the faith.

Tyndale, who remained on the continent, having heard of Fryth's labours, began to feel great anxiety about him. He knew but too well the cruel disposition of the bishops and of More. ' I will make the serpent come out of his dark den,' Sir Thomas had said, speaking of Tyndale, ' as Hercules forced Cerberus, the watchdog of hell, to come out to the light of day. . . . I will not leave Tyndale the darkest corner in which to hide his head.'* In Tyndale's eyes Fryth was the great hope of the Church in England; he trembled lest the redoubtable Hercules should seize him. ' Dearly beloved brother Jacob,' he wrote, calling him Jacob to mislead his enemies, ' be cold, sober, wise, and circumspect, and keep you low by the ground, avoiding high questions that pass the common capacity. But expound the law truly, and open the veil of Moses to condemn all flesh and prove all men sinners. Then set abroach the mercy of our Lord Jesus, and let the wounded consciences drink of him. . . . All doctrine that casteth a mist on these two to shadow and hide them, resist with all your power. . . . Beloved in my heart, there liveth not one in whom I have so great hope and trust, and in whom my heart rejoiceth, not so much for your learning and what other gifts else you may have, as because you walk in those things that the conscience may feel, and not in the imagination of the brain. Cleave fast to the rock of the help of God; and if aught be required of you contrary to the glory of God and his Christ, then stand

* *Confutation of Tyndale's Answer*, by Sir Thomas More, lord-chancellor of England (1532).

fast and commit yourself to God. He is our God, and our redemption is nigh.'*

Tyndale's fears were but too well founded. Sir Thomas More held Fryth's new treatise in his hand: he read it and gave way by turns to anger and sarcasm. 'Whetting his wits, calling his spirits together, and sharpening his pen,' to use the words of the chronicler,† he answered Fryth, and described his doctrine under the image of a cancer. This did not satisfy him. Although he had returned the seals to the king in May, he continued to hold office until the end of the year. He ordered search to be made for Fryth, and set all his bloodhounds on the track. If the reformer was discovered he was lost: when Sir Thomas More had once caught his man, nothing could save him—nothing but a merry jest, perhaps. For instance, one day when he was examining a gospeller named Silver: 'You know,' he said with a smile, 'that silver must be tried in the fire.' 'Yes,' retorted the accused instantly, 'but not quicksilver.'‡ More, delighted with the repartee, set the poor wretch at liberty. But Fryth was no jester: he could not hope, therefore, to find favour with the ex-chancellor of England.

Sir Thomas hunted the reformer by sea and by land, promising a great reward to any one who should deliver him up. There was no county or town or village where More did not look for him, no sheriff or justice of the peace to whom he did not apply, no harbour where he did not post some officer to catch him.§ But the answer from every quarter was: 'He is not

* Foxe, *Acts*, v. p. 133.   † Ibid. p. 9.
‡ Strype, i. p. 316.   § Foxe, *Acts*, v. p. 6.

here.' Indeed, Fryth, having been informed of the
great exertions of his enemy, was fleeing from place to
place, often changing his dress, and finding safety nowhere. Determining to leave England and return to
Tyndale, he went to Milton Shone in Essex with the
intention of embarking. A ship was ready to sail,
and quitting his hiding-place he went down to the
shore with all precaution. He had been betrayed.
More's agents, who were on the watch, seized him as
he was stepping on board, and carried him to the
Tower. This occurred in October 1532.

Sir Thomas More was uneasy and soured. He beheld a new power lifting its head in England and all
Christendom, and he felt that in despite of his wit and
his influence he was unable to check it. That man so
amiable, that writer of a style so pure and elegant, did
not so much dread the anger of the king; what exasperated him was to see the Scriptures circulating more
widely every day, and a continually increasing number of his fellow-citizens converted to the evangelical
faith. These new men, who seemed to have more piety
than himself—he an old follower of the old papacy!—
irritated him sorely. He claimed to have alone—he
and his friends—the privilege of being Christians.
The zeal of the partisans of the Reformation, the
sacrifice they made of their repose, their money, and
their lives, confounded him. 'These diabolical people,'
he said, 'print their books at great expense, notwithstanding the great danger; not looking for any gain,
they give them away to everybody, and even scatter
them abroad by night.* They fear no labour, no

---

* Preface to More's Confutation, *Bible Ann.* i. p. 343.

journey, no expense, no pain, no danger, no blows, no injury. They take a malicious pleasure in seeking the destruction of others, and these disciples of the devil think only how they may cast the souls of the simple into hell-fire.' In such a strain as this did the elegant utopist give vent to his anger—the man who had dreamt all his life of the plan of an imaginary world for the perfect happiness of every one. At last he had caught the chief of these disciples of Satan, and hoped to put him to death by fire.

The news soon spread through London that Fryth was in the Tower, and several priests and bishops immediately went thither to try to bring him back to the pope. Their great argument was that More had confuted his treatise on the Lord's Supper. Fryth asked to see the confutation, but it was refused him. One day the Bishop of Winchester having called up the prisoner, showed it to Fryth, and, holding it up, asserted that the book quite shut his mouth: Fryth put out his hand, but the bishop hastily withdrew the volume. More himself was ashamed of the apology, and did all he could to prevent its circulation. Fryth could only obtain a written copy, but he resolved to answer it immediately. There was no one with whom he could confer, not a book he could consult, and the chains with which he was loaded scarcely allowed him to sit and write.* But reading in his dungeon by the light of a small candle the insults of More, and finding himself charged with having collected all the poison that could be found in the writings of Wickliffe, Luther, Œcolampadius, Tyndale, and Zwingle, this

---

* 'He was so loaded with iron that he could scarce sit with any ease.'—Burnet, i. p. 161.

humble servant of God exclaimed: 'No! Luther and
his doctrine are not the mark I aim at, but the Scriptures of God.'* 'He shall pay for his heresy with
the best blood in his body,' said his enemies; and the
pious disciple replied: 'As the sheep bound by the
hand of the butcher with timid look beseeches that his
blood may soon be shed, even so do I pray my judges
that my blood may be shed *to-morrow*, if by my death
the king's eyes should be opened.'†

Before he died, Fryth desired to save, if it were
God's will, one of his adversaries. There was one of
them who had no obstinacy, no malice: it was Rastell,
More's brother-in-law. Being unable to speak to him
or to any of the enemies of the Reformation, he formed
the design of writing in prison a treatise which
should be called the *Bulwark*. But strict orders had
recently arrived that he should have neither pen, ink,
nor paper.‡ Some evangelical Christians of London,
who succeeded in getting access to him, secretly
furnished him with the means of writing, and Fryth
began. He wrote . . . but at every moment he
listened for fear the lieutenant of the Tower or the
warders should come upon him suddenly and find the
pen in his hand.§ Often a bright thought would occur to him, but some sudden alarm drove it out of his
mind, and he could not recall it.‖ He took courage,
however: he had been accused of asserting that good
works were of no service: he proceeded to explain

* Tyndale and Fryth, *Works*, iii. p. 342.
† Ibid. p. 338.
‡ The Subsidy or Bulwark; Tyndale and Fryth, *Works*, iii. p. 242.
§ 'I am in continual fear, lest the lieutenant or my keeper should espy
any such thing by me.'—Ibid.
‖ 'If any notable thing had been in my mind, it was clean lost.'—Ibid.

with much eloquence all their utility, and every time
he repeated: 'Is that nothing? is that still nothing?
Truly, Rastell,' he added, 'if you only regard that as
useful which justifies us, the sun is not useful, because
it justifieth not.'*

As he was finishing these words he heard the keys
rattling at the door, and, being alarmed, immediately
threw paper, ink, and pen into a hiding-place. However, he was able to complete the treatise and send it
to Rastell.   More's brother-in-law read it; his heart
was touched, his understanding enlightened, his prejudices cleared away; and from that hour this choice
spirit was gained over to the Gospel of Christ.   God
had given him new eyes and new ears.   A pure joy
filled the prisoner's heart.   'Rastell now looks upon
his natural reason as foolishness,' he said.   'Rastell,
become a child, drinks the wisdom that cometh from
on high.'†

The conversion of Sir Thomas More's brother-in-
law made a great sensation, and the visits to Fryth's
cell became every day more numerous.   Although
separated from his wife and from Tyndale, whom he
had been forced to leave in the Low Countries, he had
never had so many friends, brothers, mothers, and
fathers; he wept for very joy.   He took his pen and
paper from their hiding-place, and, always indefatigable, began to write first the *Looking-glass of Self-
knowledge*, and next a *Letter to the faithful Followers
of the Gospel of Christ*.'   'Imitators of the Lord,'
he said to them, 'mark yourselves with the sign of

* The Subsidy or Bulwark; Tyndale and Fryth, *Works*, iii. p. 241.
† Ibid. p. 211.

the cross, not as the superstitious crowd does, in order
to worship it, but as a testimony that you are ready to
bear that cross as soon as God shall please to send it.
Fear not when you have it, for you will also have
a hundred fathers instead of one, a hundred mothers
instead of one, a hundred mansions already in this
life (for I have made the trial), and after this life,
joy everlasting.'*

At the beginning of 1533, Anne Boleyn having
been married to the King of England, Fryth saw his
chains fall off: he was allowed to have all he asked for,
and even permitted to leave the Tower at night on
parole. He took advantage of this liberty to visit the
friends of the Gospel, and consult with them about
what was to be done. One evening in particular,
after leaving the Tower, Fryth went to Petit's house,
anxious to embrace once more that great friend of the
Reformation, that firm member of parliament, who
had been thrown into prison as we have seen, and at
last set free. Petit, weakened by his long confinement, was near his end; the persecution agitated
and pained him, and it would appear that his
emotion sometimes ended in delirium. As he was
groaning over the captivity of the young and noble
reformer, Fryth appeared. Petit was confused, his
mind wandered. Is it Fryth or his ghost? He was
like the apostles, when Rhoda came to tell them that
Peter was at the gate waiting to see them. But
gradually recovering himself, Petit said: 'You here!
how have you escaped the vigilance of the warders?'
'God himself,' answered Fryth, 'gave me this liberty

* The Subsidy or Bulwark, p. 259.

by touching their hearts.'* The two friends then
conversed about the true Reformation of England,
which in their eyes had nothing to do with the
diplomatic proceedings of the king. In their opinion
it was not a matter of overloading the external
Church with new frippery, but 'to increase that
elect, sanctified, and invisible congregation, elect
before the foundation of the world.'† Fryth did not
conceal from Petit the conviction he felt that he
would be called upon to die for the Gospel. The night
was spent in such Christian conversation, and the day
began to dawn before the prisoner hastened to return
to the Tower.

The evangelist's friends did not think as he did.
Anne Boleyn's accession seemed as if it ought to open
the doors of Fryth's prison, and in imagination they
saw him at liberty, and labouring either on the continent or at home at that real reformation which is
accomplished by the Scriptures of God.

But it was not to be so. Most of the evangelical
men raised up by God in England during the reign
of Henry VIII. found—not the influence which they
should have exercised, but—death. Yet their blood
has weighed in the divine balance; it has sanctified
the Reformation of England, and been a spiritual seed
for future ages. If the Church of that rich country,
which possesses such worldly splendour, has nevertheless witnessed the developement of a powerful
evangelical life in its bosom, it must not forget the
cause, but understand, with Tertullian, that *the blood
of the martyrs is the seed of the Church.*

* Strype.   . † Tyndale and Fryth, *Works*, iii. p. 288.

CHAPTER XIX.

A REFORMER CHOOSES RATHER TO LOSE HIS LIFE THAN
TO SAVE IT.

(MAY TO JULY 1533.)

THE enemy was on the watch: the second period
of Fryth's captivity, that which was to terminate
in martyrdom, was beginning. Henry's bishops, who,
while casting off the pope to please the king, had remained devoted to scholastic doctrines, feared lest
the reformer should escape them: they therefore undertook to solicit Henry to put him to death. Fryth
had on his side the queen, Cromwell, and Cranmer.
This did not discourage them, and they represented
to the king that although the man was shut up in the
Tower of London, he did not cease to write and act
in defence of heresy. It was the season of Lent, and
Fryth's enemies came to an understanding with Dr.
Curwin, the king's chaplain, who was to preach before
the court. He had no sooner got into the pulpit than
he began to declaim against those who denied the
material presence of Christ in the host. Having
struck his hearers with horror, he continued: 'It is
not surprising that this abominable heresy makes
such great progress among us. A man now in the
Tower of London has the audacity to defend it, and
no one thinks of punishing him.'

When the service was over, the brilliant congregation left the chapel, and each as he went out asked what was the man's name. 'Fryth' was the reply, and loud were the exclamations on hearing it. The blow took effect, the scholastic prejudices of the king were revived, and he sent for Cromwell and Cranmer. ' I am very much surprised,' he said, ' that John Fryth has been kept so long in the Tower without examination. I desire his trial to take place without delay; and if he does not retract, let him suffer the penalty he deserves.' He then nominated six of the chief spiritual and temporal peers of England to examine him: they were the Archbishop of Canterbury, the bishops of London and Winchester, the lord chancellor, the Duke of Suffolk, and the Earl of Wiltshire. This demonstrated the importance which Henry attached to the affair. Until now, all the martyrs had fallen beneath the blows either of the bishops or of More; but in this case it was the king himself who stretched out his strong hand against the servant of God.

Henry's order plunged Cranmer into the cruellest anxiety. On the one hand, Fryth was in his eyes a disciple of the Gospel; but on the other, he attacked a doctrine which the archbishop then held to be Christian; for, like Luther and Osiander, he still believed in consubstantiation. ' Alas!' he wrote to Archdeacon Hawkins, 'he professes the doctrine of Œcolampadius.'* He resolved, however, to do everything in his power to save Fryth.

The best friends of the young reformer saw that a pile was being raised to consume the most faithful Christian in England. ' Dearly beloved,' wrote Tyn-

---

* Cranmer's *Letters and Remains,* p. 246.

dale from Antwerp, 'fear not men that threat, nor trust men that speak fair. Your cause is Christ's Gospel, a light that must be fed with the blood of faith. The lamp must be trimmed daily, that the light go not out.'* There was no lack of examples to confirm these words. 'Two have suffered in Antwerp unto the great glory of the Gospel; four at Ryselles in Flanders. At Rouen in France they persecute, and at Paris are five doctors taken for the Gospel. See, you are not alone: follow the example of all your other dear brethren, who choose to suffer in hope of a better resurrection. Bear the image of Christ in your mortal body, and keep your conscience pure and undefiled. . . . *Una salus victis, nullam sperare salutem*: the only safety of the conquered is to look for none. If you could but write and tell us how you are.' In this letter from a martyr to a martyr there was one sentence honourable to a Christian woman: 'Your wife is well content with the will of God, and would not for her sake have the glory of God hindered.'

If friends were thinking of Fryth on the banks of the Scheldt, they were equally anxious about him on the banks of the Thames. Worthy citizens of London asked what was the use of England's quitting the pope to cling to Christ, if she burnt the servants of Christ? The little Church had recourse to prayer. Archbishop Cranmer wished to save Fryth: he loved the man and admired his piety. If the accused appeared before the commission appointed by the king, he was lost: some means must be devised without delay to rescue him from an inevitable death. The

---

* Tyndale to Fryth: Foxe, v. p. 132; Anderson, *Annals of Bible*, i. p. 357.

archbishop declared that, before proceeding to trial, he wished to have a conference with the prisoner, and to endeavour to convince him, which was very natural.   But at the same time the primate appeared to fear that if the conference took place in London the people would disturb the public peace, as in the time of Wickliffe.*   He settled therefore that it should be held at Croydon, where he had a palace. The primate's fear seems rather strange.   A riot on account of Fryth, at a time when king, commons, and people were in harmony, appeared hardly probable.   Cranmer had another motive.

Among the persons composing his household was a gentleman of benevolent character, and with a leaning towards the Gospel, who was distressed at the cruelty of the bishops, and looked upon it as a lawful and Christian act to rob them, if possible, of their victims. Giving him one of the porters of Lambeth palace as a companion, Cranmer committed Fryth to his care to bring him to Croydon.   They were to take the prisoner a journey of four or five hours on foot through fields and woods, without any constables or soldiers.   A strange walk and a strange escort.†

Lord Fitzwilliam, first Earl of Southampton and governor of the Tower, at that time lay sick in his house at Westminster, suffering such severe pain as to force loud groans from him.   On the 10th of June, at the desire of my lord of Canterbury, the arch-

---

* 'For that there should be no concourse of citizens.'—Foxe, *Acts,* viii. p. 696.

† The narrative from which we learn these particulars is given in the eighth volume of Foxe's *Acts,* and seems to have been written by the gentleman himself.   The circumstance that it is drawn up so as to compromise neither himself nor Cranmer is of itself a confirmation.

bishop's gentleman, and the Lambeth porter, Gallois, surnamed Perlebeane, were introduced into the nobleman's bedchamber, where they found him lying upon his bed in extreme agony.   Fitzwilliam, a man of the world, was greatly enraged against the evangelicals, who were the cause, in his opinion, of all the difficulties of England.   The gentleman respectfully presented to him the primate's letter and the king's ring. 'What do you want?' he asked sharply, without opening the letter.   'His grace desires your lordship to deliver Master Fryth to us.'   The impatient Southampton flew into a passion at the name, and cursed Fryth and all the heretics.*   He thought it strange that a gentleman and a porter should have to convey a prisoner of such importance to the episcopal court: were there no soldiers in the Tower?   Had Fitzwilliam any suspicion, or did he regret to see the reformer leave the walls within which he had been kept so safely?   We cannot tell: but he must obey, for they brought him the king's signet.   Accordingly taking his own hastily from his finger: 'Fryth,' he said, 'Fryth. . . . Here, show this to the lieutenant of the Tower, and take away your heretic quickly.   I am but too happy to get rid of him.'

A few hours later Fryth, the gentleman, and Perlebeane entered a boat moored near the Tower, and were rowed speedily to the archbishop's palace at Lambeth.   At first the three persons preserved a strict silence, only interrupted from time to time by the deep sighs of the gentleman.   Being charged to begin by trying to induce Fryth to make some compromise, he broke the silence at last.   'Master Fryth,'

* Foxe, *Acts*, viii. p. 696.

he said, 'if you are not prudent you are lost. What a pity! you that are so learned in Latin and Greek and in the Holy Scriptures, the ancient doctors, and all kinds of knowledge, you will perish, and all your admirable gifts will perish with you, with little profit to the world, and less comfort to your wife and children, your kinsfolk and friends.' . . . The gentleman was silent a minute, and then began again: 'Your position is dangerous, Master Fryth, but not desperate: you have many friends who will do all they can in your favour. On your part do something for them, make some concession, and you will be safe. Your opinion on the merely spiritual presence of the body and blood of the Saviour is premature: it is too soon for us in England ; wait until a better time comes!'

Fryth did not say a word: no sound was heard but the dash of the water and the noise of the oars. The gentleman thought he had shaken the young doctor, and after a moment's silence he resumed: 'My lord Cromwell and my lord of Canterbury feel great affection for you; they know that if you are young in years you are old in knowledge, and may become a most profitable citizen of this realm. . . . If you will be somewhat advised by their counsel, they will never permit you to be harmed; but if you stand stiff to your opinion, it is not possible to save your life, for as you have good friends so have you mortal enemies.'

The gentleman stopped and looked at the prisoner. It was by such language that Bilney had been seduced; but Fryth kept himself in the presence of God, ready to lose his life that he might save it. He thanked the gentleman for his kindness, and said that his conscience would not permit him to recede, out of respect to man, from the true doctrine of the Lord's Supper. 'If I am questioned on that point, I must answer according to my conscience, though I should lose twenty lives if I had so many. I can support it by a great number of passages from the Holy Scriptures and the ancient doctors, and if I am fairly tried I shall have nothing to fear.'—'Marry!' quoth the gentleman, 'if you be fairly tried, you would be safe, but that is what I very much doubt. Our master Christ was not fairly tried, nor would he be, as I think, if he were now present again in the world. How then should you be, when your opinions are so little understood and are so odious?'—'I know,' answered Fryth, 'that the doctrine which I hold is very hard meat to be digested just now; but listen to me.' As he spoke, he took the gentleman by the hand: 'If you live twenty years more, you will see the whole realm of my opinion concerning this sacrament of the altar—all, except a certain class of men. My death, you say, would be sorrowful to my friends, but it will be only for a short time. But, all things considered, my death will be better unto me and all mine than life in continual bondage. God knoweth what he hath to do with his poor servant, whose cause I now defend. He will help me, and no man shall prevail on me to step backwards.'

The boat reached Lambeth. The travellers landed, entered the archbishop's palace, and, after taking some refreshment, started on foot for Croydon, twelve miles from London.

The three travellers proceeded over the hills and through the plains of Surrey: here and there flocks

of sheep were grazing in the scanty pastures, and to
the east stretched vast woods. The gentleman walked
mournfully by the side of Fryth. It was useless to
ask him again to retract, but another idea engrossed
Cranmer's officer: that of letting Fryth escape. The
country was then thinly inhabited: the woods which
covered it on the east and the chalky hills might serve
as a hiding-place for the fugitive. The difficulty was to
persuade Perlebeane. The gentleman slackened his
pace, called to the porter, and they walked by themselves behind the prisoner. When they were so far
off that he could not hear their conversation, the
gentleman said: 'You have heard this man, I am
sure, and noted his talk since he came from the
Tower.'—'I never heard so constant a man,' Perlebeane answered, 'nor so eloquent a person.'—'You
have heard nothing,' resumed the gentleman, 'in
respect both of his knowledge and his eloquence. If
you could hear him at the university or in the pulpit,
you would admire him still more. England has
never had such a one of his age with so much learning. And yet our bishops treat him as if he were a
very dolt or an idiot. . . . They abhor him as the
devil himself, and want to get rid of him by any
means.'—'Marry!' said the porter, 'if there were
nothing else in him but the consideration of his
person both comely and amiable, his disposition so
gentle, meek, and humble, it were pity he should be
cast away.'—'Cast away,' interrupted the gentleman,
'he will certainly be cast away if we once bring him
to Croydon.' And lowering his voice, he continued:
'Surely before God I speak it, if thou, Perlebeane,
wert of my mind, we should never bring him thither.'

—'What do you mean?' asked the astonished porter. Then, after a moment's silence, he added: 'I know that you have a great deal more responsibility in this matter than I have; and therefore if you can honestly save this man I will yield to your proposal with all my heart.' The gentleman breathed again.

Cranmer had desired that all possible efforts should be made to change Fryth's sentiments; and these failing, he wished to save him in another way. It was his desire that the reformer should go on foot to Croydon, that he should be accompanied by two only of his servants, selected from those best disposed towards the new doctrine. The primate's gentleman would never have dared take upon himself, except by his master's desire, the responsibility of conniving at the escape of a prisoner who was to be tried by the first personages of the realm, appointed by the king himself. Happy at having gained the porter to his enterprise, he began to discuss with him the ways and means. He knew the country well, and his plan was arranged.

'You see yonder hill before us,' he said to Perlebeane; 'it is Brixton Causeway, two miles from London. There are great woods on both sides. When we come to the top we will permit Fryth to escape into the woods on the left hand, whence he may easily get into Kent, where he was born, and where he has many friends. We will linger an hour or two on the road, after his flight, to give him time to reach a place of safety, and when night approaches we will go to Streatham, which is a mile and a half off, and make an outcry in the town that our prisoner has escaped into the woods on the right hand towards

Wandsworth, that we followed him for more than a mile, and at length lost him because we were not many enough. At the same time we will take with us as many people as we can, to search for him in that direction; if necessary, we will be all night about it; and before we can send the news of what has happened to Croydon, Fryth will be in safety, and the bishops will be disappointed.'

The gentleman, we see, was not very scrupulous about the means of rescuing a victim from the Roman priests. Perlebeane thought as he did. 'Your plan pleases me,' he answered; 'now go and tell the prisoner, for we are already at the foot of the hill.'

The delighted gentleman hurried forward: 'Master Fryth,' he said, 'let us talk together a little. I cannot hide from you that the task I have undertaken, to bring you to Croydon, as a sheep to the slaughter, grieves me exceedingly, and there is no danger I would not brave to deliver you out of the lion's mouth. Yonder good fellow and I have devised a plan whereby you may escape: listen to me.' The gentleman having described his plan, Fryth smiled amiably and said: 'This then is the result of your long consultation together. You have wasted your time. If you were both to leave me here and go to Croydon, declaring to the bishops you had lost me, I should follow after as fast as I could, and bring them news that I had found and brought Fryth again.'

The gentleman had not expected such an answer. A prisoner refuse his liberty! ... 'You are mad,' he said: 'do you think your reasoning will convert the bishops? At Milton Shone you tried to escape

beyond the sea, and now you refuse to save yourself!'
—'The two cases are different,' answered Fryth;
'then I was at liberty, and according to the advice of
St. Paul I would fain have enjoyed my liberty for the
continuance of my studies. But now the higher
power, as it were by Almighty God's permission, has
seized me, and my conscience binds me to defend the
doctrine for which I am persecuted, if I would not
incur our Lord's condemnation. If I should now
run away, I should run from my God; if I should fly,
I should fly from the testimony I am bound to bear
to his Holy Word, and I should deserve a thousand
hells. I most heartily thank you both for your good
will towards me, but I beseech you to bring me
where I was appointed to be brought, for else I will
go thither all alone.' *

Those who desired to save Fryth had not counted
upon so much integrity. Such were, however, the
martyrs of protestantism. The archbishop's two servants continued their route along with their strange
prisoner. Fryth had a calm eye and cheerful look,
and the rest of the journey was accomplished in pious
and agreeable conversation. When they reached Croydon, he was delivered to the officers of the episcopal
court, and passed the night in the lodge of the primate's porter.

The next morning he appeared before the bishops
and peers appointed to examine him. Cranmer and
Lord Chancellor Audley desired his acquittal, but
some of the other judges were men without pity.

The examination began:

'Do you believe,' they said, 'that the sacrament

* Foxe, *Acts*, viii. Appendix.

of the altar is or is not the real body of Christ?' Fryth answered simply and firmly: 'I believe that the bread is the body of Christ in that it is broken, and thus teaches us that the body of Christ was to be broken and delivered unto death to redeem us from our iniquities. I believe the bread is the body of Christ in that it is *distributed*, and thus teaches us that the body of Christ and the fruits of his passion are distributed unto all faithful people. I believe that the bread is the body of Christ so far as it is *received*, and thus it teaches us that even as the outward man receiveth the sacrament with his teeth and mouth, so doth the inward man truly receive through faith the body of Christ and the fruits of his passion.'

The judges were not satisfied : they wanted a formal and complete retractation. 'Do you not think,' asked one of them, 'that the natural body of Christ, his flesh, blood, and bones, are contained under the sacrament and are there present without any figure of speech?'—'No,' he answered; 'I do not think so;' adding with much humility and charity: 'notwithstanding I would not have that any should count my saying to be an article of faith. For even as I say, that you ought not to make any necessary article of the faith of your part; so I say again, that we make no necessary article of the faith of our part, but leave it indifferent for all men to judge therein, as God shall open their hearts, and no side to condemn or despise the other, but to nourish in all things brotherly love, and to bear one another's infirmities.' *

The commissioners then undertook to convince Fryth of the truth of transubstantiation; but he

* Foxe, *Acts*, v. p. 12.

quoted Scripture, St. Augustine and Chrysostom, and eloquently defended the doctrine of the spiritual eating. The court rose. Cranmer had been moved, although he was still under the influence of Luther's teaching.* 'The man spoke admirably,' he said to Dr. Heath as they went out, 'and yet in my opinion he is wrong.' Not many years later he devoted one of the most important of his writings to an explanation of the doctrine now professed by the young reformer; it may be that Fryth's words had begun to shake him.

Full of love for him, Cranmer desired to save him. Four times during the course of the examination he sent for Fryth and conversed with him privately,† always asserting the Lutheran opinion. Fryth offered to maintain his doctrine in a public discussion against anyone who was willing to attack it, but nobody accepted his challenge.‡ Cranmer, distressed at seeing all his efforts useless, found there was nothing more for him to do; the cause was transferred to the ordinary, the Bishop of London, and on the 17th of June the prisoner was once more committed to the Tower. The bishop selected as his assessors for the trial, Longland, Bishop of Lincoln, and Gardiner, Bishop of Winchester: there were no severer judges to be found on the episcopal bench. At Cambridge Fryth had been the most distinguished pupil of the clever and ambitious Gardiner; but this, instead of

* 'Mit den Zähnen zu bissen.'—Plank. iii. p. 369.

† 'And surely I myself sent for him three or four times to persuade him.'—Cranmer, *Remains, Letters,* p. 246.

‡ 'There was no man willing to answer him in open disputation.'— Foxe, *Acts,* viii. p. 699.

exciting the compassion of that hard man, did but increase his anger. 'Fryth and his friends,' he said, 'are villains, blasphemers, and limbs of the devil.' *

On the 20th of June Fryth was taken to St. Paul's before the three bishops, and though of a humble disposition and almost timid character, he answered boldly. A clerk took down all his replies, and Fryth, snatching up the pen, wrote: 'I Fryth think thus. Thus have I spoken, written, defended, affirmed, and published in my writings.' † The bishops having asked him if he would retract his errors, Fryth replied: 'Let justice have its course and the sentence be pronounced.' Stokesley did not keep him waiting long. 'Not willing that thou, Fryth, who art wicked,' he said, 'shouldest become more wicked, and infect the Lord's flock with thy heresies, we declare thee excommunicate and cast out from the Church, and leave thee unto the secular powers, most earnestly requiring them in the truth of our Lord Jesus Christ that thy execution and punishment be not too extreme, *nor yet the gentleness too much mitigated.*' ‡

Fryth was taken to Newgate and shut up in a dark cell, where he was bound with chains on the hands and feet as heavy as he could bear, and round his neck was a collar of iron, which fastened him to a post, so that he could neither stand upright nor sit down. Truly the 'gentleness' was not 'too much mitigated.' His charity never failed him. 'I am going to die,' he said, 'but I condemn neither those

---

* Bishop Hooper, *Early Writings*, p. 245.

† 'Ego Frythus ita sentio, ita dixi, scripsi, affirmavi, &c.'—Foxe, *Acts*, v. p. 14.

‡ Ibid. p. 15.

who follow Luther nor those who follow Œcolampadius, since both reject transubstantiation.'* A young
mechanic of twenty-four, Andrew Hewet by name,
was placed in his cell. Fryth asked him for what
crime he was sent to prison. 'The bishops,' he replied,
'asked me what I thought of the sacrament, and I
answered, "I think as Fryth does." Then one of them
smiled, and the Bishop of London said: "Why Fryth
is a heretic, and already condemned to be burnt, and
if you do not retract your opinion you shall be burnt
with him." "Very well," I answered, "I am content."†
So they sent me here to be burnt along with you.'

On the 4th of July they were both taken to
Smithfield: the executioners fastened them to the
post, back to back; the torch was applied, the flame
rose in the air, and Fryth, stretching out his hands,
embraced it as if it were a dear friend whom he would
welcome. The spectators were touched, and showed
marks of lively sympathy. 'Of a truth,' said an evangelical Christian in after days, 'he was one of those
prophets whom God, having pity on this realm of
England, raised up to call us to repentance.'‡ His
enemies were there. Cooke, a fanatic priest, observing some persons praying, called out: 'Do not pray
for such folks, any more than you would for a dog.'§
At this moment a sweet light shone on Fryth's face,
and he was heard beseeching the Lord to pardon his
enemies. Hewet died first, and Fryth thanked God
that the sufferings of his young brother were over.

---

* 'All the Germans, both of Luther's side and also of Œcolampadius.'
—Tyndale and Fryth, *Works*, iii. p. 455.

† Foxe, *Acts*, v. p. 18.

‡ Becon, *Works*, iii. p. 11.   § Foxe, *Acts*, v. p. 10.

Committing his soul into the Lord's hands, he expired. 'Truly,' exclaimed many, 'great are the victories Christ gains in his saints.'

So many souls were enlightened by Fryth's writings,
that this reformer contributed powerfully to the reno-
vation of England. 'One day, an Englishman,' says
Thomas Becon, prebendary of Canterbury and chaplain to Archbishop Cranmer, 'having taken leave of
his mother and friends, travelled into Derbyshire, and
from thence to the Peak, a marvellous barren country,'
and where there was then 'neither learning nor yet
no spark of godliness.' Coming into a little village
named Alsop in the Dale, he chanced upon a certain
gentleman also named Alsop, lord of that village,
a man not only ancient in years, but also ripe in the
knowledge of Christ's doctrine. After they had taken
'a sufficient repast,' the gentleman showed his guest
certain books which he called his *jewels* and *principal
treasures*: these were the New Testament and some
books of Fryth's. In these godly treatises this ancient gentleman occupied himself among his rocks and
mountains both diligently and virtuously. 'He did
not only love the Gospel,' adds Cranmer's chaplain,
'he *lived it also*.'*

Fryth's writings were not destined to be read always
with the same avidity : the truth they contain is,
however, good for all times. The books of the
apostles and of the reformers which that gentleman
of Alsop read in the sixteenth century were better
calculated to bring joy and peace to the soul than the
light works read with such avidity in the world.

---

* Becon, *Jewell of Joy* (Parker Soc.), p. 420.

CHAPTER XX.

ENGLAND SEPARATES GRADUALLY FROM THE PAPACY.

(1533.)

WHEN Fryth mounted the scaffold, Anne Boleyn had been seated a month on the throne of England. The salvoes of artillery which had saluted the new queen had reechoed all over Europe. There could be no more doubt : the Earl of Wiltshire's daughter, radiant with grace and beauty, wore the Tudor crown; every one, especially the imperial family, must bear the consequences of the act. One day Sir John Hacket, English envoy at Brussels, arrived at court just as Mary, regent of the Low Countries, was about to mount her horse. 'Have you any news from England?' she asked him in French.—'None,' he replied. Mary gave him a look of surprise,* and added: 'Then I have, and not over good methinks.' She then told him of the king's marriage, and Hacket rejoined with an unembarrassed air : 'Madam, I know not if it has taken place, but everybody who considers it coolly and without family prejudice will agree that it is a lawful and a conscientious marriage.' Mary, who was niece of the unhappy Catherine, replied : 'Mr. Ambassador, God

---

* 'She gave me a look as to that she should marvell thereof.'—*State Papers*, vii. p. 451.

knows I wish all may go well; but I do not know how the emperor and the king my brother will take it, for it touches them as well as me.'—'I think I may be certain,' returned Sir John, 'that they will take it in good part.'—'That I do not know, Mr. Ambassador,' said the regent, who doubted it much; and then, mounting her horse, she rode out for the chase.*

Charles V. was exasperated: he immediately pressed the pope to intervene, and on the 12th of May Clement cited the king to appear at Rome. The pontiff was greatly embarrassed: having a particular liking for Benet, Henry's agent, he took him aside, and said to him privately:† 'It is an affair of such importance that there has been none like it for many ·years. I fear to kindle a fire that neither pope nor emperor will be able to quench.' And then he added unaffectedly: 'Besides, I cannot pronounce the king's excommunication before the emperor has an army ready to constrain him.' Henry being told of this *aside* made answer: 'Having the justice of our cause for us, with the entire consent of our nobility, commons, and subjects, we do not care for what the pope may do.' Accordingly, he appealed from the pope to a general council.

The pope was now more embarrassed than ever: 'I cannot stand still and do nothing,' he said.‡ On the 12th of July he revoked all the English proceedings and excommunicated the king, but suspended the effects of his sentence until the end of September.

* 'Setting forward to ride out a hunting.'—*State Papers,* vii. p. 451.
† 'Taking me aside, showed unto me secretly.'—Ibid. p. 457.
‡ 'So sore for him to stand still and do nothing.'—Ibid. p. 469.

' I hope,' said Henry contemptuously, ' that before then the pope will understand his folly.'*

He reckoned on Francis I. to help him to understand it; but that prince was about to receive the pope's niece into his family, and Henry made every exertion, but to no effect, to prevent the meeting of Clement and Francis at Marseilles. The King of England, who had already against him the Netherlands, the Empire, Rome, and Spain, saw France also slipping from him. He was isolated in Europe, and that became a serious matter. Agitated and indignant, he came to an extraordinary resolution, namely, to turn to the disciples and friends of that very Luther whom he had formerly so disdainfully treated.

Stephen Vaughan and Christopher Mann were despatched, the former to Saxony, the other to Bavaria.† Vaughan reached Weimar on the 1st of September, where he had to wait five days for the Elector of Saxony, who was away hunting. On the 5th of September he had an audience of the prince, and spoke to him first in French and then in Latin. Seeing that the elector, who spoke neither French, English, nor Latin, answered him only with nods,‡ he begged the chancellor to be his interpreter. A written answer was sent to Vaughan at seven in the evening: the Elector of Saxony turned his back on the powerful King of England. He was unworthy, he said, to have at his court ambassadors from his royal majesty; and besides, the emperor, who was his only master, might be displeased. Vaughan's annoyance was extreme. ' Strange rudeness! ' he exclaimed. ' A more

---

* *State Papers* (Henry VIII.), vii. p. 496.   † Ibid. p. 501.
‡ ' Sed tantum annuit capite.'—Ibid. p. 502.

uncourteous refusal has never been made to such a gracious proposition. And to my greater misfortune, it is the first mission of this kind with which I have ever been entrusted.' He left Weimar, determined not to deliver his credentials either to the Landgrave of Hesse or to the Duke of Lauenberg, whom he was instructed to visit: he did not wish to run the chance of receiving fresh affronts.

A strange lot was that of the King of England! the pope excommunicating him, and the heretics desiring to have nothing to do with him! No more allies, no more friends! Be it so: if the nation and the monarch are agreed, what is there to fear? Besides, at the very moment this affront was offered him, his joy was at its height: the hope of soon possessing that heir, for whom he had longed so many years, quite transported him. He ordered an official letter to be prepared announcing the birth of a prince, 'to the great joy of the king,' it ran, 'and of all his loving subjects.' Only the date of the letter was left blank.

On the 7th of September, two days after the elector's refusal, Anne, then residing in the palace at Greenwich, was brought to bed of a fine well-formed child, reminding the gossips of the features of both parents; but alas! it was a girl. Henry, agitated by two strong affections, love for Anne and desire for a son, had been kept in great anxiety during the time of labour. When he was told that the child was a girl, the love he bore for the mother prevailed, and though disappointed in his fondest wishes, he received the babe with joy. But the famous letter announcing the birth of a prince . . .

what must be done with it now? Henry ordered the
queen's secretary to add an *s* to the word *prince*, and
despatched the circular without making any change
in the expression of his satisfaction.* The christen-
ing was celebrated with great pomp; two hundred
torches were carried before the princess, a fit emblem
of the light which her reign would shed abroad. The
child was named Elizabeth, and Henry gave her the
title of Princess of Wales, declaring her his successor
in case he should have no male offspring. In London
the excitement was great: *Te Deums*, bells, and music
filled the air. The adepts of judicial astrology declared that the stars announced a glorious future.
A bright star was indeed rising over England;
and the English people, throwing off the yoke of
Rome, were about to start on a career of freedom,
morality, and greatness. The firm Elizabeth was not
destined to shine by the amiability which distinguished her mother, and the restrictions she placed
upon liberty tend rather to remind us of her father.
Yet while on the continent kings were trampling
under foot the independence of their subjects, the
English people, under Anne Boleyn's daughter, were
to develope themselves, to flourish in letters and in
arts, to extend navigation and commerce, to reform
abuses, to exercise their liberties, to watch energetically over the public good, and to set up the torch
of the Gospel of Christ.

The King of France, very adverse to England's

---

* This official document is given in the *State Papers*, i. p. 407. An
examination of the manuscript in the Harleian collection shows that the
s was added afterwards in the two following passages: 'bringing forth of
a prince*s*' and 'preservation of the said prince*s*.'

becoming independent of Rome, at last prevailed
upon Henry to send two English agents (Gardiner
and Bryan) to Marseilles. 'You will keep your eyes
open,' said Henry VIII. to them, 'and lend an attentive ear, but you will keep your mouths shut.' The
English envoys, being invited to a conference with
Clement and Francis, and solicited by those great personages to speak, declared that they had no powers.
'Why then were you sent?' exclaimed the king,
unable to conceal his vexation. The ambassadors
only answered with a smile.* Francis, who meant to
uphold the authority of the pope in France, was unwilling that England should be free: he seems to have
had some presentiment of the happy effects that independence would work for the rival nation. Accordingly
he took the ambassadors aside, and prayed them to
enter immediately on business with the pontiff. 'We
are not here for his Holiness,' dryly answered Gardiner, 'or to negotiate anything with him, but only
to do what the King of England commands us.' The
tricks of the papacy had ruined it in the minds of
the English people. Francis I., displeased at Gardiner's silence and irritated by his stiffness, intimated
to the King of England that he would be pleased
to see 'better instruments' sent.† Henry did send
another instrument to Marseilles, but he took care to
choose one sharper still.

Edward Bonner, archdeacon of Leicester, was a
clever, active man, but ambitious, coarse and rude,
wanting in delicacy and consideration towards those
with whom he had to deal, violent, and, as he showed

* Le Grand, *Hist. du Divorce*, i. p. 269.   † Ibid. iii. p. 587.

himself later to the protestants, a cruel persecutor.
For some time he had got into Cromwell's good
graces, and as the wind was against popery, Bonner
was against the pope.   Henry gave him his appeal to
a general council, and charged him to present it to
Clement VII.: it was the 'bill of divorcement' between the pope and England.   Bonner, proud of
being the bearer of so important a message, arrived
at Marseilles, firmly resolved to give Henry a proof of
his zeal.   If Luther had burnt the pope's bull at
Wittemberg, Bonner would do as much; but while
Luther had acted as a free man, Bonner was only a
slave, pushing to fanaticism his submission to the
orders of his despotic master.

Gardiner was astounded when he heard of Bonner's
arrival.   What a humiliation for him!   He hung his
head, pinched his lips,* and then lifted up his eyes
and hands, as if cursing the day and hour when
Bonner appeared.   Never were two men more dis-
cordant to one another.   Gardiner could not believe
the news.   A scheme contrived without him!   A
bishop to see one of his inferiors charged with a
mission more important than his own!   Bonner
having paid him a visit, Gardiner affected great coldness, and brought forward every reason calculated to
dissuade him from executing his commission.—'But
I have a letter from the king,' answered Bonner,
'sealed with his seal, and dated from Windsor: here
it is.'   And he took from his satchel the letter in
which Henry VIII. intimated that he had appealed
from the sentence of the pope recently delivered

* 'Making a plairemouth with his lip.'—Foxe, *Acts*, v. p. 152.

against him.* 'Good,' answered Gardiner, and taking
the letter he read : 'Our good pleasure is that if you
deem it *good* and *serviceable* (Gardiner dwelt upon
those two words) you will give the pope notice of the
said appeal, according to the forms required by law;
if not, you will acquaint us with your opinion in that
respect.'—'That is clear,' said Gardiner; 'you should
advise the king to abstain, for that notice just now
will be neither good nor serviceable.'—'And I say
that it is both,' rejoined Bonner.

One circumstance brought the two Englishmen
into harmony, at least for a time. Catherine de
Medicis, the pope's niece, had been married to the
son of Francis I., and Clement made four French
prelates cardinals. But not one Englishman, not
even Gardiner! That changed the question: there
could be no more doubt. Francis is sacrificing
Henry to the pope, and the pope insults England.
Gardiner himself desired Bonner to give the pontiff
notice of the appeal, and the English envoy, fearing
refusal if he asked for an audience of Clement, determined to overleap the usual formalities, and take the
place by assault.

On the 7th of November, the Archdeacon of
Leicester, accompanied by Penniston, a gentleman
who had brought him the king's last orders, went
early to the pontifical palace, preparing to let fall
from the folds of his mantle war between England
and the papacy. As he was not expected, the pontifical officers stopped him at the door; but the Englishman forced his way in, and entered a hall through

* Cranmer's *Memorials*, Appendix, p. 8.

which the pope must pass on his way to the consistory.

Ere long the pontiff appeared, wearing his stole,
and walking between the cardinals of Lorraine and
Medicis, his train following behind.   His eyes, which
were of remarkable quickness, immediately fell upon
the distant Bonner,* and as he advanced he did not
take them off the stranger, as if astonished and uneasy
at seeing him.   At length he stopped in the middle
of the hall, and Bonner, approaching the datary, said
to him: 'Be pleased to inform his Holiness that I
desire to speak to him.'   The officer refusing, the
intrepid Bonner made as if he would go towards the
pope.   Clement, wishing to know the meaning of
these indiscreet proceedings, bade the cardinals stand
aside, took off the stole, and going to a window recess,
called Bonner to him.   The latter, without any formality, informed the pope that the King of England
appealed from his decision to a general council, and
that he (Bonner), his Majesty's envoy, was prepared
to hand him the authentic documents of the said
appeal, taking them (as he spoke) from his portfolio.
Clement, who expected nothing like this, was greatly
surprised: 'it was a terrible breakfast for him,' says
a contemporary document.†   Not knowing what to
answer, he shrugged his shoulders, 'after the Italian
fashion;' and at last, recovering himself a little, he
told Bonner that he was going to the consistory,
and desired him to return in the afternoon.   Then
beckoning the cardinals, he left the hall.

Henry's envoy was punctual to the appointment,
but had to wait for an hour and a half, his Holiness

* 'The pope, whose sight is incredulous quick, eyed me.'—Burnet,
Records, iii. p. 38.   † Ibid. p. 51.

being engaged in giving audience. At length he and Penniston were conducted to the pope's closet. Clement fixed his eyes on the latter, and Bonner having introduced him, the pope remarked with a mistrustful air: 'It is well, but I also must have some members of my council;' and he ordered Simonetta, Capisuchi, and the datary to be sent for. While waiting their arrival, Clement leant at the window, and appeared absorbed in thought. At last, unable to contain himself any longer, he exclaimed: 'I am greatly surprised that his Majesty should behave as he does towards me.' The intrepid Bonner replied: 'His Majesty is not less surprised that your Holiness, who has received so many services from him, repays him with ingratitude.' Clement started, but restrained himself on seeing the datary enter, and ordered that officer to read the appeal which Bonner had just delivered to him.*

The datary began: 'Considering that we have endured from the pope many wrongs and injuries (*gravaminibus et injuriis*)' . . . . Clasping his hands and nodding dissent, Clement exclaimed ironically: '*O questo è molto vero!*' meaning to say that it was false, remarks Bonner.† The datary continued: 'Considering that his most holy Lordship strikes us with his spiritual sword, and wishes to separate us from the unity of the Church; we, desiring to protect with a lawful shield the kingdom which God has given us,‡ appeal by these presents, for ourselves and for all our subjects, to a holy universal council.'

---

* 'His Holiness, delivering it to the datarie, commanded him to read it.'—Burnet, *Records*, iii. p. 23.

† Ibid. pp. 37-46; Rymer, *Acta*, vi. pars ii. p. 188.

‡ 'Legitimo defensionis clypeo protegere.'—Rymer, *Acta*, vi. pars ii. p. 188.

At these words, the pope burst into a transport of passion,* and the datary stopped.   Clement's gestures and broken words uttered with vehemence, showed the horror he entertained of a council. . . . A council would set itself above the pope, a council might perhaps say that the Germans and the King of England were right. ' To speak of a general council! O good Lord!' he exclaimed.†

The pope gave way to convulsive movements, folding and unfolding his handkerchief, which was always a sign of great anger in him.   At last, as if to hide his passion, he said: ' Continue, I am listening.' When the datary had ended, the pope said coldly to his officers: ' It is well written! *Questo è bene fatto.*'

Then turning to Bonner, he asked: ' Have you anything more to say to me?' Bonner was not in the humour to show the least consideration.   A man of the north, he took a pleasure in displaying his roughness and inflexibility in the elegant, crafty, and corrupt society of Rome.   He boldly repeated the protest, and delivered the king's ' provocation ' to the pope, who broke out into fresh lamentations. ' Ha!' he exclaimed vehemently, ' his Majesty affects much respect for the Church, but does not show the least to me.' He *snarled* ‡ as he read the new document. . . . Just at this moment, one of his officers announced the King of France.   Francis could not have arrived at a more seasonable moment.   Clement rose and went to the door to meet him.   The king respectfully took off his hat, and holding it in his hand made

---

* ' He fell in a marvellous great choler and rage.'—Burnet, *Records,* iii. p. 54.
 † Ibid.   ‡ ' Wherein the pope snarling.'—Ibid. p. 42.

a low bow,* after which he enquired what his Holiness was doing. 'These English gentlemen,' said the pontiff, 'are here to notify me of certain provocations and appeals . . . and for other matters,' † he added, displaying much ill-humour. Francis sat down near the table at which the pope was seated; and turning their backs to Henry's envoy, who had retired into an adjoining room, they began a conversation in a low tone, which Bonner, notwithstanding all his efforts, could not hear.

That conversation possibly decided the separation between England and France. The king showed that he was offended at a course of proceeding which he characterised as unbecoming; and Clement learnt, to his immense satisfaction, that the English had not spoken to Francis about the council. 'If you will leave me and the emperor free to act against England,' he said to the king, 'I will ensure you possession of the duchy of Milan.'‡ The monarch promised the obedience of his people to the decrees of the papacy, and the pope in his joy exclaimed: ' *Questo è per la bontà vostra!* ' Bonner, who had not lost sight of the two speakers, remarked that at this moment the king and the pope 'laughed merrily together,' and appeared to be the best friends in the world.

The king having withdrawn, Bonner again approached the pope, and the datary finished the reading. The Englishman had not been softened by the mysterious conversation and laughter of Clement and

* 'The French king making very low *curtisie*, putting off his bonnet and keeping it off.'—Burnet, *Records*, iii. p. 42.

† ' Questi signori Inglesi sono stati quà per intimare certi provocationi et appellationi . . . . e di fare altre cose.'—Ibid.

‡ Le Grand, *Histoire du Divorce*, i. p. 268.

Francis: he was as rough and abrupt as the Frenchman had been smooth and amiable. It was long since
the papacy had suffered such insults openly, and even
the German Reformation had not put it to such torture. The Cardinal de Medicis, chief of the malcon-
tents, who had come in, listened to Bonner, with head
bent down and eyes fixed upon the floor: he was
humiliated and indignant. 'This is a matter of great
importance,' said Clement; 'I will consult the consistory and let you know my answer.'

In the afternoon of Monday, 10th of November,
Bonner returned to the palace to learn the pope's
pleasure: but there was a grand reception that day,
the lords and ladies of the court of Francis I. were
presented to Clement, who did nothing for two hours
but bless chaplets, bless the spectators, and put out
his foot for the nobles and dames to kiss.*

At last Bonner was introduced : '*Domine doctor,
quid vultis?* Sir doctor, what do you want?' said the
pope. 'I desire the answer which your Holiness promised me.' Clement, who had had time to recover
himself, replied: 'A constitution of Pope Pius, my
predecessor, condemns all appeals to a general council.
I therefore reject his Majesty's appeal as unlawful.'
The pope had pronounced these words with calmness
and dignity, but an incident occurred to put him out
of temper. Bonner, hurt at the little respect paid to
his sovereign, bluntly informed the pope that the
Archbishop of Canterbury—that Cranmer—desired
also to appeal to a council. This was going too far:
Clement, restraining himself no longer, rose, and ap-

---

* Burnet, *Records*, iii. p. 42.

proaching Henry's envoy, said to him : ' If you do not leave the room instantly, I will have you thrown into a caldron of molten lead.'*—' Truly,' remarked Bonner, ' if the pope is a shepherd, he is, as the king my master says, a violent and cruel shepherd.'† And not caring to take a leaden bath, he departed for Lyons.‡

Clement was delighted not only at the departure, but still more at the conduct of Bonner: the insolence of the English envoy helped him wonderfully; and accordingly he made a great noise about it, complaining to everybody, and particularly to Francis. ' I am wearied, vexed, disgusted with all this,' said that prince to his courtiers. ' What I do with great difficulty in a week for my good brother (Henry VIII.), his own ministers undo in an hour.' Clement endeavoured in secret interviews§ to increase this discontent, and he succeeded. The mysterious understanding was apparent to everyone, and Vannes, the English agent, who never lost sight either of the pope or the king, informed Cromwell of the close union of their minds.‖

When Henry VIII. learnt that the King of France was slipping from him, he was both irritated and alarmed. Abandoned by that prince, he saw the pope launching an interdict against his kingdom, the emperor invading England, and the people in insur-

---

* Burnet, *Records*, i. p. 130.

† ' Immitis et crudelis pastor.'—Rymer, *Acta*, p. 188.

‡ Cranmer's appeal was not written till later, except there be some error in the date. Burnet, *Records*, iii. p. 24.

§ ' Hæc omnia a pontifice cum rege amotis arbitris tractata.'—*State Papers* (Henry VIII.), vii. p. 222.

‖ ' De summa animorum conjunctione.'—Ibid. p. 523.

rection.* He had no repose by night or day: his anger against the pope continued to increase. Wishing to prevent at least the revolts which the partisans of the papacy might excite among his subjects, he dictated a strange proclamation to his secretary: ' Let no Englishman forget the most noble and loving prince of this realm,' he said, ' who is most wrongfully judged by the *great idol* and most *cruel enemy to Christ's religion, which calleth himself Pope.* Princes have two ways to attain right—the general council and the sword. Now the king, having appealed from the unlawful sentence of the Bishop of Rome to a general council lawfully congregated, the said usurper hath rejected the appeal, and is thus outlawed. By holy Scripture, there is no more jurisdiction granted to the Bishop of Rome than to any other bishop. Henceforth honour him not as an idol, who is but a man usurping God's power and authority; and a man neither in life, learning, nor conversation like Christ's minister or disciple.' †

Henry having given vent to his irritation, bethought himself, and judged it more prudent not to publish the proclamation.

At Marseilles England and France separated: the first, because she was withdrawing from the pope; the other, because she was moving nearer to him. It is here that was formed that secret understanding between Paris and Rome which, adopted by the successors of Francis I., and more or less courted by other sovereigns of Christendom, has for several centuries filled glorious countries with despotism and perse-

---

* Strype, *Eccles. Mem.* i. p. 22.   † Ibid. p. 226 (Oxf. 1822).

cution, and often with immorality. The interview at Marseilles between the pope and the King of France is the dividing point; since that time governments and nations in the train of Rome have been seen to decline, while those who separated from it have begun to rise.

CHAPTER XXI.

PARLIAMENT ABOLISHES THE USURPATIONS OF THE POPES
IN ENGLAND.

(JANUARY TO MARCH 1534.)

WHILE the papacy was intriguing with France and the empire, England was energetically working at the utter abolition of the Roman authority.* 'One loud cry must be raised in England against the papacy,' said Cromwell to the council. 'It is time that the question was laid before the people. Bishops, parsons, curates, priors, abbots, and preachers of the religious orders should all declare from their pulpits that the Bishop of Rome, styled the Pope, is subordinate, like the rest of the bishops, to a general council, and that he has no more rights in this kingdom than any other foreign bishop.'

It was necessary to pursue the same course abroad. Henry resolved to send ambassadors to Poland, Hungary, Saxony, Bavaria, Pomerania, Prussia, Hesse, and other German states, to inform them that he was touched with the zeal they had shown in defence of the Word of God and the extirpation of ancient errors, and to acquaint all men that he was himself 'utterly determined to reduce the pope's power *ad justos et*

* *State Papers* (Henry VIII.), t. vii. p. 526.

legitimos mediocritatis suæ modos, to the just and lawful bounds of his mediocrity.' *

He did not stop here. Desiring above all things to withdraw France from under the influence of Rome, he instructed his ambassadors to tell Francis I. in his name and in the name of the people : 'We shall shortly be able to give unto the pope such a buffet as he never had before.'† This was quite in Henry's style. 'Things are going at such a rate here,' wrote the Duke of Norfolk to Montmorency, 'that the pope will soon lose the obedience of England; and other nations, perceiving the great fruits, advantage, and profit that will result from it, will also separate from Rome.'‡

All this was serious: there was some chance that Norfolk's prophecy would be fulfilled. The poor pontiff could think of nothing else, and began to believe that the idea of a council was not so unreasonable after all, since the place and time of meeting and mode of proceeding would lead to endless discussions; and if the meeting ever took place, he would thus be relieved of a responsibility which became more oppressive to him every day. He therefore bade Henry VIII. be informed that he agreed to call a general council. But events had not stood still: the position was not the same. 'It is no longer necessary,' the king answered coldly. In his opinion, the Church of England was sufficient of herself, and could do without the Church of Rome.

The King of France, growing alarmed, immediately resumed his part of mediator. Du Bellay, his ambas-

---

* Burnet, *Records*, iii. p. 69.   † *State Papers*, vol. vii. p. 526.
‡ Le Grand, *Preuves*, p. 591.

sador at Rome, made indefatigable efforts to inspire
the consistory with an opinion favourable to Henry
VIII. According to that diplomatist, the King of
England was ready to reestablish friendly relations
with Clement VII., and it was parliament alone
that desired to break with the papacy for ever: it
was the people who wished for reform, it was the
king who opposed it. 'Make your choice,' he exclaimed with eloquence.* 'All that the king desires
is peace with Rome; all that the commonalty demands is war. With whom will you go—with your
enemies or with your friend?' Du Bellay's assertions,
though strange, were based upon a truth that cannot
be denied. It was the best of the people who wanted
protestantism in England, and not the king.

The court of Rome felt that the last hour had come,
and determined to despatch to London the papers
necessary to reconcile Henry. It was believed on the
Continent that the King of England was going to
gain his cause at last, and people ascribed it to the
ascendency of French policy at Rome sinee the marriage of Catherine de Medicis with Henry of Orleans.
But the more the French triumphed, the more indignant became the Imperialists. To no purpose did the
pope say to them: 'You do not understand the state
of affairs: the thing is done. . . . The King of England is married to Anne Boleyn. If I annulled the
marriage, who would undertake to execute my sentence?'—'Who?' exclaimed the ambassadors of
Charles V., 'who? . . . The emperor.'† The weak

---

* 'He eloquently declared our king's message.'—Lord Herbert, *Life
of Henry VIII.* p. 396, fol.

† 'That the emperor would be the executor.'—Ibid. p. 553.

pontiff knew not which way to turn: he had but one hope left—if Henry VIII., as he expected, should re-establish catholicism in his kingdom, a fact so important would silence Charles V.

This fact was not to be feared: a movement had begun in the minds of the people of Great Britain which it was no longer possible to stop. While many pious souls received the Word of God in their hearts, the king and the most enlightened part of the nation were agreed to put an end to the intolerable usur-pations of the Roman pontiff. 'We have looked in the Holy Scriptures for the rights of the papacy,' said the members of the Commons house of parliament, ' but instead of finding therein the institution of popes, we have found that of kings—and, according to God's commandments, the priests ought to be subject to them as much as the laity.'—' We have reflected upon the wants of the realm,' said the royal council, ' and have come to the conclusion that the nation ought to form one body; that one body can have but one head, and that head must be the king.' The parliament which met in January 1534 was to give the death-blow to the supremacy of the pope.

This blow came strictly neither from Henry nor from Cranmer, but from Thomas Cromwell.* Without possessing Cranmer's lively faith, Cromwell desired that the preachers should open the Word of God and preach it ' with pure sincereness ' before the people,† and he afterwards procured for every Englishman the right to read it. Being preeminently a statesman of

---

* For Cromwell's early history, see the *History of the Reformation*, vol. v. bk. xx. ch. xiv.

† Lord Cromwell to Parker.

sure judgment and energetic action, he was in advance of his generation; and it was his fate, like those generals who march boldly at the head of the army, to procure victory to the cause for which he fought; but, persecuted by the traitors concealed among his soldiers, to be sacrificed by the prince he had served, and to meet a tragical death before the hour of his triumph.

The Commons, wishing to put an end to the persecutions practised by the clergy against the evangelical Christians, summoned—it was a thing unprecedented *—the Lord-bishop of London to appear at their bar to answer the complaint made against him by Thomas Philips, one of the disciples of the Reformation. The latter had been lying in prison three years under a charge of heresy. The parliament, unwilling that a bishop should be able at his own fancy to transform one of his Majesty's subjects into a heretic, brought in a bill for the repression of doctrines condemned by the Church. They declared that, the authority of the Bishop of Rome being opposed to Holy Scripture and the laws of the realm, the words and acts that were contrary to the decisions of the pontiff could not be regarded as heresies. Then turning to the particular case which had given rise to the grievance, parliament declared Philips innocent and discharged him from prison.

After having thus upheld the cause of religious liberty, the Commons proceeded to the definitive abolition of the privileges which the bishops of Rome had successively usurped to the great detriment of

* 'Not fit for any of the Peers to appear and answer at the bar of the House of Commons.'—Collyers, ii. p. 83.

both Church and people.   They restored to England
the rights of which Rome had despoiled her.   They
prohibited all appeals to the pope, of what kind soever
they might be,* and substituted for them an appeal to
the king in chancery.   They voted that the election
of bishops did not concern the court of Rome, but
belonged to the chief ecclesiastical body in the diocese,
to the chapter . . . at least in appearance; for it really
appertained to the crown, the king designating the
person whom the chapter was to elect.   This strange
constitution was abolished under Edward VI., when
the nomination of the bishops was conferred purely
and simply on the king.   If this was not better, it
was at least more sincere; but the singular *congé
d'élire* was restored under Elizabeth.

At the same time new and loud complaints of the
Romish exactions were heard in parliament.   'For
centuries the Roman bishops have been deceiving us,'
said the eloquent speakers, 'making us believe that
they have the power of dispensing with everything,
even with God's commandments.   We send to Rome
the treasures of England, and Rome sends us back in
return . . . a piece of paper.   The monster which has
fattened on the substance of our people bears a hundred
different names.   They call it reliefs, dues, pensions,
provisions, procurations, delegation, rescript, appeal,
abolition, rehabilitation, relaxation of canonical penalties, licences, Peter's pence, and many other names
besides.   And after having thus caught our money
by all sorts of tricks, the Romans laugh at us in their
sleeves.'   Parliament forbade everybody, even the

---

* Collyers, ii. p. 84.

king himself,* to apply to Rome for any dispensation or delegation whatsoever, and ordered them, in case of need, to have recourse to the Archbishop of Canterbury. Then, immediately putting these principles into practice, they declared the king's marriage with Catherine to be null, for 'no man has power to dispense with God's laws,' † and ratified the marriage between Henry and Anne, proclaiming their children heirs to the crown. At the same time, wishing England to become entirely English, they deprived two Italians, Campeggi and Ghinucci, of the sees of Salisbury and Worcester, which they held.

It was during the month of March, 1534—an important date for England—that the main branches of the tree of popery were thus lopped off one after another. The trunk indeed remained, although stripped; but yet a few months, and that too was to strew the earth with its fall. Still the Commons showed a certain degree of consideration. When Clement had threatened the king with excommunication, he had given him three months' grace; England, desiring to return his politeness, informed the pope that he might receive some compensation. At the same time she made an important declaration: 'We do not separate from the Christian Church,' said the Commons, 'but merely from the usurped authority of the Pope of Rome; and we preserve the catholic faith, as *it is set forth in the Holy Scriptures.*' All these reforms were effected with great unanimity, at least in appearance. The bishops, even the most

---

* 'Neither the king, his successor, nor his subjects to apply to the see of Rome.'—Collyers, ii. p. 84.

† Ibid. p. 85.

scholastic, such as Stokesley of London, Tonstal of Durham, Gardiner of Winchester, and Rowland Lee of Coventry, declared the Roman papacy to be of human invention, and that the pope was, in regard to them, only a *bishop*, a *brother*, as his predecessors had been to the bishops of antiquity.* Every Sunday during the session of parliament a prelate preached at St. Paul's Cross 'that the pope was not the head of the Church,' and all the people said AMEN.

. Meanwhile Du Bellay, the French ambassador at Rome, was waiting for the act by which the King of England was to bind himself once more to the pope —an act which Francis I. still gave him reason to expect. Every morning he fancied it would arrive, and every evening his expectations were disappointed. He called upon the English envoys, and afterwards at the Roman chancery, to hear if there was any news; but everywhere the answer was the same—nothing.

The term fixed by Clement VII. having elapsed, he summoned the consistory for Monday the 23rd of March. Du Bellay attended it, still hoping to prevent anything being done that might separate England from the papacy. The cardinals represented to him, that as the submission of Henry VIII. had not arrived, nothing remained but for the pope to fulminate the sentence. 'Do you not know,' exclaimed Du Bellay in alarm, 'that the courier charged with that prince's despatches has seas to cross, and the winds may be contrary? The king of England waited your decision for six years, and cannot you wait six days?'†

---

* 'Solum Romanum episcopum et fratrem, ut primis episcopis mos erat. —Wilkins, *Concilia*, iii. p. 782.

† Herbert, *Life of Henry VIII.* p. 396. Burnet, *Hist. Ref.* i. p. 131.

' Delay is quite useless,' said a cardinal of the imperial faction; ' we know what is taking place in England. Instead of thinking of reparation, the king is widening the schism every day. He goes so far as to permit the representation of dramas at his court, in which the holy conclave, and some of your most illustrious selves in particular, are held up to ridicule.' The last blow, although a heavy one, was unnecessary. The priests could no longer contain their vexation; the rebellious prince must be punished. Nineteen out of twenty-two cardinals voted against Henry VIII.; the remaining three only asked for further enquiry. Clement could not conceal his surprise and annoyance. To no purpose did he demand another meeting, in conformity with the custom which requires two, and even three, consultations:* overwhelmed by an imposing and unexpected majority, he gave way.

Simonetta then handed him the sentence, which the unhappy pope took and read with the voice of a criminal rather than of a judge. ' Having invoked the name of Christ, and sitting on the throne of justice,† we decree that the marriage between Catherine of Aragon and Henry king of England was and is valid and canonical; that the said king Henry is bound to cohabit with the said queen; to pay her royal honours; and that he must be constrained to discharge these duties.' After pronouncing these words, the poor pontiff, alarmed at the bold act he had just performed, turned to the envoys of Charles V. and said to them: ' I have done my duty; it is now for the

---

* ' What could not be done in less than three consistories, was now despatched in one.'—*Herbert*, p. 397.

† ' Christi nomine invocato, in throno justitiæ pro tribunali sedentes.' —Foxe, *Acts*, v. p. 657.

emperor to do his, and to carry the sentence into execution.' 'The emperor will not hold back,' answered the ambassadors; but the thing was not so easily done as said.

Thus the great affair was ended; the king of England was condemned. It was dark when the pope quitted the consistory; the news so long expected spread immediately through the city; the emperor's partisans, transported with joy, lit bonfires in all the open places, and cannons fired repeated salvoes. Bands of Ghibelines paraded the streets, shouting, *Imperio e Espagna* (the Empire and Spain). The whole city was in commotion. The pope's disquietude was still further increased by these demonstrations. 'He is tormented,' wrote Du Bellay to his master. Clement spent the whole night in conversation with his theologians. 'What must be done? England is lost to us. Oh! how can I avert the king's anger?' Clement VII. never recovered from this blow: the thought that under his pontificate Rome lost England made him shudder. The slightest mention of it renewed his anguish, and sorrow soon brought him to the tomb.

Yet he did not know all. The evil with which Rome was threatened was greater than he had imagined. If in this matter there had been nothing more than the decision of a prince discontented with the court of Rome, a contrary decision of one of his successors might again place England under the dominion of the pontiffs; and these would be sure to spare no pains to recover the good graces of the English kings. But in despite of Henry VIII., a pure doctrine, similar to that of the apostolic times, was spreading over the different parts of the nation;

a doctrine which was not only to wrest England from the pope, but to establish in that island a true Christianity—a vast evangelical propaganda which should plant the standard of God's word even at the ends of the world. The empire of Christendom was thus to be taken from a church led astray by pride, and which bade mankind unite with it that they might be saved; and to be given to those who taught that, according to the divine declarations, none could be saved except by uniting with Jesus Christ.

BOOK VII.

MOVEMENTS OF THE REFORMATION IN ENGLAND, AT GENEVA, IN FRANCE, GERMANY, AND ITALY.

CHAPTER I.

THE BISHOP ESCAPES FROM GENEVA, NEVER TO RETURN.

(JULY 1533.)

WE have seen the Reformation advancing in the bosom of a great nation; we shall now see it making progress in one of the smallest. The fall of Wolsey in England and the flight of the bishop-prince from Geneva are two historical dates which bear a certain resemblance. After the disappearance of these two prelates, there was a forward movement in men's minds, and the Reformation advanced with more decided steps. Those two countries are now, as regards their importance, at the two extreme points in the line of nations; but in the sixteenth century the humble city of the Leman played a more important part in the Church of Christ than the mighty England. Calvin and his school did more than the Tudors, the Stuarts, and their divines, to check the reaction of the papacy and secure the triumph of true Christianity. The sixteenth and seventeenth centuries have proclaimed Geneva the

antagonist of Rome; and, in truth, the petty band
which marched under its banner held their ground
for nearly two centuries against the powerful and
well-disciplined army of the Roman pontiffs. We
have not forgotten Wittemberg, we shall not forget
Geneva. The historian is not allowed to pass by the
little ones who have had their share in the developments of the human mind. To those who repose beneath the healthful shade of the great Gospel oak, and
under its green boughs, we must relate the story of
the acorn from which it sprang. The man who despises humble things cannot understand great things.
' The Lord,' says Calvin, ' purposely made his kingdom to have small and lowly beginnings, in order that
his divine power should be better known, when we
see a progress that had never been expected.'

On the 1st of July, 1533, the bishop of Geneva had
returned to his city with the aid of the priests, the
catholics, the Friburgers, and the ' mamelukes,' with
the intention of ' burying that sect,' as he called the
Reformation. Many of the most devoted friends of
the Gospel were in exile or in the episcopal prison;
hostile bands appeared in the neighbourhood of the
city, and all expected a victory of the Roman party.
The tree was about to be violently uptorn before it
had given any shade. But when God has placed a
germ of religious, or even of political, life among a
people, that life triumphs despite all the opposition of
men. There are rocks and mountains which seem as
if they would stop the course of the mighty waters,
and yet the rivers still run on their way. The exasperated Pierre de la Baume chafed in Geneva, and

beat the earth as if to crush reform and liberty beneath his feet; but by so doing he opened a gulf, in which were swallowed up his rights as a prince, his privileges as a bishop, taxes, revenue, priests, monks, mitres, images, altars, and all the religion of the Roman pontiffs.

If the bishop was uneasy, the people were uneasy likewise. It was not only strong men who spoke against the abuses of the papacy, but even women extolled the prerogatives of the evangelical faith. One day (in June or July, 1533) there was a large party at one of their houses, and two gentlemen of the neighbouring district, the Sire de Simieux and M. de Flacien, 'besides seven or eight of their varlets,' were invited. In their presence the wife of Baudichon de la Maisonneuve professed the evangelical truth. De Simieux having reproved the Genevese lady: 'It is very clear you are a good Papist,' said she. 'And that you are a good Lutheran,' retorted De Simieux. 'Would to God,' exclaimed the lady, 'that we were all so, for it is a good thing and a good law!'* The two gentlemen had had enough; they took their leave of the ladies, and their eight 'varlets' followed them. Another incident will still better show the spirit of the times.

An evangelical named Curtet had just been murdered. Many huguenots thought it strange that, while their adversaries struck down a man—a real image of God—they must respect images made of wood, canvas, or stone. There was a deservedly celebrated place in Geneva, formerly occupied by the

---

* '.Une bonne chose et une bonne loi.' MS. du procès inquisitionnel de Lyon (Archives de Berne), pp. 200-202.

castle of Gondebaud, king of Burgundy, whence his
niece Clotilda one day escaped to marry and convert
Clovis; it was a very ancient arcade, only pulled
down within these few years,* and known as the *Porte
du Château* (the castle gate). Near this place stood
an image of the Virgin, an object of great veneration.†
On the 12th of July, 1533, some 'Lutherans,' believing it to be blasphemy against God to regard the
Virgin as 'the salvation of the world,' went to the
gate, carried away the image, broke it to pieces, and
burnt it.

The bishop, feeling that such men as these were
capable of anything, resolved to put the imprisoned
huguenots beyond their reach. A report soon spread
abroad that he was secretly preparing boats to convey
the prisoners during the night to Friburg or the castle
of Chillon, 'there to do his pleasure on them.'‡ All
the huguenot population was in commotion; each man
shouldered his arquebuse and joined his company;
Philip, the captain-general, ordered the approaches to
the lake to be guarded, so as to prevent the captive
citizens from being conveyed elsewhere.

The noble enthusiasm which the Reformation
kindles in the soul uplifts a man; while the philo-
sophic indifference of scholars and priests serves but
to degrade him. The Genevans, filled with love for
justice and liberty, were ready to risk all that they
held most dear in order to prevent innocent citizens
from being unjustly condemned, and a prelate sent
by the pope from usurping rights which belonged
to the magistrates elected by the people. An extra-

---

* About 1836.   † Registre du Conseil, *ad locum.*
‡ 'Et illic en faire à son plaisir.'

ordinary agitation prevailed in men's minds, and several huguenots proceeded to the shore of the lake. Pierre Verne, taking advantage of the darkness, got into the boats fastened to the bank, and cut the mooring-ropes as well as the cords to which the oars were lashed, so that they were made unserviceable.* Numerous patrols traversed the streets, the armed men being accompanied by citizens, both young and old, carrying *montres de feu*, that is, rods tipped with iron, having several lighted matches or port-fires at the end, which were used at that time to discharge the arquebuses. The dreaded hour when the evil use which princes make of their power accelerates their ruin, had arrived at last for the bishop of Geneva. De la Baume and his par-tisans, who watched from their windows the passage of these excited bands, were surprised at the number of arquebusiers with which the city was suddenly thronged. 'They were informed that for each arque-busier there were three or four match-men, which caused great alarm to those in the palace.' A comet that appeared during the month of July alarmed them still more.† As yet the huguenots wanted a man to lead the way: they were to find him in Baudichon de la Maisonneuve.

The Lutheranism of that citizen was of old date. He was a great friend of John Lullin, who possessed, it will be remembered, the hostelry of the Bear, at that time much frequented by German traders, who were, for the most part, Lutherans. Some Nurem-berg merchants of the name of Toquer arrived there

---

* 'Ni tirer ni nager' (neither pull nor steer), alluding to the peculiar mode of rowing employed on the lake.

† Berne MSS., *Hist. Helvet.* v. p. 125.

during the Lent of 1526.* De la Maisonneuve, who had much business with Germany, went often to see them, 'eating and drinking with them.' Their conversation was very animated, and usually turned upon religion. As early as 1523 the traders of Nuremberg had heard the Gospel from the mouth of Osiander, and they endeavoured to propagate it wherever they went. Their words struck De la Maisonneuve all the more 'because at that time there was no mention of Lutheranism in Geneva, or next to none, at least.'† There was at that time in Lullin's service a young man of Lyons, named Jean Demai, about twenty-five years of age, and very attached to the Roman Church. While waiting at table, he listened attentively to the conversation between Baudichon and the Germans, and kept it in his memory. The daring Genevese did not restrain himself, and said, sometimes at dinner, sometimes at supper,‡ 'God did not ordain Lent. It is mere folly to confess to the priests, for they cannot absolve you. It is an abuse to go to mass. All the religious orders, mendicants, and others, are nonsense.' 'What then will you do with the monks?' asked one of the party. 'Set them all to till the earth,' he replied. 'If you say such things,' observed a catholic, 'the Church will refuse you burial.' 'When I die,' he answered, 'I will have no preaching at my funeral, and no bells tolled; I will be buried wherever I please.'§ Baudichon's remarks

---

* 'About eight years ago,' says an authority of 1534 (MS. du procès inquisitionnel de Lyon). The reading of the MS. is *Toquer*, which is probably not the correct spelling of the German name.

† 'Ou du moins était-ce comme rien.'

‡ 'Soit en dînant, soit en soupant.'—*MS. de Lyon*.

§ MS. du procès de Lyon, pp. 294-297.

were not kept within the walls of the hostelry of the Bear; before.long they were repeated throughout the city and neighbourhood. ' That man,' said many, 'is one of the principal Lutherans, and in the front rank of those who set them going.' * That is what he was about to do.

On the 12th of July, 1533, Baudichon had passed the day in the country, making preparations for the harvest. Returning from the fields at night, he was surprised to see an extraordinary guard at the city gate, and on asking what it meant, he was told that the episcopalians were going to convey the prisoners to some place of strength. Immediately he determined to compel the bishop—but solely through fear— to follow the course prescribed by the laws. He desired fifty of the most resolute of his friends to take each an iron-tipped staff and to place five matches at the end; he then concealed them all in a house not far from the palace. Ere long darkness covered the city; there was nobody in the streets except a few patrols. De la Maisonneuve bade the men of his troop light their matches, and put himself at their head; in their left hands they held the staff, and the sword in their right. Entering the palace, and making their way to the prince's apartment, they appeared before him, surrounded him with their two hundred and fifty lights; and Baudichon, acting as spokesman, called upon him to surrender his prisoners to their lawful judges. The bishop stared with amazement at this band of men with their swords and flaming torches; the night season added to his terror, and he thought that if he did not give way he would be put to death. Baudichon

* ' Les mettent en train.'—MS. du procès de Lyon, p. 185.

R 2

had no such idea; but Pierre de la Baume, imagining his last hour had come,* gave the required order; upon which the troop defiled before him with their port-fires, and quitted the episcopal palace. The huguenot prisoners having been transferred to the syndics, the latter entrusted them to the gaoler of the same prison 'to keep them securely under pain of death.' They had passed from the arbitrary power of the bishop to the lawful authority of the councils. Constitutional order was restored.†

The bishop passed a very agitated night. The huguenots, and the torches, and the swords with which he had been surrounded, would not let him sleep; and when daylight came, he, as well as his courtiers, was quite unmanned. The 13th of July fell on Sunday, and what a Sunday! 'I shall leave the city,' the prelate said to his servants. A rumour of his approaching departure having got abroad, some of the canons hurried to the palace to dissuade him. 'I will go,' he repeated. To no effect did his followers represent to him, that if he left, the catholic faith, the episcopate, the authority of the prince, his revenues, would all be lost; nothing could shake him. He was determined to go. A Thomas à Becket would have died on the spot; but Pierre de la Baume, says a contemporary document, 'was very warm about his own safety, but more than cold for the Church.'‡

One thought, however, disturbed the timid bishop;

---

* Sœur Jeanne. *Levain du Calvinisme*, p. 68.

† Registres du Conseil des 10, 11, 12 Juillet. Froment, *Gestes de Genève*, pp. 62, 63. Roset MS.

‡ 'Fort échauffé pour sa propre personne, plus que froid pour l'église.'—Registre du Conseil du 13 Juillet; Froment, *Gestes de Genève*, p. 63, Berne MS.

and the proceedings of the syndics, Du Crest and Coquet, who came to beg him not to desert the city and his flock, served but to increase his distress. If the huguenots knew of his departure, he thought they might possibly stop him and bring him back to the palace. He dreamt of nothing but persecution; he saw nothing but prisons, swords, and corpses. He made up his mind to deceive the syndics, and assured them he would return in six weeks without fail; but he promised himself that Geneva should never see him again. He then asked the magistrates for six score of arquebusiers to protect his departure the next morning.

The syndics having determined to convene the council, the ushers went round the city and roused the councillors from their beds. Geneva desired to keep her bishop, while the bishop wished to desert her. The council ordered that next morning at daybreak, for fear the prelate should leave early, the syndics should go and point out the necessity for his remaining.*

The syndics had scarcely left him when he fell into fresh terrors. He thought that the mustering of six-score arquebusiers would spread abroad the news of his departure, that the huguenots would rush to arms, that he would find himself between two parties armed with spears and arquebuses. . . . He must make haste and depart alone, by night or at peep of day, without any parade, before the syndics could have time to assemble the council, which, he fancied, could not meet before the morrow. No one slept in the palace that night; all were busy preparing for the departure, and they took care that nothing should

* Registres du Conseil du 13 Juillet 1533.

betray to the outside the agitation that reigned within. That was a terrible night. Two spectres appeared to the bishop and dismayed him—the Gospel and liberty. He saw no means of escaping them but flight. But what would the duke and the pope say? To quiet his conscience, he wrote, at the last moment, a letter to the council, in which he enjoined them to oppose the evangelical meetings, and to maintain the Romish religion ' *mordicus*, tooth and nail.'

Daylight would soon appear; they were dejected in the palace, but everything was ready for flight. At that moment there was a knocking at the gate. . . . It was the four syndics; the bishop was a few minutes too late. . . . The syndics entered, and conjured Pierre de la Baume in the name of peace, country, and religion. They pointed out to him the consequences of his departure: the monarchical power crumbling away, the republic rising upon its ruins, the Church of Rome disappearing, and that of the innovators taking shape. . . .

But nothing could move the bishop; he remained insensible as a statue. They next entreated him to leave the state affairs in order; to appoint, during his absence, a vicar, an official, a judge of appeal. Pierre de la Baume refused everything. One only thought filled his mind—he wanted to get away. ' Alas!' said the moderate catholics, ' he does not set the state in order, and as for the church over which he is pastor . . . he abandons his flock.'* When the syndics had withdrawn, he gave the signal for departure. There was not a moment to lose, he thought; it will

* Le Curé Besson: *Mémoires pour l'Histoire Ecclésiastique du Diocèse de Genève*, p. 63.

soon be broad daylight, and who knows but the magistrates, who set so much upon his presence, may give orders to stop him. Let every man do his duty! Let there not be a minute's delay! The bishop took care not to leave the palace either by the principal entrance or by the ordinary gates of the city. In the vaults of the building was a passage which led to an unfrequented street—the Rue du Boule, now the Rue de la Fontaine. By following this street, the bishop could reach a secret postern in the wall of the city, which Froment calls la fausse porte du sel. Then Pierre de la Baume would be outside of Geneva; then he would be safe. Accordingly the bishop quitted his apartments, descended to the basement of the palace, and made his escape from that edifice (which is now a prison) like a malefactor escaping from his dungeon. His officers were downcast; they would have wished to crush those insolent huguenots, but were obliged to leave them a clear field. The bishop himself, forced to quit his palace and his power, felt great vexation.* He looked about him with uneasiness, and trembled lest he should see the huguenots appear at the corner of the street. The encroachments he had made on the liberties of the citizens were not of a nature to tranquillise him, and in his distress he quickened his steps.

The fugitive band reached the secret postern; the prelate had the key; he passed through and stood on the shore of the lake. There was no enemy in sight. He entered a boat which had been got ready for him, and reached the other bank. He sprang immediately upon the horse that was waiting for him, and rode

* Froment, Gestes de Genève, p. 63.

off at a gallop. He felt the weight upon his heart
grow lighter the farther he went. Now the fierce
huguenots will trouble him no more, and he will
'make good cheer.' 'He retired to the Tower of
May,' says the chronicle, 'and never returned again.' *

Baudichon de la Maisonneuve had succeeded beyond
his expectations. Not only had the prisoners been
rescued from the unlawful power of the bishop, but
the prelate himself had disappeared. A few huguenots, waving their *montres de feu*, had been sufficient to deliver Geneva. Not a drop of blood had
been shed. 'As at the sound of the trumpets of
Gideon, and at the sight of his lamps,' said the evangelists, 'the Amalekites and the Midianites fled during
the night, so did the bishop and his followers flee
away at the sound of the arms and at the sight of the
fire.' †

Early in the morning of the 14th of July, the news
of the bishop's departure circulated through the city.
The catholic members of the council, deserted by a
perjured prince, felt themselves unable henceforth to
oppose the torrent which was advancing with irresistible power. 'All the catholics,' says Sister Jeanne,
'were sorely grieved.' The pope blamed the bishop
for abandoning his church, and reproached him for his
cowardice.‡ 'That miserable city, having lost its
prince and pastor,' said people in Italy, 'will become
the asylum of every villain and the throne of heresy.' §

* Roset MS.

† Froment, *Gestes de Genève*, pp. 62, 63.

‡ Le Curé Besson, *Mémoires pour l'Histoire Ecclésiastique du Diocèse de
Genève*, p. 63.

§ Briève Relation de la Révolte de la Ville de Genève. MS. in the
Archives Générales du Royaume d'Italie, paquet 14.

But what caused so much sorrow to the papists was the source of immense joy to the evangelicals. They contended that the prince by running away abdicated his usurped power, and that the citizens resumed their rights.* The sun of Geneva was setting, according to the old style (that of the Roman court); but according to the new (that of the Gospel), it was rising; and Geneva, illumined by its rays, was to communicate that divine light to others. The 14th of July, 1533, witnessed in Geneva the fall of that hybrid power† which claims to hold two swords in its hand. Since then other bishop-kings have also disappeared, even in the most Catholic countries; and the last, that of Rome, totters on his pedestal. The people of Geneva, from the time when they lost sight of that shameless and pitiless prelate, ceased to care about him, and never asked after him. They even invented a by-word, in use to this day; and when they wish to speak of a man for whom they feel a thorough indifference, they say: *Je ne m'en soucie pas plus que de Baume* (I do not care a straw about him).‡

* Letter to Lord Townsend, by the Secretary of State Chouet. Berne MSS. vi. 57.

† It was also on the 14th of July, two centuries and a half later (1789), that the reign of the feudal system came to an end.

‡ 'I care no more for him than for Baume,' that is, *not at all.* This expression owes its origin to the name of La Baume, last bishop of Geneva. *Glossaires Genevois* de Gaudy et de J. Humbert.

CHAPTER II.

TWO REFORMERS AND A DOMINICAN IN GENEVA.

(JULY TO DECEMBER 1533.)

THE bishop had fallen from his throne, and with him had expired a despotism which offensively usurped the liberties of the people; the lawful magistrates once more sat in their curule chairs, with liberty and justice at their sides. They investigated the cases of the citizens whom Pierre de la Baume claimed to get rid of without the formality of trial. The only man who could be accused of Wernly's death was Pierre l'Hoste, and he had taken refuge in the Dominican church, where the bishop had not cared to follow him. The syndics went to the church; the poor wretch, shaking in every limb, clung vainly to the altar, and cried out: 'I claim the privileges accorded to this sanctuary.' He was arrested and the enquiry commenced. It proved the innocence of the imprisoned huguenots, and showed that the disturbance in which Wernly fell had been caused by the violence of the canon himself, who was armed from head to foot, and had taunted his adversaries with loud cries. The magistrates, however, thought that the blood of the victim called for the blood of him who had shed it. Pierre l'Hoste, the carman of the

city, denied striking the fatal blow, but confessed
that he had struck Wernly: he was condemned and
beheaded.   All the other prisoners were released.

But there was no relief to Claudine Levet's sorrow;
her husband was still confined in Castle Gaillard, and
the governor refused to release him.   The council
entreated the Bernese deputies in Geneva to intercede
in behalf of the prisoner, and on the 4th of September, one of them, accompanied by J. Lullin and C.
Savoye, having gone out to Ville-la-Grand, about a
league from the city, Aimé Levet was surrendered to
them.*

While this pious man lay in the Gaillard dungeons,
the insults heaped upon him, the harshness of the
prison, and the almost certain death which threatened
him, had given his faith a new life; so that when the
castellan had released him from his bonds, he inwardly
vowed that he would make his deliverance accelerate
the triumph of the Gospel.   He had scarcely reached
home, when he wrote to Anthony Froment, the evangelist, whose church had been the market-place, and
whose pulpit a fishwife's stall, and conjured him to
return.   The latter did not hesitate, and knowing
that the struggles which awaited him there were beyond the strength of one man, he invited one of the
brethren from Paris, and at that time in the Pays de
Vaud, to accompany him.   This was Alexander Canus,
called also Dumoulin.   One day, therefore, Aimé and
Claudine Levet saw the two evangelists arrive.   One
lodged with them at St. Gervais on the right bank,
and the other at Claude Salomon's, near the Molard,

---

* Registre du Conseil des 6, 7, 8, 12, 17 Août et 4 Septembre 1533.
—Froment, *Gestes de Genève*, p. 60. Roset MS. liv. iii. ch. xvi.

on the left bank; being thus quartered in the two parts into which the city was divided, they could share the labour.

Salomon, who shared with Levet the honour and danger of receiving the evangelists, was as gentle as his friend Maisonneuve was quick and often violent. One day, shortly after the bishop's flight, the latter saw in front of him in the street two of the bishop's partisans, whom he suspected to be getting up some conspiracy; his blood boiled at the sight, and he exclaimed: 'There are so many traitors here. . . . My fingers itch to be at them.' * A sense of duty, however, restrained him, and he did nothing. But Salomon was calm and full of charity and compassion: he felt none of these passing ebullitions, and thought only of visiting the sick and the poor, and sheltering strangers whom the Romish persecutions drove to Geneva. 'These poor refugees,' he said, 'are more destitute than all the rest.' His wife, 'neither dainty nor nice,'† lavished her cares on them. They were the Gaius and Dorcas of Scripture.

Froment and Alexander, quartered on both sides of the Rhone, preached the Word in private houses with such power that the new faith extended far and wide, 'like the layers of a vine;'‡ the old stocks producing young shoots, which took root and formed other stocks. The priests were alarmed, and exclaimed that if those doctrines continued to be so preached, all the country would soon be infested with the sect. They applied to the bishop, who was at his castle of May—restless,

* 'La main me fourmille que je n'agisse contre les traîtres!'
† 'Nullement délicate ni mignarde.'—Froment, *Gestes de Genève*, p. 68. Registre du Conseil du 12 Octobre 1535.
‡ 'A la façon des provins.'

agitated, and reproaching himself with his disgraceful flight. Wishing to redeem that fault, he replied on the 24th of October, forbidding any preaching in Geneva except according to ancient custom. The exulting priests presented these episcopal letters to the council. The bishop's cowardly behaviour had estranged the magistrates. '*Preach the Gospel*,' answered the council, '*and say nothing which cannot be proved by Holy Scripture.*' These important words, which gave the victory to the Reformation, may still be read in the official minutes.

Great was the joy among the reformed. They saw in these words a decree which made evangelical Christianity a lawful religion * at Geneva (as at Rome in the third and fourth centuries), and authorised them to form a Church which should be free without being dominant. The same fact has reappeared at other times and in other countries. From that day, all who had any leaning towards the Gospel would go to the house of Maisonneuve or of some other huguenot leader, and sit down in the largest room. Presently the preacher would enter, take his place before a table, and usually (as it would seem) under the mantelpiece of the large projecting fireplace. He would then proclaim the Word of God. These evangelists '*did not fret themselves*,' they did not speak with bitterness like some others, and make a great noise; but invited souls to approach Christ without fear, because he is *meek and lowly in heart*; and such simple genial preaching attracted all who heard it. The bishop exclaimed that it was only 'painted language,' and 'sham tenderness;' but the number of

* Religio licita.

hearers became so considerable that the two missionaries were forced to preach in the streets and crossways of the city, at the Molard, the foot of Coutance,
and other places. As soon as they appeared anywhere a numerous assembly gathered round them, the
hearers crowded one upon another, and the living
words addressed to them bore more fruit than scholastic or trivial sermons delivered in fine churches
to hearers dozing in comfortable seats. 'These
preachings in houses, streets, and crossways,' said
Froment himself, ' are not without danger to life, but
are a great advancement to the Word, and detriment to popery.'*

The catholic party became alarmed; their leaders
met, and the procurator-fiscal with the bishop's officers
and the priests, who were ' greatly envenomed against
the two reformers,'† resolved to apprehend them.
Whenever a meeting was formed, the sergeants came
upon it unexpectedly. ' But as soon as they saw
the levelled halberds, the faithful, greatly increased in
number, did their duty, surrounded their ministers,
and helped them to escape.' In consequence of this,
the episcopal police went more craftily to work: they
kept watch upon the ministers, and came upon them
when they were alone, ' aiming at nothing less than
their lives.'‡ But these efforts of the priests increased
the respect men felt for the evangelists. ' Such persecutions,' said the huguenots, ' are a sign by which
we may know that the ministers are excellent servants
of Christ.'§

* Froment, *Gestes de Genève*, p. 66.
† ' Fort envenimés contre les deux réformateurs.'
‡ ' Ne voulant pas moins que la *jacture* de leur vie.'
§ Froment, *Gestes*, p. 66.

The bishop, vexed at having left his episcopal city, could find rest nowhere.   At one time he was at the Tower of May, at another at Lons-le-Saulnier, now at Arbois, now elsewhere.   The thought that two reformers had come to take his place in Geneva disturbed him; and when he found that the citizens paid no attention to his strict prohibition of Gospel preaching sent on the 24th of October, his exasperation was at its height.   'We must apply an heroic remedy to the disease,' he said, and on the 20th of November he dictated letters patent addressed to the procurator-fiscal.

The Great Council met on the 30th of November to hear the letters read.   'We command,' said the bishop, 'that no one in our city of Geneva preach, expound, or cause to be preached or expounded, secretly or publicly, or in any manner whatsoever, the *holy page*, the *holy Gospel*,* unless he have received our express permission, under pain of perpetual excommunication and a fine of one hundred livres.'   The Two Hundred were astounded, the evangelicals were indignant, and the better catholics hung their heads.   A bishop to forbid the preaching of the *holy page*, of the *holy Gospel*! . . . to forbid it too in the very season (Advent) when it was usual to proclaim it!   To excommunicate all who preach it!   To forbid its being taught *in any manner whatsoever*!   To forbid them to talk of it in courts or gardens, or elsewhere!   Not a room, not a cellar, kitchen, or garret was excepted!   The Apostle Paul

---

* 'Neminem clam, palam, occulte vel publice sacram paginam, sacrum Evangelium exponere aut alias quomodocumque dicere.' — Gaberel, *Lettres patentes de l'Évêque.   Pièces justificatives*, i. p. 42.

declares, however, that *the Gospel of Christ must not be hindered.* The emotion of the Two Hundred was so great that all deliberation became impossible; '*the whole council rose and went out,*' we read in the minutes of the sitting. Such was the mute but energetic reply made by Geneva to its bishop.

In the city the emotion was still greater, and vented itself in murmurs and sighs, and also in ironical jests. ' Have you heard the news?' said the huguenots; ' the bishop is going to issue an order with sound of trumpet, forbidding us to speak either good or evil of God and Christ.' The silly prohibition was like oil thrown upon the fire; the preachings became more frequent, and even the indifferent began to read the Scriptures. Froment and his friends distributed evangelical books in abundance: first the New Testament, then various treatises recently composed, such as *La Vérité cachée, La Confrérie du Saint-Esprit, La Manière du Baptême, La Cène de Jésus-Christ,* and *Le Livre des Marchands.** De Vingle, the printer, and one of his men, named Grosne, helped them in this work. But the papists sometimes treated the colporteurs roughly; a gentleman of the neighbourhood, having caught Grosne on the high road, cut off his ears.† This had no effect; the people thirsted for the truth, and all were eager to hear the Word of God.

The leaders of the episcopal party, seeing that nothing could stop these *prêcheurs de cheminées* (chimney-preachers) and their hearers, looked about for a

---

* The Hidden Truth. The Brotherhood of the Holy Ghost. The Manner of Baptism. The Supper of Jesus Christ. The Tradesmen's Book.

† MS. du procès inquisitionnel de Lyon, pp. 6 et 7.

preacher whose energetic eloquence might rekindle
the expiring Roman fervour — one of those stout
champions who can deal heavy blows in serious con-
tests.   For three or four centuries the Dominicans
had played, as inquisitors, the chief parts in the papacy;
they were skilful, eloquent, shrewd in government,
persevering in their designs, inflexible in dogma, pro-
digal of threats, condemnations, and the stake.   There
was much talk in Savoy, and even in Geneva, about
one of them—a doctor of the Sorbonne, named Guy
Furbity—' a great theologian,' they said, ' an enthusiastic servant of the pope, a sworn enemy of the Reformation, daring and violent to the last degree.'*
Just then he was preaching at Chambéry and Mont-
meillan, charming all hearers.   The Genevese catholics petitioned the Sorbonne for this great preacher.
Such a rock, transported to the valley of the Leman,
would, they thought, check the devastating torrent of
reform.   Their prayer was granted, and Furbity flattered himself that he was going to win a fairer crown
than all his predecessors.   Proud of his order, his
reputation, and his Church, he arrived in Geneva with
haughty head, glaring eyes, and threatening gestures;
one might have imagined that he was going to crush
all his adversaries to powder.   ' Ah! those poor Lutherans,' he said disdainfully, ' those poor chimney-
preachers!'   ' He was in a passion,' says Froment.†
The huguenots said as they pointed him out, ' Look
at that Atlas, who fancies he carries the tottering
Church of the Roman pontiff on his shoulders.' ‡

* Berne MSS. *Hist. Helv.* v. 12.

† ' Il était enflambé.'—Froment, *Gestes.*

‡ ' Velut alter Atlas qui instanti causæ catholicæ succollaret.'—*Geneva
Restituta,* p. 63.

A plot had been formed, of which Furbity was to
be the chief instrument.   The syndics, Du Crest,
Baud, Malbuisson, and many other good Genevans
had been gained over by the priests to the cause of
the pope, and by this means the latter held in their
hands the council, the treasury, the artillery, and, in
one word, the city property, besides the ignorant populace.*   The Sorbonne doctor had hardly alighted
at the convent of his order when a deputation from
the canons came and asked him to preach in the cathedral and not in the Dominican church.   'The sermons delivered at St. Pierre's,' said the monks, 'will
produce a greater sensation.'—'Very good,' said Furbity, 'I promise you that I will cry out pretty loudly
against the modern heretics.'   It was objected that it
was contrary to the established custom to have such
preachings in the cathedral.   'We will put him there
by force of arms,' answered the churchmen, 'and he
shall say what he pleases.'

On the morning of Sunday, the 30th of November,
a certain number of priests and laymen armed themselves; and the zealous Furbity, taking his place in
the middle of the band, proceeded to the cathedral.
'Really,' said some of the Genevese with astonishment, 'he is going to preach by main force.'   But he
restrained himself that day, and he met with no opposition.   The next day, Monday, he went to work
in earnest.   His sermon was a continued declamation,
full of pompous phrases extolling the papacy, and of
invectives against the preachers.   'In the pulpit he be-
haves like a madman,' said Froment, who was present,

* Froment, *Gestes de Genève*, pp. 66-68. La Sœur Jeanne, *Levain
du Calvinisme*, p. 70.

'he roars without rhyme or reason.' But the bigots
were in ecstasies. 'Have you heard Doctor Furbity?'
they said in the city. On Wednesday an immense
crowd assembled to hear him. The Dominican went
into the pulpit resolved to crush the heretics, as his
patron, St. Dominick, had done before him.

He imagined that his great business was to lower
the Bible and then to exalt the pope, and he set to work
accordingly. 'All who read the Scriptures in the
vulgar tongue,' he said, 'are gluttons, drunkards, de-
bauchees, blasphemers, thieves, and murderers. . . .
Those who support them are as wicked as they, and
God will punish them. All who will not obey the
pope, or the cardinals, or the bishops, or the curates,
or the vicars, or the priests, are the devil's flock.
They are marked by him, worse than Jews, traitors,
murderers, and brigands, and ought to be hanged on
the gallows. All who eat meat on Friday and Saturday are worse than Turks and mad dogs. . . . Beware of these heretics, these Germans, as you would
of lepers and rottenness. Have no dealings with them
in the way of business or otherwise, and do not let
them marry your daughters. You had better give
them to the dogs.'*

Among the evangelicals who listened to this string
of abuse was one Janin, a man of small stature, a
maker of pikes, halberds, javelins, and arrows, whence
he was usually called the *collonier*, or armourer. His
activity was indefatigable; he was present everywhere; he held discussions in private and preached
'to companies, urging with all his might' those who

---

* See the documents attached to the trial, in the Registres du Conseil
du 27 Janvier 1534.

listened to him to embrace the faith which Luther had found in the Holy Scriptures.* Having gone to St. Pierre's, he sat down near some good catholics, among others Pierre Pennet, whose brothers were soon to become famous in Geneva for their zeal in behalf of the Romish faith. Janin, unable to put up with such insulting language, became restless, and exclaimed that the preacher did not know what he was saying. The catholics around him, annoyed at being disturbed in their devotions, said: 'Begone; one preacher is enough here.'† But they had some trouble to make him hold his tongue. A more telling interruption was to disturb the orator before long.

The Dominican saw clearly that abuse alone would not restore the papacy; its fundamental doctrines must be established, and this he undertook to do in other discourses. Continuing to insult the reformers as 'wretches who, instead of wearing the *robe*, are dressed like *brigands*,' he maintained that priests only, by virtue of the sacramental institution, could bring souls into communion with God. He even used language that must have sounded strange to the worshippers of Mary. 'A priest who consecrates the elements of the Sacrament,' he said, 'is above the Holy Virgin, for she only gave life to Jesus Christ once, whereas the priest creates him every day, as often as he likes. If a priest pronounces the sacramental words over a sack full of bread, or in a cellar full of wine, all the bread, by that very act, is transformed and becomes the precious body of Christ, and

* 'Prêchant à des compagnies induisant de toute sa possibilité, &c.' —MS. du procès inquisitionnel de Lyon, p. 29.
† Ibid. p. 37.

all the wine is changed into blood—which is what the Virgin never did. . . . Ah! the priest! . . . you should not merely salute him, you should kneel and prostrate yourselves before him.'

This was not enough; the Dominican thought it his duty to establish the doctrine of transubstantiation, on which the dignity of the priest is founded. He exclaimed: 'We must believe that the body of Jesus Christ is in the host in flesh and bone. We must believe that he is there as much as he was in the Blessed Virgin's womb, or on the wood of the true cross. We must believe it under pain of damnation, for our holy theological faculty of Paris at the Sorbonne, and our mother the holy Church, believe it. Yes; Jesus Christ is in the host, as he was in the Virgin's womb, . . . but small . . . as small as an ant. It is a matter that admits of no further discussion.'

Whereupon the Dominican, satisfied that he had gained a signal victory, indulged in the impetuosity of his clerical haughtiness, and, pouring out a torrent of insults, exclaimed: 'Where are those wretched Lutherans who preach the contrary? Where are these heretics, these rascals, these worse than Jews, Turks, and heathens? . . . Where are these fine *chimney-preachers*? Let them come forward, and they shall be answered. . . . Ha! ha! They will take good care not to show themselves, except at the chimney-corner, for they are only brave in deceiving poor women and such as know nothing.' *

Having spoken thus, the monk sat down, proud of his eloquence. A great agitation prevailed in the congregation; the reformers were challenged to the com-

* Froment, *Gestes de Genève*, pp. 69–71. Gautier MS.

bat; the people wondered whether they would reply
to the challenge.   There was a momentary pause,
when Froment rose, and standing in the middle of
the church, motioned them with his hand to be silent.
'For the love of God,' he said, 'listen to what I have
to tell you!'   The congregation turned their eyes on
the person who uttered these words, and the evangelist, with sonorous voice, exclaimed: 'Sirs, I offer
my life—yea, I am ready to go to the stake if I do not
show, by Holy Scripture, that what Dr. Furbity has
just said is false, and the language of Antichrist.'
He then adduced scriptural authorities against the
Dominican's assertions.   'It is the truth,' exclaimed
the reformers; and some of them, looking towards the
monk, called out: 'Let him answer that.'   Furbity,
astonished at hearing himself refuted by such plain
passages, dared not rise, but remained fixed to his
seat, hiding his head in the pulpit.   'Let him answer,'
shouted the Huguenots on all sides : their shouts
were useless.

The canons and their friends, finding their oracle
was dumb, ventured upon a controversy which was
much more in their line.   They drew their swords
(priests often wore swords in those times), and approaching Froment, exclaimed: 'Kill him—kill the
Lutheran! . . . Ah! the wretch! he has dared take
our good father to task.'   Nothing but death could
expiate the crime of a layman who had ventured to
contradict a priest.   There was only one point on
which these churchmen were not agreed: it was
whether they should *burn* or *drown* the evangelist.
Some shouted: 'Burn him—burn him!' and others:
'To the Rhone with him!'—'There was no small

commotion,' writes Froment. Just as the priests were
about to carry him off, Baudichon de la Maisonneuve,
Ami Perrin, Janin le Collonier, and others rallied
round him like a body-guard, wishing to get him out
of the church. This did not calm the tumult; the
people ran after him, and the magistrates would have
arrested him. 'They crowded upon one another,'
says Froment, 'either to see him, or to strike him,
or to carry him off.' The tumultuous crowd made a
last effort to lay hold of the evangelist, just as they
reached the great doors of the cathedral. Baudichon
de la Maisonneuve observing this, halted, drew his
sword, and, facing the rioters, cried in a loud voice:
'I will kill the first man that touches him. Let the
law prevail; and if any one has done wrong, let him
be punished.' The catholics, intimidated by Maisonneuve's look, shrank back; and Froment's friends,
taking advantage of this favourable moment, dragged
him away from his enemies. Then, 'the women, as if
they were mad, rushed after him with great fury,
throwing many stones at him.'* The huguenot
Perrin, more politic than evangelical, alarmed at the
tumult, said to Froment: 'We have spoilt the business; it was going on very well, and now all is lost.'
The other (by which words Froment indicates himself), sure of his cause, answered simply: 'All is
won!' The future showed that he was right. When
Froment arrived at Baudichon's house—the usual
asylum of the friends of the Gospel—Le Collonier
took him up to the hayloft and carefully hid him

* 'Les femmes comme enragées . . . de grande furie, lui jetant force
pierres.'—Froment, *Gestes merveilleux de Genève*, pp. 71–74. Sœur
Jeanne, *Levain du Calvinisme*, p. 70. Gautier MS.

under the hay; De la Maisonneuve and Janin had afterwards to pay dearly for their kind offices. The latter had scarcely quitted the loft when Claude Baud arrived with his officers and his halberds. 'They searched the house all over, and even thrust their spears into the hay, but finding nobody they withdrew.' *

Alexander, who had not spoken in the church, had accompanied his friend as far as the great doors. Seeing Froment led away by Janin, and believing him safe, he halted 'at the top of the steps in the midst of the people,' and, not permitting himself to be intimidated by the popular fury, he exclaimed: 'He very properly took him to task. Doctor Furbity has preached against the holy books; he is a false prophet.' The syndics, pleased to catch one at least, carried Alexander off to the town-hall, and some demanded that he should be sentenced to death. The sage Balthasar resisted this: 'It was not this man who caused the uproar,' he said. 'Besides, he is a Frenchman; and the King of France may perhaps take *some opportunity* against our city if we put his subjects to death.' The two '*mahometists*' were banished for life from the city, under pain of death; and, at the same time, it was agreed that the Advent preachers should be told 'to preach the Gospel only, in order to avoid disturbance.'

Alexander was conducted by the watch out of the city to a place called La Monnaye, where, seeing the crowd following him, he turned towards them and said: 'I shall not take my rest like a soldier whose time of service is over.' He then addressed the crowd

* Registre du Conseil du 2 Décembre 1533.

for two hours, and many were won to the Gospel. De la Maisonneuve having returned home, went in search of Froment in the hayloft; and as soon as it was night, the two friends quitted Geneva secretly, took up Alexander at La Monnaye, and then all three set off for Berne.

CHAPTER III.

FAREL, MAISONNEUVE, AND FURBITY IN GENEVA.

(DECEMBER 1533 TO JANUARY 1534.)

DE LA MAISONNEUVE was determined to uphold the liberty of Gospel-preaching. ' We are
called Lutherans,' said Froment ; 'now, *Luther* in
German means *clear*, and there is nothing clearer than
the Gospel of Jesus Christ. The Lutheran cause is
the cause of light.' And therefore De la Maisonneuve desired to propagate it.

The zealous huguenot did not lose a moment after
his arrival at Berne. He told all his friends (of
whom he had many) what was going on at Geneva.
Froment and Alexander, who stood by his side, supported his complaints and repeated the insults of the
Dominican. The Bernese were exasperated by the
abuse the monk had heaped upon the protestants,
but they were animated by a nobler motive. They
had thought that Geneva, so famous for the energetic
character of its citizens, would be a great gain for the
Reformation; and now people were beginning to say
in Savoy, in the Pays de Vaud, at Friburg, and in
France, that the reforming movement was crushed in
the huguenot city. ' A great rumour,' says Farel,
' spread everywhere touching Geneva, how that Master

Furbity had triumphed in his disputations with the Lutherans.'* The Bernese resolved to assist the threatened Reform by despatching to Geneva . . . not large battalions, but a humble preacher of the Gospel. They sent William Farel as Maisonneuve's companion.

On Sunday, December 21, the feast of St. Thomas of Canterbury, Furbity, proud at having to eulogise so heroic a saint, was more energetic than ever. 'All who follow that cursed sect,' he cried, 'are lewd and gluttonous livers, wanton, ambitious, murderers, and thieves, who live like beasts, loving their own sensuality, acknowledging neither a God nor a superior.' These words roused the enthusiasm of the catholics, the chief of whom resolved to go in a body to the bishop's palace to thank the reverend father. The noble Perceval de Pesmes, *capitaine des bons*, 'the captain of the good,' as the nuns called him, was at their head. 'Most reverend father,' said the descendant of the Crusaders, 'we thank you for preaching such good doctrine, and beg you will fear nothing.' —'Hold fast to the sword, captain; on my side I will use the spirit and the tongue.' The compact being made, the deputation withdrew.

They had scarcely quitted the episcopal palace, when a strange report circulated through the town. 'De la Maisonneuve has returned from Berne and brought the notorious William Farel with him!' Farel having re-entered Geneva, was not to leave it again until the work of the Reformation was completed there.

* *Lettres certaines d'aucuns grands troubles et tumultes advenus à Genève, avec la disputation faite l'an* 1534. This pamphlet is dated April 1, 1534, and is from the pen of Farel, though the printer describes it as being by a notary of Geneva.

'What!' exclaimed the catholics, 'that wretch, that devil whom we drove out is come back!' They were so exasperated that De Pesmes, Malbuisson, and others, meeting Farel and Maisonneuve in the street that very day, drew their swords and fell upon them; they were rescued by some huguenots. The episcopalians consulted together, and decided to take up arms to expel the reformer.

Not without reason were the catholics alarmed. Farel was a hero. A work that is beginning requires one of those strong men who, by the energy of their will, surmount all obstacles, and set in motion all the forces of their epoch to carry out the plan they have conceived. Calvin and Luther are the great men of the Reformation in the sixteenth century. Calvin defended it against dangerous enemies; he gave to the renovated Church a body of divinity and a simple powerful constitution. The scriptural faith which he has set forth is making, and will make, the circuit of the world. But when he arrived at Geneva, the Reform was already accomplished outwardly. Farel is really the reformer of that city as well as of other places in Switzerland and France. A noble and simple evangelist, his genius was less great, his name less illustrious than his successor's; but he ceased not to expose his life in fierce combats for the Saviour, and, in the order of grace, he was in that beautiful country enclosed between the Alps and the Jura what fire is in the order of nature—the most powerful of God's agents. He was not, as is sometimes imagined, a hotheaded man, liable to fits of violence and temper. With energy he combined prudence—with zeal, impartiality. 'Would to God,' he said, on the occasion of his discussion with Furbity, 'that each man would state each thing without leaning to one side more than to the other.' * But it must be acknowledged that he had more force than circumspection, and an unparalleled activity was the principal feature of his character. To venture everywhere, to act in all circumstances, to preach in every place, to brave every danger, were his enjoyment and his life. His excessive genius 'delighted in adventure,' as was said of a celebrated conqueror, and he was never so truly happy as when he was in the field. Farel began the work, and Calvin completed it.

Another man, a layman, was called to play a part not less important in the Genevan Reformation. It has been remarked † that in the great revolutions of nations, God sometimes gives not a counsellor to be listened to, but a torrent to be followed. There was indeed in Geneva a mighty torrent rushing towards Reform, and the man who personified that popular force was Baudichon de la Maisonneuve. Noble in heart as in race, at first he had been merely an independent politician and an opponent of the papacy; but, opening his house and his heart to the Gospel, he came to love it more and more every day. Certainly he did not possess all the evangelical graces ; he was somewhat of a jester, and might often be found laughing at the superstitions of his times ; occasionally also he was violent in his acts and words. But the republican energy that characterised him made him the fittest man to cope with Rome, the

* *Lettres certaines d'aucuns grands troubles et tumultes advenus à Genève, avec la disputation faite l'an* 1534, avant-propos.
† Thiers, on the Insurrection in Spain.

Duke, and the Inquisition. Strong, proud, immove-able, he was on a small stage what the Elector of Saxony and the Landgrave of Hesse were on a larger stage, the patron of evangelical doctrine. Al-though of noble descent, he was in trade, and had an extensive business. Rich and generous, he provided for the wants of the new creed. The magistrates of the cities with which he had dealings showed him much consideration, and not only did the puissant republic of Berne intercede in his favour, but King Francis I. also. De la Maisonneuve had no doubts about the triumph of the Reformation. One day, as a Lausanne dealer was buying one of his horses, the confident Genevan said to him: ' You shall pay me when no more masses are celebrated at Lausanne.' Two or three months later, when settling his accounts at Lyons, he said to one of his correspondents: ' You shall pay me when the priests in this city are what those in Berne are now.' This made the bigoted catholics exclaim: ' He is the cause of the perver-sion of Geneva: would to God he had died ten years ago!' * De la Maisonneuve had much affinity with Berthelier: the latter began the independence of the city, the former introduced the reform. They were both pioneers; but if Berthelier's death was the most heroic, Baudichon's life was the most exemplary.

De la Maisonneuve was able, in case of necessity, to unite prudence with energy. On the 21st Decem-ber, the Dominican having preached with great *éclat* in the cathedral, some of the reformed said boldly: ' Why should not our minister (Farel) preach in the

* MS. du procès inquisitionnel de Lyon. Archives de Berne, pp. 38, 198, 229, 285.

church as well as a popish doctor?' and invited the reformers to enter the building. The indignant catholics exclaimed: 'It shall cost us our lives sooner!' De la Maisonneuve calmed his friends ; he wished to try legal means and ask the magistrates for a church.

The next day he appeared before the council and handed in the letter from the chiefs of the mighty Bernese republic. 'What!' they said, 'you expel from your city our servants, people attached to the Holy Word, whom we commended to you, and at the same time you tolerate men who blaspheme against God. Your preacher has attacked us ; we shall prosecute him, and call upon you to arrest him. Moreover, we ask for a place in which Farel may preach the Gospel publicly.' The larger portion of the council was astounded at these two requests. They were about to deliberate on them, when a commotion was heard in the street : a plot had broken out.

It was near midday. Between eight and nine hundred priests and laymen were going to the bishop's palace, where they had appointed a meeting. 'In the palace everything was astir ; the cellars were open, and the servants were running about with bottles in their hands. 'They supplied wine in profusion, and every man promised to do his duty ; they were respectable-looking people and well dressed.' Two hundred men were to stop at St. Pierre's to attack the heretics in the rear; all the others were to go down to the Molard, 'burning for the cause of God,' and attack Baudichon's house, where Farel was to be found.*

* Registre du Conseil du 22 Décembre 1533. Froment, *Gestes merveilleux de Genève*, p. 78. Sœur Jeanne, *Levain du Calvinisme*, p. 71. *Lettres certaines d'aucuns grands troubles*, &c.

De la Maisonneuve, understanding what was going
on, hastily quitted the council-chamber and ran to
defend his home.* His first care was to hide Farel
as well as he could, and then, while preparations were
making to storm his house, he took steps for its defence. But the council, learning what was going on,
left the hôtel de ville, and ordered the bishop's
partisans to lay down their arms. It seemed strange
to do so, after so many protestations and so much
zeal; yet they obeyed. 'The wicked build triumphs
in the air,' said the huguenots, 'and all these reports
ended in smoke at last.'†

Farel left his hiding-place and resumed his preachings in the houses; but his audience had a singular
appearance. In front of the minister might be seen
the proud features of the huguenots, with helmets on
their heads, swords by their sides, and some were armed
with cuirass, arquebuse, or halberd; for, since the last
catholic resort to arms, they feared a surprise. Baudichon watched over the assembly. Wearing an allécret (a sort of light breastplate), and holding a staff
in his hand, he 'set the people in order,' assigning
them their places, and whenever he chanced to hear
any conversation, 'bidding them be silent;' then
Farel would begin to speak and preach the Gospel
with boldness.‡

The syndics, placed between the reformers and the

* Recent investigations indicate that this house was situated in the
Rue basse du Marché, in front of the Terraillet.

† 'Les méchants se bâtissent des triomphes en l'air, et tous ces bruits
ne sont finalement que fumée.'—Lettres certaines. Froment, Gestes de
Genève, p. 79. Sœur Jeanne, Levain du Calvinisme, p. 73.

‡ Froment, Gestes de Genève, p. 79. MS. du procès inquisitionnel
de Lyon, p. 226.

catholics, could not tell what to do.   If they arrested
Furbity they would exasperate the catholics and
Savoyards ; if they allowed him to continue his
philippics against the reformed, they would offend the
huguenots and the Bernese.   The Two Hundred
therefore resolved to leave the Dominican ostensibly
at large, at the same time treating him in reality as
a prisoner.   He might go where he pleased, but attended by six guards, who followed him even to the
foot of the pulpit.   'Alas!' exclaimed his friends,
'they have placed the reverend father in the keeping
of the watch!'   On hearing which the monk observed
haughtily: 'I am under restraint on account of a set
of people who are good for nothing.'

Christmas day arrived: the Dominican had 'a very
numerous audience, particularly of women.'   Incense
smoked on the altars ; the chants resounded in the
choir; the faithful had never shown so much fervour,
and the monk preached with such warmth that, 'within
the memory of man, there had never been so fine a
service.' *   At the same time, Farel, plainly dressed,
was preaching in a large room.   There was no incense, no tapers, no chanting, but the words of God
which stirred men's consciences.   This irritated
Furbity still more, and on the last day of the year
he exclaimed from the pulpit: 'All who follow the
new law are heretics and the most worthless of men.'†
Thus ended the year 1533.

The new year was to make the balance incline

* 'De vie d'hommes, n'avait été fait si bel office.'   Registre du
Conseil des 23 et 24 Décembre et du 27 Janvier, 1534.—La Sœur Jeanne,
Levain du Calvinisme, p. 74.

† Registre du Conseil des 27 et 28 Décembre.—Gautier MSC.—
Ruchat, iii. p. 245.

to the side of the Reformation; accordingly the clergy, as if terrified at the future, resolved to destroy the tree by the roots, and inaugurated the first day of the year 1534 by an extraordinary proclamation. 'In the name of Monseigneur of Geneva and of his vicar,' said the priests from all the pulpits, 'it is ordered that no one shall preach *the Word of God*, either in public or in private, and that all the books of Holy Scripture, whether in French or in German, shall be burnt.' * The reformed, who were present in great numbers in the church, were staggered at the new year's gift which the bishop presented to his people. The Dominican, who was preaching that day for the last time, outdid the proclamation, and bade farewell of his audience in a paltry epigram:—

> Je veux vous donner mes étrennes,
> Dieu convertisse les luthériens !
> S'ils ne se retournent à bien,
> Qu'il leur donne fièvres quartaines !
> Qui veut *si, prennent ses mitaines* ! †

Notwithstanding his invocation of the quartan ague, the catholics said, with tears in their eyes: 'With what devotion he takes leave of us!' All, however, had not been equally touched: just as the monk was preparing to depart, his guards stopped him, for he had forgotten that he was a prisoner.

Meanwhile the episcopal mandate was causing dis-

---

* MSC. de Roset, liv. iii. ch. xvii.—Registre du 1 Janvier, 1534.—Spon. i. p. 50.—Ruchat, iii. p. 244.—Roset and Farel, both contemporaries, and in a position to know the truth, report the fact that the Holy Scriptures were to be *burnt*. The minutes of the council do not mention it; but the secretary occasionally toned down what seemed too strong for a council the majority of which was at that time catholic.

† *Prendre ses mitaines*, a figurative expression for *prendre ses mesures.* —*Lettres certaines*, &c.

turbance in the city. 'Forbid the preaching of the Gospel,' said some; 'burn the holy books! What a horrible notion! The Mahometans never did anything like it with regard to the Koran, or the Ghebers with the books of Zoroaster. Those who are charged to preach the Word of God are the very men to condemn it to the flames!' Thus catholics and evangelicals took up arms—the former to destroy the Bible, the others to defend it.

They remained under arms, not only during the night of the first of January, but also during the second, the third, and a part of the fourth, bivouacking in the squares, and kindling great fires. The citizens of Geneva had often taken up arms from other motives. If any one had now gone to the catholics and asked them: 'Why are you doing this?' they would have answered: 'Because we desire to drive out the Bible;' and if the same question had been put to the reformed, they would have answered: 'Because we desire to keep it.' These poor folks had often nothing to eat or drink; and when any party sent to a house to procure provisions, the other party often seized the spoil. They were obliged to give the purveyors a strong escort.*

It was a strange sight, no doubt, to see a town filled with armed men because of the Word of peace. It was in this way that great emotions displayed themselves at that epoch, and it would be ridiculous to exhibit the men of the sixteenth century with the manners of the nineteenth. The evangelical Christians believed that, if the Bible were taken from them, Jesus would also be lost to them; it seemed that if there were

* Froment, *Actes de Genève,* p. 80.

no more Scripture, there would be no more Christ, no more salvation. The political huguenots, not troubling themselves about that matter, thought that the Bible was the best means of getting rid of the bishop. Consequently all alike passed the days and nights under arms around the watchfires, being unwilling to have the Scriptures taken from them. The reformed, desiring to appear pacific, thought it their duty to yield a little, and prevailed upon Alexander to withdraw, as he had been lawfully banished. He turned his steps in the direction of France, where he soon after found a martyr's death. But the evangelical cause in Geneva lost nothing, for, as Alexander left on one side, Froment returned on the other; and almost at the same moment an embassy from Berne, headed by Sebastian of Diesbach, appeared at the city gates. These worthy deputies, seeing what was going on—the bivouacks, the soldiers, the spears, and arquebuses—stopped their horses, examined the groups with an air of astonishment, asked what it all meant, and finally exhorted the rival parties to withdraw. The Genevese began to understand the strangeness of their position: the huguenots felt that it was a different power from that of their arquebuses which should defend the Bible; the men of both parties, therefore, yielded to the wise remonstrances of the Bernese, and every man retired to his own house.*

Diesbach and his colleagues came with the intent of prosecuting the Dominican; but while shutting the door against the monk, they desired to throw it wide open to the Reformation. Farel had been at Geneva some time; Froment had just arrived; but that was

* Froment, *Gestes de Genève*, p. 80.

not all. A man of modest appearance, who formed part of the Bernese retinue, was to be more formidable to Roman-catholicism than the illustrious ambassadors themselves. They had with them the young and gentle Viret. Weak and faint, he was still suffering from a wound inflicted by a priest of Payerne, but the deputies of Berne had insisted on his accompanying them. Thus Farel, Viret, and Froment—three men of lively faith and indefatigable zeal—were going to work together in Geneva. Everything seemed to indicate that the reformed bands of Switzerland were unmasking their batteries and preparing to dismantle those of the pope. They were about to open a sharp fire, which would beat down the thick walls that for so long had sheltered the oracles and exactions of the papacy.

Viret immediately asked after his friends Farel and Froment, who had been forced to hide themselves during the armed crisis; some huguenots went in search of them and brought them to the Tête-noire, where the embassy was quartered. ' You shall stay with us,' said the Bernese; 'we will protect your liberty, and you shall announce the Gospel.' The three reformers immediately began to preach in private houses,* proclaiming the authority and the doctrines of those Holy Scriptures which the clergy had condemned. What a strange contradiction! The bishop had just interdicted the Bible, and the three most powerful preachers in the French tongue were now publicly teaching its divine lessons. . . . So many and such good workmen had never before been

* Farellus, Fromentius, Viretus intra privatos parietes in prædicando Dei verbo. *Geneva restituta*, p. 65.

seen in Geneva. 'And the papists dared do nothing against them.' *

But the Bernese wanted more: 'You protect that Dominican who slanders our good reputation,' they said to the council; 'you despise our mode of living, you condemn the holy Gospel of God, you maltreat those who desire to understand it, and banish those who preach it: is that conducting yourselves in conformity with the treaty of alliance? Let the monk defend what he has taught; we have brought preachers who will show him the falseness of his doctrine. If you refuse these requests, Berne will find other means of vindicating her honour.' The syndics replied to the Bernese: 'It is not our business to know what concerns priests, apply to the prince-bishop.'—'That is a mere evasion,' answered Berne. 'We give you back our letters of alliance.' At these words the premier syndic, becoming alarmed, offered to let the Dominican appear before them. The Bernese accepted, but 'on condition that the monk should be obliged to answer the ministers before all the people.'†
That was the essential point.

* MSC. de Roset, *Chron.*, lib. iii. ch. xviii.—Froment, *Gestes de Genève*, pp. 80, 81.—Registre du Conseil du 5 Janvier.

† Registre du Conseil des 7 et 8 Janvier, 1534.—Froment, *Gestes de Genève*, pp. 80, 81.—Ruchat, iii. p. 245.

CHAPTER IV.

THE TOURNAMENT.

(JANUARY TO FEBRUARY 1534.)

THE 9th of January was an important date in the history of the Reformation of Geneva, and perhaps (we might add) in that of Europe. The laity were about to resume their rights: a priest was to appear before the Genevese laymen and the Bernese magistrates. As soon as the Council of Two Hundred had assembled, the ambassadors entered, followed by three persons who attracted the special attention of all present. The eyes full of fire, the bold bravery, the indomitable features of one of them marked him to be Farel. The second, less known, had, although young, the prudence of a man in years and the sweetness of a St. John—this was Viret; the third, short in stature and of mean appearance, decided in his gait, lively, and talkative—this was Froment. They all took their seats at the right of the premier syndic. The friar of the order of St. Dominic, entering in his turn, sat on the left on a raised bench. They had met to attack and defend the papacy. The tournament, at which a great crowd of gentlemen and citizens was present, resembled one of those 'solemn judgments' to which man had had recourse for ages to terminate certain controversies. The subject of

the dispute was more important than usual. Truth
and tradition, the middle ages and modern times, independence and slavery, were in the balance. All,
therefore, who were interested in divine and human
things waited with impatience. Their expectations
were disappointed.

Just as the struggle was about to begin, one of the
combatants hung back. The Dominican rose and
said: 'Messieurs, I am a monk and doctor of Paris;
I cannot appear before laymen without the license of
my prelate.' He sat down. 'You offered before all
the people,' said Sebastian of Diesbach, 'to defend your
position by the Holy Scriptures, and now you want a
license.' Farel rose and observed, that the monk and
the great apostle were of contrary opinions: 'St.
Paul refused, in such a case, to appear before the
priests at Jerusalem, and appealed to Cæsar. Now
Cæsar was certainly a layman, and what is more—a
heathen.' The monk forbore to reply to this invincible argument; but looking with pity on the
individual who had dared speak to him, said, with a
gesture of contempt, 'that he had nothing to do with
that man.' Then, remembering how the strappado
and the stake brought such cavillers to their senses in
Paris, he added: 'Let him go and speak like that in
France!' 'Good father,' said the premier syndic,
'since you will not answer when our lords of Berne
accuse you, leave that place and sit on the bench
yonder, where you shall hear the rest.' The monk of
St. Dominic had to quit his place of honour and go to
the bar; but notwithstanding this humiliation, he
again refused to speak. The syndics then sent to ask
the grand-vicar to give him leave to answer; but this
dignitary replied: 'I am ill.' The deputies made

the same request to the official, M. de Veigy, who answered: ' The bishop has forbidden me to do so.' ' Shameful!' exclaimed many ; ' all these priests refuse to give an account of their faith.' The Dominican said to the council: ' Let my lords the ambassadors select as judges two doctors from Germany; and we will select two from Paris; then I will reply not only to Farel, Viret, and Froment, but to a hundred or two hundred of such preachers. . . . Alone I will meet them all!' The Bernese declared they would entrust the matter to those only who were lawfully authorised. They wanted more. The refusal of the Dominican served but to increase their desire to see the Reformation freely preached in Geneva. Not contenting themselves with a theological discussion, they said to the syndics: ' The way to pacify the city, and to be just towards all, is to pick out one of the parish churches and appoint a preacher of the Gospel to it. Those who wish to go to the sermon, will go to the sermon; those who wish to go to mass, will go to mass. Every man is to remain free in his conscience ; no one shall be constrained, and all will be satisfied.' ' We are only laymen,' answered the astonished syndics ; 'it is not our business to choose preachers and assign them churches.' The council sent a deputation to Berne to soften the rigour of the chiefs of the state ; but it was useless. The greater the *suppleness* (to use the language of a manuscript) shown by the Genevans, the greater the inflexibility displayed by the Bernese. It was a struggle between the pliant and the rigid; and the pliant, as usual, were compelled to give way.*

* Registre du Conseil des 10, 11, 12 Janvier, 1534.—Ruchat. iii. p. 251, 252.—MSC. de Gautier.

The Bernese ambassadors pursued their plans with vigour, and demanded reparation for the insults of the Dominican, and a church for the preachers of the Gospel. 'If you refuse,' added Diesbach, 'we shall return you the seals of our alliance; we shall take back ours; we shall prosecute the monk . . . and whomsoever we think fit.' The Two Hundred were astounded, involuntary tears escaped from the eyes of some, and even the people outside were much disturbed (says the Council minute). Joining deeds to words, Sebastian of Diesbach placed the letters of alliance on the table. The whole assembly immediately rose up with indescribable emotion, and with tears begged the ambassadors to take back their letters. 'We will do our best to satisfy you!' exclaimed the premier-syndic, stout Catholic as he was. The stern Bernese noble was touched. 'We take them back,' he said at last; 'but we protest that we shall return them if you do not satisfy our demands.'* Everything was then prepared for the trial. Geneva undertook to bear the axe into the wilderness of church abuses: a priest, accused by laymen, was about to be tried by laymen. This in itself was a revolution.

On the 27th January, the Two Hundred sitting as a court of justice, Furbity was brought before them. He had taken courage; his erect head and confident look showed that he believed himself sure of victory. He called upon the Bernese to set forth their grievances, but protested against the inquiry on account of the sacerdotal character with which he

* Registre du Conseil des 25 et 26 Janvier, 1534.—MSC. de Roset, liv. ii. ch. xviii. etc.

was invested. Then the following colloquy took place : —

AMBASSADOR.—You preached publicly that four kinds of executioners divided the robe of our Saviour Jesus Christ at the foot of the cross, and that the first were Germans. That word concerns us.

MONK.—I never used such words; and I do not know to what country the executioners belonged.

AMBAS.—We will prove this charge presently. You said that those who eat meat on Friday and Saturday are worse than Jews, Turks, and mad dogs.

MONK.—I did not mean thereby to offend their Excellencies of Berne; I was preaching only to the people of this city.

AMBAS.—You said that all who read the Holy Scriptures in the vulgar tongue are no better than lewd livers, gluttons, drunkards, blasphemers, murderers, and robbers.

MONK.—I affirm that I have not abused my lords of Berne.

AMBAS.—You spoke in a general manner, and consequently included them in your accusation.

MONK.—I was speaking to the Genevese only.

AMBAS.—You said: ' Avoid these wicked modern heretics, these Germans, as you would lepers and unclean persons. Do not let them marry your daughters, you had better give them to the dogs.'

MONK.—I deny having preached that article.

AMBAS.—You said: ' That the modern heretics, who will not obey the pope or the cardinals, bishops, and curates, are on that account the devil's flock and worse than mad dogs . . . and ought to be hanged on the gallows.'

MONK.—That is an article of faith, and I have not to answer for it before you.

PREMIER-SYNDIC.—You are commanded to answer.

MONK.—I shall not answer.

PREMIER-SYNDIC.—The charge is confessed.

AMBAS.—'Most honoured lords, we belong to those who read Scripture in the vulgar tongue. We belong to those who hold our Lord as *sole head of the Church*, as its everlasting and sovereign pastor; and, moreover, we are Germans; and for this reason we believe the said articles have been uttered against us. If we were what these articles say, we should deserve corporal punishment; and therefore we demand, in terms of the *lex talionis*, that the said preacher be visited with a punishment similar to that which we should have incurred.'

The reasoning of the ambassador was not irrefutable. Envoys from Zurich, Basle, and other Evangelical cantons, even from the landgrave of Hesse or the elector of Saxony might just as well accuse the monk of having insulted them. But it is precisely this which explains the conduct of the Bernese deputies. Protestantism had been abused, its fundamental principles trampled under foot. The Bernese did not prosecute the monk in order to avenge a personal affront; what they wanted was to see the Word of God set in the place of the word of the pope, and the Reformation established in Geneva. The Gospel was on trial and not my lords of Berne; but the latter considered themselves the champions of the Reformation in Switzerland, and when enemies attacked it, they thought it their duty to defend it. To have kept out of the lists would have been disobedience

to the supreme judge of the combat. The ambassadors brought up fourteen witnesses ready to swear
that the monk had said what was ascribed to him.*

Furbity, seeing no other means of escape, determined to fight for Rome. On Thursday, 29th
January, a rumour spread through the city that the
monk would hold a discussion with the reformers.
The Two Hundred, and a certain number of other
citizens, met in the Hotel de Ville to be present at
this important struggle.

One of the tourneys of the Reformation at Geneva
was about to begin; the two combatants were in the
lists. On one side the Dominican, the champion of
Rome, came forward with scholastic learning that was
not to be despised, a front of adamant, lungs strong
enough to reduce all his rivals to silence, and a tongue
furnished with an inexhaustible flow of words.† At
once violent and skilful, he made use of every weapon,
and possessed a particular art of glozing over his
errors and rendering them less apparent.‡ On the
other side was Farel, less experienced than his rival in
the tricks of dialectics, but full of love for the truth,
firm as a warrior advancing to defend it, and ready
to confound the monk's scholastic arguments by the
invincible demonstrations of the Scriptures of God.
Possessing a manly eloquence and sonorous voice, his
clear, energetic, and at times ironical language, did
prompt justice upon the sophisms of his adversaries.§

---

* Registre du Conseil du 27 Janvier, 1534. — *Lettres certaines
d'aucuns grands troubles.*

† Furbito homine sinuoso, cui firma latera, frons ferrea.—*Geneva
restituta*, p. 68.

‡ Pictæ tectoria linguæ.—*Persius.*

§ Farello pro veritate strenue stante, etc.—*Geneva restituta.*

The reformer rose first and said: ' This is a serious
business ; let us therefore speak with all mildness.
Let not one strive to get the better of the other.   We
can have no nobler triumph than to see the truth
prevail.   So that it be acknowledged by all, I willingly consent to forfeit my life.'   Touched by his
words, the assembly exclaimed: ' Yes ! yes ! that is
what we desire.'

Furbity began by asserting the authority of the
pope.   He maintained that the heads of the Church
may ordain things that are not in Scripture, and to
prove it, he quoted Deuteronomy : ' If there arise a
matter too hard for thee in judgment, thou shalt
come unto the priests, and thou shalt observe to do
according to all that they inform thee.' *

Farel, on the contrary, maintained the authority of
the Holy Scriptures, and declared that all doctrine
must be founded on them alone.   He called to mind
that God, in this very book of Moses, had said: *Ye
shall not add. unto the Word which I command you,
neither shall you diminish aught from it.*† ' What is
said of the Levitical priest in the Old Testament (he
added) ought to be applied, not to the Romish priests,
but to Jesus Christ, who is the everlasting high-priest.
To him, therefore, we must go, him we must obey,
and not the priest.' ‡ ' Christ,' exclaimed Furbity,
' gave to St. Peter the key of the kingdom of heaven,
and St. Peter transmitted it to the priests, his successors.' ' The key of the heavenly kingdom,' answered

---

* Deuteronomy xvii. 8–10.   † Ibid. iv. 2.

‡ Farel indicated the passages taken from the following chapters :
Hebrews, v. to x ; Romans xiv. ; Matthew v. ; Luke xxiv. ; John v. viii.
xii. xiv.   Romans xv.   Galatians i.   Deuteronomy xviii.

Farel, ' is the Word of God. If any one believes in the promises of grace with all his heart, heaven opens for him. If any one rejects them, heaven is closed against him.'

As it was growing late, the discussion was adjourned to the next day, and Furbity said haughtily that he was ready. A voice from the midst of the crowd called out: ' Endeavour to hold more to the Word of God and less to the teaching of the Sorbonne.' ' I shall behave like a man,' he answered. ' If the strength of a man consists in his want of sense, then you are a true man,' rudely returned the speaker.

The next day the discussion entered upon a new phase.

Farel maintained throughout the right and duty of the Christian people to read the Scriptures, to understand them, and to submit to them alone. Furbity, on the contrary, asserted that the Scriptures should be read by the clergy only, and understood conformably with the interpretation of the councils. He proved his point by reasons which might have some force in the eyes of his friends, but they had none for Farel, who maintained the necessity of the immediate contact of each Christian soul with the Scriptures of God. It was not from councils (he contended) nor from popes, but from the Word of God itself that every Christian must receive by faith the truth which saves. The first assembly at Jerusalem (ordinarily termed the first council), was it not, according to the account in the Acts, composed of apostles, elders, and of the *whole church*, and did it not begin its letter with: ' The apostles and elders and *brethren.*' De-

fending, therefore, the rights of the lay members of
the flock, he declaimed energetically against the institution of all those dignitaries who, in the Romish
church, are *lords over God's heritage*: 'You invent
all sorts of things,' he said to the Dominican,* 'you
introduce diversities of orders, a countless number of
eminences, bishops, prelates, archbishops, primates,
cardinals, popes, and other superiorities of which Scripture makes no mention. You do everything to your
own fancy, without any regard to God or the right.
The apostles took counsel with the whole assembly of
the believers, but you . . . . you do everything, you
are everything! . . . you cut and shape as you
please. The Christian people are no more called by
you into council than dogs and brutes. Your ordi-
nances must be adored, and those of God be trodden
under foot. Your papal monarchy surpasses all
others in pride, pomp, and feasting. You want those
who are to teach the people to be princes with lordships, estates, law-courts, and governments. You
want to have a rich triumphant Jesus, who shall put
to death all who contradict Him. . . . Ah! Sirs, the
Saviour was not such here below; he was poor,
humble, put to death, and his disciples were banished,
imprisoned, stoned, and killed. . . . What similarity
is there between the Apostolic Church and yours?
. . . The supreme argument in yours is the executioner. . . . The apostles did not, like you, fulminate
fierce excommunications; they did not, like you, imprison and condemn. . . . No! Jesus is not in the
midst of you. He is in the midst of those who are

---

* *Lettres certaines*, &c., by Farel.

expelled, beaten, burnt for the Gospel, as the martyrs were in the time of the primitive Church.'

The reformer's energetic words sounded like a peal of thunder to his antagonist. Furbity was confounded and bewildered, his ideas became confused, he lost his presence of mind, and, wishing to establish the doctrine of the episcopate as it is understood at Rome, he quoted the verse in which it is said that a bishop ought to be *the husband of one wife*, which greatly amused the assembly. He did more: desiring to prove that there had been bishops of the Roman model in the apostolic times, he mentioned Judas Iscariot. 'It is written of Judas,' he said, 'his bishopric let another take: *Episcopatum suum accipiat alter*. As Judas had a bishopric, he must of necessity have been a bishop;' and he concluded that there was no salvation out of the Roman episcopate. The doctor had not kept his promise to behave *like a man*. Farel smiled at the strange argument, and began to lash the Dominican with the scourge of irony. 'As you have quoted that good bishop, Judas,' he said, 'Judas, who sold the Saviour of the world; as you have asserted that he had a diocese, pray tell me in what part of the Roman empire it lay, and how much it was worth, according to the customary language of Rome. That bishop, whose name you use, is very like certain prelates who, instead of preaching the Word of God, *carry the bag*,* and instead of glorifying Jesus Christ, sell him by selling his members, whose souls they hand over to the devil, receiving money from him in exchange.' †

* Au lieu de porter la Parole de Dieu, portent la bourse.
† *Lettres certaines.*

The monk, astonished at such boldness, again exclaimed in a threatening manner: 'Go and repeat
what you say at Paris, or any other city of France.'
So sure was he that the evangelist would be sent to
the stake there, that he could not refrain from repeating such a peremptory argument. It was all
that Farel would have desired: ' Would to God that I
were allowed to explain my faith publicly,' he said;
' I should prove it by Holy Scripture, and if I did
not, I would consent to be put to death.'

As the discussion went on, the feelings grew inflamed on both sides—some defending Furbity, others
supporting Farel.

No one was more assiduous at this verbal tournament than Baudichon de la Maisonneuve: he accompanied the evangelical champion, both as he went to
the meeting and returned from it, being unwilling to
leave to others the care of protecting his person.
The catholics did not fail to notice the constant goings
and comings of the great citizen; it quite shocked
them; his intimacy with the detested heretic seemed
to them most disgraceful. A young man of five-and-
twenty, named Delorme, who was born at Fontenay,
a league and a half from the city, and who for upwards of a year had been following his business with
a relative in Geneva, specially watched Baudichon,
and was surprised to see so great a gentleman pay
such frequent visits to the poor preacher, Farel.* He
made a note of it, which, on a future day, he made
use of.

The disputation went on all through Friday. The

* MSC. du procès inquisitionnel de Lyon, p. 80.

market on Saturday, the services on Sunday, and the Feast of the Purification which fell on Monday, interrupted it for three days. The three ministers took advantage of the leisure given them, to preach to the people with fervour. Each day they proclaimed the Gospel in the large hall of their friend's house, and Baudichon watched to see that everything went on in an orderly manner—which was very necessary, for the sensation excited by the discussion attracted large crowds. In the evening the evangelicals met in different houses and conversed together until far into the night. During the day-time they endeavoured to attract to their assemblies such as still hesitated between popery and the Reformation. ' Ah! ' exclaimed young Delorme with vexation, ' see what efforts they are making to increase their party.' * All Geneva was in a ferment.

But the sensation was not confined to that city: the anger excited by the discussions manifested itself in violent speeches in the surrounding districts. The idle, the curious, and the devout would stop and question travellers ' to learn the great news from Geneva which they so desired to know.' † Many priests and monks preached in the villages round the city against *heretics* and *heresy*; and in Geneva, as well as in other places through which Farel had passed, there was always some friar or old woman to tell strange stories about the reformer. ' He has no whites to his eyes,'

---

* MSC. du procès inquisitionnel de Lyon, p. 81.

† *Lettres certaines d'aucuns grands troubles,* &c. This work, which is dated Geneva, 1st April 1534, and consequently appeared two months after the discussion, is the principal source whence we have taken our account of these discussions.

they would say; ' his beard is red and stiff, and there is a devil in every hair of it. He has horns on his head, and his feet are cloven like a bullock's. . . . Lastly—and this seemed more horrible than all the rest—he is the son of a Jew of Carpentras.' *

All these stories, flying about the city, reached the Tête-Noire inn, where the Bernese and the three reformers lodged. The domestic life of this hostelry was not edifying. The landlord (according to the chronicle) had two wives: his lawful spouse and a servant who acted as the mistress. The former, an upright person, behaved becomingly to the preachers of the Gospel, though she did not like them; but the other woman detested them, and every time they entered the house, both master and servant scowled at them. They restrained themselves however before the illustrious lords of Berne, greeting them with forced smiles; but made up for it when they were alone with the preachers. The latter usually dined together; and the landlord and servant, while waiting on them, heard language from the lips of the evangelists which greatly provoked them. Instead of the idle stories and jests so common at the dinner-table, the three ministers would exchange words of truth with one another; and this conversation, so new to the two listeners, caused them to make wry faces (as Froment records, who saw them). The three guests had scarcely quitted the room when the servant, who had restrained herself, would cry out after them: ' Heretics! traitors! brigands! huguenots! Germans!' . . . ' I had rather,' said the landlord, ' that they went away without paying (that was saying a

* Froment, *Gestes de Genève*, p. 86.

great deal) provided it was a long way off. . . . so
long that we should never see them again.' These
two wretched people felt that the doctrine of the
Bible condemned their disorderly lives, and the hatred
they felt towards the holiness of God's Word was
vented on those who proclaimed it.

'The adulterous servant, unable to serve the
preachers as Herodias served John the Baptist,' says
Froment, 'avenged herself in another manner.' Addressing one of those women who prate at random
about everything: 'Only imagine what I have seen,'
said she; 'one night as the preachers were going to
bed, I stole up softly after them, and, approaching the
door, I peeped through a hole. . . . What did I see?
They were *feeding devils !*' The neighbour's dismay
did not hinder the servant from continuing: 'These
devils were like black cats. . . . their eyes flashed
fire, their claws were crooked and pointed. . . . they
were under the table. . . . moving backwards and
forwards. . . . Yes; I saw them through the hole.'
In a short time all the gossips of the quarter knew it;
'at which there was a great stir in the neighbourhood.' *

To this story of the servant, the priests added
theirs, and said: 'There are three devils in Geneva in
the form of men—Farel, Viret, Froment; and many
demoniacs. If ever you listen to those three goblins,
they will spring upon you, enter into your body,
and you are done for.' † Not satisfied merely with
repeating such absurdities in their conversation, the
priests began to preach to the people upon 'the three

---

* Froment, *Gestes de Genève*, p. 85. † Ibid.

devils.' Next a song was written on them; and ere
long the catholic mob went up and down the streets
singing these rude rhymes:—

> Farel farera,
> Viret virera,
> Froment on moudra,
> Dieu nous aidera
> Et le diable les emportera.*

The popular epigram was mistaken. At the very
moment when the catholics were singing it about the
city, tragic events were coming that were to change
everything in Geneva. It was the Roman Church
that was about to *veer* and popery to depart.

---

* Farel shall depart, Viret shall veer (go away); Froment (corn)
shall be ground in the mill; God will help us, and the devil shall run
away with them all. Froment's *Gestes de Genève*, pp. 84–86.

CHAPTER V.

THE PLOT.

(JANUARY AND FEBRUARY 1534.)

IN the sixteenth century a consciousness of justice, truth and liberty was awakening throughout Christendom, and men were beginning to protest everywhere, particularly in Geneva, at the lamentable perversions of social and religious life imposed by popery in times gone by. But the expiring Middle Ages rose energetically against this awakening which was to condemn them to be reckoned among the dead. The object of the struggle going on was to secure the triumph of the Reformation—or, as others expressed it, the triumph of progress and civilization. This struggle is the supreme interest of history. The intrigues of courts, and even the battles of armies, which are more pleasing to certain minds, are trifles in comparison with these mighty movements of humanity. Nevertheless, if they had their grandeur and their necessity, they had their danger also. To preserve the ship, launched into the open sea, from striking upon the treacherous shoals of disorder and libertinage, it was necessary that the Lord should command it. At the time when mankind were breaking the secular

chains of popery and the fantastic institutions of feudalism, it was necessary that they should cleave to the
sovereign Master, who alone gives the breath of life to
individuals and to nations. If England has so long
enjoyed the precious fruits of liberty, and if France
has not yet been able to secure them, it is because the
former welcomed the Reformation and the latter rejected it. One of the great evils springing out of
popery was the blunting of the moral sense; and the
revival of the sixteenth century was a moral revival.
In catholicism there were sincere men; but everything was good in their eyes, provided they attained
an end which they believed to be glorious. And
hence, strange to say, pretended preservers of order
easily became assassins.

The Bishop of Geneva watched attentively from
his silent priory all that was passing in his diocese,
at that time so strangely agitated. He desired to re-
ascend his double throne, and still hoped to reestablish the authority of the prince and the pope in the
city. Many catholics, especially at the courts of the
bishop and the duke, could really see nothing in this
reformation of doctrine but ' a popular tumult, which
would be of short duration.' ' The aspect of affairs
will soon change,' they said.* Perhaps, if Calvin had
not come, this prophecy might have been fulfilled;
but others saw things in darker colours. The *tempest
of Luther* would, in their opinion, upset everything;
the same wave that now threatened the power of the
pontiffs would ere long sweep away the power of
kings. Men did not know how to act that they might
prevent such a misfortune; and the most decided said

* Crespin, *Actes des Martyrs,* p. 114.

plainly, that the only means of saving Geneva was to set up one supreme magistrate. Did not the Romans create dictators in the hour of extreme peril? All these councils of Twenty-five, of Sixty, of Two Hundred; and, above all, the General Council of the people were (the Episcopals thought) both useless and pernicious. The administration ought to be placed in the hands of one man, and be given preferably to one of the lords of Friburg. The fervent catholicism of that canton and its resentment at Wernli's death guaranteed the fidelity with which the mission would be fulfilled. It does not appear that anything was decided about the selection; but the bishop made up his mind to attempt a bold stroke of policy. Having come to an understanding with the Duke of Savoy,* he signed at Arbois the instruments which set up in Geneva a *Lieutenant of the prince* in temporal matters *with full powers of punishing criminals*. The document was immediately forwarded to Portier, the episcopal secretary, the bishop's confidential man, who was to determine, in accordance with the heads of the party, the favourable moment and the best means of carrying it into execution. On his side the duke did not keep them waiting for assistance. Portier received blank warrants, sealed with the ducal arms, with authority to use them as he pleased, so as to bring the matter to a happy issue. The plot was skilfully devised. The court of Turin, the lords of Friburg, and the mamelukes were all to assist the bishop; but, according to the received formula, ' God was there and the republic of Berne.'†

* MSC. de Roset, liv. iii. ch. xxi.—MSC. de Gautier.
† Registre du Conseil des 8 et 10 Février, 1534.

Indeed, it seemed at first that the instrument was destined to remain mere waste-paper. The episcopal plot existed; the deed had been signed by the prince-bishop on the 12th of January, but on the 1st of February it was still a dead letter. Portier, aware of the spirit with which the citizens were animated, feared to make the episcopal ordinance known, either to magistrates or people. Privately, however, he discussed with some of his confidants the means of putting it into execution; among them were two brothers named Pennet, one of whom was the episcopal gaoler. The bishop's partisans at Geneva, as well as at Arbois and Turin, thought that logical discussions only did harm; that they should have recourse to more vigorous measures; that force only would constrain the Genevese to bend their necks to the yoke; and, finally, that a riot which disturbed the public peace would be, even if it failed, the best means of justifying the nomination of a lieutenant invested with absolute power. Some hot-headed episcopals, and particularly the two Pennets, the *séides* of the party, resolved to act immediately: 'They undertook, with several others, to spill much blood,' says a document written a few days after the affair.*

On Tuesday, 3rd February, the most excitable of the episcopal party met at the palace: Pennet the gaoler, his brother Claude, Jacques Desel, and several others. It was after dinner. Inflamed by the desire of saving the authority of the prince and the pope, excited by the ordinance which they had hitherto kept by them,

---

* *Lettres certaines,* 1534.

and irritated at seeing Furbity, the Dominican, contradicted by Farel and prosecuted by the Bernese,
perhaps also (as some have believed) acting under
positive orders emanating from the bishop, these men
armed themselves and issued from the palace, ' proposing to strike and kill the others,' says the document
which we have just quoted. These fanatics—we believe them to have been sincere, but unhappily of opinion
that to stab a heretic was one of the most meritorious
works to win heaven—these fanatics entered the court
of St. Pierre's. Just as they came in front of the
steps, and the large platform on which the white
marble portal of the cathedral opens, they met two
huguenots, Nicholas Porral, the notary, and Stephen
d'Adda.* Their blood boiled at the sight of the two
heretics: Pennet the gaoler drew his sword, sprung
at Porral, struck him; and, seeing him fall, impudently continued his way, with his band, by the Rue
du Perron to the Molard, the rallying-ground of all
rioters. D'Adda, and some other huguenots who
had come up, surrounded the wounded Porral, lifted
him up, and, wishing to stop the commencing riot as
soon as possible, carried him to the hotel-de-ville, and
laid him, all pale and bleeding, before the syndics and
the council.

The magistrates were moved at the sight as of old
—if we may compare the great things of antiquity
with the little things that inaugurated modern times—
as of old the corpse of Cæsar, gashed with wounds
and carried through the Forum, excited the indignation and cries of the startled people. D'Adda

* Froment, *Gestes de Genève*, p. 245.—*Chron. msc.* de Roset.—*Hist.
msc.* de Gauthier.—Registre du Conseil.

informed the syndics of Pennet's violent attack, and called for the punishment of the assassin. But he had scarcely ceased speaking when a great noise was heard from without: the courtyard of the hotel de ville was filled with agitated citizens; tumultuous shouts were raised, the gates of the hall were dashed open and 'incontinent (says the Register) many people rushed in furiously crying out: Justice! justice!' An estimable man, a worthy tradesman and zealous huguenot, Nicholas Berger by name, who lived in the Rue du Perron, happened to be in his shop just as the band, which had wounded Porral, was passing by. Attracted by the noise, he had probably moved towards the door: Claude Pennet observing him, stopped, and, as if jealous of his brother's exploit, sprung at the unarmed citizen, and with one blow of his dagger, laid him dead at his feet. 'All good men,' added the citizens, 'are filled with horror, and demand that the criminal be punished according to law.'

This event was not without importance. It was a new act in that obstinate struggle which, at the beginning of the sixteenth century, took place in a permanent manner in a little city on the shore of the Leman lake, and was repeated in other shapes in other countries. Combatants do not cross a frontier without marking their path by their blood. Those who were then fighting the last battles of what may be called the iron age, believed they were serving the cause of justice. Impartial history shrinks from tracing too hideous a picture of these insolent champions of Rome and feudalism. Even at Geneva, where they were perhaps more violent than elsewhere, they were not all devoid of generous sentiments. Undoubtedly many were animated by party-spirit; but there were some also who desired the good of their country. In their eyes, both religion and order were compromised by the alliance between Switzerland and the Reformation, and that sacred cause could only be upheld, they thought, by the energetic intervention of the episcopal party. They were mistaken; but their error did not lie essentially in that. The great evil consisted in the corruption of their moral sense by the principles of a fanatical bigotry, so that all means appeared good to attain their end; all—even the dagger.

While the people were demanding justice for a double murder, there was a great uproar in the city: the drums beat, and everybody ran to arms. The citizens, who wanted independence and reform, exclaimed that the bishop's followers, unable to vanquish them by words, desired to triumph over them by the *mandosse* (a sort of Spanish sword). 'It is the fifth riot the priests have got up to save the mass,' they said, as they took up their arms, not to attack but to support the established authorities.

The council was astounded at the news of Berger's death. All its members were opposed to such crimes; but three of the four syndics were catholics: Du Crest, Claude Baud, and Malbuisson, and the councillors were usually divided in the same proportion as the syndics. Besides which, Portier, who headed the band, was the accredited agent of the prince-bishop, whose authority the council desired to maintain. The syndics were discussing what was to be done, when the ambassadors of Berne demanded to speak with the council. The noble lords, who usually maintained such a cold attitude, were much excited: 'As we were coming up to the hotel-de-ville,' they said, 'all the persons we met were running to. arms. It is to be feared that there will be a great butchery (*tuerie*); we conjure you to look to it, and offer our services to appease the disturbance.' The premier syndic prayed them to do so; and, when the Bernese had left, the council continued its deliberations.

Meanwhile, the principal huguenots had met in consultation. Two of their friends had just fallen beneath the blows of their adversaries: one of them was dead; their party had taken up arms; Portier and the Pennets had fled in alarm; the catholic faction was discouraged. In this state of things it would have been easy for them to fall upon their adversaries and gain a decisive victory; but sentiments of order and legality prevailed among them. They had no desire to infringe the law, but to appeal to it; there were judges in Geneva. Blood must be avenged, not by violence but by justice. 'No disorder,' said the huguenot chiefs, 'no revenge, no attack, no fighting! . . . but let us help the magistrates that they may be able to do their duty.' Five hundred armed citizens, the most valiant men in Geneva, arrived in good order and drew up in front of the hotel-de-ville, while their chiefs—Maisonneuve, Salomon, Perrin, and Aimé Levet — went into the council-room. 'Honoured lords,' they said, 'we have assembled for no other reason than to preserve order. We fear lest the priests have prepared a fourth or fifth *émeute*; and hence we are here in a body to avoid their fury and lend assistance to the syndics. We pray that the murderers and those who counselled the riot may be punished.'* There was not a moment's hesitation: all, catholics and protestants alike, desired the guilty to be punished, and search was made for them.

It was thought that they were hiding in the bishop's palace: it was probable, indeed, that secretary Portier, who lived there, had gone thither and given a refuge to his accomplices, as being the safest place in all Geneva. 'We will go and take them there,' said Syndic Du Crest, a catholic but loyal man. The other syndics rose, and all quitted the hotel-de-ville followed by their officers. At the imposing sight of the chief magistrates of the city, demanding an entrance into the palace, the bishop's servants opened the doors, and a strict search began immediately. Not a chamber or a cellar or a garret escaped the inquisitive eyes of the magistrates and their sergeants; 'but for all the pains they took,' says the 'Council Register,' 'none of the culprits were found.' Many believed they had escaped; Perronnette alone, the episcopal secretary's wife, seeing the vigour with which the assassins were hunted after, felt her anguish doubled as to the fate of her husband. The syndics, wishing to prevent new intrigues, resolved to leave a few of their officers in the episcopal mansion, with orders to keep guard during the night. The men stationed themselves in the vestibule to wait for the morning; but no one in the city knew they were there.

These brave men were talking of what was going on in Geneva, when a little before eight o'clock at

* Registre du Conseil du 3 Février, 1534.—MSC. de Roset, *Chron.*, liv. iii., ch. xix.—MSC. de Gautier.

night (it had been dark for some time, as it was the
beginning of February), a low smothered voice was
heard in the street, as if some one was speaking
through the key-hole. The guards listened. The
voice was heard again and pronounced several times
in a distinct manner the name of the portress. 'It
was a priest softly calling to the servant,' says the
'Council Register.' The huguenots, understanding
instantly the advantage they could derive from this
unexpected circumstance, desired a young man who
was with them to imitate a woman's voice and
answer. Disguising his tones, he said : 'What do
you want?' The priest having no doubts about the
sex and functions of the speaker, said (still in a low
voice) that he wanted certain keys for Mr. Secretary
Portier and Claude Pennet. It is probable they
wished to use them to hide in some safer place, and
perhaps leave the city by a secret gate. The young
man, again assuming a female voice, said: 'What
will you do with them?' 'I shall take them to St.
Pierre's church, where they are hidden,' answered the
priest. It was just what the guard wanted to know.
One of them got up, opened the gate, and the priest,
seeing an armed man instead of a woman, fled in
affright. The guard, without stopping to pursue
him, ran to the hotel-de-ville, where the council was
sitting *en permanence*, and told the whole story to
the syndics. The murderers whom they were looking for were hidden in the cathedral. The magistrates determined to go there immediately.

It was no slight task to seek the assassins in the
vast cathedral, all filled with chapels, altars, and other
places where men could hide. The syndics entered

between eight and nine o'clock at night with a certain number of officers carrying flambeaux. The doors were shut immediately, so that no one could get out, and a dead silence prevailed in the nave. Under the flickering light of the torches, this pile, one of the finest monuments of the twelfth century, displayed all its august majesty. But that splendour of byzantine and gothic architecture, those graceful proportions, that admirable unity so well calculated to produce a deep impression of grandeur and harmony, did not strike My Lords of Geneva, who were thinking of other matters. Du Crest and his colleagues were not occupied with architectural decorations and holy images. . . . They were hunting for murderers.

The search began: the magistrates and their officers went over the chapels of the Holy Cross, the Virgin, St. Martin, St. Maurice, St. Anthony, and nine others in the interior; they examined carefully the eighteen altars, so richly adorned with all that the catholic worship requires. The sergeants took their flambeaux into every corner, they lifted up the carpets, they stooped to search for the culprits. The apse, the transept, the sanctuary, they searched them all; they examined the vestry, the stalls, the aisles, the galleries, the stairs—they found nothing. They next went into the chapel of the Maccabees, adjoining the cathedral, and which the cardinal-bishop, Jean de Brogny, had built a century before, adorning it with magnificent carvings, gorgeous paintings, and mouldings enriched with beads of gold. They passed by those tables where might still be seen a young man keeping swine under an oak, the cardinal desiring in this manner to recall the humble recollections of his early life; but neither Portier, nor Pennet, nor any of their accomplices could be found. The search had lasted nearly three hours, and the magistrates and their officers were beginning to lose all hope, when the idea occurred to one of them that possibly the murderers they were looking after might be hidden in one of the three towers. The syndics and their suite resolved to examine them, beginning with the south tower, one hundred and fifty feet high. As they climbed the numerous steps, they thought that, if the evidence of the priest was true, the criminals must be there, and they might perhaps find not only Portier and the Pennets, but a band of their friends well armed. The stairs being very narrow, it would have been easy for the episcopals to close the passage and even to kill some of those who were looking after them. The men who executed the syndics' orders ascended slowly and steadily, and approached the great steeple with its four gothic windows surmounted by semicircular arches. The steps of this numerous party re-echoed through the winding staircase. The officer of the Council, who marched at the head of the band, having reached the top of the tower, carefully put forward his torch and saw arms glittering and eyes sparkling in one corner. He drew near, followed by his friends, and discovered the crafty Portier and the violent Pennet, crouching down, ' armed,' says the Register, ' with swords, iron pikes, axes, and daggers, and covered with coats of mail.' The two malefactors, although armed to the teeth, did not think of defending themselves: they were more dead than alive. The officers of the State seized them and shut them up in the prison of the hôtel de ville.*

While these things were going on at St. Pierre's, the guard which the syndics had left at the palace, encouraged by the success of their stratagem, had resolved to take advantage of the opportunity to get at the secrets of the house; and, assuming a simple good-natured air, they entered into conversation with the servants, questioning them so skilfully that they soon knew all they wanted. ' The bishop's secretary, alone and without support, is too weak,' they said, ' to withstand the will of the council and people.' ' But he is not so *alone* as you think,' answered one; ' he has with him my lord the bishop, his highness the Duke of Savoy,' and then he continued proudly, ' he has even received letters from them!' The independent citizens, affecting incredulity, exclaimed: ' What! Portier receive secret messages from such great personages!' . . . One of the episcopals, piqued by the disdainful sneer, declared aloud, ' that the letters were in existence, *in buffeto* (says the Council Register, in its classic Latin), in the secretary's buffet.' At these words, the sly huguenots started up suddenly, and hurrying in great glee to Portier's room, broke open the cupboard, took out the papers lying there, and carried them to the syndics. This discovery was still more important than the other.

The magistrates hastened to open the packet, and found a bundle of papers all having reference to the plot which the bishop had contrived for the subjugation of Geneva. They examined the contents and

* Registre du Conseil du 3 Février 1534. Spon, i. p. 516. Ruchat, iii. p. 276. Blavignac, *Mém. d'Archéologie*, iv. pp. 101–102.

were alarmed. 'Here is an act signed by the bishop on the 12th of January last—only twenty days ago—appointing a governor for the temporalities, with power to punish rebels. The prince, of his mere caprice, establishes an unconstitutional agent, who is to have no other law than his own will. Here are blank warrants sealed with the arms of the Dukes of Savoy. It is a downright conspiracy, a crime of high-treason.' The date of the act made it sufficiently clear that Pierre de la Baume was the instigator of the troubles which had been on the point of throwing the city into confusion. It was determined that Portier, the recognised agent of this revolutionary intrigue, should be tried before the syndics; and a public prosecutor, Jean Lambert, a sound huguenot, was elected to conduct the proceedings.[*]

However, before commencing this trial, that of Pennet, less complicated than the other, was to be concluded. The case was clear, provided for by the law, and not pardonable. Claude Pennet stood forward boldly like a man enduring persecution for the Christian religion. He was convicted of having murdered Nicholas Berger in his shop at the Perron, and Syndic du Crest, a catholic but a wise man, pronounced the sentence of death. This made no change in Pennet's manner: he did not repent the deed he had done, fanaticism stifled the voice of conscience in him. It was the same with all his friends, zealots of the Roman party. In them passion took the place of reason, and they boasted of the murder as an honourable, holy, and heroic act. Pennet asked to see Furbity,

[*] Registre du Conseil des 3 et 8 Février 1534. Ruchat, iii. p. 277. Mém. de Gautier.

the Dominican, who was detained in prison for having insulted the adversaries of Rome. The monk of the order of the Inquisition was conducted to the murderer's cell, ' and when they saw each other they could not forbear from weeping,' says the nun of St. Claire.*
Pennet wished to die piously: ' therefore this good catholic made his confession.' . . . ' I am condemned to the scaffold for the love of Jesus Christ,' he said to the Dominican, 'and I entreat your holy prayers.'
The reverend father, moved to tears by the piety and wretched fate of this precious son of the Church, kissed him and said: ' Sire Claude, go cheerfully and rejoice in your martyrdom, nothing doubting, for the kingdom of heaven is open and the angels are waiting for you.' †

The murder of which Pennet was guilty, was, in the Dominican's eyes, the work of a saint. Most of the episcopals thought the same; and it was feared that their party, which had the populace with them, would oppose the execution of the sentence. De la Maisonneuve, determining to support the law by force, collected a certain number of armed men in his house.‡
But their intervention was not necessary; nothing disturbed the course of justice, and the executioner cut off the murderer's head, and hung his body on a gibbet. Before long, the populace was in commotion. ' Have you heard the news?' people said. ' Miracles are worked at the place where Pennet's body hangs. His face is as ruddy and his lips as fresh as if he was

* ' Quand se virent l'un l'autre, ne se purent tenir de pleurer.'—La Sœur Jeanne, Levain du Calvinisme.

† Ibid. pp. 82-83.

‡ MS. du Procès inquisitionnel de Lyon, p. 32.

alive, and a white dove is continually hovering over his head.' The devout made pilgrimages to the place of execution.

The other Pennet, the gaoler who had wounded Porral, and who, says Sister Jeanne, 'was not less ardent than his brother in upholding the holy catholic religion,' was all this time lying hid in the house of a poor beggar-woman, where the nuns of St. Claire, who alone were in the secret, stealthily carried him food. The execution of his brother alarmed him; so one night, when it froze hard, he left his hiding-place barefoot, and arrived stealthily at the convent of St. Claire, where the nuns provided him with a disguise, in which he escaped to Savoy.

The third delinquent, the State criminal, Portier, remained. The matter appeared so serious to the procurator-general that he desired it should be communicated to the people. The Council General having met on the 8th February, Lambert ordered the letters found at the palace, as well as the duke's blank warrants, to be read to the assembly. 'What! a governor of Geneva invested with the temporalities of the sovereign power, with authority to punish citizens who maintain their political and religious rights; the constitution of the State trampled under foot by the prince-bishop; and the Duke of Savoy, that eternal enemy of Genevan independence, forcibly aiding this usurpation and violence!' All this constituted a guilty plot, even in the eyes of right-minded catholics. The voice of the people and the voice of justice were in harmony; the procurator-general demanded that Portier should be brought before his judges. The trial was much slower than that of the two Pennets had been, for the Roman-catholics made every effort to save him, and even offered large sums of money. But the procurator general and the huguenots represented continually that ' there was a conspiracy against the liberties of the city; ' it was not possible to save the episcopal secretary.

Yet Portier and his agents had merely begun to carry out the orders they had received: the bishop was the real criminal. His quality of prince covered his person, so that even had he been in Geneva, not a hair of his head would have fallen. But Pierre de la Baume was to receive the punishment which, by the will of God, falls upon unjust princes. He had de-sired to employ his power for the purpose of oppres-sion; and God shattered that power. When the sealed letters of the bishop which gave Geneva a dictator were read in the assembly of the people, the citizens were shocked; a sullen silence betrayed their indig-nation; they seemed to hear the funeral knell of an ancient dynasty that had departed. The Genevese de-termined to break with the episcopal traditions, and to raise to the government none but men known by their attachment to the union of Geneva with Switzerland and to the cause of the Reformation. While, among the syndics retiring from offiee, there was only one who belonged to this category, four friends of inde-pendence were called by the people to the first posi-tion in the State. They were Michael Sept, one of the huguenots who, in 1526, had fled to Berne, and had brought back the Swiss alliance; Ami de Chapeau-rouge, Aimé Curtet, and J. Duvillard. The execu-tive council thus became a huguenot majority. It was the episcopal conspiracy that struck the decisive blow, that threw wide open the hitherto half-open door, and permitted the victorious Reformation to enter the city.*

* Registre du Conseil des 8 et 10 Février 1534.

CHAPTER VI.

A FINAL EFFORT OF ROMAN-CATHOLICISM.

(FEBRUARY 10 TO MARCH 1, 1534.)

UNEQUIVOCAL tokens soon made known the change that had taken place. Every one knew that the critical moment had arrived; but that it should be salutary, it was necessary to enlighten the people and set distinctly before them the end which it was proposed to attain. In all that concerns religious questions, the first point is to understand them thoroughly: vagueness always does injury to true religion. The magistrates determined to make clear the points on which the discussion turned, and accordingly the new syndics ordered Furbity to appear before the Council. This body, which had called to their aid the deputies of Berne and the three reformers, invited the monk to prove by the Holy Scriptures, as he had promised, the doctrines he advanced. 'In the first place,' they said, 'you have accused those who eat meat, *which God hath created to be received*,* of being worse than *Turks*.'—'Sirs,' answered the monk, 'I confess that our Lord did not make the prohibition of which I spoke; I will, therefore, prove my statement by the decrees of St.

* 1 Timothy iv. 3.

Thomas.'—'Ho! ho!' said Farel, 'you pretended to prove everything by the Word of God; you even consented, in the opposite case, to be burnt at the stake, and now . . . you give up the Scriptures!'

They did not confine themselves to this question: the lords of Berne proved by fourteen witnesses the other errors preached by Furbity; for instance, that God will punish those who read the Scriptures in the vulgar tongue, and that Christ had given the papacy to St. Peter. They proved, also, the reality of the abuse uttered by the Dominican against the reformed Christians, except, however, that a *German* (a Swiss-German) was among the executioners of our Lord: it appeared that some wag had invented the story to ridicule the monk. The Bernese declared that, as the monk was, according to his own confession, only 'a preacher of the decrees of St. Thomas' and a story-teller, justice ought to have its course.

The Dominican began to be afraid, and offered to apologise in the cathedral for the outrage to God and the lords of Berne. 'We accept,' said the premier syndic, 'and you will afterwards quit Geneva and never return, under pain of death.' The Dominican desired nothing better than to get away as soon as possible.*

In consequence of this decision, the Dominican, attended by his guard, was led quietly to St. Pierre's on Sunday, the 15th of February. He was much agitated, walked hurriedly, and his mind was distracted with contending emotions. On reaching the foot of the pulpit, he went into it hastily, and, casting his eyes on the crowd which filled the church, his confusion and embarrassment increased. He saw himself

---

* *Lettres certaines,* &c. Registre du Conseil des 11, 12, 13, 15 Février 1534. Froment, *Gestes,* p. 87.

between two powers—the horrible Bernese and the terrible Dominicans—and felt himself unable to satisfy one without offending the other. He tried, however, to recover himself, made the sign of the cross, said the *Ave Maria*, and invoked the Virgin. . . . The Bernese looked surprised; but it was much worse when, instead of reading the retractation which the syndics had given him, he began to skim it over, to wander from it, and, finally, to say something quite different. One of the Bernese called to him: 'Sir Doctor, you have nothing to do here but to retract,' and numerous voices immediately seconded the remark. But the monk rambled wider than ever from the question, hesitated, and became confused; * many of the huguenots left their places, a great agitation pervaded the church, and the patience of the congregation was becoming exhausted. 'You are making fools of us,' they cried out to the monk. 'Do not stuff our ears with your usual nonsense. Come! a good *peccavi*!' † But there was no retractation. A great uproar then arose; some violent men went up into the pulpit, seized the disciple of St. Dominic, and dragged him down roughly.‡ 'They made the chair fall after him,' says Sister Jeanne, 'and he was nearly left dead on the spot' (the good sister often colours too highly). The catholics quitted the church in alarm, and the doctor of the Sorbonne, having broken his promise, was led back to prison.§

* 'Vagans et vacillans, sententiæ satisfacere neglexit.'—Registre du Conseil du 15 Février 1534.

† 'Nugis solitus plebis aures suspendere satageret.'—*Geneva restituta*, pp. 6–9.

‡ 'Impostor suggestu deturbatus.'—*Geneva restituta*, pp. 6–9.

§ Registre du Conseil des 15, 16, 20 Février. Froment, *Gestes de Genève*, p. 88. La Sœur Jeanne, *Levain du Calvinisme*, p. 78.

The Bernese ambassadors next appeared before the Council, and asked permission for the Gospel to . be publicly preached in one of the churches. The syndics replied that it was just what they wanted, and that they would require the Lent preacher to conform his sermons to the Gospel.

The fanatical Dominican, empowered to deliver the Advent lectures, having compromised catholicism, and the Council having declared against every preacher who should not preach according to God's Word, the Genevan clergy determined to make a last effort. They said they must choose a monk of another sort for the Lent course, and consequently turned to the Franciscans, who had often dreamt of a transformation of religious society. There were great differences between these two mendicant orders: the Dominicans were rich, the Franciscans poor; the Dominicans aimed at dominion, the Franciscans at humility; the Dominicans were fossilised in their doctrines and customs, the Franciscans were flexible and had a taste for innovations. They knew how to catch the multitude by their enthusiasm and flagellations, by their insinuating manners and miraculous visions. It is a man of this sort, said the oldest of the catholics, that we want after the Dominican. If Geneva had resisted the roughness of the one, it would be captivated by the flatteries of the other. In this manner the clergy hoped to lead Geneva insensibly back into the arms of Rome.

Father Courtelier, superior of the Franciscans of Chambery, renowned for his eloquence and wit, was invited to come and preach at Geneva during Lent. He arrived on Saturday, the 14th of February: next morning (it was the Sunday preceding Shrove Tuesday) he appeared before the Council. The premier syndic, assuming a duty that was somewhat episcopal, said to him: 'Reverend father, you must preach nothing but the pure Gospel of God.'—'I undertake to do so,' replied the monk, who had been well tutored; 'you will be satisfied.' And then, desiring to show how accommodating he was, he presented nine articles, saying: 'This is what I desire to preach;' adding, as if he was before the college of cardinals: 'Strike out what you do not approve of.' The Council, in great part Lutheran, finding themselves converted by the priest into a court of doctrine, ordered the paper to be read. *Invocation of the Virgin Mary* was one of the articles; *Purgatory* was another ; *Prayer for the dead; Invocation of the Saints*. . . . The huguenots objected, and these four points were struck off the list; but he was allowed to make the sign of the cross in the pulpit, to repeat the salutation of the angel to Mary, which is recorded in the Gospel of St. Luke, and to celebrate mass. The priest returned to his convent with the revised articles.*

On Ash Wednesday the reverend superior went into the pulpit and laboured skilfully to retain Geneva in the orbit of the papacy. The two chiefs of the Reformation—the layman Baudichon de la Maisonneuve and the reformer Farel—with many of their *accomplices* (as Father Courtelier styles them),† desirous of hearing how the monk would manage to make the pope and Luther agree, had gone to the Franciscan church at Rive (Courtelier had not been admitted to the honour

* Registre du Conseil des 15 et 16 Février 1534.
† MS. du Procès inquisitionnel de Lyon, p. 331.

of the cathedral).   The monk began by repeating in
a sonorous voice the invocation to the Virgin: *Ave
Maria . . .*, at which Farel and the huguenots called
out so that all could hear them: 'It is a foolish thing
to salute the Virgin Mary!'—'I do it *by permission of
the Council*,' answered the monk ingenuously, and all
the catholics in the congregation, desiring to support
their champion, began to cry out: *Ave Maria, gratia
plena!*   There was such a loud and universal mur-
mur, that Farel, Maisonneuve, and their friends were
obliged to hold their tongues.*

Courtelier continued, endeavouring to speak at
once according to the pope and the Gospel.   One
sentence contradicted another; what was white one
moment was black the next; his sermon was a muddle
of ideas without issue, a strain of music without harmony.   Farel and his friends soon understood the
manœuvre.   'He is using a cloak to entrap us,' they
said, 'and will take care not to show his teeth at
starting. He gives us drink . . . as they did at Babylon, poison in a golden chalice.'   Disgusted with such
trimming, Farel stood up and said: 'You cannot teach
the truth, for you do not know it.'   The poor friar
stopped short: resuming his courage by degrees and
wishing to please the friends of the Gospel, he began to
inveigh against both priests and popes.   It was now
the turn of the catholics; and the Franciscan, no-
ticing their anger and desiring to regain their favour,
began once more to vituperate the reformers.   Without doctrine, without opinions, he fluctuated between
Rome and Wittemberg, and instead of satisfying

* MS. du Procès inquisitionnel de Lyon, pp. 331-332.

everybody, he exasperated both parties. 'We cannot serve God and the devil,' said Froment with disgust.

The reverend superior now changed his tactics, knowing, as all good Franciscans did, that flies are to be caught with honey, and began to praise the Genevans in extravagant language: 'Ladies and gentlemen,' he said from the pulpit, 'beware how you suffer yourselves to be seduced by the people (Farel and his two friends) who teach you that you and your fathers were idolaters, and that you are being led away to hell. No! you are a noble and mighty city . . . you are of good repute . . . and worthy people. . . . Ladies and gentlemen, always preserve your glorious title, and make yourselves worthy of the great name borne by your noble city. Is it not called *Geneva*, *Gebenna*,* that is to say, *gens bona*, *gens benigna*, *gens sancta*, *gens præclara*, *gens devota*? . . . a good, merciful, holy, illustrious, and devout people . . . Your name declares it.' The monk was inexhaustible in extravagant compliments, although he knew very well what he ought to think of the 'holiness' of the Genevese, and particularly of the monks and priests.

This final effort of Roman-catholicism in Geneva did not succeed. On the contrary, the huguenots, provoked by his fawning, said: 'We do not desire to please either gentlemen or ladies,'† and moved with firm steps in the path of Reform. Farel, setting aside the manifold ceremonies with which Rome had overburdened public worship, desired to re-esta-

---

* The word *Gebenna* occurs frequently in ancient documents.

† 'Nous ne voulons plaire, nous, ni à Monsieur ni à Madame.'—Froment, *Gestes de Genève*, pp. 83–84.

blish baptism in conformity with the Gospel institution, as a sign of regeneration.   The news spread,
and excited great curiosity even among the strangers
who were in Geneva.   On the 22nd of February, the
first Sunday in Lent, two Savoyards, Claude Theve-
non of the mountains of the Grand-Bornand, and
Henry Advreillon of the parish of Thonon, were in
the Molard, where also a number of Genevans, both
catholics and Lutherans, had assembled.   ' Have you
heard,' said one of them, ' that there is going to be a
baptism at Baudichon's house? '—' Let us go and see
what it is like,' said the Savoyards ; and, following
some huguenots, they entered a large hall, which had
been contrived by removing the partitions.*   Some of
the seats were already occupied; the two strangers
were able to find room, but the later arrivals were
compelled to stand near the door.   ' There must be
three hundred and more present,' said Advreillon to his
friend.   On a raised chair sat a young man with mild
countenance and sharp eyes: they were told it was
Viret of Orbe; right and left of him were Farel and
Froment.   A gentleman of the city of good appearance, who seemed to be between forty and fifty years
old, showed the people to their seats and watched to
see that everything was conducted with propriety.
' That is Baudichon de la Maisonneuve,' the Savoyards
were informed, ' the master of the house, and the
greatest Lutheran in Geneva.' †

The service then began.   Viret's gentle eloquence
charmed his hearers; the two strangers, however,
would gladly have seen themselves outside of the

* MS. du Procès inquisitionnel de Lyon, pp. 231, 232, 236.
† Ibid. pp. 233, 234.

assembly into which they had impudently crept; but
all the passages were blocked up: 'We cannot get
out,' said Advreillon, 'because of the great crowd of
people;' so they made up their minds to stay till the
end. As soon as the sermon was over, the two Savoyards were about to leave, when De la Maisonneuve
said aloud: 'Let no one move, a baptism is going
to be celebrated here.' The baptism took place,
and Viret added: 'It was with pure fair water that
John baptized Jesus Christ; to baptize with oil, salt,
and spittle as the hypocrites do, is wrong.' The two
strangers, offended by such language, got away as
fast as they could.

As many persons had been unable to take part in
the service, the huguenots, whose patience was exhausted, resolved to be no longer satisfied with narrow halls, which did not permit all who loved the
Word of God to hear it. 'Jesus Christ commands
the Gospel to be preached in all the world,' said
Farel, 'it must therefore be preached in Geneva;'
whereupon he asked for a church. The Bernese ambassadors undertook to present the petition. 'Most
honoured lords,' they said to the Council, 'when we
and our ministers pass along the streets, people shout
after us: " Holla! heretics, you do not dare appear in
public, you preach your heresies in holes and corners
like pigsties." * We have long put up with this, and
now we come to ask you for a church. No one will
be constrained to hear our preacher; every man will
go to the worship he prefers, and thus everybody will
be satisfied.' The syndics, greatly embarrassed, de-

* MS. du procès inquisitionnel de Lyon, pp. 235, 236.

clared they were grieved at the *ignominies* heaped upon the Bernese, but said it was not in their jurisdiction to assign a pulpit to a Lutheran preacher; that it belonged to the prince-bishop and his vicars. ' Still,' they added, ' if you take of your own accord some edifice in which you can preach your doctrines . . . you are strong . . . we cannot resist you . . . we dare not.'

The refusal of the syndics annoyed the evangelicals ; Farel resolved to have an interview with the father-superior.   Did he wish to convince Courtelier, at times so accommodating, that the evangelical doctrine ought to be preached in the churches; or else, convinced, like Luther, that the papacy was a power of Antichrist which resisted the kingdom of God, did he desire to tell the cordelier his mind?   We cannot say: perhaps it was partly both. Accompanied by the intrepid Maisonneuve and the wise councillor Balthasar, Farel proceeded to the Franciscan convent. Courtelier received them in his cell, and the reformer having complained that the Gospel truth could not be preached, the monk, instead of making the least concession, took refuge behind the authority of the pope, extolling his holiness's infallibility and power.   Had not Alvarus Pelagius, a Franciscan like himself, declared that ' the jurisdiction of the pope is universal, embracing the whole world, its temporalities as well as its spiritualities? ' * Had not another monk taught that ' the pope is in the place of God? ' †   But Farel,

---

* 'Jurisdictionem habet universalem in toto mundo papa, nedum in spiritualibus sed temporalibus.'—*De planctu ecclesiæ*, lib. i. cap. xiii.

† 'Papa vice Dei, est omnium regnorum provisor.'—Aug. Triumphus, *Summa de potestate ecclesiastica*, Qu. xlvi. art. 3.

instead of seeking his ideas about Rome in the writings of the monks of the middle ages, derived them from the Holy Scriptures, and particularly from the Revelation of St. John. ' Your holy Father,' he said to the superior, ' is the beast whom the ignorant worship. John the Evangelist tells us of a beast with seven heads,* which "devoureth them which dwell upon the earth," and makes war upon the saints, and he adds: *the seven heads are seven hills*, on which it sits. *Seven hills*, do you hear? Everybody knows that Rome is built on *seven hills*. Therefore the holy see is not apostolical but diabolical.' Courtelier was moved. He remonstrated with Farel ' as well as he could,' he says ; but the reformer replied, the conversation grew warm, and at last the evangelists, unable to convince the monk, took leave of him. Maisonneuve quitted the cell, annoyed at Courtelier's blindness, and all three left the convent together.

This energetic argument, which applied the prophecies of the Bible respecting Antichrist to the pope, had already been employed by Luther. No proof excited more anger among the Romanists or inspired the evangelicals with more firmness.

---

* Revelation xiii.—xx.

CHAPTER VII.

FAREL PREACHES IN THE GRAND AUDITORY OF THE CONVENT AT RIVE.

(MARCH 1 TO APRIL 25, 1534.)

THE interview with the father-superior had been useless ; the churches remained closed. The evangelicals could wait no longer: the majority of the inhabitants were for the Word of God, but not a church was opened to them. The walls of St. Pierre, St. Gervais, St. Germain, and the Madelaine contained merely the external and barren forms of the Roman worship; life and movement were there no longer; they had passed into the hearts of the resolute men and pious women who gathered round Farel. Neither the hall in Maisonneuve's house, nor any other sufficed for the *lovers of the Word.* Every day numbers of hearers had to remain in the street. 'Alas!' said they, 'the Gospel can find nothing in Geneva but *secret chambers,* and we can only whisper of the grace of Christ. And yet grace ought to be proclaimed all through the city and spread even to the ends of the world.' They were about to take measures accordingly.

On the second Sunday in Lent (1st of March, 1534), after the evangelicals had heard Farel in one

of the usual halls, twenty-nine of the most notable
huguenots remained behind and began to enquire
what ought to be done. ' The Council,' reported one
of them, 'told my lords of Berne to take any place
they liked for their preacher . . . well, suppose we
take one. It is God's will to have the Gospel published. But the pope, with his people, care no more
about it than the priests of Bacchus, Jupiter, and
Venus did of old. Without any further petitioning
let us do what God commands.' At these words Maisonneuve and the other huguenots proceeded to the
convent at Rive.· Father Courtelier was preaching
there: he had just finished his sermon and the crowd
were leaving the church. The daring Baudichon informed the monks, to their great surprise, that Farel
was going to preach there, and also that the bells
would be rung, which did not astonish them less.
Two or three huguenots, going into the belfry, rang
three loud peals at intervals during an hour. Meanwhile De la Maisonneuve took his measures. Instead
of taking possession of the church, he selected a part
of the convent named the *grand auditory*, or the
cloister. This part of the monastery was constructed
in the shape of a gallery, and had a court in the
middle: it was more spacious than the church, and
would hold four or five thousand persons.*

* Froment, an eye-witness, says (*Gestes de Genève*, p. 82) that Farel
preached 'in the grand auditory of the convent of Rive, without entering
the church.' Father Courtelier, in his evidence at Lyons (*Procès inquisitionnel*, p. 322), says that Farel preached 'in the same church and
pulpit as himself.' But Froment's evidence is corroborated by the
Register of the Council of Geneva, which says, that the meeting was
held in the cloister or auditory. Courtelier no doubt only meant to say
that Farel preached in the same edifice as himself, without strictly designating the place.

The sound of the bells at an unusual hour was heard all through the city. Each note, as it rang in the ears of the Genevese, announced to them that the Gospel, with which all Christendom was then agitated, was at last about to be publicly proclaimed within their walls. 'Master Farel,' they said, 'is going to preach in the cloister at Rive,' and a crowd collected from all sides. People of every sort had assembled to hear him: evangelicals, political huguenots, the indifferent and bigoted. Certain priests gnashed their teeth and even attempted to turn away some of their parishioners; but it was labour in vain: the number increased every minute. Some Franciscan monks, who stared at the sight of such an extraordinary multitude, could not resist the desire of going to the grand auditory and hearing what was said.

De la Maisonneuve gave the necessary orders for placing the people. The assembly, although respectful, was profoundly agitated. In the place where they had met, men of different parties crowded together: the opportunity of hearing the famous Farel, and the object which such meetings were to attain, namely, a change in the religion of Geneva—all stirred their minds deeply. But if there was any unbecoming movement, Maisonneuve, from his elevated place, imposed silence by his hand. At length the reformer appeared. The catholics were astonished when they saw him: 'What!' they said, 'no sacerdotal ornaments! He is dressed like a layman, with a Spanish cloak and brimmed cap.' * But under that cap and cloak lay hid what was rarely found beneath the robes of priests—an ardent soul, a heart overflowing

* MS. du procès inquisitionnel de Lyon, p. 323.

with love, and such eloquence that the hearers exclaimed, as Calvin did once: 'Your thunders have
caused an indescribable trouble in my soul.'*   Farel
began to speak: borrowing his fire from the writings
of the prophets and apostles, says one of his bio-
graphers, he enlightened and inflamed the heart.†
He excited in many a lively feeling of love for Christ.
God, as Calvin says, was at work in his own through
the ministry of the reformer.   Some began to consider and to relish the grace which they had formerly
swallowed without tasting.‡   The assembly was
charmed and enraptured; the souls of many were
inflamed by the ardour of the divine spirit.

Among the Franciscans who listened to Farel was
Jacques Bernard, belonging to one of the best families in Geneva.   He was lively, intelligent, learned,
and defiant, and had long been a sincere worshipper
of the Virgin.   He had often spoken violently against
the reformers, and a few days before, meeting Farel
and Viret, he told them with a scowl: 'In times past
there were schismatics enough who forbade men to
salute the Virgin and make the sign of the cross.'
Then, without another word, he rudely turned his back
on them.   But on this occasion no one in the grand
auditory was more attentive than Jacques.   God gave
him *new eyes* and *new ears*.   It has been said that the
convent at Rive was to him as the road to Damascus
—that there this new Saul became a new Paul.§
This first preaching of Farel's contributed at least to

* 'Sane me tam vehementer conturbarunt tua illa fulgura.'—Calvini
Epp.
† Ancillon, *Vie de Farel.*
‡ 'Savourer la grâce . . . avalée sans la goûter.'
§ M. Archinard: *Edifices religieux de l'ancienne Genève*, p. 108.

Bernard's conversion, and ere long he maintained courageously the truths he had once so much attacked.

But this light, which had enlightened some, blinded others. The wrath of the men devoted to the papacy knew no bounds; they indulged in terrible bursts of passion, and their followers spread the flames through the city. The conflagration broke out the next day. The Two Hundred were hardly met, when Nicholas du Crest, the three Malbuissons, Girardin, and Philip de la Rive, with several others, appeared before them and said: A minister preached the new law yesterday in the cloister at Rive; we wish to know if it was with your consent. At the same moment the ambassadors of Berne arrived and held very different language: ' What we have so long asked for,' they said, ' has been accomplished *by the inspiration of God*, without our knowing anything of it. The place which you had refused us has been given by the Lord himself. Yes, God, by the inspiration of the Holy Ghost, has put it into the hearts of your citizens to have the Gospel preached in the grand auditory. Permit the minister to continue his preaching in that place, and give no annoyance to such as may go to hear him.'

Although, to satisfy the catholics, the Council had at first hinted to the Bernese that as they were returning home, it would be very natural that they should take their ministers with them, Farel continued to preach every day to numerous congregations. His hearers were more convinced than ever of the errors of Rome and of the truth of the evangelical doctrine —things which appeared to them as clear as the day. Many threw aside their supineness; their contrite hearts joyfully received the Saviour's pardon, and, 'caring no longer for the frivolous things so esteemed by the papists,' devoted themselves to works of true innocence and charity. There was great cheerfulness in Geneva. Bands of people paraded the city with songs of joy; groups assembled at the Molard and conversed of the extraordinary things that were taking place. The evangelicals no longer doubted of the victory. A young Savoyard, named Henry Percyn, approaching one of these groups, recognised Baudichon de la Maisonneuve, who, surrounded by several Lutherans, 'was talking to some catholics who were there.' The latter defended their Church: 'Are these three chimney-preachers better than pope, bishop, canons, priests, and monks?' Maisonneuve replied: 'I will bet one hundred crowns to fifty, that next Easter not a single mass will be celebrated in Geneva.' None of the catholics would accept the wager. Baudichon was mistaken, but by a few months only.*

On Saturday, the 7th of March, the Bernese ambassadors attended the evangelical assembly for the last time. They were leaving Farel, Viret, and Froment without protection in the midst of deadly enemies, and without force to resist them alone. Accordingly, as soon as the service was ended, they rose and said: 'Farewell, gentlemen of Geneva, we commend our preachers to you.' †—'It is not necessary to commend them,' answered a Genevese, 'we know the danger they incur in trying to rescue the people from the slavery into which they have fallen.' As he left the hall, Claude Bernard took the three evangelists

---

* MS. du procès inquisitionnel de Lyon, pp. 226–227.

† Registre du Conseil du 6 Mars 1534. Froment, *Gestes de Genève,* p. 91. MS. de Gautier.

home to his house, where they lived thenceforward.

De la Maisonneuve departed about the same time as the Bernese, on his way to Frankfort on business. At a date we cannot fix he took Farel and Viret to Lausanne to 'similarly seduce' the inhabitants of that city; but the Lausannese, the priests and their friends (for the middle-class was favourable to the Reform), 'drove the preachers away.' It is scarcely probable that the two reformers should have chosen to leave Geneva at the important epoch of which we are treating; and yet a contemporary document would lead us to believe so. When De la Maisonneuve reached Frankfort, he conversed with the Lutherans and communicated, as it would seem, according to the ritual of Luther.*

Shortly after this, Portier was convicted of having conspired with the bishop against the liberty of the city, and condemned to lose his head. The law having punished the guilty, the public conscience was satisfied. It is necessary that justice should reign among nations; when it is trampled under foot and the guilty are held to be innocent, there rises in the breasts of the good a cry of sorrow, we will not say of revenge. But that condemnation was big with important consequences for Geneva; it was, says the chronicler, 'a terror to the creatures of the bishop.' As Portier had only carried out the orders of the prince, the condemnation of the servant was that of the master. The episcopal agents began to understand that they must obey the laws and pay respect

---

* MS. du procès inquisitionnel de Lyon, pp. 199, 200, 204.

to lay tribunals. The power of the episcopal faction was broken.*

Farel became more energetic, while, on the other hand, the Franciscan preacher did all he could to support the tottering papacy. It was not only in the same country that these two .contrary systems were then in conflict: it was in the same city, in the same house—the monastery at Rive. One day the cordelier taught in the church that ' the wafer ceases to be bread, and that the *mouth* receives the body of Jesus Christ;' while Farel said in the cloister: ' It is true that the life is *enclosed* in the body of Christ, but we have no communion with him except by a true faith. Faith is the mouth of the soul to receive the Saviour.' In the church the cordelier encouraged the purchase of indulgences, the practice of penances and satisfactions; but in the grand auditory Farel exclaimed: ' All our sins are pardoned *freely*. How dare the monks, then, set up their satisfactions, which the Word of God has shattered to pieces?' † Gradually the cordelier lowered his tone, the powerful voice of Farel was reducing him to silence. ' You must know,' wrote Madame de la Maisonneuve to her husband, who was at Frankfort, ' you must know that Master William does his duty bravely in announcing the Word of God.' She added: ' We have had no prohibitions; nobody contradicts us. Our business increases greatly.' ‡

---

* Registre du Conseil du 10 Mars 1534.

† MS. de Gautier. Registre du Conseil du 18 Mars 1534.

‡ She dated her letter: *De Genève, trois semaines avant Pâques*, and signed it: *La toute votre femme chérie, Baudichone.*—MS. du procès inquisitionnel, pp. 23–24.

Roman-catholicism was falling: Friburg hurried to
its support. 'Alas!' replied the syndics to the ambassadors, 'we do not set Farel to preach, it is the
people. We could sooner stop a torrent than prevent people going to hear them. So far as we are
concerned, we have abolished no ceremony, pulled
down no church.' Thus, at Geneva, as in mighty
England, it was the nation rather than its leaders
who desired the Reform; and it was the same everywhere. The Friburgers, calm and reserved, then
stepped forward in the midst of the assembly of the
people, coldly laid their letters of alliance before
the premier syndic, and asked for those of Geneva.
'Keep them! keep them!' was the cry on all sides;
and the citizens rushed towards the deputation, lavish-
ing on them marks of affection and prayers. Messieurs of Friburg, sternly shaking off their em-
braces, departed leaving the letters of alliance on the
table.

The alarmed Council now resolved to do all in
their power to appease the catholics and Friburgers.
Every year at Easter a grand procession took place,
in which the images and relics of the saints were
carried through the city. The Council ordered the
usual honours to be paid them. Aimé Levet having
declared that he would not forsake the living God for
that multitude of *petty gods*, the syndics served him
with a special order through the police. But still
the Levets would hang no drapery upon their house
and kept the shop open as on an ordinary day. For
this offence, Aimé was kept three days in prison on
bread and water.

The consideration due to Friburg had led the magistrates to this act of severity, but the evangelical

movement was not checked by it. The Christian meetings increased in number after Easter. Farel energetically urged forward the car of Reform, and his voice by turns alarmed like the thunders of Sinai, or consoled like the Beatitudes of the Gospel. Yet, in the midst of these numerous works, he was often observed to pause, overcome with sadness. The persecution continued in France: three hundred Lutherans were in prison at Paris. 'What restive horses are these!' he exclaimed. 'They shrink back instead of advancing! What adversaries are springing up against the Redeemer, who reigns with glory in heaven! But God will not forsake his work.' * He had still keener sorrows than these: his own brothers, Daniel, Walter, and Claude, had been seized by the enemy from a desire to avenge upon them the *evil* which the reformer was doing. One of the three, who was younger than himself, had been condemned to imprisonment for life, and his mother, already a widow, was shedding tears of bitterness. 'Alas!' said William Farel, 'her son, who was born after me, has long been in prison, and has greater sorrows to endure than I have.' The reformer applied to friends in high station to obtain his brother's release from the king, but the strictness of the prison had only been increased. 'I know not,' he said on the 28th of April, 1534, 'who has so stirred the fire. . . . May it please God that the poor prisoner hold firm and declare fearlessly what ought to be said of the good Saviour.'† Farel possessed that filial affection

---

* MS. du procès inquisitionnel de Lyon, pp. 11-12.

† 'Puisse à Dieu seulement que le pauvre prisonnier pousse outre et déclare sans crainte ce qui doit être dit du bon Sauveur.'—Lettre aux fidèles de Paris. (MS. du procès inquisitionnel de Lyon.)

which is serious and respectful towards the father,
tender and gentle towards the mother; it made him
exclaim in his anguish: 'Alas! the poor widow!
Oh, my anguish-stricken mother!' The love he felt
for Christ had increased his natural affections.

De la Maisonneuve, having returned to Geneva
after Easter, was about to start again for Lyons.
Farel, knowing that his friend, De la Forge, the
merchant of Paris, would be going also to that city at
this season of the year, gave Baudichon a letter for
his Paris brethren, at that time so afflicted, directing
his letter *to the holy vessel elect of God.* 'Jesus,' he
wrote to this little flock in the capital, 'is the rock of
offence against which the world has fought since the
beginning of time, and will always fight: but its
efforts are vain. No council can withstand God, and
if the wicked lift their horns, they shall be broken.'
He then solicited the intercession of the members of
the Church in behalf of his brother. 'I pray you,'
he said, 'speak of my brother in that quarter where
you know better than myself that it is expedient to
do so. What! a protracted detention, the confiscation of his property, six hundred crowns which the
bishop has extracted from him—is not that enough?
Oh! that the poor fellow could be set at liberty!
All here who fear the Lord entreat you to exert
yourselves for him.' * The evangelicals of Geneva
were interested in the fate of their reformer's brothers.
At the same time Farel wrote also to De la Forge, com-
mending his brother to him, and knowing the perils
with which the Parisian merchant was threatened, he

---

* Geneva, April 25, 1534.   MS. du procès inquisitionnel de Lyon.

added: ' If we have Jesus, that heavenly treasure cannot be taken from us; let us march onwards, though
all the world should rise against Him.'

In treating of our reformers, we naturally bestow
attention on their labours, struggles, writings, and
trials; it is well, however, to enter sometimes into the
inner sanctuary of their hearts and of their domestic
lives. We are touched and rejoice to find there such
abundance of the most legitimate and tenderest of
human affections. They were men as well as Christians. This fact is a proof of the sincerity of their
piety; it is like a spring of pure water gushing
up on a field of battle, refreshing and-reviving those
whom so many struggles might have wearied.

CHAPTER VIII.

A BOLD PROTESTANT AT LYONS.

(1530 TO 1534.)

FAREL, who was so distressed by the long captivity of one of the members of his family, little
suspected that a friend, loved by him as a brother,
would ere long be in a dungeon.   De la Maisonneuve,
who traded in all sorts of merchandise, but particularly in silk fabrics, jewellery, and furs, had been in
the habit of attending the fairs of Lyons for twenty
years, and went there as often as three or four
times a year.   Of late, the frankness with which he
maintained the evangelical doctrines had offended
many persons, and thus paved the way for a cata-
strophe which now seemed inevitable.   Courted by the
merchants, esteemed by the magistrates, he was, on
the other hand, in the bad books of the priests, and
the priests were powerful.

One day, in the year 1530, when he was at Nuremberg on business, a rich merchant of that city, a sound
protestant, who had no love for relics, had given him
a valuable reliquary in payment of a debt.*   As Lyons

---

* MS. du procès inquisitionnel de Lyon, p. 147.

was noted for its devotion, Baudichon, who cared little for the object and looked at it only as an article of merchandise, thought it might fetch a good price in that city, and happening to go there not long after, offered the little box to a money-changer. He would have done better to have refused it at Nuremberg, but Christian wisdom was then only dawning upon him. The money-changer took up the article and examined it devoutly. On the top was an image of St. James in silver, 'carefully wrought,' and weighing about four marks. Underneath was the reliquary: a box of silver with a glass allowing the inside to be seen, and some little parchment labels indicating the names of the saints whose relics were contained within. The Lyons money-changer looked with adoration on the precious remains of St. Christopher, St. Syriac, and another. He took off his cap, made a bow to the relics, and kissed them devoutly ; and as his wife and children had clustered round him with pious curiosity, he made each of them kiss the sacred remains. Turning to Maisonneuve, he said: ' Sir Baudichon, I am surprised that you should bring me this relic in such a manner.' Maisonneuve replied: ' It is very likely they are the bones of some ordinary body which the priests give the people to kiss to deceive them.' At these words, an apprentice, of the age of eighteen, a very bigoted youth, left the shop indignant, and sat down on a bench in the street. The changer having paid Baudichon seventy livres tournois for his merchandise, the huguenot departed. But as he was passing in front of the bench, the apprentice, unable to restrain his anger, insulted him. Maisonneuve was content to reply that if he was in Geneva, ' he would give him relics for nothing.' This affair began to make Baudichon suspected.*

Next year (1531), when Maisonneuve was again at Lyons, and dining at the table-d'hôte of the Coupe d'Or, he met with some merchants from the neighbouring provinces, and particularly from Auvergne, whose inhabitants, upright and charitable, but ignorant and vindictive, were distinguished at that time by a credulous devotion, as excessive as it was superstitious. The Genevan did not scruple to declare his religious convictions boldly before them, and the bigoted Auvergnats were much surprised to hear him speak ' *after his manner about the Gospel and 'faith during all the meal.*' 'Hold your tongue,' they said angrily, 'if you were in our country, *you would be burnt.*' †

A year later (in 1532), also at fair time, De la Maisonneuve, Bournet, a broker, to whom he had confided an article of jewellery for sale, Humbert des Oches, and other tradesmen, were supping at the table-d'hôte of the Coupe d'Or. It was one of those days on which the Church forbids the eating of meat: Bournet had brought some fish, of which they all partook, and Baudichon among them. This surprised one of the guests, who asked him whether they eat meat at Geneva on fast days. 'Certainly they do,' he answered, 'and if I were in a place where it could be got, I should make no difficulty about it, for

---

* All these particulars, as well as those which follow, are taken literally from the depositions of the witnesses, made on oath, before the court of Lyons, and are to be found in pages 132–147 of the official manuscript.

† MS. du procès inquisitionnel de Lyon, déposition de Pécoud, pp. 159–163.

God does not forbid it.'—' The pope and the Church forbid it,' returned Bournet sharply. Baudichon declared that he did not acknowledge the pope's power to forbid what God permits. ' God said to St. Peter,' rejoined Bournet, ' *Whatsoever thou shalt bind on earth shall be bound in heaven* (Matthew xvi. 19). The pope is now in the place of St. Peter; therefore ' . . .—' The pope and the priests,' retorted Maisonneuve, ' are so far from being like St. Peter that there are many among them who lead evil lives, and require to be set in order and reformed. The Word of God alone brings grace to the sinner.' He then began to repeat ' some passages from the Gospels *in the French language,*' selecting those which announce Jesus Christ and the complete pardon He gives. Every Christian who proclaims the Gospel might, he declared, be God's instrument to liberate souls from sin and condemnation ; and then growing bolder, he exclaimed: ' I am *Petrus*; you (turning to Bournet) are *Petrus*. Every man is Peter, provided he is firm in the faith of Jesus Christ.' All present were much struck with his observations, and the strange man became still blacker in their eyes.*

At the feast of the Epiphany in the year 1533, the brother of Lyonnel Raynaud, priest of the order of St. John of Jerusalem, and Messire Jean Barbier, of the cathedral of Vienne, arrived at the Coupe d'Or, with a clerk in attendance upon the latter. They sat down to table with the company. Everybody was speaking at once ; one of the guests, however—and he was usually among those who talked the most— seemed absorbed in thought. De la Maisonneuve (for

* MS. du procès inquisitionnel de Lyon, pp. 209, 211, 217, 218.

it was he) fixed his eyes on the priests of Vienne, and, after a few moments, said to them: 'Can you explain to me why they put a certain cordelier to death at Vienne a few years ago?' He alluded to Stephen Renier, of whom we have spoken elsewhere.* 'He was a heretic,' said Barbier, 'and had taught endless errors at Annonay and elsewhere.' De la Maison- neuve boldly undertook his defence: 'You did wrong to put him to death,' he said, 'he was a truly good man, of sound learning, and one likely to produce great fruits.' The strife began immediately. Baudi- chon affirmed that we were not required to keep the commandments of the Church, but only those of God; while the priest tried with all his might to prove that Baudichon was wrong. The Genevan grew more animated, and spoke with great boldness. This new kind of tournament absorbed all attention: the guests left off eating and drinking, fixed their eyes on the two champions, and opened their ears wide. A mer- chant of Vienne, one Master Simon de Montverban, an acquaintance of Baudichon's, and whom the latter had often soundly beaten, observed to him: 'You have found a man at last to answer you.' But the Genevan replied so forcibly to the arguments of the Viennese, and the contest became so animated, that the three priests, suddenly rising from table, quitted the room hastily, and went into a separate chamber. 'If this man were at Vienne,' said Barbier, 'I would have him sent to prison.' The prison and the stake which followed it were safer arms than discussion.†

* Vol. i. p. 576.

† MS. du procès inquisitionnel de Lyon. There are three deposi- tions with regard to these facts: those of Barbier the priest, pp. 267– 270; of the furrier Simon de Montverban, pp. 274–278; and of friar Lyonnel, pp. 305–312.

De la Maisonneuve, having returned to Lyons for the fairs of Easter and of August, met a considerable number of merchants at the Coupe d'Or, and immediately undertook to enlighten them, feeling that language was given for such purposes; but as he feared also that his scattered remarks, if not followed up, would be insufficient to correct the tardiness of certain men, he determined to make use of various stimulants. Accordingly, he spared neither toil nor weariness. Simon de Montverban, who was there again, was struck with his zeal, and complained of it. 'Whenever the merchants take their meals,' he said, 'whenever he meets them in the common hall; when they come in or go out, everywhere and always, Baudichon gets talking and disputing about the Gospel.' No longer confining himself to questions of fasting or images, he went straight to what was essential; he put forward Scripture as the fountain of truth, and declared that every sinner, even the greatest, was saved through uniting himself by faith to Jesus Christ. People censured him in vain; in vain did two merchants, one named Arcon and the other Hugues, repeat to everybody, and to Baudichon himself, that if he was in their country he would be burnt; the latter, who did not doubt them, continued his arguments. Lyons was a free city during the fair, and he took advantage of it to make the pure Gospel known. Simon de Montverban complained to the Genevan huguenot's brother-in-law, an ardent papist, who made answer: 'I wish that Baudichon had died ten years ago; he is the cause of all the troubles at Geneva.' *

* MS. du procès inquisitionnel de Lyon, pp. 282-285.

De la Maisonneuve was again at Lyons at the feasts of All Saints (November 1533) and Epiphany (1534). One evening, when a numerous company was supping at the inn, the conversation turned on the religious circumstances of the times. After listening awhile, he exclaimed: 'It is nonsense to pray to the saints, to hear mass, and confess to the priests!' and proceeded to quote *the Gospels and the Apostles* to prove what he said. 'In our country,' again asserted some who heard him, 'at Avignon, at Clermont, you would be sent to the stake!' It was the burden of the old song, and they were only surprised that he was not burnt at Lyons. De la Maisonneuve, knowing well that it was out of their Roman piety that they wished to burn him, was content to smile. But his calmness excited the wrath of his fellow-guests; the merchants of Auvergne rose from the table in a fit of anger, and addressing the hostess, desired that she would not receive Maisonneuve in future. 'If we find him here when we come again,' they said, 'we shall go and lodge elsewhere.' The landlady promised the Auvergnats not to receive him in future.*

The Easter fair of 1534 was drawing near, and as it was the most considerable in the year, Maisonneuve did not want to miss it. But circumstances had become more threatening, and rendered the journey dangerous. There were, as we have seen, in the castle of Peney on the Lyons road, and other strong places, traitors who had fled from Geneva and carried off all the Genevans they could lay hands on. Baudichon's friends wished him to put off this journey. 'The fair is free (*franche*) to every one,'

---

* MS. du procès inquisitionnel de Lyon, pp. 298–300, 413–414.

he answered. ' Aye!' said Froment, ' under the papacy there are many franchises for thieves, robbers,
and murderers ; but for the evangelicals all the liberties, franchises, and promises of princes are broken.'*
Maisonneuve knew this well, yet he was not a man to
be frightened. The report of his intentions having
gone abroad, certain *traitors* (as Froment terms the
fanatical partisans of the bishop and pope) hastened
to give their Lyons friends notice of Baudichon's
approaching arrival, conjuring them to get him put
to death. ' He was spied and *recommended* to their
care.'†

De la Maisonneuve, bearing Farel's letters, started
from Geneva in the morning of the 25th of April, and
arrived at Lyons on the 26th, having no suspicion that
his enemies were waiting for him and preparing his
scaffold. He had with him Janin the armourer, his
aide-de-camp in religious matters, who had supplied
himself with evangelical books printed at Neufchatel
to circulate them in Lyons. Baudichon, as usual,
had alighted at the Coupe d'Or near St. Pierre-les-
Nonnains, and was cordially received by the landlady
notwithstanding the promise she had made the Auvergnats some months before. Janin stopped there
also, and stored his evangelical books away in the
room that had been assigned him.

The next day there was a great disturbance at the
inn. The merchants had arrived from Auvergne,
and one of the first persons they saw was the famous
heretic! . . . The colour rushed to their cheeks, and
they had words with the hostess because she did not

* Froment, *Gestes de Genève*, p. 241.
† ' Iceluy fut épié et recommandé.'—Froment, *Gestes de Genève*, p 241.

keep her promise. That they did not content themselves with mere words, is clear from events which followed. The bigots of France wished to share with the bigots of Geneva the honour of putting to death the captain of the Lutherans.*

Maisonneuve immediately began to look after Étienne de la Forge, in order to hand him the reformer's letters ; but on going to his house in the Place de l'Herberie, he learnt, to his great disappointment, that the Parisian merchant had not yet arrived.

The enemies of the Reformation lost no time. Informations were sworn against Maisonneuve on the 27th of April, the day after his arrival, and the following morning, the 28th, the officers of justice arrested him and his friend Janin ' by authority of the seneschal's court of Lyons,' and shut him up in the king's prison. But this was not what the priests wanted. ' These two men,' they said, ' being charged with offences against our holy faith, the interest of the king our lord, and the common weal, we demand that they be sent to the prison of the archiepiscopal see, and that they be tried before the ecclesiastical judges.' † The two prisoners were accordingly transferred to the archbishop's prison. The great huguenot saw that he had fallen into a trap, and prepared to meet his enemies.

There was great agitation in the episcopal palace. That church of Lyons which had been the church of the primate of all the Gauls—of which thirty bishops had been canonised—which had supplied so many cardinals, legates, statesmen, and ambassadors—whose chapter, consisting of seventy canons, had included

* MS. du procès inquisitionnel de Lyon, p. 424.　　† Ibid. p. 1.

the sons of emperors, kings, and dukes among their number, and of which the kings of France were honorary canons—that church was about to have the glory of trying and putting to death the layman who was Farel's right arm, as Jerome of Prague had been that of John Huss. All its dignitaries—the deans, chamberlains, wardens, provosts, knights, theologians, and schoolmen—all were talking of this fortunate circumstance. The clergy of the metropolitan church of St. John the Baptist, in particular, took an active part in the business, and the walls of that vast Gothic building echoed to the oft-repeated name of the captain of the Lutherans. On the 29th of April the members of the *inquisitional court* assembled in the hall of justice of the episcopal prison, and, wearing their robes of office, took their seats on the judicial benches. They were Stephen Faye, official of the primacy, and Benedict Buatier, ordinary official of Lyons—both of them vicars-general of the primate of France. The third judge was John Gauteret, inquisitor of 'heretical pravity.' Ami Ponchon, notary public, was to act as secretary; * and Claude Bellièvre, king's advocate, was to aid them by his presence. The court being thus formed, they summoned before them Baudichon de la Maisonneuve, who declared his name, age (forty-six years), and condition, and the trial began.†

* All the procès-verbaux or minutes have his signature, with a curious flourish (*parafe*) exactly alike on each.

† MS. du procès inquisitionnel, pp. 5–6.

CHAPTER IX.

BAUDICHON DE LA MAISONNEUVE BEFORE THE INQUISITIONAL
COURT OF LYONS.

(FROM 29TH OF APRIL TO 21ST OF MAY, 1534.)

THE tribunal of priests wished to mark distinctly at the very outset that the Romish doctrine was in question : it was necessary to proclaim anew that *in instanti*, at the very moment, at the priest's word, there was no longer in the host either bread or wine, but only the body and blood of the Saviour. 'What do you think of the sacrament of the altar?' was the first question put by the court to Maisonneuve. He rejected the Roman error; but his protestantism, as we have seen, came from Germany, and the Lutherans taught that 'in the sacrament of the altar, in the bread and wine, were the true body, the true blood of Christ;' * and as, according to the Lutheran doctrine, the presence was spiritual, supernatural, and heavenly,† Maisonneuve, who professed this faith and had taken the sacrament at Frankfort in the Lutheran church, answered: 'I believe that the real body of Christ is in the blessed host,' ‡ but knowing the axiom

* 'Panem et vinum in cœna esse verum corpus et sanguinem Christi.'
Ant. Smalcad. Catech. major, &c.

† 'Intelligimus spiritualem, supernaturalem, cœlestem modum.'—*Formula Concordiæ*.

‡ MS. du procès inquisitionnel, pp. 6-9.

of jurisprudence, that no accused person is bound to criminate himself, he would not declare his faith more precisely.

If this doctrine interested the court, the connection of the accused with the chiefs of what they called *heresy* had also a great importance in their eyes, and a doctor well known in France had given them great umbrage. 'Do you know *Pharellus*?' they asked Maisonneuve, who calmly replied : 'He is from Dauphiny; he was brought to Geneva by my lords of Berne; and when I hear him, I believe as much of his sermons as seems right, and no more.' These two answers might have led some to hope that they would exercise clemency towards the accused; but such was not the intention of the canons of St. John. The court declared that the witnesses would be examined on the following day. They were all to be for the prosecution; they might invent, add, or exaggerate, and the prisoner would not have it in his power to produce any witnesses for the defence.

The first who gave evidence was a young working-man, twenty-two years of age, by name Philip Martin, and by trade a weaver. 'I lived three years in the city of Geneva,' he said, 'and during that time the Lutheran sect multiplied exceedingly. I witnessed many armed assemblies and riots, papists against evangelists, by day as well as by night. Among the most prominent of the Lutheran party was Baudichon, and after him Jean Philippe, Jean Golaz, Ami Perrin, who commonly were present at the armed meetings, directing everything and providing for the expenses. About a year ago a canon named Wernli was run through the body; Baudichon was there, armed, and wearing a cuirass.' * De la Maisonneuve calmly interrupted him : ' The witness does not speak the truth. When the canon was wounded, I was in this very city of Lyons. I therefore charge him with perjury, and desire that he be taken into custody.' Martin had borne false witness; this all who knew Maisonneuve at Geneva and Lyons could declare. It was a bad beginning.

On the 1st of May a fanatical youth, named Pierre, brother of the two Pennets, who had been condemned for assassinating a citizen and conspiring against the liberties of the city, gave his evidence. ' Baudichon entirely supports this Lutheran sect,' he said; ' he is their captain. One day last year he assembled all the Lutherans and armed them to plunder the churches, which ended in the death of four persons and the wounding of many others.' † This also was false: Vandel, a huguenot, had been wounded in a riot got up by the priests; but there had been no deaths. ' The witness hates me,' said Maisonneuve, ' because one of his brothers was executed by judicial authority.'—' Baudichon,' continued Pennet, in greater excitement, ' instead of fearing the syndics, constrains them to humble themselves before him.' —' I submit to lose my head,' exclaimed Maisonneuve, ' in case the syndics declare that I have ever done them any displeasure.' ‡ The court rose.

All this time Geneva was greatly agitated : the news of Baudichon's arrest had caused uneasiness

---

* ' Embastonné et muni d'un allécret.'—MS. du procès inquisitionnel.

† MS. du procès inquisitionnel, pp. 34–41.   ‡ Ibid. p. 46.

among his friends.   Men spoke about it 'in the city
and in the fields,' everywhere, in short.   When friends
met one another, they asked : ' Have you heard that
Baudichon has been brought before the archiepiscopal
court of Lyons for being a Lutheran?'   The devout
(if we may use the words of the manuscript) ' con-
signed him to Satan, as being the principal cause of
heresy in Geneva ; '* while the huguenots, agitated
and alarmed at the dangers that threatened their
friend, considered what was to be done.   They determined to act immediately and simultaneously at
Lyons, Berne, and even at Paris, if they could.
Thomas, Baudichon's brother, started for Lyons at
once, and asked for an audience with Monseigneur
du Peyrat, the king's lieutenant-general.   ' For what
reason,' he said, ' and by what authority has my
brother, Baudichon de la Maisonneuve, been sent to
prison?'—' I do not detain him,' answered Du Peyrat; ' apply to the vicars general.'   Thomas, learning
that his brother was in the hands of the priests, and
his danger therefore greater, resolved to make every
effort to save him.

Thomas and the Genevans were not the only persons interested in this matter.   Baudichon's imprisonment was an attack upon the rights of the foreign
merchants, and compromised the fairs at Lyons.
What German Lutheran would come there in future?
The inhabitants, especially the innkeepers, trades-
people, and merchants, foresaw great pecuniary loss,
and the princes of commerce felt the injury done to
one of their number.   There was, consequently, a great
commotion in the city, and many merchants, ' as well

* ' Le donnaient au diable.'—MS. du procès inquisiticnnel, pp. 87-88.

of the city as foreigners,' determining to complain of it, proceeded to the *consulate* (or town-council), to whom they represented, 'with much grief,' * that the imprisonment of Baudichon de la Maisonneuve was an infringement of the privileges of the fairs; and that many merchants had to receive from him certain sums which it was impossible for him to pay now, because he could not collect the money which other merchants owed him. 'We pray you, therefore,' they said, in conclusion, 'not to suffer our privileges to be violated.'—'Release my brother, *à pur et à plein*, without reserve,' added Thomas de la Maisonneuve. Four of the consuls seconded the remonstrance.† The municipality resolved that Jean de la Bessie, procurator-general of Lyons, and one councillor should demand Baudichon's liberation of the inquisitional court. 'My brother,' said Thomas, 'is a burgess of Berne and of Friburg, and by virtue of the treaties between the king and the lords of the League, he cannot be made a prisoner in this kingdom.' ‡ The priests were determined to pay no regard to the request of the magistrates: a serious incident roused them from their listlessness.

A despatch had just arrived, addressed to Monseigneur the king's lieutenant-general: it was from the lords of Berne. The lieutenant-general knew well the value of Swiss intervention. Had not four hundred of them, at the battle of Sesia, after Bayard's death, checked, by their impetuosity and the sacrifice

---

* 'Fort dolosés.'—MS. du procès inquisitionnel, pp. 52, 53.

† Henri Guyot, Benoît Rochefort, Pierre Manicier, and Simon Penet. MS. du procès inquisitionnel.

‡ Ibid. pp. 47–50.

of their lives, the army of the allies? Monseigneur du Peyrat determined, therefore, to support the prayer of the Bernese, and gave the city secretary the necessary instructions. The effect of the despatch was still greater upon Thomas de la Maisonneuve. Now there could be no more delays! Impatient to see his brother at liberty, imagining that he would succeed better by hurrying the affair, he would not wait a day or an hour. He should have considered that haste increases the chances of failure, and that the impatient man compromises both his character and his cause; but he could see nothing but Baudichon's sufferings and the injury done to the Genevese reformation by his captivity. He was no longer master of himself: he wanted that very instant to deliver his brother from the jaws of the lion. 'Set him free immediately,' he said, 'so that we may be able to answer the lords of Berne by the courier who is ready to return.' The vicars-general answered curtly: 'We are in course to order it, as is right.' * This cold formula appeared of evil omen to Thomas, and from that hour his fears increased.

On the other hand, Baudichon, informed of what was going on, took courage; and the judges, fully aware that it would not do to condemn on suspicious evidence a man who had such powerful supporters, determined to entice Maisonneuve craftily into some heretical declaration.

On the 5th of May the sergeants once more brought in their prisoner. 'What are your opinions in regard to faith?' asked the court. De la Maisonneuve answered: 'I am a good Christian; if you do not think

---

* MS. du procès inquisitionnel, pp. 59–61.

so, deliver me over to my superiors (the magistrates
of Geneva) to examine me.'   But instead of doing so,
the vicars-general tried to induce him to explain his
ideas on the subject of transubstantiation, feeling sure
of catching him in an error. The prisoner only replied:
'I am not bound to answer you.'   The court tried in
vain to induce him to speak: 'I will not make any
reply,' he repeated.   They read to him Janin's answer on the sacrament, which was (it would appear)
very shocking to Roman ears, and asked him what he
thought of it; but Baudichon did not fall into the
snare. 'I am no judge,' he said, 'and it is not my
business to decide whether the answer is good or
bad.'*   Then taking the offensive, he added : 'If
Frenchmen were imprisoned at Geneva for cases ana-
logous to mine, would you be pleased?'—'You have
Pharellus and other Frenchmen there,' answered the
judges, 'and have not surrendered them to the king.'
The officials of Lyons complained to the man whom
they kept in prison because people were left at liberty
in Geneva.   Baudichon retorted proudly: 'Ours is a
free city,' and withdrew.†   'They set their traps in
vain,' said a reformer, speaking of the attacks of the
papacy.   'God has victories abundantly in his hands
to triumph over them and their chief.' ‡

The judges were greatly embarrassed : they desired, not to release Maisonneuve, but (as he had
often been told) to burn him; and yet, as it was
impossible for them not to reply, at least by some
formalities, to such high and mighty lords as Messieurs of Berne, they gave a certain solemnity to their

* MS. du procès inquisitionnel, pp. 62-65.
† Ibid. pp. 66, 67.   ‡ Calvin.

answer. On Wednesday, the 6th of May, the officials, vicars-episcopal, inquisitors, and other ecclesiastical dignitaries, took their seats in front of the main door of the archiepiscopal palace. In public and in the open air they were about to hear the demand of the Swiss, supported by the lieutenant-general of the king. The city clerk, delegated by the councillors of Lyons, set forth the contents of the letters from Berne, and at the same time Thomas de la Maison-neuve presented two substantial merchants of the city as bail for his brother.* The cause of the Gene-vese prisoner was growing in importance: a sovereign state, which the king had every reason to treat cour-teously, had taken up his defence ; the trial was be-coming an international matter. The court knew that Francis I. was susceptible, and that it was dangerous to thwart him, as he had shown in the case of Beda. After full examination, therefore, they decreed that they 'would amply inform the king *our sire*, in order that he may make known his good pleasure, and until his answer arrives, the said Baudichon shall not be liberated; at the same time, he shall be permitted, on account of his business, to speak with those who have dealings with him, in the presence of the gaolers of the archiepiscopal prison, who are enjoined to treat him well and discreetly, according to his station.'†

Two points were gained : Baudichon was to be treated like a prisoner of mark, and his case was to be laid before the king. The memory of the *estrapades* of Paris was too recent for the evangelicals to enter-

* Thomas Javellot and Loys de la Croix. MS. du procès inquisi-tionnel, p. 72.
† MS. du procès inquisitionnel, pp. 69-76.

tain very lively hopes: it was, however, a gleam of
light.   The judges themselves, feeling that the matter
was becoming difficult and success doubtful, undertook to obtain a recantation from Baudichon, which
would, besides, be more glorious for Rome (they
thought) than a sentence of death.   On the 21st of
May, therefore, the court having called to their aid
two inquisitors skilful in controversy, Nicholas
Morini and Jean Rapinati, summoned Maisonneuve
before them; when Father Morini endeavoured to
prove to him out of Scripture the material presence
of Christ in the Sacrament.   Baudichon understood
the passages quoted differently from the doctors.
Refusing to stop at the material substance, the flesh
(as they did, and also the people of Capernaum who
are blamed in the Gospel), he held to our Saviour's
words: *It is the spirit that quickeneth; the flesh pro-
fiteth nothing : the words that I speak unto you, they
are spirit, and they are life.**—'I understand these
words as well as you, and better, but I will not enter
into any discussion.   I am not bound to answer inquisitors.' †   The court, provoked by these refusals,
resolved to put the grand question to him: 'Do you
yield obedience to our holy father the pope of
Rome?'   To the great disappointment of the vicars-
general and inquisitors, he simply replied: 'I am not
bound to answer.'—'We are your judges in this
matter,' they exclaimed with irritation; 'we order
and summon you to answer.'‡   But he would not;
and then, recovering from their emotion, they tried
to surprise him by an insidious question.

* St. John vi. 63.
† MS. du procès inquisitionnel, pp. 91–94.
‡ Ibid. pp. 95-96.

Alexander, who had preached the Gospel at Lyons with such energy, had just been thrown into prison. If De la Maisonneuve acknowledged him for his friend, they might easily class them together. The judges therefore asked him insidiously, 'whether Jacques de la Croix, *alias* Alexander, had not in former times eaten and drunk at his house?'—'If he has eaten and drunk at my house,' responded Baudichon, 'I hope it did him good.' And that was all. It was impossible to make the prisoner fall into the trap: his good sense foiled all the plots of his adversaries.

Thus did the judges hunt down an innocent man. At that time men set themselves up between God and the soul of man. This was not only an outrage upon human liberty, it was high-treason against Heaven. Such a grave consideration imparts a tragic interest to this trial, and encourages us conscientiously to reproduce all its painful phases. The judge has no concern with the relations of the soul with its Creator. 'The dominion of man ends where that of God begins.' * God does not give his glory to another. Whoever desires to exercise authority over the conscience is a madman; nay, more, he is an atheist. He presumes to move God from his throne and sit in his place.

* Said by Napoleon I. to a deputation from the Consistory of Geneva.

CHAPTER X.

THE TWO WORSHIPS IN GENEVA.

(MAY TO JULY 1534.)

WHILE they were prosecuting Maisonneuve on the banks of the Rhone and the Saône, the struggle between catholicism and reform became more active on the shores of Lake Leman: an evangelical was threatened with death at Lyons, but Roman-catholicism was on the point of expiring at Geneva. It was crumbling away beneath its own weight: the religious orders, and especially the Franciscans, which had been founded to support it, were now shaking its foundations. Notorious abuses and scandalous disorders were making the protest against monkery and popery more necessary every day. At the very moment when the trial was beginning at Lyons (3rd of May), an honourable lady of Geneva, Madame Jaquemette Matonnier, passing near the Franciscan convent, observed a woman noted for her disorderly life stealthily entering the building. 'It would be better for you,' she said, 'to stay with your husband.' At these words, two monks who were standing at the door rushed violently upon Madame Matonnier and beat her until the blood came. This incident, which soon became known, aroused the whole city. The syndics went to the convent, shut up the

two monks in the prison, and took away the key.
' Men who live in convents,' said the people, ' ought
not to be stained with such depravity; and yet it is
hard to find one monastery out of ten that is not a
den of wantonness rather than the home of chastity.'

Sin begat death. The Romish clergy destroyed
themselves by the abominable manners of a great
number of their members. But better times were
beginning: morality was springing, in company with
faith, from the tomb in which they had been buried
so long, and were spreading through Christendom the
potent germs of a new life. A sad spectacle was that
presented by the Church at the beginning of the sixteenth century! There were magnificent cathedrals,
wealthy pontiffs, sumptuous rites, admirable paintings, and harmonious chants; but in the midst of all
these pomps yawned an immense void: faith and life
were wanting. Religion was at that time like those
winter trees whose frost-covered branches glitter with
a certain brightness under the rays of the sun, but
are all frozen. A new season was beginning, which,
by bringing back the sap into their sterile branches,
would cover them with rich foliage and make them
produce savoury fruit. We do not say, as an eminent Christian has said, that the reaction of morality
against formalism is the great fact of the Reformation, its glory and its appropriate title. Such an
assertion omits one essential element. The grand
title of the Reformation is to have restored to Christendom religion in its entirety, the truth with the
life, doctrine with morality. If one had been wanting, the other would not have sufficed, and the Reformation would not have existed.

While Roman-catholicism was falling lower through
the disorders of the monks, evangelical Christianity
was rising through the zeal of the reformers.   Farel,
Viret, and Froment preached every day, either publicly or in private houses, 'to the great advancement of the Word of God, which increased much.'   The
Reformation was no longer a mere teaching; it entered into the manners and worship, and produced
life.   On the Sunday after Easter, Farel gave his
blessing to the first evangelical marriage.

When sincere catholics, and even those who were
not so, saw these strange contrasts, they imagined
that the last hour of the papacy in Geneva had arrived.   A final effort must be made, but unfortunately
the remedies employed were not much better than the
disease.   One day a report spread instantaneously
through the whole city that the Blessed Virgin, ar-
rayed in white robes, had appeared to the curate in
the church of St. Leger, and ordered a grand procession of all the surrounding districts.   She added that
if this were done, 'the Lutherans would all burst in
the middle; but if the order was not obeyed, the city
would be swallowed up.' *   The huguenots smiled,
enquired into the matter, and at the end of authentic
investigations, discovered 'that the fine lady was the
curate's housemaid.'   But many catholics in Geneva,
and almost all in Savoy, were convinced of the
reality of the apparition.   The clergy mustered their
forces.   'It depends upon you,' they said in many
places, 'to put all the heretics in Geneva to death.'
The devotees of the neighbouring parishes began

---

* 'Les luthériens crêveraient par le milieu . . . la ville s'abymerait.'—
Froment, Gestes de Genève, pp. 92, 93.

to stir in this pious work, and on the 15th of May a long procession of men, women, and children arrived before the city. They were heard singing lustily in the Savoyard tongue—

Mare de Dy, pryy pou nous!
(Mother of God, pray for us!)

The Council, fearing a disturbance, would not let them enter, and they had to be content with going to Our Lady of Grace, near the Arve bridge. As the poor people had eaten nothing on the road, and were exhausted, the syndics sent them bread; and after taking some refreshments, the assemblage turned homewards. Many Genevese, anxious to see them close, went out of the city, and collected on their road, and as the Savoyards passed before them singing *Mare de Dy, pryy pou nous!* the bantering huguenots answered to the same tune: *Frare Farel, pregy toujours!* Brother Farel, preach for ever! *

All was not over: the story of the apparition of the Virgin and of her commandment having reached as far as the capital of the Chablais, the heights of Cologny were soon crowned by a numerous and compact procession, in appearance more formidable than the first: it was the men of Thonon and the adjoining places, who, carrying banners, crosses, and relics, were descending the hill with a firm step. The stalwart pilgrims boldly passed the gates of the city, the huguenots, who were listening to Farel, not being there to prevent them; and on reaching the Bourg de Four, halted before the church of St. Claire. The alarm spread immediately: some citizens en-

* Registre du Conseil du 15 Mai 1534. Froment, *Gestes de Genève.*

tering the auditory where Farel was preaching, announced this Romish invasion.   The reformer did
not disturb himself; but some of his hearers, the
fiery Perrin, the energetic Goulaz, and others, went
out, and, charging the head of the procession, drove
back at the point of the sword the Savoyards who
had entered Geneva as if it were a village of the Chablais. The startled pilgrims threw away their banners
with affright, and fled from the city.   Froment sup-
poses that as the enemy from within had not had
time to join with those from without, the plot had
failed; but we rather believe that these devout pilgrims
calculated only on their litanies in their war against
the Lutherans.   Those processions, those banners of
the Virgin, those paltry relies, inspired the reformed
with a still deeper disgust for Roman-catholicism:
even the pomps of St. Pierre's touched them little
more than the fetichism of the Savoyards. They were
beginning to understand that public worship ought
not to be a spectacle, and that to burden the Church
with a multitude of rites is to rob her of the presence
of Christ.

The audacity displayed by these catholic bands emboldened some of the huguenots. If Savoyards came
to strengthen their faith in Geneva, ought they to hesitate to show theirs?   Some hot-headed members of
the Reform permitted themselves to be carried away
to the committal of reprehensible acts. Whenever
they went to the Franciscan cloister, the first object
that struck their eyes was the image of St. Anthony
of Padua, a miracle-monger of the thirteenth century,
having eight other saints on each side of it.   These
pious figures, ranged over the convent gate, irritated

the huguenots. It was vain to tell them that pictures are *the books of the ignorant*: the reformers answered that if the catholic prelates left the duty of teaching the people to *idols*, they would prefer remaining at home in their chairs. 'If you had not taken the Bible from the Church,' said the huguenots, 'you would have had no necessity to hang up your paintings.' Accordingly, between eleven and twelve o'clock one Saturday night, nine men carrying a ladder approached the convent, raised it silently against the porch, and then, with hammers and chisels, began to destroy the images. They cut off the head and limbs of the saint, leaving only his trunk; they did the same to the others, and threw the fragments into the well of St. Claire. The night passed without any disturbance, but in the morning there was a great uproar in the city. 'What a piteous sight!' said the devout assembled before the porch of St. Francis. The iconoclasts, who were discovered after a little time, were punished, but the images were not restored.

'Alas!' said the Friburgers, 'Geneva is about to pull down the altars of the Romish faith!'—'It is,' answered the Bernese, 'because upon these very altars the bishop desired to burn the venerable charters of her people, and has sprinkled them with the blood of her most illustrious citizens.' * . . . Sensuous worship no longer pleased the Genevans. Those laboured pictures, those sculptured angels, those dazzling decorations, that charm of ceremonies and edi-

* Registre du Conseil des 4, 11, 13, 30 Avril; 5, 14, 15, 17, 24, 26 Mai, and 12 Juin. Sœur Jeanne, *Levain du Calvinisme*, p. 89. MS. de Berne, *Hist. Helv.*, v. 12. Froment, *Gestes de Genève*, pp. 119, 120.

fices, those shafts and pediments, those unintelligible chants, those intoxicating perfumes, those mechanical performances of the priests, with their gold and lace— all these things disgusted them exceedingly. Since God is a spirit, they said, those who worship him must worship him in spirit, by the inward faith of the heart, by purity of conscience, and by offering themselves to God to do his will.

The hour had come when this spiritual worship was to be really celebrated in Geneva: the Feast of Pentecost had arrived. On that day a large crowd had assembled in the Great Auditory. It was not only such as Vandel, Chautemps, Roset, Levet, with their wives and friends, who resorted thither, but new hearers were added to the old ones. Farel preached with fervour. He was accustomed to say that 'God sends rain upon one city when he pleases, while another city has not a single drop;' and therefore he conjured 'all hearts thirsting with desire for the preaching of the Gospel' * to pray that the Spirit might be given them. We have not his Whitsunday sermon, he preached extempore; but we know that he ended it by giving glory *to the Father, Son, and Holy Ghost, the only true God,* and that his discourse bore good fruit. Several circumstances had prepared his audience. The plot of the bishop and the duke which God had frustrated, the nomination of the huguenot syndics, the rupture with Friburg, Maisonneuve's imprisonment—all these events had stirred their hearts, had cleft them as the ploughshare cleaves the

---

* Farel's words. See p. 242 of the volume recently published in commemoration of the tercentenary of his death (*Du vrai usage de la croix de Jésus-Christ,* Neuchâtel, 1865).

earth, and opened them to the seed from heaven. What now shone before the eyes of those who filled the Grand Auditory ' were not the petty flames of human candles, but Christ, the great sun of righteousness, as if at noonday.'* While the priests were chanting words that sounded only in the air, the voice of the reformer had penetrated to the very bottom of men's hearts. The proof was soon visible.

When the sermon was over, Farel prepared to celebrate the Lord's Supper publicly, according to the Gospel form, and standing with his brethren Viret and Froment before a table, he gave thanks, took the bread, broke it, and said: ' *Take, eat;*' and then, lifting up the cup, he added: ' *This is the blood of the New Testament, which is shed for the remission of sins.*' The believers were beginning to draw near to receive the communion of the Lord,† when an unexpected circumstance fixed their attention. A priest of noble stature, wearing his sacerdotal robes, left the place where he had been sitting among the congregation, and approached the table. It was Louis Bernard, one of the twelve *habilités* of the cathedral, possessor of a wealthy benefice, and brother of him who had been touched at the time of Farel's first preaching. Was he going to say mass? did he want to dispute with Farel? or had he been converted? All were anxious to see what would happen. The priest went up to the table, and then, to the general surprise, he took off his sacerdotal vestments, flung away cope, alb, and stole, and said aloud: ' I throw off the old

---

* *Du vrai usage*, &c.

† 'Gebennis hac Pentacoste cum innumeri cœnam peragerent dominicam.'—Haller to Bullinger, 4th June, 1534. MS. Arch. Eccl. Tigur.

man, and declare myself a prisoner to the Gospel of
the Lord.'*   Then turning to the reformers and
their friends, he said: 'Brethren, I will live and die
with you for Jesus Christ's sake.'   All imagined they
say a miracle; † their hearts were touched.   Farel received Bernard like a brother; he broke bread with
him, gave him the cup, and eating of the same morsel,
the two adversaries thus signified that they would in
future love one another 'with a sincere and pure
affection.'   The priest was not the only person who
threw off the foul robes of his ancient life and put on
the white robe of the Lord.   Many Genevans from
that day began to think and live differently from
their fathers; but Louis Bernard was a striking type
of that transformation, and the crowd, as they quitted
the church, could not keep their eyes off him.   They
saw him returning full of peace and joy to his father's
house, wearing a Spanish cape instead of the usual
priest's hood.   All the evangelicals, 'men, women,
and children, went with great joy to greet him and
make their reverence.' ‡

Another circumstance, quite as extraordinary, still
further increased the beauty of this festival.   During
the rejoicings of that first evangelical Pentecost, a
knight of Rhodes came to Geneva in search of liberty
of faith.   A knight of Rhodes was a strange visitor
in that city.   It was known confusedly that those
warlike monks, instituted to defend the pilgrims in

* 'Veterem hominem exuens et se Evangelii captivum exhibens.'—
Haller, ibid.

† 'Est in miraculum.'—Haller to Bullinger, 4th June, 1534. MS.
Eccl. Tigur.

‡ The Spanish cape was a cloak with a hood, in common use at that
time.—La Sœur Jeanne, Levain du Calvinisme, p. 89.

the Holy Land, had been expelled from Jerusalem by
Soliman, and had finally settled in Malta! But why
should this one come to Geneva? The ex-knight,
whose name was Pierre Gaudet, related how, being
born at St. Cloud, near Paris, he had heard the
Gospel, and that having chosen for his glory the
cross of the Son of God, he held the world in contempt. The scandal he had thus occasioned had
forced him to flee. Having an uncle living about
a league from Geneva—the commander of Com-
pesières—he had taken refuge with him; but feeling
the need of Christian communion, he had come to his
brethren that he might enjoy it. The huguenots
received him like a friend. That city which had seen
in Berthelier and Lévrier the martyrs of liberty, was
to have in Gaudet the first martyr of the Gospel.*

While the Word of God was forming new manners,
the contrast of the old manners asserted itself more
boldly. The people of the lower classes—men and
women, youths and maidens—danced, according to
custom, in the public square on the evening of Whit-
sunday. The *tabarins* played their music in the
streets, and merry-andrews made the people laugh.
The women of St. Gervais, disguised and carrying
bunches of box, set the example to those of the other
quarters. The young men united with them, and the
joyous troops paraded the streets in long files, singing, capering, and sometimes attacking the passers-
by. George Marchand, a huguenot no doubt, who
was very ready with his hands, being caught hold of
by a woman who wanted to make him dance with her,
gave her a slap on the face. There was a fierce dis-

* Registre du Conseil du 29 Juin 1535. Crespin, *Martyrologue*, p. 114.

turbance; and the Council consequently forbade these
dancing promenades, and ordered that every one
should be content 'to dance before his own house:'
and this was surely enough. From that time such
idle processions were not repeated. While the
catholic common people were indulging in wanton
sports, not perceiving that they were dancing round
the open grave of Roman-catholicism, the evangelicals
increased in zeal and faith to extend the teaching of
the Word of God; and a gentler and more Christian
life was about to be naturalised in that small but
important city. The Whitsuntide procession of 1534,
with its coarse jests, was, in Geneva, the funeral procession of popery.*

Indeed, the laity were then learning better things
than those which the monks had taught them. It
was not the ministers alone who laboured: simple
believers practised the ministry of charity. If there
chanced to be in any house a man 'very rebellious,'
opposing the doctrine of Scripture, his friends, neighbours, and relations, who had tasted of its excellence,
would go to him, and without offending him, without
returning him evil for evil, 'admonish him with
great mildness.' The evangelicals invited certain of
their friends, even strangers and enemies, to their
houses to eat and drink, in order that they might
speak more familiarly with them. All their study
was 'to gain some one to the Word.'†

In the neighbouring countries, in Savoy, Gex,
Vaud, and the Chablais, not only did the enemies of
Geneva use threats, but made preparations to attack

---

* Registre du Conseil des 31 Mai et 2 Juin 1534.

† 'Gaigner quelqu'un à la Parolle.'—Froment, Gestes de Genève, p. 127.

it.   There was much talk in the city of the assaults that were to be made by the *forains*, the aliens ; and accordingly there was always a number of citizens kept under arms.   Farel, Viret, and Froment often joined these soldiers of the republic during their night-watches, and, sitting near the gates of the city or on the ramparts, by the glare of the bivouac fires or the torches, they would converse together about the truth, questioning and answering one another.   ' Each man familiarly and freely objected and replied to what the preacher said ; ' and sometimes before they left their posts, the citizens were resolved in heart upon religious points about which they had hitherto been in doubt.   Not without reason are these ' conversations of the bivouac ' recorded here.   In later times, one of the evangelists of Geneva, calling to mind the nocturnal meetings he had held at the military posts, exclaimed : ' At these assemblies and watches more people have been won to the Gospel than by public preaching.' *

* Froment, *Gestes de Genève*, pp. 126, 127.

CHAPTER XI.

BOLDNESS OF TWO HUGUENOTS IN PRISON AND BEFORE
THE COURT OF LYONS.

(MAY TO JUNE, 1534.)

IN the midst of these dangers and struggles the
Huguenots were not to be consoled for the imprisonment of Maisonneuve. So long as the intrepid
captain of the Lutherans was threatened with extreme
punishment, the triumph of the evangelicals could not
be complete. They feared generally a fatal termination,
for Baudichon and Janin, far from yielding anything
to their adversaries, were boldly spreading the knowledge of the Gospel in their prison. Janin was as
much at his ease as if he had been in the streets of
Geneva: at the gaoler's table, in the halls and galleries and elsewhere, the armourer argued about the
faith. One day, meeting Jacques Desvaux, a priest of
the diocese of Le Mans, Janin took him to task and
tried to convert him to the Gospel. He spoke to him
of the Apostles and the saints, and showed him how
they had always taught doctrines opposed to those of
Rome. He did more. A garden was attached to the
prison, and the prisoners were allowed to walk in it
at certain hours. One day, shortly before the festival
of the Rogations, Janin went into it, taking a French

Testament with him, and began to read it. When
he had done he left the book, not unintentionally, on
a low wall, and went away. A priest named Delay
(there was no lack of ecclesiastics in the archiepiscopal prison) passing near, observed the book, took it
up, and, opening it, read: *The New Testament.* A
Testament in French! Delay began to examine it:
a number of prisoners, priests and others, gathered
round him; he turned over the pages in search of the
First Epistle of St. John, 'because on that day the
Church mentioned it,' but could not find it.*

From the place in the garden to which he had retired, Janin saw Delay looking for something. Going
up to him, the Genevese asked what he wanted. On
being told, he took the book, immediately found the
epistle (those laymen of Geneva knew their Bible
better than the priests), and began to read the first
chapter aloud, dwelling upon the words: *The blood
of Jesus Christ his Son cleanseth us from all sin.*
He stopped, and addressing the prisoners, explained
the words, and drew their attention to two doctrines
which, he said, can never be made to harmonize:
that of the Bible, according to which we are cleansed
by the blood of Christ; and that of Rome, according
to which we are cleansed by meritorious works.
'You explain the passage wrongly,' exclaimed
some of his hearers: 'we must not follow the letter,
but the moral meaning.' It is an argument we have
seen revived in more recent times. 'You cannot
understand that epistle,' said a priest, 'since you are
obliged to read it in French.'—'Surely I must read

* MS. du procès inquisitionnel de Lyon. Déposition Desvaux, pp.
99, 100; Déposition Delay, pp. 112, 113.

it in my own language,' answered Janin, ' for I do not understand Latin. God commanded his Apostles to preach the Gospel to all creatures, and therefore in all languages.'—' That is true,' answered the priests: '*prædicate Evangelium omni creaturæ*; but it is also true that all good Christians draw near our mother, the Holy Church, to hear Scripture explained by the mouths of priests and doctors who, in this world, hold the place of the Apostles.' Janin, who, though honouring the special ministry of the Word, firmly believed in the universal priesthood taught by St. Peter,[*] exclaimed boldly: ' I am just as much a priest as any man, and can give absolution. God has made us all priests. I can pronounce the sacramental words, like the other priests.' And, if we are to believe his accusers, he added: ' You may even utter them in the house, in the kitchen.' He then began to repeat aloud: *Hoc est corpus meum*.[†] Janin was one of those daring spirits who imagine that the more they startle their hearers, the more good they do. Still, the ministers, Farel and Viret, had no warmer friend.

The prisoners who listened to him, wishing, perhaps, to prolong a discussion that amused them, started the huguenot again. ' The Virgin Mary,' began one. Janin, interrupting him, said: ' The Virgin Mary was the noblest woman that ever existed in the world, inasmuch as she bore in her bosom Him who has washed us from our sins. But we must not pray to her or to the saints in paradise.'—' And prayers for the dead,' suggested another.—' There is no need of

---

[*] 1 St. Peter ii. 9.

[†] MS. du procès inquisitionnel de Lyon. Déposition Desvaux, pp. 100-103; Déposition Delay, pp. 114, 115, 124.

them,' said the armourer, 'for as soon as we are dead, we are saved or condemned for everlasting, and there is no purgatory.'*

On Monday, the 11th of May, the festival of the Rogations afforded the prisoners a spectacle calculated to break the uniformity of their lives. They proceeded to the garden, and presently a noisy crowd gave indications of the grand procession, which was now returning to St. John's church, adjoining the archiepiscopal prison, whence it had started. The priests went first, with crosses and banners, reciting prayers or singing hymns; after them came the people. De la Maisonneuve and Janin said that such a ceremony was an abuse, and that it would have been far better to have given to the poor the money which those fine banners had cost. The procession having at last re-entered the church of St. John, the singing, shouting, and noise became insupportable, even in the garden. Baudichon, according to the evidence of one of his accusers, withdrew, saying: 'Those people must be fools and madmen, or do they imagine that God is deaf?'†

The next day the festival continued, and just as the prisoners were going to dinner, the noise of singing was heard. It was a new procession. 'Where do they come from?' asked Maisonneuve. The gaoler's wife answered: 'From the church of St. Cler.' 'And what have they been doing there?' said Baudichon; 'have they been looking for St. Cler? They will not find him or God either, for they are in

---

* MS. du procès inquisitionnel. Déposition Desvaux, pp. 104, 105; Déposition Delay, pp. 116, 117.

† Ibid. Déposition Desvaux, pp. 106, 107; Déposition Delay, pp. 118, 119.

paradise; and it is great nonsense to look for them elsewhere.' *

On the 28th of May, the depositions made by the prisoners with reference to the language used on the Rogation days were read. ' I would sooner be torn in pieces,' said De la Maisonneuve, ' than have uttered the words contained in that deposition.' † The Court having summoned the priest Delay before them, the latter declared that he adhered to the main points, *with the exception* of the words ascribed to Baudichon. ' He only said,' continued Delay, ' that it would have been better to give the poor the money paid for the banners. I did not hear him use the other words.' ‡

Janin, who had hitherto been the most ardent of the two prisoners, now began to grow dispirited, as is usual with such temperaments. He looked upon his condemnation to death as certain; and was quite unmanned by the thought that he would never see Geneva again. On Whitsunday, a turnkey having gone to fetch him from his dungeon to hear a mass which the other prisoners had asked for, Janin, far from refusing, did not betray the least sign of opposition during the service, but behaved himself decently, ' which he had not been accustomed to do before,' said one who was present. He quitted the chapel, dejected and silent. Just as he was about to re-enter his narrow cell, De la Maisonneuve came up : he knew the state of his friend's soul and desired to cheer him. Leaning against the door, he said to Janin, who was

---

* MS. du procès inquisitionnel. Déposition Galla, pp. 148-151; Déposition de Gynieux dit Nego, pp. 154-156.

† Ibid. p. 121.　　　　　　　　　　‡ Ibid. p. 124.

already inside: ' Do not fret yourself; be firm, and make no answer. I would sooner it cost me five hundred crowns, than that any harm should come to you or me. My lords of Berne will not suffer them to do us any mischief.' *

Janin's alarm was not, however, without foundation: false evidence multiplied. Louis Joffrillet accused De la Maisonneuve of having said to him at the door of his master's shop: ' Pshaw! if you were at Geneva I would give you a horse-load of relics for a dozen *aiguillettes. . . .* They sell relics there at the butchers' stalls.' † On hearing the unbecoming words ascribed to him, Baudichon exclaimed: ' That witness is a little brigand, a young thief; he has told a lie. I demand that he be detained, and (he added in great anger) I will have him hanged!' Manicier, Joffrillet's master, deposed that he had no recollection of such words being used by De la Maisonneuve.‡

All these depositions, De la Maisonneuve's courage, and the interest felt for him in high places, created a greater excitement every day in the second city of France. ' There was much noise in Lyons about those two Lutherans of Geneva.' § Some eagerly took their part; others, who detested them, hoped to see them burnt. But as the two protestants had powerful protectors, the clergy dared not proceed to extremities without sufficient proof. The canons of St. John sent M. de Simieux, a gentleman of

* MS. du procès inquisitionnel. Déposition de Billet, pp. 127–129; Déposition de Mochon, pp. 130, 131.

† Ibid. Déposition de Joffrillet, pp. 136, 137.

‡ ' Recors de tels propos et paroles.'—MS. du procès inquisitionnel, pp. 138–140; Déposition de Manicier, p. 144.

§ Froment, *Gestes de Genève*, p. 241.

Dauphiny, who was related to one of them, to Geneva to try and hunt up some capital charge against Baudichon. De Simieux alighted at the Hôtel de la Grue, in the Corraterie, and immediately entered into conversation with the landlord, who promised to introduce him to some worthy people, from whom he would receive accurate information about that wretched Baudichon.*

Meanwhile, the gentleman amused himself by walking up and down in front of his lodging. Presently he saw fifteen persons, ' of the most respectable of the city,' approaching, who saluted him and said: 'We have heard that you are come from Lyons; is it true that Baudichon is about to be released?' De Simieux asked the gentlemen what they thought of the prisoner. 'If he is discharged,' said one of them, 'we and all the catholics in Geneva will be totally ruined and lost. His accomplices, the Lutherans of the city, have prepared their plan, and the only thing they are waiting for, before putting it into execution, is Baudichon's release.' ' Yes, yes,' said all the fifteen, ' we are sure of it.' †

De Simieux asked them to specify some overt act. ' On Corpus Christi day,' said one, 'as the procession was passing Baudichon's house, his wife was at the window with her maid, and both were spinning with their distaffs. When Madame de la Maisonneuve saw the priests marching before her *all in white*, she exclaimed: " Look what fine *goats*! " . . . as if a flock of

---

* Froment, *Gestes de Genève*. The inn of La Grue was, it would seem, the projecting corner house on the left as you go from the Rhône, before reaching the Museum.

† MS. du procès inquisitionnel, pp. 194–196.

those animals had been passing by twos before her.'*
As this remark of the wife was not sufficient to burn
the husband, De Simieux asked for something more.
'It is notorious,' they told him, 'that Baudichon is
the person most employed in seducing the city of
Geneva to the Lutheran heresies; that it was he who
caused the preachers to come; and that, if he is liberated, everybody will go over to his faith.' †

While this conversation was going on in a narrow
street, an official interview of far greater importance
was taking place not far off. Two ambassadors from
the king of France had just arrived at Geneva, and
the syndics who waited upon them declared they
thought it very strange that messieurs of Lyons should
presume to give them the law. The ambassadors
promised to speak to the king on the subject.‡

Meantime, matters were looking worse at Lyons.
On Thursday, the 18th of June, Florimond Pécoud,
the merchant, seasoned his deposition with some
piquant expressions which he falsely ascribed to
Baudichon. 'Telling him one day that I had just
come from mass,' said Pécoud, 'Baudichon made the
remark: "And what did you see there? . . . a slice
of turnip. . . . nothing more." '§ At these words the
prisoner rose indignantly, and said to the judges:
'I will not make any reply, I have made too many
already,' and proceeded to leave the hall. 'We order
you to stay,' said the judges; but De la Maisonneuve
would not stop. 'Positively,' said the judges, looking at

* MS. du procès inquisitionnel, pp. 197, 198.
† Ibid. pp. 198-200.
‡ Registres du Conseil du 10 Juin 1534.
§ Maisonneuve compared the host to a slice of turnip—one of the
commonest of things.—MS. du procès inquisitionnel, p. 162.

each other, ' he flees our presence.' To the gaoler
who was sent after him to bid him return, he answered haughtily: 'I am not disposed at present;
let them wait until after dinner.' Baudichon reappeared in the afternoon, but his anger had not
cooled down. ' I· know that Pécoud,' he said; ' he
has cheated the merchants, he has been a bankrupt,
and his wife and he live by the debauchery of others.
I guarantee to prove what I say.'

The next day there was a scene quite as lively.
Maisonneuve having contradicted a witness: ' I command you to sit in the dock,' said the president.
' I will not sit in the dock,' answered the citizen of
Geneva, 'I have sat there too long.' This was too
much for the judges. The procurator-fiscal ordered
Baudichon to be taken away and put in solitary confinement: no one was to speak to him. The prisoner
was accordingly removed and locked up.*

The Court immediately increased the number of
witnesses for the prosecution: it is useless to name
them. De la Maisonneuve, more indignant than ever,
thought it enough to say: ' They are false witnesses,
tutored to procure my death.'†

Such was indeed the intention of the Court, and,
considering the power of the ecclesiastical tribunals,
it seemed impossible they should fail to attain their
end. De la Maisonneuve was not prepared to die.
His knowledge of the Gospel had stripped death of its
terrors in his eyes, but the work of his life was not
terminated: the reformation of Geneva was not accomplished, there was still many a tough contest to be

* MS. du procès inquisitionnel, pp. 189–191.
† Ibid. pp. 222–238.

fought for liberty.   A man of resolution was wanted at Geneva—a man to launch the bark with energy towards the happy shores it was to reach.   That man was De la Maisonneuve.

On the 1st of July, seeing the eagerness of his adversaries, he petitioned the Court to grant him an advocate.   The judges would not consent: the prosecution was difficult enough already.   'The case does not require it,' said the procurator-fiscal, 'the accused must answer by his own mouth.   The said Baudichon is not an ignorant man; he is prudent and *astute* enough in his business.' *

De la Maisonneuve could indeed speak freely in the uprightness of his heart; but a formal defence alarmed him.   Anticipating, however, the unjust refusal of his judges, he had resolved to protest against it.   Producing certain papers, he said, as he pointed to them: 'This document was written by my own hand; I desire that it be inserted among the minutes of the trial, and propose to read it word for word.'   He was permitted to do so; upon which Baudichon, standing before his judges with the paper in his hand, reminded them of the fact of his unjust imprisonment, which had already lasted three months; contended that his judges had no authority to take cognizance of anything he had done out of the kingdom, and added: 'I call upon you to do me speedy justice; if you refuse, I will prosecute each one of you, and force you to make compensation and reparation for the injuries I have suffered. . . . I appeal to his Majesty.' †

---

* MS. du procès inquisitionnel, p. 246.
† Ibid. pp. 247–250.

The vicars-general could not believe their ears. What impudence ! The accused presumes to attack the members of the Court, and his judges are to be put on their defence. Are they not the representatives of the Church? 'You have no cause to complain of your long detention,' they said. 'It proceeds solely from your having refused to answer us. We cannot send you before the syndics of Geneva, because, as laymen, they have no cognizance of such matters. Besides, the king understands that you demur concerning the offences committed by you in the kingdom of France.' Then pressing him with questions, they said: 'Are you a Christian? What is your faith? Do you believe in the holy catholic Church? Do you obey our holy father the pope? We are judges of your faith, and we require you to answer, under pain of excommunication and other lawful penalties.' 'I will not answer,' returned Maisonneuve, quite as determined as they, 'and I appeal from your order to every court in the kingdom.' After this answer, Baudichon, in the eyes of the Court, was nothing but an obstinate heretic. The inquisitor, Morini, conjured him to return to the catholic faith. It was useless.*

A man who struggled with so much courage against unreasonable judges, who, in their despotism, claimed the right to forbid him to display before God the faith, homage, and obedience which his conscience imposed upon him—a man who, in the first half of the sixteenth century, bearded the inquisitors even in sight of the stake, as if his forehead had been made *of*

---

* MS. du procès inquisitionnel, pp. 251-259.

adamant, harder than flint, deserves some respect from an easier age, which is no longer called to such combats, and which perhaps would be unable to sustain them.

CHAPTER XII.

SENTENCE OF DEATH.

(JULY, 1534.)

THE judges and priests, though determined to free the Church from such a dangerous enemy by pronouncing the capital sentence upon him, resolved to make a last effort to obtain a condemnatory confession from him. The procurator-fiscal, looking at Baudichon, said: 'Considering the arrogance and temerity of the accused, considering that he is not sufficiently attainted by the witnesses, we order that he be *constrained* to answer *concerning his faith*, and to that end be put to the torture.' The noble-minded citizen was to be exposed to the horrible torments practised by the inquisitors, but there were no instructions as to the kind of torture to be employed.* De la Maisonneuve was imprisoned under the roof. Was the order of the Court carried out? That is more than we can tell; we have discovered nothing relative to his punishment; we can only find that he was treated in a harsh and cruel manner. Appearing before the Court on the 13th of July, he complained

---

* MS. du procès inquisitionnel, pp. 260–262.

strongly of the indignities to which he had been exposed. 'They have behaved tyrannously to me,' he said, 'and shown me much rudeness and cruelty.' The judges answered that he had no grounds of complaint, and that if he wished any favour he had only to answer concerning his faith. 'If I were to remain here a prisoner all my life,' said Baudichon, 'I would never answer you, for you are not my judges.'*

The Court then resolved to try if they could not obtain from him some semi-catholic formula which would authorise them to publish his recantation, or, in default of that, some very heretical declaration which would justify their burning him. A few words uttered with the lips were enough for certain judges to give life or death. Evangelical Christianity prescribes an opposite way; words will not satisfy it: truth must penetrate into the depths of the heart and abide there by means of a thorough assimilation which transforms man to the image of God. But, above all, it protests against constraint; and to those officials, those inquisitors who imagine they are helping the cause of truth, it exclaims: 'Leave to God what belongs to God!' This was Maisonneuve's opinion.

The Court and the canons of St. John having failed to obtain any confession from Baudichon, resolved to call a witness before them who, they thought, must crush him. At their request, the bishop of Geneva, who was then at Chambéry, desired father Coutelier, superior of the Franciscan convent, to proceed to Lyons and give evidence against the prisoner. On the 18th of July the monk appeared before the

* MS. du procès inquisitionnel, pp. 303, 304.

Court, and declared that 'he had preached daily at
Geneva all through Lent, doing the best he could;
that he had known Baudichon, notoriously reputed as
a favourer of the Lutheran sect, and one Farellus, a
very bad man, who preached that heresy, and others
more execrable still, of which he was the inventor;
that one day, being unable to obtain a license for
Farellus to preach, Baudichon came up with his
accomplices; that, in the presence of a very great
multitude of people, he declared he would have
Farellus preach; that thereupon some of his party
went and rang the bell three different times, and that
in the same monastery where he, Coutelier, had
preached in the morning, the said Farellus preached
publicly, according to his accursed doctrine, which he
continued to do all through Lent, wearing a secular
dress.' Then, speaking of the visit made him by
Maisonneuve and Farel, the father superior continued: 'They asserted that the pope is the beast of
the apocalypse, and that the holy see is not apostolical but diabolical; . . . and Baudichon was so transported with rage and anger, that he would have set
the monastery on fire.' *

De la Maisonneuve was then brought in. The two
great adversaries met face to face and kept their eyes
fixed on each other. The energetic huguenot, speaking
with calmness, almost with disdain, said: 'I know
that witness; he is a bad man. . . . He preached
several heresies at Geneva, and excited much disturbance among the people.'—'Heresies!' exclaimed the
astonished judges. 'What heresies?' An heretical
father superior! that was strange indeed!—'If I was

* MS. du procès inquisitionnel, pp. 324–327.

at Geneva,' answered the accused, 'I would tell you, but here I shall say no more.'*

At the same time the crafty monk had with him a weapon which, he thought, must infallibly procure Baudichon's death. Pierre de la Baume, in his quality of bishop and prince, had given him a sealed letter addressed to the judges, praying them to send the culprit to him, or at least to treat him with all the rigour of justice. Coutelier handed it to the Court. The bishop informed his ' good brothers and friends' that Maisonneuve had already been convicted of Lutheran heresy (this was five or six years back), that he had done penance, and promised him, his bishop, that he would not go astray again. 'Cum nemini gremium ecclesia claudat,' continued La Baume, ' as the Church shuts her bosom against no one, I was content to pardon him, but threatened him with the stake in case of relapse.' It is possible that De la Maisonneuve may formerly have had some conversation of this sort with the bishop, who took advantage of it. The law threatened very severe penalties against such as relapsed; they were not allowed a trial, and were delivered up immediately to the secular arm to be put to death. ' I beg you to transfer him to me,' continued the bishop, ' to execute justice upon him to the contentment of *God and the world,* and the maintenance of our holy faith.' But a rivalry worthy of Rome existed between the bishop of Geneva and the primate of France: each wished to have the honour of burning the Genevan.†

The struggle was natural. The affair had all the more

* MS. du procès inquisitionnel, pp. 335–338.
† Ibid. pp. 345–349.

importance in the eyes of the bishops and priests inasmuch as Maisonneuve was guilty of a blacker crime in their opinion than that of Luther and of Farel. He was a *layman*, and yet he presumed to reform the Church. The clergy believed that the intervention of the laity was the most menacing circumstance possible. A great transformation was going on: opinion was changing; as the understanding became enlightened, it condemned abuses and reformed errors. One of the evils introduced by catholicism, aggravated still further by the papacy, had been to nullify the faithful in religious matters. It was endurable that a bishop should go to war; but for a layman to have anything to say in the Church was inadmissible. This perversion of the primitive order was pointed out by the reformers: in their eyes the despotism of priests was still more revolting than the despotism of kings. A man might, they thought, give up to another man his house, his fields, his earthly existence; but to give up to him his soul, his eternal existence, . . . impossible! One of the forces of protestantism was the influence of the laity; one of the weaknesses of Roman-catholicism was their exclusion from the direction of religious interests.

The bishop of Geneva thought that, by putting that powerful layman, Maisonneuve, to death, he was dealing the Reformation a heavy blow. The officials of the archbishop-primate of France thought the same. There was no doubt what would be the fate of the proud Baudichon: it was only a question whether the flames of his funeral pile should be kindled at Lyons or Chambéry. The judges consequently asked him if he desired to be sent to Chambéry to be tried by the bishop of Geneva; and the prisoner declared that he preferred remaining in the kingdom of France. De la Baume gave way, but insisted that the Court should make haste and punish such a turbulent man. 'Chastise him,' said the bishop, 'according to the good pleasure of the king, who has shown in his letters that he is quite inclined that way. Nay more, you will do a very meritorious work before God.' The Court accordingly began their preparations for offering up the sacrifice.*

The magistrates of Geneva had not remained inactive. On the 23rd of June the syndics and council of the city wrote three letters: one to the king's lieutenant, another to the burgesses of Lyons, and a third to Diesbach and Schœner, ambassadors of Berne at the Court of Francis I., declaring they thought it 'very strange that Messieurs of Lyons should wish to give the law to Geneva.'† The vicars-general were not much alarmed: they hoped that the intervention of Francis I. would be limited to forbidding Baudichon de la Maisonneuve to be tried for acts committed in his own country. Still they judged it prudent to make haste.

The Court now resorted to its final, solemn, and triple summons.‡ 'Baudichon de la Maisonneuve,' said the president, 'we adjure you to answer concerning your faith under pain of excommunication.' The Genevan was silent. Thrice the same question was put, thrice there was the same silence. At last, when the president added: 'Are you a Christian?' he re-

---

* MS. du procès inquisitionnel, p. 338.

† Registres du Conseil des 10 et 23 Juin et 7 Juillet 1534.

‡ Friday, 17th July, 1534.

plied: ' You are not my judges, and never will be. If I were before the syndics of Geneva, I should answer so that every one would be satisfied.' He declared, however, that he was ready to enter into explanations immediately concerning any offence he was accused of committing in France; thus showing that he desired merely to maintain the rights of his people and of their magistrates. The Court would not consent: they no doubt understood that mere table-talk was not sufficient to cause a man to be burnt. Once more they refused him a counsel. ' If you can write,' they told him, ' we permit you to set down with your own hand whatever you please, and we will hear you to-morrow.' He declared he could not do it without access to the minutes of the proceedings; to which the Court answered, that the proceedings must be well known to him.*

The enquiry was over: De la Maisonneuve was returned to the care of the archbishop's procurator-general, and the next day, the 18th of July, he was taken before him. That personage rose and said : ' Baudichon de la Maisonneuve, being manifestly con- victed of the crimes and offences mentioned in the indictment, is by us pronounced heretical, a great abettor, defender, and protector of the heretics and heresies which at present swarm so greatly, and as such he is remitted to the secular arm.' †

They were in haste to finish. There was a rumour that the king would deliver the prisoner: they must, therefore, hurry on the sentence and execution. On the 28th of July the Court held its last sitting. Two

---

* MS. du procès inquisitionnel, pp. 339–343.

† MS. du procès inquisitionnel, pp. 350–354.

inquisitors were on the bench, and the final sentence was pronounced:

'Baudichon de la Maisonneuve,' said the Court, ' you have been fully convicted of having affirmed at Geneva and elsewhere many heretical propositions of the Lutheran or Œcolampadian faction;

' Of having been the chief promoter and defender of that sect;

' Of having protected the impure Farel and other persons, própagators of that perverse doctrine;

' Of having refused to answer in our presence concerning your faith;

' We therefore declare you to be heretical, and the chief fautor and defender of heresy and heretics; *

' Consequently we deliver you over as such to the secular arm.'

This was the formula employed by the ecclesiastical tribunals in pronouncing the capital sentence. De la Maisonneuve appealed to the king, to the legate, to any proper authority, and was led back to prison.

The Church, having a horror of blood, delivered Baudichon to the civil magistrates that they might take the life of that high-minded man: the captain of the Lutherans was condemned to death.† For a long while people at Geneva, Lyons, and elsewhere, had been every day expecting that he would be burnt.‡ Now there could no longer be any doubt about his fate: the sentence was lawfully pronounced. The

---

* 'Hæreticæ pravitates et hæreticorum maximum defensorem et factorem.'—The sentence is in Latin in the MS. du procès inquisitionnel, pp. 431-435.

† See the letter of Francis I. to the Council of Geneva in the archives of that city.

‡ Froment, *Gestes de Genève*, p. 242.

priests triumphed, and the evangelicals awaited a great sorrow.

Many burning piles had already been erected in France, Germany, and elsewhere, and Christians more earnest than Maisonneuve, but not freer or more courageous, had perished on them for their faith. Were the persecutors always influenced by cruelty and hatred? Were the vicars-general, the canons of St. John, the archbishop-primate of France—all of them thirsting for blood? No doubt there were malignant fanatics among them, but it would be unjust to form so severe a judgment of all. Some of them were upright and perhaps benevolent men, to whom the words uttered upon the cross might be justly applied: *Forgive them, for they know not what they do.* Atrocious as are the deeds of the persecutors in the sixteenth century, they easily admit of explanation. A religion convinced of the truth of its dogmas considers it to be its right and duty to combat the errors which destroy souls (as it believes); and, if it is allied with the civil power, makes it a virtue and a law to borrow the secular sword to purify the Church from contagion. The fault of such judges—and it is a great fault—is to put themselves in the place of God, to whom alone belongs the dominion over conscience; to forget that religion, being in its nature spiritual, has nothing to do with constraint, and can be propagated and received by moral convictions only. The sword, when religion determines to grasp it, easily becomes insensate and ruthless in her hands. *Put up thy sword into the sheath,* said Jesus to Peter; and those who call themselves Peter's successors have been always drawing it. The ground is so slippery, the gulf so near, that, besides the thousands of cases in which the Church of Rome during the sixteenth century suffered that great fall, two or three instances may be quoted in which even protestants have stumbled.

Three centuries have corrected such lamentable aberrations; we no longer erect scaffolds, but tribunals, dungeons, and exile still coerce religious convictions. What must we do to destroy for ever such evils in all their ramifications? The most effectual remedy would seem to be the separation of the spiritual and temporal power, the destruction of the links which still unite the ecclesiastical with the civil power. The doctrine which condemns those fanatical murders has long prevailed all over evangelical Christendom; at Rome, the acts are tempered, but the principles remain. Modern civilization is waiting for the time when salutary modifications between the Church and the State will take from the former, everywhere and for evermore, the possibility of again grasping the unholy sword which has poured forth such torrents of the most generous blood.

CHAPTER XIII.

THE NIGHT OF JULY THIRTY-FIRST AT GENEVA.

(JULY, 1534.)

BY imprisoning Maisonneuve, the priests had desired to check the progress of the Gospel, but it
had the contrary effect. The courage of the accused
and the injustice of the accusers increased the deter-
mination of the Genevans. The work of the Reformation was not a work without forethought; it had
been long preparing, and advanced step by step towards the goal by paths which the hand of God had
traced for it. The rich harvests which were to cover
the shores of Lake Leman and to feed so many hungry
souls, were not to spring from the earth in a day; the
soil had long been ploughed and dressed, the seed had
been sown, and therefore the crop was so abundant.
The Reformation was the fruit of a long travail: at
one time the secret operations of divine influence, at
another, deeds done by men in the light of day,
was transforming by slow degrees a somewhat restless but still energetic and generous people.

The festival of Corpus Christi was approaching,
and the catholics hoped by that imposing ceremony
to bring back some of those who had left them;
but their expectations were · disappointed. The

most enlightened and honourable men of Geneva had
no longer any taste for these feasts—not because of
their antiquity, but because they were in their opinion
founded on serious errors, and shocked their enlightened sentiments.   The thought that a wafer,
consecrated by a priest, was about to be paraded
through the city to receive divine honours, revolted
evangelical Christians.   They determined not to join
in the procession, or to shut up their houses, but to
work as on ordinary days.   When the priests and
their adherents heard of this, they imagined that the
Lutherans intended attacking them during their progress; but on being reassured, they took courage and
the devout began to file off.   There was not the least
act of violence, but only a silent protest; many houses
before which the procession passed were without hang-
ings, and through the open windows 'the Lutheran
dames were seen in velvet hoods busily spinning with
their distaffs or working with their needles.'   Vainly
did the priests sing and the splendid cortège defile
through the streets: the velvet-hooded ladies remained motionless.   Gross insults would not have
enraged the devotees so much.   One of them seeing
a window open on the ground-floor and a protestant
lady filling her distaff, reached into the room, snatched
away the distaff, struck her violently on the head
with it, threw it into the mud, trampled on it, and
disappeared among the crowd.   The startled lady
screamed out, and (says Sister Jeanne) nearly died
of fright.   Notwithstanding this act of violence, the
protestants remained quiet.   Everything helped the
cause of Reform: neither the grotesque nor unseemly
dances of the populace, nor the sanctimonious proces-

sions of the clergy, were able to paralyze in Geneva the power of the doctrine from on high.*

An act of a new convert still further increased the murmurs. When Louis Bernard threw off the surplice he returned to civil life: he soon became a member of the Two Hundred, and afterwards of the Executive Council. Being an upright man and desirous of leading a Christian life, he married a widow of good family, and Viret blessed their union. The marriage created a great sensation. 'What!' exclaimed the catholics, 'priests and monks with wives!' 'Yes!' rejoined the reformers, 'you think it strange they should have lawful wives, but you were not surprised when they had unlawful wives, the practice was so general. What foxy consciences are yours! You confess to brushing off the dew with your tail as you crossed the meadows, but not of having stolen the poor man's poultry!' Bernard justified by his conduct the step that he had taken. The men who had been dissolute priests became good fathers,† and society was a gainer by the exchange.

But the priests did not think so. Master Jean, the vicar of St. Gervais, a zealous man and noisy talker, having heard of Bernard's marriage, exclaimed from the pulpit: 'Where is the discipline prescribed by the Church, where are the commandments of the pope? O horror! priests marry after they have taken the vow of chastity!' The question of marriage and celibacy was discussed before the Council; the priest

---

* Registres du Conseil du 2 Juin 1534.—La sœur Jeanne, *Levain du Calvinisme,* pp. 89, 90.

† Froment, *Gestes de Genève,* pp. 127–129; MS. de Gautier.

and Viret, who had given the nuptial benediction, were summoned to the Hôtel de ville. The reformer maintained that marriage is honourable to all men. St. Paul, when directing that the minister of the Lord should not have several wives, shows that we must not constrain him to have none at all, and if the Apostle insists that he must be a good father, it follows evidently that he should be married. 'Those who issue from the dens of the solitary and idle life called monkery or celibacy,' said one of the reformers, 'are like savages; while the government of a household is an apprenticeship for the government of the Church of God.' The vicar supported his opinion by bad arguments,' says the 'Register,' 'and wandered far from the truth.' 'Do not corrupt the Gospel, or else we shall take proceedings against you,' said the premier-syndic. The poor dumbfounded vicar stammered out a few excuses and retired, promising to teach in future in conformity with their Lordships' instructions.*

But they had no sooner shut his mouth on the question of marriage, than he opened it on that of baptism. 'Do these heretics imagine,' he exclaimed, 'that the Holy Ghost can descend into the heart by other channels than the priests? . . . They baptise in rooms, in gardens, without blowing upon the child to drive away the wicked one . . . They are *ipso facto* excommunicate.'

The independence of Church and State was not understood in the sixteenth century. Farel complained to the Council, and the priest was about to

---

* Registres du Conseil du 8 Juin 1534.—MS. de Gautier; La sœur Jeanne; *Levain du Calvinisme*, p. 88.

yield, when some laymen, irritated by the defeat of
Rome, came to his assistance. 'Are these heretics
already giving us the law in Geneva?' they said to
the council. 'Only the other day they were satisfied to speak, and now they want to hinder us from
doing so. We demand that it be as permissible for
Master Jean to preach as it is for Master Farel.' The
syndic replied frankly:—'We have not forbidden the
vicar to preach: on the contrary, we order him to
preach the Gospel.'* It was not then understood
that to command a man to preach what he did not
believe was more tyrannical than to silence him.

Farel, Viret, and the vicar were in attendance;
they were led into the council chamber, and the discussion began immediately. 'The Holy Ghost,' said
Farel, 'can act without the aid of priests. It is
faith in the power of Christ's blood that cleanseth us
from our sins, and baptism is the evidence of that absolution. But where have you read that it must be
celebrated with oil, salt, and other rubbish?† . . . I
know very well that this strange trumpery is of
ancient origin. . . . The devil very early began to
indulge in heavy jokes, and all these baubles come
from him. Let us put aside these pomps and shows
that dazzle the eyes of the simple, but brutalize their
understanding, and let us celebrate the rite of baptism
simply, according to the Gospel form, with fair water,
in the name of the Father, Son, and Holy Ghost.' The
embarrassed vicar quoted the authority of the pope in
his defence, and highly extolled the two swords that
are in his hand. 'That is an idle allegory,' said

* Registres du Conseil des 20 et 24 Juillet 1534.—MS. de Gautier.
† 'Aliis unguentis.'—Registres du Conseil du 24 Juillet 1534.

the reformer, 'and a sorry jest. . . . There are two powers, indeed: one in the Church, the other in the State. The only power in the Church is the Word of Christ, and the only power in the State is the sword.' That distinction gave much pleasure, and the secretary entered it on the minutes. An important transformation was going on: the civil power was lifting its head and beginning to brave that spiritual power which had humbled it for so long. The syndic kindly entreated Farel 'to take it all in good part;' but turning with severity towards the vicar, ordered him again 'to preach in accordance with the truth.' 'Do you forbid me to preach any more?' asked the priest, abashed. The syndic answered him a little harshly: 'You are forbidden nothing, except lying.' This marks a new phase of the Reformation in Geneva. The monks who remained faithful to St. Francis were alarmed in their convent at Rive, and said: 'Let us make haste to carry away our altar-ornaments and jewels.' . . . The Council opposed this, and ordered those precious objects to be kept in safe custody.*

While the magistracy of Geneva held back from catholicism, the partisans of the pope in the surrounding country were preparing to support it. An alarming rumour had been circulating in the city for some days; and the vicar and the reformer had scarcely withdrawn, when several members of the Council expressed their fears. 'The bishop, in concert with the duke, has formed the design of invading us,' they said. 'At a banquet, at which two hundred persons were present,

* Registres du Conseil des 30 Juin et 24 Juillet 1534.—MS. de Gautier.

a formidable conspiracy was planned against our liberties. Wherever you go, you hear nothing but threats
against the city. Many of our fellow-citizens have
gone out to join the enemy, and are preparing to attack
us, with the gentry of the neighbourhood.' Captain-
General Philippe was ordered 'to be on the look-out,'
and many placed their hands and their lives at his disposal. It was true that Pierre de la Baume, having
formed a new plot, had come to an understanding
with the Genevese episcopals and the Lords of Friburg;
and, quitting, not without reluctance, his delightful
residence at Arbois, he had gone to Chambéry to concert measures with the duke. A Romish camarilla
stimulated the two princes. The most fervid of the
mamelukes, and of the Lords of Savoy and of Vaud,
had arranged a meeting for a grand hunting match at
the foot of the Voirons, and there arrangements had
been made for 'hunting down' the heresy of Geneva.
'Every one there is running after this new word,'
they told the duke. 'There is but one means of
safety left, and that is, to destroy the city and the
heretics by making war upon them, and then restoring the prelate by force.' Forthwith the plan
was arranged 'of the most dangerous treason that
had yet been aimed at Geneva.' The duke hoped to
become master of the city, and to re-establish the
papal power in it. He had no doubt that catholicity,
far from being jealous of his conquest, would be
eager to applaud it. To ensure success, he determined to ask the help of France, and to that end
applied to the Cardinal de Tournon. It was proposed
that Pierre de la Baume should resign his see to one
of the duke's sons, the young Count of Bresse, and a

handsome compensation was offered him. Maisonneuve, the captain of the Lutherans, a man so generally
dreaded, being then in prison at Lyons, it was de-
sirable to take advantage of his absence, and the last
day of July was fixed for the execution of the enterprise.*

The Councils of Geneva, in great alarm, sent John
Lullin and Francis Favre to Berne to ask the advice
and assistance of those powerful allies. At the same
time they ordered the bells of the convent of St.
Victor and others to be cast into cannon, and directed
the captains of the city to take the necessary measures
for putting it into a state of defence. And, lastly,
wishing to deprive the enemies of Geneva of every
pretext, the Council determined to punish those who
had ' ill-advisedly broken the images of the convent
at Rive;' and declared, that *though such images ought
to be taken down and destroyed, according to God's
law,* yet ' those persons' ought not to have done it
without order and permission, because it was *an act
pertaining to the magistracy.* In consequence of this,
six men, of whom little was known, were imprisoned
on the 26th July.†

Great was the enthusiasm in Geneva. The citizens
were ready to give up everything ' to follow the right
path,' and the Reformation still advanced, notwithstanding the great danger with which it was threatened.
Some even chose this moment to confess their faith.
The last Sunday in July, a few hours before the day
when the enemy intended to enter Geneva, a member

---

* Registres du Conseil des 23 Juin et 7 Juillet 1534.—Froment,
Gestes de Genève, p. 123 ; Ruchart, iii. p. 334.—MS. de Gautier.

† Registres du Conseil des 24, 26 Juin, 17, 26, 27, 28 Juillet, 1534.

of the Dominican order, that pillar of the papacy,
'after the bell had bidden the people to the sermon,'
appeared before the congregation, took off his monastic
dress, went into the pulpit, and then, 'like a madman,'
prayed God to have pity on him. He bewailed himself, asked pardon of his listeners for having 'lived so
ill in times past, and so monstrously deceived everybody. 'I have preached indulgences,' he continued,
'I have praised the mass, I have extolled the sacraments and ceremonies of the Church. Now I renounce them all as idle things. I desire to find but
one thing—the grace of Christ crucified for me. After
which he preached an heretical sermon.'*

These conversions increased the dangers of Geneva,
by exciting the wrath of the catholics. Four days
after the touching confession of the Dominican the
projected plot was to be carried out. The Savoyard
troops, assembling at a little distance from the city,
were to approach it under cover of the darkness. One
detachment would arrive by the lake, and the tower
guard, bribed by ten crowns, would let the boats pass
without firing on them. Within the city, more than
three hundred foreigners had entered separately and
stealthily, and were hidden in catholic houses. In the
middle of the night F. du Crest was to go to the
Molard with firearms and hoist a red flag. The firing
of a heavy culverine would be the signal for the priests
to come to the support of their friends. Certain episcopals would mount to the roofs of their houses with
lighted torches to summon the foreign troops to approach. The catholics of Geneva and their allies would
then leave their houses; three of the city gates were

* La sœur Jeanne, *Levain du Calvinisme*, p. 94.

to be forced by a locksmith of their party, the troops would enter, and Genevans and strangers would advance shouting: ' Long live our prince, monseigneur of Geneva!' The friends of independence and reform, thus caught between two fires, would be unable to make any resistance. Then would begin the execution of the judgment of God: if it had been waited for long, it would only be the more terrible now. The pious soldiers of the Church would fall upon the Lutherans and put them to death. The city would be purged of all those seeds of the Gospel and liberty which were choking, within its walls, the ancient and glorious plants of feudalism and popery. Finally, to complete their work, the conquerors would share the property of the vanquished, which the bishop had in anticipation confiscated for their benefit, and Geneva, for ever bound to Rome, would thus become its slave and never its rival.*

On the 29th and 30th July all began to move round the city. On the north, the Marshal of Burgundy, the bishop's brother, was to descend into the valley of the Leman, with six thousand men, raised in imperial Burgundy. On the south, the Duke of Savoy had obtained permission of the king of France to enlist in Dauphiny, ' persons experienced in war.' Numerous soldiers—some coming by land, others by water—were expected from Chablais, Faucigny, Gex, and Vaud. A galley and other boats had been fitted out near Thonon, to which place the artillery of Chillon

* *Chron.* MS. de Roset, liv. iii. ch. xxvii.—MS. de Gautier.—Froment, *Gestes de Genève*, pp. 123, 124.—Procès aux Archives.—Gaberel, Pièces Justificatives.—Papiers Galiffe, communiqués par M. A. Roget, ii. 115.

had been removed. Several corps were marching on Geneva. The bishop, who was anything but brave, did not wish to leave Chambéry; but the duke, to encourage him, gave him a body-guard of two hundred well-armed men, and Pierre de la Baume quitted, not without alarm, the capital of Savoy early in the morning of the 30th July, and halted at Léluiset, a village situated about two leagues from Geneva, where he intended to wait in safety the issue of the affair.

The corps nearest to Geneva appeared. Savoyard troops under the command of Mauloz, castellan of Gaillard, reached their station in front of the St. Antoine Gate. Armed men from Chablais advanced along the Thonon road as far as Jargonnant, in front of the Rive gate. Other bands prepared to enter by the gate on the side of Arve and Plainpalais. Barks and boats filled with soldiers arrived in the waters that bathe the city. The army that was to cross the Jura, and other corps, did not appear; but the assembled forces were sufficent for the coup-de-main.*

While these manœuvres were going on without, everything seemed going on well within. The man entrusted with the care of the artillery, and who was called Le Bossu (the Hunchback), had been bribed. In the evening Jean Levrat, 'one of the most active of the traitors,' had prowled about his dwelling, and the keeper, not wishing to be compromised, had handed him through a loophole the keys of the tower of Rive, where the cannons had been stored. Levrat and his accomplices spiked several, and Le Bossu had

---

* *Chron.* de Roset.—Registre du Conseil des 17, 28, 31 Juillet 1534.—Ruchat, iii. p. 325.—Vulliemin, *Histoire de la Suisse*, xi. p. 89.—Froment, *Gestes de Genève*, pp. 123–125.

filled others with hay. The locksmith had counterfeited the keys of the city, and made iron implements to break down the gates.* The most lively
emotion prevailed in the houses of all the catholics.
Party walls had been broken through, so that they
could go from one to another and concert matters
secretly. Michael Guillet, Thomas Moine, Jacques
Malbuisson, De Prato, Jean Levrat, and the Sire de
Pesmes, went to and fro, watching that no man
shrank back.

Throughout the whole of the 30th of July the Councils and the reformed remained in complete ignorance of the blow that was impending. They knew of
the threats, but did not believe there was any danger,
so that in the evening of the 30th they had gone to
rest as quietly as usual. In the early part of the
night a stranger desired to speak with the premier
syndic on urgent business. Michael Sept received
him. 'I am from Dauphiny,' said the man: 'I am
a hearer of the word of God, and should grieve to see
Geneva and the Gospel brought to destruction. The
duke's army is marching upon your city; a number of
soldiers are already assembled all round you, and
very early this morning the bishop left Chambéry
to make his entrance among you.' It was a fellow-
countryman of Farel and Froment that undertook
to save Geneva. But was there still time? The
premier syndic immediately communicated the intelligence to his colleagues, and it was resolved
to arrest some of those who were always ready to
make common cause with the enemy outside. The
syndics questioned them, confronted them with one

---

* Froment, *Gestes de Genève*, p. 123.

another, and gradually saw the horrible plot un-
ravelled, of which they had until that moment been
ignorant.* All the citizens upon whom they could
rely were called to arms. It was not yet midnight.

The episcopals, who had not gone to bed, waited
in excitement for the appointed hour. A great number of canons and priests had assembled in the house
of the canon of Brentena, seigneur of Menthon, belonging to an illustrious family of Savoy. They
congratulated one another that the plot had been so
well arranged, and nothing in that assembly of ecclesiastics was talked of but torches, banners, and artillery. In a short time, however, one of their party
came in, and told them that the huguenots were
arming everywhere. The reverend members of the
chapter ran to the window, and saw with affright a
numerous patrol marching by. The alarm spread; not
an episcopal dared venture out: they hid the red flag,
the signal for the murder of the huguenots. One
hope only remained; the troops round Geneva were
amply sufficient to secure the triumph of the bishop.†

And indeed the number of soldiers round the city
was very great. Playing on the word *Geneva*, *gens
nova*, the leaders had chosen for their watchword this
cruel phrase: *Nous ferons ici gent nouvelle*,‡ that is to

---

* Our account of the manner in which the plot was discovered is
founded on the testimony of many witnesses. Froment, *Gestes de Genève*,
p. 125; Roset (*Chron.* MS. liv. iii. ch. xxvii.), and the minutes or
Register of the Council which were drawn up by Roset's father. Other
versions, differing from this narrative, do not appear to us to repose upon
such solid foundations.

† Registre du Conseil du 31 Juillet 1534.—*Chron.* MS. de Roset.

‡ 'Faciemus hic gentem novam.'—*Geneva restituta*, p. 73. 'We will
make a new people here.'

say, they would extirpate the evangelicals from Geneva and replace them by catholic Savoyards. They waited for the appointed signal, and turned their eyes to the roofs of the houses from which the torches were to be waved. They fancied that some had been seen, but had soon disappeared. While the anxious officers were asking what was to be done, some of the soldiers noticed a simple-looking boy walking about on the hill, peering innocently about him, but constantly getting nearer to the city gates. He was taken before Mauloz the castellan and M. de Simon, another of the leaders, who asked him what he was doing there at such an hour of the night. The boy, who seemed greatly embarrassed, answered, ' I am looking for the mare I lost.' It was not the case.

Three of the best citizens of Geneva, Jean d'Arlod, auditor, the zealous Étienne d'Adda, and Pontet, happening to be at La Roche, three or four leagues from Geneva, in the evening, had heard the enterprise talked of, and had immediately mounted their horses in order to reach the gates before the enemy.* Pushing rapidly along the bye-roads, they stopped at a farm-house a short distance from the city, where they learnt that the Savoyard troops were already under the walls. D'Arlod directed one of the farm-servants to go and see if they could enter. M. de Simon and Mauloz the castellan, impatient to know the cause of the delay, determined to make use of this poor boy, of whose innocence they felt no doubts. 'Hark ye!' they said to him; 'go and see whether the Rive and St. Antoine gates are open.' The lad, who was very unwilling to serve as a scout to the

* Registre du Conseil *in loco.*

Savoyards, replied: 'Oh! I should be afraid they would kill me.' At that instant Mauloz, whose attention was divided between the youth and the houses on which the torches were to be displayed, exclaimed, ' There is one!' A brilliant light appeared over the city: the whole force hailed it with joy, and the two captains could not turn away their eyes. The light appeared and disappeared, returned, and was again eclipsed, and every time it came in sight, strange to say, it looked more elevated. Higher and higher it rose; already it overtopped the tallest chimneys. There was something extraordinary about it, and the Savoyards began to grow uneasy. 'Why, can it be so?' said those who knew Geneva; 'the light is ascending the spire of St. Pierre! . . . Yes, it is so . . . that is where the main watch of the city is stationed in time of danger.' At last the light ceased to move; it halted at the top of the spire, which was built on the crest of the hill. It thus brooded over the city, and seemed turned upon the Savoyard army, like the glaring eye of the lion shining through the midnight darkness of the desert. Then a panic terror seized the soldiers of Charles III.; their features were disturbed, their hearts quaked. Mauloz, who had kept his eyes fixed on the threatening apparition, turned in despair towards M. de Simon, who was already moving off, and exclaimed: 'We are discovered: we are betrayed! We shall not enter Geneva to-night.' The young messenger, finding that nobody took heed of him, ran off to the farm to tell D'Arlod and his friends what had taken place.*

* Registre du Conseil du 25 Janvier 1537. It was not until then that D'Arlod related to the Council of Two Hundred what had happened to him three years before. *Chron.* MS. de Roset, liv. iii. ch. xxvii.

Yet the lion's eye still glared above the city. ' The sugar-plums are all ready for our supper,' said the men-at-arms.* Every one thought of retiring: Mauloz and Simon gave orders for the retreat. As day was beginning to break, the Genevese look-outs stationed on the tower saw the Savoyards filing off in the direction of Castle Gaillard, with drums beating and colours flying.

The Genevan catholics were in suspense no longer : their enterprise had miscarried. They were stupefied and furious against their allies. One of them, Francis Regis, said with a great oath: ' We are ruined and undone: those gentlemen are not worth a straw. We made the signals, everything was in good order, but the gentry deceived us.'† As for the bishop, he was more frightened than disappointed. When the terrible beacon shone out from the steeple of St. Pierre's, some men, commissioned to keep him informed of what was going on, had started off full gallop, and reported to him the ominous words of the ferocious Mauloz: ' We are betrayed!' Instantly the poor prelate mounted his horse, and rode hastily away to join the duke.

When the sun rose, not an enemy was to be seen about the city. The Genevans could not believe their eyes: the events of that memorable night seemed almost miraculous, and they were transported with joy, like men who have been saved from death. All the morning the streets were filled with people; they exchanged glances, they shook hands with each other;

* The soldiers played upon the word *dragée*—which means small-shot as well as sweetmeats.

† Déposition de Jacques Maguin. Papiers Galiffe. A. Roget, ii. p. 116.

many blessed God; some could not believe that their catholic fellow-citizens were cognisant of the plot. One little incident removed every doubt.

As some citizens happened to be passing the house of the keeper of the artillery, they heard the shrill voice of a woman screaming in great emotion: 'Ha! traitor! you are betraying me as you betrayed the city!' . . . A man replied with abuse and blows; the screams of the wretched creature became louder and louder, and the coarse voice of another woman was mingled with hers. It was the Bossu, his wife, and servant: the keeper of the artillery had been surprised by his wife in flagrant infidelity. The huguenots, hearing the uproar, stopped and entered the house. 'Yes,' screamed the wife louder than ever; 'yes, traitor, you gave Jean Levrat the keys through the loop-hole.' Levrat, the Bossu, and the locksmith were immediately arrested.*

The leaders of the conspiracy remained, as usual, at liberty. Skulking in their houses, Guillet, De Prato, Perceval de Pesmes, the two Du Crests, the two Regis, and many others, knew well that they merited death more than Portier; and, affrighted like the hare in its form, which pricks up its ears to listen for the pursuing huntsman, they started at the slightest noise, and fancied every moment that the syndics or their officers were coming. As no one appeared, they formed a desperate resolution: disguising themselves in various ways, they left their houses and escaped; 'and never returned to the city again,' says Froment. The bishop's conspiracy with Portier and the Pennets

---

* Froment, *Gestes de Genève*, p. 125. Registre du Conseil du 31 Juillet 1534. *Chron.* MS. de Roset.

had forced several catholics to leave the council; the project of a night attack obliged many to leave Geneva. Every effort made by catholicism to rise helped it to descend, and every blow aimed at the Reformation for its destruction raised it still higher. The citizens remarked to one another, reports a contemporary, who has recorded the words: ' It was God who brought down the hearts of our enemies, both without and within, so that they could not make use of their strength.'*

Meanwhile Geneva was not at ease. The marshal of Burgundy and the governor of Chablais had not appeared; and the enemy might have withdrawn only to wait for these powerful reinforcements. All the citizens were called to arms. ' Throughout that week a strong guard was kept up, and the gates of the city were closed.' As the episcopals had often had recourse to the bells to summon their partisans, 'it was forbidden to ring the church-bells either day or night.' A silence, accompanied with meditation and vigilance, prevailed through the city. The inhabitants were ready to sacrifice their lives, and showed their resolution by a deep earnestness, and not by idle boasts. The preachers would converse with the soldiers, speaking familiarly to them of *the good fight*, and the soldiers never grew tired of listening to them. ' What a new way of making war,' said many. ' In old times the soldiers used to have dissolute women with them at their posts, but now they have preachers, and instead of debauchery and filthy language, everything is turned to good.'†

---

* Michel Roset, MS. Froment, *Gestes de Genève*, pp. 123-125. Registre du Conseil du 7 Août 1534.

† La sœur Jeanne, *Levain du Calvinisme*, p. 92. Froment, *Gestes de Genève*, p. 126. MS. de Gautier.

Could such generous zeal save the city from the attacks of Savoy supported by France, Friburg, Burgundy, and the mamelukes? There were men who
shook their heads with sorrow and ' lived in fear and
despondency.' But ' a friend sticketh closer than a
brother.' On the morning after the enterprise, a
delegate from Lausanne arrived in Geneva, and although the Duke had given orders that the Estates
of Vaud should make common cause with him, the
messenger said : ' We are ready, brethren, to send you
a hundred arquebusiers if you want them.' Neuchâtel
made a similar offer. Berne commissioned Francis
Nägeli the treasurer, the banneret Weingarten, and
two other citizens, to exhort the duke and marshal
of Burgundy to desist from hostilities. The Swiss
cantons, assembled at Baden, forwarded a similar
message to Charles III.

The partisans of the pope and of the bishop saw
that as their enterprise had miscarried, their cause
was lost. The leaders had escaped at first: now the
flight became general. Even the friends of the
Genevese franchises began to leave the city ; it was,
therefore, natural that the fanatics should depart to
swell the ranks of the mamelukes. They took with
them all they could carry, and used various stratagems
to get out of the city, stealing away cautiously by night.
Some took refuge on the left shore of the lake ; a greater
number in the castle of Peney, on the right bank of
the Rhone, whence they kept the Genevese population
continually on the alert. Their wives and children,
left behind in the city, held secret interviews with them
at the foot of the steep cliffs which line the banks of
the river, and told them all the news. No Genevan

citizen could start for Lyons without the refugees at Peney being informed of it; they were always on the look-out for travellers. It was a strange phenomenon, of which history presents, however, more than one example, this opposition of the papists and feudalists to civil and religious liberty degenerating into brigandage.*

The flight of the episcopalian laity destroyed the power of the clergy, whose support they were, and made the reformers masters of the situation. Geneva was resolved to keep within her walls none but those who were ready to shed their blood for her. One night when the drum called the citizens to arms, a timid man bade his wife say he was absent; some of his neighbours, however, forced their way into his chamber and found him hidden in bed, pretending to have the fever: he shook, indeed, but it was with fear. The coward was banished from the city for life, under pain of being flogged if he returned; a year later, however, he was indulgently readmitted, 'because it is not given to every man to have the courage of a Cæsar,' says the Register; but he was always looked upon as an alien. Courage was at that time one of the qualifications necessary for Genevese citizenship.†

While the mamelukes were indulging in highway robbery without the city, the weaker members of the episcopal party who still remained within it were living in fear. Their persons, their worship, their convents

---

* Registre du 20 Septembre 1534. The ruins of the castle of Peney were still to be seen a few years ago near Satigny, between the Lyons and Geneva railway and the Rhone.

† Registre du Conseil des 4, 12, 13 Août, 4 Septembre 1534; 27 Janvier 1535.

were respected; not a hair of their heads was touched;
but they trembled lest the outrages of the refugees
at Peney should excite the huguenots to take their
revenge.   The nuns especially were in perpetual
alarm.   One night, between eleven and twelve o'clock,
the sisters of St. Claire were startled from their slum-
bers by a loud knocking at the door: scared at the
noise, they listened with beating hearts.   Then other
knocks were heard.   Faint and trembling, they crept
from their beds.   The huguenots are surely coming
to avenge on them the perfidious night of the 31st
of July!   'The heretics,' they whispered one to another, 'have broken down the gates of the convent.'
The nuns, ascribing guilty intentions to them, ran to
the abbess in dismay: 'My dear children,' said she,
'fight valiantly for the love of God.'   They waited,
but nobody came.

The youngest of the nuns, who had been at service
over-night with the rest of the community, and made
drowsy by the long prayers, had fallen into a
sound sleep; the under-superior had locked her in
the church without observing her.   About eleven
o'clock the unlucky sister awoke: she looked round,
and could not make out where she was. . . . At last
she recognised the chapel; but the darkness, the
loneliness, the place itself—all combined to frighten
her.   She fancied she could see the dead taking advantage of that silent hour to quit their graves and
wander through the church. . . . Her limbs refused
to move.   At length she summoned up courage and
rushed to the door.   It was locked.   In her fright,
she gave it a violent blow.   It was this which woke
the sisters.   Then she listened, and as no one

came, she knocked again three times as loud as she could.

While this was going on, the abbess prepared to receive the wolves who were about to devour her innocent lambs. She first desired to know if all her flock were present, and to her great anguish discovered that one was missing. Then another knock, louder than all the rest, was heard. 'Let us go forth,' said the abbess, 'and enter the church, for it will be better for us to be before God than in the dormitory.' They descended the stairs; the abbess put the key into the lock, opened the door . . . and found before her the young nun, who, pale as death, fainted away at her feet.*

The tales that men took pleasure in circulating, and sometimes even printing, about the reformers and the reformed, about Calvin and Luther in particular, often had no more reality than the imaginations of the nuns of St. Claire as to the designs of the huguenots, which had given the poor girls such a terrible fright; and they were less innocent.

* La sœur Jeanne, *Levain du Calvinisme*, pp. 92–94.

CHAPTER XIV.

AN HEROIC RESOLUTION AND A HAPPY DELIVERANCE.

(AUGUST AND SEPTEMBER 1534.)

THE friends of independence and of the Reformation had better grounded anxieties than those of the nuns of St. Claire: they understood that the attack had only been adjourned, and that they must hold themselves ready for severe struggles. Accordingly, Geneva mustered all. her forces. ' Let those who are abroad return home,' said the Council; but alas! two of the most intrepid were in the prisons of the French primate, and about to be sent to the stake. The sentence condemning Baudichon de la Maisonneuve and his friend to death had been pronounced, as we have seen. They had been delivered by the priests to the secular arm, and were about to be executed, when a fresh attempt was made in their behalf.

There was a patrician family in Berne, illustrious for its ancient nobility and valour, some of whose members had rendered signal services to France. In the fifteenth century, Nicholas of Diesbach, the avoyer, allied that puissant republic with Louis XI. against Charles the Bold, and had gained several victories over the Burgundian forces. At Pavia, in 1525,

another of the family, John of Diesbach, commanded
the Swiss auxiliary troops of France. Stationed on
the right wing, at the head of 2,000 Helvetians,
at first he drove back the imperialist infantry and
cavalry. Francis I. was on the point of gaining the
victory; but meanwhile his left wing had been an-
nihilated; in that quarter Suffolk, the heir of the
White Rose, the Duke of Lorraine's brother, Nassau,
Schomberg, La Tremouille, San Severino, and the
veteran La Palisse, fell on the field of battle, and
Montmorency was made prisoner. Nevertheless, the
Swiss still held their ground manfully, when Alençon,
the king's brother-in-law, fleeing shamefully, and
carrying after him part of the French men-at-arms,
caused Diesbach's soldiers, who were fighting at his
side and already shouting victory, to waver. At that
moment the lansquenets, commanded by the redoubtable Freundsberg, fell furiously on the Swiss and
broke them. The Helvetians, seeing the Frenchmen
retiring, believed they were to be sacrificed to the
hatred of the Germans. John of Diesbach conjured
and threatened them in vain; nothing could stop
them. Then the valorous captain rushed forward
alone against a battalion of lansquenets and fell dead.
Bonnivet, in despair, stretched out his neck to the
spears of the enemy, and was killed; and Francis I.,
who was the last to fight, yielded up his sword with
a shudder to Lannoy.*

John of Diesbach had married a French lady,
Mademoiselle de Refuge, to whom the king had pro-

---

* Narrative of Pescara and Freundsberg. *Histoire de la Suisse*, by
Jean de Muller, continued by MM. Gloutz-Blotzheim, J. J. Hottinger,
Monnard, and L. Vulliemin.

mised a dowry of 10,000 livres, but had afterwards given her husband, as an equivalent, the lordship of Langes, which the latter had bequeathed to his wife. But in 1533 Francis I. had taken back the estate, without giving the promised dowry. The widow of the hero of Pavia, finding herself thus deprived of her property by the man for whom her husband had died, implored the intervention of Berne, and the chiefs of that republic had commissioned another Diesbach, Rodolph, to proceed to the court of France to support the just claims of his relation. Rodolph departed on the 12th of January, 1534, accompanied by George Schœner. This mission was destined to be of more importance to Geneva than to Berne.*

Rodolph of Diesbach himself was highly esteemed in France. He had passed his youth there, had studied at the University of Paris, and from 1507 to 1515 had taken part in the wars of Louis XII., and honourably distinguished himself. On his return to Berne, he was one of those who embraced the evangelical faith, and was often called to defend the interests of Geneva and the Reformation. While Rodolph was in France pleading the cause of his cousin, De la Maisonneuve and Janin were imprisoned at Lyons, and Diesbach received instructions from the lords of Berne to do all in his power to obtain their liberation from the king. He set about it with all the energy of a Bernese and a warrior; went to Blois, where Francis I. was then holding his court, and earnestly solicited the enlargement of the two evangelicals.† He regarded Baudichon de la Maisonneuve as his co-burgher and co-religionist,

---

* MS. chronicles of the Diesbach family at Berne.
† Registre du Conseil de Genève, 17 Septembre 1534.

and saw clearly how useful his presence would be in Geneva. But, on the other hand, the catholic nobles and ultramontane priests urged the king to suffer the two Genevans to be burnt. How could Francis I., who had recently become the pope's friend, and who had ordered the heretics in his kingdom to be brought to trial*—how could he save the heretics of Geneva? The friends as well as the enemies of the Reformation were in the keenest suspense. Weeks, and even months elapsed, without obtaining a decisive answer from the king.

Geneva was greatly agitated during this long delay; but the absence of the two energetic huguenots did not hinder the work from being pursued with resolution. The magistrates desired to take and execute promptly the supreme measures rendered necessary by the danger of the country. A terrible and inexorable necessity continually rose before their minds. To save Geneva, a great portion of it must be destroyed.

The city was at that time composed of two parts: the city proper and the four suburbs. The suburb of the Temple, or *Aigues Vives* (Eaux Vives), stood on the left shore of the lake, and took its name from the church of St. John of Rhodes, which stood there.† The suburb of Palais lay to the left, on the picturesque banks of the Rhone; that of St. Leger extended from the city to the bridge thrown over the icy torrent of the Arve; and that of St. Victor, in which the monastery of that name was situated, stretched from Malagnou to Champel. This town beyond the walls

---

* '*Faire et perfaire le procès des hérétiques.*'—Letter to the Bishop of Paris.

† Near the Pré l'Évêque.

not only had as many houses as the one within, but covered a far more extensive surface, and contained over six thousand inhabitants.

On the 23rd August the Two Hundred members of the Great Council received a summons, bearing the words: 'In consequent of urgent affairs of the city.'* Everyone understood what they meant. The premier syndic proposed to build up some of the gates, and to set a good guard; but added, that such measures alone were not sufficient; that, as the suburbs were very extensive, the enemy could establish himself in them; and that it was necessary unhesitatingly to knock down all the houses, barns, and walls, beginning with the nearest. Many were struck with grief when they heard the proposition. What a resolution! what a disaster! With their own hands the citizens were to destroy those peaceful homes in which their childhood had played, where they had been born, and where those whom they loved had died; and a great part of the population would have no other shelter left them than the vault of heaven. Yet the Two Hundred did not hesitate. The friends of the Reformation, in whose eyes the Gospel had shone with all its brightness, were prepared for the greatest sacrifices so that they might preserve it. Those who were not touched by religious motives were carried away by patriotic enthusiasm. 'It is better to lose the hand than the arm . . . the suburbs than the city,' exclaimed the citizens. The resolution was agreed to; and without any delay—for the matter was urgent—the very same day, after dinner, the four syndics, accompanied by Aimé Levet and five other

* Registre du Conseil *ad diem*.

captains of the city, ' ' went to give orders for the
destruction of the suburbs.' There were cries and
tears here and there, but nearly all had formed the
resolution to lay their goods, although with trembling hands, upon the altar of their country and their
faith.

, It must be done, for every day the danger appeared
to draw nearer. The Genevese ambassadors at Berne
wrote to the Council: ' Be on your guard.' Acts
of violence and trifling skirmishes announced more
serious combats. On the 14th of August, Richerme,
a. merchant of Geneva, returning from Lyons, was
seized, dragged successively to three of the bishop's
castles, and put to the torture. On the 25th, Chabot,
another citizen, was stopped at the Mont de Sion,
taken to the castle of Peney, and also put to the
torture; but the judges, wishing to give a proof of
their good nature, added: ' Do not let his bones be
broken or his life endangered.' They soon brought
in a new prisoner.

There was an embroiderer at Avignon, ' so superstitious in fasting,' that he had sometimes gone several
days without eating or drinking. The poor artisan,
having received the Gospel, had ceased to attend
mass, and had consequently been sent to prison. The
churchmen asked him how long it was since he had
been present at the sacrifice of the altar. ' Three
years,' he replied; ' and with my own will neither
myself nor any of my family would ever have gone
there.' When they heard him talk in this way, the
priests did not dare put him to death, for they thought
him mad. Six months afterwards there came a great
pestilence; everyone fled, and the prison-doors were

left open: 'seeing which the pious embroiderer went
out.' He thirsted for the Gospel, and knowing that
there were great preachers at Geneva, he took the
road to that city. His travelling expenses were not
great: 'he had been accustomed to go from Avignon
to Lyons, more than sixty French leagues, for a *sol-
de-roi*,' says Froment. At last he reached the valley
of the Lemàn, alone and a fugitive, but joyfully anticipating the words of life that he was soon to hear.
Suddenly he was surrounded by a troop of horsemen,
who asked him roughly: 'Where are you going?'
'To Geneva.' 'What to do?' The embroiderer answered frankly and courteously, as was his custom,
'I am going to hear the Gospel preached; will you
not go and hear it also?' 'No, indeed,' answered the
men. He began to press them: 'Go, I entreat you,'
he said. 'I am surprised at you: you are so near,
and I am come expressly all the way from Avignon
to hear it. I entreat you to come.' 'March, rascal!'
they cried, 'and we will teach you to hear those
devils of Geneva.' They took him to Peney, and, on
reaching the castle, said to him: 'We will give you
three strappadoes in the name of the three devils you
wished to go and hear preach.' Having tied his
hands behind his back, they raised him to the top of
a long beam of wood, and let him fall suddenly to
within two feet of the ground. 'That is in the name
of Farel,' they cried; then came one for Froment, and
another for Viret. The poor fellow, all bruised as
he was, getting on his legs as well as he could,
again looked at his tormentors, and, touched with
love for them, repeated, in a persuasive tone: 'Come
along with me and hear the Gospel.' The indignant

Peneysans answered roughly : ' March back quickly
to the place from whence you came,' which he would
not do for anything they could do to him.   ' He is out
of his mind,' they said; and, taking him for an idiot,
they let him go.   The poor man reached Geneva at
last, and was ' lodged for nearly two months,' says
Froment, ' with the author of this book, to whom he
related the whole matter.'*

Such deeds of violence showed the Genevans that
there was no time to lose.   In the month of August
the resolutions of the Council followed one another
rapidly.   On the 18th they ordered that the church
and priory of St. Victor should be demolished; on
the 23rd, that all the houses, barns, and walls in the
suburbs should be pulled down ; and that a certain
number of Swiss veteran soldiers should be enrolled
who should be fed and lodged by the rich in turn; on
the 24th, that all absentees should be summoned to
return for the defence of the city; on the 1st of
September, that it should be fortified on the side of
the lake; on the 11th, that the trees round the walls
which might screen the approach of the enemy should
be cut down; and on the 13th, that every man should
begin to pull down his house within two days, that is,
by the 15th of September.†

The calamity then appeared before them as imminent and inexorable, and with all its coarser and sad
realities. The weaker minds were distressed, the more
excitable gave way to anger.   In the suburbs there
was much clamour. What! the houses to be levelled

* Froment, *Actes et Gestes Merveilleux de la Cité de Genève*, pp. 174,
175.

† Council Registers under the dates mentioned.

to the ground, like those of traitors, and that too by the very hands of the inhabitants! The priests shuddered at the thought that the churches of St. Victor, St. Leger, and of the knights of Rhodes were to be destroyed. Discontented citizens pointed coolly to the solidity of the condemned edifices, and declared that it would not be possible to pull them down. And finally, the chiefs of the catholic party, foreseeing that the measures which were to be the salvation of Reform would be the ruin of popery, determined to make a vigorous demonstration against them.

Thirty of the most notable catholics, headed by Anthony Fabri, one of the family of the celebrated Bishop Waldemar, and Philip de la Rive, waited upon the council. Fabri, who had been elected spokesman, was calm, but by his side stood De Muro (du Mur), who was much excited. 'We demand that the suburbs be left in their present condition, as being beautiful, convenient, and more useful to the city than if they were destroyed.' The council, whom it pained to impose such a sacrifice, reserved the power of compensating the greatest sufferers, but held to their orders. 'I crave permission to leave the city,' said De Muro, 'with eight hundred of my co-burghers, for this demolition is an act of hostility against us.'*

At the very time when certain of the citizens were threatening to leave Geneva, the friends of independence desired all the more to see the return of those who were away. There was one in particular whose decision and courage were appreciated by all. Suddenly, on the 26th of September, the very day when De Muro had used that threatening language, a report

* Registre du Conseil du 14 Septembre 1534.

circulated through the city that Baudichon de la Maisonneuve and his companion had been set at liberty.

Rodolph of Diesbach and George Schœner had not ceased to implore the king's intervention. Although the prince, who in a few months was to fill the streets of his capital with strappadoes and burning piles, did not feel any very sincere compassion for the two heretics, still, he desired to conciliate the favour of the Swiss, and perhaps not being much inclined to restore her estates to John of Diesbach's widow, he was not sorry to give the Bernese some other satisfaction. The cause of justice triumphed at last. Moved by Diesbach's earnest solicitations, Francis I. granted the release of the prisoners. The two Bernese, instead of 'tarrying to turn from side to side to the helps of this world,' acknowledged the protection of God. 'We have obtained their liberty,' said the ambassadors, 'God having given them to us.'* They started immediately for Lyons, furnished with letters under his Majesty's seal, which they presented to the authorities in whose guard the prisoners were kept 'until they should be burnt, as was the practice in those days.'† The gates of the prison were opened; De la Maisonneuve and Janin were given up to the Bernese. At the news of such an unprecedented act, the officials, inquisitors, and canons of St. John were amazed; 'all the priests of Lyons were sorely vexed, and the archbishop of Geneva still more

---

* 'Deo dante illorum relaxationem obtinuerunt.' Registres du Conseil du 14 Septembre 1534.

† Note by Flournois on the corresponding passage of the Council Registers.

so ; but they were forced to be patient.'* As for the prisoners, they knew that if God delivers his servants, it is not with the intent that they should abandon what they have begun. Instead of saying, when they were restored to liberty, Let us remain for a time in the shade, lest we be exposed to new dangers, they desired to work with greater zeal at the emancipation of their country. They travelled from Lyons to Geneva with the two lords of Berne, and were once more within the walls of that ancient city.

There was still so much uneasiness felt about them, that on the 16th September, when the news spread that some Bernese gentlemen had arrived at the hostelry of the Tour Perse † with Baudichon and Collonier, many persons would hardly believe it. God gave the Genevans more than they had hoped for. When friends who have been supposed lost are found again, those who had sorrowed over their bereavement run to meet them, and feel an inexpressible satisfaction as they look at them. So it happened at Geneva when the two prisoners returned. There was great joy in the city : many gave thanks to God that 'the violent course of the wolves who would have devoured the best sheep of the flock had been frustrated,' and praised the king of France because he valued the arquebusses of the Swiss more than the paternosters of the priests.

Desirous of showing the ambassadors a mark of respectful gratitude, the four syndics and the councillors, with their ushers and serjeants, proceeded on

---

* Froment, *Gestes de Genève*, p. 244.

† Registre du Conseil du 17 Septembre 1534.

the 17th of September to the Tour Perse* to hold an official sitting, at which the transfer of the prisoners was to be made. The chief magistrates of the republic having taken their seats in one of the large rooms, according to the usual order, Rodolph of Diesbach and G. Schœner entered, accompanied by the captives. Those noble gentlemen explained that they had come from Lyons and the court of France; that with God's aid they had obtained the release of the two Genevans; that, according to rule, they ought to deliver the prisoners into the hands of the magnificent lords of Berne, to whose intervention their deliverance was due ;† that they yielded, however, to the wishes of Baudichon and Collonier, who preferred to remain in the city of Geneva;‡ and that they only wanted a guarantee that the Council would be willing to produce them before Messieurs of Berne, whenever the latter demanded them.§ The Genevese magistrates thanked the lords of Berne, and gave the required guarantee in writing.‖

At last De la Maisonneuve was free: he could return to his wife and children, and converse with his friends. The latter were never tired of listening to him: the particulars of his imprisonment, his examinations, and his dangers possessed the liveliest interest for them. Froment especially, who was fond of a gossip,¶ asked him many questions. 'As

* 'In domo turris Perse.' Registre du Conseil du 17 Septembre 1534.

† 'Illos debere magnificis Dominis Bernatibus præsentari.'—*Ibid.*

‡ 'Dicti Baudichon et Collonier optant potius in hac civitate expectare, quod alibi.'—*Ibid.*

§ 'Petunt cautionem de repræsentando eosdem.'—*Ibid.*

‖ 'Super quo factum remersiationibus.'—*Ibid.*

¶ Bonnet, *Lettres Françaises de Calvin,* ii. p. 575.

Baudichon told me,' we read in his *Gestes*, 'all that could not be done without great expense, and his captivity cost him one thousand and fifty crowns of the sun.' *

A letter from Francis I. completed this episode in the history of the Reformation. Four days after the prisoners had been restored to their homes, that prince wrote to the syndics of Geneva:—†

' To our very dear and good friends the lords of Geneva:

Very dear and good friends,—You know how, at your earnest prayer and request, and also at that of our very dear and great friends, confederates, allies, and gossips, the lords of the city and canton of Berne, we have restored and sent back certain prisoners who had, in this our kingdom, used words respecting the faith, such and of such consequence, that therefore they had been condemned to death. This we were right willing to do; for the affection we have to gratify you and the said lords of Berne, as well in this respect as in all others that may be possible to us, having perfect confidence that you are willing to do the like for us. For this cause, having been advertised that you have detained in prison in your city a monk our subject, Guy Furbity by name, of the order of Preaching Friars, for having held certain language and dogmatised things touching the faith of the Church, which did not seem good to you, and for which he is about to be brought to trial, we desire to pray you right affectionately by these presents, that,

---

* Froment, *Gestes de Genève*, p. 244.
† Archives of Geneva, No. 1054, year 1534.

showing towards us reciprocal pleasure, you would immediately release the said Furbity our subject, without further proceedings against him, for the reasons aforesaid. By so doing you will please us very agreeably. Praying the Creator to guard you, our very dear and good friends, in his most holy keeping. Written at Blois the xxist day of September one thousand v hundred xxxiiij.

FRANÇOYS.   BRETON.'

Francis I. said: I send you back two prisoners, return me one. That seemed just and natural, yet the petty republic did not yield to the demand of the puissant king of France. The Council desired to follow conscientiously the legal course, and the rules of diplomacy. They found that the two cases were not identical; and as the Dominican had been imprisoned at the instance of the lords of Berne, it was agreed to ask their opinion first. The favour of the house of Valois could not make the magistrates of Geneva yield, even after the extraordinary boon they had just received: they desired, above all things, to follow the principles admitted in politics, and act justly towards the Bernese. Furbity was set at liberty at the beginning of 1536.

To have imprisoned the Dominican at all for preaching was a fault, and to keep him in prison was another; but in each case the fault was that of the age. With this reserve, we may pay to the courage of the weak the honour that is due to them. It is a noble thing in small states to hold firm to their principles in the presence of powerful empires, when they do so without presumption. And not only is it noble, it is salutary also, and invests them with a moral force which guarantees their existence. The petty republics of Switzerland and Geneva in particular have given more signal examples than that which has just been recorded.

CHAPTER XV.

THE SUBURBS OF GENEVA ARE DEMOLISHED AND THE ADVERSARIES MAKE READY.

(SEPTEMBER 1534 TO JANUARY 1535.)

BAUDICHON DE LA MAISONNEUVE and Janin re-entered Geneva the day after that on which the final order to demolish the suburbs was given. The captain of the Lutherans was restored to his country at the very moment when the deadliest blows were aimed at it. The coincidence is remarkable. The return of these two energetic citizens could not but give a fresh impetus to the resolution to sacrifice one half of the city in order to save the other. The first walls destined to fall were those of the monastery of St. Victor, which, as it stood at the gate of the city, might easily be occupied by the enemy's army as an advanced post.* There were no tears shed over the destruction of that building, except such as might have been drawn down by the thought of its antiquity. Ever since Bonivard the prior had been a prisoner at Chillon, the monks had shaken off every kind of restraint, and the monastery had become a sty of scandals and disorders. The friars had been in the habit of frequenting certain houses of ill fame in their suburbs; but now the

* It was situated nearly on the spot where the Russian church now stands.

convent was the scene of their continual orgies.   No sooner was there a talk of destroying that nest of de- bauchery than the reprobates exhibited the most in- satiable greediness.   The monks and their mistresses began to pillage the monastery: they tore down and carried away everything that was of any value; at night, and sometimes even during the day, they were seen leaving the monastery with bundles, and hiding their plunder in the adjoining houses. The priory was thus not only emptied, but almost stripped to the bare walls.* What an ignoble fall was that of these pre- tended religious orders!   Notwithstanding their rob- bery, the Council assigned the monks a residence in the city, and even a chapel, which was more than they deserved.

Then every man put his hand to the work.   All was life and animation on those beautiful heights whence the eye takes in the lake, the Alps, the Jura, and the valley lying between them.   First, the church was pulled down, and then the priory; and nothing was left but rubbish which encumbered the ground.   That building, the most ancient in Geneva, was founded at the beginning of the sixth century by Queen Sedeleuba, sister of Queen Clotilda, in memory of the victories of her brother-in-law, Clovis;†—that temple where the body of St. Victor had been deposited during the night, and which (as it was said) a light from heaven pointed out to strangers — that sanc- tuary to which the great ones of the earth had gone. as pilgrims, was now an undistinguishable ruin.

* Registre du Conseil du 18 Août 1534. The expression in the Re- gister is much more energetic.

† 'Ecclesia quam Sedeleuba regina in suburbano Genevensi con- struxerat.'—Fredegarius, Chron. cap. xxii. La sœur Jeanne, Levain du Calvinisme, p. 94.

That monument, erected to commemorate the triumph of orthodoxy defended by Clovis over Arianism professed by Gondebald, crumbled to the ground, after lasting more than a thousand years, in the midst of the libertinism of its monks. A crown had been placed on the cradle of St. Victor—a rod should have been placed upon its ruins.

Yet things that have been great in the eyes of men do not always end like those that have been vulgar. One day a strange report, set afloat by the monks and nuns, circulated through the city. During the night, voices, groans, and lamentations had been heard among the ruins of St. Victor. The wind, when it blows strong over those heights, often resembles the human voice. The devotees listened: again the plaintive tones were heard, and agitated them. ' Ah!' they exclaimed, 'it is the dead groaning, and not without reason, because their repose has been disturbed.' The crowd increased, and ere long ' the ghosts were plainly heard lamenting, not only. by night, but by day.' If the dead lamented over the fall of St. Victor, the living had reason to weep still more over the Church, whose monks had been its disgrace instead of its glory.

After the priory, the houses nearest to the city were pulled down one by one. When the citizens, wearied by their labours, sat down on the ruins to rest, they asked what was to become of them. ' Where shall I store my goods, where shelter my wife and children?' said Jean Montagnier. ' And where shall I go myself?' A poor mason, an infirm old man, burst into tears when he saw his wretched home demolished: the Council gave him a measure of

wheat, and promised to pay his rent. But if the
magistrates showed kindness to the wretched, they
were inflexible to the rebels. Magdalen Picot, a
widow, having insulted the syndics in a fit of passion,
was sentenced to three days' imprisonment. If the
poor lamented their hovels, the rich regretted their
beautiful houses, the pleasant gardens round them,
the smiling meadows watered by running streams
and overshadowed by majestic trees, the fountains
and the temple of the Crusaders, whose Gothic walls
imparted an antique and religious character to the
pleasing picture. A poet gave utterance to their
thoughts in these lines:—

> Urbe fuere mihi majora suburbia quondam,
> Templis et domibus nec speciosa minus,
> Quinetiam irriguis pratis, hortis et amœnis;
> Pascebant oculos hæc animosque magis.*

Amid such lamentations, all good citizens and
zealous evangelicals remained firm; but De Muro
with a great number of catholics quitted Geneva, and
passed over to the enemy's camp. Henceforward
they were to fight no longer against the Reformation
with secret conspiracies; they would attack it in open
war: *aperto bello patriam oppugnaturi.*†

At the same time that the houses were demolished,
ramparts were built. Tribolet, captain of Berne, and

---

* 'Great suburbs at one time surrounded the city, not less beautiful
with churches and houses than with well-watered meadows and pleasant gardens; which feasted the eyes and the heart still more.' The
lines from which our extract is taken are in Gautier's manuscript. He
ascribes them to an anonymous writer who had seen the suburbs.

† Registre du Conseil des 11, 14, 15, et 19 Septembre 1534. Gautier,
MS. La sœur Jeanne, *Levain du Calvinisme*, pp. 97, 98. MS. de Tur-
rettini; Berne, *Hist. Helvet.*

one of the envoys from that republic, a man of experience, quick and compassionate at the same time,
directed the construction of the earthworks and
masonry intended to fortify the city. Towards the
end of September, he began to plot out the lines in a
garden adjoining the convent of St. Claire. Rich and
poor, great and small, wheeled their barrows filled with
earth and stones. When the work was done, Tribolet
decided that it must be continued into the next
garden, that of the nuns; and on the 30th September,
as early as four in the morning, they were politely
requested to remove from the garden everything they
wished to keep. Sorely distressed at this terrible
message, they began to call upon God through the
intercession of the Virgin and the saints. 'We are
secluded from the world for the love of God,' said the
abbess to the Bernese captain; 'forbear from breaking
into our holy cloister.' Tribolet explained to her
that the safety of the city required it, and added that
he would do his work, 'whether they liked it or not.'
Thereupon the frightened sisters threw open the convent, and running into the church, fell prostrate to
the earth, weeping bitterly. When the captain opened
the door, and saw the poor women stretched on the
pavement, he said kindly to them: 'Do not be afraid,
we shall do you no harm.' The sisters were much
surprised to find a heretic could be so good-natured.*

Meanwhile the work of destruction continued, and
as the materials were employed to build the fortifi-
cations and repair the breaches in the walls, we may

Registre du Conseil des 21, 25 Septembre 1534. La sœur Jeanne,
Levain du Calvinisme, pp. 97–100.

say with Bonivard, '*Etiam periere ruinæ :*' 'the very ruins have perished.'

But what was to be done with the six thousand citizens expelled from their homes? Were they to be left to wander about, exposed to the robbers of the neighbourhood? There would have been room for a great portion of them in the convents, but those buildings were kept closed. On the other hand, the houses of the huguenots were thrown open, even to catholics. The citizens had incurred debts through long wars, their trade was ruined and their fields laid waste. . . . Nevertheless, he that possessed two rooms gave up one, and he who had a loaf of bread shared it with his brother. Syndic Duvillard was empowered to lodge provisionally, either in the state buildings or in private houses, such as had been deprived of their homes. If any destitute persons were seen loitering in the streets, benevolent men and pious women would accost them, take them home, sit them down at the family table, and every place, however small, was fitted up with sleeping accommodation. The Council even gave aid and comfort to the rich. Butini of Miolans was lodged, says the Register, in the house of the curate of St. Leger.

The activity of the Genevese was constantly stimulated by the news which reached them from without. 'The Duke of Savoy,' said letters from Berne, 'is collecting an army of brigands, and preparing perpetual troubles for you.' Towards the end of September, the two Gallatins (John the notary and his son Pierre), having gone to their estate at Peicy for the vintage, were on their return summoned before the Council on a charge of communicating

.with the people in the castle of Peney, which was half
a league distant.   The father said that, while he
was in the press-house pressing the grapes, Nicod
de Prato and other Peneysans had called on him.
Did anyone ever refuse a visit paid in the press-
house ?   They had taken a glass of wine together,
and that was all.   'As for me,' said the son, 'I confess that I went to Peney and drank with the episcopal fugitives there; they told me that ere long we
should have a *stout war*; that it would not be a little
one like De Mauloz' night-attack on the 31st of July;
that they would come in great force, and that I should
do well to leave the city.   When I returned (continued
Pierre) I reported it all to my captain.'   The two
Gallatins were immediately discharged without any
remark.*

The first enemy which the bishop loosed against
his flock was famine: he gave orders to intercept the
provisions all round the city.   The market-place was
deserted, the stores in the houses were gradually exhausted, and the episcopals flattered themselves that
before long none but hungry phantoms would be seen
in Geneva, instead of valiant citizens.   'O insensate
shepherd! he robs even his sheep of their food, when
he should feed them,' said one who was among the
number confined within the city walls.   Unhappy
bishop! unhappy Geneva!†

As if starvation were not enough, the unnatural

---

* Registre du Conseil du 21 Septembre 1534.   The Gallatin family,
after serving this republic, furnished devoted citizens to the United
States.   Abraham Albert Alphonse Gallatin, who emigrated to America at the end of the eighteenth century, became Secretary of State.

† Froment, *Gestes de Genève*, p. 115.   Registre du Conseil, 29 Septembre 1534

pastor surrounded Geneva with a circle of iron. His
castle of Jussy to the east, at the foot of the Voirons;
that of Peney to the west, on the banks of the
Rhone; the duke's castle of Galliard to the south-
west, on the heights overlooking the Arve; and to
the north on the lake, the village of Versoix, at that
time well defended: all these fortresses, filled with
mamelukes and soldiers, hemmed in the city, and left
no issue but by the lake. 'In this way no one can
leave Geneva,' they said, 'except at the risk of his
life.' The bishop followed the example given by
dispossessed princes—nay, even by ecclesiastical authorities, and connived more or less at the brigands.
Many gentlemen of those districts, returning with
delight to a trade their fathers had formerly prae-
tised, kept watch in their eyries for the little merchant caravans, to pounce upon them. One day some
devout catholics of Valais, on their way to France with
a long file of well-laden mules, were stripped by these
rough episcopals. Beyond the Fort de l'Ecluse was
situated a castle—a thorough den of robbers—belonging to the Seigneur of Avanchi, 'the cunningest and
cruellest man ever known.' Accompanied by a few
savage mercenaries, he would lie in ambush near the
high-road, and when travellers appeared, spring from
the rocks like a wild beast, 'tearing out the eyes of
some, and cutting off the ears of others.' D'Avanchi
treated in this manner a poor tradesman who had
printed some New Testaments;* and when the judge
of the castle remonstrated with him for his cruelty, the
seigneur killed him on the spot. He showed no pre-

* Procès Inquisitionnel de Baudichon de la Maisonneuve. MS. de
Berne, p. 7.

ference, however, so far as religion was concerned. Having fallen in with some nuns one day, he graciously invited them to enter his mansion under pretence of giving them alms, and then maltreated them. The fierce and sensual wild-boar of the Jura was taken to Dôle, and there put to death by order of a catholic tribunal.*

The bishop now took another step: he ordered the episcopal see to be transferred from Geneva to the town of Gex, at the foot of the Jura, and gave instructions ' that his council, court, judges, and all other officers should proceed thither.' In the night of the 24th of September the episcopal officers escaped stealthily, and the city was left not only without prelate, but also without civil judges or courts of appeal. When the news of this flight got abroad in the morning, De la Maisonneuve, Levet, Salomon, and their friends felt an immense relief. At last they were free from that episcopal crew, who had so often caught the Genevese in their toils ' by frauds and snares.'† The Council forbade the seals, the symbol of supreme authority, to be taken from Geneva.‡ The prince bishop assembled at Gex a great number of priests from the surrounding districts. ' We must crush that Lutheran sect,' he told them, ' by war or otherwise. It is not enough to remain entrenched in our camp, we must force the enemy in theirs.'

Pierre de la Baume launched his thunderbolts at last. In every parish of the Chablais, Faucigny, Gex,

* Froment, *Gestes de Genève*, pp. 117, 118, 121, 174. Registre du Conseil du 29 Septembre 1534. Roset MS.

† ' Par fraudes et pipées.'

‡ Froment, *Gestes de Genève*, p. 115. Registre du Conseil du 25 Septembre 1534. Gautier MS.

and Bugey, in every abbey, priory, and convent, the great excommunication was pronounced in his name, not only against the councils and citizens of Geneva, but against all who should hear the preachers or talk with them, and even against any persons who should enter the city for any purpose whatsoever. Hereafter, the superstitious rural population looked upon Geneva as a place inhabited by devils. Some men of Thonon, more curious than the rest, ventured to pay it a visit, and on their return declared 'that the preachers were really men and not demons.' These rash individuals were arrested and taken to Gex, where the bishop sent them to prison;[*] and after that time no one dared go to Geneva.

The friends of the Reformation were not discouraged by these hostile acts. 'By Christmas, at the latest,' they said, 'all the churches will be empty, and the whole city of one faith.'[†] 'It is all for the best,' added many. 'Once upon a time the bishops usurped the franchises of the city; now they return them to us and go away. Well, then, let us do without bishops, and govern ourselves.' The Council did not think fit to proceed so quickly, and merely resolved 'that everything should be written down which the bishop had done against the city, by way of precaution against him.'[‡] When the canons, the representatives of the prelate, assembled for their usual monthly meeting,[§] the syndics and council appeared before them: 'Forsaken by our bishop, who is exciting cruel

---

* Froment, *Gestes*, p. 116.
† La sœur de Sainte Claire, *Levain du Calvinisme*, p. 97.
‡ Registre du 18 Sept. 1534.
§ 'Die calendæ suæ.'—Registre du Conseil du 1ᵉʳ Octobre 1534.

soldiers against his flock, what shall we do, reverend
sirs?' they asked. ' The see is vacant: we pray you
to recognise the fact, and to elect, as is your privilege, the necessary functionaries for the city, in the
place of those who have deserted their office.'*

The canons having answered in a dilatory manner,
the councils, who were always rigid observers of precedent, resolved to apply to the only authority that
could decide between them and the bishop. The
Genevese appealed to the pope. It was a strange
step, but appeals to the Roman pontiff as head of
the catholic world, partly founded on the forged
decretals of the pseudo Isidore,† were then in full
vigour. That petty people followed the path of
legality, and by this means attained their end. The
men who have succeeded, remarks an historian, are
those who, in the very midst of a revolution, have
neither accepted nor adopted a revolutionary policy.‡
On the 7th of October 1534 the syndics and council
entered an appeal at Rome, complaining that their
bishop had deprived them of their franchises and jurisdiction. It was not a matter of religion, but of policy.
The prince of the Vatican was called upon to fulfil
his obligations. It was Rome who broke the bond:
no answer was returned, which greatly delighted the
evangelicals.§

But as the pope laid down the crosier the duke took
it up. He succeeded in gaining over some Bernese

* Registre du Conseil du 1er Octobre 1534. MS. de Gautier. MS.
de Roset, liv. iii. ch. xxix.

† 'Episcoporum judicia et cunctorum majorum negotia causarum eidem
sanctæ sedi reservata esse liquet.'—Canon 12.

‡ M. Guizot.

§ *Chrom.* MS. de Roset, liv. iii. ch. xxix. MS. de Gautier.

ambassadors who had been sent to him, and these men, enraptured with the prince's courteous manners, tried to convince the people of Geneva of his goodness. 'We know him,' said the huguenots, 'he has an ass's head and a fox's tail.' * The Bernese continued: 'Everything will be forgiven, but on condition that you send away these new preachers; that you permit such preachings no longer; that the bishop be restored to his former estate, and finally that you live in the faith of our holy mother, the Church.' † The Genevans could hardly believe their ears. The Little and the Great Council having sent for the ambassadors of Berne, told them plainly and curtly: 'You ask us to abandon our liberties and the Gospel of Jesus Christ. We would sooner renounce father and mother, wife and children, we would sooner lose our goods and our life! Tell the duke we will set fire to the four corners of the city, before we dismiss the preachers who announce the Word of God. . . . . . Nevertheless, they offer to endure death, if it can be shown by scripture that they are wrong.' The men of Berne were greatly astonished at such a reply.‡

The duke was still more astonished; the measure was full, the insolence of that handful of friends to the evangelical doctrine must be severely punished. 'Seeing this, the duke and all his following (*sequelle*), more inflamed than ever with anger against Geneva, consulted together to make war upon it.' From every quarter the heads of the clergy (and Bishop du Bellay

---

* Froment, *Gestes de Genève*, p. 110. Registre du Conseil du 1er Septembre 1534.

† Froment, *Gestes de Genève*, pp. 110, 111.

‡ Ibid. p. 112.

in particular) conjured him 'to support the authority of the holy faith in the city of Geneva.'* The persuasion of these prelates inflamed the prince with such zeal for the maintenance of the papacy, that, unmindful of every treaty, he sent letters to Valais and the catholic cantons, demanding their assistance *propter fidem*, in behalf of the true faith, against the cities of Geneva, Lausanne, and others.† At the same time he despatched orders to his governors, gentlemen, provosts and other officers, 'to ruin and destroy Geneva.' ‡ On the 20th of November a diet was held at Thonon to decide upon the fate of the city; and as the aristocratic influence prevailed just then at Berne, the Bernese deputies adopted the sinister resolutions of Savoy. Even Charles V. declared through an ambassador his support of the duke's demands, and required that, prior to any other measure, the bishop should be restored to all his rights.

Happily the citizens of Geneva were not without timely warning of the storm that was about to burst upon them. The messengers, commissioned by Charles III. to carry his rigorous orders to his agents, had to pass through certain villages, where they would sometimes halt at the inn. Everybody noticed their embarrassed manner, and in some places there were well-disposed persons who stopped and searched them, and discovering their letters took them away and sent them to the syndics. The latter comprehended the

* 'Soutenir l'autorité de la sainte foy dans la ville de Genève.'— Archives of the kingdom of Italy at Turin, bundle xiii. No. 19.

† Archives of the kingdom of Italy at Turin, bundle xiii. No. 19.

‡ 'Nuire et détruire Genève.'

danger impending over the city, and accordingly took
the measures necessary for its defence.*. The friends
of independence and of the Reformation, instead of
being dejected by such news, felt their courage increased.   It was as if a spark had fallen upon powder;
their spirits caught fire.   The hour of sacrifices and
energetic resolutions had arrived ; there were no
more paltry scruples, evasions or delays, no more
timid compromises.   For a thing to succeed, it must
be done with decision. The Genevese therefore boldly
grasped the hammer, and with fresh strength began to
demolish the suburbs and popery at the same time.
At the Pré l'Evêque, they took down a stone cross
because (as they said) 'it turned men away from
the true cross of Jesus Christ.' †   At St. Leger, as
the church had been demolished, they destroyed the
images also.   Still the Roman worship remained free ;
while Rome was attacking Geneva, Geneva protected
Rome.   The canons having timidly asked the Council,
on the 24th of December, if they might celebrate the
Christmas matins next day, the syndics posted themselves at the doors of the different churches ' with
men-at-arms to prevent annoyance,' until divine
service was over.‡

Geneva had still one hope remaining.   Would those
same Switzers, who had shaken off the oppression of
Austria, permit Savoy to place Geneva under the
yoke?   Would the protestant republic of Berne,

* Froment, *Gestes de Genève*, p. 113.   Registre du Conseil dès 1er, 13
Octobre 1534.   MSC. de Roset, liv. iii. ch. xxx.

† Registre du Conseil des 28 Novembre, 3 Décembre 1534, et 9 Mars
1535.   La sœur Jeanne, *Levain du Calvinisme*, pp. 100–104.

‡ Registre du Conseil du 24 Décembre 1534.   La sœur Jeanne,
Levain du Calvinisme, p. 104.

which had done so much to sow the good seed
in this allied city—which to this end had brought
thither and protected Farel, Viret, and Froment
—would that republic turn away, now that the
grain was beginning to shoot forth, and the harvest
was at hand? It seemed impossible. A diet was
to meet at Lucerne in January, to deliberate what
Switzerland should do in this conjuncture. All the
ideas of the Genevans were concentred on that one
point. Not only did a majority of the cantons, but
the Bernese themselves, consent to the restoration of
the duke and the bishop. They required, indeed,
that liberty of conscience should be respected; 'for,'
said they, 'it does not depend upon man to believe
what he wishes; faith is the gift of God.' But the
duke and the bishop had the frankness to reject such
a condition : 'We claim,' they said, 'the right of
ordering everything that concerns religion in our
states.'—'We mean,' added their representatives,
'that the preachers shall be expelled from the city,
and that Berne shall break off her alliance with it.'
At these words grief and indignation pierced the
Genevan deputies like a sword. 'What!' they said;
'the bishop complains of being robbed of his jurisdiction, and it is he who is the robber! He has been
always wishing to strip Geneva of her franchises;
and not long ago he transferred the officers of justice,
the courts, and the tribunals, to a foreign country.'
The diet was inexorable. They resolved that the duke
and the bishop should be reinstated in the possession
of all their lordships and privileges. To no purpose did
Syndic Claude Savoie and Jean Lullin, who were
alarmed at this decision, hasten to Lucerne and declare

that Geneva would never accept the articles voted. ' You ought to thank us,' answered the Swiss—was it in irony or in sincerity?—' instead of which you insult us. Accept the mandate.'—' We cannot,' proudly answered the deputies. ' In that case,' resumed the cantons, ' we have only to place the matter in the hands of God.'*

Geneva was abandoned by all, even by Berne. The news filled the citizens with the liveliest emotion. There was nothing left them but God, and God is mighty. ' Yes,' said they, ' be it so, let God decide.' Men worked at the walls and prepared their arms, the women prayed, and the children in their games defied Savoy and the bishop. The bells of the demolished churches were melted down to make cannon. Every night, men on guard stretched - the chains across the streets, and the watchword was to make ' good ward and sure ward.' Everything was carried out with order, calmness, and courage.†

Their enemies smiled at this activity, and asked how it could be possible for such a small city to resist the numerous forces about to march against it. But wiser men were not ignorant that in the world faith often prevails over superstition, wisdom over strength, piety over anger, and that the great mission falls ultimately to the just and the calm. Charles V., who aspired to place his sword in the balance, and other great and ambitious men, have had something gigantic in them ; extraordinary ideas have flashed across their minds like lightning, and they have often

* MS. de Roset, liv. iii. ch. xx. Registre du Conseil des 5, 28 Janvier, 20 et 21 Février 1535. MS. de Gautier.

† Registre du Conseil des 29 Décembre 1534 ; 8, 12, 15 Janvier 1535.

cast a wide and sombre light over history; but they have founded nothing lasting. All great and solid creations belong to justice, perseverance, and faith.

The spirit of self-sacrifice and firmness with which the Genevans demolished one half of their city was a pledge of victory. At the beginning of 1535 the work was almost ended. A few, however, of the remoter buildings did not come down until 1536, and even 1537. Everything was levelled round the walls, the approaches to the place were free, the artillery could play without obstruction, the lines intended to cover the city were formed, the ramparts were built, and Geneva, witnessing the labours of her children, and her sudden and marvellous transformation, might well exclaim by the mouth of one of her poets :—

> . . . . . Incepit tentandi causa pudoris
> Alliciens varios hæc mea forma procos ;
> Qui me cum blandis non possent fallere verbis,
> Ecce minas addunt, denique vimque parant.
> Tunc ego non volui pulchrum præponere honesto,
> Diripui rigida sed mea pulchra manu
> Templa, domos, hortos, in propugnacula verti,
> Arcerent stolidos quæ procul inde procos.
> Diripui pulchrum certe, ut tutarer honestum.
> *E pulchra et fortis facta Geneva vocor.* *

Geneva was then passing through the arduous ordeal of transformation. Rough blows assailed her, groans

---

* 'My beauty attracted many suitors who sought to seduce me. When they saw that their flattering could not make me faithless, they had recourse to threats, and at last prepared to overcome me by force. Then I, unwilling to set my beauty above my virtue, destroyed with inflexible hand my temples, gardens, and houses, and converted them into ramparts, to keep my insensate suitors at a distance. I destroyed my beauty to preserve my honour. I was once Geneva the fair; now I am called Geneva the valiant.' These lines are preserved in Gautier's manuscript history.

burst from her bosom, and on her features was the
pallor of death.   But in the hour when the sacrifice
was thus accomplished on the altar, when riches and
beauty were immolated to save independence and faith,
when these proud thoughts agitated men's hearts
and made their presence known by a cry of agony
or by words of high-mindedness, a mysterious light
shone forth, in the midst of the darkness; liberty,
morality, and the Gospel had appeared.   Hopeful eyes
had seen a new edifice, radiant with immortal glory,
rising above the ruins of the old.   The song then
heard was not the song of death, but of resurrection.

CHAPTER XVI.

THE KING OF FRANCE INVITES MELANCHTHON TO RESTORE UNITY AND TRUTH.

(END OF 1534 TO AUGUST 1535.)

WHILE the work of the Reformation appeared exposed to great dangers in a small city of the Alps, it had in the eyes of the optimists chances of success in two of the greatest countries of Europe—France and Italy. The two finest geniuses of the reform, Melanchthon and Calvin, had been summoned to those two countries respectively. Luther, their superior by the movements of his heart and the simplicity of his faith, was inferior to them as a theologian, and they probably surpassed him in their capacity to comprehend in their thoughts all nations and all churches.

The first half of the sixteenth century was the epoch of a great transformation to the people of Europe ; there had been nothing like it since the introduction of Christianity. During the middle ages, the pope was the guardian of Christendom, and the people were infants, who, not having attained the necessary age, could not act for themselves. The pontifical hierarchy opened or shut the gates of heaven, laid down what every man ought to believe and do, dominated in the councils of princes, and exercised a powerful influence over all public institutions.

But a wardship is always provisional. When a man attains his majority, he enters into the enjoyment of his property and rights, and having to render an account to none but God, he walks without guardians by the light which his conscience gives him. There is also a time of majority for nations, and Christian society attained that age in the sixteenth century. From that moment it ceased to receive blindly all that the priests taught; it entered into a higher and more independent sphere. The teaching of man vanished away; the teaching of God began again. Once more those words were heard in Christendom which Paul of Tarsus had uttered in the first century: '*I speak as to wise men; judge ye what I say.*'* But it must be carefully observed that it was by throwing open the Bible to their generation that the reformers realised this sentence. If they had not restored a heavenly torch to man, if they had left him to himself in the thick shadows of the night, he would have remained blind, uneasy, restless, and unsatisfied. The holy emancipation of the sixteenth century invited those who listened to it to draw freely from the divine Word all that was necessary to scatter the darkness of their reason and fill up the void in their hearts. Elevating them above the goods of the body, above even arts, literature, science, and philosophy, it offered to their soul eternal treasures—God himself. The Gospel, then restored to the world, gave an unaccustomed force to the moral law, and thus conferred on the people who received it two

* 1 Corinth. x. 15.

boons—order and liberty—which the Vatican has never possessed within its precincts.

All men, however, did not understand that the majority which each must necessarily attain individually is at the same time essential to them collectively, and that the Church in particular must inevitably attain it. There were many, among those who were interested in the prosperity of nations, who felt alarm at the abolition of the papal guardianship. They saw that this stupendous act would work immense changes in the sphere of the mind; that society as a whole, literature, social life, politics, the relations of foreign countries with one another, would be made new. This prospect, which was a subject of joy to the greater number, excited the liveliest apprehensions in others. Those especially who had not learnt that man, as a moral being, can only be led by free convictions, imagined that all society would run wild and be lost if that power was suppressed which had so long intimidated and restrained it by the fear of excommunications and the stake. These men, alarmed at the sight of the free and living waters of reform, and wishing at any cost to save the nations of Europe from the deluge which appeared to threaten them, thought it their duty to confine them still more, to restore, strengthen and raise the imperilled dikes, and thus keep the stagnant waters in the foul canals where they had stood for ages.

Notwithstanding his liberal tendencies with regard to literature and the arts, Francis I. was not exempt from these fears, and gave a helping hand to a restoration—often a cruel restoration of the Romish jurisdiction. Henry VIII., of little interest as an in-

dividual, though great as a king, and who was truly
the father, predecessor, and forerunner of Elizabeth
and her reign, even while striving ineffectually to
preserve the catholic doctrines in his realm, separated
it decisively from the papacy, and by so doing laid the
foundations of the liberty and greatness of England.
Francis I., on the other hand, maintained the papal
supremacy in his dominions, and laboured to restore
it in the countries where it had been abolished. In
1534 and 1535 we see him making great exertions
to that end, and finding numerous helpers to back
him up.

The idea of restoring unity in the Christian Church
of the West, not only engrossed the attention of those
who were actuated by despotic views, but also of
noble-minded and liberal men. ' By what means can
we succeed ? ' they asked. The violent answered,
' By force ; ' but the wise represented that Christian
unity could not be brought about by the sword.
Those who were occupied with this great question
determined to examine whether they could not solve
it by means of mutual concessions ; and they set
about their task with different motives and in different tempers. They formed three categories.

There existed at that time in all parts of Europe
men of wit and learning, children of the Renaissance,
who disliked the superstitions and abuses of Rome,
as well as the bold doctrines and severe precepts
of the Reformation. They wanted a religion, but it
must be an easy one, and more in conformity (as
they held) with reason. Between Luther and the
pope, they saw Erasmus, and that elegant and judi-
cious writer was their apostle : hence the Elector of

Saxony called them Erasmians.*   They thought that
by melting popery and protestantism together they
might realise their dreams.

In like manner, too, there were persons to be found
of greater or less eminence in whom the desire prevailed to maintain Europe in that papal wardship
which had lasted through all the middle ages:
they feared the most terrible convulsions if that
supreme authority should come to an end.   At their
head in France was the king.   Francis I. had also a
more interested object: he desired, from political
motives, to unite protestants and catholics, because
he had need of Rome in Italy to recover his prepon-
derance there, and of the protestants in Germany to
humble Charles V.   To this class also belonged, to a
greater or less extent, William du Bellay, the king's
councillor and right hand in diplomacy.   So far as
concerns doctrine, both were on the side of Erasmus;
but, in an ecclesiastical point of view, while the
prince inclined to a moderate papal dominion, the
minister would have preferred a still more liberal
system.

. Finally, there were, particularly in Germany, a few
evangelical Christians who consented to accept the
episcopalian form, and even the primacy of a bishop,
in the hope of obtaining the transformation of the
doctrine and manners of the universal Church.   Melanchthon at Wittemberg, Bucer at Strasburg, and
Professor Sturm at Paris, were the most eminent men
of this school.   Melanchthon went farther than his
colleagues.   He believed that the great revolution

* 'Die Leute die die Sache fordern, mehr Erasmich als Evangelisch
sind.'—Bretschneider, *Corpus Reformatorum*, ii. p. 909.

then going on was salutary and even necessary; but he would have liked to see it limited and directed. Former ages had elaborated certain results which ought, in his opinion, to be handed down to ages to come; and he imagined that if the pope could be induced to receive the Gospel, that despot of old times might still be useful to the Church. Another and a still more urgent interest animated these pious men: it was necessary to rescue the victims of fanaticism, to extinguish the burning piles. The bloody and solemn executions which had taken place in Paris on the 21st of January 1535, in presence of the king and court, had excited an indescribable horror everywhere. One might have imagined that those noble-hearted men foresaw the miseries of France, the battle-fields running with blood, and the night of St. Bartholomew with its murders ushered in by the death-knell from the steeple of St. Germain l'Auxerrois; that they saw pass before them those armies of fugitives whom the revocation of the Edict of Nantes scattered over the wide world.

One common feature characterised all three classes. Those who composed them were in general of an accommodating disposition, an easy manner, ready to sacrifice some part of what they thought true, in order to attain their end. But there were in Europe, on the side of Rome many inflexible papists, and on the side of the Reformation many determined protestants, who set truth above unity, and were resolved to do everything ' so that the talent which God had entrusted to them might not be lost through their cowardice, or taken from them on account of their ingratitude.'*

* Calvin.

The famous placards posted up in the capital and all over France on that October night of 1534 had carried trouble into the hearts of the peacemakers. They had seen, as they imagined, the torch suddenly applied to the house in which they were quietly labouring to reconcile Rome and the Reformation. 'Such a seditious act agitates the whole kingdom, and exposes us to the greatest dangers,'* wrote Sturm from Paris to Melanchthon. 'The authors of those placards are men of a fanatical turn, rebels who circulate pernicious sentiments, and who deserve chastisement,' wrote Melanchthon to the bishop of Paris. But at the same time the most energetic of the German protestants, revolted by the cruelty of Francis I., refused to join in union with a prince who burnt their brethren. The king of France had formed the plan of a congress, destined to restore peace to Christendom; but an imprudent hand had applied the match to the mine, and the friends of peace were struck with terror and confusion. From that moment there was nothing heard but recriminations, reproaches, and altercations.

Francis I. saw clearly that, if his project was on the brink of failing, the fault was due mainly to his own violence; he therefore undertook to set straight the affairs he had so imprudently damaged. On the 1st February 1535 he wrote to the evangelical princes of the empire, assuring them that there was no similarity between the German protestants and the French *heretics*, his victims. The contriver of the strappadoes of the 21st January assumed a lofty tone, as if he

.   * 'Stultissimis et seditiosissimis rationibus regna et gentes perturbarunt.'—*Corp. Ref.* ii. p. 855.

were innocence itself. '' I am insulted in Germany,'
he said, 'in every place of assembly, and even at
public banquets. It is said that people dressed
like Turks can walk freely about the streets of Paris,
but that no one dares appear there in German costume. People say that the Germans are looked
upon here as heretics, and are arrested, tortured,
and put to death. We think it our duty to reply to
these calumnies. Just when we were on the point of
coming to an understanding with you, certain madmen endeavoured to upset our work. I prefer to
bury in darkness the paradoxes they have put forth ;
I am loth to set them before you, most illustrious
princes, and thus display them in the sight of the
world.* I think it sufficient to say that even you
would have devoted them to execration. I wished to
prevent the pestilence from spreading over France,
but not a single German was sent to prison.† The
men of your nation, princes and nobles, continue
to be graciously received at my court; and as for
the German students, merchants, and artisans who
work in my kingdom, I treat them like my other subjects, and, I may say, like my own children.' The
letter produced some little effect, and there was a
reaction on the other side of the Rhine. Melanchthon
resumed his schemes of reunion.

---

* 'Quorum ego paradoxa malo iisdem sepelire tenebris, unde subito
emerserant, quam apud vos, amplissimi ordines, hoc est, in orbis terrarum
luce memorari.' In the *Corpus Reformatorum*, ii. pp. 828-835, Bretschneider gives only the German translation of this letter. The original
Latin, whose existence we were ignorant of when our third volume was
published, will be found in Freheri *Script. Rerum German.* iii. p. 295.

† It appears certain that some Germans were imprisoned; but they
were afterwards released and sent back to Germany by the king's order.
—*Corpus Reformatorum*, ii. p. 857.

But a new change then occurred: suddenly, and with greater violence than ever, new difficulties arose, which threatened to make shipwreck of the whole business. Francis I. had caused the conciliatory opinions of Melanchthon, Hedio, and Bucer to be circulated in Germany.* Some unwise and by no means upright adherents of catholicism mutilated and abridged those opinions,† and then proclaimed with an air of triumph that the heretics, with Melanchthon at their head, were about to return into the bosom of the Church! . . . Excessive was the irritation in the evangelical flocks, and loud cries arose from every quarter against the temporisers and their weakness. They called to mind that truth is not a merchandise which can be cheapened; but a chain, of which if but one link be broken, all the rest is useless. ' Melanchthon is of opinion,' said some, ' that a single pontiff, residing at Rome, would be very useful to maintain harmony of faith between the different nations of Christendom. Bucer adds that we must not overthrow all that exists in popery, but restore in the protestant churches many of the practices observed by the ancients. The men who speak thus are deserters and turncoats. They betray our cause, they commit a crime.'‡ If such protests as these were heard among the Lutherans, doctors such as Farel and Calvin spoke out still more plainly against all attempts at union with popery. ' It is wrong,' wrote Calvin afterwards to

---

* For these opinions see *supra,* vol. ii. p. 353.

† 'Mutilati et excerpti . . . . . mala fide decerpti.'—*Corpus Reformatorum,* ii. p. 976.

‡ 'Vocor transfuga, desertor . . . . . me totam causam prodidisse.' —Melanchthon to Du Bellay. *Corpus Reform.* ii. p. 915.

some English friends, ' to preserve such paltry rubbish, the sad relics of papal superstition, every recollection of which we ought to strive to extirpate.'* The thought that Francis I. was at the head of these negotiations filled the Swiss theologians in particular with ineffable disgust. ' What good can be expected of that prince,' said Bullinger, ' that impure, profane, ambitious man?† He is dissembling: Christ and truth are of no account in his projects. His only thought is how to gain possession of Naples and Milan. What does this or that matter, so that he makes himself master of Italy?' These honest Swiss were not wanting in common sense. Alarmed at the trap that was preparing for Reform, Bullinger, Blaarer, Zwick, and other reformed divines wrote to Bucer: 'It is of no use your contriving a reunion with the pope; thousands of protestants would rather forfeit their lives than follow you.'

At the same time the Sorbonne and its followers raised their voices still higher against all assimilation with Lutheran doctrines. The storm swelled on both sides, and burst upon the moderate party. Poor Bucer, driven in different directions, succumbed under the weight of his sorrow. ' Would to God,' he exclaimed, ' that, like the French martyrs, I were delivered from this life to stand before the face of Jesus Christ!'‡

Every hope of union seemed lost. The ship which

---

* ' C'est un vice d'entretenir des menus fatras.'—Calvin, *Lettres Françaises*, i. p. 420.

† ' De Gallo, homine impuro, profano et ambitioso.'—Bullinger to Myconius, 12 March 1534. *Corp. Ref.* p. 122.

‡ ' Ego velim . . . . cum Gallis martyribus Christum adire.'—Bucer, *Zeitschrift für Hist. Theol.* 1850, p. 44.

the politic King of France had launched, and to
which the hand of the pious Melanchthon had fastened
the banners of peace, had been carried upon the
breakers; all attempts to get her out to sea again
appeared useless; there was neither water enough to
float her, nor wind enough to move her. She was
about to be abandoned, when a sudden breeze extri-
cated her from the shallows, and launched her once
more upon the wide ocean.

Clement VII. having died of chagrin, occasioned by
the prospect of a future in which he could see nothing
but deception and sorrow,* the King of France
considered himself thenceforward liberated from the
promises made to Catherine's uncle. Ere long the
choice of the Sacred College gave him still greater
liberty. Alexander Farnese, who, under the title of
Paul III., succeeded Clement, was a man of the
world; he had studied at Florence in the famous
gardens of Lorenzo de' Medici, and from his youth
had lived an irregular life. On one occasion, being
imprisoned by his mother's orders in the castle of St.
Angelo, he took advantage of the moment when the
attention of his gaolers was attracted by the procession
of Corpus Christi to escape through a window by
means of a rope. Although he had two illegitimate
children, a son and a daughter, he was made cardinal,
and from that hour kept his eyes steadily fixed upon
the triple crown. He obtained it at last, at the age
of sixty-seven, and declared that in religious matters
he would follow very different principles from those of
his predecessors. This man, who had so much need of

---

* 'E fu questo dolore ed affanno che lo condusse alla morte.'—Soriano,
in Ranke, i. p. 127.

reformation for himself and his family, was engrossed wholly with reforming the Church. We shall find not only a king of France, but a pope of Rome also, making advances to Melanchthon. Leo X. bequeathed schism to Christendom. Paul III. undertook to restore unity, and thus hoped to acquire a greater glory than that of the Medicis. He promised the ambassadors of Charles V. to call a council, and four days after his election declared his intentions in full consistory. 'I desire a reform,' he said; 'but before we attempt to change the universal Church, we must first sweep out the court of Rome;' and he nominated a congregation to draw up a plan of reform. Proud of his skill, he thought that everything would be easy to him, and already triumphed in imagination over the Germans, who were, in his opinion, so boorish, and the Swiss, who were so barbarous. Francis I., satisfied with this disposition of the pope, was not unaware, besides, that he had private means of communicating with him. The first secretary of his Holiness was Ambrosio, an influential man and by no means averse to presents. A person who had need of his services having given him sixty silver basins with as many ewers, 'How is it,' said a man one day, 'that with all these basins to wash in, his hands are never clean?'*

But the work of union was not to be so easy as the conjunction of two such stars as Farnese and Valois seemed to promise. While the Romish Church was being toned down at Rome, popery became stricter in France. The fanatical party that was to acquire a horrible celebrity by the crimes of the Bartholomew massacre and of the League, was beginning to take

* Warchi, *Istorie Fiorentine*, p. 636. Ranke.

shape round the dauphin, the future Henry II. That youth of eighteen, who had not long returned from Madrid, was far from being lively, talkative and independent, like a young Frenchman, but gloomy and silent, and appeared to live only to obey women. There were two at his side, admirably calculated to give him a papistical direction : first, his wife, Catherine de Medicis, and next his mistress, Diana of Poitiers, a widow, still beautiful in despite of her age, and who would not (as it has been said) have spoken to a heretic for an empire. The mistress and the wife, who were on the best of terms, and all of the dauphin's party, endeavoured to thwart the king's plans. The most influential members of that faction were continually repeating to him that the protestants of Germany were quite as fanatical and seditious as those of France. At the same time, the emperor's agents, animated by the same intentions, told the German protestants that Francis I. was an infidel in alliance with the Turks. The obstacles opposed in France and Germany to the reconciliation of Christendom were such that its realisation appeared a matter of difficulty.

But in the midst of these intrigues the moderate party held firm. The Du Bellays belonged to one of the oldest families in France; their nobility could be traced back to the reign of Lothaire,* and their mother, Margaret de la Tour-Landry, reckoned among her ancestors a man who had occupied himself with laying down the rules of a good education. After a life of busy warfare, the Chevalier de la Tour-Landry, seignior of Bourmont and Clermont, who lived in the fourteenth century, wrote two

* Moreri, art. *Du Bellay.*

works on education: one for his sons, the other for
his daughters, copies of which became numerous.
The treatise intended for the girls was printed in
1514, perhaps by the direction of the parents of the
Du Bellays. 'Out of the great affection I bear to
my children,' wrote the old cavalier, 'whom I love as
a father ought to love them, my heart will be filled
with perfect joy if they grow up good and honourable, loving and serving God.'* William and John
particularly seemed to have responded to this prayer.
William, the elder, was not void of Christian sentiments. 'I desire,' he said, 'that nothing may happen
injurious to the cause of the Gospel and the glory of
Christ;'† but he was specially one of the most distinguished generals and diplomatists of his epoch. He
knew, says Brantome, the most private secrets of the
emperor and of all the princes of Europe, so that
people supposed him to have a familiar spirit.
Although maimed in his limbs—the consequence of
his campaigns—he was a man of indefatigable activity. His brother John, bishop of Paris, who was
also 'another master-mind,' professed like him an
enlightened catholicism; and hence it happened that
on the accession of Henry II. he was deprived of his
rank by the intrigues of the papist party, and driven
from France. Still, to show that he remained a
catholic, he took up his residence at Rome.

---

* *Livre du Chevalier de la Tour-Landry qui fut fait pour l'enseignement
des femmes mariées et à marier.* It was reprinted in 1854 by Jannet, in
the 'Bibliothèque Elzevirienne.' There are seven manuscript copies in
the Bibliothèque Impériale. See also Burnier, *Histoire littéraire de l'Education,* i. p. 11.

† 'Quod Evangelii causam et Christi gloriam perturbaret.'—*Corp. Ref.*
ii. p. 887.

In 1535 the moderate catholic party, at the head of which were these two brothers, seeing the chances of success at Rome as well as at Paris, resolved to take a more decided step, and to invite Melanchthon to France. The proposal was made to Francis I., and supported by all the members of the party. They knew that Melanchthon was called 'the master of Germany,' and thought that if he came to France he would conciliate all parties by the culture of his mind, by his learning, wisdom, piety, and gentleness. One man, if he appears at the right moment, is some-times sufficient to give a new direction to an entire epoch, to a whole nation. 'Ah, sire,' said Barnabas Voré de la Fosse, a learned and zealous French nobleman, who knew Germany well, and had tasted of the Gospel, 'if you knew Melanchthon, his up-rightness, learning, and modesty! I am his disciple, and fear not to tell it you. Of all those who in our days have the reputation of learning, and who deserve it, he is the foremost.' *

These advances were not useless : Francis I. thought the priests very arrogant and noisy. His despotism made him incline to the side of the pope ; but his love of letters, and his disgust at the monks, attracted him the other way. Just now he thought it possible to satisfy both these inclinations at once. Fully occu-pied with the effect of the moment, and inattentive to consequences, he passed rapidly from one extreme to another. At Marseilles he had thrown himself into the arms of Clement VII., now he made up his mind to hold out his hand to Melanchthon. 'Well!' said the

* 'Cum rege diu de te locutus est, ita ut te omnibus, qui nostris tem-poribus docti et habentur et sunt, prætulerit.'—*Corp. Ref.* ii. p. 857.

king, 'since he differs so much from our rebels, let him come: I shall be enchanted to hear him.' This gavè great delight to the peacemakers: ' God has seen the affliction of his children and heard their cries,' exclaimed Sturm.*   Francis I. ordered De la Fosse to proceed to Germany to urge Melanchthon in person.

A king of France inviting a reformer to come and explain his views was something very new.   The two principal obstacles which impeded the Reformation seemed now to be removed.   The first was the character of the reformers in France, the exclusive firmness of their doctrines, and the strictness of their morality.   Melanchthon, the mild, the wise, the tolerant, the learned scholar, was to attempt the task. The second obstacle was the fickleness and opposition of Francis I.; but it was this prince who made the advances.   There are hours of grace in the history of the human race, and one of those hours seemed to have arrived.   ' God, who rules the tempests,' exclaimed Sturm, ' is showing us a harbour of refuge.'†

The friends of the Gospel and of light set earnestly to work.   It was necessary to persuade Melanchthon, the Elector, and the protestants of Germany, which might be a task of some difficulty.   But the mediators did not shrink from before obstacles; they raised powerful batteries; they stretched the strings of their bow, and made a great effort to carry the fortress.   Sturm, in particular, spared no exertions.   The free courses he was giving at the Royal College, his lectures on Cicero, his logic, which, instead of preparing his dis-

---

* ' Sentio respici a Deo calamitatibus affectas et afflictas hominum conditiones.'—*Corpus Reformatorum*, ii. p. 858.

† ' Deus portum aliquem profugium ostendit.'—*Ibid.* p. 856.

ciples (among whom was Peter Ramus) for barren
disputes, developed and adorned their minds—nothing
could stop him. Sturm was not only an enlightened
man, a humanist, appreciating the Beautiful in the
productions of genius, but he had a deep feeling of the
divine grandeur of the Gospel. Men of letters in those
times, especially in Italy, were often negative in regard
to the things of God, light in their conduct, without
moral force, and consequently incapable of exercising
a salutary influence over their contemporaries. Such
was not Sturm : and while those *beaux-esprits*, those
wits were making a useless display of their brilliant
intelligence in drawing-rooms, that eminent man exhibited a Christian faith and life : he busied himself
in the cultivation of all that is most exalted, and
during his long career, never ceased from enlightening
his contemporaries.* 'The future of French protestantism is in your hands,' he wrote to Bucer; 'Melanchthon's answer and yours will decide whether the
evangelicals are to enjoy liberty, or undergo the most
cruel persecutions. When I see Francis I. meditating
the revival of the Church, I recognise God, who in-
clines the hearts of princes. I do not doubt his
sincerity; I see no hidden designs, no political motives; although a German by birth, I do not share
my fellow-countrymen's suspicions about him. The
king, I am convinced, wishes to do all he can to
reform the Church, and to give liberty of conscience
to the French.'† Such was, then, the hope of the

---

* See Schmidt's *Vie de Jean Sturm, premier recteur de Strasbourg.*

† 'Da Franz I. aüf Erneürung der Kirche sinne . . . . bereit sei zur
Kirchenverbesserung, das seine zu thun, und die Gevissen frei zu lassen.'
—Sturm to Bucer. Schmidt, *Zeitschrift für die Hist. Theol.* 1850, i. p. 46;
Strobel, *Hist. du Gymnase de Strasbourg,* p. 111 &c.

most generous spirits—such the aim of their labours.

Sturm, wishing to do everything in his power to give France that liberty and reformation, wrote personally to Melanchthon. He was the man to be gained, and the professor set his heart upon gaining him. 'How delighted I am at the thought that you will come to France!' he said. 'The king talks much about you; he praises your integrity, learning, and modesty; he ranks you above all the scholars of our time, and has declared that he is *your disciple*.* I shed tears when I think of the devouring flames that have consumed so many noble lives; but when I learn that the king invites you to advise with him as to the means of extinguishing those fires, then I feel that God is turning his eyes with love upon the souls who are threatened with unutterable calamities. What a strange thing! France appeals to you at the very time when our cause is so fiercely attacked. The king, who is of a good disposition at bottom, perceives so many defects in the old cause, and such imprudence in those who adhere to the truth, that he applies to you to find a remedy for these evils. O Melanchthon! to see your face will be our salvation. Come into the midst of our violent tempests, and show us the haven. A refusal from you would keep our brethren suspended above the flames. Trouble yourself neither about emperors nor kings: those who invite you are men who are fighting against death. But they are not alone: the voice of Christ, nay, the voice of God

* 'Non rogatus se discipulum tuum esse dixit.'—*Corpus Reformatorum*, ii. p. 857.

himself, calls you.'*· The letter is dated from Paris, 4th March, 1535.

The Holy Scriptures, which were read wherever the Reform had penetrated, had revived in men's hearts feelings of real unity and christian charity. Such cries of distress could not fail to touch the protestants of Germany; Bucer, who had also been invited, made preparations for his departure. 'The French, Germans, Italians, Spaniards, and other nations, who are they?'† he asked. 'All are our brethren in Jesus Christ. It is not this nation or that nation only, but all nations that the Father has given to the Son. I am ready,' he wrote to Melanchthon; 'prepare for your departure.'

What could Melanchthon do? that was the great question. Many persons, even in Germany, had hoped that France would put herself at the head of the great revival of the Church. Had not her kings, and especially Louis XII., often resisted Rome? Had not the university of Paris been the rival of the Vatican? Was it not a Frenchman who, cross in hand, had roused the West to march to the conquest of Jerusalem? Many believed that if France were transformed, all Christendom would be transformed with her. To a certain point, Melanchthon had shared these ideas, but he was less eager than Bucer. The outspoken language of the placards had shocked him; but the burning piles erected in Paris had afterwards revolted him; he feared that the king's plans were a mere trick, and his reform a phantom. Nevertheless,

---

* 'Sed advocari te Dei Christique voce.'—*Corp. Ref.* ii. p. 859.

† 'Qui sunt Germani, qui Itali, qui Hispani et alii?'—Schmidt, *Zeitschr. für Hist. Theol.* 1850, p. 47.

after reflecting upon the matter, he concluded that the conquest of such a mighty nation was a thing of supreme importance. His adhesion to the regenerating movement then accomplishing might decide its success, just as his hostility might destroy it. He must do something more than open his arms to France, he must go to meet her.

Melanchthon understood the position and set to work. First, he wrote to the bishop of Paris, in order to gain him over to the proposed union, by representing to him that the episcopal order ought to be maintained. The German doctor did not doubt that even under that form, the increasing consciousness of truth and justice, the living force of the Gospel, which was seen opening and increasing everywhere, would gain over to the Reformation the fellow-countrymen of St. Bernard and St. Louis. 'France is, so to speak, the head of the Christian world,' he wrote to the bishop of Paris.* 'The example of the most eminent people may exercise a great influence over others. If France is resolved to defend energetically the existing vices of the Church, good men of all countries will see their fondest desires vanish. But I have better hopes; the French nation possesses, I know, a remarkable zeal for piety.† All men turn their eyes to us; all conjure us, not only by their words, but by their tears, to prevent sound learning from being stifled, and Christ's glory from being buried.'

On the same day, 9th of May, 1535, Melanchthon

---

* 'Cum regnum gallicum, si licet dicere, caput christiani orbis sit.'— *Corpus Reformatorium*, ii. p. 869.

† 'Gallica natio eximium habet pietatis studium.'—*Ibid.*

wrote to Sturm: 'I will not suffer myself to be prevented either by domestic ties or the fear of danger.
There is no human grandeur which I can prefer to
the glory of Christ. Only one thought checks me:
I doubt of my ability to do any good; I fear it will
be impossible to obtain from the king what I consider
necessary to the glory of the Lord and the peace of
France.* If you can dispel these apprehensions, I
shall hasten to France, and no prison shall affright me.
We must seek only for what is fitting for the Church
and France. You know that kingdom. Speak. If
you think I should do well to undertake the journey,
I will start.'

Melanchthon's letter to the bishop of Paris was not
without effect. That prelate had just been made a
cardinal; but the new dignity in nowise diminished
his desire for the restoration of truth and unity in
the Church; on the contrary, it gave him more power
to realise the great project. The Reformation was
approaching. Delighted with the sentiments expressed to him by the *master* of Germany, he communicated his letter to such as might feel an interest
in it, and among others, no doubt, to the king. 'There
is not one of our friends here,' he said, 'to whom
Melanchthon's mode of seeing things is not agreeable.
As for myself, it is pleasant far beyond what I can
express.'† It was the same with his brother William.
While the new cardinal especially desired a union
with Melanchthon in the hope of obtaining a wise

* 'Vereor ut impetrari ea possint quæ ad gloriam Christi et tranquil-
litatem Galliæ et Ecclesiæ necessaria esse duco.'—*Corpus Reformatorum*,
ii. p. 876.

† 'Mihi vero etiam supra quam dici potest jucundum.'—*Ibid.* p. 880.

and pious reform, the councillor of Francis I. desired, while leaving to the pope his spiritual authority, to make France politically independent of Rome. The two brothers united in entreating the king to send for Luther's friend. De la Fosse joined them, and all the friends of peace, in conjuring the king to give the German doctor some proof of his good-will. 'He will come if you write to him,' they said.

Francis I. made up his mind, and instead of addressing the sovereign whose subject Melanchthon was, the proud king of France wrote to the plain doctor of Wittemberg. This was not quite regular; had the monarch written to the elector, such a step might have produced very beneficial results; not so much because the susceptibility of the latter prince would not have been wounded, as because the reasons which Francis, with Du Bellay's help, might have given him, would perhaps have convinced a ruler so friendly to the Gospel and to peace as John Frederick. It is sometimes useful to observe the rules of diplomacy. This is the letter from the king of France to the learned doctor, dated 23rd of June, 1535.

'Francis, by the grace of God king of the French,
to our dear Philip Melanchthon, greeting:
'I have long since been informed by William du Bellay, my chamberlain and councillor, of the zeal with which you are endeavouring to appease the dissensions to which the Christian doctrine has given rise. I now learn from the letter which you have written to him, and from Voré de la Fosse, that you are much inclined to come to us, to confer with some of our most distinguished doctors on the means of

restoring in the Church that divine harmony which
is the first of all my desires.*   Come then, either in
an official character, or in your own name; you will
be very acceptable to me, and you will learn, in either
case, the interest I feel in the glory of your Germany
and the peace of the universe.'

These declarations from the king of France forwarded the enterprise; before taking such a step, he
must have been very clear in his intentions.   We
may well ask, however, if the letter was sincere.   In
history, as in nature, there are striking contrasts.
While these things were passing in the upper regions
of society, scenes were occurring in the lower regions
which ran counter to those fine projects of princes
and scholars.   The Swiss divines maintained that the
whole affair was a comedy in which the king and his
ministers played the chief parts.   That may be ques-
tionable, but the interlude was a blood-stained tragedy.
In the very month when Francis I. wrote to Melanchthon, a poor husbandman of La Bresse, John Cornon,
was arrested while at work in the fields, and taken to
Macon.   The judges, who expected to see an idiot
appear before them, were astonished when they heard
that poor peasant proving to them, in his simple
patois, the truth of his faith, and displaying an extensive knowledge of Holy Scripture.   As the pious
husbandman remained unshaken in his attachment to
the all-sufficient grace of Jesus Christ, he was condemned to death, dragged on a hurdle to the place
of execution, and there burnt alive.†

* 'Quo resarciri possit pulcherrima illa ecclesiasticæ politiæ harmonia,
qua una re cum ego mihi nihil unquam quicquam majori cura, studio
complectendum esse duxerim.'—*Corp. Ref.* ii. p. 880.

† Crespin, *Actes des Martyrs*, p. 116.

In the following month of July, Dennis Brion, a humble barber of Sancerre, near Paris, and a reputed heretic, was taken in his shop. He had often expounded the Scriptures, not only to those who visited him, but also to a number of persons who assembled to hear him. Nothing annoyed the priests so much as these meetings, where simple Christians, speaking in succession, bore testimony to the light and consolation they had found in the Bible. Brion was condemned, as the husbandman of La Bresse had been, and his death was made a great show. It was the time of the *grands jours* at Angers; and there he was burnt alive, in the midst of an immense concourse of people from every quarter.† It is probable that these executions were not the result of any new orders; but a mere sequel to the cruelties of the 21st of January, the influence of which had only then reached the provinces.

These two executions, however, made the necessity of labouring to restore peace and unity still more keenly felt. Those engaged in the task saw but one means: to admit on one side the evangelical doctrine, and on the other the episcopal form with a bishop *primus inter pares*. Western Christendom would thus have a protestant body with a Roman dress. The Church of the Reformation (it was said) holds to doctrine before all things, and the Church of Rome to its government; let us unite the two elements. The Wittemberg doctors hoped that the substance would prevail over the form; the Roman doctors that the form would prevail over the substance; but many on

---

* Crespin, *Actes des Martyres*, p. 126.

both sides honestly believed that the proposed combination would succeed and be perpetual.

At the same time as De la Fosse started for Wittemberg, the new cardinal Du Bellay departed for Rome: two French embassies were to be simultaneously in the two rival cities. The ostensible object of the cardinal's journey was not the great matter which the king had at heart, but to thank the pope for the dignity conferred upon him; still it was the intention and the charge of the bishop of Paris to do all in his power to induce the catholic Church to come to an understanding with the protestants. Before quitting France, he wrote to Melanchthon: 'There is nothing I desire more earnestly than to put an end to the divisions which are shaking the Church of Christ. My dear Melanchthon, do all you can to bring about this happy pacification.* If you come here, you will have all good men with you, and especially the king, who is not only in name, but in reality, *most Christian*. When you have conferred with him thoroughly, which will be soon, I trust, there is nothing that we may not hope for. God grant that at Rome, whither I am going with all speed, I may obtain, in behalf of the work I meditate, all the success that I desire.'†

The cardinal's journey was of great importance. The party to which he belonged, which desired one sole Catholic church, in which evangelical doctrines and Romish forms should be skilfully combined, was acquiring favour in the metropolis of catho-

---

* In hanc pacificationem, mi Melanchthon, per Deum quantum potes incumbe.'—*Corp. Ref.* ii. p. 881.

† The letter is dated: ' Ex fano Quintini (St. Quentin) in Viromanduis, die 27 Jun. anno 1535.'—*Ibid.*

licism. The new pope raised to the cardinalate Contarini and several other prelates who were known for their evangelical sentiments and the purity of their lives. He left them entire liberty; he permitted them to contradict him in the consistory, and even encouraged them to do so. The hope of a reform grew greater day by day in Italy.* It thus happened that Cardinal du Bellay found himself in a very favourable atmosphere at Rome: he would be backed by the influence of France, and to a certain point by the imperial influence also, for no one desired more strongly than Charles V. an arrangement between catholics and protestants. The bishop of Paris, an enlightened and skilful diplomatist and pious man, had a noble appearance, and displayed in every act the mark of a great soul.† He thus won men's hearts, and might, in concert with Melanchthon, be the chosen instrument to establish the so much desired unity in the Church.

While he was on his way to confer with the pope and cardinals, others were canvassing Melanchthon and the protestants. De la Fosse left for Wittemberg, bearing the king's letter, and William du Bellay, an intelligent statesman, who was determined to spare no pains to bring the great scheme to a successful issue, wrote to the German doctor, explaining motives and removing objections. In his eyes the cause in question was the greatest of all: it was the cause of religion and of France. 'Let us beware,' wrote the

---

* 'Molti anni inanzi, li prelati non erano stati in quelle riforma di vita; li cardinali havevono libertà maggiore di dire l' opinione loro, in consistorio . . . . Si poteva sperare di giorno in giorno maggiore riforma.'— *Tre libri delli Commentarj delli Guerra,* 1537. Ranke.

† De Thou; Sainte-Marthe.

councillor of Francis I. to Melanchthon, 'let us beware of irritating the king, whose favour you will confess is necessary to us. If, after he has written to you with his own hand, after you have almost given your consent, after he has sent you a deputation, in whose company you could make the journey without danger—if you finally refuse to come to France, I much fear that the monarch will not look upon it with a favourable eye. It is necessary both to France and religion that you comply with the king's request.* Fear not the influence of the wicked, who cannot endure to be deprived of anything in order that the glory of Jesus Christ should be increased.† The king is skilful, prudent, yielding, and allows himself to be convinced by sound reasons. If you have an interview with him, if you talk with him, if you set your motives before him, you will inflame him with an admirable zeal for your cause.‡ Do not think that you will have to dissemble or give way. . . . No; the king will praise your courage in such serious matters more than he would praise your weakness. I therefore exhort and conjure you in Christ's name not to miss the opportunity of doing the noblest of all the works which it is possible to perform among men.'

As we read these important letters, these touching solicitations, and the firm opinions of the councillor of Francis I., we are tempted to enquire what is their date. Is it in reality only five months after the strappadoes? One circumstance explains the start-

---

* 'Necessarium esse religioni et Galliæ ut regiæ exspectationi satisfacias.'—*Corp. Ref.* ii. p. 888.

† 'Non enim est quod metuas iniquorum potentiam.'—*Ibid.*

‡ 'Mirabiliter eum inflammares.'—*Ibid.*

ling contrast. France might say : 'I feel two natures in me.' Which of them shall prevail? That is the question. Will it be the intelligence, frankness, love of liberty, and presentiment of the moral responsibility of man, which are often found in the French people? or the incredulity, superstition, sensuality, cruelty, and despotism, of which Catherine de Medicis, her husband, and her sons were the types? Shall we see a people, eager for liberty, submitting in religious things to the yoke of a Church which never allows any independence to individual thought? Strange to say, the solution of this important question seemed to depend upon a reformer. Should Melanchthon come to France, he would, in the opinion of the Du Bellays and the best intellects of the age, inaugurate with God's help in that illustrious country the reign of the Gospel and liberty, and put an end to the usurpations of Rome.

If the great enterprise at which some of the best and most powerful personages were then working succeeded—if the tendency of Catherine and her sons (continued unfortunately by the Bourbons) were overcome, France was saved. It was a solemn opportunity. Never perhaps had that great nation been nearer the most important transformation.

In addition to the appeals of Du Bellay, no means were spared to persuade Germany. Sturm wrote another letter to the Wittemberg doctor, telling him that the king was not very far from sharing the religious ideas of the protestants, and that if his views were laid clearly and fearlessly before him, the reformer would find that the sovereign agreed with him on

many important points.   And more than this, Claude
Baduel, who, after studying at Wittemberg, was in
succession professor at Paris, rector at Nismes, and
pastor at Geneva, was entrusted by the queen of
Navarre with a mission to Melanchthon.   Francis I.,
wishing to pass from words to deeds, published an
amnesty on the 16th July, 1535, in which he declared
that ' the anger of our Lord being appeased, persons
accused or suspected should not be molested, that all
prisoners should be set at liberty, their confiscated
goods restored, and the fugitives permitted to re-enter
the kingdom, provided they lived as good catholic
christians.' *

As Francis I. did not wish to alarm the court of
Rome, and desired to prevent it from interfering and
seeking to disturb and thwart his plans, he called
Cardinal du Bellay to him a short time before his
departure, and said: ' You will give the Holy Father
to understand, that I am sending your brother to the
protestants of Germany to get what he can from
them ; at the very least, to prevail on them to
acknowledge the power of the pope as head of the
Church universal.   With regard to faith, religion,
ceremonies, institutions, and doctrines, he will preserve such as it will be proper to preserve—at least,
what may reasonably be tolerated, while waiting the
decision of the council. . . . Matters being thus
arranged, our Holy Father will then be able earnestly
and joyfully to summon a council to meet at Rome,
and his authority will remain sure and flourishing;
for if the enemies of the Holy See once draw in their

* Isambert, xii. p. 405 ; Sismondi, xvi. p. 459.

horns in Germany, they will do the same in France, Italy, England, Scotland, and Denmark.'*

The opinions of Francis I. come out clearly in these instructions. The only thing he cared about was the preservation of the pope's temporal power. As for religion, ceremonies, and doctrines, he would try to come to an understanding; he would get what he could; but the protestants must pull in their horns— must renounce their independent bearing. The king declared himself satisfied, provided the people of Europe continued to walk beneath the Caudine forks of Romish power.

It was not long before the king showed what were his real intentions, and towards what kind of reconciliation a council would have to labour, if one should ever be assembled, which was very doubtful. On the 20th July, the Bishop of Senlis, his confessor, requested the Sorbonne to nominate ten or twelve of its theologians, to confer with the reformers. If a bombshell had fallen in the midst of the Faculty, it could not have caused greater alarm. 'What an unprecedented proposal!' exclaimed the doctors; 'is it a jest or an insult?' For two days they remained in deliberation. 'We will nominate deputies,' said the assembly; 'but for the purpose of remonstrating with the king.' 'Sire,' boldly said these delegates, 'your proposal is quite useless and supremely dangerous. Useless, for the heretics will hear of nothing but Holy Scripture; dangerous, for the catholics, who are weak in faith, may be perverted by the objections of the heretics. . . . Let the Germans communicate to

* Instructions des rois très chrétiens et de leurs ambassadeurs (Paris, 1654), p. 7.

us the articles on which they have need of instruction, we will give it them willingly; but there can be no discussion with heretics. If we meet them, it can only be as their judges. It is a divine and a human law to cut off the corrupted members from the body. If such is the duty of the State against assassins, much more is it their duty against schismatics who destroy souls by their rebellion.' *

These different movements did not take place in secret; they were talked about all over the city, and far beyond it. Enlightened minds were much amused by the fear which the doctors of the Sorbonne had of speaking. There was no lack of remarks on that subject. 'We must not chatter and babble overmuch about the Gospel; but it is absurd that, when anybody enquires into our faith, we should say nothing in defence of it. Let us discourse about the mysteries of God peaceably and mildly: to be silent is a supineness and cowardice worthy of the sneers of unbelievers.' † When Marot the poet heard of the answer of the Sorbonne, he said:

Je ne dis pas que Mélanchthon
Ne déclare au roi son advis ;
Mais de disputer vis-à-vis . . .
Nos maîtres n'y veulent entendre.

The politicians were not silent. The prospect of an agreement with the protestants deeply moved the chiefs of the Roman party, who resolved to do all in their power to oppose the attempt. Montmorency, the grand master, the Cardinal de Tournon, the Bishop of Soissons, de Chateaubriand, and others exerted all

---

* Ballue et Bouchigny. Crevier, *Hist. de l' Université*, v. pp. 2–4.
† Calvin.

their influence to prevent Melanchthon from coming to
France, Cardinal du Bellay from succeeding at Rome,
and catholics and protestants from shaking hands
together under the auspices of Francis I.   This fanatical party, which was to make common cause with
the Jesuits, already forestalled them in cunning.
'One morning,' say Roman-catholic historians,* 'Cardinal de Tournon appeared at the king's *lever*, reading a book magnificently bound.'   'Cardinal, what a
handsome book you have there!' said the king.   'Sire,'
replied De Tournon, 'it is the work of an illustrious
martyr, Saint Irenæus, who presided over the Church
of Lyons in the second century.   I was . reading the
passage which says that John the Evangelist, being
about to enter some public baths, and learning that
the heretic Cerinthus was inside, hastily retired, exclaiming: "Let us fly, my children, lest we be swallowed up with the enemies of the Lord."   That is
what the apostles thought of heretics; and yet you,
Sire, the eldest son of the Church, intend inviting to
your court the most celebrated disciple of that arch-
heretic Luther.'   De Tournon added that an alliance
with the Lutherans would not only cause Milan to
be lost to France, but would throw all the catholic
powers into the arms of the emperor.†   Francis I.,
though persisting in his scheme, saw that he could not·
force those to speak who had made up their minds to
be silent; and wishing to give De Tournon some little
satisfaction he let the Faculty know that he would
not ask them to confer with the reformers.   The king
intended to hear both parties; he sought to place

* Pallavicini, Maimbourg, Varillas, &c.
† Maimbourg, *Calvinisme*, p. 28.   Varillas, ii. p. 449.

himself between the two stormy seas, like a quiet channel, which communicates with both oceans, and in which it was possible to manœuvre undisturbed by tempests.

The refusal of the Sorbonne, at that time more papistical than the pope himself, does not imply that a conference between protestant and catholic theologians was impossible; for six years later such a conference really did take place at Ratisbon, and nearly succeeded. A committee, half protestant, half Romanist, in which Melanchthon and Bucer sat, and in which the pious Cardinal Contarini took part as papal legate, admitted the evangelical faith in all essential points, and declared in particular that man is justified not by his own merits, but by faith alone in the merits of Christ, pointing out, however, as the protestants had always done, that the faith which justifies must *work by love*. That meeting of Ratisbon came to nothing: it could come to nothing. A gleam of light shone forth, but a breath from Rome extinguished the torch, and Contarini submitted in silence. The conference, however, remains in history as a solemn homage, paid by the most believing members of the Roman-catholic Church to the christian doctrines of the Reformation.*

* 'Acta in conventu Ratisbonensi, 1541,' by Melanchthon and Bucer.

CHAPTER XVII.

WILL THE ATTEMPT TO ESTABLISH UNITY AND TRUTH SUCCEED?

(AUGUST TO NOVEMBER 1535.)

WAS the union desired by so many eminent men to be for good or for evil? On this question different opinions may be, and have been, entertained. Certain minds like to isolate themselves, and look with mistrust and disdain upon human associations. It is true that man exists first as an individual, and that before all things he must be himself; but he does not exist alone: he is a member of a body, and this forms the second part of his existence. Human life is both a monologue and a dialogue. Before the era of Christianity, these two essential modes of being had but an imperfect existence: on the one hand, social institutions absorbed the individual, and on the other, each nation was encamped apart. Christianity aggrandised individuality by calling men to unite with God, and at the same time it proclaimed the great unity of the human race, and undertook to make into one family all the families of the earth, by giving the same heavenly Father to all. It imparts a fresh intensity to individuality by teaching man that a single soul is in God's eyes of more value than the whole universe; but this, far from doing society an injury, becomes the source of great prosperity to it.   The more an individual is developed in a Christian sense, the more useful a member he becomes of the nation and of the human race.   Individuality and community are the two poles of life; and it is necessary to maintain both, in order that humanity may fulfil its mission in revolving ages.   The mischief lies in giving an unjust pre-eminence to either of the two elements.   Romish unity, which encroaches upon individuality, is an obstacle to real christian civilisation; while an extreme individuality, which isolates man, is full of peril both to society and to the individual himself.   It would therefore be unreasonable to condemn or to approve absolutely the eminent men who in 1535 endeavoured to restore unity to the Church.   The question is to know whether, by reconstructing catholicity, they intended or not to sacrifice individual liberty.   If they desired a real christian union, their work was good; if, on the contrary, they aimed at restoring unity with a hierarchical object, with a despotic spirit, their work was bad.

There was another question on which men were not more agreed.   Would the great undertaking succeed?   France continued to ask for Melanchthon; would Germany reply to her advances?   We must briefly glance at the events which had taken place in the empire since the agreement between the catholics and protestants concluded, as we have seen, in July 1532.*   These events may help us to solve the question.

It had been stipulated in the religious peace that

* *Supra,* vol. ii. ch. xxi. bk. 2,

all Germans should show to one another a sincere and christian friendship. In the treaty of Cadan (29th June, 1534), Ferdinand, who had been recognised as king of the Romans, had undertaken, both for himself and for Charles V., to protect the protestants against the proceedings of the imperial court. Somewhat later, the city of Münster, in Westphalia, had become the theatre of the extravagances of fanaticism. John Bockhold, a tailor of Leyden, setting himself up for a prophet, had made himself master of the city, and been proclaimed king of Zion. He had also established a community of goods, and attempted, like other sectarians, to restore polygamy. He used to parade the city, wearing a golden crown; to sit in judgment in the market-place, and would often cut off the head of a condemned person. A pulpit was erected at the side of the throne, and after the sermon the whole congregation would sometimes begin to dance. The Landgrave, Philip of Hesse, one of the leaders of the protestant cause, marched against these madmen, took Münster on the 24th June, 1535, and put an end to the pretended kingdom of Zion.* These extravagances did not injure the Protestant cause, which was not confounded with a brutal communism, reeking with cruelty and debauchery; besides, it was the protestants, and not the catholics, who had put them down. But from that hour, the evangelicals felt more strongly than ever the necessity of resisting the sectarian spirit: this they had done at Wittemberg as early as 1522. At last it appeared clearer every day that the free and christian general council, which

* *Historia belli Anabaptistarum monasteriensis*, by H. von Kerssenbroeck.

they had so often demanded, would be granted them. All the events, which we have indicated, seemed to have prepared protestant Germany to accept the proposals of France.

Voré de la Fosse, bearing letters from Francis I., William du Bellay, and other friends of the union, was going to Germany to try and bring it to a successful issue. De la Fosse was not such a distinguished ambassador as those who figured at London and at Rome, and the power to which he was accredited was a professor in a petty town of Saxony. But Germany called this professor her 'master,' and De la Fosse considered his mission a more important one than any that had been confided to dukes and cardinals. Christendom was weakened by being severed into two parts; he was going to re-establish unity, and revive and purify the old member by the life of the new one. The christian Church thus strengthened would be made capable of the greatest conquests. On the success of the steps that were about to be taken, depended, in the opinion of De la Fosse and his friends, the destiny of the world.

The envoy of Francis I. arrived at Wittemberg on the 4th of August, 1535, and immediately paid Melanchthon a visit, at which he delivered the letters entrusted to him, and warmly explained the motives which ought to induce the reformer to proceed to France. De la Fosse's candour, his love for the Gospel, and his zeal, gained the heart of Luther's friend; by degrees a sincere friendship grew up between them; and when Melanchthon afterwards wanted to justify himself in the eyes of the French, he appealed to the testimony of the 'very good and very excellent Voré.'* But if the messenger pleased him, the message filled his heart with trouble: the perusal of the letters from the king, Du Bellay, and Sturm brought the doubts of this man of peace to a climax. He saw powerful reasons for going to France, and equally powerful reasons for staying in Germany. To use the expression of a reformer, there were two batteries firing upon him by turns from opposite quarters, now driving him to the right, now to the left. What would Charles V. say if a German should go to the court of his great adversary? Besides, what was to be expected from the Sorbonne, the clergy, and the court? Contempt. . . . He would not go. On the other hand, Melanchthon had before him a letter from the king, pressing him to come to Paris. An influential nation might be gained to the Gospel, and carry all the West along with it. When the Lord calls, must we allow ourselves to be stopped by fear? . . . He hesitated no longer: he would depart. Voré de la Fosse was delighted. But erelong other thoughts sprang up to torment the doctor's imagination. What was there not to be feared from a prince who had sworn, standing before the stake at which he was burning his subjects, that to stop heresy, he would, if necessary, cut off his own arm and cast it into the fire? . . . In that terrible day of the strappadoes, a deep gulf had opened in the midst of the Church: was it his business to throw himself, Curtius-like, into the abyss, in order that the gulf should close over him? . . . Melanchthon would willingly leave to the young Roman the glory of devoting himself to the infernal gods.

* 'Viri optimi et fidelissimi Voræi testimonium.'—Melanchthon G. Bellaio, *Corp. Ref.* ii. 315.

De la Fosse visited the illustrious professor daily, and employed every means to induce him to cross the Rhine.* 'We will do whatever you desire,' he said. ' Do you wish for royal letters to secure to you full liberty of going to France and returning? You shall have them. Do you ask for hostages as guarantees for your return? You shall have them also. Do you want an armed guard of honour to escort you and bring you back? It shall be given you.† We will spare nothing. On your interview with the king depends not only the fate of France, but (so to speak) of the whole world.‡ Hearken to the friends of the Gospel who dwell in Paris. Threatening waves surround us, they say by my mouth; furious tempests assail us; but the moment you come we shall find ourselves, as it were, miraculously transported into the safest of havens.§ If, on the contrary, you despise the king's invitation, all hope is lost for us. The fires now slumbering will instantly shoot forth their flames, and there will be a cruel return of the most frightful tortures.‖ It is not only Sturm, Du Bellay, and other friends like them who invite you, but all the pious Christians of France. They are silent, no doubt—those whom the cruellest of punishments have laid among the dead, and even those who, im-

* 'Cum eo locutus de profectione ad Regem.'—Camerarius, *Vita Melanchthonis*, p. 148. Camerarius was an intimate friend of Melanchthon's.

† 'Obsides qui darentur dum abesset. . . . . Præsidia quibus deduceretur.'—*Ibid.*

‡ 'Pæne orbis terrarum fortunam esse positam.'—*Ibid.*

§ 'In illis fluctibus et sævissimis tempestatibus, jam portum et tutissimam stationem.'—*Ibid.*

‖ 'Sopiti ignes rursum suscitarentur, et suppliciorum immanitas recrudesceret.'—*Ibid.*

mured in dungeons, are separated from us by doors of iron; but if their voices cannot reach you, listen at least to one mighty voice, the voice of God himself, the voice of Jesus Christ.'*

When Melanchthon heard this appeal, he was agitated and overpowered.† What an immense task! these Frenchmen are placing the world on his shoulders! Can such a poor Atlas as he is bear it? How must he decide? what must he do? In a short time his perplexity was again increased. The French gentleman had hardly left the room, when his wife Catherine, daughter of the burgomaster of Wittemberg, her relations, her young children, and some of his best friends, surrounded him and entreated him not to leave them. They were convinced that if Melanchthon once set foot in that city 'which killeth the prophets,' they would never see him again. They described the traps laid for him; they reminded him that no safe-conduct had been given him. They shed tears, they clung to him, and yet he did not give way.

Melanchthon was a man of God, and prayed his heavenly Father to show him the road he ought to take: he thoroughly weighed the arguments for and against his going. 'The thought of myself and of mine,' he said, 'the remoteness of the place to which I am invited, and fear of the dangers that await me, ought not to stop me.‡ Nothing should be more sacred to me than the glory of the Son of God, the

* 'Advocari ipsum Dei Christique Jesu voce.'—Camerarius, *Vita Melanchthonis*, p. 148.

† 'Afficiebatur atque perturbabatur.'—*Ibid.*

‡ 'Non respectus ad se aut suos, non longiquitas loci, non periculorum metus.'—*Ibid.* p. 149.

deliverance of so many pious men, and the peace of the Church troubled by such great tempests. Upon that all my thoughts ought to be concentred; but this is what disturbs me: I fear to act imprudently in a matter of such great importance, and to make the disease still more incurable through my precipitancy. Will not the French, while giving way on some trivial points, which they must necessarily renounce, retain the most important articles in which falsehood and impiety are especially found?* Alas! such patchwork would produce more harm than good.'

There was much truth in these fears; but De la Fosse, returning to his friend, sought to banish his apprehensions, and assured him that the disposition of Francis I. was excellent at bottom. 'Yes,' replied Luther's friend, 'but is he in a position to act upon it?'† He expected nothing from a conference with fanatical doctors; besides, the Sorbonne refused all discussion. 'The king,' he said, 'is not the Church. A council alone has power to reform it; and therefore the prince ought to set his heart upon hastening its convocation. All other means of succouring afflicted Christendom are useless and dangerous.'

De la Fosse turned Melanchthon's objection against him. 'At least we must prepare the way for the council,' he said, 'and it is just on that account that the king of France wishes to converse with you.' Then, desiring to strike home, the envoy of Francis I.

---

* 'In quibus potissimum falsitas impietatis resideret.'—Camerarius, *Vita Melanchthonis*, p. 150.

† 'Quid ipse tamen rex posset efficere—non sine causa dubitabat.'—*Ibid.* p. 150.

continued: 'The king never had anything more at heart than to heal the wounds of the Church: he has never shown so much care, anxiety, and zeal.* If you comply with his wishes, you will be received with more joy in France than any stranger before you. Will you withhold from the afflicted Church the hand that can save her? Let nothing in the world, I conjure you, turn you aside from so pure and sacred an enterprise.'† De la Fosse was agitated. The idea of returning to Paris without Melanchthon —that is to say, without the salvation he expected— was insupportable. 'Depart,' he exclaimed; 'if you do not come to France. . . . I shall never return there.'‡

Melanchthon was touched by these supplications. He thought he heard (as they had told him) the voice of God himself. 'Well, then,' he said, 'I will go. My friends in France have entertained great expectations and apply to me to fulfil them: I will not disappoint their hopes.' Melanchthon was resolved to maintain the essential truths of Christianity, and hoped to see them accepted by the catholic world. Francis I. and his friends had not rejected Luther's fundamental article—justification solely by faith in the merits of Christ, by a living faith which produces holiness and works. According to the most eminent and most christian orator of the Roman Church, 'Melanchthon combined learning, gentleness, and ele-

* 'Nullam enim rem unquam majore Regem cura, studio, sollicitudine animi complectendam duxisse.'—Camerarius, *Vita Melanchthonis*, p. 151.

† 'Neque se abduci ullius persuasione sineret ex tam pio sanctoque instituto.'—*Ibid.*

‡ 'Er wollte nicht in Frankreich wiederkommen, so ich nicht mit zöge.'—*Corp. Ref.* ii. p. 905.

gance of style with singular moderation, so that he was regarded as the only man fitted to succeed in literature to the reputation of Erasmus.'* But he was more than that: his convictions were not to be shaken; *he knew where he was*, and far from seeking all his life for his religion, as Bossuet asserts, he had found it and admirably explained it in his *Theological Commonplaces.*† Still he constantly said to his friends: 'We must contend only for what is great and necessary.'‡

Melanchthon, who was full of meekness, was always ready to do what might be agreeable to others. Sincere, open, and exceedingly fond of children, he liked to play with them and tell them little tales. But with all this amiability he had a horror of ambiguous language, especially in matters of faith; and although a man of extreme gentleness, he felt strongly, his anguish could be very bitter, and when his soul was stirred, he would break out with sudden impetuosity, which, however, he would soon repress. His error, in the present case, was in believing that the pope could be received without receiving his doctrines: every true Roman-catholic could have told him that this was impossible. At all events De la Fosse had decided him. For the triumph of unity and truth, this simple-hearted bashful man was resolved to brave the dangers of France and the bitter reproaches of Germany. 'I will go,' he said to the envoy of Francis I. It was the language of a Christian ready

* Bossuet, *Hist. des Variations*, t. i. liv. v. ch. ii. et xix.

† *Loci communes theologici.* They went through sixty-seven editions, and were translated into several languages.

‡ 'Non puto contendendum esse, nisi de magnis et necessariis rebus.'—Melanchthon Sturmio, *Corp. Ref.* ii. p. 917.

to sacrifice himself. In history we sometimes meet
with characters who enlarge our ideas of moral greatness: Melanchthon was one of them.

But would his prince allow him to go? The prejudices of Germany against France, besides numerous
political and religious considerations, might influence
the elector. These were difficulties that might cause
the enterprise to fail. Still the noble-minded professor resolved to do all in his power to overcome
them. The university had just removed from Wittemberg to Jena on account of the plague. Melanchthon, quitting Thuringia, directed his course hastily
towards the banks of the Elbe, and arriving at
Torgau, where the court was staying, at the old
castle outside the city, was admitted on Sunday, the
15th of August, after divine service to present his
respects to the elector.

John Frederick was attended by many of his councillors and courtiers, and notwithstanding the esteem
he felt for Melanchthon, an air of dissatisfaction and
reserve was visible in his face. The elector was
offended because the king of France, instead of
applying to him, had written direct to one of his
subjects; but graver motives caused him to regard
the Wittemberg doctor's project with displeasure.

It was no slight thing for Melanchthon, who was
naturally timid and bashful, to ask his sovereign for
anything likely to displease him. Without alluding
to the letter he had received from Francis.I., which
he thought it wiser not to mention, he said: ' Your
Electoral Grace is aware that eighteen Christians have
been burnt in Paris, and many others thrown into
prison or compelled to fly. The brother of the bishop

of Paris has endeavoured to soften the king, and has written to me that that prince has put an end to the executions, and desires to come to an understanding with us in regard to religious matters. Du Bellay invites me to mount my horse and go to France.* If I refuse, I appear to despise the invitation or to be afraid. For this reason I am ready in God's name to go to Paris, as a private individual, if your Highness permits. It is right that we should teach great potentates and foreign nations the importance and beauty of our evangelical cause. It is right that they should learn what our doctrine is and not confound us with fanatics, as our enemies endeavour to do. I do not deceive myself as to my personal unimportance and incapacity; but I also know, that if I do not go to Paris, I shall appear to be ashamed of our cause, and to distrust the words of the king of . France, and the good men who are endeavouring to put an end to the persecution will be exposed to the displeasure of their master. I know the weight of the task imposed upon me . . . it overwhelms me . . . but I will do my duty all the same, and with that intent I conjure your Grace to grant me two or three months' leave of absence.'

Melanchthon, according to custom, handed in a written petition.† John Frederick was content to answer coldly that he would make his pleasure known through the members of his council.

The ice was broken; France and Germany were face to face in that castle on the banks of the Elbe. The opposition immediately showed itself. The

* 'Ich wollte einen Ritt in Frankreich thun.'—*Corp. Ref.* ii. p. 904.
† *Ibid.* ii. pp. 903-905.

audience given to Melanchthon set all the court in motion. The Germanic spirit prevailed there more than the evangelical spirit, and the knowledge that Germans could be found who were willing to hold out their hands to Francis I. irritated the courtiers. They met in secret conference, looked coldly upon Melanchthon, and addressed him rudely. Gifted with the tenderest feelings, the noble-hearted man was deeply wounded. 'Alas!' he wrote to Jonas, 'the court is full of mysteries, or rather of hatreds! . . . I will tell you all about it when I see you.' *

He awaited with anxiety the official communication from the elector. The next day, 16th of August, he was informed that John Frederick's councillors had a communication to make to him on the part of their master. If the interview with the Elector had been cold, this was icy. Chancellor Bruck— better known as Pontanus, according to the fashion of latinising names—had been intrusted with this mission. Bruck, who at the famous diet of Augsburg had presented the Evangelical Confession to Charles V. in the presence of all the princes of Germany, was an excellent man, more decided than Melanchthon, and in some respects more enlightened; he saw that it was dangerous to accept the pope, if they desired to reject his doctrines. He received the doctor with a severe look, and said to him in a harsh tone: 'His Highness informs you that the business you have submitted to him is of such importance, that you ought not to have engaged yourself in it without his consent. As your intentions

---

* 'Aulica quædam μυστήρια vel potius odia sunt.'—*Corp. Reform.* ii. p. 903.

were good, he will overlook it; but as to permitting you to make a hasty and perilous journey to France, all sorts of reasons are against it. Not only his Highness cannot expose your safety; but as he is on the point of discussing with the emperor several questions which concern religion, he fears that if he sent a deputy to Paris, his Imperial Majesty, and the other princes of Germany, would imagine that he was charged with negotiations opposed to the declarations we have made to them. That journey might be the cause of divisions, quarrels, and irreparable evils.* You are consequently desired to excuse yourself to the king of France in the best way you can, and the elector promises you he will write to him on the subject.'

Melanchthon withdrew in sorrow. What a position was his! His conscience bade him go to Paris, and his prince forbade him. Do what he would, he must fail in one of his most important duties. If he departs in defiance of the elector's prohibition, he will not only offend his prince, but set Germany against himself, and sacrifice the circle of activity which God has given him. If he remains, all hope is lost of bringing France to the light of the Gospel. Hesitating and heartbroken, he went first to Wittemberg, desiring to confer with Luther, and did not conceal from his friend the deep indignation with which he was filled.† He was called to raise the standard of the Gospel in an illustrious kingdom, and the elector opposed it on account of certain diplomatic negotiations. He declared to Luther that he would not

---

* 'Zerrüttung, unwiederbringlicher Nachtheil, Beschwerung und Schade zu erfolgen.'—*Corp. Ref.* ii. p. 908.

† 'Subindignabundus hinc discessit,' said Luther. *Ep.* iv. p. 621.

renounce the important mission, and he was fortified in this opinion by the sentiments which that
reformer entertained. The two friends could speak
of nothing but France, the king, and Du Bellay.
' As you have consulted me,' said Luther, ' I declare
that I should see you depart with pleasure.'* He also
made a communication to Melanchthon which gave the
latter some hope.

Having been informed of the audience of the 15th,
the reformer had just written to the elector. The
cries of his brethren in France, delivered to the flames,
moved Luther at Wittemberg, as they moved Calvin
at Basle. The French reformer addressed an admirable letter to Francis I., and the German reformer endeavoured to send Melanchthon to him. The two men
were thus unsuspectingly ' conjoint together in opinion
and desires.' ' I entreat your Grace,' wrote Luther to
John Frederick, in the most pressing manner, ' to
authorise Master Philip to go to France. I am
moved by the tearful prayers made to him by pious
men, hardly rescued from the stake, entreating him
to go and confer with the king, and thus put an end
to the murders and burnings. If this consolation be
refused them, their enemies, thirsting for blood,† will
begin to slay and burn with redoubled fury. . . .
Francis I. has written Melanchthon an exceedingly
kind letter, and envoys have come to solicit him on
his behalf. . . . For the love of God, grant him three
months' leave. Who can tell what God means to do?
His thoughts are always higher and better than ours.

* 'Philippus . . . . me consule libens proficisceretur.'—Lutheri *Ep.*
iv. p. 621.

† 'Bluthünde,' bloodhounds. *Ibid.* p. 620.

I should be greatly distressed if so many pious souls who invite Melanchthon with cries of pain, and reckon upon him, should be disappointed and conceive untoward prejudices against us.   May God lead your Grace by his Holy Spirit!'

Such was Luther's affection for his brethren in France. He did more than write. The reformer was not in good health just then ; he complained of losing his strength, and of being so *decrepid* that he was compelled to remain idle half the day.*   Notwithstanding this, he made the journey from Wittemberg to Torgau, where he had an interview with the prince.†   Perhaps this journey was anterior to Melanchthon's.

The simultaneous efforts of these two great reformers ought to have produced a favourable effect upon a prince like the elector.   John Frederick, who had succeeded his father John in August 1532, was true and high-minded, a good husband, and a good prince. A disciple of Spalatin and the friend of Luther, he venerated the Word of God, and was full of zeal for the cause of the Reformation.   Less phlegmatic than his father, he united judgment and prudence with an enterprising spirit.   Such qualities must have led him to favour Melanchthon's journey to France. But he was susceptible and rather obstinate; so that if a project, not originating with him, but with

---

* 'Ego non annis, sed viribus, decrepitus fio, ad labores antemeridianos pene totus inutilis factus.'—Lutheri *Ep*. iv. p. 623 (23rd August, 1535).

† 'Nachdem aber Dr. Martinus bey uns zu Torgau auch gewest, so haben wir Ihm solches ungefährlich vermeldet.' This declaration of the elector incontestably proves the fact of Luther's journey to Torgau with this object. The time cannot be fixed, but the elector speaks of it in a paper addressed to Bruck on the 19th August. *Corp. Ref*. ii. p. 908.

another, displeased him in any way, the probability
of its success was not great. And hence Luther's
letter did not make a great impression upon him: it
merely increased the excitement. The prejudices of
Germany rendered Melanchthon's journey less popular
every day; at the court of Torgau, in Saxony, and
in the other protestant countries, it was regarded
as madness. 'We at Augsburg,' wrote Sailer, the
deputy of that city, 'know the king of France well:
he cares very little, as everybody knows, about religion, and even morality. He is playing the hypocrite
with the pope, and cajoling the Germans, thinking
only how he can disappoint the expectations he raises
in them. His sole thought is to crush the emperor.'[*]
Some even of the best disposed were full of horrible
apprehensions, and fancied that they saw an immense
pile constructing on which to burn *the master of Germany.* Passions were roused; a violent tempest
stirred men's minds; the most gloomy opinions
arrived at Torgau every day from all quarters.
Others did not look upon the matter so tragically,
but employed the weapons of ridicule. German susceptibility was wounded because Francis I. had not
selected some great personage for this mission. They
looked down upon Barnabas Voré, called De la Fosse:
'A fine ambassador!' they said; 'all the pawn-
brokers in France would not advance twenty crowns
upon his head.'—'Even the Jews,' said another, 'would
not have such a Barnabas, if they could buy him for
a penny.'[†]

Before long the people grew tired of jests and sup-

---

[*] Seckendorf, *Historie des Lutherthums,* p. 1497.
[†] *Ibid.* p. 1498.

positions, and circulated extraordinary stories. Many prophesied that Melanchthon would be assassinated, even before he had crossed the Rhine. It was reported that the papists had killed the real ambassador on the road, that they had substituted De la Fosse for him, and given him forged letters with a view to influence Melanchthon, for whom they had prepared an ambuscade. 'If he departs, he is a dead man.' * Albert of Mayence, the ecclesiastical elector, in particular gave umbrage to the protestants. When these rumours reached Luther, he said : 'In this I clearly recognise that bishop and his colleagues; of all the devil's instruments, they are the worst; my fears for Philip increase. Alas! the world belongs to Satan, and Satan to the world.' Then, remembering an anecdote, he continued : 'The archbishop of Mayence, after reading Melanchthon's commentary on the Epistle to the Romans, exclaimed: "The man is possessed!" and throwing the volume on the ground, trampled upon it.' If the prince, through whose states Melanchthon would probably have to pass, treated the book thus, what would he do to the author? Luther was shaken. In 1527, George Winckler, the pious pastor of Halle, having been summoned before this very Archbishop Albert, had been murdered by some horsemen as he was returning by the road Melanchthon must take. The great reformer began to change his mind.

The elector, perceiving this, put more solid arguments before him: 'I fear,' he said, 'that if Melanchthon goes to France, he will concede to the papists far more than what you, doctor, and the other theologians

* Luther to Jonas, 1 Sept. 1535. *Ep.* iv. p. 628.

would grant, and hence there would arise a disunion
between you and him that would scandalise Christians
and injure the Gospel.   Those who invite him are
more the disciples of Erasmus than of the Bible.
Melanchthon will infallibly incur the greatest danger .
at Paris—danger both to body and soul.   I would
rather see God take him to Himself than permit him
to go to France.   That is my firm resolve.'*

These communications seriously affected Luther:
the elector attacked him on his weakest side.   The reformer venerated Melanchthon, but he knew to what
sacrifices his desire for union had more than once
been on the point of leading him.   If Melanchthon
was the champion of unity, Luther was the champion
of truth: to guard the whole truth with a holy
jealousy was his principle.   The Reformation, he
thought, must triumph by fidelity to the Word of
God, and not by the negotiations of kings.   Recovering from his first impressions, he said to Melanchthon:
'I begin to suspect these ambassadors.'†   From that
moment he never uttered a word in favour of the
journey.   Still the dangers of the protestants of France
were never out of his thoughts.   'Must we abandon
our brethren?' he asked himself perpetually.   A
luminous idea occurred to him: Suppose the evangelicals were to leave France, and come to Germany
in search of liberty.‡   He engaged to receive them
well: Luther anticipated *the Réfuge* by a century
and a half.

* *Corpus Reformat.* ii. p. 909.   Seckendorf, *Historie des Lutherthums*,
p. 1458.
    † 'Ego suspectos cœpi habere istos legatos tuos.'—Lutheri *Ep.* iv.
p. 627.
    ‡ 'Invenirent loca in quibus viverent.'—*Ibid.*

By degrees the elector gained ground, and the extraordinary adventure proposed to Melanchthon became more doubtful every day. From the first the prince had had the politicians and courtiers with him; then the men of letters and citizens, alarmed by the sinister reports, had gone over to his side; and now Luther himself was convinced. Melanchthon remained almost alone. His sympathetic heart longed to remove the sword hanging over the heads of the French evangelicals, and it seemed as if nothing could stop him. John Frederick endeavoured to convince him. Beyond a doubt, the French reformation, driven at this moment by contrary winds, must reach the haven; but the task must be left to its own crew. Every ship must have its own pilot. John Frederick, therefore, wrote a severe letter to Melanchthon, and the tender-hearted divine had to drink the cup to the dregs. 'You declared that you were ready to undertake a journey to France,' said the elector, 'without consulting us. You should, however, have thought of your duty to us, whom God has established as your superior. We were greatly displeased to see that you had gone so far in the matter. You know the relations existing between the king of France and the emperor, and you are not ignorant that we are obliged to respect them. We desire that foreign nations should be brought to the Gospel; but must we go to them to effect their conversion?* The undertaking is of great extent, and the success very doubtful. The letters we receive from France are well calculated to make us despair of seeing the evangelical seed bear fruit there.

---

* 'Wir viel mehr fördern wollten dasz fremde *nationes* zu dem Evangelio gebracht wurden.'—*Corp. Reform.* ii. p. 911.

*Do you desire to disturb the public peace of the German
nation, and while we have a right to expect that you will
second us, do you presume on the contrary to vex us
and thwart our plans?'*

This was too much. Melanchthon stopped; the
arrow, aimed by the elector, had pierced his heart.
His decision was soon made: 'Because of these
words,' he said, 'I will not go.' He afterwards un-
derlined the passage, and wrote in the margin the
words we have just quoted.* The elector had been
still more severe, when he dictated the despatch. 'Go,'
were his words, 'go and do as you please; engage in
this adventure. But we leave all the responsibility
with you. Consider it well.' He suppressed this
paragraph at the chancellor's desire.†

Melanchthon's simple and tender heart was crushed
by his sovereign's dissatisfaction. Surmounting his
natural shyness, he had determined to brave danger,
in the hope of seeing the Reformation triumph, and
now disgrace was his only reward. The courtiers
maintained that he and the other theologians were
obstinate and almost imbecile, and would do much
better to be content with their schools and leave the
government of the Church to others. Melanchthon
lightened his grief by sharing it with his friends; he
wrote to Camerarius, to Sturm, and even to William
du Bellay. The great hellenist, who had lived much
among the ancient republics of Greece, imagined that
Europe was already overrun by the evils under which

---

* 'Propter hæc verba nolui proficisci.'—*Corp. Ref.* ii. p. 911, in note.
The italics in the text indicate the lines underscored by Melanchthon.

† The passage is found in Bruck's copy (Weimar Archives), but not in
Melanchthon's.

those states had perished. 'I have never known
a more cruel.prince,' he said to them: 'with what
harshness he treats me! * He not only does not permit me to depart, but he insults me besides. My
fault is in being less obstinate than others. I confess that peace is so precious in my eyes that it ought
not to be broken except for matters really great and
necessary. Oh! if the elector did but know those
who take advantage of this proposed journey to sow
discord! It is not the learned who do it, but the
ignorant and the fools. They call me deserter and
runaway. . . . O my friend, we live under the *régime*
of the democracy, that is to say, under the tyranny
of the unlearned,† of people who quarrel about old-
wives' stories, and think of nothing but gratifying
their passions. How great is the hatred with which
they are inflamed against me! . . . They slander
me and say that I am betraying my prince.' Theramenes was condemned to drink hemlock because he
had substituted an aristocracy or government of the
worthiest for a democracy, and governed the state
with wisdom. 'I do not deceive myself,' he exclaimed; 'the fate of Theramenes awaits me.'‡

Melanchthon was not the only sufferer; his faithful friend, Luther, did not fail him. Although he
was now opposed to the French journey, John Frederick's letter disturbed him seriously; it appeared to
him that great changes were necessary, and a stormy
future loomed before him. 'My heart is sad,' he

---

* 'Nunquam sensi asperiorem principem.'—*Corpus Reformat.* ii. p. 915.

† 'Nunc autem est democratia aut tyrannis indoctorum.'—*Ibid.*
p. 917.

‡ 'Plane fatum mihi Theramenis impendere videtur.'—*Ibid.* p. 918.

wrote to Jonas, ' for I know that such a severe letter,
will cause Philip the keenest anguish. . . . All this,
awakens thoughts which I would rather not have.*
Another time I will tell you more . . . at present
I am overwhelmed with sorrow.'   Then, feeling
uneasy about Melanchthon, he wrote to him: ' Have
you *swallowed* our prince's letter? †   I was exceedingly agitated by it from love to you.   Tell me how
you are.' . . .

What were the thoughts that occurred to Luther
involuntarily? There is some difficulty in deciding.
Perhaps the reformer thought that this business might
occasion a difference between Church and State. ' Admire the wisdom of the court,' he said; 'see how it
boasts of being an actor in this adventure! As for
us, we much prefer being merely spectators, and I
begin to congratulate myself that the court despises
and excludes us.‡   It all happens through the goodness of God, so that we should not be mixed up with
these disturbances, which we might perchance have
to lament hereafter very sorely.   Now we are safe, for
whatever is done is done without us. What Demosthenes desired too late, we obtain early—namely, not
to be concerned in the government.§   May God
strengthen us therein! Amen.'   Luther appeared to
foresee a time when the evangelical Church would
have no other support but God, and rejoiced at the
prospect.

- As John Frederick had not yet despatched his letter

---

* 'Cogito varia, quæ utinam non cogitarem.'—Lutheri *Epp.* iv. p. 626.

† ' An devoraveris litteras istas principis.'—*Ibid.* p. 627.

‡ 'Incipio enim unice gaudere, nos ab aula contemni et excludi.'—*Ibid.*

§ ' Scilicet ne ad rempublicam adhibeamur.'—*Ibid.* p. 628.

to Francis I., his councillors delicately advised him to suppress it. 'Since the king has not written to the elector about the proposed journey,' said Luther, 'it would be better for the elector also not to write. A letter from him would perhaps give the king an opportunity of answering, and that should be avoided.'* John Frederick still hesitated, for although his letter was written on the 18th of August, it was not despatched until the 28th. 'Most serene and illustrious king,' he said, 'we should have been willing to do your majesty a pleasure, by permitting Melanchthon to go to France, especially as it was for an extraordinary propagation of the Gospel, so as to make it yield the most abundant and the richest fruit.† But we had to take into consideration the difficulties of the present times.' Then, as a final reason, the elector added: 'Lastly, we do not remember for certain . . . that your Majesty has written to us about Melanchthon. If in any future contingency you should write to us for him,' continued John Frederick, 'and should assure us that he will be restored safe and sound, we will permit him to proceed to you. Be assured that we shall always readily do whatever we can to propagate the Gospel of Christ in every place, to favour the temporal and spiritual interests of your Majesty, your kingdom, and its church, and to hasten the deliverance of the Christian commonwealth.'

Melanchthon, to whom the elector communicated

---

* Lutheri *Epp.* iv. p. 627.

† 'Ad insignem propagationem, uberrimum et amplissimum fructum Evangelii.'—Johannes Fredericus ad Franciscum regem Galliæ. *Corpus Reform.* ii. p. 906.

this letter,* feared that instead of quieting the king
of France, it would only irritate him still more.   He
could not bear the idea of answering ungratefully a
powerful monarch who had shown such kindness
towards him.   This thought engrossed him from
morning to night.   On the very day when the Elector Frederick's letter was despatched, Melanchthon
sent off three, the first of which was for the king.
He feared, above all things, that Francis I. would
relinquish the great enterprise that was to restore
unity and truth to the Church.   He therefore wrote
to him, suppressing the indignation he felt at the
elector's refusal.   ' Most christian and most mighty
king,' he said, ' France infinitely excels all the kingdoms of the world, in that it has continually been a
vigilant sentinel for the defence of the christian religion.†   Wherefore, I humbly congratulate your
Majesty for having undertaken to reform the doctrine
of the Church, not by violent remedies but by reasonable means ;‡ and I beseech your Majesty not to cease
bestowing all your thoughts and all your care upon
this matter.   Sire, do not allow yourself to be stopped
by the harsh judgments and rude writings of certain
men.   Do not suffer their imprudence to nullify a
project so useful to the Church.   After receiving
your letter, I made every effort to hasten to your
Majesty ; for there is nothing I desire more than
to aid the Church according to my poverty.   I had

---

* *Corpus Reform.* ii. p. 903.

† ' Pro religionis christianæ defensione præcipue velut in statione per-
petuo fuit.'—*Ibid.* p. 913.

‡ ' Suscipit curam sanandæ doctrinæ christianæ ; non tamen violentis
remediis, sed vera ratione.'—*Ibid.*

conceived the best hopes, but great obstacles keep me back. . . . Voré de la Fosse will inform you of them.'

If the doctor of Germany was reserved when writing to the king, he allowed the emotions of his heart to be seen in the letters he wrote the same day to Du Bellay and Sturm : ' Could anything be more distressing,' he said to Du Bellay, 'than to be exposed at one and the same time to the anger of the most christian king, the harsh treatment of the elector, and the calumnies of the people ? . . . But the injustice of men shall not rob me of moderation of spirit or zeal for religion.   Touching the journey, I have promised Voré de la Fosse to go to Frankfort shortly, whence, if it be desired, I will hasten to you.'   He had not, therefore, entirely given up France.   ' I hope,' he said in conclusion, 'that the king's mind will be so guided by your advice and by that of your brother the cardinal, that he will henceforward employ all his powers in setting forth the glory of Christ.' *

The work of union to which Francis I. invited Melanchthon, had struck deep root in the doctor's mind.   Sadolet, bishop of Carpentras (who was raised to the cardinalate the year after), having published a treatise on the matter under discussion, the reformer wrote to Sturm that Sadolet advocated the very points he was resolved to defend, but he regretted to see him indulge in such bitter attacks upon the protestants.†   A little later, when the illustrious

---

* ' Ut potius (rex) det operam, ut illustretur gloria Christi.'—*Corpus Reformat.* ii. p. 916.

† ' Sadoleti scriptum . . . . . eadem dicit quæ nos defendimus.'— *Ibid.* p. 917.

Budæus, on whom he had counted, praised Francis for his zeal in expiating and punishing the assaults of the heretics,* Melanchthon was hurt, but not disconcerted. ' I have read his treatise,' he said to Sturm, ' but what does it matter? All these things inflame rather than cool me; they fan my desire to go to you, to make my ideas known to all those learned men, those friends of what is good, and to learn theirs. Let us unite all our forces to save the Church: no injustice of man shall check my zeal.'†

In this respect Melanchthon did not stand alone: Francis I. showed no less energy, and was careful not to be offended at the elector's refusal. The alliance of the protestants became more necessary to him every day. The prince who did so much in France for the arts, and who, as the patron of scholars, received the title of *Father of Letters*, desired a reform after Erasmus's pattern. There was a very marked distinction, which it is impossible to overlook, between Francis I. and his son Henry II.; but the love of knowledge was not the king's chief motive: he entertained certain political designs which greatly increased his eagerness for an alliance with the protestants. The duke of Milan was just dead, and the ambitious Francis desired to conquer the duchy for his second son. Moreover, the evangelical party was not without influence at court: Margaret queen of Navarre, Admiral Chabot, and many noblemen favoured the Gospel: and they were supported by the Du Bellays and others of the moderate party. The men of the

---

* See his treatise: *De transitu Hellenismi ad Christianismum*, dedicated to the king in 1535.

† 'Hoc studium nulla mihi eripiet hominum iniquitas.'—*Corp. Ref.*

Romish faction rallied round Diana of Poitiers and Catherine of Medicis.

The king had discovered that John Frederick had felt hurt at seeing a foreign monarch address one of his subjects on a matter touching the cause of which the elector was regarded as the head. Francis probably thought the prince's susceptibility to be very natural, and therefore, instead of breaking with him, determined to profit by the lesson he had received. He would resume his plans, but he would write no more to Melanchthon: he would address the elector in person, or rather all the protestant princes united, according to the usual forms ; and to avoid reminding them of his first fault, the name of Melanchthon should not be mentioned. The zeal of the learned professor and of the powerful monarch came, we may be sure, from different sources ; one proceeded from on high, the other from below ; but the same desire animated both of them.

The Romish party were greatly agitated when they heard of the king's intentions, and again attempted to thwart a project they regarded as highly pernicious. The Sorbonne represented to Francis I. that no concession ought to be made, and proceeded to demonstrate, after an extraordinary fashion, the articles rejected by the Lutherans. ' They deny the power of the saints to heal the sick,' said the theologians; ' but is not this miraculous power proved by the virtue the kings of France possess of healing the *evil* by a touch?' Francis I. was an extraordinary saint, and such an argument probably amused him more than it convinced him. The cardinal De Tournon proceeded more wisely, by reiterating to the monarch

that he could not have Milan without the help of the
pope.   But even this argument did not shake Francis I.: he highly appreciated the pope's friendship,
but he valued still more highly the spears of the
lansquenets.

The protestants were about to assemble at Smalcalde; two powerful princes, the dukes of Wurtemberg
and of Pomerania, had joined the evangelical alliance,
and steps had been taken by the confederates to have
a large army constantly on foot.   When he heard of
this, the king of France felt new hopes, and began a
second campaign, which he planned better than the
first.   Instead of employing an obscure gentleman
like Voré de la Fosse, he selected the most illustrious
of his diplomatists, and ordered William du Bellay to
start for Germany.   The latter was still more zealous
than his master, and fearing he should arrive too late,
wrote from Lorraine (where he happened to be staying) to the elector of Saxony, praying him to prolong the meeting for a few days, 'as the king of
France had intrusted him with certain propositions
touching the peace of Christendom.'*   The news of
such a mission delighted the friends of the Reformation,
and filled the Roman party with indignation.   'Never,'
said Sturm, 'never before now has the cause of the
Gospel been in such a favourable position in France.'†
The elector, Melanchthon, and Du Bellay arrived at
Smalcalde in the middle of December.

The ambassador of Francis I. immediately de-

* 'Ad publicam christianæ reipublicæ pacem spectantibus.' 2 Dec.
1535.   Corp. Ref. ii. p. 1015.

† 'Nunquam in meliori loco fuit res Evangelii, quam sit hoc tempore
in Gallia.' Sturm to Bucer.

manded a private audience of the elector, and on the
16th December handed him the letters in which the
king, with many professions of zeal for the pacification
of the Christian Church, besought the elector to
co-operate earnestly 'in so pious and holy a work.'*
John Frederick was not convinced; he always set religion before policy, but he knew that Francis I. adopted
the contrary order.   Fearing, accordingly, that behind this *pious work*, the king concealed war with the
emperor, he immediately pointed to the insurmountable barrier which separated them: 'Our alliance,' he
said, 'has been formed solely to maintain the pure
Word of God, and propagate the holy doctrine of
faith.'   The diplomatist was not to be baffled: there
were two pockets in his portfolio—one containing religious, the other political matters.   Opening the former,
he said: 'We ask you to send us doctors to deliberate
on the union of the Churches.'   Germany spoke of
the *Word* and *doctrine*: France of *union* and of the
Church: this was characteristic.   John Frederick
replied that he would consult his allies.   The audience came to an end, and the 19th December was
appointed by the princes and deputies of the cities
to receive the ambassador of France.

To gain this assembly was the essential thing, and
this the king had felt.   Accordingly, in the letter he
addressed to that body, he made use of every plea,
and spoke 'of the ancient, sacred, and unbroken

---

* 'Maximopere obtestantes ut pro virili nobiscum incumbatis in tam
pium sanctumque opus.'   *Corp. Ref.* ii. p. 1010.   Seckendorf says (*Hist.
Luth.* p. 1146) that this letter had been sent to the Elector beforehand;
but in the documents of the State Paper Office at Weimar we read:
'Hæc locutus reddidit principi litteras quas vocant credentiales.'   And
the *Corpus* gives in a note the letter we have just quoted.

friendship which united France and Germany, and
of the unalterable affection and good-will he entertained towards the princes.'*　Francis I. hoped that
these worthy Germans would allow themselves to be
caught by his words; but they were more clear-sighted
than he imagined.　Du Bellay had observed this: he
had ascertained the unfavourable prepossessions of
Germany, and when he rose to speak, he described
the pious and peaceable evangelicals put to death by
Francis as seditious persons who desired to stir up the
people. ' Most illustrious and most excellent princes,'.
he continued, ' certain persons, moved by hatred, pretend that the states of the empire ought to be on their
guard when foreign kings send them embassies, seeing
that those monarchs speak in one way and act in
another.†　The French have not been named, I must
confess, but they are clearly pointed at. Who has
been more strictly faithful to his friendships than the
king of France?　Who has. been more prompt to
brave danger for the good of Germany?　What nations
have ever been more united than the. Germans and
the French?　The king is convinced that you think very
soundly on. many things; but he could have desired
a little more moderation in some of them.　Like
yourselves, he feels that the negligence and superstition of men have introduced many useless ceremonies
into the Church; but he does not approve of their
suppression without a public decree.‡　He. fears lest

* 'Quæ voluntas, quam amica, quam benevola, quam constans.'—*Corp.
Ref.* ii. p. 1010.

† 'Ut aliud agentibus et aliud significantibus.'　Bellaii ad principes
Oratio.—*Ibid.* p. 1012.

‡ Sleidan, *Mémoires sur l'État de la Religion et de la République*, i.
p. 389.

a' diversity' of rites should engender dissension of minds, and be the cause of civil strife throughout Christendom. Reconciliation is the dearest of his wishes. If you are willing to receive him into your association, you will find him a sure friend. Diversity of opinion has separated you from him hitherto, but similitude of doctrine will henceforward unite him.'*
In conclusion, Du Bellay renewed his demand for a congress of French and German doctors, to confer on the matters in dispute.

· This clever oration did not convince the protestants; they had remained cold, while Du Bellay was pleading his cause so warmly. The point on which Francis I. and his ambassador wished to touch lightly was that which the Germans had most at heart: They could not forget what they had heard about Du Bourg and the cripple, and other martyrs, prisoners, and fugitives. They were shocked at the idea of entering into alliance with the man who had shed the blood of their brethren. They determined to 'open their mouths for the dumb, and to support the cause of all such as were appointed to destruction.' 'We will not suffer in our states,' they answered, 'any stirrers-up of sedition, and we cannot, therefore, condemn the king of France for putting them down in his kingdom. But we beseech him not to punish all without distinction. We ask him to spare those who, having been convinced of the errors with which religion is infected, have embraced the pure doctrine of the Gospel, which we ourselves possess. Merciless men, who wish to save their in-

---

· * 'Ut quos diversitas opinionum sejunxerit, similitudo doctrinæ conjungat.'—*Corp. Ref.* ii. p. 1013.

terests and their power, have cruelly defended their impious opinions, and, in order to exasperate the king's mind, have supposed false crimes, which they impute to innocent and pious Christians. It is the duty of princes to seek God's glory, to cleanse the Church from error, and to stop iniquitous cruelties; and we earnestly beseech the mighty king of France to give his most serious attention to this great duty only.'*

This noble answer was not encouraging. The ambassador was not disconcerted, but dexterously eluding the subject, merely assured the assembly once more of his master's firm resolution to labour at the reformation of the Church. The great point was to know what would be the nature of this reformation. Why assemble a congress of learned men to discuss it, if it was certain beforehand that they could not come to an understanding? The protestants present did not all think alike; the religious men, who were very incredulous on the subject of the king's evangelical piety, thought that nothing ought to be done; on the other hand, the men of expediency said it was worth looking into; and the proposition having been made to hold a preliminary consultation (at Smalcalde), it was resolved that next day (20th of December) there should be a meeting between Du Bellay, Bruck the electoral chancellor, Melanchthon, John Sturm deputy from Strasburg,† the delegates of the Landgrave of Hesse, in whose states the conference was held, and Spalatin, the elector's chaplain, who was ap-

---

* Sleidan, i. p. 392.

† He must not be confounded with Professor Sturm, who was then in Paris.

pointed secretary.   The opposing parties were now to try if they could come to some arrangement.   It was no slight task assumed by the minister of Francis I., who came forward, according to his master's instructions, as the representative of the catholic party; but no one knew better than Du Bellay how far, in the king's opinion, France could then be reformed, if the protestants consented to enter into alliance with her. This explanation is important: it is worth our while to learn the plan conceived by the French government.

At daybreak * on the 20th of December, the members of the conference assembled.   They had chosen that early hour, probably because important business still demanded their attention.   An ambassador from the pope, the famous legate Vergerio, who afterwards came over to the side of the reformers, was then in the town.   He had been sent to propose a council, and was to receive the answer of the protestants on the following morning.   The delegates having taken their seats, the French ambassador explained what was the nature of the reform to which the kingdom of France would lend a helping hand.   'Firstly,' he said, 'with regard to the primacy of the Roman pontiff, the king of France thinks, as you do, that he possesses it by human, and not by divine right. We are not inclined to loose the rein too much in this respect; hitherto the popes have employed the power they claim, in making and unmaking kings— which is certainly going too far.   True, some of our theologians maintain that the papacy is of divine right; but when the king asked for proofs, they could

* 'Sub diluculum.'—*Corp. Ref.* ii. p. 1014.

not give him any.' Melanchthon was satisfied; the chancellor less so; Bruck shared the opinion of the king of England, who, says Du Bellay, would not concede any authority to the pope, whether coming from God or from man.

'As for the sacrament of the Eucharist,' continued the ambassador, 'your opinions on the matter please the king, but not his theologians, who support transubstantiation with all their might. His Majesty seeks for arguments to justify your way of thinking, and is ready to profess it, if you will give him sound ones. Now you know that the king is the only person who commands in his realm.' *

'As for the mass,' continued Du Bellay, a little uneasy, like a man walking over a quicksand, 'there are great disputes about it. The king is of opinion that many prayers and silly impious legends have been foisted into that portion of divine worship; and that those absurd and ridiculous passages must be expurgated, and the primitive order restored.'† As Francis I. was particularly averse to masses celebrated in honour of the saints to obtain their intercession with God, Du Bellay repeated one or two of the king's expressions on that point. 'One day the king said: "I have a prayer-book, written many years ago, in which there is no mention of the intercession of saints. I am assured that Bessarion ‡ himself said:

---

* 'Esse enim solum qui in suo regno imperet.'—*Corp. Ref.* ii. p. 1015.

† 'Orationes et legendas multas ut ineptas et impias abrogandas, aut saltem emendandas; multa enim in his absurda, multa ridicula.'—*Ibid.* p. 1015.

‡ Bessarion, born at Trebizond in 1395, Greek bishop of Nicæa, and afterwards Cardinal of the Roman Church, endeavoured to unite the two Churches, and was on the point of being elected pope.

' As for me, I am more concerned about live saints than dead ones.' ' "

' The king thinks, however,' added Du Bellay, ' that we must preserve the celebration of mass; only there must not be more than three a day in every parish church ; one before daybreak, for working men and servants; the second and third for the other worshippers.' If transubstantiation and the *silly legends* were rejected, the moderate protestants were ready to concede the daily celebration of the Eucharist. Du Bellay continued :—

' As for the images of the saints, the king thinks, with you, that they are not set up to be worshippèd, but to remind us of the faith and works of those whom they represent; and that is what the people ought to be taught.

' His Majesty is also pleased with your opinions on free-will.'

The discussion—the great struggle in France— turned on purgatory ; the ambassador slily pointed out the reason: ' Our divines obstinately defend it,' he said, ' for upon that doctrine depends the payment of masses, indulgences, and pious gifts. Put down purgatory, and you take away from them all opportunity of acquiring wealth and honour ;* you cut off the limbs that supply their very life-blood! The king gave -them some months to prove their doctrine by Scripture; they accepted the terms, but made no answer, and when the king pressed them, they exclaimed: " Ah, Sire, do not furnish our adversaries with weapons that they will afterwards turn against

---

* ' Videre enim eos, alioqui sibi tolli omnes occasiones acquirendi opes, honores, et omnia.'—*Corp. Ref.* ii. p. 1015.

us." It therefore appears to me that it would be proper for one of your doctors to write a treatise on the subject and present it to his Majesty.

'As for good works, our theologians stoutly maintain their opinion; namely, that they are necessary. I told them that you thought the same, and that all you assert is, that the necessity of works cannot be affirmed so as to mean that we are justified and saved by them. An inquisitor of the faith has declared his agreement with Melanchthon on this point.* I think, therefore, that we may come to an understanding on that matter.

'You do not like monasteries: well! The king hopes to obtain from the Roman party that no one shall be at liberty to take monastic vows before the age of thirty or forty; and that the monks shall be free henceforth to leave their convents and marry, if opportunity offers. The king thinks that not only the good of the Church requires it, but also the good of the State, for there are many capable men in the cloisters who might be usefully employed in divers functions and duties. His Majesty is therefore of opinion, not that monasteries should be destroyed, but that vows should be no longer obligatory. It is by taking one step after another that we shall come to an understanding. . . . It is not convenient to pluck off a horse's tail at one pull.† Monasteries ought to be places of study, set apart for the instruction of those who are to teach the young. It is useful and

---

* 'De fide quoque inquisitorem fidei recte sentire.'—*Corp. Ref.* ii. p. 1016.

† 'Sicut etiam cauda equina non statim et commode tota evelli possit.' *Corp. Ref.* ii. p. 1016.

even necessary to proceed with moderation. . . . His Majesty hopes to bring the Roman pontiff himself gradually to this idea.

'As for the marriage of priests, the French theologians do not approve of it; but here the king holds a certain medium. He desires the toleration of those of your ecclesiastics who have wives; as for the others, he wishes they should remain in celibacy. If, however, there are any priests who desire to be married, let them marry; only they must at the same time quit holy orders.

'As for the communion, the king hopes to obtain from the pope permission for every man to take the sacrament under one or both kinds, as his conscience may dictate. He declares that he has heard old men say that both kinds used to be given to the laity in France a hundred and twenty years ago; not indeed in the churches but in private chapels. And even to this day, the kings of France communicate under both kinds.'

This explanation of the reform projected for France, and the exchange of ideas which it had occasioned, occupied some time. The day was already advanced, and the protestant delegates were making ready to depart.* The ambassador hastened to add a few words to prove the sincerity of his proposals. 'Cardinal Santa Croce,' he said, 'has already substituted psalms for the silly and ungodly hymns in the liturgy. True, the theologians of Paris have condemned the change. You see the Sorbonne claims such authority that it not only calls you heretics, but does not fear

* 'Nobis jam abituris.'—*Corp. Ref.* ii. p. 1017.

to condemn the cardinals and the pope himself.'*
Thus, according to Du Bellay, protestants, king, cardinals, and pope were on one side, and the Sorbonne on the other. The Lutherans, being in such
good company, had nothing to fear. To encourage
them still more, he informed them that Francis I.
admitted the point which they put forward as the very
life-spring of their doctrine. ' The king,' he continued,
'thinks highly of the doctrine of justification, as
you explain it. It would please him much, if two or
three of your learned men were sent to France to
discuss these several points in his presence. We must
take precautions that the best and soundest part of
the Church be not conquered and crushed by numbers.† Lastly, it would be very beneficial,' Du Bellay
adroitly added, as he finished his speech, ' if the princes
and deputies of the cities here assembled were to
intercede in behalf of those who are exiled on account
of religion, and to ask that no one should hereafter
suffer any injury for what he thinks, says, or does
with respect to his faith.'‡ How could the protestants, after such a compassionate solicitation, speak
any more of the scaffolds of the 21st of January?

Such was the Reformation which Francis I. declared himself willing to give France. As concerns
doctrine, it was much more complete than the hybrid
system which Henry VIII. was at that time endeavouring to set up in England. The protestants found

---

* 'Sed etiam cardinales, papam quoque ipsum, condemnare non dubi-
tant.'—*Corp. Ref.* ii. p. 1017.

† 'Melior et sanior pars a majore vincatur et opprimatur.'—*Corp. Ref.*
ii. p. 1018.

‡ 'Nequid fraudi sit, quod quisque senserit, dixerit, egerit.'—*Corp. Ref.*
ii. p. 1018.

these propositions acceptable enough in general, with
som.: modifications, doubtless, which could not fail to
be introduced: the imperfect reform of the French
king would be completed by degrees. Had not his
ambassador just said that it was dangerous to pull out
a horse's tail at once, giving them to understand that
it would be pulled out hair by hair?   The Reformation
proclaimed, the evangelical doctrine professed, the
frivolities of public worship put away, the Sorbonne
placed under ban, the sounder part of Christendom
preponderating over the more numerous part—the
cardinals and the pope himself (as Du Bellay hinted)
aiding in this transformation—what important advantages! One thing, however, was still wanting;
many asked not only whether the catholics would
carry out the Reformation to an end, as they hinted,
but even whether they would maintain the conces·
sions they had made.

This thought engrossed the attention of the protestant delegates.   They made their report, however, to
their principals, and amid the doubts by which they were
agitated, one thing only appeared urgent to the men
of the Augsburg Confession—the duty of interceding
in favour of their brethren in France.   They commissioned Melanchthon to draw up the answer to Du
Bellay, and on the 22nd of December, the French envoy having been once more admitted into the assembly
of the princes and deputies, the vice-chancellor said
to him: ' That the most puissant king of France by
sending them an ambassador as illustrious by his
virtues as eminent by his rank, and the duty imposed on him to treat concerning matters of faith, the
importance of which was paramount in their eyes,

manifestly showed them the Christian zeal with which
the king was animated—a zeal most worthy of so
good a prince; that the reports circulated with respect
to certain punishments that had taken place in France
could not in truth authorise the States of Germany
to form a judgment on the puissant monarch of that
kingdom; however, they besought him not to allow
himself to be carried away by the cruelty of men
who, ignorant of the truth, desire to act severely
against good and bad without distinction; that idle
opinions having crept into the Church, it was necessary
to apply a remedy, but those who endeavoured to do
so became objects of the bitterest hatred—the papists,
who clung to their abuses, striving by a thousand
artifices to inflame the hearts of kings and to arm
them against the innocent.* For this reason the
States assembled at Smalcalde conjured his Majesty to
prohibit such iniquitous cruelty, and to advance the
good of the Church and the glory of God.'

The evangelicals having discharged this duty passed
rapidly over the rest. They represented to the ambassador that the proposal to send learned men into
France was of such importance, that it was impossible
to give him an immediate answer, but that the deputies
would report thereon to their chiefs as soon as they
returned home. 'We assure you, however,' they said
in conclusion, 'that nothing would please us more
than to see the doctrines of piety and the concord of
nations propagated more and more by means in conformity with the Word of God.'†

---

* 'Variis artificiis regum animos incendunt atque armant adversus eos.'
—Corp. Ref. ii. p. 1024.

† 'Nihil enim optatius quam ut latissime propagetur pia doctrina et
multarum gentium concordia.'—Corp. Ref. ii. p. 1026.

After a postponement, which seemed almost a refusal, Du Bellay felt embarrassed, for he had still to discharge the principal mission that his master had entrusted to him. He could not, however, leave Smalcalde without fulfilling it. He did not make it known distinctly in his public speeches, but solicited the protestants in private conversations to make an alliance with the king his master. The latter answered that the first condition of such a union would be that the allies should undertake nothing against the emperor, the head of the Germanic Confederation. Now it was precisely for the purpose of acting against Charles V. that Francis I. sought the friendship of evangelical Germany. Du Bellay left Smalcalde dissatisfied.

The distrust of the Lutheran princes was not unreasonable. While the king was acting the protestant beyond the Rhine, he was acting the papist beyond the Alps ; if the emperor would consent to yield Milan to him, Francis I. would bind himself to reduce Germany under the yoke of the house of Austria. ' I will spare nothing,' he said, ' for the greatness of the said emperor and his brother the king of the Romans.' * He went further than this: ' Let the pope say the word, and I will constrain England by force of arms to submit to the Church.' The cruel paw peeped out from beneath the skin of the lamb, and the lion suddenly appeared, ready to attack, seize, and devour, as a delicate morsel, those whom he treated as friends and companions.

The cause of truth and unity was not to triumph by means of a congress at Smalcalde, by diplomatic

* Mémoires de Du Bellay, p. 243.

negotiations, or by the instrumentality of Francis I. He who said, *My kingdom is not of this world*, did not choose men of the world to establish his kingdom, and will not permit a monotonous uniformity to take the place of unity in his empire. Treaties, constitutions, and forms prescribed by monarchs are human elements which the kingdom of heaven repudiates. True unity does not proceed from an identical administration, a clerical organisation, or a pompous hierarchy: it is essentially moral and spiritual, and consists in community of thoughts, faith, affections, works, and hopes. Diversity of forms, far from injuring it, gives it more intensity. In the sixteenth century the world was far, and is still far, from seeing the realisation of this divine unity. Some steps, however, have been taken, and the time no doubt will come when, according to the scriptural prophecy, all the families of the earth will be blessed in Christ Jesus.* But there will be no real, free, evangelical catholicity until Christians understand and realise those elementary words of the primitive Church: *I believe in the communion of saints.*

* Genesis xii. 3.

CHAPTER XVIII.

THE GOSPEL IN THE NORTH OF ITALY.

(1519 TO 1536.)

THE Reformation had also commenced in Italy. As the knowledge of the ancient languages, literary pursuits, and cultivation of the intellect, flourished more in that country than elsewhere, it seemed natural that it should be among the first to open itself to the light of the Gospel. In the midst of superstition, many elevated minds were to be found whom the formalism of the Roman Church could not satisfy. The corruption of the clergy and of religion had sunk deeper in Italy than in the rest of Christendom, so that the magnitude of the evil made the necessity of a remedy more keenly felt. Accordingly, although many obstacles appeared to close the peninsula against the entrance of evangelical doctrine; although national pride, the interest which the Italians of every class seemed to have in the continuance of the papacy, the hostility of the governments, and above all the overwhelming power of the pontifical hierarchy, erected barriers everywhere, which seemed more insurmountable than the Alps, there was at that time an electric current between Italy and the reformed countries that nothing could stop. The Reformation had hardly sent forth its first beams of light, the

flame had hardly risen over Germany and Switzerland, when in the regions beyond the mountains, from
Venice and Turin to Naples, isolated spots of light
gleamed out amidst the darkness. The evangelical
doctrine, in general not much appreciated by the
people, found an easy access to the hearts of many cultivated men. Italy was a vast plain in which were
numerous uncultivated fields and barren heaths;
but a liberal hand having been opened over it,
the seeds of life which fell from it found here and
there good soil, and at the breath of spring the
blade and the ear sprang forth. A fierce storm,
mingled with thunder and lightning, afterwards burst
upon those fields; the light of day was hidden, and
the obscurity of darkness once more covered the
country. But the light had been beautiful, and its
appearance, although fugitive, deserves to be remembered, if only as a pledge to make us hope for
better days. The positive results of the Italian
Reformation seem to escape us entirely; and yet it
possesses quite as many of those characteristics which
charm the mind, captivate the imagination, and
touch the heart, as other Reformations do. The new
and varied plants which that ancient land began to
produce, the brilliant flames which for a moment shed
such beautiful light, the men of God at that time
scattered all over Italy, deserve to be known, and we
must now turn to them.

At Pavia, on the Ticino, there lived a bookseller
named Calvi, ' who cultivated the muses.' Frobenius,
the celebrated printer of Basle, having as early as 1519
sent him Erasmus's Testament and the early writings
of Luther, he began to study the Gospel more than

the poets. Wishing to help, in proportion to his ability, in 'the revival of piety,'* he undertook to circulate the writings of the reformers not only in his immediate neighbourhood, but through all the cities of Italy.† Pavia possessed a celebrated university, and the precious volumes were first distributed among its professors and their pupils. The students might often be seen reading these absorbing pages under the porticoes of the university and beneath the walls of the cathedral or of the old castle. Other printers and booksellers joined with Calvi in the work of dissemination, and before long a book entitled *I Principii della Theologia di Ippolito di Terranigra* was read all over Italy, even in Rome. *Terranigra* was Melanchthon, and these *Principles of Divinity* were his *Theological Commonplaces*. This admirable book was to be found even in the Vatican, along with the works of *Coricius Cogelius* (Zwingle) and *Aretius Felinus* (Bucer). Bishops and cardinals pompously extolled them; none of them suspecting that the breath of evangelical piety which animated those writings must necessarily dissipate the false piety of the confessional. *Terranigra*'s book was read with such eagerness at Rome, that it soon became necessary to ask for a fresh supply. A learned Franciscan of the metropolis, who possessed the Latin edition, struck with the unknown name *Terranigra*,‡ desired to procure the Italian work so much talked of.

* 'Cupit renascenti pietati suppetias ferre.'—Frobenius to Luther, February 14, 1519.

† 'Per omnes civitates sparsum.'—*Ibid.*

‡ Gerdesius, *Specimen Ital. Ref.* ii. p. 11. The words *Schwarzerd, Melanchthon,* and *Terranigra* have the same meaning in German, Greek, and Italian, namely, *black earth.*

It soon began to call up certain recollections: he fancied he had seen the work before. He rose from his seat, took down his Latin *Melanchthon*, compared it with the Italian, and to his great horror found the two works were the same. Without delay he made known the stratagem of the booksellers, and the volume, which the cardinals had extolled to the skies one day, was condemned to the flames on the next.

But the propaganda did not cease. The young Germans who came to study law and medicine at Bologna, Padua, and other universities of the peninsula, the young Italians who began to frequent the schools of Germany and Switzerland, helped alike to diffuse evangelical faith beyond the Alps. Many of the Lutheran lansquenets whom Charles V. marched into Italy, and of the Swiss soldiers whom Francis I. drew thither, professed in the houses where they lodged the doctrines of the Reformation, and did so with thorough military frankness. Some praised Luther, others Zwingle, and all contrasted the purity of the reformers' lives and the simplicity of their manners with the irregularities, luxury, and pride of the Roman prelates.

The Italians have an open and quick understanding, precision in their ideas, clearness of expression, an instinct of the beautiful, and great independence of character; and hence they were tired of living in ignoble subjection to ignorant, lazy, and dissolute priests. Conscientious men of eminent mind joyfully welcomed a doctrine which put God's Word in the place of papal bulls, briefs, and decretals, and substituted the spirit and the life for the ecclesiastical mechanism of the Latin ritual. Italy was charmed with Luther's character and work.   In 1521 a voice from Milan exclaimed: ' O mighty Luther! who can paint thy features so full of animation, the godlike qualities of thy mind, thy soul inspired with a will so pure?   Thy voice, which rings through the universe and utters unaccustomed sounds, terrifies the vile hearts of the wicked,* and bears an unexpected balm to diseases which appeared beyond remedy. Take courage, then, venerable father, whose mouth makes salvation known to all, and whose word destroys more monsters than ever Hercules rent in pieces.'

The dignitaries of Rome were alarmed at this enthusiasm.   At the diet of Nuremberg in 1524, Cardinal Campeggi exclaimed: ' The Germans take up a new opinion quickly, but they soon abandon it; while the Italians obstinately persist in what they have once adopted.'†   It was rather the contrary that was to take place.   The Italians showed themselves still more prompt than the Germans; the number of Lutherans increased every day.‡   The converted catholics began by degrees to explain the Gospel and to refute the errors of the Roman Church in private houses: this was done even in the Papal States. Before long, several priests and monks were enlightened, and the Reformation took a new step: its principles were taught in the churches.   Clement VII. felt great alarm, when all of a sudden the doctrine,

---

*   ' Vocis, quæ totum penitus diffusa per orbem,
          Terruit insolito pectora tetra sono.'

These verses have been preserved by Schelhorn in his *Amœnitates Eccl.* ii. p. 624.

† Seckendorf, *Hist. du Luthéranisme,* p. 613.

‡ Sarpi, *Hist. du Concile de Trente,* i. p. 85.

attacked by him and his legates in distant countries, broke out all over his dear Italy and threatened the walls of the papacy. He uttered a cry of terror: 'To our exceeding sorrow,' he said, 'Luther's pestilential heresy has been spread among us, not only among the laity, but also among the priests and monks.* Heresy is increasing, and in every place the catholic faith has to suffer the cruellest assaults.' The cry was useless. In that very year (1530) the New Testament was translated by Bruccioli, printed at Venice, and the much dreaded contagion thenceforward made still more rapid progress.

It was in this latter city, on the hundred islets and amid the lagunes of the queen of the Adriatic, that the doctrine of the Gospel first raised its standard. There was no power in Europe more jealous of its independence and authority than Venice; the winged lion of St. Mark braved the priest of Rome; the senate rejected the Inquisition, practised freedom of inquiry, and did not license the pope's edicts until after serious study and strict examination. Protestants were soon to be found at Venice who, strange to say, were more protestant than those of Augsburg. 'I am delighted,' said Luther, on the 7th of March, 1528, 'to hear that they have received the Word of God at Venice.'† A report having got abroad that Melanchthon appeared inclined, at the diet of 1530, to recognise the primacy of the bishop of Rome, the new evangelicals of Venice were

---

* 'Pestifera hæresis Lutheri non tantum apud sæculares personas, sed etiam ecclesiasticas et regulares, tam mendicantes quam non mendicantes.' *Brief to the Inquisitors,* Raynald *ad annum.*

† 'Læte audio de Venetis quod Verbum Dei receperint.'—Luther, *Ep.* iii. p. 289.

troubled and alarmed; one of them, Lucio Paolo Rosselli, although only a beginner in the Christian doctrine, determined to write, respectfully but frankly, to the illustrious doctor of Germany: 'There are no books by any author,' he said to Melanchthon, 'which please me more than those you have published. But if the reports which the papists circulate about you are true, the cause of the Gospel and those who, taught by the writings of yourself and Luther, have embraced it, are in great danger. All Italy awaits the result of your meeting at Augsburg.* O Melanchthon! let neither threats, nor fears, nor prayers, nor promises make you desert the standard of Jesus Christ! Even if you must suffer death to maintain His glory, do not hesitate. It is better to die with honour than to live with ignominy.'

It was much worse when the Venetian ambassador at the court of Charles V. forwarded to the senate the letter which Melanchthon had written on the 6th of July to Cardinal Campeggi, and in which he went so far as to say that the protestants did not differ from the Roman Church in any important dogma, and were disposed to acknowledge the papal jurisdiction.† The evangelical Christians of Venice, who wanted a decided position, were dismayed. Most of them denied that the letter was Melanchthon's; Rosselli, in particular, with generous enthusiasm, took up the doctor's defence, and on the 1st of August sent him a copy of the letter, 'to the end that he might carefully scrutinise the wickedness of those who ascribed to him words

---

* 'Scias igitur Italos omnes expectare Augustensis hujus vestri decreta.' Venetiis, 3 calend. Aug. anno 1530. *Corp. Ref.* ii. p. 227.

† *Corp. Ref.* ii. p. 170.

calculated to disgrace the true defenders of the cause of Christ and Christ himself.* Now that we have discovered their malice,' added the Venetian, 'resist their iniquity with greater zeal, and let the emperor and all Christian princes know the shameless practices of the enemy.'

What seemed impossible to the Italians was but too true : Melanchthon had carried his concessions too far. When he declared, however, that he would not recognise the bishop of Rome until he became evangelical, he had put a stipulation to his compact which rendered it impossible.

From Venice we pass to Turin. The Italian revival did not present that simple historical and continuous advance which we meet with in other European countries. It was not like a single river whose deep and mighty waters, as they flowed along, ran calmly in the same channel ; but like little streams, issuing from the earth in various places, whose bright and limpid waters glittered in the sunbeam and fertilised the soil around them. They disappeared ; they were lost in the ground, oftentimes, alas! imparting to it a sanguine hue, and the earth returned to its former barrenness. Yet many a plant had been revived by them, and their sweet remembrance may still cause joy to others.

The works of the reformers had reached Turin. Piedmont, from its vicinity to Switzerland, France, and Germany, was among the first to receive a glimpse of the sun which had just risen beyond the Alps. The Reformation had already appeared in one

---

* 'Tibi ea adscribent, quæ Christo, verisque Christi defensoribus, dedecori sunt.'—*Corp. Ref.* ii. p. 243.

of its cities—at Aosta—and most of its doctrines had
for ages been current among the Waldensian valleys.
Monks of the Augustine convent at Turin, Hieronimo Nigro Foscianeo in particular, were among the
number of those who first became familiar with the
evangelical writings. Celio Secundo Curione, a young
man still at college, received them from their hands
in 1520.

About three leagues and a half from Turin, and at
the foot of the Alps, was situated the town of Cirié,
with its two parochial churches and an Augustine
monastery. Higher up there stood an old castle
named Cuori, and the family to which it belonged
was called from it Curione or Curioni.* One of its
members, Giacomino Curione, who lived at Cirié, had
married Charlotte de Montrotier, lady of honour to
Blanche, duchess of Savoy, and sister to the chief
equerry of the reigning duke. On the 1st of May,
1503, a son was born to them at Cirié; he was named
Celio Secundo,† and was their twenty-third child.‡
He lost his mother as he came into the world, and
his father, who had removed to Turin, and afterwards
to Moncaglieri, where he had property, died when
Celio was only nine years old.

The elder Curione possessed a Bible, which in the
hour of death he put into his son's hands. That act
was perhaps the cause of the love for Scripture by

---

* Celio Secundo writes his name both ways, but more frequently
Curioni.

† 'Natus anno MDIII. calendis Maii, Cyriaci Taurinorum.'—*Curionis
Historia* a Professore Stupano, 1570, in Schelhorn, *Amœnitates Litte-
rariæ*, xiii. p. 330.

‡ 'Vicenos ternosque liberos suscepit, ex quibus Cœlius ultimus natus
fuit.'—*Curionis Historia*, p. 329.

which the heir of the Curiones was afterwards distinguished: the depth of his filial piety made him
look upon the book as a treasure before he knew
the value of its contents. Celio having begun his
education at Moncaglieri, went to Turin, where his
maternal grandmother, Maddalena, lived. She received him into her house, where the anxious love of
the venerable lady surrounded him with the tenderest
care.* He is said to have dwelt on that pleasant hill
which overlooks Turin, whence the summits of the
Alps are visible, and whose base is washed by the
slow and majestic waters of the Po.† Celio had
applied with his whole heart to the study of the
classical orators, poets, historians, and philosophers;
when he reached his twentieth year he felt deeper
longings, which literature was incapable of satisfying.
The old Bible of his father could do this: a new
world, superior to that of letters and philosophy—the
world of the Spirit—opened before his soul.

There was much talk just then, both in university
and city, of the Reformation and the reformers.
Curione had often heard certain priests and their partisans bitterly complaining of the 'false doctrines' of
those *heretics*, and making use of the harshest language
against Luther and Zwingle. He listened to their
abuse, but was not convinced. He possessed a nobler
soul than the majority of the people around him, and
his generous independent spirit was more disposed in
favour of the accused than of the accusers. Instead
of joining in this almost unanimous censure, Celio

---

* 'Taurinum se contulit, ubi per aliquos annos apud Magdalenam
proavam suam agens.'—*Curionis Historia*, p. 330.

† Bonnet, *Récits du seizième Siècle*, p. 248.

said to himself: 'I will not condemn those doctors before I have read their works.'* It would appear that he was already known in the Augustine convent, in which, as in that of Wittemberg, some truly pious men were to be found. The grace of his person, the quickness of his intellect, and his ardent thirst for religious knowledge, interested the monks. Knowing that they possessed some of the writings of the reformers, Curione asked for them, and Father Hieronimo lent him Luther's *Babylonian Captivity*, translated into Italian under a different title. The young man carried it away eagerly to his study. He read those vigorous pages in which the Saxon doctor speaks of the lively faith with which the Christian ought to cling to the promises of God's Word; and those in which he asserts that neither bishop nor pope has any right to command despotically the believer who has received Christian liberty from God. But Celio had not yet obtained light enough; he carried the book back to the convent, and asked for another. Melanchthon's *Principles of Theology* and Zwingle's *True and False Religion* were devoured by him in turn.

A work was then going on in his soul. The truths he had read in his Bible grew clearer and sank deeper into his mind; his spirit thrilled with joy when he found his faith confirmed by that of these great doctors, and his heart was filled with love for Luther and Melanchthon. 'When I was still young,' he said to the latter afterwards, 'when first I read

---

* 'Non esse sibi damnandos hosce, priusquam illorum libros legisset.' —*Curionis Historia*, p. 331.

your writings, I felt such love for you that it seemed
hardly capable of increase.'*

Curione was not satisfied with the writings merely
of these men of God : his admiration for them was
such that he longed to hear them; an ardent desire
to start immediately for Germany was kindled in his
heart.† He talked about it with his friends, especially with Giovanni Cornelio and Francesco Guarino,
whom the Gospel had also touched, and who declared
their readiness to depart with him.

The three young Italians, enthusiastic admirers of
Luther and Melanchthon, quitted Turin and started
for Wittemberg. They turned their steps towards the
valley of Aosta, intending to cross the St. Bernard,‡
where for more than five centuries a house of the
Augustine order had existed for the reception of the
travellers who made use of that then very frequented
pass. They conversed about their journey, their
feelings, and their hopes; and not content with this,
they spoke of the truth with simple-hearted earnestness to the people they met with on the road or at
the inns. In the ardour of their youthful zeal, they
even allowed themselves to enter into imprudent discussions upon the Romish doctrines.§ They were
'bursting to speak'—they could not wait until they
had crossed the Alps; the spirit with which they

---

* 'Adolescens adhuc, cum prima tua monimenta legissem, te ita amavi
ut vix ulterius progredi meus in te amor posse videretur.'—*C. S. Curionis, Epist.* i. p. 71.

† 'Ita est illa (opera) admiratus, ut statim decreverit in Germaniam
transire.'—*Curionis Historia*, p. 331.

‡ 'Institutum iter per Salassorum regionem ingreditur.'—*Ibid.*

§ 'Cum juvenes in itinere, minus caute, de rebus ad religionem perti-
nentibus disputarent.'—*Ibid.* p. 332.

were filled carried them away. They had been cautioned, and had resolved to be circumspect; but 'however deep the hiding-places in the hearts of men,' said a reformer, 'their tongues betray their hidden affections.'* One of those with whom these Piedmontese youths had debated went and denounced them to Boniface, cardinal-bishop of Ivrea, and pointed out the road they were to take. The prelate gave the necessary orders, and just as the three students were entering the valley of Aosta,† the cardinal's satellites, who were waiting for them, laid hold of them and carried them to prison.

What a disappointment! At the very time they were anticipating the delights of an unrestrained intercourse with Melanchthon and Luther, they found themselves in chains and solitary imprisonment. Curione possessed friends in that district who belonged to the higher nobility; and contriving to inform them of his fate, they exerted themselves in his behalf. The cardinal having sent for him, soon discovered that his prisoner was not an ordinary man. Struck with the extent of his knowledge and the elegance of his mind, he resolved to do all he could to attach him to the Roman Church. He loaded him with attentions, promised to bear the necessary expenses for the continuation of his studies, and with that intent placed him in the priory of St. Benignus. It is probable that Cornelio and Guarino were soon released: although less celebrated than their fellow-traveller, they afterwards became distinguished by their evangelical zeal.

* Calvin.
† 'Cum essent vallem prætoriam ingressuri.'—*Curionis Historia*, p. 332.

Although shut up in a monastery, Curione's soul
burnt with zeal for the Word of God. He regretted
that Germany on which he had so much reckoned, and
unable to increase his light at the altar of Wittemberg, he wished at least to make use of what he had for
the benefit of the monks commissioned to convert him.
He was grieved at the superstitious practices of their
worship, and would have desired to enfranchise those
about him. A shrine, put in a prominent place on
the altar, enclosed a skull and other bones reported
to be those of St. Agapetus and St. Tibur the martyr,
and which during certain solemnities were presented
to the adoration of the people. Why set dry bones
in the place which should be occupied by the living
Word of God? Are not their writings the only authentic remains of the apostles and prophets? Curione
refused to pay the slightest honour to these relics, and
in his private conversation he went so far as to speak
to some of the monks against such idolatrous worship, instructing them in the true faith.* He resolved
to do something more. In the convent library he
had found a Bible, to which no one paid any attention; he had, moreover, noticed the place where the
monks kept the key of the shrine they held so dear.†
One day—probably in 1530—taking advantage of a
favourable opportunity when the monks were occupied
elsewhere,‡ he went into the library, took down the
holy Word of which David said it was *more to be
desired than gold*, carried it into the church, opened

---

* 'Privatim multos contraria hisce docebat et in vera fide erudiebat.'
—*Curionis Historia*, p. 332.

† 'Itaque, observato clavium loco, capsam aperit.'—*Ibid.* p. 333.

‡ 'Cum cæteri aliis rebus intenti essent.'—*Ibid.*

the mysterious coffer, removed the relics, put the Bible in their place, and laid this inscription upon it: ' *This is the ark of the covenant, wherein a man can enquire of the true oracles of God, and in which are contained the true relics of the saints.*' Curione, with emotion and joy, closed the shrine and left the church without being observed. The act, rash as it was, had a deep and evangelical meaning: it expressed the greatest principles of the Reformation. Some time after, at one of the festivals when the relics were to be presented to the adoration of the worshippers, the monks opened the shrine. Their surprise, emotion, and rage were boundless, and they at once accused their young companion of sacrilege. Being on the watch, he made his escape, and, quitting Piedmont, took refuge at Milan.

In that city Curione zealously devoted himself to lecturing; but, being at the same time disgusted with the unmeaning practices of the monks, he gave himself with his whole heart to works of Christian charity. As famine and pestilence were wasting the country, he soon after occupied himself wholly in succouring the poor and the sick; he solicited the donations of the nobility, prevailed on the priests to sell for the relief of the wretched the precious objects which adorned their churches, consoled the dying, and even buried the dead.* In the convent, he had appeared to be struggling for faith only; in the midst of the pestilence, he seemed to be living for works only. He remembered that Jesus had come *to serve*, and following his Master's example, he was eager to console

---

* ' Ipse omnibus aderat, consolabatur, atque etiam mortuos ipsos sepeliebat.'—*Curionis Historia,* p. 335.

every misery. 'Christ having become the living root of his soul, had made it a fruitful tree.' As soon as the scourge abated, everyone was eager to testify a proper gratitude to Celio, and the Isacios, one of the best families in the province, gave him the hand of one of their daughters, Margarita Bianca, a young woman of great beauty, who became the faithful and brave companion of his life.*

Some time after this, Curione, believing that he had nothing more to fear, and desiring to receive his patrimony, to revisit his native country, and to devote his strength and faith to her service, returned to Piedmont. His hopes were disappointed. Cruel family vexations and clerical persecutions assailed a life that was never free from agitation. He had lost all but one sister, whose husband, learning that he intended claiming his inheritance, determined to ruin him. A dominican monk was making a great noise by his sermons in a neighbouring city.† Celio took a book from his library, and went with some friends to hear him. He expected that the monk, according to the custom of his class, would draw a frightful picture of the reformers. Curione knew that the essence of the preaching of the evangelical ministry was Christ, justification by faith in his atoning work, the new life which He imparts, and the new commandments which He gives. According to him, the task of the servant of God, now that all things were made new, was to exalt, not the Church, but the Saviour; and to make known all the preciousness

---

* 'Ei uxorem dederunt Margaritam Blancam, puellam elegantissimam.'—*Curionis Historia*, p. 335.

† 'In vicinum locum, Castelleviolonem nomine.'—*Ibid.*

of Christ rather than to stun his hearers by furious declamations against their adversaries. Such were not the opinions entertained at that time—we will not say by the great doctors of the Romish Church, but by the vulgar preachers of the papacy. Laying down as a fundamental principle that *there was no salvation out of the Church*, they naturally believed themselves called to urge the necessity of union—not with Christ, but—with Rome ; to extol the beauties of its hierarchy, its worship, and its devout institutions. Instead of feeding the sheep, by giving them the spiritual nourishment of faith, they thought only of pronouncing declamatory eulogies of the fold and drawing horrible pictures of the devouring wolves that were prowling about it. If there had been no protestants to combat, no Luther or Calvin to calumniate, many popish preachers would have found the sermon a superfluous part of the service, as had been the case in the Middle Ages.

The *good monk*, whom Curione and his friends had gone to hear, preached according to the oratorical rules of vulgar preachers. 'Do you know,' he exclaimed, 'why Luther pleases the Germans? . . . Because, under the name of Christian liberty, he permits them to indulge in all kinds of excess.* He teaches, moreover, that Christ is not God, and that He was not born of a virgin.' And continuing this monkish philippic with great vehemence, he inflamed the animosity of his hearers.

When the sermon was over, Curione asked the

---

* 'Lutherum Germanis placere, quod sub libertate christiana omnis generis libidines concederet.'—*Curionis Historia.*

prelate who was present for permission to say a few
words. Having obtained it, and the congregation
being silent and expectant, he said: 'Reverend father,
you have brought serious charges against Luther: can
you tell me the book or the place in which he teaches
the things with which you reproach him?' The
monk replied that he could not do so then, but if
Curione would accompany him to Turin, he would
show him the passages. The young man rejoined
with indignation: 'Then I will tell you at once the
page and book where the Wittemberg doctor has
said the very contrary.' And opening Luther's *Commentary on the Galatians*, he read aloud several passages which completely demonstrated the falseness
of the monk's calumnies. The persons of rank present at the service were disgusted; the people went
still further; some violent men, exasperated by the
dominican's having told them such impudent lies,
rushed upon him and struck him. The more reasonable had some trouble to rescue him and send him
home safe and sound.*

This scene made a great noise. The bishop and
the inquisitors looked upon it as a revolt against
the papacy. Curione was a firebrand flung by Satan
into the midst of the Church, and they felt that if
they did not quench it instantly, the impetuous wind
which, crossing the Alps, was beginning to blow in
the peninsula, would scatter the sparks far and wide,
and spread the conflagration everywhere. The valiant
evangelist was seized, taken to Turin, thrown into
prison, and in a moment, as soon as the news circu-

---

* 'Ut vix intercedente Præfecto, vivus Taurinum redire potuerit.'—
Curionis Historia, p. 339.

lated, all his old enemies set to work.   His covetous
brother, and even his sister, as it would appear,
made common cause with the priests to destroy
him.*   Fanaticism and avarice joined together; one
party wished to deprive him of his property only, but
the others wanted his life.   It was not the first time
Curione had been in prison for speaking according
to the truth: he did not lose courage, he preserved
all the serenity of his mind, and remained master
of himself.   The ecclesiastic charged with the examination overwhelmed him with questions.†   He
was reminded of the relics taken away from the
monastery of St. Benignus, the journey he had
wished to take to Germany, and the conversations he
had held on the road, and was threatened with the
stake.‡

The bishop, knowing that Curione had protectors
among the first people in the city, started for Rome,
in order to obtain from the pope in person his condemnation to death.   Before leaving, he transferred
the prisoner to his coadjutor David, brother of the
influential cardinal Cibo.   David, wishing to make
sure of his man, and to prevent its being known
where he was detained, removed him by night from
the prison in which he had been placed, took him
to one of those mansions, not very unlike castles,
that are often to be found in Italy, and locked him
up in a room enclosed by very thick walls.§   His

* ‘In causa propemodum ipsi fuerunt (soror et maritus) quod captus
fuerit, vitam quoque fere amiserit.’—*Curionis Historia*, p. 336.

† ‘Hic examinatur, quæstiones adhibentur.’—*Ibid.* p. 339.

‡ ‘Ignem flammasque minantur.’—*Ibid.* p. 339.

§ ‘Ex prioribus carceribus noctu deducit, et in conclavi quodam for-
tissimis parietibus munito . . . asservari curat.’—*Ibid.*

officers attached heavy chains to poor Celio's feet, riveted them roughly, and fastened them into the wall; and finally, two sentries were placed inside the door of the house.   When that was done, David felt at ease, sure of being able to produce his prisoner when the condemnation arrived from Rome.   There was no hope left the wretched man of being saved.   Curione felt that his death could not be far off; but though in great distress he still remained full of courage.

The different operations by which David had secured his prisoner had been carried on during the night; when the day came, Curione looked round him: the place seemed to bring to his memory certain half-effaced recollections.   He began to examine everything about him more carefully, and by degrees remembered that once upon a time, when a boy, he had been in that house, in that very room—it had probably been the house of some friend.   He called to remembrance exactly the arrangement of the building, the galleries, the staircase, the door, and the windows.* But ere long he was recalled from these thoughts by a feeling of pain: his gaolers had riveted the fetters so tightly that his feet began to swell and the anguish became intolerable.   When his keeper came as usual to bring him food, Curione spoke to him of his pain, and begged him to leave one of his feet at liberty, adding that, when that was healed, the gaoler could chain it up again and set the other free.   The man consented, and some days passed in this way, during which the prisoner experienced by turns severe pain and occasional relief.

* 'Recreatque in memoriam singularum domus partium situm.'—
Curionis Historia.

This circumstance did not prevent him from making the most serious reflections. He should never see his wife, his children, or his friends again; he could no longer take part in that great work of revival which God was then carrying on in the Church. He knew what sentence would be delivered at Rome. When St. John saw the woman seated on the seven hills, he exclaimed: '*Babylon!* .... *drunken with the blood of the saints and martyrs of Jesus.*' Death awaited Curione on the bishop's return: of that he had not a doubt. But was it not lawful to defend one's life against the violence of murderers? An idea suddenly crossed his inventive mind; the hope of escaping, of seeing his dear ones again, of again serving the cause of the Gospel, flashed upon him. He reflected and planned; the expedient which occurred to his mind was singular: possibly it might not succeed, but it might also be the means of saving him from the hands of his persecutors. When Peter was in prison, the angel of the Lord opened the door and led him out. Celio did not expect a miracle; but he thought it was man's duty to do all in his power to thwart the counsels of the ungodly. He was not, however, very sanguine of success. God holds the lives of his children in his hand; the Lord will restore him to liberty or send him to the scaffold, as He shall judge best.

Curione delayed no longer: he proceeded at once to carry out the curious and yet simple expedient which had occurred to his lively imagination. He took the boot off his free leg and stuffed it with rags;*

---

* 'Extrahit caligam pedis liberi, eamdem lineis quibusdam pannis infarcit.'—*Curionis Historia,* p. 341.

he then broke off the leg of a stool that was within his reach, fastened the sham foot to it, and contrived a wooden leg which he fixed to his knee in such a way that he could move it as if it were a real leg. His Spanish robe, reaching down to his heels, covered everything, and made the matter easier. Presently he heard the footsteps of his gaolers: luckily, everything was ready. They entered, did what they were accustomed to do every day, loosed the chained foot, and then, without examining too closely—for they had no suspicions—they put the fetters on the sham leg, and went away.

Celio was free; he rose, he walked: surprised at a deliverance so little expected, he was almost beside himself . . . he was rescued from death. But all was not over; he had still to get out of that strong mansion, where so close a watch was kept over him. He waited until night, and when darkness brooded over the city and his keepers were sunk in sleep, he approached the door of the chamber. The gaolers, knowing that the prisoner was chained to the wall, and that sentinels were posted at the outer gate, had only pushed it to without locking it. Curione opened it, and moved along with slow and cautious steps, avoiding the slightest noise for fear of giving the alarm. Although it was quite dark, he easily found his way by the help of his memory: he groped his course along the galleries, descended the stairs; but on reaching the door of the house, he found it closely shut. What was to be done now? The *sbirri* were asleep, but he dared not make any noise, lest he should wake them. Recollecting that there was a window placed rather high on one side of the door, he contrived to reach it, leapt into the court-yard, sealed the outer wall, fell into the street, and began to seek for a hiding-place as fast as his wounded feet would permit him.* When the morning came, there was great surprise and agitation in the house. The fidelity of the gaolers was not suspected; and as no one could explain the prisoner's flight, his enemies circulated the report that he had had recourse to magic to save himself from death.

Curione himself was surprised. The thought that he had escaped not only from the hands of his guards, but also from the terrible condemnation of the sovereign pontiff, whose support the bishop had gone to solicit, still further magnified in his eyes the greatness of his deliverance. He had felt, and severely too, the power of his enemies; but he saw that however keen the hatred of the world, a breath of heaven was sufficient to frustrate its plots. He hastened to leave Turin, and took refuge in a secluded village in the duchy of Milan, where his family joined him. His reputation as a man of letters had spread through that country, and certain Milanese gentlemen, who came to pass the summer in the villas near the lonely house which he inhabited, entertained a high opinion of him. One of them, happening to meet him, recognised him; he spoke of him to others of his friends, who made his acquaintance, and all of them, delighted with his amiable character and cultivated mind, were unwilling that such fine talents should remain buried in a sequestered village. They got him invited to the university of Pavia, where he was

---

* His feet never recovered their strength.

soon surrounded by an admiring audience. The inquisition, for a time at fault, discovered at last that the daring heretic who had escaped from his prison at Turin was teaching quietly at Pavia: it issued an arrest against him, being determined to put an end to the harassing warfare which this independent man was waging against the darkness of the Middle Ages. The familiars of the Holy Office lay in ambush with the intention of seizing the Piedmontese professor as he was leaving his house to go to the lecture-room. But the plot got wind; the students, who were very numerous, supported by some of the chief people of the town, formed a battalion which surrounded Curione as he left his house, conducted him to the Academy, and when the lecture was over, escorted him home again.* Public opinion declared itself so strongly in favour of liberty of teaching and against Romish tyranny, that three years elapsed without the inquisitors being able to seize the professor, which caused great joy all over the city. The pope, irritated at such resistance, threatened to excommunicate the senate of Pavia; and Curione, unwilling to imperil his friends, quitted that town for Venice, whence he proceeded to Ferrara to live under that enlightened protection which the duchess Renée extended to all who loved the Gospel.

Ferrara was in truth a centre where the Gospel found a firm support. Renée, who was daughter of Louis XII., and would have succeeded him if (as she used to say) ' she had had a beard on her chin,' had inherited, not the catholic ardour of her mother, Anne

---

* 'Magna studiosorum caterva, eum a sua domo in auditorium deducebat, et ex eo iterum domum comitabatur.'—*Curionis Historia*, p. 343.

of Brittany, but the reforming and anti-popish spirit of
her father, who had taken for his device: *Perdam
Babylonis nomen.*   Deprived of the throne by 'that
accursed Salic law'—to use her own words—but
brought up at the court of Francis I., she was closely
attached to her cousin Margaret, and although her
junior by eighteen years, had eagerly embraced the
Gospel which that 'elder sister' had preached to her
with so much earnestness.   Renée was not one of
those people who are simply the disciples of others.
Less beautiful than Margaret, she resembled her in
possessing a great soul, a generous heart, and, more
than that, a sound judgment and firm will.   While
clouds gathered round the mild and brilliant luminary
which presided over the destinies of Navarre and
obscured the end of its course, hardly a passing vapour
dimmed for an instant the pure star of Ferrara and
Montargis.

There had been a talk of marrying Renée, as there
had been of marrying Margaret, to Charles V., and
also to Henry VIII.; but the politic Francis had
preferred giving his predecessor's daughter to a
prince who would cause him no umbrage.   She was
therefore married to Hercules of Este, duke of Ferrara,
grandson of pope Alexander VI. by Lucrezia Borgia,
and vassal of the Holy See.   Such gloomy antecedents
did not promise a sympathetic union to the friend
of Margaret of Valois.

Although surrounded at Ferrara with all the splendours of a court, Renée delighted in the associations
of literature and art, and loved above every thing
to retire to her closet and seek for 'the one thing
needful.'   There was in her piety at this period of

her life a slight trace of Margaret's mystical spirit. A contemplative life, however, was not in keeping with her active character; she had rather a practical turn; she loved to attract to her small court the learned men of Italy, and particularly welcomed the evangelicals who had been driven out of France. She was thus beginning to be the object of the most opposite remarks. All were agreed as to her extreme beneficence; but the adherents of the papacy complained that her intellect, which enabled her to excel in philosophy, inclined her, unfortunately, to investigate religious questions; they added, however, that if she came to the aid of certain persons in bad odour among Roman catholics, it was because her inexhaustible goodness filled her with compassion for those whom she thought unjustly treated.* 'She desires to do good to everybody,' it was said; 'in one year she assisted ten thousand of her fellow-countrymen. And when the stewards of her household represented to her the excessive expense of this, she only answered: "What would you have?—they are poor people of my own country, all of whom would be my subjects but for that wicked Salic law!"'† She was at once a Mæcenas and a Dorcas.

The time had gone by in Italy when the fanaticism of pagan antiquity had misled the mind, and preachers were to be heard speaking from the pulpit of Minerva, Christ, and Jupiter in the same breath. At the very moment when celebrated professors, commissioned to teach philosophy even at the university of Ferrara,

---

* Maimbourg, *Histoire du Calvinisme,* liv. i. p. 61.

† Varillas, *Histoire des Hérésies,* ii. p. 499. Brantôme, *Dames Illustres.*

were exclaiming, as Voltaire and others did after him: 'Christianity is dying out, and its end is near!' Christianity on the contrary was reviving at Wittemberg, Zurich, Cambridge, and even in France, and the cry which it uttered as it issued from the tomb, reechoed through Italy and awoke many souls there. In 1528, and perhaps earlier, the evangelical doctrines had been professed at Ferrara. In 1530 the inquisition of that city wrote to the pope that there were many Lutherans, both laymen and ecclesiastics, within its walls.* In fact, the duchess was calling round her, either for the education of her children, or simply for love of learning and the Gospel, professors skilled in the study of the classics, among whom were men enlightened about the superstitions of the Roman Church, and often sincerely attached to the Gospel. Of their number were Celio Calcagnini, Lilio Giraldi, Bartholomeo Riccio, Marzello Palingenio, and the two brothers Sinapi. Giovanni Sinapi in particular was full of zeal to spread around him the doctrine of the Scriptures. Many of the most eminent men of Italy, such as Curione, Occhino, Peter Martyr, and the famous poet Flaminio, lived for a time at Ferrara. From that centre evangelical doctrines were propagated in the neighbouring cities; and particularly in Modena, where they spread so widely in the university and among the townspeople, that it was soon called *the Lutheran city.*†

* *P. Martyr Vermigli,* par C. Schmidt, p. 11.
† 'Città lutherana.'—Poli, *Epist.* iii. p. 84.

CHAPTER XIX.

THE GOSPEL IN THE CENTRE OF ITALY.

(1520 TO 1536.)

WHILE Venice, Turin, Milan, Ferrara, Modena, and other cities of Upper Italy were listening to the voice of the Gospel, the centre and south of the peninsula had also their witnesses to the truth.

Bernardino Occhino, born at Sienna in 1487, four years younger than Luther and Zwingle, and twenty-one years older than Calvin, was the most famous preacher of the age. In his sermons were to be found that elegance, that choice of words and those turns of expression which produce clearness, grace, and facility of style; but at the same time he was not void of imagination or enthusiasm, and possessed a boldness of language which surprises and carries away those who listen to it. Without being one of those firm solid spirits who search into all knowledge, and weigh and measure all thoughts, he had strong religious cravings, and as he was moved himself, he moved his hearers. 'From the very beginning of my life,' he said, 'I had a great longing for the heavenly paradise.' He determined to win it, but went astray on the road. His studies were imperfect; he knew little Greek and no Hebrew; his knowledge of

Christian doctrine was neither deep nor extensive; he sometimes allowed himself to descend to trifles and even to contradictions; and without denying the essential doctrines of faith, he was found in the latter part of his life employing obscure and equivocal expressions concerning them. He inopportunely defended customs tolerated under the old covenant, but manifestly forbidden under the new, and thus drew down much affliction on his old age. Occhino was a great orator, but not a great divine.

Sienna, the rival of Florence in the Middle Ages, still possessed sufficient attractions to induce a young man to follow the career of letters or of honours; but Occhino's mind took another direction. From his earliest youth, his religious feelings had inclined him to an ascetic life, and he sought peace for his soul in exercises of devotion. 'I believe in salvation through works,' he said, 'through fasting, prayer, mortifications, and vigils. With the help of God's grace we can, by means of these practices, satisfy the justice of God, obtain pardon for our sins, and merit heaven.'* Erelong his private macerations proved insufficient for him, and he became a monk. Every religious society approved of by Rome was holy in his eyes; but he joined the Observantine Franciscans, because that order was reputed to be stricter than the others. The youthful Bernardino soon found, like Luther, that the life of the cloister could not satisfy his need of holiness. He was discouraged, and, renouncing the pursuit of an object which he seemed unable to attain, he turned to the study of medicine, without, however, leaving the convent. Some Franciscans,

* B. Occhino, 'Responsio qua rationem reddit discessus ex Italia.'

having separated from the order with the intention of forming a still stricter rule, under the name of Capuchins, Occhino thought he had found what he wanted, and, having joined them, gave himself up with all his strength to voluntary humiliation and the mortification of the senses. *Eat not, touch not, taste not.* If any new and stricter laws were drawn up by the chiefs of the order, he hastened to conform to them. He threw himself blindfold into a complicated labyrinth of traditions, disciplines, fastings, mortifications, austerities, and ecstasies. And when they were over, he would ask himself whether he had gained anything? Remaining ill at ease and motionless in his cell, he would exclaim: 'O Christ! if I am not saved now, I know not what I can do more!' The moment was approaching when he would feel that all these macerations were but 'running knots, which bind at first and strangle at last.'*

This was in 1534, when Occhino was forty-seven years old. The agitations of his soul often inspired him, during his sermons, with those pathetic impulses which touch the heart; his superiors, wishing to turn his gifts to account, called him to the functions of the pulpit, and as he thus entered upon a new phase of life, a revolution was also effected in his thoughts. He turned away from the superstitious practices and paltry bonds of the monks and devotees, and approached the Holy Scriptures. Monastic discipline had increased his darkness: the Word was to bring him light. He felt the necessity of conscientiously preparing his sermons, and began to study the Bible. But, strange to say, Scripture, instead of

* Calvin.

making his work easier, embarrassed him at the very outset, made him uneasy, and even paralysed him. A striking contrast presented itself to his mind. 'I believe,' he said, 'that we must merit heaven by our works, while Scripture tells me that heaven is given by grace, because of the redemption through Jesus Christ.' He tried for some time to reconcile these contradictory views; but, do what he would, Rome and the Bible remained diametrically opposed to each other: he determined in favour of Rome. To doubt that the pope's teaching was divine would have been a crime. 'The authority of the Church,' he said in after years, 'silenced my scruples.' He applied again to his mortifications. It was all in vain : peace was a stranger to his soul.

Then he turned once more to what he had abandoned. He said to himself that, according to the universal opinion of Christendom, the Scriptures were given by God to show the path to heaven ; and that if there was anywhere a remedy for the disease under which he felt himself suffering, it must be in God's Book. He read its holy pages with entire confidence, and made every exertion to understand them. Erelong a new light broke upon him ; a heavenly brightness was poured upon the mystery of Golgotha, and he was filled with unutterable joy. 'Certainly,' he said, 'Christ by his obedience and death has fully satisfied the law of God and merited heaven for his elect. That is true righteousness, that is the true salvation.'* He did not advance any farther just then; for some time longer the Roman-Catholic Church was in his eyes the true Church, and the religious orders were

* B. Occhino, 'Responsio qua rationem reddit discessus ex Italia.'

holy institutions. He had found that peace which he had sought so long, and was satisfied.

The activity of his life increased, the fervour of his zeal augmented, his preaching became more spiritual and more earnest. He continued his itinerant ministry, and attracted still more the attention of the people of Italy. He always went on foot, though weak in body. His name filled the peninsula, and when he was expected in any city a multitude of people and even nobles and princes would go out to meet him. The principal men of the city would display a deep affection for him, pay him every honour, and not permit him to go and lodge in the wretched cell of a monastery, but force him to accept the brilliant hospitality of their mansions. The magnificence of these dwellings, the costly dresses of their inhabitants, and 'all the pomp of the age,' made no change in his humble and austere life. Sitting at the luxurious banquets of the great ones of this world, he would drink no wine and eat but of one dish, and that the plainest. Being conducted to the best chamber, and invited to repose in a soft and richly-furnished bed, in order to recruit himself after the fatigue of his journey, he would smile, stretch his threadbare mantle on the floor, and lie down upon it.

As soon as the news of his arrival became known, crowds of people would throng round him from all parts. 'Whole cities went to hear him,' says the bishop of Amelia, 'and there was no church large enough to contain the multitude of hearers.' * All eyes were

---

* Ant. M. Gratiani, bishop of Amelia: see *Hist. du Cardinal Commendon,* liv. ii. ch. ix.

fixed on him as soon as he entered the pulpit. His age, his thin pale face, his beard falling below the waist, his grey hair and coarse robe, and all that was known of his life, made the people regard him as an extraordinary man, indeed as a saint. Was there any affectation in these strange manners? Probably there was, for though a new creation had begun in him, the old nature was still very strong. He was not insensible to the glory that comes from man, and perhaps did not seek alone that which comes from God.

At length the great orator began to speak, and all the congregation hung upon his lips. He explained his ideas with such ease and grace, that even from the very beginning of his ministry, he charmed all who heard him. But after he had studied Scripture, there was more elegance, originality, and talent in his discourses. He made use of evangelical language, which penetrated the heart; and yet no one, unless he were a very subtle theologian, would dare ascribe new doctrines to him. The inward power which he had received touched their hearts; the movements of his eloquence carried away his hearers, and he led them where he pleased.* At Perugia, enemies embraced one another as they left the church, and renounced the family feuds which had been handed down through several generations. At Naples, when he preached for some work of charity, every purse was opened: one day he collected five thousand crowns—an enormous sum for those times. Even princes of the Church, such as Cardinal Sadolet and Cardinal Bembo,

---

* 'Ut auditorum animos quocumque vellet raperet.'—Bzovius, ad annum 1542.

adjudged him the palm of popular eloquence: all voices hailed him as the first preacher of Italy.* We shall see him presently producing a religious revival at Naples. He was preceded and aided in that work by men who although inferior to him in eloquence, were his superiors in knowledge and faith.

At the time when the Word was thus sown, and was everywhere bearing fruit more or less, Florence, the land of the Medici, so illustrious from its attachment to letters and liberty, was not to be a barren soil. In the year 1500, the year in which Charles V. was born, a rich patrician named Stephen Vermigli had a son whom he named Peter Martyr in honour of Peter of Milan whom the Arians are said to have put to death for maintaining the orthodox faith, and to whom a church was dedicated near the house in which the child was born.† His mother, Maria Fumantina, an educated woman of meek and tranquil piety, devoted herself to her only son, taught him Latin in his earliest years, and poured into his heart that incorruptible spirit, which is of such great value before God. The boy early attended the public schools established for the Florentine youth, and was distinguished for the quickness of his understanding, the extent of his powers, the strength of his memory, and above all by such a thirst for learning that no difficulties could stop him. If Occhino possessed liveliness of feeling and imagination, Peter Martyr possessed solidity of judgment and depth of mind.

* 'Ut unus optimus totius Italiæ concionator haberetur.'—Bzovius, ad annum 1542.

† 'Ex voto quodam quod fuerunt Petro Martyri Mediolanensi, qui quondam ab Arianis occisus est.'—Simler, *Vita Petri M. Vermilii*, Tiguri, 1569.

Before long the youth was involved in a painful struggle. His father—either because he disapproved of a monastic life, the abuses of which, even at Florence, had been exposed by Dante and afterwards by Savonarola; or because he was ambitious and desired to see his son attain a brilliant position—intended giving him an education calculated to advance him in the service of the State. Peter Martyr, on the contrary, inspired by the pious feelings which he had inherited from his mother, wished to dedicate himself to God. His greatest ambition was to learn: his glory was to know: knowledge, and especially the knowledge of divine things, was in his eyes superior to all the world besides. His father commanded in vain and disinherited him in vain; in 1516 the young man entered the monastery of regular canons of St. Augustine at Fiesole near Florence. After a certain interval of time Peter Martyr felt that he did not learn much in the cloister. He was penetrated with the thought that man ought to make it his object to propagate around him solid knowledge and true light, especially in all that relates to the immortal soul; but to propagate them, he must first possess them. He obtained permission to visit Padua, the seat of a celebrated university. Quiet, steady, diligent, affectionate, and respectful, he was loved and esteemed by all. He venerated the aged as if they were his fathers, and displayed such modesty, affection, and eagerness to do what was pleasing to his comrades, that he always found them, in times of trial, his surest friends.*

---

* 'Æquales suos quamvis plerosque ingenio excelleret, ita tamen amabat, ita modestia sua sibi devinciebat, ut . . . amicissimos semper habuerit.'—Simler, *Vita Petri M. Vermilii*, Tiguri, 1569.

Although he was in the age of passions, and lived in cities where temptations were numerous, he was able to preserve that chastity of thought and that purity of conduct so necessary to the happiness and real success of a young man.   He studied philosophy, and in the public disputations acquired a singular dialectic skill, of which he afterwards gave striking proofs.   But he was in search of something better, namely, divine truth; and therefore began to attend the lectures of the theological professors.   He was soon disgusted with them, for they taught nothing but scholastics, and he resolved to seek the road by himself.   He frequently spent the greater part of the night in the library of his monastery; he read the Greek authors, and then took up the Fathers of the Church, Tertullian, Athanasius, and Augustine, and began to have a perception that the theology of primitive catholicism was quite different from that of the papacy.

In 1526, his superiors, struck with his talents, called him to the ministry.   Peter Martyr preached at Rome, Bologna, Pisa, Venice, Mantua, Bergamo, and other cities.   At the same time he gave public lessons in literature and philosophy, particularly on Homer.   But he determined to go farther, and no longer contenting himself with the poets, philosophers, and Fathers of the Church, he desired to know the Holy Scriptures.   He was enraptured with them; as the Latin text was not sufficient for him, he read the New Testament in Greek; he next resolved to read the Old Testament also in the original, and meeting with a Jewish doctor named Isaac at Bologna, he learnt Hebrew of him.   Then it was that a new light illumined his fine genius.   While he was studying the letter of the Holy Scriptures, *the Spirit of God opened his understanding*, and displayed before him the mysteries concealed within them.* His learning, labours, and administrative ability had already attracted general consideration; and the pious sentiments he now displayed helped to increase it. He was appointed abbot of Spoleto, and in 1530 was summoned to a larger theatre, to Naples, as prior of St. Peter's *ad Aram*, where we shall meet him erelong.

In 1534, there lived in Sienna a friend of Greek and Latin literature, an enthusiast for Cicero, whose elegant and harmonious periods he translated better than any other scholar, and who was particularly distinguished among the professors of the university for his elevation of soul, love of truth, boldness of thought, and the courage with which he attacked false doctors and sham ascetics. He made a sensation in the world of schools, and though he had no official post, the students crowded to his lectures. His name was Antonio della Paglia, which he latinised according to the fashion of the age into Aonius Palearius. This again was Italianised into Aonio Paleario. Among the hills which bound the Roman Campagna, near the source of the Garigliano, stands the ancient city of Veroli; here he was born in 1503, of an old patrician house according to some, of the family of an artisan according to others. In 1520 he went to Rome, where the love of art and antiquity was then much cultivated, and from the lessons of illustrious teachers he learnt to admire Demosthenes, Homer, and Virgil.

---

* 'Dum litteram aliquandiu sectatur, patefaciente Spiritu Dei, abdita et spiritualia mysteria salutariter cognovit.'—Simler, *Vita Petri M. Vermilii*, Tiguri, 1569.

A rumour of war disturbed his peaceful labours.   In 1527 the imperial army descended the Alps, and like an avalanche which, slipping from the icy mountain-tops, rushes down into the valley, it overthrew and destroyed everything in its course.   Milan had been crushed, and when the news reached Rome at the same time with the furious threats uttered by the imperialists against the city of the pontiffs, the young student exclaimed, 'If they come near us, we are lost!'   Paleario hastily took refuge in the valley where he was born, but even there the spray of the avalanche reached him.   When he returned to the papal city, alas! the houses were in ruins, the men of letters had fled.   He turned his eyes towards Tuscany, quitted Rome in the latter part of 1529, and after spending some time at Perugia, went on to Sienna, where he arrived in the autumn of 1530.

That ancient city of the Etruscans, transformed into a city of the Middle Ages, at first delighted the friend of letters.   Its position in the midst of smiling hills,* the fertility of its fields, the abundance of everything, the beauty of the buildings, the cultivated minds of its inhabitants—all enraptured him.   But erelong he discovered a wound which wrung his heart: the state was torn by factions; an ignorant, impetuous, turbulent democracy had the upper hand; the strength of a people who might have done great things, was wasted in idle and barren disputes.   The most eminent men wept over the sorrows of their country, and fled with their wives and children from the

---

* 'Urbs situ, natura, et ingeniis nobilis, inter amœnos colles conclusa, fertilis et copiosa.'—*Oratio de Concordia Civium*, p. 380. (*Palearii Opera*, Wetstein, Amsterdam.)

desolated land. ' Alas !' exclaimed Paleario, ' the city wants nothing but concord between the citizens.'* He met, however, with an affectionate welcome in the families of a few nobles; and, after visiting Florence, Ferrara, Padua and Bologna, he returned in 1532 to Sienna, to which his friends had invited him.

Paleario was a poet: his fancy was at work where-ever he went; and, either during his travels or on his return to the Ghibeline city, he composed a Latin poem on the immortality of the soul.† We find traces of the Roman doctrine in it, especially of purgatory‡ and of the queenship of the Virgin:§ his eyes, how-ever, were already turned towards the Reformation. He desired to have readers like Sadolet, and also the sympathy of Germany.‖ The poem evidences a soul which, without having yet found God and the peace He gives, sighs after a new earth, a rejuvenated humanity, and a happiness which consists in contemplating the Almighty, the King of men, as the eternal and absolute goodness and supreme happiness.¶

Ere long Paleario took another step. The religious questions by which Italy was so deeply agitated,

---

* ' Nihil unquam enim civitati defuit nisi concordia civilis.'—*Oratio de Concordia Civium.*

† De Immortalitate Animarum. The poem was published by Gryphius, at Lyons, in 1536, through the instrumentality of Cardinal Sadolet, bishop of Carpentras.

‡ ' Tres igitur sedes statuit pater optimus ipse.'

§ 'Teque, optima Virgo,
Victricem, præclare acto *Regina* triumpho.'

‖ 'Quales nunc habet ingeniis Germania florens.'.

¶ 'Oculos defigite in unum,
Unus ego omnipotens, ego Rex hominumque Deumque,
Æternumque bonum simplexque, et summa voluptas.'
(*Ad finem.*)

engrossed that eminent mind. He commenced reading not only Saint Augustin, but the Reformers and the Holy Scriptures, and began to speak in his lectures with a liberty that enraptured his hearers, but so exasperated the priests, that his friend and patron Sadolet recommended him to be more prudent. Paleario, however, boldly crossed the threshold which separates the literary from the Christian world. He received thoroughly the doctrine of justification by faith, and found in it a peace which was to him the warrant of its truth. 'Since He in whom the Godhead dwells,' he said, 'has so lovingly poured out his blood for our salvation, we must not doubt of the favour of heaven. All who turn their souls towards Jesus crucified, and bind themselves to him with thorough confidence, are delivered from evil, and receive forgiveness of their sins.'

Paleario loved the country. Having noticed a villa which had belonged to Aulus Cecina, the friend of Cicero, situated between Colle and Volterra, at the summit of a plateau, whence flowed a stream, watering the slopes, and where a pure air and the tranquillity of the fields could be enjoyed,* the Christian poet bought it, and there, in his beloved *Cecignana*, on the terrace before the house or among the forest oaks, he passed many a peaceful day, consecrated to serious meditation. He knew that the world on which he fixed his eyes was the creation of the supreme, the free will of God; that an inward and uninterrupted bond existed between the Creator and his creatures, and rejoiced that, owing to the redemp-

* The villa is now the property of Count Guicciardini.

tion of Jesus Christ, there would be formed out of its inhabitants a kingdom of God, from which evil would be for ever banished.

Paleario's tender soul needed domestic affections, and at Sienna he was alone. He married Marietta Guidotti, a young person of respectable parentage; who had been brought up with holy modesty.* She bore him two sons, Lampridius and Phædrus, and two daughters, Aspasia and Sophonisba, whom he loved tenderly, and who were, after God, the consolation of a life agitated by the injustice of his enemies. Family affections and a love for the beauties of nature were in Paleario, as they often are, the marks of an elevated soul. At a later period, when his life had become still more bitter; when he had lost his health, and his faith had made him an object of horror to the fanatical; when he exclaimed: 'All men are full of hatred and ill-will towards me;'† when he foresaw that he must ere long succumb beneath the blows of his adversaries; even then he sighed after the country, and wrote to one of his friends, with a simplicity reminding us of ancient times:—'I am weary of study; fain would I fly to you and pass my days under the warm bright sky of your fields. At early morn, or when the day begins to wane, we will wander through the country, around the cottages, with Lampridius and Phædrus, my darling boys, and with your wife and mine.‡ Get ready the garden, that we may live on herbs,

* 'Adolescentulam optimis parentibus bene et pudice educatam ducam in uxorem.'—Palearii *Epist.* p. 61.

† 'Malevolorum et invidorum plena sunt omnia.'—*Ibid.* p. 209.

‡ 'Mane aut inclinato in pomeridianum tempus die, cum Lampridio et Phædro, suavissimis pueris, et cum mulieribus nostris circum villulas errabimus.'—*Ibid.* p. 209.

for I am utterly disgusted with the luxurious tables
of our cities. The farm shall supply us with eggs
and poultry, the river with fish. Oh! how sweet
are the repasts at which we eat the fruit we
gather from our own garden, the fowls fed by our
own hands, the birds caught in our nets,—sweeter
far than those where you see nothing on the table
but provisions bought in the market! We will work
in the fields, we will tire ourselves. Make your
preparations; get ready a saw, a hatchet, a wedge to
cleave the wood, pruning-shears, a harrow, and a hoe.
If these implements fail us, we will be content with
planting trees, that shall serve for ages yet to come.'
It is pleasing to see the disciple of Cicero and especially of the Bible, at a time when he was tormented
by sickness and the hatred of the wicked, rejoicing like a child at the thought of planting trees
that should give a cool shade and welcome fruit to
coming generations. We shall now describe the
end of his stay at Sienna, and what brought his
great sorrow upon him, although it will lead us
beyond the limits of time we have prescribed for
ourselves.

The best friend Paleario possessed was Antonio
Bellantes, president of the Council of Nine, a grave
and benevolent man, generally loved and respected;
in a time of difficulty he had assisted the State by the
gift of two million golden crowns. Bellantes esteemed
Paleario very highly, and Paleario loved him above
all other men. In the course of the popular disturbances, the members of the Council of Nine had been
banished; but the senate and people had entreated
Bellantes to remain at Sienna—a circumstance which

had greatly enraged his enemies. Ruffians broke into his house one night and plundered it. Somewhat later Bellantes died, leaving all his ready money to his mother, that she might deliver it to his sons when they came of age. The good lady was a great friend of the monks; every day the capuchins used to visit her,* and when she fell sick they crowded round her bed. After her death, no property could be found in her house, except some torn bags which appeared to have held money. The sons of Bellantes accused the monks of having stolen their inheritance, and Paleario supported them with his eloquence. The monks denied the fact, and were acquitted upon their solemn oath. Inflamed with anger against Paleario, they resolved upon his destruction.

At the head of his adversaries was the senator Otto Melio Cotta, a rich, powerful, and ambitious man of a domineering spirit. At first he had been mixed up in political affairs, but he afterwards enlisted under the banners of the clergy, and made common cause with the monks. A plot was formed in the Observantine convent, situated about a mile from Sienna, in the midst of woods, grottoes, and holy places. Three hundred members of the Joanelli, a brotherhood formed for certain exercises of piety, swore upon the altar to destroy Paleario. Not confining themselves to attacks upon his teaching, Cotta and his other adversaries began to pry into his private life, to watch all his movements, and to catch up every word. They soon found fresh subjects of complaint

---

* 'Lignipodas, qui in aviæ conclave quotidie cursabant.'—Faustus Bellantes to Paleario, *Epist.* p. 97.

against him. Paleario had ridiculed a wealthy priest who was to be seen every morning devoutly kneeling before the shrine of a saint, but who refused to pay his debts; and the keen irony with which he had spoken of him had occasioned a great scandal among the clergy. That, however, was not enough; they must have a palpable mark of heresy. His adversaries endeavoured, therefore, to entrap him, and some of them, presenting themselves as if they wanted to be instructed, put questions to him calculated to lead him into the snare. 'What,' they asked, 'is the first means of salvation given by God to man?' He an-swered ' *Christ.*' That might pass; but, continuing their questions, Paleario's enemies added: 'What is the second?' In their opinion, he should have indi-cated meritorious works; but Paleario replied: ' *Christ.*' Continuing their enquiry, they said: 'And what is the third?' They thought that Paleario should answer, The Church; out of the Church there is no salvation; but he still replied, ' *Christ.*'* From that moment he was a lost man. The monks and their friends reported to Cotta the answer which they deemed so heretical.

Paleario had no suspicion of danger. Cardinal Sadolet and some other friends invited him to come and see them at Rome, and he went. He had not been there long before he received a very excited letter from Faustus Bellantes. 'There is a great agitation in the city,' he said: 'an astounding con-

---

* 'Rogatus quid primum esset generi hominum a Deo datum, in quo salutem collocare mortales possent? Responderim CHRISTUM. Quid secundum? CHRISTUM. Quid *tertium*? CHRISTUM.'—Palearii *Epist.* p. 99.

spiracy has been formed against you by the most criminal of men.* We do not know upon what the accusation is founded; we are ignorant of the names of your adversaries. The report runs that the chiefs of the state have been excited against you in consequence of calumnious charges concerning religion. It is said that some wretched monks have sworn your ruin; but the plot must have deeper roots. I shall go to Sienna to-morrow, and shall speak to my friends and relations about it. I am ready for everything, even to lose my life in your defence. Meantime I conjure you, let your mind be at peace.'

Bellantes was not deceived. Cotta, without loss of time, appeared in the senate and reported to his colleagues the monstrous language of Paleario, and exclaimed, that if they suffered him to live, ' there would be no vestige of religion left in the city.'† Every man was silent: such was the alarm caused by a charge of heresy, that no one dared take up the defence of that courageous Christian.

Paleario heard of this, and was distressed but not surprised. One truth was deeply engraved in his heart: All power of salvation is given to Jesus Christ; He is the only source whence the new life can be drawn. It seemed to him that the priests had forged so many means of acquiring pardon, that they hardly left Christ the hundredth part. He could well understand how irritated the clergy must be against a man who set so little store by all their paltry contrivances;

---

* 'Incredibilem conspirationem scelestissimorum hominum contra te esse factam.'—Palearii *Epist.* p. 97.

† 'Cotta asserebat, me salvo, vestigium religionis in civitate reliquum esse nullum.'—*Ibid.* p. 99.

but although he saw clearly the danger that threatened him, he remained firm. ‘The power of the conspirators is immense,’ he said; ‘the more fiercely a man attacks me, the more pious he is reckoned. But what matters it? Jesus Christ, whom I have always sincerely and religiously adored, is my hope.* . . . I despise the cabals of men, and my heart is full of courage.’† Christ was his king. He knew that that great Sovereign, who is achieving the conquest of the world, preserves at the same time all those who have found reconciliation with God through him.

His wife was not so calm. Marietta, his virtuous and devoted partner, so ardent in her affection, was filled with uneasiness and trouble; her imagination called up before her not only the misfortunes of the moment, but also those of the future; she was the most unhappy of women.‡ Her agony was greater than her strength; she passed whole days in tears.§ Distressed and exhausted, she lost her health; and everyone might see in her face the sorrow which was consuming her. When her husband heard of this at Rome, he was heart-broken, and conjured his mother and Bellantes to visit Marietta, in order to distract the afflicted wife from her sorrow.

Paleario would have desired to hasten to her in person and confront his accusers; but his friends at Sienna and at Rome alike dissuaded him. The citizens who were then at the head of the state were

---

* ‘Christus tamen meus mihi spem facit, quem sancte et auguste semper colui.’—Palearii *Epist.* p. 100.

† ‘Sed ego jam humana contemno, fortissimo animo sum.’—*Ibid.*

‡ ‘Miserrima est omnium mulierum.’—*Ibid.* p. 103.

§ ‘In lacrymis jacet totos dies et mærore conficitur.’—*Ibid.*

violent men, of no morality, and as ready to condemn the innocent as to acquit the guilty. It was hoped that a new election would bring upright men into power: they conjured Paleario to wait, and he did so. But there was no change: the denunciations, charges, and murmurs only increased. The enemies of the Gospel attacked not merely Paleario, but the re-formers, the *Germans*, as they said: they tried to involve all the friends of the Bible, both German and Italian, in the same condemnation. At last, what had been hoped for came to pass; an important change took place in the government of the republic; order and liberty were restored. Paleario thought he could no longer remain away; he left Rome and joined his family at his country-house near Colle.

As soon as his adversaries were informed of his return, they laid a charge of heresy before the senate of Sienna and the court of Rome. Determined to employ all means to destroy Paleario, they resolved to constrain the ecclesiastical authority to go along with them by the strong pressure they would bring to bear upon it. With this intent twelve of them met, and, bent on prevailing upon the archbishop to demand that Paleario should be put upon his trial, they marched through the streets of the city to the prelate's palace. In this excited band there was the senator Cotta with five others, distinguished among whom was Alexis Lucrinas, an impetuous and foolish man; then three priests, people of little importance, but very violent, grossly ignorant, and untiring babblers;* and lastly, three monks. The

* 'Tenues homines sed arrogantes, imperiti, loquacissimi.'—Palearii *Opera*, p. 86.

archbishop happened just then to be at his villa in the suburbs, for the sake of the purer air ; the delegates went there after him, accompanying their march with such shouting, threats, and disputes, that the women, attracted by the unusual noise, ran to the windows, fancying they were taking some criminal to punishment. Some of the conspirators said: ' The witnesses will be heard, the motives of his condemnation will be declared, and then Paleario will be thrown into the fire;' but others wanted to proceed more quickly, so that the punishment should follow immediately upon the statement of the offence, without any form of trial and without permitting the accused to be heard.*   Archbishop Francesco Bandini, of the illustrious house of Piccolomini, was a friend of letters, and consequently of Paleario. It was afternoon; the prelate, who was taking his siesta, being awoke by the noise, called a servant, and asked him who were vociferating in that manner. Being informed that they were men of consideration, he ordered them to be admitted. He rose from his couch, took his seat, and waited for the strange deputation. They entered: Lucrinas, who had been sometimes invited to his lordship's table, was full of confidence in himself, and accordingly had begged that they would allow him to speak. Looking round him with a satisfied and boasting air, he began to pour out against Paleario a long string of insults and maledictions in a passionate tone. The bishop, a wise and grave man, had some difficulty to contain himself, and said that the whole proceeding

---

* 'Alii . . . auditis testibus, mox in ignem conjiciendum censebant, indicata causa. Alii, causa dicta pœnam sequi oportere putabant.' —Palearii *Opera.*

appeared to him full of levity. ' There can be no
question of levity,' impudently exclaimed Lucrinas,
' when three hundred citizens are ready to sign the
accusation.' ' And I could produce six hundred witnesses,' rejoined the prelate, ' who have sworn that
you are a merciless usurer. I did not, however, give
effect to their denunciation. Did I do well or ill?
tell me.' . . . The poor wretch was silent; the fact
was too notorious to be denied, and too scandalous
to be confessed. But his companions were not to be
put out by such a trifle; they explained the motives
of their prosecution, threw themselves at the prelate's
feet, and conjured him in the name of religion to
support the charge against Paleario. The archbishop,
considering that it was a question of heresy, thought
that it was a matter for the courts to decide, and consented to their prayer.

  Paleario's enemies set to work immediately; they
endeavoured to prejudice the most notable persons in
Sienna against him; and picked out individuals from
among the populace, who were without light and
without conscience, whom they induced to testify
before the court to things of which they knew nothing.*
It was in vain that the famous Sadolet, summoned to
Rome by the pope, stopped at Sienna, and undertook
Paleario's defence. It was in vain that the cardinal,
the archbishop, and Paleario had a consultation in
which Sadolet commended the accused to the archbishop, and gave touching proofs of his esteem and
affection for him; the conspirators were able to turn
the interview against the man whom they had sworn to

* ' Testes partim e plebecula tenues, rerum de quibus testimonium
dixerunt imperiti.'—Palearii *Epist.* p. 116.

sacrifice to their hatred. A number of people who had assembled in the public square began to talk about the conference: 'When Paleario was accused by the prelate,' said some, 'he was silent through shame.' 'No,' said the others, 'he answered, but was sharply reprimanded by Sadolet.'* Impatient to see their victim handed over to death, happy at having already caused doubt in the mind of the archbishop, and imagining they had convinced Sfondrati the president of the republic, and Crasso the prætor, the twelve obtained an order for Paleario to be summoned before the senate on a charge of heresy.

That innocent and just man was not blind to the danger and difficulty of his position. He felt that the calumnies of his enemies would check the good he hoped to do, would break up old friendships, and destroy the peace that the city was beginning to enjoy. Ere long, perhaps, his wife would be a widow and his children orphans: a veil of sadness covered his face. Oh! how bitter was such a trial! He knew full well that afflictions awaken heavenly life in the Christian; that it is a privilege of the child of God; but he was for some time without comfort, and his soul was bowed down. 'My adversaries,' he said, 'heap wrong upon wrong, hatred upon hatred:† they have done nothing else these six months. Has there ever been a man saintly enough not to give way under the attacks of such a perverse zeal? I will not speak of Socrates, Scipio, Rutilius, or Metellus; certain failings might

---

* 'Alii respondentem graviter objurgatum a Sadoleto.'—Palearii *Epist.* p. 118.

† 'Injuriam augere injuria, et odio cumulare odium.'—*Ibid.* p. 119.

have laid them open to the attacks of their enemies. But even He than whom none was so good, none so holy, even the all-innocent Jesus Christ himself, was assailed on every side.* Alas! where can the righteous man turn? whom can he implore?'

Paleario soon learnt to answer this. When he found himself summoned to appear before the senate, his courage revived. He was not only strong in his innocence, but the faith which inspired his heart told him that God loves his servants, and that with Him they are free from every danger. He went to the palace of the Signiory, and entered the hall, leaning on the arm of the youthful Faustus Bellantes, son of his old friend, accompanied by some faithful men who were unwilling to forsake him in the day of his distress. He stood in the presence of those who held his life in their hands. Sfondrati the president, Crasso the prætor, the senate, and the Nine were seated in their judicial chairs. His adversaries were there also; Cotta especially, full of presumptuous assurance, and feeling certain that the time had come at last when he could fall upon his prey. Paleario recognised him; he was agitated and indignant at seeing him quietly taking his seat in the senate, at the very time he was bent on carrying out an infamous plot. He contained himself, however; and, first addressing the senators, to whom he gave the title employed in ancient Rome, he said:† 'Conscript

---

* 'Quo nemo melior, nemo sanctior circumventus est innocentissimus Christus.'—Palearii *Epist.* p. 116.

† *Oratio tertia pro se ipso.* This is the speech which the ecclesiastical authorities of Naples cut out of all the copies of Paleario's works that fell into their hands, but which we have found complete in the edition of Amsterdam, pp. 73-97.

fathers, when there was a talk about me in former years, I was not seriously moved by it: the times were times of desolation; all human and divine rights were confounded in the same disorder. But now, when, by the goodness of God, men of wisdom have been placed at the head of the republic, when the sap and the blood circulate afresh through the state,* why should I not lift up my head?'

By degrees Paleario grew warm; his eyes fell again upon his insolent enemy whom he apostrophised as Cicero did Catiline: 'Cotta, you wicked, arrogant, and factious man,' he said, 'who practise not that religion in which God is worshipped in spirit and in truth, but that which plunges into every super-stition, because it is the best adapted to impose upon mankind: Cotta, you imagine you are a Christian, because you bear the image of Christ upon your purple robe; while by your calumnies you are crushing an innocent man, who is also an image, a living image, of Jesus Christ. When you accused me falsely of a crime, did you obey Jesus Christ? When you went to the house of the Nine to utter falsehoods against me, did you think, Cotta, you were making a pilgrimage to Jerusalem? I am surprised that you do not crucify innocent persons. . . . You would do it—yes, you would do it, if you could do all that your pride suggests.' †

Paleario then passed on to a more important subject.

---

* 'Cum succus et sanguis Reipublicæ sit restitutus.'—Palearii *Opera*, edit. Amsterdam, p. 73.

† 'Homines innocentes in crucem tollas. . . . Tolleres, tolleres quidem si quantum furor iste, superbia, iracundia affert, tautum tibi liceret.' —*Ibid.* p. 80.

In attacking him, his adversaries really attacked the Gospel, the Reformation, and those excellent men whom God was making use of to transform Christian society. Paleario defended the reformers in the presence of all Italy.

'You bring impudent reproaches against me, Cotta,' he continued; 'you assert that I think wrongly on religious matters, that I am falling into heresy, and you accuse me of having adopted the opinions of the *Germans*. What a paltry accusation! Do you pretend to bind all the Germans in the same bundle? Are all the Germans bad? Do you not know that the august Emperor is a German? Will you say that you mean only the theologians? What noble theologians there are in Germany! But though your accusations are unmeaning in appearance, there is a sting lying under them. I know the venom they contain. . . . The *Germans* that you mean are Œcolampadius, Erasmus, Melanchthon, Luther, Pomeranus, Bucer, and their friends. But is there a single theologian in Italy so stupid as not to know that there are many things worthy of praise in the works of those doctors? . . . Exact, sincere, earnest, they have professed the truths which we find set forth by the early fathers. To accuse the Germans is to accuse Origen, Chrysostom, Cyrillus, Irenæus, Hilary, Augustin, and Jerome. If I purpose imitating those illustrious doctors of Christian antiquity, why repeat perpetually that I think like the Germans? What! because the learned professors of the German schools have followed the footsteps of those holy men of the first centuries, may not I follow them also? You would like me to imitate the folly of those who, to obtain good preferments,

fight against even that which is good in Germany. . . .
Ah! conscript fathers, rather than strive after those
delights which lead many astray, I prefer to live
honestly. My circumstances may be narrow, but my
conscience is at liberty.* Let those vile flatterers
sit on the doctor's seat or the bishop's throne, let them
put mitres or tiaras on their heads, let them wear the
purple.† . . . Not so for me, I will remain in my
library, sitting on a wooden stool, wearing a woollen
garment against the cold, a linen garment in the heat,
and with only a little bed on which to taste the repose
of sleep.

'But, Cotta, you still continue your attacks; you
reproach me for praising all the Germans say and do.
No! there are some things I approve of in them and
others that I do not. When I meet with thoughts
which for ages had been obscured by a barbarous
style, hidden under the brambles of scholasticism, and
sunk into the deepest darkness—when I see these
brought into the full light of day, placed within the
reach of all, and expressed in the choicest Latinity, I
not only praise the Germans, but I heartily thank
them. Sacred studies had fallen asleep in convent cells,
where the idle men who should have cultivated them
had hidden themselves as if in gloomy forests, under
the pretence of applying to work. But what happened?
They snored so loud that we could hear them in our
cities and towns.‡ Now, learning has been restored

---

* 'Res domi angusta est; at conscientia in animi penetralibus
augusta, læta, alacris.'—Palearii *Opera*, edit. Amsterdam, p. 84.

† 'Sedeant illi in cathedra, diademata imponunt, dibaphum vestiant.'
—*Ibid.*

‡ Jacebant divina studia, strata in cellulis hominum otiosorum, qui

to us; Latin, Greek, and Chaldee libraries have been
formed; assistance has been honourably extended to
the theologians; precious books have been multiplied
by means of the wonderful invention of printing. Can
there be anything more striking, more glorious, or
more deserving our eternal gratitude?'

After this defence of the literary and reforming
movement of Germany, Paleario came to what is
grander than all—to Christ: ' Are they not insuffer-
able men,' he said, 'nay, wicked men, before whom
we dare not praise the God of our salvation, Jesus
Christ, the King of all nations, by whose death such
precious boons have been conferred upon the human
race? And yet for this, conscript fathers, yes, for
this I am reproached in the accusation brought against
me. On the authority of the most ancient and most
faithful documents, I had declared that the end of all
evils had arrived, that all condemnation was done away
with for those who, being converted to Christ crucified,
trust in him with perfect confidence. These are the
things that appeared detestable to those twelve . . .
shall I say to those twelve *men* or twelve wild beasts,
who desire that the man who wrote these things
should be thrown into the fire! If I must suffer
that penalty for the testimony I have borne to the Son
of God, believe me that no happier fate could befall
me; in truth, I do not think that a Christian in our
times ought to die in his bed. Ah! conscript fathers,
to be accused and cast into prison is a trifle; to be
scourged, to be hanged, to be sewn up in a sack, to

licet in sylvas se abstrusissent, ut in hæc incumberent; ita stertebant
tamen, ut nos in urbibus et vicis audiremus.'—Palearii *Opera*, edit.
Amsterdam, pp. 81-85.

be thrown to wild beasts, to be consumed by fire, all these are trifles, if only by such punishments truth is brought into the light of day.' *

Aonio Paleario did not speak as a rhetorician; he was no maker of Ciceronian periods. The man who at this time professed so energetically the supreme importance of truth and did so again in his *Beneficio di Gesù Cristo crocifisso*,† gave his life for it. If he *spoke* at Sienna, he was to *act* at Rome. In each of these phases we recognise the noble victim of 1570.

After speaking like a martyr, he spoke like a man. He looked round him: some of the most eminent citizens, the Tancredis, the Placidis, the Malevoltas were near him full of emotion. Egidio, superior of the Augustines, and his monks—men abounding in piety and modesty—strengthened him by their approbation and their prayers. His two young friends, Faustus and Evander Bellantes, keeping their eyes fixed upon him, could not restrain their tears. Presently a more moving sight met his eyes: he beheld Marietta, pale and weeping. 'What do I see?' he exclaimed. 'Thou also, my wife, art thou come dressed in mourning weeds, accompanied by the noblest and most pious of women—art thou come with thy children, to throw thyself at the feet of the senators? O my light, my life, my soul! return home, train up our children; do not be afraid, Christ who is thy spouse

---

* 'Parum est accusari et deduci in carcerem, virgis cædi, reste suspendi, insui in culeum, feris objici, ad ignem torreri nos decet, si his suppliciis veritas in lucem est proferenda.'—Palearii *Opera*, edit. Amsterdam, p. 91.

† The fact that Paleario was the author of this book seems clearly established by Mr. Babington, as well as by M. J. Bonnet and Mrs. Young.

will be their father.* . . . Alas! she is half killed with grief.† O mother, support her, take her away; take her to your own home, if you can . . . and let your love dry up her tears.'

The impression produced by this address was so profound, that the senate declared Paleario innocent. But such a striking triumph served only to enrage his enemies the more: he saw that he could not remain at Sienna, and therefore took leave of his friends. Bellantes, on his death-bed, had commended his children to him, and Paleario exhorted them to aspire to something great. It is probable that he went to Rome for a short time, where his friends had got the proceedings set aside which his enemies had commenced against him; and afterwards to Lucca, where the chair of eloquence was given him. He left a great void at Sienna, and his friends were grieved. Faustus Bellantes seemed to express the feelings of all when he wrote: 'Since you left, such a torpor has come over me that I am scarcely able to write.' ‡

Besides these lights—a Curione or a Paleario, scattered here and there over Italy—there were societies of Christian men in several cities who courageously professed evangelical truth. Bologna in particular —a city in the neighbourhood of Ferrara, and whose university was, along with that of Paris, the first of the great schools of Europe—counted a large number of lay-

---

* 'Nunquam iis sponsore Christo deerit pater.'—Palearii *Opera*, p. 97.

† 'Præ dolore misere exanimatam.'—*Ibid.*

‡ 'Postquam in urbem profectus es, ita nescio quomodo animus meus torpuit, ut difficillimum mihi fuerit scribere epistolam hanc.'—Palearii *Epist.* p. 93.

men and ecclesiastics who, like those of Venice, showed much zeal and decision for the great principles of the Reformation. When John of Planitz, ambassador from Saxony to the emperor, crossed the Alps in 1533, the evangelical Christians of Bologna addressed him with thorough Italian ardour. 'We know,' they said, ' that the Germans have thrown off the yoke of antichrist and have attained to the liberty of the children of God. We know that they are but little troubled because the hateful name of heretics has been given them, and that, on the contrary, they rejoice because they are thought worthy of enduring shame, imprisonment, fire, and sword for the cause of Christ. We know that if they demand a council, it is not in their own interest, but with a view to the salvation of other people. For this reason all the nations of Christendom owe a deep debt of gratitude both to them and to you, most honoured lord; but there is no nation more indebted to you than our own. Of all countries subject to the tyrant, Italy, being the nearest to him, as it is his seat,*experiences the liveliest joy and special gratitude, because through the goodness of God redemption has drawn nigh to her at last. We entreat you to employ every means for the convocation of a council. In all the towns of the peninsula, and in Rome itself, as the emperor knows, a great number of pious, wise, and distinguished men desire it, are waiting for it, and loudly demanding it. If the pope should summon a council, he will easily remedy the abuses that have crept into the Church through the neglect of his pre-

---

* 'Besonders Italien, welches dem Tyrannus am nähesten unterworfen; ja, dessen Sitz sey.'—Seckendorff's translation, p. 1366.

decessors; and for that excellent work he will receive appropriate honour from men, and from Jesus Christ life eternal.   Let every one be at liberty to read the books in which learned doctors (the reformers) have explained their faith.   At least let priests, monks, and laity be at liberty to possess the Bible without incurring the reproach of heresy, and even to quote the words of Christ and of St. Paul without being reviled as sectarians.   If, on the contrary, Rome tramples under foot the commandments of the Lord, his grace, his doctrine, his peace, and the liberty which He gives—has not the reign of Antichrist begun? . . . If you need our help, speak! we are ready.   If necessary, we will sacrifice our fortunes and our lives in the Redeemer's cause; and as long as we live we will commend it daily to God by fervent prayer.' * Such was the decision of the Christians of Italy, even in the cities subject to the pope.

About the time when this eloquent address reached the lord of Planitz, John Mollio, a Franciscan from the neighbourhood of Sienna, arrived at Bologna as professor in the university.   Convinced by the teaching of the Holy Scriptures and of the reformers, he professed with great freedom the Christian truth according to the writings of St. Paul; but the pope forbade him to lecture on the epistles of that Apostle. Mollio then took up the other books of the New Testament; but he drew from them the same doctrine, and his hearers, delighted at seeing the pope's pro-

* The Italian original, which is dated 5th January, 1533, is preserved in the archives of Weimar.   Seckendorff gives a German translation in his 'History of Lutheranism,' pp. 1365–1367.

hibition thus evaded, enthusiastically applauded him. The court of Rome, finding that there was no means of turning grace out of the Bible, gave orders to turn Mollio out of the university—which was much easier. However, the number of evangelical Christians in Bologna continued to increase.*

* Mac Crie, *History of the Reformation in Italy*, p. 88.

CHAPTER XX.

THE Gospel had made noble conquests in the north and centre of the peninsula: it did the same at Naples, and even at Rome.

It was not the Italians alone who spread the Gospel in Italy. Among the contemporaries and acquaintances of Paleario, Peter Martyr, and Occhino, were two twin brothers, descended from one of the oldest families of Leon in Spain, Juan and Alfonso di Valdez. They were so much alike, that Erasmus, who knew Alfonso, wrote to Juan: 'They tell me you are so like your brother, both in figure and in talent, that when people see you they do not take you for twins, but for the same person. I shall regard you, then, as one, and not two individuals.'[*] And, indeed, some historians, understanding literally what Erasmus merely intended for a pleasant jest, have converted the two brothers into one person. One of them disappears, and it is usually Alfonso: his actions are recorded, but they are ascribed to Juan. The two Valdez were born in 1500, at Cuença, in

---

[*] 'Tu vero, ut audio, sic illum (Alfonsum) refers et corporis specie et ingenii dexteritate, ut non duo gemelli, sed idem prorsus homo videri possitis.'—Erasmi *Epist*. 938 et 1030.

New Castile, of which their father was corregidor in 1520. Charles V. made Alfonso his secretary,* and took him with him when he left Spain in 1520 to receive the imperial crown at Aix-la-Chapelle. In the following year the young Spaniard was among the gentlemen who attended the emperor at Worms, when Luther made his famous appearance before the Diet. Luther's writings having been condemned by imperial decree to be burnt, Alfonso, whom all these events interested in the highest degree, desired to be present at the execution of the sentence. When the monks who surrounded and fed the fire saw all the heretical paper converted into black ashes, as thin as a spider's web, and blown to and fro by the wind, they exclaimed: ' There is nothing more to fear now: it is all over;' and then went away. But such was not Alfonso's opinion. ' They call it the end of the tragedy,' he wrote to his friend Peter Martyr of Anghiera (who must not be confounded with Vermigli), ' but I believe we are only at the beginning of it.' Valdez, whom everybody looked upon as a youth of great expectations,† became intimate with Erasmus; perhaps at the suggestion of the emperor, who, like Francis I., would willingly have united with the prince of the schools, in order to become master of Luther and the pope, and if possible to reconcile them. Alfonso, who was a great admirer of Erasmus, was considered to be more Erasmian than Erasmus himself; but the disciple

---

* 'Fue secretario de la Magestad del Emperador.'—*Hist. de la Ciudad de Cuenza*, quoted by E. Bœhmer.

† 'Ab Alfonso Valdesio, magnæ spei juvene.'—Petri Martyris Anghierii *Epist.* p. 689.

went further and higher than the teacher. Erasmus was the bridge by which Alfonso crossed the river, and passed from Rome to the Gospel.

In May 1527 the emperor and his court were at Valladolid, where the empress awaited her confinement. Valdez was there also. On a sudden the news arrived of the famous Sack of Rome by the troops of Charles V. The indignation of the clergy, the agitation of the people, and the emotion of the courtiers were extreme. Although grieved by the excesses of which the capital of Romanism had been the theatre, Alfonso believed it was the season to say what he thought of the papacy, and consequently he wrote and published a ' Dialogue on the Things which happened at Rome.'* The afflictions of the metropolis of catholicism, he says, have dispersed a great number of its inhabitants; a Roman archbishop, escaping from the disaster, arrives at Valladolid, and in the town where a prince (the future Philip II.) had just been born, he meets one of the emperor's knights, by name Lactontio. The guilt of these disasters, says the knight, lies with the pope, who, as instigator of the war and unfaithful to his oaths, has dishonoured his holy calling. Lactontio draws one of those contrasts of light and darkness, between Christ and the pontiff, which Luther's pen could describe so well, but which were quite new in the ' most catholic' kingdom. He goes even further, and declares for the separation of the spiritual from the temporal power. ' Is it useful, is it advantageous,' he asks, ' for the high priests of Christendom to possess

---

* *Dialogo sulle Cose accadute in Roma.*

temporal power? We believe they could occupy themselves much more freely with spiritual interests if they
had not this great burden of secular things.   In all
Christendom there is not a state worse governed than
the States of the Church.   Erasmus pointed out the
faults of the court of Rome, but his gentle remonstrances did not touch you. . Then God permitted
Martin Luther unsparingly to expose all your vices
in broad daylight, and to detach many churches
from their obedience to you.   It was all of no use;
neither the respectful advice of Erasmus nor the
irreverent language of Luther could convince Rome
of its errors.   God therefore had recourse to other
appeals, and 'permitted the calamities of war to fall
upon your impenitent city.'   Here the archdeacon,
much more sensitive about the punishment of
Rome than about its faults, exclaims with mingled
sorrow and naïveté: 'Alas! the sacking of the city
has occasioned a loss of fifteen millions of ducats.
Rome·will never become Rome again, even in half a
century.   The holy church of St. Peter has been
turned into a stable.   For forty days not a single
mass has been said in the metropolis of Christendom.
Even the bones of the Apostles were scattered about.'
'The relics of the saints should be honoured,' remarks the knight.   'Let us understand one another,
however; I do not speak of those which require believers to solve some very thorny problems—to
decide, for instance, whether the mother of the
Virgin had two heads, or the Virgin had two
mothers. . . . : We should place all our hope in
Jesus Christ alone.   Honour images, if you like, but
do not dishonour Jesus Christ, and do not let

Paradise be shut against the man who has no money in his purse.' *

This sharp attack, levelled at the papacy, was the more important, as before the dialogue was published and circulated in Spain, Italy, and Germany, it had been submitted by Valdez to several men of mark: to Don Juan Manuel, formerly ambassador of the emperor at Rome, to the celebrated imperial chancellor Gattinara, to Doctor Carrasco, and to several other theologians, who, with a few unimportant observations, had approved of it. Count Castiglione, the papal nuncio, was not to be deceived; he made a violent attack upon the imperial secretary, called him a Lutheran, and declared that he could already see him wearing the ignominious costume of the *autos da fé.*

Alfonso was silent; but a voice was raised in his defence—it was that of his twin brother. In 1528 † Juan published a *Dialogue*, half serious and half in jest, *between Mercury and Charon*, which bears the mark of a young writer. While the ferryman of Hades is busy taking over the souls which come to him on the banks of the Styx, he is accosted by the messenger of heaven, who makes use of strong language about the papacy. 'So great is the corruption of those who call themselves Christians,' he

---

* Mr. Bœhmer, of the university of Halle, has done good service to literature and to the history of religion by reprinting at Halle, in 1860, the *Cento e dieci divine Considerazioni di Giovanni Valdesso*, and by carefully studying the history of the two brothers. He has communicated the result of his researches in his *Cenni Biografici*, and in the conscientious paper he has contributed to the Encyclopædia of our learned friend M. Herzog.

† It has been stated that this dialogue was written in 1521; but it begins with the history of the challenge sent by Francis I. to Charles V., which occurred at the beginning of 1528.

says, 'that I should consider it a great insult if they
wanted to change their name and be called *Mercurians.*
One day,' he continues, 'seeing a number of people
approaching the altar to receive the host, I followed
them, with the pious design of partaking one of the
wafers the priests were distributing. But I was refused; and why? Solely because I would not pay for
it.' Then, turning to the relics, whose dispersion was
considered to be the greatest outrage in the sack of
Rome, Juan introduces St. Peter, and puts wiser
words into his mouth on this subject than those of
Mercury. According to the fervent apostle, the
plunder of Rome teaches Christians that they ought to
set more value upon one of the epistles of St. Paul or
of himself than upon all the *relics* of their bodies.
'The homage hitherto paid to our bones,' he continues, 'must now be paid to the spirit which, for
the good of Christians, we have enshrined in our
writings.' But the satire immediately begins again.
At the thought of the sack of Rome, Mercury bursts
out into an 'Olympian laugh.' 'Behold the judgment of God!' he says; 'the sellers have been sold,
the robbers have been robbed, and the ill-doers ill-
done!' And when Charon complains that the pretended vicars of heaven often forget to keep their
word: 'It is quite the rule,' answers Mercury, 'that
at the place where the best wine grows you drink
the worst; that the cobbler is always ill shod, and the
barber never shaved.' The dialogues of the twin
brothers, so full of wit and yet of Christian truth,
excited loud recriminations; for the moment, however, persecution did not touch them. It is true, the
priests raised a violent storm against them; but they

were protected by the name of Charles V. In March 1529, Erasmus wrote to Juan, congratulating him on having escaped safe and sound from the tempest.*

When the emperor returned to Germany, Alfonso accompanied him. At Augsburg, in 1530, as we have said in another place,† he played the part of mediator between Charles V. and the protestants, and immediately translated the celebrated evangelical confession into Spanish. But in April 1533, when Charles V. embarked at Genoa on his return to Spain, Valdez remained in Italy. If he had accompanied his master, even that powerful monarch, it was said, could not have preserved him from the death the monks were preparing for him. From this period Alfonso seems to have shared his time between Germany and Italy: henceforward his brother occupies the foremost place. He was converted to the Gospel after Alfonso, but eventually outstripped him.

Juan had been forced to leave his native country.‡ He did not go to Germany, as some have said, confounding him with his brother; but henceforward he occupies an important position in Italy. In 1531 he went to Naples, thence he proceeded to Rome, returning again to Naples in 1534, where he spent the remainder of his days. Some zealous protestants, who formed part of the German army, and had been sent in 1528 to drive off the French, who were be-

---

* These two dialogues, which have been recently reprinted in Spanish, were translated into Italian and German, and the last (*Charon and Mercury*) into French.

† History of the Reformation of the Sixteenth Century, vol. iv. bk. xiv. ch. v.

‡ 'In disciplina fraterna præclare institutus, in Hispania vivere non potuit.'—*Francisco Enzinas to Melanchthon.*

sieging that city, were the first to propagate the knowledge of the Gospel in that district. . But when Juan
Valdez arrived,' says the Roman-catholic Caracciolo,
' he alone committed greater ravages among souls than
many thousands of heretic soldiers had done.' *   Some
have thought that he occupied the post of secretary to
the viceroy of Naples.   But if he had an office at court,
he soon resigned it to enjoy his independence.   ' He
did not frequent the court very much,' says Curione,
' after Christ was revealed to him.' †

Persecution had made Juan more serious; the
experiences of his inner life had matured him; he was
still busy with literature and languages,‡ but he loved
the Gospel above everything, and sought to make it
known by his conversation as well as by his writings.
There was such grace in his mind, such peace and
innocence in his features, such attraction in his character, that he exercised an irresistible charm over
all who came near him.   He soon gathered a circle of
scholars and gentlemen about him; he strove to extri-
cate them from their worldliness, to convince them of
the nothingness of their own righteousness, and to lead
them to the salvation that is in Christ Jesus.   He was
even a torch to enlighten some of the most celebrated
preachers of Italy.   ' I know it,' says Curione, ' for I
have heard it from their own mouths.'   But at the
same time he had so much love in his heart and so

* 'Longe majorem mentium stragem dedit, quam multa illa hæreticorum militum millia.'—Ant. Caracciolo, de Vita Pauli IV. p. 239.

† 'Non però ha egli seguito molto la corte dopo che gli fu rivelato
Cristo.'—Epist. de Curione at the end of the Cento e dieci divine Considerazioni of J. Valdez, p. 433.

‡ His Dialogo de la Lengua was first printed at Madrid in 1737, and
again in 1860.

much simplicity in his manners, that he put the poor
at their ease, and won the confidence even of the rudest
men, the lazzaroni of that day.　He became all things
to all men to bring souls to Christ.*　Valdez was not
robust; he was thin, and his limbs were weak ; and it
would appear that the state of his health induced
him to settle at Naples.　'But,' said his friends, 'one
part of his soul served to animate his delicate and
puny nature, while the greater part of that clear bright
spirit was devoted to the contemplation of truth.'　He
generally collected his friends together at Chiaja, near
Pausilippo and Virgil's tomb, in a villa whose gardens
looked over the wide sea, in front of the island of
Nisida.　In that delightful country, 'where Nature
exults in her magnificence and smiles on all who
behold her,' Juan Valdez, and such as were attracted
by the loveliness of his doctrine and the holiness of
his life, passed hours and days never to be forgotten.
He was not content to admire with them the magnificence of nature; he introduced them to the
magnificence of grace.　'An honoured and brilliant
knight of the emperor,' says Curione, 'he was a still
more honoured and brilliant knight of Jesus Christ.'†

Among the eminently gifted men who gathered
round him was Peter Martyr Vermigli, abbot of St.
Peter's *ad aram*.　Peter Martyr, as we have said, had
gone from Spoleto to Naples in 1530, where he had
made great progress in the knowledge of the Gospel.
Nothing could divert him from the search after truth;

---

* 'Era di tanta benignità e carità, che a ogni piccola e bassa e rozza
persona si rendeva debitore.'—Curione, *Epist.* p. 433.

† 'Ma più onorato e splendido cavaliere di Cristo.'—Curione, *Epist.*
p. 433.

neither fear of the world, nor the great income he
possessed, nor the high dignity with which he was
invested. That earnest soul, that profound mind,
pursued after the knowledge of God with indefatigable
zeal. Being called to give drink to the sheep which,
attracted by his voice, crowded to the sheepfold, he
was thirsty himself, and alas! he had no water. He
experienced that tormenting, that bitter, that violent
thirst under which the strongest men sometimes give
way. It was then he heard those words of Christ:
If any man thirst, let him come unto me and drink.
He knew that man *comes* to Christ by faith—by
believing in his holiness, in his love, in his promises,
and in his almighty power to save. Putting scholasticism aside, and no longer contenting himself with
the Fathers of the Church, he hastened to the fountain
of Scripture and drank of the cup of salvation.* He
knew the fulness of grace which is in the Redeemer,
and understood how those who seek consolation elsewhere labour in vain. Growing more enlightened
every day by the Spirit of God, he discovered the
grievous errors of the Church and the simple grandeur
of the Gospel. It was at Naples that the light of
the divine Word shone into his soul with increasing
glory and splendour.† Vermigli admired the beauties
of creation,‡ the sea glittering in the sunshine, and
the graceful promontories of the bay; but he loved
still better to plunge into the mysterious splendours
of grace. He did not confine himself to the writings

---

* 'Ad ipsos fontes se totum contulit.'—Simler, *Vita Vermilii.*

† 'In hac urbe gratia divinæ illuminationis illustrius ac clarius illi
effulgere.'—*Ibid.*

‡ 'Loci amœnitatem.'—*Ibid.*

of the Apostles, but added those of the reformers—of Bucer, Zwingle, Luther, and Melanchthon. Zwingle's treatise on *False and True Religion* showed him the necessity of returning to the simplicity and primitive customs of the Church. Almost every day he conversed upon Holy Scripture with friends who, like himself, loved religion pure and undefiled, and principally with Flaminio and Valdez.* But above all things he sought to impart by preaching the light which he had received.

To this end Vermigli undertook to preach on the First Epistle to the Corinthians, which he did in the presence of a large audience, including even bishops. When he came to the third chapter,† he first showed what was the foundation upon which the whole of Christian doctrine must be built: *For other foundation can no man lay than that is laid, which is Jesus Christ,* says the Apostle. But what is built on that stone? When the architect has laid the foundations of the edifice he intends to raise, he employs various materials to complete the work. Marble, porphyry, and jasper shall form the pillars, the mantle-pieces, the pavement, and the statues; gold and silver will serve for the internal decorations; but there will also be wood and paper, stubble, and other coarse materials employed in the structure. It is so with the edifice of God. On the foundation, which is Christ, we must build sound doctrines which flow from Christ himself, from his divinity, truth, grace, and spirit. If false doctrines are substituted for them

* 'Quotidie pæne cum amicis qui puræ religionis studiosi erant aliquid ex sanis litteris commentabatur.'—Simler, *Vita Vermilii.*
† 1 Corinth. iii. 13-15.

—doctrines proceeding from man's own righteousness
and from the darkness with which sin has overshadowed
his understanding, what will happen? When a conflagration breaks out, the fire makes manifest the
divers materials with which the house was built: the
flame consumes the wood and the stubble; but it
attacks in vain the marble and the jasper, the silver
and gold: these it cannot destroy. So it will be with
the doctrines taught in the Church. ' False teachings
cannot eternally pass for true,' said Peter Martyr.
' There is nothing hidden which shall not be revealed;
if the falsehood of the dogmas put forth is not detected
at the first, time will make it known.* The day will
come when every error hidden under an appearance of
truth shall be declared to be error in the most striking
manner; all darkness shall be scattered, everything
will be valued in conformity with its strict reality.†
The eternal judgment of God is *the fire that shall try
every man's work*. It is not enough that the doctrines
should be approved by the judgment of men, they
must be able to stand before the fire of God's trial.‡
The day and the fire of which the Apostle speaks are
the piercing investigation, the sure touchstone, which
will enable us at last to distinguish between true
doctrines and false.§ *Gold, stubble, fire*—they are all
metaphors.'

* 'Quod si e vestigio prava dogmata non patefiant, accessione tem
poris declarantur.'—Petri Martyris *Loci Communes; de Purgatorio Igne*,
p. 440.

† 'Dies ergo accipitur, cum tenebræ depellentur, ut de re, prout ipsa
est, judicium feratur.'—*Ibid.* p. 441.

‡ 'Ad ignem divini examinis perstare illas oportet.'—*Ibid.*

§ 'Est itaque ignis et dies, clara inspectio, certa probatio, perspicua
revelatio, qua tandem cognoscemus doctrinarum veritatem, earum denique

Peter Martyr's audience, and especially the ecclesiastics, were unable to conceal their surprise. The passage which he thus explained was that on which the Romish Church based the doctrine of purgatorial fire ; but the learned doctor found something quite different in it. The priests and monks not only saw that precious fire taken away from which they had derived so much profit, but saw another fire substituted for it, which threatened to consume their traditions and practices, *their hay and stubble*. And hence the sermon aroused a storm in the hitherto calm waters of Naples. The monks accused the prior of St. Peter's *ad aram*, and his friends of Chiaja defended him. His enemies succeeded in closing the pulpit against him; but on the intervention of the powerful protectors he possessed at Rome, his liberty of preaching was restored.

This petty persecution was salutary to the Christian circle at Chiaja. It grew wider, and its meetings were attended by nobles and scholars, among others by Benedetto Gusano de Verceil, and a Neapolitan nobleman, Giovanni Francesco Caserta.* The latter had a young relative, at that time living in the midst of the splendours of the world. The Marquis Caraccioli, one of the grandees of Naples, had an only son, Galeazzo. Ardently desiring to perpetuate his name, he married him early to a wealthy heiress, Vittoria, daughter of the duke of Nocera, who bore him four

fallaciam.'—Petri Martyris *Loci Communes: de Purgatorio Igne*. These may not be the exact words used by Peter Martyr in his sermon, but the sense was the same.

* This is the person whom Flaminio mentions in a letter to Galeazzo, printed in Schelhorn's *Amœnit. Eccles.* ii. p. 132 : 'Johannes Franciscus magna lætitia affecit me,' &c.

sons and two daughters.   As soon as the old marquis
saw that his desire for posterity would be satisfied,
he turned his ambition in another direction, and sent
his son to the court of the emperor, who invested him
with one of the great offices of his household.   As
Galeazzo was not always on service, he returned from
time to time to Naples, where he gave himself up
entirely to the vanities of the world, to the pleasures
of the earth, and to projects of ambition.   A close
friendship, however, bound him to the pious Caserta.
The Christian, taking advantage of this intimacy,
spoke to the worldling about the Word of God and
the only way of salvation which is Christ Jesus;
but after these conversations, the youthful chamberlain of Charles V. would hurry off to theatre or ball.
Caserta took him to hear Peter Martyr; and then
thinking that a society so cultivated as that which
met at Chiaja might perhaps win over his friend,
he introduced him to Valdez.   For some time longer
the seed continued to fall among thorns; but a little
later the young marquis received with joy the salvation of the Gospel, and desiring to remain faithful to
it, he took refuge at Geneva.   Calvin, who welcomed
him like a son, dedicated one of his writings to
him, to show his respect for the firmness of his
faith.   Although Caraccioli 'did not court the applause of men, and was content to have God alone
for a witness,' the reformer, when he saw the illustrious Neapolitan refugee, exclaimed with emotion:
'Here is a man of ancient house and great parentage,
flourishing in honours and in goods, having a noble
and virtuous wife, a family of children, quiet and
peace in his house, in short, happy in everything

that concerns the state of this life, but who has voluntarily abandoned the place of his birth to stand beneath the banner of Christ. He made no difficulty in leaving his lordship, a fertile and pleasant country, a great and rich patrimony, a convenient, comfortable, and cheerful palace; he broke up his household, he left father, wife, children, relations, and friends, and after abandoning so many allurements of the world, he is content with our littleness, and lives frugally according to the habits of the commonalty—neither more nor less than any one of us.' *

In the select society which gathered round Valdez, there were also, as at Thessalonica in the days of St. Paul, *of the chief women not a few.* Among these high-born dames was Vittoria Colonna, widow of that famous general the marquis of Pescara, a woman illustrious for her beauty, her virtues, and her talent, whose poems were much admired at the time, and in whose society, the poet Bernardo Tasso, father of him who wrote the 'Jerusalem Delivered,' and Cardinal Bembo, learned some of the truths of the Gospel. There also might be seen Isabella di Bresegna, to whom Curione dedicated the works of Olympia Morata; but above all Giulia di Gonzaga, widow of Vespasiano Colonna, duke of Trajetto,† the most beautiful woman in Italy. So great was the reputation of her beauty in Europe, and even beyond it, that Barbarossa the corsair determined to carry her off. Having under-

---

* Calvin to Signor Galeazzo Caraccioli, a man of noble birth, and still more renowned for the excellence of his virtues than for the nobility of his family, the only son and lawful heir to the marquis of Vico.— Dédicace de la 1ère Épître aux Corinthiens : *Commentaires.*

† Trajetto, the ancient Minturnæ, where Marius hid himself.

taken in 1534 to terrify Naples, he suddenly appeared before that city with a hundred sail, and landing near Fondi, between Gaeta and Terracina, where the duchess was living on her estate, he tried to surprise her; but she escaped the bird of prey, though not without difficulty. This attempt was one of the motives which determined Charles to undertake the expedition to Tunis. It is thus that men and women, of whom the sixteenth century is proud, adorned the evangelical circle of Chiaja.

While Valdez reposed on the beautiful hills of Pausilippo, in the midst of orange and fig-trees, and in front of the wide sea, he loved to indulge peacefully in religious meditations, and not unfrequently the thoughts with which he was busy formed the subject of interesting conversations with his friends. Certain topics — *Considerazioni*, as he called them — occupied a mind at once eminently original and Christian. Virgil's tomb, which was situated a few paces off, might have suggested other thoughts: the dying poet had ordered the following words to be carved on his sepulchre:

Parthenope, cecini pascua, rura, duces.

The country life and the warlike exploits which the prince of Latin poets sang have great attractions to many minds; but the visitors at Pausilippo, whose history we are relating, had higher aspirations, and conversed on topics which it is our duty to record.

'In what do the sons of God differ,' they asked, 'from the sons of Adam?—Why is the state of a Christian who believes with difficulty better than that of him who believes with ease?—Why does God give a child to a Christian and suddenly take it away?—The man from whom God takes away the love of the world, and to whom He gives the love of God, experiences nearly the same thing as he who ceases to love one woman and becomes enamoured of another.*—To believe with difficulty is the sign of a call from God.—Those who tread the Christian path without the inward light of the Holy Spirit, are like those who walk by night without the light of the sun.—How can God make himself *felt*, and how can He permit himself to be *seen*?—The evils of curiosity, and how we ought to read the Scriptures without curiosity.—Why are the superstitious severe, while true Christians are merciful?—How God reigns by Christ, and Christ is the head of the Church.— The three kinds of conscience: that of the natural law, that of the written law, and that of the Gospel.—Is justification the fruit of piety, or piety the fruit of justification?—How does it happen that the wicked cannot believe, that the superstitious believe easily, and that pious men believe with difficulty?—How to resist the imaginations which confuse our Christian faith.' —Such are some of the thoughts with which the noblest minds were then busy on the enchanting shores of the bay of Naples.†

The sermons of the celebrated Occhino helped to give a wider circulation to the thoughts which

* 'Che a colui, il quale Dio disinnamora del mondo ed innamora di se, avvengano quasi tutte le medesime cose che a colui che si disinnamora d' una donna e s'innamora d' un' altra.'—23ᵉ *Considerazione*: Valdez, *Cento e dieci divine Considerazioni.*

† The *Cento e dieci divine Considerazioni* of Giovanni Valdesso (Juan Valdez) were published at Halle in Saxony in 1860 by Ed. Bœhmer. Each of the meditations occupies from two to ten pages. They have been reprinted recently at Madrid in Spanish.

engrossed the evangelicals of Chiaja. In the early part of 1536, the great orator of Italy was invited to Naples to preach the Lent course. Valdez immediately felt the living faith by which the orator was animated: he became intimate with him, and introduced him to the Christian circle around him. The well-known name of Occhino, his strange appearance, his coarse dress, and his reputation for holiness, attracted an immense crowd to the church of S. Giovanni Maggiore. He seemed called to scatter among the people the religious ideas which Valdez and Peter Martyr were propagating among the noble and the learned. De Vio, cardinal of Gaeta, before whom Luther had appeared, was a man of singular perspicacity, and he immediately suspected heresy.* Struck with the power of the three doctors, he fancied he saw the formation of a league, one of those triumvirates which destroyed the Roman republic. 'These triumvirs of the republic of Satan,' † he said, 'are circulating doctrines of startling novelty, and even of detestable impiety about purgatory, the power of the sovereign pontiff, freewill, and the justification of the sinner.' The cardinal protested in vain: not only the Christian society of Naples, but a great crowd of the nobility and people, attended Occhino's sermons.

The beautiful duchess of Trajetto did not miss one of them. She was at that time suffering under great domestic trouble: her brother Luigi, wishing to recover a castle that had been taken from his sister, perished in the assault, and Luigi's widow, Isabella

---

* 'Cajetanus, perspicaci vir ingenio, rem odorari cœpit.'—Caracciolo, *Vita Pauli IV.*

† 'Illi Satanicæ reipublicæ triumviri.'—*Ibid.*

Colonna, who was also the duchess's daughter-in-law, went to law with her for a portion of her inheritance. Giulia, roused by her vexations from the worldly indifference in which she had lived, sought consolation in God, and hoped to find in Occhino's words a relief from her sorrow. An event which at this time gave splendour to Naples might have diverted her from these thoughts: the emperor arrived, and held a brilliant court. It was natural that the monarch and the daughter of Gonzaga should meet, for he had desired to avenge her when he gave up Tunis to be pillaged; but Giulia would willingly have dispensed with the honour done to her in Africa. Besides, her troubles and the awakening of her mind estranged her from the court: the great lady, the ornament of every fête, did not appear at those which were given to Charles V. If they did not meet at court or ball, they probably met at church. The emperor having heard much of the great orator of Italy, went like the rest to the church of S. Giovanni Maggiore. He was surprised and struck by Occhino's eloquence, and said as he went out: ' That monk would make the very stones weep.'*

It was easier to draw tears from Giulia Gonzaga's eyes. That young woman, whose heart was wrung by sorrow, was agitated more and more every day by the powerful words of the great preacher; and it was at this time that the Christian life truly began in her. One day, as she was leaving the church of S. Giovanni Maggiore, Juan Valdez observed her emotion, and accompanied her to her palace. The stricken and

---

* Sadoleti *Epist.* p. 558. Schröck, *Kirchengeschichte*, ii. p. 780.

agitated widow begged him to stay and enlighten her, and made known to him the distress, the hopes, and the struggles of her soul. Valdez felt that he was called to disperse the darkness in the midst of which Giulia was struggling, and the conversation lasted till evening. The duchess of Trajetto desired to have nothing more to do with the world, but as yet she had not tasted the peace of God. 'Ah!' she exclaimed to Valdez 'there is a combat within me. The monk's words fill me with fear of hell, but I fear evil tongues also. Occhino inspires me with love for paradise, but I feel at the same time a love for the world and its glory. How can I escape from the contest under which I am sinking? Is it by harmonising these two tendencies, or by rejecting one of them? Pray show me the way; I promise to follow it.' Valdez replied that the agitation she felt was occasioned by the renewing of the image of God in her. 'The Law has wounded you,' he said, 'the Gospel will heal you; for if the Law gives death, the Gospel gives life.* What I fear,' he continued, 'is lest you should attempt to regulate your Christian life in such a manner that those about you should not remark any change in you.' The duchess confessing that such was her secret wish, Valdez told her to choose between God and the world, add-

---

* *Abecedario espiritual,* fols. 11-12. Valdez gives a full report of this conversation in his *Spiritual Abecedary,* which he so called because it was intended to teach the elements of Christian perfection. There is no doubt as to the genuineness of the dialogues he reports, for the duchess asked him to commit what he had said to her to paper. Did Valdez, when doing so, complete any of his answers? It is very possible. In Herzog's *Encyclopædia,* M. Bœhmer has given an extract from this dialogue, much longer than the limits of this history will permit us to do.

ing: 'I will show you the path of perfection: Love
God above everything, and your neighbour as yourself.'
—'Your words surprise me,' she said; 'I have heard
all my life that monastic vows alone lead to perfection.'—'Let them say on,' replied Valdez firmly;
'the monks have no Christian perfection except so
far as they possess the love of God, and not an atom
more.' Valdez then tried to make her understand
the only means by which that charity, which is perfection, is produced in the heart. 'Our works are
good,' he said, 'only when they are done by a justified person. Fire is needed to give warmth, a living
faith to produce charity. Faith is the tree, charity
the fruit. But when I speak of faith, Madam, I
mean that which lives in the soul, that which proceeds
from God's grace, and which clings with boundless confidence to every word of God. When Christ says: *He
that believes shall be saved*, the disciple who believes
must not have the slightest doubt of his salvation.'*
—'Ah!' exclaimed the duchess, 'I will yield to no one
in faith.'—'Take care,' rejoined Valdez; 'if you were
asked whether you believed in the articles of the
faith, you would reply, Yes! but if you were asked
whether you believed God had pardoned all your
sins, you would say that you think so . . . that
you are not quite sure, however. . . . Ah! Madam,
if you accept with full faith the words of Christ,
then, even while suffering under the pain caused by
your sins, you would not hesitate to say with perfect
assurance: *Yes, God himself has pardoned all my
sins.*†

---

* *Abecedario espiritual*, fol. 26. On this point Valdez is quite in harmony with the reformers.

† *Ibid.* fol. 27.

Such evangelical sentiments, uttered by a Spaniard in a palace at Naples, and received with humility by a Gonzaga, are a feature of the Reformation. We must humble ourselves before we can be exalted. Conscience spoke in Giulia. We have here a woman whose family had given many sovereigns to Italy and princesses to royal houses, the widow of a Colonna, the chief of the most ancient family in the peninsula, which has counted among its members cardinals, illustrious generals, and the celebrated pope Martin V.; and this Gonzaga, touched by grace, lent an ear to the truth with more humility than her own servants: she had become a little child. If the Acts of the Apostles remark more than once that among the persons converted to Christ in Asia and in Greece, where St. Paul preached, were women of distinction, history will also remark that at the epoch of the Reformation of the sixteenth century the wave mounted from the lowest levels of the shore to the highest peaks. Or rather, *the hills did bow* before it.

Valdez having spoken of a '*path*,' the duchess manifested a desire to know it. 'There are three paths,' he answered, 'which lead to the knowledge of God: the natural light which teaches us the omnipotence of God; the Old Testament, which shows us the Creator as hating iniquity; and lastly, Christ, the sure, clear, and royal way. Christ is love; and accordingly, when we know God through him, we know him as a God of love. Christ has made satisfaction for sin. An infinite God alone could pay an infinite debt. But it is not sufficient to believe it, we must experience it also.' *

---

* *Abecedario espiritual*, fols. 36, 37, 38.

'Devote some time every day,' continued Valdez, 'to meditation on the world, on yourself, on God, and on Jesus Christ, without binding yourself to it in a superstitious manner; do it in liberty of spirit, selecting any of your rooms that may seem most convenient, perhaps even as you lie awake in bed. Two images should be continually before your eyes: that of Christian perfection and that of your own imperfection. These books will cause you to make greater progress in a day than any others would in ten years. Even the Holy Scriptures, if you do not read them with that humility which I point out to you, might become poison to your soul.'*

'Listen to preaching with a humble mind,' continued Valdez.—'But,' said Giulia, 'if the preacher is one of those who, instead of preaching Christ, give utterance to vain and foolish things, drawn from philosophy or some empty theology—one of those who tell us dreams and fables—would you have me follow him?'—'In that case, do what seems best. The worst moments of all the year are to me those which I waste in listening to preachers such as you have described; and hence it rarely happens to me.'†

The day was coming to an end when Valdez rose: the duchess was like a person who has discovered the road to happiness, and fears to go astray in the new path. Valdez desired to leave, but she detained him: 'Only two words more before you go,' she said; 'what use must I make of Christian liberty?'—'The true Christian,' replied the Spanish gentleman, 'is free from the tyranny of sin and death; he is the absolute

---

* *Abecedario espiritual,* fols. 44, 45, 47, 50, 52, 53.
† *Ibid.* fols. 57, 58.

master of his affections ; but at the same time he is
the servant of all. . . . Farewell, Madam, from this
very moment pray follow my advice, and to-morrow I
will ask how you have found yourself after it.' He
withdrew.*

It was during these solemn hours, when Valdez
traced out for her the order of salvation, that the
daughter of the Gonzagas sat in spirit at her Saviour's
feet, and gave herself to him with all her soul. It is
possible that in the instructions given by this pious
layman we may here and there discover some slight
shades not strictly evangelical, tinged either with a
mystic or a Roman colour; and possibly the Holy
Scriptures do not occupy a place sufficiently prominent; yet the two great Christian facts—the work
of Christ on the cross, and that which He aecom-
plishes in the heart—were clearly laid down by the
Spanish gentleman, and that was the essential thing.

The religious awakening then going on in the
duchess of Trajetto and in many others at Naples,
happened at a difficult moment. Some days before,
Charles V., excited by the priests who were growing
alarmed at a movement which they could not understand, had published an edict forbidding all intercourse
with those infected with or only suspected of Lutheranism. When the emperor left Naples shortly after
(22 March, 1536), the viceroy, driven onwards by the
same influence, and ascribing to Occhino's eloquence
a religious agitation which was so novel in the Par-
thenopean city, interdicted the preaching of that great
orator; but his eloquence and energy, backed by his
numerous friends and the protests of those who so

* *Abecedario espiritual,* fol. 68.

liked to hear him, prevailed.   He was able to continue
the course of his sermons, and did not end them until
Easter (April 16).   The duchess of Trajetto, without
leaving the Church, endeavoured more and more to
walk in that new path which Valdez had shown her;
the latter zealously directed her, and not long after
dedicated to her a translation of the Psalms from the
Hebrew, with a practical explanation.   Somewhat
later he published *Commentaries* on the Epistles of
Paul to the Romans and to the Corinthians.*

In this charming circle at Chiaja, and among the
habitual guests of Valdez, Vittoria Colonna, and Giulia
Gonzaga, was a patrician of Florence, as distinguished
by his person as by the important offices he had filled:
he was Pietro Carnesecchi.† Although for a long
time placed as near as possible to the pontifical throne,
he found a strange and indefinable charm in the conversations of Valdez, attended with pleasure the sermons of Occhino, drew light from the lamp of Peter
Martyr, formed a close friendship with Galeazzo
Caraccioli, and was touched by that mixture of grace,
intelligence, humility, faith, and good works then to
be found in some of the most distinguished women of
Italy.   As soon as Charles V. arrived at Naples, he
desired Carnesecchi to come and see him.   The noble
Florentine was surprised at the order, but the emperor's motive was this.   Carnesecchi, a native of the
city of the Medicis,‡ was early distinguished by his

---

* These *Commentaries* have recently been reprinted in Spain.

. † 'Convictus quod in Italia, cum Victoria Colonna Marchionis Piscarii
vidua et Julia Gonzaga, lectissimis alioquin feminis, de pravitate sectaria
suspectis, amicitiam coluisset, tandem ad ignem damnatus.'—De Thou,
ad annum 1567. Schelhorn, *Amœnitates Ecclesiasticæ*, ii. p. 187.

‡ The name of Carnesecchi still exists in Florence; the Latin documents which we use give it under the form of Carneseca.

knowledge of polite literature, by his talent in the art
of writing, and particularly by that penetrating mind
which can discern the secret springs of events and see
clear in the obscurest matters.   From his early youth
he had felt a desire for great things,* and had placed
himself in connexion with the most eminent men, with
the view of running a more useful career.   His fine
countenance struck observers all the more because
with nobility of features he combined modesty, purity,
sobriety, and admirable mildness tempered by imposing gravity.   By these qualities he gained the
favour of the Medicis, and when Julius became pope,
under the name of Clement VII., Carnesecchi received
a message appointing him secretary to the new pontiff.
Having at that time no evangelical convictions, he
thought that the invitation would open a noble career
before him; he therefore accepted it, and soon found
himself in possession of great influence.   Clement, who
had so much to do with politics, with Charles V., Francis I., and Henry VIII., committed the direction of
the Church to Carnesecchi, and it was generally said
that 'the pontificate was at that time filled by Pietro
Carnesecchi rather than by Clement.'†   The pope
several times offered him a cardinal's hat, which he
always refused.   This is surprising, for he was naturally
ambitious; but after he had seen the papacy closely,
he probably feared to ally himself too intimately with
it; possibly, also, the first beams of evangelical light
were dawning upon his soul.

* 'Literarum bonarum scientia ... ad perspiciendum acerrimi sensus ...
cupiditas verum magnarum.'—Notice of *Camerarius,* the friend of Melanchthon, in Schelhornii *Amœnit. Literar.* x. p. 1201.

† 'Pontificatum illius temporis magis a Petro Carneseca geri quam a
Clemente.'—*Camerarius* in Schelhorn, *Amœnit. Literar.* x. p. 1202.

The death of Clement VII. broke the golden chains which were beginning to oppress Carnesecchi. He quitted Rome, and, attracted by the mild light which was shining over the hills of Chiaja, he went to Naples with the desire of remaining for a time in the society of those men of God who were so much talked about in Italy.* The treasures of truth and life which he found there surpassed his expectations. But suddenly the command of Charles V. disturbed him in the midst of the Christian joy by which his soul was filled. What did the puissant emperor want with him? Did he design to open once more that career of politics and glory which he, Carnesecchi, had renounced for ever? Was there some political scheme brewing, or did Charles V. desire to become a disciple of the Gospel? Carnesecchi could not make it out, but he went to the palace all the same. The emperor had a very different object: knowing full well that the Florentine had been initiated into all the thoughts of Clement VII., he desired to learn what schemes that pope had formed with Francis I. at Marseilles.† In that interview Carnesecchi did not forfeit the confidence which Clement had reposed in him; he did not violate the fidelity he had sworn, ‡ but answered the emperor with a nobleness and respect which quite won the esteem of that prince. Francis I., however, when he heard of this conference at Naples, was

* 'Carneseca commoratus aliquantulum in regno Neapolitano.'—Camerarius in Schelhorn, *Amœnit. Literar.* x. p. 1203.

† 'Carolum V. accercisse Carnesecam, ut ex ipso eliceret arcana consilia pontificis Clementis, quæ hic credebatur cum Francisco rege Galliarum Massiliæ inivisse.'—*Ibid.*

‡ 'Tunc etiam boni viri officium neutiquam violavit.'—*Ibid.*

exasperated; it seemed to him that the kindness he had shown Carnesecchi during the famous interview at Marseilles should have led him to refuse his rival's invitation, and he confiscated the revenues of an abbey which Carnesecchi possessed in France. The Medicis, however, and even Catherine, having known this excellent man well, never withdrew their esteem from him, although he was everywhere decried as a heretic.

However great was the honour of a conference with Charles V., Carnesecchi much preferred those he had with Valdez, Peter Martyr, and Occhino. These pious men were not content with *vain babbling*: they read the Holy Scriptures together, enlightened each other on their meaning, and carefully compared one passage with another.* Carnesecchi had that love of truth and that boldness of thought which make rapid progress in the knowledge of Christ. A gleam of light shone into his heart. He did not oscillate for years in doubt between light and darkness; he was one of those noble spirits who attain their end at a bound. Ere long, the influential secretary of Clement VII., by turns the object of the attentions of the two greatest monarchs in Europe, sat humbly at the foot of the cross. He believed in those truths which he afterwards confessed before the college of cardinals, and on account of which he was put to death by the pope. Looking unto Christ, he could say: 'Certainly justification proceeds from faith alone in the work and love of a crucified Saviour. We can have the assurance of sal-

* 'Cum quibus de sacrarum literarum lectione et intelligentia disserere conferreque accurate solebat.'—Schelhorn, *Amœnit. Literar.* x. p. 1204.

vation, because it was purchased for us by the Son of
God at so great a price. We must submit to no
authority except the Word of God, which has been
handed down to us in Holy Scripture.'* These doctrines formed from that hour the happiness of his eminent spirit, and filled with sweetness the intercourse
he enjoyed at Naples with Valdez and Peter Martyr.

Two groups of pious men took part at this time in
the revival of Italy: the independent Christians, all
of whom ended their lives in exile or at the stake;
and men of a hierarchical tendency who, though religious, still remained in Romanism, some of them even
rising to the highest posts in the Church. Carnesecchi and Paleario belonged to the first group, and
no doubt Valdez also; and if his life had been much
prolonged, it is probable that he also would have come
to a tragic end. As for the second group, it included
many of those who had belonged to the oratory of *Divine Love*, the most distinguished of whom (Contarini)
we shall mention presently. One of them, Caraffa,
who became pope under the name of Paul IV., fell
lower than all the others, and became a persecutor.
These two groups, however, did not include all the
Italians who were touched by the Reformation. Between them were many truly Christian people, who,
as regards faith, were with the evangelicals, but as
regards the Church, clung to Rome through dread of
falling into what they called schism. Of this number
was Flaminio, one of Valdez' best friends. He was
born between Ferrara and Florence, but we meet with

---

* 'Justificatio per solam fidem . . . Gratiæ et salutis certitudo
habetur . . . Nulli credendum, nisi Verbo Dei, in Sacris Scripturis
tradito.'—Schelhorn, *Amœnit. Eccles.* ii. pp. 197–205.

him in the south.   Political disturbances having
broken out at Imola in the early part of the sixteenth
century, one of the burgesses of that city, named
Flaminio, who had acquired a reputation in literature, fled hastily, carrying with him a very young
child, and took refuge in a castle in the Venetian
territory.*   That child was Marco Antonio Flaminio, and his flight was almost a type of what
his whole life would be—one of anguish, and often of
pressing want.   When he grew older, he went to
study at Padua, where he displayed very remarkable
poetic talents.   'His poems,' it was afterwards said,
'possess all the simplicity and grace of Catullus, but
untainted with his licence.   They penetrate into the
soul with their wonderful sweetness.'   With the gifts,
Flaminio also shared the adversities of the poet.   He
was often greatly straitened during his studentship,
and his university friends had to subscribe to supply
him with clothes.†   Whatever were the hardships of
his position and the weakness of his health, he worked
assiduously and made great progress in philosophy and
the study of languages, and attained a thorough knowledge of the poets and orators.   At the same time,
trial was telling upon his soul: his literary and philosophical studies could not satisfy him.   Shut up in
his little room, he said to himself 'that there was a
science higher than that of Cicero and Plato, the
science of the sacred writings, the knowledge of
divine things handed down to us by the everlasting

---

* 'Puerum parvulum cum patre fugiente turbulentam dissentionem
civium suorum.'—*Camerarius* in Schelhorn, *Amœnit. Literar.* x. p. 1149.

† 'Adolescentem tueamur, in vestiario tantum laboramus.'—Longoli
Epist. lib. iv. fol. 271.

Word.'* Such was the only treasure he longed for in the midst of his poverty. 'The study of heavenly truth is the goal I set before me,' he said. 'I desire to adore the eternal God with fervour, and devote my life to the salvation of souls.'† He might have received considerable sums for his writings; but he could not bear the idea of making a trade of his books, as if they were merchandise. He might, as he grew older, have attained high ecclesiastical dignity and earthly distinction; but he loved the spiritual heights of faith more than the elevations of the world, and disdaining empty decorations, preferred a life hidden with Christ in God. He visited in succession Rome, Venice, and Verona, and was received in the last city by the bishop Giovanni Matteo Giberto, who esteemed learning, had published the *Homilies of Chrysostom on St. Paul*, and 'thus revived the doctrine of the Greek fathers in Europe.' This prelate, perhaps from devotion, but perhaps also because he wished to be made a cardinal, had adopted an exceedingly austere life; Flaminio, who cared nothing for the hat with its red cords, followed, however, the rough paths by which Giberto hoped to attain his end. The bishop, combining labour with ascetic practices, desired his guest to make a translation and commentary of the Psalms. The latter applied zealously to his work, and endeavoured to make the labour attractive; ‡ but his constitution

---

* 'Veram et salutarem sapientiam esse statuisset cognitionem sacrarum literarum, id est, rerum divinarum Verbo Dei æterno proditarum.'— *Camerarius* in Schelhorn, *Amœnit. Literar.* x. p. 1150.

† *Ibid.* p. 1152.

‡ 'Cum Gibertus pontifex Veronensis, homo literarum divinarum amantissimus, a me summo studio contenderet, ut hymnos Davidis

being too weak to bear up against the severities of
the ascetic prelate, he fell ill and nearly died.[*]

Flaminio went into the Venetian campagna to
recover his strength, and entered, as soon as he
was well, the household of another future cardinal,
Giovanni Pietro Caraffa, bishop of Chieti.   Caraffa,
a violent and impetuous man, and afterwards, when
pope, under the name of Paul IV., the restorer of the
inquisition and of the strictest Roman-catholicism,
had had his seasons of struggle and even of faith in
the truth.   Oppressed by the agitation caused within
him by his ardent and fanatical nature, he often felt
that he would never find peace except by sacrificing
his will to that of God; and this it was that bound
him to Flaminio.   Unhappily, his evil nature afterwards prevailed.   Caraffa being made cardinal, went
to Rome, and Flaminio to Naples, at the time when
Valdez, Peter Martyr, Carnesecchi, and their friends
were there.

Association with these pious men was of great use
to Flaminio: he had been prepared to seek God
by adversity, by sickness, and by the approach of
death; in his intercourse with the Christians of
Pausilippo he learnt the way of peace.   'God,' he
said, ' does not call those happy who are clear from
every stain; alas! there is not one! but those whom
his mercy pardons, because they believe with all
their heart that the blood of our Lord Jesus Christ
is the atonement for all sin.   If our conscience

breviter ac dilucide interpretarer, studiose istum laborem suscepi.'—
Flaminii *Psalmorum Explanatio,* Lugduni, 1576, præf. 12.

   * 'Et tum factum est ut in periculosum morbum incideret.'—
Camerarius in Schelhorn, *Amœnit. Literar.* x. p. 1158.

accuses us before the tribunal of God, if death is imminent, let us still be full of hope, for the mercy of the Supreme Ruler infinitely exceeds the wickedness of the whole human race.' Flaminio having dedicated his book on the *Psalms* to the famous cardinal Farnese, he boldly confessed his faith before that grandson of Paul III. 'Herein will be found,' he said, 'many things about Christ, our Lord and our God; his bitter death and his everlasting kingship;—his death, by which, sacrificing himself on the cross and blotting out all our sins by his most precious blood, He has reconciled us with God—his kingship, by which He defends us against the eternal enemy of the human race, and, governing us by his Spirit, leads us to a blessed and immortal life.'*

Valdez, charmed by the simplicity of Flaminio's character, the beauty of his genius, and the liveliness of his faith, was accustomed to say: ' Of all men, Flaminio is the one for whom I feel the greatest love and admiration.'† Carnesecchi also appreciated Flaminio, but without being so enthusiastic in his affection as Valdez. He had a less glowing imagination than the poet of Imola, and perhaps his feelings were less quick, but his understanding was clearer, more logical, and more practical. While Flaminio desired to remain in the Roman Church, Carnesecchi was still more resolved to walk in the paths of the Gospel. These two eminent men had serious discussions about universal consent

* 'Nos Deo reconciliavit, se ipsum in cruce immolans, et omnia peccata nostra suo purissimo sanguine delens.'—Flaminii *Psalmorum Explicatio* (Epistola nuncupatoria Alex. Farnesio, Cardinali amplissimo), p. 9.

† 'Hunc enim, præ cæteris omnibus, magnopere dilexit et admiratus est.'—*De religione* Flaminii. Schelhorn, *Amœnit. Eccles.* p. 50.

(*catholicus consensus*) and the sacrifice of the mass, which Flaminio defended, but to which Carnesecchi opposed the sacrifice offered once for all at Golgotha, as the only real one. Still, it was not until later that these two Christians entered into a correspondence on the subject which shows us the diversity of their faith.[*] Notwithstanding their differences, they remained united in close affection; and when they were forced to separate, Flaminio addressed his friend in a graceful little poem, the very first lines of which indicate the charms of the sweet and serious conversations of the Chiaja.[†] 'Although I must now depart far from thee, O dear Carnesecchi,' he said in conclusion, 'neither time, nor distance, nor death itself, shall deprive me of the sweetness of thy friendship. I shall remain with thee; I shall be ever with thee; I shall leave thee always the greater half of my soul.'

Flaminio returned to Rome, and Reginald Pole, cousin to Henry VIII., who was then in the city, endeavoured to gain for the papacy a man whose value he appreciated. The intercourse of Flaminio with Caraffa and Pole had an unfortunate influence upon him. Somewhat later he said to Carnesecchi: 'O my friend, if we do not wish to be wrecked in the midst of the dangerous breakers that surround us, let us bend humbly before God, and permit no motive,

---

[*] This correspondence took place in the year 1543, and is found in Schelhorn's *Amœnitates Ecclesiasticæ,* ii. pp. 146–179.

[†]   ' O dulce hospitium! O lares beati!
         O mores faciles! O Atticorum
         Conditæ sale collocutiones!
         Quam vos ægro animo et laborioso
         Quantis cum lacrymis miser relinquo !'
            Schelhorn, *Amœnit. Literar.* x. p. 1199.

however lawful it may appear, to separate us from the catholic Church.' * Since that time, Romish and evangelical writers have continually disputed posses- sion of him, each affirming that he belonged to them: he belonged entirely to neither. He was able to keep himself evenly balanced between the two powers that then disputed the sovereignty of Christendom, and did not fall into the abyss. But, whatever men may say, if the reformers had desired to follow that middle path which pleases certain minds, it would assuredly have been fatal to truth and liberty. Christendom would have fallen back into the servility of the middle ages; and if the yoke had appeared too heavy, it would have plunged into the licence of incredulity. The narrow path of evangelical truth runs between these two gulfs : it is a refuge to those whom they threaten to swallow up.

Among the Italians affected by the religious move- ment there were many who clung to the papacy still more than Flaminio did. The scepticism which had been fashionable at the pontifical court had brought about a reaction, to which, no doubt, the writings of the reformers contributed. The wave, uplifted at Wittemberg, Zurich, and Cambridge, descending gra- dually towards the south, reached as far as Rome, and touched the gates of the Vatican. The men who there received the doctrine of grace in their hearts, seeing religion weakened and public worship decayed, united to found in the Trastevere—in the very spot where it was said the first Christians had assembled, and where St. Peter had dwelt—that *Oratory of Divine*

---

* 'Protonotario Carnesecæ.'—Schelhorn, *Amœnit. Eccles.* p. 154.

Love which was to be a kind of citadel in which
they could rally their forces to preserve the divine
law in its purity.* They were between fifty and
sixty in number, ecclesiastics and laymen, and Julio
Bathi, rector of the church of St. Silvester, in which
their meetings were held, was the centre of that
Christian association. They were not all alike. In
some, the hierarchical tendency ultimately stifled the
evangelical spirit; but there were others whose living
piety endured unto the end. On certain days they
might be seen crossing the Tiber and ascending the
Trastevere. Among them were two priests, who
were afterwards Flaminio's patrons—Giberto and
Caraffa; Gaetano di Thiene, who founded in 1524
the order of Regular Clerks or Theatines, and was
canonised; Sadolet, born at Modena, secretary to
Leo X., who made him bishop of Carpentras in 1517,
and Lippomano, who attained a high reputation by
his writings. They were afterwards joined by a
number of eminent men, among whom were Reginald
Pole, whose opposition to the work of Henry VIII.
had forced him to leave England; Pietro Bembo,
whose house at Padua was the resort of men of
letters; Gregorio Cortesi, abbot of San Giorgio Maggiore, near Venice, and many more, among whom
was one whom we must soon speak of at greater
length.

These men, most of whom were called to play important parts, were not the only persons who felt the
influence of the revival; many a monk shut up in his

---

* 'Cosi maltrato il culto divino, si unirono in un' oratorio chiamato
del *Divino Amore.*'—Caracciolo, *Vita di Paolo IV. Vita Cajetani
Thienæi*, i. pp. 7–10.

convent shared in it.   These were to be found particularly in the Benedictine monasteries, and among
their number was Marco of Padua, who appears to
have been the monk from whom Pole says he had
drawn the spiritual milk of the Word.   But the most
striking example of this semi-evangelical, semi-monas-
tic life was Giovanni-Battista Folengo.   In his cell
in the cloister of St. Benedict, he passed days and
nights in the study of Scripture, and plainly ascribed
the justification of the sinner to grace alone.   The
good Benedictine was punctual in attending matins,
in fasting, in singing mass, and in confessing; but he
earnestly exhorted the faithful not to put their trust
in fasts, or in the mechanical repetition of the prayers
prescribed by the Church, or in confession, or in the
mass.   He was a monk and a priest, in subjection to
the dignities of the Church; but, like a prophet, he
hurled the flashes of his burning eloquence against the
priesthood, the tonsure, and the mitre.   He called
for the reform of the Church; he loved evangelical
Christians; he would have wished, in his profound
charity, to reunite them *with the flock*.   He published commentaries on the Epistles of St. Peter, St.
James, and St. John; and his noble style, as well as
the elevation of his Christian thoughts, caused them
to be read with eagerness; but the court of Rome,
irritated by the liberty with which he expressed his
faith, put his book in the Index Expurgatorius.   The
truth of the Latin saying—*habent sua fata libelli*—
was then manifested.   Folengo having written a
commentary on the Psalms, expressed in it his evangelical views with great decision, especially in his
remarks on the Sixty-eighth Psalm.   Strange to say,

while his first work had been put in the Index by one
pope, the second was reprinted by another pope
(Gregory XIII.), with some corrections indeed, but
with nothing that changed the general spirit of the
work.   More than one infallible pontiff has condemned
what another infallible pontiff has approved of.   The
pious Folengo died at the age of sixty, in the same
convent where he had taken the vows in his youth.*
A man of piety less lively than Folengo's was destined
to play a more important part in the affairs of the
Church at the epoch of the Reformation.

At that famous sitting of the Diet of Worms in 1521,
before which Martin Luther appeared, there was present among the ambassadors from the different states
of Europe, who had come to congratulate the young
emperor, a senator of Venice, by name Gaspar Contarini.   Eldest son of one of the noble families of the
republic, possessing an elevated mind formed by the
study of philosophy and literature, delicate taste,
exquisite judgment, elegant in his life and manners,
Contarini was not favourably impressed with the celebrated reformer.   These two men, who held many
principles of religion and morality in common, were
widely separated from each other as regards cultivation, character, and mode of life.   Luther was dis-
pleasing to Contarini, and the Reformation of Germany
itself, stamped with the character of the nation, did
not suit the Venetian's taste.   Noble impulses acted
on the reformer, order prevailed with the diplomatist.
Contarini devoted three hours every day to study,
never more, never less, and each time began by re-

* De Thou, *Histoire*, liv. xxiii. *Le Mire de Scriptor. sæculi* xvi., &c.

peating what he had done the day before.   He never abandoned the study of a science until he had mastered it.*   One of his first writings was directed against his master the celebrated Pomponatius, who passed for an atheist.   That philosopher having affirmed the impossibility of proving the immortality of the soul by reason, Contarini established it by philosophical arguments.   His birth called him to the first offices of the republic, and while still young he became a member of the Venetian senate.   At first he sat and listened to the deliberations ⸺of his colleagues: his modesty, and perhaps his timidity, prevented him from speaking.   At length he took courage, and though he did not speak with much wit, grace, or animation, he expressed himself with such simplicity and showed such thorough knowledge of the questions under discussion, that he soon acquired great consideration.   His mission to Charles V. was not limited to the embassy of Worms; he accompanied the emperor to Spain, and was there when the ship *Vittoria* returned from the first voyage ever made round the world.   People were surprised that the hardy sailors arrived a day later than the one marked in their log; it was Contarini, as it would appear, who discovered the cause.   Being sent as ambassador to the pope, after the sack of Rome, he effected a reconciliation between the pontiff and Charles V., and officiated at the coronation of the emperor by Clement VII.†

Every one present at these pomps took notice of the

---

* Joannis Casæ *Vita Gasparis Contarini*, p. 88.   Ranke, *Römische Päpste*, i. p. 152.   Herzog, *Encyclopédie Théologique*.

† Beccatello, *Vita del Contarini*, p. 103.   Ranke, *Römische Päpste*, i. p. 153.

Venetian ambassador, and a brilliant career seemed to lie before him. Men admired the rich gifts of his mind, the firmness and mildness of his character, the moral dignity and gravity which challenged respect. This was not all: a deep religious feeling had been developed early in his soul. At Rome he had joined the pious men who assembled at the Oratory of Divine Love on the Trastevere: he was fond of the meetings which so reminded him of those held by the disciples at Jerusalem in Mary's house.

One day, in the year 1535, when the senate of Venice had assembled for the elections, Contarini, at that time invested with one of the most important offices of the republic, was sitting near the balloting urn. On a sudden he was told that the pope had appointed him cardinal. The news surprised him exceedingly, and at first he would not believe it: he, a layman, the magistrate of a republic, and not known to the sovereign pontiff . . . to be nominated a cardinal, a prince of the Church! It appeared like a dream, and yet it was a reality. Paul III., having undertaken the task of bringing the protestants back to the Church, saw that he must employ for that purpose, not worldly prelates of the school of Leo X., but men of sincere piety; besides, Contarini had rendered services to the papacy, and hence he was invited to Rome. The report of his nomination circulated in a moment through the assembly, and his colleagues, leaving their places, gathered round to congratulate him. Even the senator who was at the head of the party opposed to him, his every-day antagonist, exclaimed, 'The republic has lost her best citizen.'

But in the midst of these congratulations Contarini remained undecided and silent. There was a struggle in his soul. He felt it difficult to leave his friends, the country of his fathers, a free city, where he was among equals, and where he might aspire to the highest dignity, that of doge—an honour enjoyed by seven of his family; he shrank from putting himself at the service of an autocrat, often the slave of passion, of living in the midst of a corrupt clergy, in a world of simony and intrigue. However, he believed he could see the finger of God in his appointment. The Church was exposed to unprecedented danger. Could he, in such a critical hour, refuse his services and his life to that militant assembly which then claimed the support of all the servants of God? He accepted the offer.* Such catholics as desired to see the Church animated by a new spirit were filled with joy, which they expressed to Contarini: ' I congratulate you,' wrote Sadolet, ' because you can now employ your genius and wisdom more profitably for the necessities and advantage of the Christian republic.' †

In becoming a cardinal, he did not intend that the golden chain should bind him to the foot of the pontifical throne: he desired to preserve his independence. Ready to devote to the catholic Church all the powers he had hitherto employed in the service of his country, he was determined to remain himself;

---

* Jean de la Case, *Vie du cardinal Contarini*, Lettere Volgari, i. 73. Moreri, art. *Contarini.*

† ' Gratulor tibi quod habiturus sis locum tui et ingenii et animi in Christianæ reipublicæ utilitate et commodis uberius explicandi.'— Sadoletus Contareno, 3 Novemb. 1535, *Epist.* p. 330.

to obey the voice of God in his conscience more than
the varying caprices of the Vatican.   He desired to be
faithful to that internal truth which gave him sweet
and constant peace.   One day, when he opposed the
nomination of a certain ecclesiastic to the cardinalate,
the pope, who was of a contrary opinion, exclaimed:
'Yes, yes! we know how men sail in these waters;
the cardinals do not like to see another made equal
to them in dignity.'   Contarini turned to the pontiff,
and observed calmly: 'I do not think the cardinal's
hat constitutes my highest honour.' *

Opposed to the deplorable elections which were
customary at Rome, the Venetian ardently desired to
bring men of sound morals, learning, and piety into
the sacred college.   The pope, therefore, following
his advice, gave the purple in succession to Sadolet,
Caraffa, Giberto bishop of Verona, Fregoso archbishop
of Salerno, and Reginald Pole.   These new and
strange elections seemed as if they would be favourable to the Gospel, but, on the contrary, they became
the principle of a restoration of Romanism, and of
a serious and ere long cruel resistance to the Reformation.

Contarini, the Melanchthon of the papacy, set to
work at once: he sincerely wished to reform the
doctrines and morals of the Church, but to maintain
it still under a sole chief.   Like the reformers he
laid great stress in religious matters on the positive side, but remained faithful to Roman-catholicism,
by extenuating the negative side.   'Assuredly, the
sinner is justified by grace through faith,' he would
say to the evangelicals.   'But why pronounce so

* Ranke, *Die Römische Päpste*, i. p. 155.

harshly against meritorious works?'—'A frank opposition to those practices,' they replied, 'can alone destroy the numberless abuses of popular superstition.'
—' Predestination,' said the cardinal again, ' belongs
undoubtedly to God's mercy; by his grace He prevents
all our movements, but at the same time the will
must oppose no resistance. God has known from all
eternity the predestined and the reprobate, but that
knowledge does not take away either contingency or
liberty.' *—' We recognise man's responsibility,' answered the reformers; ' we believe that man must
will to be saved, and yet we say with St. Paul: *God
worketh in us both to will and to do.*' †

Contarini followed the same principle in his conversations with the champions of the papacy. ' The
unity of the Church is necessary,' he said; ' to separate from it is the wildest error; but the cause of
the sufferings of Christendom, the root of all the evil,
is the unlimited authority ascribed by its adulators to
the pontifical legislation. A pope ought not to govern
just as he pleases, but only in accordance with God's
commandments, the rules of reason, and the laws
of charity.' Convinced that unity of faith would
gradually be restored, he devoted all his efforts to
remove from the Church everything that shocked
the moral sentiment; he resolutely fought against
simony, and advocated the marriage of priests. He
entertained no doubt that success would crown the
holy work he had commenced. We shall see hereafter what became of it.

* Contarini, *De Prædestinatione. De Libero Arbitrio.* Contarini's theological, philosophical, and political treatises were printed at Paris in 1571.
† Philippians ii. 13.

At the dawn of the Reformation, when the first gleams heralding the rising of the sun began to appear, they were probably nowhere more brilliant than in Italy, and nowhere foretokened a brighter day. Men's souls were moved by a spirit from on high, and a new life sanctified their hearts: the primitive relation of man to God, and his personal relation to Him, which sin had destroyed, were restored. It was in the very stronghold of formalism that the adoration of God was manifested with most liberty and grace. From the Alps to Sicily, burning lights had everywhere appeared, and many rejoiced in their brightness.

Rome still remained seated on her seven hills—with her excommunications and her burning piles; but it seemed as if a new invasion—that of the Gospel and of liberty—would repair all the mischiefs committed by the inroads of the barbarians and the papacy. Two camps were formed, one to the north, the other to the south of that ancient city. On one side was Naples and the camp of Pausilippo, where a small but gallant army was assembled. A gentle light gilded the hills of Chiaja : no formidable enemy appeared in sight, and everything led to the hope that a final and successful victory would ere long be gained.

The other camp was to the north. It could not boast of such eminent men as those who watched in the ancient city of Parthenope. The throne of Ferrara was occupied by an earnest woman and devoted Christian, the daughter of Louis XII., who gave a welcome to all the fugitive soldiers of Christ; and who had made it her business to build up the city of God in Italy, and thus to work out, in a Christian manner, her father's device: *Perdam Babylonis nomen.* About this time she was expecting at her court a young divine, who had confessed Jesus Christ in France with energy, who had just written to Francis I. an eloquent and forcible letter, and published a book in which he had set forth the great doctrines of the faith in admirable order and in language of unequalled beauty. What would be the effect of his presence beyond the Alps? No one could say; but if the duchess had influence enough over her husband to make religious liberty prevail at Ferrara; if Calvin should settle in the birthplace of Savonarola, his faith, his talents, and his activity among a people already moved by the power of God, might gain a glorious victory for the truth.

Thus two great forces met face to face—Rome and the Gospel. Curione, Paleario, Peter Martyr, and many others, asked themselves what would be the issue of the struggle then preparing in Italy. Experiencing in themselves the power of God's Word, and seeing its marvellous effects around them, they doubted not that the Gospel would triumph in their country, as it had triumphed in other countries more to the north, and where, perhaps, less of light and life were to be found. The Reformation in Italy would doubtless present peculiar features, which, without disturbing Christian unity, would manifest national individuality. Episcopacy existed in England; the primate, archbishop of Canterbury, remained on his throne, while submitting to the Word of God. Why might not a similar reform be effected in Rome itself? Not only evangelicals, such as Curione and Carnesecchi, but pious catholics were full of hope.

'Ah!' they said; 'at the beginning of his reign the pope wonderfully excited all our expectations.* Putting aside institutions established by preceding popes, he resolved to conduct the supreme pontificate in a holier manner;† and to accomplish that task, he gathered round him men whom fame had pointed out as doctors excellent in wisdom and integrity.' Contarini believed in a reformation which, beginning with the head, would purify all the members. 'God,' he said, 'will not permit the gates of hell to prevail against his Holy Spirit. He is about to accomplish something great in the Church.' ‡ The flames which had been kindled in the peninsula, and which rose higher and higher every day, appeared as if they would soon reduce to ashes the scaffolding of dead works which the papacy had set up, and to purify the temple of God.

But the times of Rome were not accomplished. The malady, with which the body of the Church was affected in Italy, was (to use the words of Cardinal Sadolet) one of those which incline the sick man to reject the remedies prescribed for him.§ Pope Paul III., who consulted the stars more than he did the Gospel, finding at last that his attempts ended in nothing; that the Reformation was advancing, and

---

* 'Is Paulus [tertius], sui pontificatus initio, spem atque expectationem omnium mirabiliter erexit.'—Florebelli *Vita Sadoleti cardinalis,* p. 708.

† 'Sublatis eis quæ a superioribus pontificibus Romanis instituta, sanctiorem gerendi summi pontificatus rationem instituere.'—*Ibid.* p. 709.

‡ Contarini, Weizsæcker, *Theol. Encyclop.*

§ ' Ægrotat enim corpus republicæ, et eo morbi genere ægrotat quod præscriptam medicinam respuit.'—*Sadolet to Contarini,* March 1536. Sadoleti *Epist.* p. 342.

threatening to regenerate and deliver the Church, suddenly turned upon it and endeavoured to crush it. Those men who would have been the regenerators of Italy, with minds of such activity, with such varied learning and exquisite cultivation, who held converse in the finest parts of the world with the best and most illustrious of their time—those men, the flower of their nation, soon found themselves constrained to escape beyond the Alps, or saw themselves condemned by cruel pontiffs, insulted by ignorant priests, and conducted ignominiously to some public square in Rome, there to be beheaded and have their bodies cast into the fire. . . . The heart shrinks at the thought, and an inner voice seems to say: ' If Carnesecchi, Paleario, and all the noble army of martyrs were disowned by their contemporaries; if coarse monks jeered at them, if they were covered with opprobrium ; there are now thousands of Christians in the world who love them as fathers, honour them as victorious heroes of the Gospel of peace, and preserve a grateful remembrance of them in their hearts.'

END OF THE FOURTH VOLUME.

LONDON
PRINTED BY SPOTTISWOODE AND CO.
NEW-STREET SQUARE

39 Paternoster Row, E.C

London, *March* 1866.

GENERAL LIST OF WORKS

PUBLISHED BY

Messrs. LONGMANS, GREEN, READER, and DYER.

———◆◇◆———

———oo∘o∘oo———

Historical Works.

Lord Macaulay's Works. Complete and uniform Library Edition. Edited by his Sister, Lady Trevelyan. 8 vols. 8vo. with Portrait, price £5 5s. cloth, or £8 8s. bound in tree-calf by Rivière.

The History of England from the Fall of Wolsey to the Death of Elizabeth. By James Anthony Froude, M.A. late Fellow of Exeter College, Oxford.

Vols. I. to IV. the Reign of Henry VIII. Third Edition, 54s.

Vols. V. and VI. the Reigns of Edward VI. and Mary. Second Edition, 28s.

Vols. VII. & VIII. the Reign of Elizabeth, Vols. I. & II. Third Edition, 28s.

The History of England from the Accession of James II. By Lord Macaulay.

Library Edition, 5 vols. 8vo. £4.

Cabinet Edition, 8 vols. post 8vo. 48s.

People's Edition, 4 vols. crown 8vo. 16s.

Revolutions in English History. By Robert Vaughan, D.D. 3 vols. 8vo. 45s.

Vol. I. Revolutions of Race, 15s.

Vol. II. Revolutions in Religion, 15s.

Vol. III. Revolutions in Government, 15s.

An Essay on the History of the English Government and Constitution, from the Reign of Henry VII. to the Present Time. By John Earl Russell. Third Edition, revised. Crown 8vo. 6s.

The History of England during the Reign of George the Third. By the Right Hon. W. N. Massey. Cabinet Edition, 4 vols. post 8vo. 24s.

The Constitutional History of England, since the Accession of George III. 1760—1860. By Thomas Erskine May, C.B. Second Edition. 2 vols. 8vo. 33s.

Brodie's Constitutional History of the British Empire from the Accession of Charles I. to the Restoration. Second Edition. 3 vols. 8vo. 36s.

Historical Studies. I. On Precursors of the French Revolution; II. Studies from the History of the Seventeenth Century; III. Leisure Hours of a Tourist. By Herman Merivale, M.A. 8vo. 12s. 6d.

Lectures on the History of England. By William Longman. Vol. I. from the Earliest Times to the Death of King Edward II. with 6 Maps, a coloured Plate, and 53 Woodcuts. 8vo. 15s.

History of Civilization. By HENRY THOMAS BUCKLE. 2 vols. £1 17s.

VOL. I. *England* and *France*, Fourth Edition, 21s.

VOL. II. *Spain* and *Scotland*, Second Edition, 16s.

Democracy in America. By ALEXIS DE TOCQUEVILLE. Translated by HENRY REEVE, with an Introductory Notice by the Translator. 2 vols. 8vo. 21s.

The Spanish Conquest in America, and its Relation to the History of Slavery and to the Government of Colonies. By ARTHUR HELPS. 4 vols. 8vo. £3. VOLS. I. & II. 28s. VOLS. III. & IV. 16s. each.

History of the Reformation in Europe in the Time of Calvin. By J. H. MERLE D'AUBIGNÉ, D.D. VOLS. I. and II. 8vo. 28s. and VOL. III. 12s. VOL. IV. nearly ready.

Library History of France, in 5 vols. 8vo. By EYRE EVANS CROWE. VOL. I. 14s. VOL. II. 15s. VOL. III. 18s. VOL. IV. nearly ready.

Lectures on the History of France. By the late Sir JAMES STEPHEN, LL.D. 2 vols. 8vo. 24s.

The History of Greece. By C. THIRL-WALL, D.D. Lord Bishop of St. David's. 8 vols. 8vo. £3; or in 8 vols. fcp. 28s.

The Tale of the Great Persian War, from the Histories of Herodotus. By GEORGE W. COX, M.A. late Scholar of Trin. Coll. Oxon. Fcp. 7s. 6d.

Greek History from Themistocles to Alexander, in a Series of Lives from Plutarch. Revised and arranged by A. H. CLOUGH. Fcp. with 44 Woodcuts, 6s.

Critical History of the Lan-guage and Literature of Ancient Greece. By WILLIAM MURE, of Caldwell. 5 vols. 8vo. £3 9s.

History of the Literature of Ancient Greece. By Professor K. O. MÜLLER. Translated by the Right Hon. Sir GEORGE CORNEWALL LEWIS, Bart. and by J. W. DONALDSON, D.D. 3 vols. 8vo. 36s.

History of the City of Rome from its Foundation to the Sixteenth Century of the Christian Era. By THOMAS H. DYER, LL.D. 8vo. with 2 Maps, 15s.

History of the Romans unde the Empire. By CHARLES MERIVALE, B.D Chaplain to the Speaker. Cabinet Edition with Maps, complete in 8 vols. post 8vo. 48s

The Fall of the Roman Re public : a Short History of the Last Cen tury of the Commonwealth. By the sam Author. 12mo. 7s. 6d.

The Conversion of the Roma Empire; the Boyle Lectures for the yea 1864, delivered at the Chapel Royal, White hall. By the same. 2nd Edition. 8vo. 8s. 6

The Conversion of the Norther Nations; the Boyle Lectures for 1865. B the same. 8vo. 8s. 6d.

Critical and Historical Essay contributed to the *Edinburgh Review*. B the Right Hon. Lord MACAULAY.

LIBRARY EDITION, 3 vols. 8vo. 36s.
TRAVELLER'S EDITION, in 1 vol. 21s.
CABINET EDITION, 3 vols. fcp. 21s.
PEOPLE'S EDITION, 2 vols. crown 8vo. 8

Historical and Philosophica Essays. By NASSAU W. SENIOR. 2 vol post 8vo. 16s.

History of the Rise and Influenc of the Spirit of Rationalism in Europe. B W. E. H. LECKY, M.A. Second Editio 2 vols. 8vo. 25s.

The History of Philosophy, fro Thales to the Present Day. By GEORG HENRY LEWES. Third Edition, partly re written and greatly enlarged. In 2 vol VOL. I. *Ancient Philosophy*: VOL. II. *M< dern Philosophy*. [*Nearly ready.*

History of the Inductive Science By WILLIAM WHEWELL, D.D. F.R.S. la Master of Trin. Coll. Cantab. Third Editio 3 vols. crown 8vo. 24s.

History of Scientific Ideas; bein the First Part of the Philosophy of th Inductive Sciences. By the same Autho Third Edition. 2 vols. crown 8vo. 14s.

Egypt's Place in Universal Hi tory; an Historical Investigation. B C. C. J. BUNSEN, D.D. Translated t C. H. COTTRELL, M.A. With many Illu trations. 4 vols. 8vo. £5 8s. VOL. V. nearly ready, completing the work.

Maunder's Historical Treasury comprising a General Introductory Outli of Universal History, and a Series of Sep rate Histories. Fcp. 10s.

Historical and Chronological Encyclopædia, presenting in a brief and convenient form Chronological Notices of all the Great Events of Universal History. By B. B. WOODWARD, F.S.A. Librarian to the Queen. [*In the press.*

History of the Christian Church, from the Ascension of Christ to the Conversion of Constantine. By E. BURTON, D.D. late Regius Prof. of Divinity in the University of Oxford. Eighth Edition. Fcp. 3s. 6d.

Lectures on the History of Modern Music, delivered at the Royal Institution. By JOHN HULLAH. FIRST COURSE, with Chronological Tables, post 8vo. 6s. 6d. SECOND COURSE, the Transition Period, with 26 Specimens, 8vo. 16s.

History of the Early Church, from the First Preaching of the Gospel to the Council of Nicæa, A.D. 325. By the Author of 'Amy Herbert.' Fcp. 4s. 6d.

The English Reformation. By F. C. MASSINGBERD, M.A. Chancellor of Lincoln. Fourth Edition, revised. Fcp. 8vo. [*Nearly ready.*

History of Wesleyan Methodism. By GEORGE SMITH, F.A.S Fourth Edition, with numerous Portraits. 3 vols. crown 8vo. 7s. each.

Sketch of the History of the Church of England to the Revolution of 1688. By the Right Rev. T. V. SHORT, D.D. Lord Bishop of St. Asaph. Seventh Edition. Crown 8vo. 10s. 6d.

Biography and *Memoirs.*

Extracts of the Journals and Correspondence of Miss Berry, from the Year 1783 to 1852. Edited by Lady THERESA LEWIS. Second Edition, with 3 Portraits. 3 vols. 8vo. 42s.

The Diary of the Right Hon. William Windham, M.P. From 1783 to 1809. Edited by Mrs. H. BARING. 8vo. 18s.

Life of the Duke of Wellington. By the Rev. G. R. GLEIG, M.A. Popular Edition, carefully revised; with copious Additions. Crown 8vo. with Portrait, 5s.

Life of the Duke of Wellington, partly from M. BRIALMONT, partly from Original Documents (Intermediate Edition). By Rev. G. R. GLEIG, M.A. 8vo. with Portrait, 15s.

Brialmont and Gleig's Life of the Duke of Wellington (the Parent Work). 4 vols. 8vo. with Illustrations, £2 14s.

History of my Religious Opinions. By J. H. NEWMAN, D.D. Being the Substance of Apologia pro Vitâ Suâ. Post 8vo. 6s.

Father Mathew: a Biography. By JOHN FRANCIS MAGUIRE, M.P. Popular Edition, with Portrait. Crown 8vo. 3s. 6d.

Rome; its Rulers and its Institutions. By the same Author. New Edition in preparation.

Letters and Life of Francis Bacon, including all his Occasional Works. Collected and edited, with a Commentary, by J. SPEDDING, Trin. Coll. Cantab. VOLS. I. and II. 8vo. 24s.

Life of Amelia Wilhelmina Sieveking, from the German. Edited, with the Author's sanction, by CATHERINE WINKWORTH. Post 8vo. with Portrait, 12s.

Mozart's Letters (1769-1791), translated from the Collection of Dr. LUDWIG NOHL by Lady WALLACE. 2 vols. post 8vo. with Portrait and Facsimile, 18s.

Beethoven's Letters (1790-1826), from the Two Collections of Drs. NOHL and VON KÖCHEL. Translated by Lady WALLACE. 2 vols. post 8vo. with Portrait.

Felix Mendelssohn's Letters from *Italy and Switzerland,* and *Letters from* 1833 to 1847, translated by Lady WALLACE. With Portrait. 2 vols. crown 8vo. 5s. each.

Recollections of the late William Wilberforce, M.P. for the County of York during nearly 30 Years. By J. S. HARFORD, F.R.S. Second Edition. Post 8vo. 7s.

Memoirs of Sir Henry Havelock, K.C.B. By JOHN CLARK MARSHMAN. Second Edition. 8vo. with Portrait, 12s. 6d.

Thomas Moore's Memoirs, Journal, and Correspondence. Edited and abridged from the First Edition by Earl RUSSELL. Square crown 8vo. with 8 Portraits, 12s. 6d.

Memoir of the Rev. Sydney Smith. By his Daughter, Lady HOLLAND. With a Selection from his Letters, edited by Mrs. AUSTIN. 2 vols. 8vo. 28s.

Essays in Ecclesiastical Biogra- phy. By the Right Hon. Sir J. Stephen, LL.D. Fourth Edition. 8vo. 14s.

Biographies of Distinguished Sci- entific Men. By François Arago. Translated by Admiral W. H. Smyth, F.R.S. the Rev. B. Powell, M.A. and R. Grant, M.A. 8vo. 18s.

Vicissitudes of Families. By Bernard Burke, Ulster King of Ar First, Second, and Third Series. 3 vo crown 8vo. 12s. 6d. each.

Maunder's Biographical Tre sury: Memoirs, Sketches, and Brief Notice of above 12,000 Eminent Persons of Ages and Nations. Fcp. 8vo. 10s.

Criticism, Philosophy, Polity, &c.

The Institutes of Justinian; with English Introduction, Translation, and Notes. By T. C. Sandars, M.A. Barrister-at-Law, late Fellow of Oriel Coll. Oxon. Third Edition. 8vo. 15s.

The Ethics of Aristotle. Illustrated with Essays and Notes. By Sir A. Grant, Bart. M.A. LL.D. Director of Public Instruction in the Bombay Presidency. Second Edition, revised and completed. 2 vols. 8vo.

On Representative Government. By John Stuart Mill, M.P. Third Edition. 8vo. 9s. crown 8vo. 2s.

On Liberty. By the same Author. Third Edition. Post 8vo. 7s. 6d. crown 8vo. 1s. 4d,

Principles of Political Economy. By the same. Sixth Edition. 2 vols. 8vo. 30s. or in 1 vol. crown 8vo. 5s.

A System of Logic, Ratiocinative and Inductive. By the same. Sixth Edition. 2 vols. 8vo. 25s.

Utilitarianism. By the same. 2d Edit. 8vo. 5s.

Dissertations and Discussions. By the same Author. 2 vols. 8vo. 24s.

Examination of Sir W. Hamilton's Philosophy, and of the Principal Philosophical Questions discussed in his Writings. By the same Author. Second Edition. 8vo. 14s.

Lord Bacon's Works, collected and edited by R. L. Ellis, M.A. J. Spedding, M.A. and D. D. Heath. Vols. I. to V. *Philosophical Works,* 5 vols. 8vo. £4 6s. Vols. VI. and VII. *Literary and Professional Works,* 2 vols. £1 16s.

Bacon's Essays, with Annotations.

Elements of Logic. By R. Whatel D.D. late Archbishop of Dublin. Nin Edition. 8vo. 10s. 6d. crown 8vo. 4s. 6d.

Elements of Rhetoric. By the sam Author. Seventh Edition. 8vo. 10s. crown 8vo. 4s. 6d.

English Synonymes. Edited by Ar bishop Whately. 5th Edition. Fcp. 3s

Miscellaneous Remains from t Common-place Book of Richard Whate D.D. late Archbishop of Dublin. Edited Miss E. J. Whately. Post 8vo. 7s. 6d.

Essays on the Administrations Great Britain from 1783 to 1830. By t Right Hon. Sir G. C. Lewis, Bart. Edit by the Right Hon. Sir E. Head, Bart. 8 with Portrait, 15s.

By the same Author.

Inquiry into the Credibility of t Early Roman History, 2 vols. 30s.

On the Methods of Observation a Reasoning in Politics, 2 vols. 28s.

Irish Disturbances and Irish Chur Question, 12s.

Remarks on the Use and Abuse some Political Terms, 9s.

The Fables of Babrius, Greek Te with Latin Notes, Part I. 5s. 6d. Part 3s. 6d.

An Outline of the Necessa Laws of Thought: a Treatise on Pure a Applied Logic. By the Most Rev. Thomson, D.D. Archbishop of York. Cro 8vo. 5s. 6d.

The Elements of Logic. By Thom

Analysis of Mr. Mill's System of Logic. By W. STEBBING, M.A. Second Edition. 12mo. 3s. 6d.

The Election of Representatives, Parliamentary and Municipal; a Treatise. By THOMAS HARE, Barrister-at-Law. Third Edition, with Additions. Crown 8vo. 6s.

Speeches of the Right Hon. Lord MACAULAY, corrected by Himself. Library Edition, 8vo. 12s. People's Edition, crown 8vo. 3s. 6d.

Lord Macaulay's Speeches on Parliamentary Reform in 1831 and 1832. 16mo. 1s.

Dictionary of the English Language. By R. G. LATHAM, M.A. M.D. F.R.S. Founded on the Dictionary of Dr. S. JOHNSON, as edited by the Rev. H. J. TODD, with numerous Emendations and Additions. Publishing in 36 Parts, price 3s. 6d. each, to form 2 vols. 4to.

Thesaurus of English Words and Phrases, classified and arranged so as to facilitate the Expression of Ideas, and assist in Literary Composition. By P. M. ROGET, M.D. 18th Edition, crown 8vo. 10s. 6d.

ectures on the Science of Lan- guage, delivered at the Royal Institution. By MAX MÜLLER, M.A. Taylorian Professor in the University of Oxford. FIRST SERIES, Fourth Edition, 12s. SECOND SERIES, 18s.

hapters on Language. By FREDERIC W. FARRAR, M.A. late Fellow of Trin. Coll. Cambridge. Crown 8vo. 8s. 6d.

he Debater; a Series of Complete Debates, Outlines of Debates, and Questions for Discussion. By F. ROWTON. Fcp. 6s.

Course of English Reading, adapted to every taste and capacity; or, How and What to Read. By the Rev. J. PYCROFT, B.A. Fourth Edition, fcp. 5s.

anual of English Literature, Historical and Critical: with a Chapter on English Metres. By THOMAS ARNOLD, B.A. Post 8vo. 10s. 6d.

outhey's Doctor, complete in One Volume. Edited by the Rev. J.W. WARTER, B.D. Square crown 8vo. 12s. 6d.

Historical and Critical Commen- tary on the Old Testament; with a New Translation. By M. M. KALISCH, Ph. D. VOL. I. *Genesis*, 8vo. 18s. or adapted for the General Reader, 12s. VOL. II. *Exodus*, 15s. or adapted for the General Reader, 12s.

A Hebrew Grammar, with Exercises. By the same. PART 1. *Outlines with Exercises*, 8vo. 12s. 6d. KEY, 5s. PART II. *Exceptional Forms and Constructions*, 12s. 6d.

A Latin-English Dictionary. By J. T. WHITE, M.A. of Corpus Christi College, and J. E. RIDDLE, M.A. of St. Edmund Hall, Oxford. Imp. 8vo. pp. 2,128, price 42s.

A New Latin-English Dictionary, abridged from the larger work of *White* and *Riddle* (as above), by J. T. WHITE, M.A. Joint-Author. 8vo. pp. 1,048, price 18s.

The Junior Scholar's Latin-English Dictionary, abridged from the larger works of *White* and *Riddle* (as above), by J. T. WHITE, M.A. surviving Joint-Author. Square 12mo. pp. 662, price 7s. 6d.

An English-Greek Lexicon, containing all the Greek Words used by Writers of good authority. By C. D. YONGE, B.A. Fifth Edition. 4to. 21s.

Mr. Yonge's New Lexicon, En- glish and Greek, abridged 'from his larger work (as above). Square 12mo. 8s. 6d.

A Greek-English Lexicon. Compiled by H. G. LIDDELL, D.D. Dean of Christ Church, and R. SCOTT, D.D. Master of Balliol. Fifth Edition, crown 4to. 31s. 6d.

A Lexicon, Greek and English, abridged from LIDDELL and SCOTT's *Greek-English Lexicon*. Eleventh Edition, square 12mo. 7s. 6d.

A Sanskrit-English Dictionary, The Sanskrit words printed both in the original Devanagari and in Roman letters; with References to the Best Editions of Sanskrit Authors, and with Etymologies and Comparisons of Cognate Words chiefly in Greek, Latin, Gothic, and Anglo-Saxon. Compiled by T. BENFEY. 8vo. 52s. 6d.

A Practical Dictionary of the French and English Languages. By L. CONTANSEAU. 10th Edition, post 8vo. 10s. 6d.

Contanseau's Pocket Dictionary, French and English, abridged from the above by the Author. 3d Edition. 18mo. 5s.

New Practical Dictionary of the German Language; German-English, and English-German. By the Rev. W. L. BLACKLEY, M.A. and Dr. CARL MARTIN FRIEDLANDER. Post 8vo. [*Nearly ready.*]

Miscellaneous Works and Popular Metaphysics.

Recreations of a Country Parson. By A. K. H. B. FIRST SERIES, with 41 Woodcut Illustrations from Designs by R. T. Pritchett. Crown 8vo. 12s. 6d.

Recreations of a Country Parson. SECOND SERIES. Crown 8vo. 3s. 6d.

The Commonplace Philosopher in Town and Country. By the same Author. Crown 8vo. 3s. 6d.

Leisure Hours in Town; Essays Consolatory, Æsthetical, Moral, Social, and Domestic. By the same. Crown 8vo. 3s. 6d.

The Autumn Holidays of a Country Parson; Essays contributed to *Fraser's Magazine* and to *Good Words*, by the same. Crown 8vo. 3s. 6d.

The Graver Thoughts of a Country Parson, SECOND SERIES. By the same. Crown 8vo. 3s. 6d.

Critical Essays of a Country Parson, selected from Essays contributed to *Fraser's Magazine*, by the same. Post 8vo. 9s.

A Campaigner at Home. By SHIRLEY, Author of 'Thalatta' and 'Nugæ Criticæ.' Post 8vo. with Vignette, 7s. 6d.

Studies in Parliament: a Series of Sketches of Leading Politicians. By R. H. HUTTON. (Reprinted from the *Pall Mall Gazette*.) Crown 8vo. 4s. 6d.

Lord Macaulay's Miscellaneous Writings.

LIBRARY EDITION, 2 vols. 8vo. Portrait, 21s.

PEOPLE'S EDITION, 1 vol. crown 8vo. 4s. 6d.

The Rev. Sydney Smith's Mis- cellaneous Works; including his Contributions to the *Edinburgh Review*.

LIBRARY EDITION, 3 vols. 8vo. 36s.

TRAVELLER'S EDITION, in 1 vol. 21s.

CABINET EDITION, 3 vols. fcp. 21s.

PEOPLE'S EDITION, 2 vols. crown 8vo. 8s.

Elementary Sketches of Moral Philo- sophy, delivered at the Royal Institution. By the same Author. Fcp. 7s.

The Wit and Wisdom of the Rev. SYDNEY SMITH: a Selection of the most memorable Passages in his Writings and Conversation. 16mo. 5s.

Epigrams, Ancient and Modern: Humorous, Witty, Satirical, Moral, and Panegyrical. Edited by Rev. JOHN BOOTH, B.A. Cambridge. Second Edition, revised and enlarged. Fcp. 7s. 6d.

From Matter to Spirit: the Result of Ten Years' Experience in Spirit Manifestations. By SOPHIA E. DE MORGAN. With a Preface by Professor DE MORGAN. Post 8vo. 8s. 6d.

Essays selected from Contribu- tions to the *Edinburgh Review*. By HENRY ROGERS. Second Edition. 3 vols. fcp. 21s.

The Eclipse of Faith; or, a Visit to a Religious Sceptic. By the same Author. Eleventh Edition. Fcp. 5s.

Defence of the Eclipse of Faith, by its Author. Third Edition. Fcp. 3s. 6d.

Selections from the Correspondence of R. E. H. Greyson. By the same Author. Third Edition. Crown 8vo. 7s. 6d.

Fulleriana, or the Wisdom and Wit of THOMAS FULLER, with Essay on his Life and Genius. By the same Author. 16mo. 2s. 6d.

An Essay on Human Nature; showing the Necessity of a Divine Revelation for the Perfect Development of Man's Capacities. By HENRY S. BOASE, M.D. F.R.S. and G.S. 8vo. 12s.

The Philosophy of Nature; a Systematic Treatise on the Causes and Laws of Natural Phenomena. By the same Author. 8vo. 12s.

The Secret of Hegel: being the Hegelian System in Origin, Principle, Form, and Matter. By JAMES HUTCHISON STIRLING. 2 vols. 8vo. 28s.

An Introduction to Mental Phi- losophy, on the Inductive Method. By J. D. MORELL, M.A. LL.D. 8vo. 12s.

Elements of Psychology, containing the Analysis of the Intellectual Powers. By the same Author. Post 8vo. 7s. 6d.

Sight and Touch: an Attempt to Disprove the Received (or Berkeleian) Theory of Vision. By THOMAS K. ABBOTT, M.A. Fellow and Tutor of Trin. Coll. Dublin. 8vo. with 21 Woodcuts, 5s. 6d.

The Senses and the Intellect. By ALEXANDER BAIN, M.A. Prof. of Logic in the Univ. of Aberdeen. Second Edition. 8vo. 15s.

The Emotions and the Will, by the same Author. 8vo. 15s.

On the Study of Character, including an Estimate of Phrenology. By the same Author. 8vo. 9s.

Time and Space: a Metaphysical Essay. By SHADWORTH H. HODGSON. 8vo. pp. 588, price 16s.

The Way to Rest: Results from a Life-search after Religious Truth. By R. VAUGHAN, D.D. [Nearly ready.

Hours with the Mystics: a Contribution to the History of Religious Opinion. By ROBERT ALFRED VAUGHAN, B.A. Second Edition. 2.vols. crown 8vo. 12s.

The Philosophy of Necessity; or, Natural Law as applicable to Mental, Moral, and Social Science. By CHARLES BRAY. Second Edition. 8vo. 9s.

The Education of the Feelings and Affections. By the same Author. Third Edition. 8vo. 3s. 6d.

Christianity and Common Sense. By Sir WILLOUGHBY JONES, Bart. M.A. Trin. Coll. Cantab. 8vo. 6s.

Astronomy, Meteorology, Popular Geography, &c.

Outlines of Astronomy. By Sir J. F. W. HERSCHEL, Bart, M.A. Eighth Edition, revised; with Plates and Woodcuts. 8vo. 18s.

Arago's Popular Astronomy. Translated by Admiral W. H. SMYTH, F.R.S. and R. GRANT, M.A. With 25 Plates and 358 Woodcuts. 2 vols. 8vo. £2 5s.

Saturn and its System. By RICHARD A. PROCTOR, B.A. late Scholar of St. John's Coll. Camb. and King's Coll. London. 8vo. with 14 Plates, 14s.

Celestial Objects for Common Telescopes. By T. W. WEBB, M.A. F.R.A.S. With Map of the Moon, and Woodcuts. 16mo. 7s.

Physical Geography for Schools and General Readers. By M. F. MAURY, LL.D. Fcp. with 2 Charts, 2s. 6d.

A General Dictionary of Geography, Descriptive, Physical, Statistical, and Historical ; forming a complete Gazetteer of the World. By A. KEITH JOHNSTON, F.R.S.E. 8vo. 31s. 6d.

M'Culloch's Dictionary, Geographical, Statistical, and Historical, of the various Countries, Places, and principal Natural Objects in the World. Revised Edition, printed in a larger type, with Maps, and with the Statistical Information throughout brought up to the latest returns. By FREDERICK MARTIN. 4 vols. 8vo. price 21s. each. VOL. I. now ready.

A Manual of Geography, Physical, Industrial, and Political. By W. HUGHES, F.R.G.S. Prof. of Geog. in King's Coll. and in Queen's Coll. Lond. With 6 Maps. Fcp. 7s. 6d.

The Geography of British History; a Geographical Description of the British Islands at Successive Periods. By the same Author. With 6 Maps. Fcp. 8s. 6d.

Abridged Text-Book of British Geography. By the same. Fcp. 1s. 6d.

Maunder's Treasury of Geography, Physical, Historical, Descriptive, and Political. Edited by W. HUGHES, F.R.G.S. With 7 Maps and 16 Plates. Fcp. 10s. 6d.

Natural History and *Popular Science.*

The Elements of Physics or Natural Philosophy. By NEIL ARNOTT, M.D. F.R.S. Physician Extraordinary to the Queen. Sixth Edition, rewritten and completed. 2 Parts, 8vo. 21s.

Volcanos, the Character of their Phenomena, their Share in the Structure and Composition of the Surface of the Globe, &c. By G. POULETT SCROPE, M.P. F.R.S. Second Edition. 8vo. with Illustrations, 15s.

Heat Considered as a Mode of Motion. By Professor JOHN TYNDALL, F.R.S. LL.D. Second Edition. Crown 8vo. with Woodcuts, 12s. 6d.

A Treatise on Electricity, in Theory and Practice. By A. DE LA RIVE, Prof. in the Academy of Geneva. Translated by C. V. WALKER, F.R.S. 3 vols. 8vo. with Woodcuts, £3 13s.

The Correlation of Physical Forces. By W. R. GROVE, Q.C. V.P.R S. Fourth Edition. 8vo. 7s. 6d.

Manual of Geology. By S. HAUGHTON, M.D. F.R.S. Fellow of Trin. Coll. and Prof. of Geol. in the Univ. of Dublin. Revised Edition, with 66 Woodcuts. Fcp. 6s.

A Guide to Geology. By J. PHILLIPS, M.A. Prof. of Geol. in the Univ. of Oxford. Fifth Edition. Fcp. 4s.

A Glossary of Mineralogy. By H. W. BRISTOW, F.G.S. of the Geological Survey of Great Britain. With 486 Figures. Crown 8vo. 12s.

Phillips's Elementary Introduc-tion to Mineralogy, re-edited by H. J. BROOKE, F.R.S. and W. H. MILLER, F.G.S. Post 8vo. with Woodcuts, 18s.

Van Der Hoeven's Handbook of ZOOLOGY. Translated from the Second Dutch Edition by the Rev. W. CLARK, M.D. F.R.S. 2 vols. 8vo. with 24 Plates of Figures, 60s.

The Comparative Anatomy and Physiology of the Vertebrate Animals. By RICHARD OWEN, F.R.S. D.C.L. 3 vols. 8vo. with upwards of 1,200 Woodcuts. VOLS. I. and II. price 21s. each, now ready. VOL. III. in the Autumn.

Homes without Hands: a Description of the Habitations of Animals, classed according to their Principle of Construction. By Rev. J. G. WOOD, M.A. F.L.S. With about 140 Vignettes on Wood (20 full size of page). Second Edition. 8vo. 21s.

The Harmonies of Nature and Unity of Creation. By Dr. G. HARTWIG, 8vo. with numerous Illustrations.

The Sea and its Living Wonders. By the same Author. Second (English) Edition. 8vo. with many Illustrations, 18s.

The Tropical World. By the same Author. With 8 Chromoxylographs and 172 Woodcuts. 8vo. 21s.

Manual of Corals and Sea Jellie By J. R. GREENE, B.A. Edited by J. GALBRAITH, M.A. and S. HAUGHTON, M. Fcp. with 39 Woodcuts, 5s.

Manual of Sponges and Animalcula with a General Introduction on the Prin ples of Zoology. By the same Author a Editors. Fcp. with 16 Woodcuts, 2s.

Manual of the Metalloids. By J. APJOH M.D. F.R.S. and the same Editors. 2 Edition. Fcp. with 38 Woodcuts, 7s. 6d.

Sketches of the Natural Histor of Ceylon. By Sir J. EMERSON TENNEN K.C.S. LL.D. With 82 Wood Engraving Post 8vo. 12s. 6d.

Ceylon. By the same Author. 5th Editio with Maps, &c. and 90 Wood Engraving 2 vols. 8vo. £2 10s.

A Familiar History of Bird By E. STANLEY, D.D. late Lord Bishop Norwich. Fcp. with Woodcuts, 3s. 6d.

Marvels and Mysteries of I stinct; or, Curiosities of Animal Life. B G. GARRATT. Third Edition. Fcp. 7s.

Home Walks and Holiday Ra bles. By the Rev. C. A. JOHNS, B.A. F.L. Fcp. with 10 Illustrations, 6s.

Kirby and Spence's Introductio to Entomology, or Elements of the Natur History of Insects. Crown 8vo. 5s.

Maunder's Treasury of Natur History, or Popular Dictionary of Zoolog Revised and corrected by T. S. COBBOL M.D. Fcp. with 900 Woodcuts, 10s.

The Elements of Botany fo Families and Schools. Tenth Edition, re vised by THOMAS MOORE, F.L.S. Fc with 154 Woodcuts, 2s. 6d.

The Treasury of Botany, o Popular Dictionary of the Vegetable King dom; with which is incorporated a Glos sary of Botanical Terms. Edited b J. LINDLEY, F.R.S. and T. MOORE, F.L. assisted by eminent Contributors. P 1,274, with 274 Woodcuts and 20 Stee Plates. 2 Parts, fcp. 20s.

The British Flora; comprising th Phænogamous or Flowering Plants and th Ferns. By Sir W. J. HOOKER, K.H. an G. A. WALKER-ARNOTT, LL.D. 12mc with 12 Plates, 14s. or coloured, 21s.

The Rose Amateur's Guide. By THOMAS RIVERS. New Edition. Fcp. 4s.

The Indoor Gardener. By Miss MALING. Fcp. with Frontispiece, 5s.

Loudon's Encyclopædia of Plants; comprising the Specific Character, Description, Culture, History, &c. of all the Plants found in Great Britain. With upwards of 12,000 Woodcuts. 8vo. £3 13s. 6d.

Loudon's Encyclopædia of Trees and Shrubs; containing the Hardy Trees and Shrubs of Great Britain scientifically and popularly described. With 2,000 Woodcuts. 8vo. 50s.

Bryologia Britannica; containing the Mosses of Great Britain and Ireland, arranged and described. By W. WILSON. 8vo. with 61 Plates, 42s. or coloured, £4 4s.

Maunder's Scientific and Lit rary Treasury; a Popular Encyclopædia Science, Literature, and Art. Fcp. 10s.

A Dictionary of Science, Liter ture, and Art. Fourth Edition, re-edit by the late W. T. BRANDE (the Autho and GEORGE W. COX, M.A. assisted gentlemen of eminent Scientific and Lit rary Acquirements. In 12 Parts, each co taining 240 pages, price 5s. forming 3 vo medium 8vo. price 21s. each.

Essays on Scientific and oth subjects, contributed to Reviews. By Sir I HOLLAND, Bart. M.D. Second Editio 8vo. 14s.

Essays from the Edinburgh an *Quarterly Reviews*; with Addresses ar other Pieces. By Sir J. F. W. HERSCHE Bart. M.A. 8vo. 18s.

Chemistry, Medicine, Surgery, and the Allied Sciences.

A Dictionary of Chemistry and the Allied Branches of other Sciences. By HENRY WATTS, F.C.S. assisted by eminent Contributors. 5 vols. medium 8vo. in course of publication in Parts. VOL. I. 31s. 6d. VOL. II. 26s. and VOL. III. 31s. 6d. are now ready.

Handbook of Chemical Analysis, adapted to the Unitary System of Notation: By F. T. CONINGTON, M.A. F.C.S. Post 8vo. 7s. 6d.—TABLES of QUALITATIVE ANALYSIS adapted to the same, 2s. 6d.

A Handbook of Volumetrical Analysis. By ROBERT H. SCOTT, M.A. T.C.D. Post 8vo. 4s. 6d.

Elements of Chemistry, Theore- tical and Practical. By WILLIAM A. MILLER, M.D. LL.D. F.R.S. F.G.S. Professor of Chemistry, King's College, London. 3 vols. 8vo. £2 13s. PART I. CHEMICAL PHYSICS, Third Edition, 12s. PART II. INORGANIC CHEMISTRY, 21s. PART III. ORGANIC CHEMISTRY, Second Edition, 20s.

A Manual of Chemistry, De- scriptive and Theoretical. By WILLIAM ODLING, M.B. F.R.S. PART I. 8vo. 9s.

A Course of Practical Chemistry, for the use of Medical Students. By the same Author. Second Edition, with 70 new Woodcuts. Crown 8vo. 7s. 6d.

Lectures on Animal Chemistry Delivered at the Royal College of Physicians in 1865. By the same Author. Crown 8vo. 4s. 6d.

The Toxicologist's Guide: a Ne Manual on Poisons, giving the Best Metho to be pursued for the Detection of Poison By J. HORSLEY, F.C.S. Analytical Chemis

The Diagnosis and Treatment the Diseases of Women; including t Diagnosis of Pregnancy. By GRAIL HEWITT, M.D. &c. 8vo. 16s.

Lectures on the Diseases of I fancy and Childhood. By CHARLES WES M.D. &c. 5th Edition, revised and enlarge 8vo. 16s.

Exposition of the Signs an Symptoms of Pregnancy: with other Pape on subjects connected with Midwifery. B W. F. MONTGOMERY, M.A. M.D. M.R.I./ 8vo. with Illustrations, 25s.

A System of Surgery, Theoretica and Practical, in Treatises by Variou Authors. Edited by T. HOLMES, M.A Cantab. Assistant-Surgeon to St. George' Hospital. 4 vols. 8vo. £4 13s.

Vol. I. General Pathology, 21s.
Vol. II. Local Injuries: Gun-shot Wounds Injuries of the Head, Back, Face, Neck Chest, Abdomen, Pelvis, of the Upper an Lower Extremities, and Diseases of th Eye. 21s.
Vol. III. Operative Surgery. Disease of the Organs of Circulation, Locomotion &c. 21s.
Vol. IV. Diseases of the Organs o Digestion, of the Genito-Urinary System and of the Breast, Thyroid Gland, and Skin with APPENDIX and GENERAL INDEX. 30s

Lectures on the Principles and Practice of Physic. By Thomas Watson, M.D. Physician-Extraordinary to the Queen. Fourth Edition. 2 vols. 8vo. 34s.

Lectures on Surgical Pathology. By J. Paget, F.R.S. Surgeon-Extraordinary to the Queen. Edited by W. Turner, M.B. 8vo. with 117 Woodcuts, 21s.

A Treatise on the Continued Fevers of Great Britain. By C. Murchison, M.D. Senior Physician to the London Fever Hospital. 8vo. with coloured Plates, 18s.

Anatomy, Descriptive and Sur- gical. By Henry Gray, F.R.S. With 410 Wood Engravings from Dissections. Third Edition, by T. Holmes, M.A. Cantab. Royal 8vo. 28s.

The Cyclopædia of Anatomy and Physiology. Edited by the late R. B. Todd, M.D. F.R.S. Assisted by nearly all the most eminent cultivators of Physiological Science of the present age. 5 vols. 8vo. with 2,853 Woodcuts, £6 6s.

Physiological Anatomy and Phy- siology of Man. By the late R. B. Todd, M.D. F.R.S. and W. Bowman, F.R.S. of King's College. With numerous Illustrations. Vol. II. 8vo. 25s.

A Dictionary of Practical Medi- cine. By J. Copland, M.D. F.R.S. Abridged from the larger work by the Author, assisted by J. C. Copland, M.R.C.S. and throughout brought down to the present state of Medical Science. Pp. 1,560, in 8vo. price 36s.

Dr. Copland's Dictionary of Practical Medicine (the larger work). 3 vols. 8vo. £5 11s.

The Works of Sir B. C. Bro Bart. collected and arranged by Cha Hawkins, F.R.C.S.E. 3 vols. 8vo. Medallion and Facsimile, 48s.

Autobiography of Sir B. C. Bro Bart. printed from the Author's mate left in MS. Second Edition. Fcp. 4s.

A Manual of Materia Me and Therapeutics, abridged ' from Pereira's Elements by F. J. Farre, assisted by R. Bentley, M.R.C.S. an R. Warington, F.R.S. 1 vol. 8vo. 90 Woodcuts, 21s.

Dr. Pereira's Elements of Mat Medica and Therapeutics, Third Editio A. S. Taylor, M.D. and G. O. Rees, 3 vols. 8vo. with Woodcuts, £3 15s.

Thomson's Conspectus of British Pharmacopœia. Twenty-fo Edition, corrected and made conform throughout to the New Pharmacopœi the General Council of Medical Educa By E. Lloyd Birkett, M.D. 18mo. 5s

Manual of the Domestic Pract of Medicine. By W. B. Keste F.R.C.S.E. Second Edition, thorou revised, with Additions. Fcp. 5s.

The Restoration of Health; the Application of the Laws of Hygiei the Recovery of Health: a Manual for Invalid, and a Guide in the Sick R By W. Strange, M.D. Fcp. 6s.

Sea-Air and Sea-Bathing Children and Invalids. By the s Author. Fcp. 3s.

Manual for the Classificati Training, and Education of the Fee Minded, Imbecile, and Idiotic. By Martin Duncan, M.B. and Will Millard. Crown 8vo. 5s.'

The Fine Arts, and Illustrated Editions.

The Life of Man Symbolised by the Months of the Year in their Seasons and Phases; with Passages selected from Ancient and Modern Authors. By Richard Pigot. Accompanied by a Series of 25 full-page Illustrations and numerous Marginal Devices, Decorative Initial Letters, and Tailpieces, engraved on Wood from

The New Testament, illustrated Wood Engravings after the Early Mas chiefly of the Italian School. Crown 63s. cloth, gilt top; or £5 5s. morocco.

Lyra Germanica; Hymns for Sundays and Chief Festivals of the Chris Year. Translated by Catherine W

Cats' and Farlie's Moral Emblems; with Aphorisms, Adages, and Proverbs of all Nations : comprising 121 Illustrations on Wood by J. Leighton, F.S.A. with an appropriate Text by R. Pigot. Imperial 8vo. 31s. 6d.

Shakspeare's Sentiments and Similes printed in Black and Gold and illuminated in the Missal style by Henry Noel Humphreys. In massive covers, containing the Medallion and Cypher of Shakspeare. Square post 8vo. 21s.

Moore's Irish Melodies. Illustrated with 161 Original Designs by D. Maclise, R.A. Super-royal 8vo. 31s. 6d. Imperial 16mo. 10s. 6d.

The History of Our Lord, as exemplified in Works of Art. By Mrs. Jameson and Lady Eastlake. Being the concludin Series of 'Sacred and Legendary Ar Second Edition, with 13 Etchings and 2 Woodcuts. 2 vols. square crown 8vo. 42s.

Mrs. Jameson's Legends of the Sain and Martyrs. Fourth Edition, with 19 Etc ings and 187 Woodcuts. 2 vols. 31s. 6d.

Mrs. Jameson's Legends of the Monast Orders. Third Edition, with 11 Etchin and 88 Woodcuts. 1 vol. 21s.

Mrs. Jameson's Legends of the Madonn Third Edition, with 27 Etchings and 1 Woodcuts. 1 vol. 21s.

Arts, Manufactures, &c.

Drawing from Nature; a Series of Progressive Instructions in Sketching, from Elementary Studies to Finished Views, with Examples from Switzerland and the Pyrenees. By George Barnard, Professor of Drawing at Rugby School. With 18 Lithographic Plates and 108 Wood Engravings. Imp. 8vo. 25s.

Encyclopædia of Architecture, Historical, Theoretical, and Practical. By Joseph Gwilt. With more than 1,000 Woodcuts. 8vo. 42s.

Tuscan Sculptors, their Lives, Works, and Times. With 45 Etchings and 28 Woodcuts from Original Drawings and Photographs. By Charles C. Perkins. 2 vols. imp. 8vo. 63s.

The Grammar of Heraldry: containing a Description of all the Principal Charges used in Armory, the Signification of Heraldic Terms, and the Rules to be observed in Blazoning and Marshalling. By John E. Cussans. Fcp. with 196 Woodcuts, 4s. 6d.

The Engineer's Handbook ; explaining the Principles which should guide the young Engineer in the Construction of Machinery. By C. S. Lowndes. Post 8vo. 5s.

The Elements of Mechanism. By T. M. Goodeve, M.A. Prof. of Mechanics at the R. M. Acad. Woolwich.

Ure's Dictionary of Arts, Man factures, and Mines. Re-written and e larged by Robert Hunt, F.R.S., assiste by numerous gentlemen eminent in Scien and the Arts. With 2,000 Woodcuts. 3 vol 8vo. £4.

Encyclopædia of Civil Enginee ing, Historical, Theoretical, and Practic By E. Cresy, C.E. With above 3,0 Woodcuts. 8vo. 42s.

Treatise on Mills and Millwor By W. Fairbairn, C.E. F.R.S. With Plates and 322 Woodcuts. 2 vols. 8vo. 3

Useful Information for Engineers. the same Author. First and Secon Series, with many Plates and Woodcu 2 vols. crown 8vo. 10s. 6d. each.

The Application of Cast and Wroug Iron to Building Purposes. By the sa Author. Third Edition, with 6 Plates a 118 Woodcuts. 8vo. 16s.

Iron Ship Building, its Histo and Progress, as comprised in a Series Experimental Researches on the Laws Strain; the Strengths, Forms, and oth conditions of the Material; and an Inqui into the Present and Prospective State the Navy, including the Experiment Results on the Resisting Powers of Armo Plates and Shot at High Velocities. B the same Author. With 4 Plates and 13 Woodcuts, 8vo. 18s.

The Practical Mechanic's Jour nal: An Illustrated Record of Mechanic

The **Practical Draughtsman's** Book of Industrial Design. By W. JOHNSON, Assoc. Inst. C.E. With many hundred Illustrations. 4to. 28s. 6d.

The **Patentee's Manual**: a Treatise on the Law and Practice of Letters Patent for the use of Patentees and Inventors. By J. and J. H. JOHNSON. Post 8vo. 7s. 6d.

The **Artisan Club's Treatise on** the Steam Engine, in its various Applications to Mines, Mills, Steam-Navigation, Railways, and Agriculture. By J. BOURNE, C.E. Seventh Edition; with 37 Plates and 546 Woodcuts. 4to. 42s.

A **Treatise on the Screw Pro**peller, Screw Vessels, and Screw Engines, as adapted for purposes of Peace and War; illustrated by many Plates and Woodcuts. By the same Author. New and enlarged Edition in course of publication in 24 Parts, royal 4to. 2s. 6d. each.

Catechism of the Steam Engine, in its various Applications to Mines, Mills, Steam Navigation, Railways, and Agriculture. By J. BOURNE. C.E. With 199 Woodcuts. Fcp. 9s. The INTRODUCTION of 'Recent Improvements' may be had separately, with 110 Woodcuts, price 3s. 6d.

Handbook of the Steam Engine, by the same Author, forming a KEY to the Catechism of the Steam Engine, with 67 Woodcuts. Fcp. 9s.

The **Theory of War Illustrated** by numerous Examples from History. By Lieut.-Col. P. L. MacDOUGALL. Third Edition, with 10 Plans. Post 8vo. 10s. 6d.

The **Art of Perfumery**; the Histor and Theory of Odours, and the Methods Extracting the Aromas of Plants. E Dr. PIESSE, F.C.S. Third Edition, wit 53 Woodcuts. Crown 8vo. 10s. 6d.

Chemical, Natural, and Physical Magi for Juveniles during the Holidays. By t same Author. Third Edition, enlarg with 38 Woodcuts. Fcp. 6s.

Talpa; or, the Chronicles of a Cl Farm. By C. W. HOSKYNS, Esq. With Woodcuts from Designs by G. CRUI SHANK. Sixth Edition. 16mo. 5s. 6d.

Loudon's Encyclopædia of Agr culture: Comprising the Laying-out, Is provement, and Management of Lande Property, and the Cultivation and Econom of the Productions of Agriculture. Wit 1,100 Woodcuts. 8vo. 31s. 6d.

Loudon's Encyclopædia of Gardenin Comprising the Theory and Practice Horticulture, Floriculture, Arboricultur and Landscape Gardening. With 1,0 Woodcuts. 8vo. 31s. 6d.

Loudon's Encyclopædia of Cottage, Far and Villa Architecture and Furniture. Wit more than 2,000 Woodcuts. 8vo. 42s.

History of Windsor Great Par and Windsor Forest. By WILLIAM ME zies, Resident Deputy Surveyor. With Maps and 20 Photographs. Imp. folio, £8 8

Bayldon's Art of Valuing Rent and Tillages, and Claims of Tenants upc Quitting Farms, both at Michaelmas ar Lady-Day. Eighth Edition, revised b J. C. MORTON. 8vo. 10s. 6d.

Religious and *Moral Works.*

An Exposition of the 39 Articles, Historical and Doctrinal. By E. HAROLD BROWNE, D.D. Lord Bishop of Ely. Seventh Edition. 8vo. 16s.

The **Pentateuch and the Elohistic** Psalms, in Reply to Bishop Colenso. By the same. Second Edition. 8vo. 2s.

Examination-Questions on Bishop Browne's Exposition of the Articles. By the Rev. J. GORLE, M.A. Fcp. 3s. 6d.

Five Lectures on the Character of St. Paul; being the Hulsean Lectures for 1862. By the Rev. J. S. HOWSON, D.D. Second Edition. 8vo. 9s.

The **Life and Epistles of S** Paul. By W. J. CONYBEARE, M.A. la Fellow of Trin. Coll. Cantab. and J. HOWSON, D.D. Principal of Liverpool Co

LIBRARY EDITION, with all the Origin Illustrations, Maps, Landscapes on Ste Woodcuts, &c. 2 vols. 4to. 48s.

INTERMEDIATE EDITION, with a Selectic of Maps, Plates, and Woodcuts. 2 vol square crown 8vo. 31s. 6d.

PEOPLE'S EDITION, revised and co densed, with 46 Illustrations and Map 2 vols. crown 8vo. 12s.

The **Voyage and Shipwreck of**
St. Paul; with Dissertations on the Ships and Navigation of the Ancients. By JAMES SMITH, F.R.S. Crown 8vo. Charts, 8s. 6d.

Fasti Sacri, or a Key to the
Chronology of the New Testament; comprising an Historical Harmony of the Four Gospels, and Chronological Tables generally from B.C. 70 to A.D. 70: with a Preliminary Dissertation and other Aids. By THOMAS LEWIN, M.A. F.S.A. Imp. 8vo. 42s.

A Critical and Grammatical Com-
mentary on St. Paul's Epistles. By C. J. ELLICOTT, D.D. Lord Bishop of Gloucester and Bristol. 8vo.
Galatians, Third Edition, 8s. 6d.
Ephesians, Third Edition, 8s. 6d.
Pastoral Epistles, Third Edition, 10s. 6d.
Philippians, Colossians, and Philemon, Third Edition, 10s. 6d.
Thessalonians, Second Edition, 7s. 6d.

Historical Lectures on the Life of
Our Lord Jesus Christ: being the Hulsean Lectures for 1859. By the same Author. Fourth Edition. 8vo. 10s. 6d.

The **Destiny of the Creature**; and other Sermons preached before the University of Cambridge. By the same. Post 8vo. 5s.

The **Broad and the Narrow Way**; Two Sermons preached before the University of Cambridge. By the same. Crown 8vo. 2s.

Rev. T. H. Horne's Introduction
to the Critical Study and Knowledge of the Holy Scriptures. Eleventh Edition, corrected, and extended under careful Editorial revision. With 4 Maps and 22 Woodcuts and Facsimiles. 4 vols. 8vo. £3 13s. 6d.

Rev. T. H. Horne's Compendious In-
troduction to the Study of the Bible, being an Analysis of the larger work by the same Author. Re-edited by the Rev. JOHN AYRE, M.A. With Maps, &c. Post 8vo. 9s.

The **Treasury of Bible Know-**
ledge; being a Dictionary of the Books, Persons, Places, Events, and other Matters of which mention is made in Holy Scripture; intended to establish its Authority and illustrate its Contents. By Rev. J. AYRE, M.A. With Maps, 15 Plates, and numerous Woodcuts. Fcp. 10s. 6d.

The **Greek Testament; with Notes,**
Grammatical and Exegetical. By the Rev. W. WEBSTER, M.A. and the Rev. W. F. WILKINSON, M.A. 2 vols. 8vo. £2 4s.
VOL. I. the Gospels and Acts, 20s.

Every-day Scripture Difficulti
explained and illustrated. By J. E. PRE COTT, M.A. VOL. I. *Matthew* and *Mar* VOL. II. *Luke* and *John*. 2 vols. 8vo. 9s. eac

The **Pentateuch and Book**
Joshua Critically Examined. By the Righ Rev. J. W. COLENSO, D.D. Lord Bishop Natal. People's Edition, in 1 vol. crow 8vo. 6s. or in 5 Parts, 1s. each.

The **Pentateuch and Book**
Joshua Critically Examined. By Prof. . KUENEN, of Leyden. Translated from t Dutch, and edited with Notes, by the Rig Rev. J. W. COLENSO, D.D. Bishop of Nat: 8vo. 8s. 6d.

The **Church and the World:** Essa
on Questions of the Day. By vario Writers. Edited by Rev. ORBY SHIPLE M.A. 8vo. [*Nearly ready.*

The **Formation of Christendon**
PART I. By T. W. ALLIES. 8vo. 12s.

Christendom's Divisions; a Phi
sophical Sketch of the Divisions of t Christian Family in East and West. EDMUND S. FFOULKES, formerly Fellow an Tutor of Jesus Coll. Oxford. Post 8vo. 7s. 6

Christendom's Divisions, Part I
Greeks and Latins, being a History of the Dissentions and Overtures for Peace dov to the Reformation. By the same Autho [*Nearly ready.*

The **Life of Christ**, an Eclectic Go
pel, from the Old and New Testamen arranged on a New Principle, with Analytic Tables, &c. By CHARLES DE LA PRYM M.A. Revised Edition. 8vo. 5s.

The **Hidden Wisdom of Chri**
and the Key of Knowledge; or, History the Apocrypha. By ERNEST DE BUNSE 2 vols. 8vo. 28s.

The **Temporal Mission of t**
Holy Ghost; or, Reason and Revelatic By the Most Rev. Archbishop MANNIN Second Edition. Crown 8vo. 8s. 6d.

Essays on Religion and Liter
ture. Edited by the Most Rev. Archbish MANNING. 8vo. 10s. 6d.

Essays and Reviews. By the Re
W. TEMPLE, D.D. the Rev. R. WILLIAN B.D. the Rev. B. POWELL, M.A. the Re H. B. WILSON, B.D. C. W. GOODWIN, M. the Rev. M. PATTISON, B.D. and the Re

Mosheim's Ecclesiastical History. MURDOCK and SOAMES's Translation and Notes, re-edited by the Rev. W. STUBBS, M.A. 3 vols. 8vo. 45s.

Bishop Jeremy Taylor's Entire Works: With Life by BISHOP HEBER. Revised and corrected by the Rev. C. P. EDEN, 10 vols. £5 5s.

Passing Thoughts on Religion. By the Author of 'Amy Herbert.' New Edition. Fcp. 5s.

Thoughts for the Holy Week, for Young Persons. By the same Author. 3d Edit on. Fcp. 8vo. 2s.

Night Lessons from Scripture. By the same Author. 2d Edition. 32mo. 3s.

Self-examination before Confirmation. By the same Author. 32mo. 1s. 6d.

Readings for a Month Preparatory to Confirmation from Writers of the Early and English Church. By the same. Fcp. 4s.

Readings for Every Day in Lent, compiled from the Writings of Bishop JEREMY TAYLOR. By the same. Fcp. 5s.

Preparation for the Holy Communion; the Devotions chiefly from the works of JEREMY TAYLOR. By the same. 32mo. 3s.

Principles of Education drawn from Nature and Revelation, and Applied to Female Education in the Upper Classes. By the same. 2 vols. fcp. 12s, 6d.

Morning Clouds. Second Edition. Fcp. 5s.

The Wife's Manual; or, Prayers, Thoughts, and Songs on Several Occasions of a Matron's Life. By the Rev. W. CALVERT, M.A. Crown 8vo. 10s. 6d.

Spiritual Songs for the Sundays and Holidays throughout the Year. By J. S. B. MONSELL, LL.D. Vicar of Egham. Fourth Edition. Fcp. 4s. 6d.

The Beatitudes: Abasement before God: Sorrow for Sin; Meekness of Spirit; Desire for Holiness; Gentleness; Purity of Heart; the Peace-makers; Sufferings for Christ. By the same. 2nd Edition, fcp. 3s. 6d.

Lyra Domestica; Christian Songs for Domestic Edification. Translated from the *Psaltery and Harp* of C. J. P. SPITTA, and from other sources, by RICHARD MASSIE. FIRST and SECOND SERIES, fcp. 4s. 6d.each.

Lyra Sacra; Hymns, Ancient Modern, Odes, and Fragments of Sa Poetry. Edited by the Rev. B. W. SAV M A. Third Edition, enlarged. Fcp.

Lyra Germanica, translated from German by Miss C. WINKWORTH. F SERIES, Hymns for the Sundays and C Festivals; SECOND SERIES, the Chris Life. Fcp. 5s. each SERIES.

Hymns from Lyra Germanica, 18mo

Lyra Eucharistica; Hymns Verses on the Holy Communion, Anc and Modern; with other Poems. Edite the Rev. ORBY SHIPLEY, M.A. Sec Edition. Fcp. 7s. 6d.

Lyra Messianica; Hymns and Verses the Life of Christ, Ancient and Mode with other Poems. By the same Edi Second Edition, enlarged. Fcp. 7s. 6d.

Lyra Mystica; Hymns and Verses on Sac Subjects, Ancient and Modern. By same Editor. Fcp. 7s. 6d.

The Chorale Book for Englan a complete Hymn-Book in accordance the Services and Festivals of the Churc England: the Hymns translated by Mis WINKWORTH; the Tunes arranged by P W. S. BENNETT and OTTO GOLDSCHMI Fcp. 4to. 12s. 6d.

Congregational Edition. Fcp. 2s.

The Catholic Doctrine of t Atonement; an Historical Inquiry into Development in the Church: with an Int duction on the Principle of Theologi Developments. By H. N. OXENHAM, M formerly Scholar of Balliol College, Oxfc 8vo. 8s. 6d.

From Sunday to Sunday; an atte to consider familiarly the Weekday and Labours of a Country Clergyman. R. GEE, M.A. Fcp. 5s.

First Sundays at Church; Familiar Conversations on the Morning a Evening Services of the Church of Engla By J. E. RIDDLE, M.A. Fcp. 2s. 6d.

The Judgment of Conscienc and other Sermons. By RICHARD WHATE D.D. late Archbishop of Dublin. Cro 8vo. 4s. 6d.

Paley's Moral Philosophy, w Annotations. By RICHARD WHATELY, D. late Archbishop of Dublin. 8vo. 7s.

Travels, Voyages, &c.

Outline Sketches of the High Alps of Dauphiné. By T. G. BONNEY, M.A. F.G.S. M.A.C. Fellow of St. John's Coll. Camb. With 13 Plates and a Coloured Map. Post 4to. 16s.

Ice Caves of France and Switzerland; a narrative of Subterranean Exploration. By the Rev. G. F. BROWNE, M.A. Fellow and Assistant-Tutor of St. Catherine's Coll. Cambridge, M.A.C. With 11 Woodcuts. Square crown 8vo. 12s. 6d.

Village Life in Switzerland. By SOPHIA D. DELMARD. Post 8vo. 9s. 6d.

How we Spent the Summer; or, a Voyage en Zigzag in Switzerland and Tyrol with some Members of the ALPINE CLUB. From the Sketch-Book of one of the Party. Third Edition, re-drawn. In oblong 4to. with about 300 Illustrations, 15s.

Beaten Tracks; or, Pen and Pencil Sketches in Italy. By the Authoress of 'A Voyage en Zigzag.' With 42 Plates, containing about 200 Sketches from Drawings made on the Spot. 8vo. 16s.

Map of the Chain of Mont Blanc, from an actual Survey in 1863—1864. By A. ADAMS-REILLY, F.R.G.S. M.A.C. Published under the Authority of the Alpine Club. In Chromolithography on extra stout drawing-paper 28in. × 17in. price 10s. or mounted on canvas in a folding case, 12s. 6d.

Transylvania, its Products and its People. By CHARLES BONER. With 5 Maps and 43 Illustrations on Wood and in Chromolithography. 8vo. 21s.

Explorations in South - west Africa, from Walvisch Bay to Lake Ngami and the Victoria Falls. By THOMAS BAINES, F.R.G.S. 8vo. with Maps and Illustrations, 21s.

Vancouver Island and British Columbia; their History, Resources, and Prospects. By MATTHEW MACFIE, F.R.G.S. With Maps and Illustrations. 8vo. 18s.

History of Discovery in our Australasian Colonies, Australia, Tasmania, and New Zealand, from the Earliest Date to the Present Day. By WILLIAM HOWITT. With 3 Maps of the Recent Explorations from Official Sources. 2 vols. 8vo. 28s.

The Capital of the Tycoon; a Narrative of a 3 Years' Residence in Japan. By Sir RUTHERFORD ALCOCK, K.C.B. 2 vols. 8vo. with numerous Illustrations, 42s.

Last Winter in Rome. By C. R. WELD. With Portrait and Engravings on Wood. Post 8vo. 14s.

Autumn Rambles in North Africa. By JOHN ORMSBY, of the Middle Temple. With 16 Illustrations. Post 8vo. 8s. 6d.

The Dolomite Mountains. Excursions through Tyrol, Carinthia, Carniola, and Friuli in 1861, 1862, and 1863. By J. GILBERT and G. C. CHURCHILL, F.R.G.S. With numerous Illustrations. Square crown 8vo. 21s.

A Summer Tour in the Grisons and Italian Valleys of the Bernina. By Mrs. HENRY FRESHFIELD. With 2 Coloured Maps and 4 Views. Post 8vo. 10s. 6d.

Alpine Byways; or, Light Leaves gathered in 1859 and 1860. By the same Authoress. Post 8vo. with Illustrations, 10s. 6d.

A Lady's Tour Round Monte Rosa; including Visits to the Italian Valleys. With Map and Illustrations. Post 8vo, 14s.

Guide to the Pyrenees, for the use of Mountaineers. By CHARLES PACKE. With Maps, &c. and Appendix. Fcp. 6s.

The Alpine Guide. By JOHN BALL, M.R.I.A. late President of the Alpine Club. Post 8vo. with Maps and other Illustrations.

Guide to the Eastern Alps. [Just ready.

Guide to the Western Alps, including Mont Blanc, Monte Rosa, Zermatt, &c. price 7s. 6d.

Guide to the Oberland and all Switzerland, excepting the Neighbourhood of Monte Rosa and the Great St. Bernard; with Lombardy and the adjoining portion of Tyrol. 7s. 6d.

A Guide to Spain. By H. O'SHEA. Post 8vo. with Travelling Map, 15s.

Christopher Columbus; his Life, Voyages, and Discoveries. Revised Edition, with 4 Woodcuts. 18mo. 2s. 6d.

Captain James Cook; his Life, Voyages, and Discoveries. Revised Edition, with numerous Woodcuts. 18mo. 2s. 6d.

Humboldt's Travels and Disco- veries in South America. Third Edition, with numerous Woodcuts. 18mo. 2s. 6d.

Mungo Park's Life and Travels in Africa, with an Account of his Death and the Substance of Later Discoveries. Sixth Edition, with Woodcuts. 18mo. 2s. 6d.

Narratives of Shipwrecks of the Royal Navy between 1793 and 1857, compiled from Official Documents in the Admiralty by W. O. S. GILLY; with a Preface by W. S. GILLY, D.D. 3d Edition, fcp. 5s.

A Week at the Land's E By J. T. BLIGHT; assisted by E. H. R(R. Q. COUCH, and J. RALFS. With and 96 Woodcuts. Fcp. 6s. 6d.

Visits to Remarkable Plac Old Halls, Battle-Fields, and Scenes il trative of Striking Passages in Eng History and Poetry. By WILLIAM HOW 2 vols. square crown 8vo. with Wood gravings, 25s.

The Rural Life of Engla By the same Author. With Woodcut: Bewick and Williams. Medium 8vo. 12s

Works of Fiction.

Atherstone Priory. By L. N. COMYN. 2 vols. post 8vo. 21s.

Ellice : a Tale. By the same. Post 8vo. 9s. 6d.

Stories and Tales by the Author of 'Amy Herbert,' uniform Edition, each Tale or Story complete in a single volume.

AMY HERBERT, 2s. 6d.	KATHARINE ASHTON,
GERTRUDE, 2s. 6d.	3s. 6d.
EARL'S DAUGHTER,	MARGARET PERCI-
2s. 6d.	VAL, 5s.
EXPERIENCE OF LIFE,	LANETON PARSON-
2s. 6d.	AGE, 4s. 6d.
CLEVE HALL, 3s. 6d.	URSULA, 4s. 6d.
IVORS, 3s. 6d.	

A Glimpse of the World. By the Author of 'Amy Herbert.' Fcp. 7s. 6d.

The Six Sisters of the Valleys : an Historical Romance. By W. BRAMLEY-MOORE, M.A. Incumbent of Gerrard's Cross, Bucks. Third Edition, with 14 Illustrations. Crown 8vo. 5s.

Icelandic Legends. Collected by JON. ARNASON. Selected and Translated from the Icelandic by GEORGE E. J. POWELL and E. MAGNUSSON. SECOND SERIES, with Notes and an Introductory Essay on the Origin and Genius of the Icelandic Folk-Lore, and 3 Illustrations on Wood. Crown 8vo. 21s.

The Warden : a Novel. By ANTHONY TROLLOPE, Crown 8vo. 3s. 6d.

Barchester Towers : a Sequel to 'The

The Gladiators : a Tale of Rome Judæa. By G. J. WHYTE MELVI Crown 8vo. 5s.

Digby Grand, an Autobiography. By same Author. 1 vol. 5s.

Kate Coventry, an Autobiography. By same. 1 vol. 5s.

General Bounce, or the Lady and the custs. By the same. 1 vol. 5s.

Holmby House, a Tale of Old Northamp shire. 1 vol. 5s.

Good for Nothing, or All Down Hill. the same. 1 vol. 6s.

The Queen's Maries, a Romance of H rood. By the same. 1 vol. 6s.

The Interpreter, a Tale of the War. the same Author. 1 vol. 5s.

Tales from Greek Mytholo By GEORGE W. COX, M.A. late Sch of Trin. Coll. Oxon. Second Edition. Sqi 16mo. 3s. 6d.

Tales of the Gods and Heroes. By same Author. Second Edition. Fcp. 5s.

Tales of Thebes and Argos. By the s Author. Fcp. 4s. 6d.

Gallus ; or, Roman Scenes of the T. of Augustus: with Notes and Excursi illustrative of the Manners and Custom the Ancient Romans. From the Germa: Prof. BECKER. New Edition. [Nearly re(

Charicles ; a Tale illustrative of Priv Life among the Ancient Greeks : with N and Excursuses. From the German of P

Poetry and The Drama.

Goethe's Second Faust. Translated by JOHN ANSTER, LL.D. M.R.I.A. Regius Professor of Civil Law in the University of Dublin. Post 8vo. 15s.

Tasso's Jerusalem Delivered, translated into English Verse by Sir J. KINGSTON JAMES, Kt. M.A. 2 vols. fcp. with Facsimile, 14s.

Poetical Works of John Edmund Reade; with final Revision and Additions. 3 vols. fcp. 18s. or each vol. separately, 6s.

Moore's Poetical Works, Cheapest Editions complete in 1 vol. including the Autobiographical Prefaces and Author's last Notes, which are still copyright. Crown 8vo. ruby type, with Portrait, 6s. or People's Edition, in larger type, 12s. 6d.

Moore's Poetical Works, as above, Library Edition, medium 8vo. with Portrait and Vignette, 14s. or in 10 vols. fcp. 3s. 6d. each.

Moore's Lalla Rookh. 32mo. Plate, 1s. 16mo. Vignette, 2s. 6d.

Tenniel's Edition of Moore's Lalla Rookh, with 68 Wood Engravings from Original Drawings and other Illustrations. Fcp. 4to. 21s.

Moore's Irish Melodies. 32mo. Portrait, 1s. 16mo. Vignette, 2s. 6d.

Maclise's Edition of Moore's Irish Melodies, with 161 Steel Plates from Original Drawings. Super-royal 8vo. 31s. 6d.

Maclise's Edition of Moore's Irish Melodies, with all the Original Designs (as above) reduced by a New Process. Imp. 16mo. 10s. 6d.

Southey's Poetical Works, with the Author's last Corrections and copyright Additions. Library Edition, in 1 vol. medium 8vo. with Portrait and Vignette, 14s. or in 10 vols. fcp. 3s. 6d. each.

Lays of Ancient Rome; with Ivry and the Armada. By the Right Hon. LORD MACAULAY. 16mo. 4s. 6d.

Lord Macaulay's Lays of Ancient Rome. With 90 Illustrations on Wood, Original and from the Antique, from Drawings by G. SCHARF. Fcp. 4to. 21s.

Poems. By JEAN INGELOW. Tenth Edition. Fcp. 8vo. 5s.

Poetical Works of Letitia Elizabeth Landon (L.E.L.) 2 vols. 16mo. 10s.

Playtime with the Poets : a Selection of the best English Poetry for the use of Children. By a LADY. Crown 8vo. 5s.

Bowdler's Family Shakspeare, cheaper Genuine Edition, complete in 1 vol. large type, with 36 Woodcut Illustrations, price 14s. or, with the same ILLUSTRATIONS, in 6 pocket vols. 3s. 6d. each.

Arundines Cami, sive Musarum Cantabrigiensium Lusus Canori. Collegit atque edidit H. DRURY. M.A. Editio Sexta, curavit H. J. HODGSON, M.A. Crown 8vo. price 7s. 6d.

The Iliad of Homer Translated into Blank Verse. By ICHABOD CHARLES WRIGHT, M.A. late Fellow of Magdalen Coll. Oxon. 2 vols. crown 8vo. 21s.

The Iliad of Homer in English Hexameter Verse. By J. HENRY DART, M.A. of Exeter College, Oxford; Author of 'The Exile of St. Helena, Newdigate, 1838.' Square crown 8vo. price 21s. cloth.

Dante's Divine Comedy, translated in English Terza Rima by JOHN DAYMAN, M.A. [With the Italian Text, after Brunetti, interpaged.] 8vo. 21s.

Rural Sports, &c.

Encyclopædia of Rural Sports ; a Complete Account, Historical, Practical, and Descriptive, of Hunting, Shooting, Fishing, Racing, &c. By D. P. BLAINE. With above 600 Woodcuts (20 from Designs by JOHN LEECH). 8vo. 42s.

Notes on Rifle Shooting. By Captain HEATON, Adjutant of the Third Manchester Rifle Volunteer Corps. Fcp. 2s. 6d.

Col. Hawker's Instructions to Young Sportsmen in all that relates to Guns and Shooting. Revised by the Author's SON. Square crown 8vo. with Illustrations. 18s.

The Rifle, its Theory and Practice. By ARTHUR WALKER (79th Highlanders), Staff, Hythe and Fleetwood Schools of Musketry. Second Edition. Crown 8vo. with 125 Woodcuts, 5s.

The Dead Shot, or Sportsman's Complete Guide; a Treatise on the Use of the Gun, Dog-breaking, Pigeon-shooting, &c. By MARKSMAN. Fcp. with Plates, 5s.

Hints on Shooting, Fishing, &c. both on Sea and Land and in the Fresh and Saltwater Lochs of Scotland. By C. IDLE, Esq. Second Edition. Fcp. 6s.

The Fly-Fisher's Entomology. By ALFRED RONALDS. With coloured Representations of the Natural and Artificial Insect. Sixth Edition; with 20 coloured Plates. 8vo. 14s.

Hand-book of Angling: Teaching Fly-fishing, Trolling, Bottom-fishing, Salmon-fishing; with the Natural History of River Fish, and the best modes of Catching the . By EPHEMERA. Fcp. Woodcuts, 5s.

The Cricket Field; or, the History and the Science of the Game of Cricket. By ES PYCROFT, B.A. 4th Edition. Fcp. 5s.

The Cricket Tutor; a Treatise exclusively Practical. By the same. 18mo. 1s.

Cricketana. By the same Author. With 7 Portraits of Cricketers. Fcp. 5s.

Youatt on the Horse. Revised and enlarged by W. WATSON, M.R.C.V.S. 8vo. with numerous Woodcuts, 12s. 6d.

Youatt on the Dog. (By the same Author.) 8vo. with numerous Woodcuts, 6s.

The Horse-Trainer's and Sportsman's Guide: with Considerations on the Duties of Grooms, on Purchasing Blood Stock, and on Veterinary Examination. By DIGBY COLLINS. Post 8vo. 6s.

Blaine's Veterinary Art: a T tise on the Anatomy, Physiology, Curative Treatment of the Diseases o Horse, Neat Cattle, and Sheep. Sev Edition, revised and enlarged by C. St M.R.C.V.S.L. 8vo. with Plates and W cuts, 18s.

The Horse's Foot, and how to k it Sound. By W. MILES, Esq. 9th Edi with Illustrations. Imp. 8vo. 12s. 6d.

A Plain Treatise on Horse-shoeing the same Author. Post 8vo. with Illu tions, 2s. 6d.

Stables and Stable Fittings. By the s Imp. 8vo. with 13 Plates, 15s.

Remarks on Horses' Teeth, address Purchasers. By the same. Post 8vo. 1

On Drill and Manœuvres Cavalry, combined with Horse Artil By Major-Gen. MICHAEL W. SMITH, Commanding the Poonah Division o Bombay Army. 8vo. 12s. 6d.

The Dog in Health and Dise By STONEHENGE. With 70 Wood gravings. Square crown 8vo. 15s.

The Greyhound. By the same Au Revised Edition, with 24 Portraits of G hounds. Square crown 8vo. 21s.

The Ox, his Diseases and their T ment; with an Essay on Parturition i Cow. By J. R. DOBSON, M.R.C.V.S. C 8vo. with Illustrations, 7s. 6d.

Commerce, Navigation, and Mercantile Affairs.

A Dictionary, Practical, Theoretical, and Historical, of Commerce and Commercial Navigation. By J. R. M'CULLOCH. 8vo. with Maps and Plans, 50s.

Practical Guide for British Shipmasters to United States Ports. By PIERREFONT EDWARDS, Her Britannic Majesty's Vice-Consul at New York. Post 8vo. 8s. 6d.

A Manual for Naval Cadets. By J. M'NEIL BOYD, late Captain R.N. Third Edition; with 240 Woodcuts, and 11 coloured Plates. Post 8vo. 12s. 6d.

The Law of Nations Conside as Independent Political Communities. TRAVERS TWISS, D.C.L. Regius Prof of Civil Law in the University of Ox 2 vols. 8vo. 30s. or separately, PART I. 12s. PART II. War. 18s.

A Nautical Dictionary, de the Technical Language relative t Building and Equipment of Sailing V and Steamers, &c. By ARTHUR Yo Second Edition; with Plates and 150 W cuts. 8vo. 18s.

Works of Utility and General Information.

Modern Cookery for Private Families, reduced to a System of Easy Practice in a Series of carefully-tested Receipts. By ELIZA ACTON. Newly revised and enlarged; with 8 Plates, Figures, and 150 Woodcuts. Fcp. 7s. 6d.

The Handbook of Dining; or, Corpulency and Leanness scientifically considered. By BRILLAT-SAVARIN, Author of 'Physiologie du Goût.' Translated by L. F. SIMPSON. Revised Edition, with Additions. Fcp. 3s. 6d.

On Food and its Digestion; an Introduction to Dietetics. By W. BRINTON, M.D. Physician to St. Thomas's Hospital, &c. With 48 Woodcuts. Post 8vo. 12s.

Wine, the Vine, and the Cellar. By THOMAS G. SHAW. Second Edition, revised and enlarged, with Frontispiece and 31 Illustrations on Wood. 8vo. 16s.

A Practical Treatise on Brewing; with Formulæ for Public Brewers, and Instructions for Private Families. By W. BLACK. Fifth Edition. 8vo. 10s. 6d.

How to Brew Good Beer: a complete Guide to the Art of Brewing Ale, Bitter Ale, Table Ale, Brown Stout, Porter, and Table Beer. By JOHN PITT. Revised Edition. Fcp. 4s. 6d.

Short Whist. By MAJOR A. The Sixteenth Edition, revised, with an Essay on the Theory of the Modern Scientific Game by PROF. P. Fcp. 3s. 6d.

Whist, What to Lead. By CAM. Third Edition. 32mo. 1s.

Two Hundred Chess Problems, composed by F. HEALEY, including the Problems to which the Prizes were awarded by the Committees of the Era, the Manchester, the Birmingham, and the Bristol Chess Problem Tournaments; accompanied by the SOLUTIONS. Crown 8vo. with 200 Diagrams, 5s.

Hints on Etiquette and the Usages of Society; with a Glance at Bad Habits. Revised, with Additions, by a LADY of RANK. Fcp. 2s. 6d.

The Cabinet Lawyer; a Popul Digest of the Laws of England, Civil a Criminal. 21st Edition, extended by t Author; including the Acts of the Sessio 1864 and 1865. Fcp. 10s. 6d.

The Philosophy of Health; or, ɛ Exposition of the Physiological and Sanita Conditions conducive to Human Longevit and Happiness. By SOUTHWOOD SMIT M.D. Eleventh Edition, revised and e larged; with 113 Woodcuts. 8vo. 15s.

Hints to Mothers on the Manag ment of their Health during the Period Pregnancy and in the Lying-in Room. T. BULL, M.D. Fcp. 5s.

The Maternal Management of Childr in Health and Disease. By the sa Author. Fcp. 5s.

Notes on Hospitals. By FLOREN(NIGHTINGALE. Third Edition, enlarge with 13 Plans. Post 4to. 18s.

The Law relating to Bene Building Societies; with Practical Obse vations on the Act and all the Cases decid thereon, also a Form of Rules and Forms Mortgages. By W. TIDD PRATT, Barriste 2nd Edition. Fcp. 3s. 6d.

C. M. Willich's Popular Table for Ascertaining the Value of Lifehol Leasehold, and Church Property, Renew Fines, &c.; the Public Funds; Annu Average Price and Interest on Consols fro 1731 to 1861; Chemical, Geographica Astronomical, Trigonometrical Tables, & Post 8vo. 10s.

Thomson's Tables of Interes at Three, Four, Four and a Half, and Fiv per Cent, from One Pound to Ten Thousan and from 1 to 365 Days. 12mo. 3s. 6d.

Maunder's Treasury of Know ledge and Library of Reference: comprisin an English Dictionary and Grammar, Uni versal Gazetteer, Classical Dictionary, Chrc nology, Law Dictionary, Synopsis of th Peerage, useful Tables, &c. Fcp. 10s.

General and School Atlases.

An Atlas of History and Geography, representing the Political State of the World at successive Epochs from the commencement of the Christian Era to the Present Time, in a Series of 16 coloured Maps. By J. S. BREWER, M.A. Third Edition, revised, &c. by E. C. BREWER, LL.D. Royal 8vo. 15s.

Bishop Butler's Atlas of Modern Geography, in a Series of 33 full-coloured Maps, accompanied by a complete Alphabetical Index. New Edition, corrected and enlarged. Royal 8vo. 10s. 6d.

Bishop Butler's Atlas of Ancient Geography, in a Series of 24 full-coloured Maps, accompanied by a complete Accentuated Index. New Edition, corrected and enlarged. Royal 8vo. 12s.

School Atlas of Physical, Ptical, and Commercial Geography, in full-coloured Maps, accompanied by scriptive Letterpress. By E. HUG F.R.A.S. Royal 8vo. 10s. 6d.

Middle-Class Atlas of Gene Geography, in a Series of 29 full-colo Maps, containing the most recent T torial Changes and Discoveries. By WAI M'LEOD, F.R.G.S. 4to. 5s.

Physical Atlas of Great Brit and Ireland; comprising 30 full-colo Maps, with illustrative Letterpress, form a concise Synopsis of British Physical graphy. By WALTER M'LEOD, F.R. Fcp. 4to. 7s. 6d.

Periodical Publications.

The Edinburgh Review, or Critical Journal, published Quarterly in January, April, July, and October. 8vo. price 6s. each No.

The County Seats of the Noblemen and Gentlemen of Great Britain and Ireland. Edited by the Rev. F, O. MORRIS, B.A. Rector of Nunburnholme. In course of publication monthly, with coloured Views, in 4to. price 2s. 6d. each Part.

Fraser's Magazine for Town Country, published on the 1st of Month. 8vo. price 2s. 6d. each No.

The Alpine Journal: a Recor Mountain Adventure and Scientific Ob vation. By Members of the Alpine C Edited by H. B. GEORGE, M.A. Publi Quarterly, May 31, Aug. 31, Nov. 30, 28. 8vo. price 1s. 6d. each No.

Knowledge for the Young.

The Stepping Stone to Knowledge: Containing upwards of 700 Questions and Answers on Miscellaneous Subjects, adapted to the capacity of Infant Minds. By a MOTHER. 18mo. price 1s.

The Stepping Stone to Geography: Containing several Hundred Questions and Answers on Geographical Subjects. 18mo. 1s.

The Stepping Stone to English History: Containing several Hundred Questions and Answers on the History of England. 1s.

The Stepping Stone to Bible Knowledge: Containing several Hundred Questions and Answers on the Old and New Testaments. 18mo. 1s.

The Stepping Stone to Biography: Containing several Hundred Questions and Answers on the Lives of Eminent Men and

Second Series of the Stepp Stone to Knowledge: containing upw of Eight Hundred Questions and Ans on Miscellaneous Subjects not containe the FIRST SERIES. 18mo. 1s.

The Stepping Stone to French Pronciation and Conversation: Containing s ral Hundred Questions and Answers. Mr. P. SADLER. 18mo. 1s.

The Stepping Stone to English Grmar: containing several Hundred Quest and Answers on English Grammar. Mr. P. SADLER. 18mo. 1s.

The Stepping Stone to Natural Hist VERTEBRATE or BACKBONED ANIM PART I. *Mammalia*; PART II. *Birds*, .

D

INDEX.

CPSIA information can be obtained
at www.ICGtesting.com
Printed in the USA
BVHW090917261118
534012BV00017B/303/P